RECONSIDERING
AMERICAN
LIBERALISM

RECONSIDERING AMERICAN LIBERALISM

The Troubled Odyssey of the Liberal Idea

JAMES P. YOUNG

Routledge
Taylor & Francis Group
New York London

First published 1996 by Westview Press

Published 2018 by Routledge
711 Third Avenue, New York, NY 10017, USA
2 Park Square, Milton Park, Abingdon, Oxon OX14 4RN

Routledge is an imprint of the Taylor & Francis Group, an informa business

Library of Congress Cataloging-in-Publication Data
Young, James P., 1934–
   Reconsidering American liberalism : the troubled odyssey of the
liberal idea / James P. Young.
      p. cm.
   Includes bibliographical references and index.
   ISBN 0-8133-0647-7.—ISBN 0-8133-0648-5
   1. Liberalism—United States—History.   2. United States—Politics
and government.   I. Title.
JC574.2. U6Y68   1996
320.5'1'0973—dc20   95-37950
                                                                                          CIP

ISBN 13: 978-0-8133-0648-3 (pbk)

Once again for Gladys
and this time for
Jim and Susan
too

It's a complex fate,
being an American.

—Henry James

Contents

Preface
and Acknowledgments

ALTHOUGH I HOPE the argument of this book will speak for itself, a few words about its analytical point of view may be helpful. Though the approach is historical, this work is intended to be a piece of political theory; historians may find it too "present minded." Richard Hofstadter once commented that he wrote history out of his engagement with the present, and I, though not a historian, share his motivation. However, much of the history of American political thought is the product of important political actors, and one must avoid doing violence to history when trying to theorize about it. I believe the close connection of politics and history in American political thought to be at least as much a virtue as a defect in that it helps to avoid the excessively high level of abstraction characteristic of so much contemporary political thinking.

In a tribute to Judith Shklar, Rogers Smith wrote: "She found most if not all metaphysical pretensions intellectually silly and politically pernicious. . . . She studied political thought chiefly as a way of revealing the characteristic meaning that different political institutions, commitments, and ways of life expressed and fostered" *(Yale Journal of Law and the Humanities* [Winter 1993], p. 188). I find this appraisal compelling; it states my aim far better than I can myself.

The goal then is interpretation, but the starting point is a particular interpretation of American politics and history. For this reason I have tried to take into account the best available scholarship; that does not always mean the most recent scholarship, since, in my view, too much recent work ignores intellectual and political history and shies away from attempts at theoretically oriented narratives. My excessively immodest ambition is to contribute to those attempts, that is, to try to make sense of the complex body of thought and practice that constitute American political culture. In fact, my hope is to extend and revise that narrative tradition.

The interpretation I begin with is that of a dominant liberal consensus, an idea developed above all by Richard Hofstadter and Louis Hartz. Neither theory has fared very well with recent critics, though the Hartz thesis seems to be making a comeback. My belief is that Hofstadter was on the mark in general terms more often than contemporary historians allow. Still, the theory of a hegemonic liberal consensus *is* flawed, and liberal theory itself is under attack. In this book I assess the value of the consensus theory and of the liberal tradition itself.

I have wrestled with Hartz and Hofstadter for my entire professional career; though I often disagree with them, this book would not exist without their ideas. I am also indebted to others who have attempted holistic interpretations of the American experience. I have tried to discharge specific obligations in the notes, but I am sure that there is a more general influence that cannot be documented, so I would like to acknowledge its forerunners here: Wilson Carey McWilliams, *The Idea of Fraternity in America;* John P. Diggins, *The Lost Soul of American Politics;* and Russell Hanson, *The Democratic Idea in America.*

I was also lucky in my teachers at the University of Michigan. Frank Grace and George Peek showed a sometimes resistant student that his virtually hereditary commitment to social democratic reform liberalism was not *automatically* correct. Roy Pierce, in what was probably the greatest seminar I ever took, taught an important lesson about the essential inseparability of the great works in the history of political theory and the study of politics itself by assigning Aristotle's *Politics* as the first reading in a course on comparative European government. Sidney Fine taught me the basics of U.S. history since Reconstruction and gave me a vivid sense of the historian's craft—I regret that he will probably find much to disagree with here. Finally, the great James Meisel, a refugee from Hitler's Germany, showed by example—since he *never* wasted time talking about method—the richness of the Central European tradition of social thought and demonstrated the essential irrelevance of the disciplinary distinctions between political science, political theory, history, sociology, and even philosophy and economics properly understood. More generally, he showed me what the life of the mind was about.

I also learned more than I can say from the discussions that went on with my graduate school friends. They included Dave Smeltzer, Larry Berlin, Larry Scheinman, Fred Jellison, Jane Thompson Schneider, Bill Steslicke, and Jim Herndon.

For years I have tried out ideas that appear here (often in primitive form) in both graduate and undergraduate courses in political theory. In particular I would like to thank Maeve Kim, Ron Bayer, Barry Shapiro, Harriet Zuckerman, Jim Knauer, Jon Plebani, Sam Martineau, Debbie Rosenthal, Sherri DeWitt, Mike Turner, Dave Schultz, Gary Shiffman, Bob Rosh, Kent Trachte, Jeff Wengrofsky, Rainer Forst, who made a special contribution as a visitor from Germany, Kathy Doherty, Martin Hwang, Frank Cohen, Kristin Broderick, John Camobreco, Theresa Wilson, Michael Andrew, Shawna

Sweeney, and Jonathan Spence. Their comments, questions, and arguments made this a better book than it would otherwise be. Kimberly Maslin-Wicks also belongs on this list and for the past two years has been an invaluable research assistant, rummaging through the library, proofreading, checking footnotes, and attempting to teach me to spell several common English words. In the spring of 1995, she, along with Michelle Barnello, Therese Caruso, and Scott Pandich, participated in a seminar on Tocqueville. That seminar shaped my treatment of him and, because of the range and sweep of his work, influenced many other aspects of the final version of this study. Roy Cager, Jennifer Willower, and Dawn McKibben also made useful contributions on this subject. I am also indebted to Michelle Barnello, who keyed the end notes to the appropriate text pages. My deep apologies to anyone inadvertently omitted.

I also owe a general debt of gratitude to Jim and Sondra Farganis. For thirty years we have talked and often argued about politics and society. They will find things to disagree with here too, but this book would not be what it is without our endless conversation. Now we will have something new to argue about.

This study has had a long genesis; it is tempting to say that it began in the back of my mind with my first encounter with Louis Hartz in spring 1957. More formally, it started in 1981 with the draft of several chapters for a book on liberalism and its critics; the discussion of Locke here is a much revised version of one of those pieces. In the same year I was invited to give a paper on "Equality and the Welfare State" at the meeting of the Northeast Political Science Association and to appear on a panel on authority at the American Political Science Association convention. These opportunities set my thinking off in some new directions, and fragments of what I wrote then are scattered throughout this work. Before returning to the larger study of liberalism in general, I was diverted by an invitation to write a long chapter on American political thought from the Revolution to the Civil War. It would be translated into German as "Amerikanisches politisches Denken: Von der Revolution bis zum Bürgerkrieg" and included in *Piper's Handbuch der Politischen Ideen,* Band 3, edited by Irving Fetscher and Herfried Münkler, pp. 617–653. In much expanded and revised form, this article forms the basis for Chapters 3 through 7 of this book.

Two other articles are closely related to what appears here. The first offered me a chance to publish a preliminary overview of the argument in a Memorial Festschrift for my friend John Lees: "The Hartz Thesis Revisited," in *Studies in U.S. Politics,* edited by David Adams (Manchester: Manchester University Press, 1989), pp. 24–45. It is a matter of deep regret that I could not discuss the themes of this book with John. The other is also a Festschrift piece in honor of my dear friend Kurt Shell, whose imprint is also on this book: "The Theory of the Liberal Consensus and the Politics of Interpretation," in *Liberale Demokratie in Europa und den USA,* edited by Franz Gress and Hans Vorländer (Frankfurt: Campus Verlag, 1990), pp. 34–48.

A number of friends have read all or part of the manuscript in various stages. Isaac Kramnick and George Armstrong Kelly both read the *Handbuch* article in its original English version. Both provided needed encouragement to go on with the larger project and gave me valuable advice. I owe a special debt to George Kelly, whose well-known generosity was very much in evidence in the time and care he took to read the early thoughts of someone he barely knew. Those who knew him would not be surprised by the quality of his advice. I am sure the book is the poorer since he did not live to see its final form.

Isaac Kramnick did read the entire manuscript as it developed, even when he had pressing commitments of his own. I owe much to him, particularly, but by no means exclusively, for sharing with me his unexcelled knowledge of eighteenth-century Anglo-American thought.

Wilson Carey McWilliams also read the entire manuscript, to my great benefit, drawing on his enormous understanding of American thought and politics to raise questions, open up new problems, and guide me through literature I would otherwise have overlooked.

The last six chapters were read in draft by George Kateb and Michael Walzer, each of whom may have had a clearer idea of what I was trying to do there than I did myself. In any event, both of them led me to state more clearly my own theoretical aims. George Kateb saved me from at least one foolish error, and his pointed questions forced me to clarify the argument in several places. Michael Walzer tried to teach me to curb my penchant for what he aptly called "diversionary inclusiveness." If the arguments march in anything like a straight line, he deserves much of the credit. My debt to his writings will be evident throughout.

To my great benefit, Westview Press wisely commissioned Robert Booth Fowler to read the penultimate draft, a feat he accomplished in startlingly short time. His mix of warm support and penetrating observation led me to deepen the historical background in a number of places and above all to keep the argument sharply focused on the consensus theory. If this book reads like a coherent whole, much of the credit goes to him.

At Westview Press, I owe an enormous debt to Spencer Carr, who encouraged the project from the start and then patiently put up with the progress of an overlong, overdue manuscript. His faith in this book has meant more to me than he can imagine. For any readability I have achieved I am deeply obligated to my marvelous copy editor, Marian Safran. I also thank Libby Barstow and Beth Partin for their excellent editorial assistance.

It goes with saying that none of these generous people are responsible for the errors of omission and commission that doubtless remain.

Finally my family. This study has been a long time in the making, and there have been many ups and downs. My wife, Gladys, has been through all of them with me. I can only say that without her, there would be no book. Many years ago, I thanked Jim and Susan, who were then small, for their unwitting help on a previous study. Now they are grown and their presence in my mind still urges me on. So too does my feeling for the new members of my family, Ellen Ward and Andrew Schmidt. For all their sakes, I hope one day to be able to paint a less bleak portrait of the condition of American democracy.

James P. Young
June 1995

RECONSIDERING AMERICAN LIBERALISM

Introduction:
The Role of Liberalism
in American Politics

WILLIAM FAULKNER told us that the past was not dead; it was not even past. This insight is politically important because, as Thomas Hobbes wrote, "Out of our conceptions of the past we make a future."[1] That implied that the past was not simply *there;* it was not just an inert object waiting to be discovered. In order for us to understand our past and thus to shape our future, we must first interpret it. What we must come to understand, in Sheldon Wolin's term, is our *birthright*, that is, those "historical moments when collective identity is collectively established or reconstituted."[2] Such moments are historically ambiguous, and their meanings are often contested. Therefore they must be interpreted if we are to be "able to reconnect past and present experience." And that, in turn, "calls for a citizen who can become an interpreting being, one who can interpret the present experience of the collectivity, reconnect it to past symbols, and carry it forward."[3] It is our theoretical understanding of past and present that helps to make us a people. Thus, the Constitution is part of our political inheritance, but the interpretation of its origins and its substantive meaning is highly contested.[4] The understanding we achieve of this and other aspects of our history shapes our politics and culture in the most direct way. It is with interpretation of this sort that this book is concerned.

There is also another, connected, interpretive concern. If, somewhat tendentiously, we translate Wolin's vocabulary into that of Michael Walzer, then birthright seems, on the surface, closely related to the idea of "shared understandings," which is central to the latter's work. Citizens, Walzer tells us, share a world of meanings. Precisely what those meanings are and how they require us to act politically are not always clear and indeed may be a source of conflict. It is perhaps not too much to say that that kind of interpretive

1

question is what much of politics is about in a democratic society and that those debates are vital, particularly if, as Walzer says: "Justice and equality can conceivably be worked out as philosophical artifacts, but a just or an egalitarian society cannot be. If such a society isn't already here—hidden, as it were, in our concepts and categories—we will never know it concretely or realize it in fact."[5] In this view too, then, political ideas and their interpretation are not matters of abstract, purely academic interest but are instead questions of the highest political importance. Democratic politics and, particularly, democratic leadership—Lincoln in the crisis of the Civil War period is an especially apt example—involve an attempt to interpret the often submerged logic of the shared understandings that hold a society together.

Since 1955, when Louis Hartz published *The Liberal Tradition in America*, the dominant interpretation of American political thought and culture has been the one advanced in that great book.[6] Hartz's study represents the high point of the "consensus school" in American historiography, which was initiated in 1948 by Richard Hofstadter's pioneering and iconoclastic work, *The American Political Tradition*. The paradigm stemming from the Progressive period in the early years of the twentieth century had focused on a series of presumably epic conflicts: agrarian versus commercial interests, haves versus have-nots, Jeffersonians versus Hamiltonians. But, Hofstadter argued, these conflicts masked an unusually high level of consensus, a commitment, as he put it, to an "ideology of self-help, free enterprise, competition, and beneficent cupidity." He went on, "However much at odds on specific issues, the major political traditions have shared a belief in the rights of property, the philosophy of economic individualism, the value of competition; they have accepted the economic virtues of capitalism as necessary qualities of man."[7] These ideas not only have political resonance but also, as Hofstadter noted, are among the central tenets of the liberal capitalism that has been so vital a part of American culture.

The contribution of Louis Hartz was to cast this argument in more explicitly political and more general, theoretical terms; at the same time he tried to explain the origins of this consensus. Hartz proposed that we should take seriously the often repeated observation that America is a historically unique nation. Fruitfully using Marxian categories to arrive at Tocquevillian conclusions,[8] Hartz contended that America has experienced a kind of inverted Law of Combined Development, skipping the feudal stage of history, as Leon Trotsky had argued that Russia had leaped over the bourgeois, middle-class interlude. The latter is, by contrast, the heart of the American worldview. Since we have not had a history of an organic, hierarchically organized, feudal society, Hartz, following Tocqueville, noted that the result was that Americans were "born equal" rather than having had to become so.[9]

Consequently, American thought is profoundly middle-class liberal in its basic orientation. Americans have never seriously considered any ideological or philosophical alternatives, a fact that has led to a certain intellectual rigidity—noticed particularly by Tocqueville—and that has raised the specter of massive pressures to conform to the universally held tenets of liberal culture. Hartz described this consensus as deeply, even irrationally, "Lockean" in character. As he put it: "Locke dominates American political thought, as no thinker anywhere dominates the political thought of a nation. He is a massive national cliché." It is not, of course, that the political theory of John Locke as such was irrational; it is rather the way in which it was absorbed into the American mind without conscious thought that Hartz found notable and also troubling. Still, the meaning of "Lockeanism" was never precisely defined in Hartz's book, although he did refer to "the reality of atomistic social freedom" as the "master assumption" of American political thought.[10] This last point, I will argue, is a great overstatement, though such a concept of freedom is a powerful recurrent force in U.S. politics. However, to insist on this concept as the essence of the tradition is to give way to a misleading simplification. But beyond this very contestable and contested theory of human nature, liberalism clearly stood in Hartz's work for such basic ideas as constitutionalism, capitalism, and a formal commitment to political and legal, if not economic, equality. Moreover, at least in Hartz's version, liberalism was clearly democratic in character. Surely these ideas are near the heart of American political thought.

According to Hartz, the depth of these attachments has frozen American thought and politics at the center of the political and ideological continuum. The result is that America has not experienced the development of a traditionalist, European-style conservatism or, still less, any politically significant form of socialism. Further, American politics has been notable for a distinctively lower level of class conflict than has been typical of other advanced capitalist, industrial societies. These are compelling considerations, and there is no doubt that the Hartz thesis explains a great deal about the politics and history of the United States. At the minimum, the liberal tradition, if it does not cause the peculiarities of American politics, acts as a powerful limiting factor on its development.[11] If we cannot seriously contemplate ideas or policies that fall outside the liberal framework, then the system has a powerful tendency toward self-perpetuation, both politically and economically, though the rigidities inherent in the narrow range of allowable ideas may well threaten that perpetuation in the long run.

However, in spite of its power, the Hartz thesis is flawed and has not gone without critical scrutiny. First, Hartz began his analysis with the Revolution, thus leaving out 168 years of colonial history. The result, of course, was that the profoundly formative experience of Puritanism was almost entirely ignored. This is unfortunate because, although it can be argued that Puritanism, in a nice example of the law of unintended consequences, might well have contributed to the development of liberalism, it certainly was not in itself liberal and therefore did not fit easily with the thesis of the absolute dominance of the liberal creed.

Second, although it is certainly true that the United States never passed through a feudal period, an analysis of colonial life suggests that there were significant vestiges of hierarchy. Those vestiges, which took particularly deep root in the slave South, were a source of some tension.

Third, according to significant research carried out in the years since Hartz wrote, the ideas of neoclassical republicanism were very important in the Revolution and perhaps for a considerable time thereafter. This theory stemmed ultimately from Aristotle and reached these shores by way of Machiavelli, the English republicans of the seventeenth century, and the "Country" opposition to the Walpole government in eighteenth-century England. Like Puritan thought, neoclassical republicanism, in its rejection of individualism and the pursuit of self-interest, is not a liberal theory. Proponents of Hartz's view must take republicanism into account, even if, in the end, they treat it as less important than the "republican synthesis," which has been advanced by some as a fundamental alternative to the thesis of liberal dominance. Although I believe that the significance of the republican synthesis has been much exaggerated, it nonetheless provides an interesting complication for the theory of liberal ideological hegemony.

Fourth, a theory of consensus must face the fact of the ubiquity of conflict in American history. There are severe limits to a model that offers a consensual interpretation of the history of a nation, when the central event of that history is a civil war. And the Civil War is not the only problem, for, as Robert Dahl has pointed out, there has been intense, seriously disruptive conflict approximately once a generation through the course of U.S. history. Aside from the Civil War, the Revolution, and the framing of the Constitution, the disruptive events include the struggle over the Alien and Sedition Acts in the Washington administration, the crisis over the Hartford convention in 1815, the battle over the tariff and nullification during the Jackson presidency, the trauma of Reconstruction, the adjustment to the rapid post–Civil War emergence of large-scale industrial capitalism that transformed the structure of the economy, the Great Depression of the 1930s, and the civil rights revolution of the 1960s.[12] And to those must be added the deeply wounding conflict over the Vietnam War and the continuing crisis in race relations, which has now taken on a new dimension as part of the controversy over multiculturalism. Because the particularist advocates of the latter have claimed that the universalism of liberalism was a sham—merely empty words—the idea of multiculturalism is not easy to reconcile with the individualism of liberal principles. Nor should the deep conflicts over the "social issues"—abortion, crime, drugs, the family, sexual orientation—be ignored. This is a long list of conflicts for a "consensual" society to display.

Surely Richard Hofstadter was right when he argued that "consensus, to be effective, must be a matter of behavior as well as thought, of institutions as well as theories."[13] Further, if, as in Wolin's term, it is events such as these and their assimilation into the culture that constitute the "birthright" of Americans, the historical inheritance that shapes the national identity,[14] then conflict as much as consensus appears to be central to the tradition of American politics. Put differently, it is obvious that major conflict can occur within a framework of widely shared ideas.

Two other points require further notice. The first is that although Americans may have the social attitudes of a people "born equal," the nation is by no means egalitarian as a matter of empirical reality, regardless of how one understands equality. However, if one looks at the question in the comparative perspective of a Tocqueville, the point behind his observation about Americans being born equal becomes clear. Nonetheless, the manifest inequalities in American society have been, and no doubt will continue to be, sources of serious political conflict.

The second point is that for Hartz, liberalism and democracy were so closely intertwined as to be virtually indistinguishable. However, this is a somewhat problematic assumption. Liberalism and democracy are terms and movements that have separate histories. Essentially, as Russell Hanson succinctly pointed out, democracy has to do with a conception of the people as the ultimate authority, whereas liberalism is concerned with limitations on that authority. The suggested opposition is by no means necessary or absolute, but there is a potential tension here.[15] For example, Hanson argued that at the present time democracy is threatened by an excess of liberalism in the area of economics. In contrast, Jennifer Hochschild, in her study of contemporary race relations, argues very forcefully that our difficulties lie in democratically based hostility to blacks, which could be curbed only by the imposition of liberal controls over the inclinations of racist white majorities.[16] Here is not the place to enter into that interesting dispute, which fully illustrates the complexities inherent in the compound notion of liberal democracy. To the extent that the United States is somehow ineradicably liberal and also aspires to be more democratic, a reconciliation of democracy and liberalism is of continuing theoretical and political importance.

Hanson argues that democracy is an essentially contested concept, that is, not only that its meaning was, in fact, in dispute, but that in principle there could be no resolution to the argument.[17] Much of the history of American politics can be told in terms of a struggle to control the meaning of this central notion. The side in a political dispute that can successfully claim the democratic label has a tremendous rhetorical advantage. I would suggest that something analogous can be said about liberalism. At this writing *liberalism* is surely not an honorific term on a par with *democracy*. Still, even when there has been the most conflict in American history, liberalism broadly conceived has been a vital, even if not the only, tradition in American thought.

One thing that is clearly illustrated by Hartz's *Liberal Tradition in America* is the great plasticity of its central term. The history he recounted in his book was a tale of the "pragmatic" adaptation of the liberal tradition while politics remained within the framework outlined by the basic ideas of individualism, capitalism, constitutionalism, and some measure of a rather vaguely defined and often formulaic or even mythological equality. In this perspective, the meaning of the essential elements of liberalism has been a source of much contestation. Given the high level of abstraction of such terms as *liberty, equality,* and *democracy,* the specification of their meaning is in itself a significant source of conflict. Further, a good deal of what is at stake in American politics today is rooted in the question of the continued adaptability of the liberal tradition. In the view of many, liberal ideas have exhausted whatever vitality they might have had. If that is true, then the basic character of U.S. politics is due for a profound change.

Perhaps it is useful to suggest more fully than Hartz the range of meanings attached to the idea of liberalism. At least three major currents of thought have been fitted under the rubric. Common to all is an image of human beings as essentially equal, rights-bearing, interest-oriented individuals— individuals who are entitled to have those rights defended, particularly against governmental intrusion. I call this the liberal idea. It is the foundation of the liberalism of constitutional limitations; its patron saint, so to speak, is John Locke, and its contemporary advocates range from Robert Bork on the "conservative" Right to Lawrence Tribe on the liberal Left. The centrality of this image of human nature is a major part of what allowed Hartz to argue for the critical role of Lockeanism in American political culture.

A second form of liberal theory is economic, free market, or laissez-faire liberalism; its lineage may be traced back to Adam Smith, and its best-known contemporary advocate is economist Milton Friedman, not to mention former president Ronald Reagan. That is the intellectual source of much of the opposition to government regulation of the economy in the Republican Party. This theory is also individualistic and rests on the assumption that the economic laws of the market—supply and demand and so on—will lead to benign outcomes through the self-equilibrating guidance of a "hidden hand." Those outcomes will develop only if government does not interfere with the pursuit of self-interest, on which the system supposedly rests. That is also the version of liberalism that most clearly rests on a theory of "atomistic social freedom."

The third form can be called reform liberalism; its intellectual roots can be seen in the work of John Stuart Mill and Thomas Hill Green in England, and in the thought of John Dewey and the political ideas of the populist and Progressive movements late in the nineteenth and early in the twentieth centuries, the New Deal, Fair Deal, New Frontier, and Great Society programs, and then on to contemporary philosophers such as John Rawls and political leaders such as Edward Kennedy and Bill Clinton. The focus continues to be on the free, equal, rights-bearing individual, but now, it is argued, those individuals may best be served by an active government, though one that, in economics, still adheres to the theory of the market, albeit in regulated form. That view often generates conflict with laissez-faire liberals, who, much to the despair of those who prize neat ideological labels, have come to be known as "conservatives." In any case, the reform tradition dominated American politics for most of this century and lasted until the onset of the Reagan revolution.

It is important to remember that to insist on the relative narrowness of the ideological spectrum is not to assert the unimportance of ideas in the United States. On the contrary, in fact. On one level, as I have argued, the absence of both traditionalist conservatism and any politically viable form of socialism serves as a profoundly limiting factor on the permissible range of sociopolitical alternatives that may plausibly be discussed. On another level, as Hartz observed, "law has flourished on the corpse of philosophy in America."[18] It is that which helps to explain the striking tendency of Americans to turn political questions into matters of constitutional law, to the extent that law often becomes a form of applied political theory. American law is permeated by sometimes confining assumptions rooted in liberal thought, and law is often a major focus of ideological debate, as can be illustrated by the sometimes fierce confirmation battles over nominations to the Supreme Court.

Finally, more important still, Samuel Huntington argues persuasively that the tenacity with which we hold to the liberal creed is, in itself, a major source of political conflict, because when values are so widely held, any deviation from them is bound to receive critical attention.[19] The civil rights movement, for example, certainly gained much of its moral and political force from its ability to appeal to what were presumably among the most deeply held values in the culture, even, or perhaps especially, when they were largely being observed in the breach. One need not share Huntington's distrust of what he rather disdainfully refers to as political "moralism" to feel the force of much of his analysis of American history. In fact, our finest hours probably come when we ask ourselves to live up to the highest principles in liberalism. It is precisely that sort of criticism Walzer has in mind when he tries to show how the "shared values" of a society become powerful weapons in the quest for justice.

A further note of caution must be introduced. Huntington is certainly correct to insist on the importance of the "liberal creed." However, as Rogers Smith observed, he overestimated both the unchanging nature of the consensus and the highly abstract nature of the ideas that it included.[20] Much of this critique, as I have already implied, can be applied to Hartz as well. Although Hartz was fully aware of the continual transformations of the liberal tradition, he did overstress, I think, a politics of "pragmatic" adaptation and, as Dahl and Wolin suggest, downplay the significance of intense conflict in the course of U.S. history. Once again, one reason for conflict is surely the abstract nature of the principles that make up the liberal tradition. It is one thing, for example, to endorse liberty and equality, but many will argue that there is an inevitable tension, if not direct conflict, between the two ideas when we try to implement them. I would prefer to argue, as does Michael Walzer, that liberty and equality stand best when they stand together,[21] but that argument only reinforces the point that these concepts are highly abstract and that the attempt to apply them is likely to breed conflict and debate. I am not denying the earlier assertion that liberalism acts as a powerful limiting force on U.S. politics, but rather insisting that there is ample room for serious conflict even within the confines of the tradition.

A few general thoughts on the relation of conflict and consensus in politics and culture are in order. There can be no perfectly consensual politics; the very idea of politics implies conflict. An essential aspect of the political problem is to find a way to resolve those conflicts peacefully, generally within a framework of rules that are part of a regime's consensus. Theorists may differ over the source of the rules. For those with ancestors as diverse as Thomas Hobbes and Karl Marx, the focus is on conflict. Either by nature or because of the structure of the preexisting society, society is seen to be essentially noncooperative, so that it is force rather than a system of shared values that ultimately holds it together. Any apparent consensus reflects the power of the dominant elites to impose their will on others so as to create a system of ideas supportive of the status quo. A second view, often associated with the implicitly conservative Parsonian sociology that was dominant in the 1950s, and before Parsons, with turn-of-the-century French sociologist Emile Durkheim, finds it impossible to imagine a society held together largely by force, so that consensus rests on a more or less spontaneously generated set of commonly held values. A social system without such a set of social values would be seen by theorists of the consensus school to be in danger of self-destruction.[22]

Neither of these views is entirely adequate by itself, and thus the mix between consensus and coercion is one of the defining characteristics of any political regime. This mixture is one of the theoretical issues at stake in the attempt to ascertain the broad outlines of American politics and history. Richard Hofstadter, who in some sense started it all, drew back from many of the implications of the consensus model. There surely can be no doubt, he wrote in one of his last works, that the consensus theory was a needed corrective to the Progressive model, since even the most devoted Marxist should be able to perceive the "pervasively liberal-bourgeois character of American society in the past." (In fact, some Marxists have come to insist on this point.) And yet, Hofstadter went on, the consensus framework has some "intrinsic limitations *as history.*" He said that the proposition was essentially negative in that its primary use was to outline the limits of conflict in U.S. history.[23] The criticism is fair, but such a use is still an important, though sometimes overlooked, function of a historical theory. Louis Hartz displayed his own sense of this when he wrote, apropos the relation between conflict and consensus, "You do not get closer to the significance of an earthquake by ignoring the terrain on which it takes place."[24]

Hartz was fully aware that his was a single-factor analysis of the American tradition. Such an analysis can have great utility. It is like sitting in a darkened room and aiming a flashlight at the wall. If the beam is direct, it will illuminate a small area with great clarity, though leaving much of the wall in darkness. If the beam is aimed at an angle, the area covered will be greater, though the light will be less intense. So it is in the use of a theory. *The Liberal Tradition in America* illuminates some important aspects of our politics with great intensity, but nevertheless, and with all due respect to Hartz's masterpiece, conflict recedes into the background and what often seem to be intricate but rather arcane variations on the consensus theme come to the fore. There is no question of the great, perhaps unique, importance of liberalism in U.S. politics and history, but surely there is more to be said.

What I think needs to be recovered is a greater feeling for complexity and subtlety in our sense of the past, such as that suggested by Lionel Trilling. Focusing his attention on Progressive historian V. L. Parrington's *Main Currents in American Thought,* Trilling suggested that the title metaphor needed modification. "A culture," he wrote, "is not a flow, nor even a confluence; the form of its existence is struggle, or at least debate—it is nothing if not a dialectic."[25] For Parrington, history consisted of pitting the good guys against the bad guys in the most Manichaean way. But for Trilling, history was filled with "variousness, possibility, complexity, and difficulty,"[26] not to mention, one might add, a great deal of ambiguity. For him the dialectic was neither Marxist nor Hegelian—in fact, dialogue might have been a better term—but the tension and conflict were there, as was a strong sense of the centrality of liberalism, combined with an equally strong sense that the tradition needed criticism, from within if necessary.[27]

In recent years there has been no shortage of criticism. Beset by the unpopular war in Vietnam, deteriorating race relations, stagflation, and the hostage crisis in Iran, the reform liberal New Deal coalition, which had, even in its dotage, remained a vital force in American electoral politics, finally self-destructed, and Ronald Reagan was elected president in 1980. Current policy battles take place on terms largely defined by the conservative Right, though a chastened reformism was elevated to power with the election of Bill Clinton in 1992. On another level, the formal legal consensus seemed somewhat more secure with the appointment of Justices Ginsburg and Breyer, though the meaning of the Bill of Rights is constantly debated and changes in the membership of the Supreme Court and congressional action could lead to alteration. Moreover, the court is deeply divided, and important decisions in the spring of 1995 create significant ambiguity about its position on issues such as affirmative action, or more precisely, minority set-aside provisions, in federal contracting procedures. They also appear to be in retreat from the historic commitment to school desegregation, and a decision on congressional districting reinterprets the Voting Rights Act in a way that threatens recently created black majority seats. Conflict over this issue will be prolonged and intense.

It may be the conflicts over the rights associated with social issues that threaten consensus most, but there are ominous signs of a deep discontent with the major social institutions that goes beyond mere rejection of any specific policies. We have seen a decline in the intangible thing that Richard Hofstadter referred to as "comity," the condition that

> exists in a society to the degree that those enlisted in its contending interests have a basic minimal regard for each other: One party or interest seeks the defeat of an opposing interest on matters of policy, but at the same time seeks to avoid crushing the opposition, denying the legitimacy of its existence or its values, or inflicting upon it extreme and gratuitous humiliations. . . . The basic humanity of the opposition is not forgotten, civility is not abandoned; . . . an awareness that the opposition will someday be the government is always present.[28]

As perhaps in all nations, the level of comity rises and falls in America. At present it is at a low ebb. The intensification of social, racial, and religious tensions, combined with the growth of single-issue politics, points strongly in this direction. Perhaps the clearest example is the intense sociocultural-religious conflict over the abortion question. But the conduct of the 1994 congressional elections is perhaps an even better indicator. Turnout was low and electioneering was accompanied by uniquely vicious negative television advertising on both sides. A climax of sorts was reached when the incoming speaker of the House blamed the moral climate established by the Democratic Party for the tragic murder of two small children by their mother and announced that liberal Democrats were enemies of "normal Americans." This is not a sign of health in a liberal democracy.

Such conditions can erode the legitimacy of a regime. Concerning the religious crisis of early modern Europe, Michael Walzer writes:

> The process of destruction is very complex. What occurs is a slow erosion of the old symbols, a wasting away of the feelings they once evoked, an increasingly disjointed and inconsistent expression of political ideas, a nervous insistence upon the old units and references—all this accompanied, willy-nilly, by a more and more arbitrary and extravagant manipulation of them—until finally the units cease to be accepted as intellectual givens and the references cease to be meaningful. But . . . the systems are replaced even as they are called into question. And the more profound the questioning, the more adventurous is the search for replacements.[29]

If Walzer is right that a just society cannot be created unless its outlines are already present in the shared understandings that underlie it, then there is enough evidence of the symbolic disorder he described in earlier times to disquiet observers of contemporary U.S. politics. His critics, such as J. Peter Euben, suggest that is the case, and Sheldon Wolin's work on American collective identity also seems predicated on a sense of greater political and cultural division than Walzer might see, though the latter is surely not devoid of a sense of social conflict. (In any case, it is my view that a revival of the democratic Left is most likely to occur somewhere within the range of ideas demarcated by Wolin's populism and Walzer's social democratic theory.)

Those are among the themes to be explored in what follows. In brief, I will argue that Hartz overstated a good case by insisting that liberalism has been dominant in American culture from the very start. America, to adapt Hartz and Tocqueville, instead of being born liberal, became so through the course of its frequently stormy history, though Hartz was surely correct to insist on the early importance of liberal ideas. I will sketch this development and try to show the ways the liberal consensus has narrowed the range of choice in U.S. politics, as well as the nature of the conflicts to which it has given rise. My aim will be to restore some of the sense of complexity Trilling suggested was missing from much interpretation of American life.[30]

Since this study is not a comprehensive interpretation of all of American politics and thought, I will focus particularly, though not exclusively, on political economy in the broadest sense, including the central place of capitalist, free market liberalism, attempts to reform and control it, the intellectual, political, and constitutional framework in which its development has taken place, its relation to democracy, and also the critical role of conflicts over race, ethnicity, and gender that are so central to contemporary politics and that have such deep roots in our past.

I want also to explore what is commonly taken to be a crisis in liberal thought and politics today. That crisis may be taken somewhat schematically to revolve around the question of whether the liberal tradition has at long last been exhausted. Historically, American liberalism has displayed great flexibility, which allowed it to adapt to changing conditions while remaining within the admittedly loose confines of the framework spelled out by the Hofstadter/Hartz theory of consensus. Is it possible to renew the vitality of the tradition yet again? In the concluding chapters, I will explore this problem. Is there life left in liberalism in any of its forms? As part of my answer, I will attempt to synthesize a new liberalism, developed as I go along, which, though not currently politically popular, seems to me to give some prospect of revitalizing liberal politics and democratic thought. If it cannot do so, then Americans may be at a truly momentous turning point in their history.

To set the stage for an analysis of the present discontents there is need for an extensive historical discussion. In the next two chapters I will first consider the Puritan heritage and then briefly sketch the political theory of John Locke to serve as a point of reference for the Hartz thesis. After that I will discuss the complex thought of the American founding, including the Revolution, the debates over the ratification of the Constitution, and the political battle to interpret and define the meaning of the constitutional text, once it was adopted. It is this founding period that provides the framework within which much of subsequent U.S. politics takes place.

• 1 •

The Ambiguous Legacy of Puritanism

IT IS EXTRAORDINARILY DIFFICULT for secularized, twentieth-century Americans to understand the Puritan inheritance. They see the Puritans through a haze of competing mythologies. On the one hand there is the famous remark of H. L. Mencken to the effect that Puritanism was the nagging fear that someone, somewhere, might be happy, and on the other there is the pietistic hagiography to which all are subjected each year at Thanksgiving. Each, of course, is a gross caricature, and neither begins to come close to capturing the intellectual sophistication of Puritan theology and political theory. The difficulty is that the Puritans seem to have inhabited another, long-gone world.

This last point is especially important in discussing the Hartz thesis. One implication of that theory is that since liberalism is an essentially modern ideology, it follows that from the very beginning the United States has been a quintessentially modern nation. But Puritanism was a complex mix of the modern and the premodern, so that Hartz's thesis, although still very powerful, is oversimplified. A brief exploration of Puritan theological and political ideas illustrates the problem.

Puritan Doctrine

It would be hard to overestimate the importance of the fact that the most dynamic settlements in the American colonies were populated by dissenting Protestants. Of course, the earliest colonial beachhead was at Jamestown, Virginia, in 1607. But from an intellectual and cultural point of view, the northern colonies, founded by accident by settlers aiming for Virginia, were much more important. The first wave came in 1620 with the sailing of the

Mayflower and the establishment of Plymouth by the Pilgrims. However, the creation of the Massachusetts Bay Colony by the Puritans in 1630 was to have even more important repercussions. Though also, like their predecessors, in revolt against the authority of the Church of England, the Puritans were more worldly and more intellectually sophisticated than their brethren in Plymouth. For various reasons, they rapidly dispersed throughout much of New England. And, of course, they spread a body of doctrine.

In somewhat formal, schematic terms, Puritanism can be defined as "theocratic, congregational-presbyterian, Calvinistic, protestant, medieval Christianity."[1] Medieval Christianity implies the dominance of religion and an Augustinian belief in two worlds—the City of God and the City of Man. The City of Man is corrupt, but it can be saved by faith and faith alone. The dominance of religion implies a theocratic state, but a state influenced by the Protestant revolt against the hierarchy of the medieval Catholic church in the interest of a purification intended to restore the once pristine condition of the faith. But if Protestantism represents an attempt to "purify and conserve" traditional Christianity, then Calvinism is something more, an effort, as Ralph Barton Perry put it, to "save protestantism both from its enemies and from itself."[2] Protestantism contains within itself profound disintegrative tendencies, and John Calvin proposed a set of rules, ranging far beyond theology, to bring order to this potential chaos. The Calvinists were militants, the "shock troops" of Protestantism, as Perry called them. Having formed a mass movement, they have been called the prototype of the modern revolutionary party.[3] Congregationalism and Presbyterianism represent alternatives not only to the papacy but also to the Episcopalian hierarchy of the Anglican church, which was the principal target of Puritan discontent. It is not important to distinguish here between those two forms of Protestant church government; it is sufficient to note that for both, the authority of the church stems from the community of the church membership. This need not necessarily imply a democratic form of church organization, since the clergy may still be vested with a great deal of power. However, both Presbyterian and Congregationalist forms insist on the principle that authorities are chosen by and responsible to believers, who are equal at least before God, even if not in their social relations.[4]

This is a complex body of ideas that must be further explored, but enough has been said to suggest that Puritanism presents a difficult historical problem for the Hartz thesis, since, while having clear roots in an earlier time, it equally clearly looks forward to some of the most significant aspects of modernity. It is this paradox that may account for the wide range of responses to the ideas and institutions of Puritanism.

Perry Miller's remarks suggest the interpretive range. In the 1930s, he pointed out, it was common, as a reaction to the pietistic writers who insisted on making the Puritans into prophets of the Constitution and the Bill of Rights, to stress that they were not at all liberal and to underline the "authoritarian, the totalitarian elements in a complex and sophisticated philosophy." Later, a contrary disposition took hold, and it became more usual to "dwell upon the inherent individualism, the respect for private conscience, the implications of revolution, nurtured by Puritan doctrine." Neither interpretation, Miller hastened to add, constituted more than a "partial apprehension of the reality."[5]

To see Puritanism more clearly, it is necessary to penetrate the clouds of myth that tend to obscure the subject. First, and perhaps most contrary to the historical pieties, the Puritans were not advocates of religious toleration but, rather, "professed enemies of it."[6] Their purpose was to worship as they pleased and not to allow others in their community to worship as *they* pleased. Nor were the Puritans concerned in any modern sense with the separation of church and state: Their government was a *theocracy*. To use that term is somewhat controversial, since the civil magistrates were not ministers. However, the Puritans themselves used the concept of theocracy to suggest the coming together of the sacred and the secular. There was thus a "harmony between minister and magistrate in church and state affairs." Moreover, Perry Miller wrote, at that time "very few men would even have grasped the idea that church and state could be distinct. For the Puritan mind it was not possible to segregate a man's spiritual from his communal life."[7]

Society was conceived as an organic whole, in which government was to play an active part. There was no Jeffersonian liberal ideal of the minimal state. The Hobbesian conception of liberty as the absence of external restraints is at the center of the liberal tradition, but it was simply not in evidence among the Puritans. Rather, as John Winthrop put it, there was "liberty to that only which is good, just and honest."[8] This is much closer to the idea of positive liberty, the concept that we are truly free only when we obey our true will, a will that is always for the good, even though we may not recognize it, than it is to any liberal version of the theory of liberty. From here it is only a step to the famous formula of Rousseau that held, in words that to a liberal mind seem supremely paradoxical at best, that we might legitimately be "forced to be free."[9]

The Puritans had a very strong community bound together by a powerful sense of religious fellowship.[10] Individuals were expected to subordinate their personal interests to the common good. Again Winthrop was to the point: "The care of the public must oversway all private respects . . . for it is a true rule that particular estates cannot subsist in the ruin of the public."[11] There was thus an almost civic republican sense of what we today would call the primacy of the public interest—a primacy that is quite at variance with the liberal stress on the pursuit of self-interest.

Puritanism, Michael Walzer tells us, was a "revolution of the saints,"[12] and it is perhaps not too much to add that the governmental result was a dictatorship of the saints. Nonetheless it was "a dictatorship, not of a single tyrant, or of an economic class, or of a political faction, but of the holy and regenerate."[13] Still, active participation in the governance of the community was restricted to members of the church, and nonmembers were expected to hold their silence. Even for the "saved," it was not an egalitarian society in the usual sense of the word. "In all times," Winthrop preached, "some must be rich, some poor, some high and eminent in power and dignity, others mean and in subjection."[14] Nor was there any question that the magistrates were to be obeyed: "Liberty is maintained and exercised in a way of subjection to that authority." As a result, men should "quietly and cheerfully" submit to those in office.[15] That they should do so was simply to give due recognition to the fallen state of man, for which government was a just punishment.

Obviously these are not the typical principles of a modern liberal democratic society. Yet they are part of the foundation of American political culture. But Puritanism is more complex in its implications than those ideas alone suggest. Whatever the predilections of the Puritan divines, their theories, in a superb illustration of the law of unintended consequences, often contributed to some of the basic ideas and practices of liberal democracy.

Some Consequences of Puritanism

First, it is important to stress that the "dictatorship" of the saints was not absolute. Puritanism took over the position of the parliamentary side in the English Civil War that held that even government had to be subordinated to a law more fundamental than its own statutes.[16] In New England, of course, the source of such law was the Bible, but the idea itself was capable of surviving into a more secular age and contributed to the development of constitutionalism. In addition, the idea of a fundamental law was closely related to the idea of a social contract. And after all, there are few documents with greater symbolic resonance in all of American history than the Mayflower Compact, concluded at the very outset of the Puritan experiment. It was a founding document outlining the high ideals that were presumably to guide and indeed structure society. Although the Puritans did not think of the theory of social contract in the same formal terms as Thomas Hobbes and John Locke had, it is not hard to imagine that the Puritan mentality was susceptible to the use of these formal doctrines in a later, more secular period.

Second, in spite of the strong communitarian impulse of the Puritans, there was also, at the same time, a genuinely individualistic, voluntarist side to both theory and practice. Because of the Calvinist emphasis on a determinist theology of predestination, that other side of Calvinism is often overlooked. Nevertheless, Protestantism in general involves a stripping away of the intermediaries between the individual and God. Individual "saints" entered into the church voluntarily in pursuit of their calling, and at the end of time they still had to face God alone.[17] This individualistic voluntarism naturally enough carried over into politics. Citizens were indeed expected to submit to authority, but submission was also to be a matter of willed choice, just as in the case of the church.[18] The similarity of this voluntarism to the underpinnings of liberal contract theory, to the idea that the authority of the state rests on individual consent, is apparent.

Third, for the citizens, in spite of lack of commitment to any modern form of egalitarianism, there was an expectation of a high degree of political participation. As George Armstrong Kelly wrote: "One can recognize in early Massachusetts and Connecticut the sprouting germs of republican civic cooperation. Citizenship and mutual help were strict duties in these communities."[19] Even in the face of the pervasiveness and power of the religious creed, it is still possible to argue that "the clergy had less control over politics than anywhere in Europe."[20]

Fourth, and very much more controversial, there is the much debated question of the relation of Protestantism to the origins of capitalism. By all odds, the most powerful statement of the connection between the two was in Max Weber's great study, *The Protestant Ethic and the Spirit of Capitalism*. No such large-scale historical generalization is ever likely to be established beyond doubt. However, Weber's theory, especially when applied to the United States, is wonderfully suggestive.

It is vitally important to remember that Weber was at pains to distinguish the three central concepts: modern Western capitalism, the Protestant ethic, and the spirit of capitalism.[21] Weber's lifelong project was to explain the historical uniqueness of the modern, rationalized, bureaucratized Western world. To this end he focused on the unique Western form of capitalist economic organization. The capitalist adventurer, avid for material gain, has always existed, said Weber. What was unique was "the rational capitalistic organization of (formally) free labour."[22] It was this rational, systematized organization of labor and the origin of the peculiarly Western middle class that, in Weber's view, needed to be explained. The spirit of capitalism is something quite different from this form of organization. It is an ethos, a way of looking at the world in which the key feature is the disciplined pursuit of the summum bonum, a pursuit of more and more money, combined with the sort of asceticism that often goes with highly disciplined behavior.[23] Of great interest to this inquiry is the fact that Weber used extended examples from the works of

Benjamin Franklin to illustrate the spirit of capitalism at work.[24] Time is money, A penny saved is a penny earned, and other familiar axioms of Poor Richard pass in review before us.

The Protestant ethic is still another thing and must not be confused with the spirit of capitalism. It is rooted in the central Calvinist tenet of predestination, which holds that the fate of each person in the afterlife is already determined at birth, that no effort he or she can make will alter that fate, and that there is no way to know in advance what is to happen in the life to come. In Weber's view, the "extreme inhumanity" of this doctrine must have led to "a feeling of unprecedented inner loneliness" for the individual believer.[25] Inevitably the question arose in his mind as to whether he was one of the saved, and his natural instinct was to search for external signs of salvation. In this view the true saint presumably would lead a life designed to serve the glory of God. A life of asceticism and hard work might be such a sign. "Thus," Weber wrote, "the Calvinist, as it is sometimes put, himself creates his own salvation, or, as would be more correct, the conviction of it."[26] As Edmund Morgan has summed up, "Although Weber seems to have believed, erroneously, that Calvinists thought consistent good behavior a sufficient proof of salvation, and although he exaggerated the degree of self-denial that was demanded, he was certainly correct in perceiving that a Calvinist had powerful motives to behave consistently as though he were saved, if only to persuade himself that he was."[27]

Weber's great and controversial move was to link this disciplined, ascetic way of life to the spirit of capitalism. The point is not that Puritans explicitly set out to become capitalists or, still less, to grow rich. It is rather that the Puritan ethic created habits of mind and behavior that proved to be an unintentional seedbed for a radical transformation of the economic order. In Weber's words:

> Asceticism looked upon the pursuit of wealth as an end in itself as highly reprehensible; but the attainment of it as a fruit of labour in a calling was a sign of God's blessing. And even more important: The religious valuation of restless, continuous, systematic work in a worldly calling, as the highest means to asceticism, and at the same time the surest and most evident proof of rebirth and genuine faith, must have been the most powerful conceivable lever for the expansion of that attitude toward life which we have here called the spirit of capitalism.[28]

This theory is powerful in general, and when applied to the American scene, it is, as I have said, extremely suggestive. In particular, it is difficult to avoid the conclusion that the fact that Puritanism took root in New England in a way that it never did in the South played a significant role in the profoundly different economic and cultural development of the two regions.[29] Little in American history is more important and more paradoxical. As

Weber said, "The early history of the North American Colonies is dominated by the sharp contrast of the adventurers, who wanted to set up plantations with the labour of indentured servants, and live as feudal lords, and the specifically middle-class outlook of the Puritans."[30] And yet, of course, it is true that it was in the northern colonies that a full-scale capitalism took root and flourished.

The development of Puritanism was marked by simultaneous processes of secularization and the emergence of capitalism. The societies were dependent on a high degree of religious enthusiasm, and as secularism inexorably advanced, aided and abetted by a developing capitalist economy, a degree of cultural stress was virtually inevitable. There were inroads on the religious commitments required for the system to function, so that, quite unsurprisingly, the dictatorship of the saints began to find that saints were in short supply.[31]

This was a genuine problem for a social system based on a set of religious and political ideals and possessed by a high sense of moral mission. Nonetheless, the conflict between these standards and the self-perceived behavior of the Puritans posed difficulties almost from the very start. John Winthrop had announced, before setting foot on land, "We must consider that we shall be as a city upon a hill, the eyes of all people are upon us."[32] But as early as 1662, Michael Wigglesworth cried out that "God has a controversy with New England." In general, the Puritan ministers seemed to be saying, as Perry Miller wrote, "that New England was sent on an errand and that it had failed."[33]

This disappointment becomes clear when one reads the passionate sermons, lamenting the falling away from the true faith whose pursuit was the essence of the Puritan sense of mission. One may stress the dark side of these jeremiads, as they have come to be called, as did Perry Miller, or, with Sacvan Bercovitch, one may find in them a message of hope, but on either reading they have become one of the most characteristic forms of American political rhetoric.[34] And on either reading, one can sense the feeling of a special calling that pervaded Puritan thought. Winthrop's sermon "A Model of Christian Charity," with its famous reference to the City on the Hill, is redolent of the sense that all history is heading, in Loren Baritz's apt phrase, toward the "cosmic climax of Boston's founding."[35] Such expectations could hardly fail to be disappointed; hence the jeremiad, the "mounting wail of sinfulness, this incessant and never successful cry for repentance."[36]

The jeremiad is an important key to the peculiar ambivalence of Puritan culture. Men enjoined to work hard in a calling dedicated to the greater glory of God began—some of them at least—to grow rich and also to appear to their fellows to be living wealthy and ostentatious lives. Moreover, though the Puritans were not egalitarians, they could not help but be disturbed by the reduction to poverty of some of their number. Slowly, over time, Puritans were being converted into "grasping Yankees."[37] The resulting tensions were inherent in the theoretical self-understanding of the society. The Puritans were much concerned with selfishness, but they were caught up in a society that since early in the eighteenth century had placed great stress on economic motivations. Referring to the "ministerial nagging of the worldlings," Perry Miller captured the dilemma with epigrammatic brilliance. The jeremiads "were releases from a grief and a sickness of the soul which otherwise found no surcease. They were professions of a society that knew it was doing wrong, but could not help itself, because the wrong thing was also the right thing."[38] Waiting in the wings was John Locke, descendant of Puritans, devout Protestant, and, much more directly than the Calvinist clergy, a predecessor of liberal capitalism.

The rhetorical style created by the ambiguities of Puritan doctrine has deep resonance in American thought and politics. Arthur Schlesinger, Jr., sees two conflicting tendencies. On the one hand is "the idea of America as an experiment, undertaken in defiance of history, fraught with risk, problematic in outcome."[39] For Schlesinger, this is an admirable tradition, suffused with a salutary sense of the limits of human action rooted in the profound insights of Augustinian Christianity; it is the "realist" tradition of American politics, the tradition of the framers of the Constitution. But there is a considerably less benign countertradition: a messianic sense of Americans as a chosen people, "a geopolitical specification of the millennium," as Schlesinger wryly puts it.[40] In his view, it is this aspect of the Puritan heritage that has led to the often noted outbursts of a feeling that only America could save the world from communism, make it safe for democracy, or accomplish whatever other prodigious historical mission seemed momentarily to be required.

Samuel Huntington offers a similar, though rather less nuanced view. Huntington places great stress on Protestantism as one of the major sources of the American tradition and points out, "The United States is the only country in the world in which a majority of the population has belonged to dissenting Protestant sects." Indeed, he goes as far as to claim that the English Puritan revolution was "the single most important formative fact of American history." That is because it is the source of our intermingling of religion and politics and "of the moral passion that has powered the engines of political change in America."[41] It is this very moralism that troubles Huntington, since it is a major source of tension as the inevitable gap between the high ideals of the system and the actual performance of its institutions appears. The persistent attempt to close the gap generates a threat to the stability and firm authority needed to govern effectively and particularly to conduct foreign affairs. There is, then, real danger in the politics of "creedal passion." And yet, even Huntington concedes that without these outbursts of moral intensity, it would be hard for the political system to avoid stagnation and decay.[42] Though one may reject Huntington's political views, to which I shall return later, there is little doubt that he accurately identifies one major source of the continuing appeal to high moral principles, real or specious, that is so characteristic of U.S. politics, both at its best and at its worst. And, once again, it is the ambivalence of the Puritan legacy that must be made clear.

Finally, this has been a rights-oriented political culture. It is abundantly clear that the Puritans conceived of a regime in which the individual had to give way to the claims of the community. And yet, the individualism at the heart of their theological convictions has provided a base for the commitment to the rights of the person, which are so central to American thought, even when—perhaps particularly when—those rights are being ignored in practice. There is no situation more likely than this to cause the descendants of Puritans to proclaim their contemporary jeremiads.

In sum then, Puritanism looked both ways. It was not modern, but it paved the way, no doubt unwittingly, for much that is modern. It was certainly neither liberal nor democratic and thus does not fit easily with the Hartz thesis. At the same time, in some aspects of church government, it contained seeds of democracy, and it helped lay the groundwork for what, in secular form, became liberal constitutionalism. Again unintentionally, it provided a basis for the growth of the capitalist economy whose essential hedonism has done so much to undermine Puritan moral values. The Protestant ethic, transformed into the work ethic, is central to the whole of American culture and politics. Puritan ideas were also part of the intellectual background of the American Revolution. And finally, though certainly not least important, they inspired a peculiarly American form of political morality that is very much in evidence to this day. For all their strangeness to us, the Puritans represent a form of idealism, which, though open to abuse, often shows us U.S. politics at its best. As Carey McWilliams writes, "The duty to establish the best city, short of which no failure is adequate or excusable; is that not the definition of the American dream?"[43] Furthermore, although it is clear that the Puritans were not liberals, it is still interesting to note that John Locke, the progenitor of classical liberalism, a profound influence on the Revolution, and the great symbolic heart of the Hartz thesis, was, though not a conventional Calvinist, very much a product of the radical Protestant milieu of seventeenth-century England. I now turn to an analysis of Locke so as to gain insight into the source of the "Lockeanism" that is said to pervade U.S. politics.

· 2 ·

John Locke
and the Theory of
Liberal Constitutionalism

Fʀᴏᴍ ᴛʜᴇ ᴛɪᴍᴇ of the Mayflower Compact, the American colonies had had experience with the practice of government based on an agreement to certain specified principles. It was therefore natural that they would turn toward the social contract tradition in political theory as a device for the legitimation of their political actions. And for reasons to be explored in Chapter 3, it was equally natural that they would turn to John Locke as a model contractarian. However, hovering in the background behind Locke was Thomas Hobbes, the prototypical contract theorist in the Anglo-American tradition. Hobbes presented an altogether harsher view of the problems of politics than did Locke, and a brief sketch of his views is useful as a counterpoint to the work of his successor.

The central idea of all social contract theory is an agreement among free, equal individuals existing in a presocial state of nature to establish society and/or government according to some set of principles rooted in a particular conception of human nature. The idea is to picture human nature as it exists naturally, uncontaminated by the influences of society. It is this conception that is of crucial importance. For Hobbes, the picture was dark indeed. Men were restless, asocial, if not antisocial, atoms, driven by their desires and aversions in a relentless pursuit of the power that made possible such fleeting felicity as was conceivable in the absence of social and political order. The result was the notorious war of all against all, which tended to render felicity—the necessarily impermanent achievement of one's desires—impossible and to generate such a deep fear of violent death that it motivated human beings to enter into a social contract. The social contract obligated them to obey an all-powerful, unlimited sovereign for as long as the sovereign achieved the supreme goal of preserving peace. It should be carefully noted that the social contract creates a society and a state, but it by no means creates a meaningful sense of community. Instead, what is provided is the minimal degree of order that makes it possible for the Hobbesian man to pursue his self-defined personal interests with at least some minimum hope of achieving a modicum of success. Locke, although neither a follower of Hobbes nor an author writing to refute Hobbes, surely had this theory in the back of his mind while he was composing his political writings.

If John Locke is at the core of American political thought, then we need a clearer picture of his theory than the somewhat cryptic allusions offered by Louis Hartz in *The Liberal Tradition in America*. This is by no means easy, for Locke was a complex and perhaps confused thinker. *The Second Treatise of Civil Government* often appears to rest on a series of unresolved tensions and ambiguous formulations. It speaks of majority rule *and* minority rights, a natural right to property, combined with a power to regulate that property that is, by implication, quite extensive, and a theory of consent that, to say the least, requires interpretation. Some critics have been tempted simply to throw up their hands.

The situation is further confused because in the past scholarly generation a number of major studies attempted reassessments of Locke's work and its place in the history of political thought.[1] The extent to which the traditionally received understanding of Locke can be reconciled with the new interpretations or, for that matter, the new views with themselves is a cause of no little controversy. It is well beyond the scope of the present study to attempt a full-scale synthesis, but a few tentative steps in that direction may be possible.

The Theory Outlined

As a point of reference, it may be useful to sketch the outline of Locke's familiar theory as it is set forth in the *Second Treatise*. Like Thomas Hobbes before him, Locke also placed men in a state of nature, but one that was considerably less grim than the terrifying image of his great predecessor. The state of nature was clearly distinct from the state of war; the latter was but a possible situation of man in the presocial condition.[2] "One great reason" to enter society was to avoid the state of war.[3] More generally, the state of nature was beset by certain "inconveniences," the most important of which was perhaps the fact that in nature each man was necessarily judge in his own case in a situation in which the natural law was ambiguous because undeclared.[4]

But, above all, one left the state of nature in order to provide security for property, defined broadly as "lives, liberties, and estates."[5]

Government was created in two steps. Men first contracted with one another to leave nature and create society. In the second step government was established and placed in a fiduciary relationship to the society. Thus the community retained a "supreme power" to remove or alter the legislative power. The supreme power protected the community from the "attempts and designs of anybody, even of their legislatures, wherever they shall be so foolish, or so wicked, as to lay and carry on designs against the liberties and properties of the subject."[6] The ultimate sanction for defending the rights of the people was revolution. Therefore, when the trust was violated, power "devolves to the people who have a right to resume their original liberty."[7] Of course such circumstances were exceptional, and normal political activity took place by means of a consensual process based on the principle of majority rule. It was through such processes that property was not only preserved and protected but also regulated when necessary. Then, "when any number of men have so consented to make one community or government, they are thereby presently incorporated and make one body politic wherein the majority have a right to act and conclude the rest."[8] That, in brief form, is the familiar outline of the most basic arguments of the *Second Treatise*. It is now possible to explore some of the hidden complexities and implications of the theory.

The Individual in Society

The individual is critically important in Locke's political thought, as in liberal theory generally. However, Locke's natural man was profoundly different from the creature theorized earlier by Hobbes, and the differences were vital to the development of the liberal theory of politics. Locke's individualism, unlike that of Hobbes, was deeply rooted in religious convictions. The fundamental source of the individualism of Locke, a descendant of Calvinists, was the belief that salvation itself was ultimately individual. It is important not to exaggerate this point, since Locke's Christianity was very unorthodox. Still, he was very much a theist and very much a Protestant. John Calvin's understanding of the early modern world "reveals his profound affinity with the rationalistic materialism commonly associated with such authors as Hobbes and Locke."[9] The burden of salvation was placed on all men as individuals and was placed on them equally.[10] Implicit and explicit religious commitments permeate Locke's work. Men, in Locke's view, are owned by God.

In his words, "Men being all the workmanship of one omnipotent and infinitely wise maker, all the servants of one sovereign master, sent into the world by his order and about his business, they are his property, whose workmanship they are, made to last during his, not one another's pleasure."[11] It was for this reason that men were "bound" to preserve themselves and insofar as possible "to preserve the rest of mankind."[12]

Thus the right of self-preservation is based on grounds radically different from the fear and prudence that Hobbes saw as motivating men. It is a serious error to try to equate Locke's state of nature to that of Hobbes. The state of nature was one of liberty but not license,[13] and it is important to stress again that the state of nature is not necessarily one of war. Locke was not Hobbes in disguise; the differences are real and they are politically important.[14] For Locke, in the words of Richard Ashcraft, "the natural condition of man is one of uncertain peace."[15] War is a condition that may arise in the state of nature, but it is not the defining condition of that state. Locke's vocabulary is carefully chosen; nature has its inconveniences, but men need not be driven in their desperate fear of violent death to subordinate themselves to an all-powerful and in principle unlimited Leviathan.

Locke's image of man is thus very different from Hobbes's conception of antisocial atoms engaged in mortal conflict. At the least, humans have some tendency toward sociality. At the most, they might be said to be endowed with what Peter Laslett called "natural political virtue." This doctrine "lays it down that all individuals, whether grouped together formally or informally, or even when alone, will have some tendency to allow for the existence, the desires, actions and needs of other men." That is what "accounts for the quasi-social character of the state of nature."[16] In fact, in Laslett's view, the main theme of the *Second Treatise* is "the development of the implications of this doctrine of natural political virtue, defined, checked and safeguarded by the concept of trust."[17] And the common bond that unites human beings is reason.[18] Whatever individual differences exist—and they are real—men do hold this bond in common. There is even a sense of a common good of a sort inconceivable to Hobbes, though still of a powerfully individualistic nature. Thus, in the *First Treatise,* Locke wrote that the public good was "the good of every particular member of that society, as far as by common rules it can be provided for."[19]

There is much to be said for Laslett's interpretation. It can account for the peculiar character of the Lockean state of nature and for some of the critically significant differences that exist between Locke and Hobbes. At the same time, one must be careful not to exaggerate the explanatory power of this doctrine. It should not be used to obliterate Locke's strong sense of the potential for human conflict. It should also be remembered that natural political virtue is an idea nowhere expressly stated by Locke. Finally, and most important, the concept of natural political virtue should not be confused with the Aristotelian idea that man is by nature a political animal. To do so would be to ignore the symbolism of the state of nature—a symbolism that is rendered meaningless if a distinction between the political and the prepolitical condition is not retained. What can be granted is Laslett's point that the distinction is by no means sharp,[20] particularly if one's point of reference is Hobbes.

What Locke's view of the human nature of man offered, for all its ambiguity, was the possibility of developing a rationally based theory for the protection of human rights, which was something Hobbes's anthropological atomism could not do. The claim here is not that Locke was successful in his effort, but that he moved usefully in that direction. We now know that Locke certainly did not write for the purpose of refuting Hobbes; rather, as the *First Treatise* makes clear, his true opponent was Sir Robert Filmer and his doctrine of patriarchal domination.[21] However, this fact should not blur the distinctions between Hobbes and Locke nor make Locke into a covert proponent of Hobbes's ideas. There are elements of liberalism in the thought of Hobbes, particularly in his portrait of individual men in hot pursuit of their interests, but certainly not in his picture of a sovereign in principle unlimited in power. One could say, in effect, that Hobbes started from many of the premises of liberalism, but that he did not use them to reach liberal conclusions. Liberalism is a complex body of ideas, and part of that complexity is captured in the real differences between the antisocial atomism of Hobbes and the incipient, if underdeveloped, sociality of Locke.

Property and the Economy

Locke's theory of property is the central aspect—and one of the most ambiguous and controversial aspects—of his political thought. The first thing to note is that the meaning of *property*, in Locke's most common usage, is much wider than the contemporary sense, limited to material possessions. As we have already seen, for Locke, property comprised life, liberty, and estate. Men had a natural right to the preservation of these goods. However, they might be abridged or regulated, but only with the consent of the governed.[22] The doctrine of consent is highly problematic, but this issue may be deferred for the time being. At present the point to be made is that the right to property is both presocial and prepolitical. Men enter into society and then establish government so that these rights may be secured. It may also be said that life, liberty, and estate are on the same footing analytically. Karen Iverson Vaughn observed: "By defining property as he does, Locke is implying that the government's charge to protect estate is no less important than its charge to protect life and liberty. In this sense, then, government as an institution is subordinate to the requirements of economic activity."[23] The logic is inescapable, although to redress the balance somewhat, one must add that the same logic may require the subordination of government to life and liberty as well. The general point to be made is that Locke called for a downgrading of government, politics, and the political that can best be conceptualized by saying that he made the state subordinate to society. This too is a vital distinction that has important implications in liberal political theory. For the moment, however, let us focus on material property, the component known to Locke as *estate*.

It has long been understood that Locke's doctrines on material property give him a significant place in the development of liberal political economy. Thus, Marx wrote, "Locke's view is all the more important because it was the classical expression of bourgeois society's ideas of right as against feudal society, and more over, his philosophy served as the basis for all the ideas of the whole of subsequent English political economy."[24] C. B. Macpherson, writing under the influence of Marx, labeled Locke a prophet of unlimited capitalist appropriation, and neoclassicist conservative Leo Strauss largely agreed and referred to Locke as an apostle of a Weberian "spirit of capitalism."[25] Certainly, it requires a peculiarly bourgeois cast of mind to consider all rights as property rights,[26] and it is appropriate to note that the definition of property in the "extended" sense—that is, life, liberty, and estate—is not introduced until after the lengthy discussion of material goods that is the subject of Locke's critically important fifth chapter.[27]

Locke's initial problem was to show "how men might come to have a property in several parts of that which God gave to mankind in common."[28] The problem was the individuation or particularization of what had been held by all in common.[29] The earth and everything in it was "given to men for the support and comfort of their being."[30] In particular, it was there for the use of the "industrial and the rational."[31] Consistent with the extended definition of property, "every man has a property in his own person." At least initially, material property was an extension of the individual self, so conceived. Thus the "labour of his body and the work of his hands" belonged to him, so that "whatsoever then he removes out of the state that nature has provided, and left it in, he has mixed his labour with and joined it to something that is his own and thereby makes it his property."[32] However, the accumulation of property was not strictly limited to what a man could create by means of his own labor, for Locke added in a much noted passage that "the grass my horse has bit" and "the turfs my servant has cut . . . become my own property without the assignation or consent of anybody."[33] Thus, Macpherson seems to have been correct in saying that Locke clearly assumed a wage relationship as part of the economic structure of his theory.[34]

The question then arises whether limitations existed as to what could be extracted from the commons and thus become part of a man's private estate. At first Locke cited the existence of certain natural law limitations on property accumulation that had their roots in medieval economic thought. The same natural law that gave us property also bound property. Men were not given the earth to spoil or destroy, and consequently no one might take more of the commons as part of his estate than he could use before it spoiled—the so-called spoilage limitation.[35] Further, men, in accumulating estate, had to leave "enough and as good" for others—the sufficiency limitation.[36]

However, both Strauss and Macpherson argued that these limits were superseded by the invention of money. In this connection, the great virtue of money was that it was "some lasting thing that men can keep without spoiling, and that by mutual consent men would take in exchange for the truly useful but perishable supports of life."[37] Given the existence of money, then, men accumulated differential quantities of property not only because they differed in industry but also because money gave them the opportunity to enlarge their possessions.[38]

It is obvious that the creation of a monetary system has important consequences, among which is the removal of at least some of the natural law limits on property accumulation, most obviously those relating to spoilage. The real question is whether *all* limitations are removed. To argue the strong position is to fly in the face of Locke's text, for he insisted that "the obligations of the law of nature cease not in society but only in many cases are drawn closer."[39] Moreover, it is by no means clear that Locke simply celebrated the invention of money, as the readings of Strauss and Macpherson asked us to believe. Thus, in a somewhat ambiguous passage, Locke referred to a golden age before acquisitiveness and love of luxury had corrupted man.[40] At the least, as John Dunn notes, this suggests a certain disquiet with the development Locke described, although, as Dunn concedes, there is a positive side to the situation. That positive side stems from the generally improved standard of living produced by the new system of incentives,[41] which in turn lends support to the claim that the benefits of economic development supersede the limits of the sufficiency limit. James Tully goes further and argues that in Locke's view money disrupted the natural order that was conducive to the just society; thus government was required to intervene in order to "constitute a new order of social relations."[42] However, it is certain, in spite of all the ambiguities, that Locke believed the existence of a monetary system to be pregovernmental, that this system was conducive to the unequal distribution of material property, that the unequal distribution has been accepted by men, was ratified by the social contract, and that after the contract, "in governments the laws regulate the right of property, and the possession of land is determined by positive constitutions."[43]

The extent of permissible regulation is not specified, nor is it clearly implied. Peter Laslett and Ramon Lemos have both suggested that it could be very extensive. Laslett sums up his view of the logic of Locke's position by saying: "If not complete communism, certainly redistributive taxation, perhaps nationalization could be justified on the principles we have discussed: All that would be necessary is the consent of the majority, regularly and constitutionally expressed, and such a law would hold even if all the property holders were in the minority."[44]

Three important caveats must be added. The first is that it is one thing to note the logical force of Locke's theory, but it is quite another to confuse that logic with his intent, which is a good deal less clear. One may be permitted to doubt, given Locke's close ties to the landholding aristocracy, that this quasi-socialist reading is compatible with what he had in mind. Second, Laslett's last point is a logical artifact of Locke's argument, but it is questionable at the very least, given seventeenth-century suffrage requirements, that the propertied elite ever would, in fact, have been in such a minority position. Laslett's reading seemed to suggest a level of democracy that did not then exist, though Locke's own beliefs on the suffrage question are today in much dispute. However, it can be said with certainty that if Locke was a democrat in any meaningful sense, then he was certainly far in advance of his Whig colleagues. Finally, Locke's majoritarianism must be qualified by his belief in natural law and natural rights; therefore, these additional limits on permissible regulation of property must be considered. These qualifications aside, it is clear that Lockean liberalism is not a theory of laissez-faire and that the logical form, if not the actual substance, of his thought can lend itself to the service of policies often bitterly opposed by contemporary conservatives who are devotees of the unfettered free market and who sometimes embrace Locke's work.

A further observation should be made about the role of the market. Economic markets certainly existed in the time of Locke, but it is important to keep in mind Karl Polanyi's insistence that we not confuse this fact with an assertion that a society entirely permeated by market-oriented decision-making procedures and principles was in place. Such a development was still a hundred years or more away.[45]

However, the preceding discussion should not be taken to mean that Locke cannot properly be seen as a contributor to the development of the political economy of liberal capitalism. Even John Dunn, who is very wary of attempts to connect Locke to the history of capitalism, is very much aware of Locke's view of the positive benefits that flowed from economic development. Leo Strauss stressed this point with particular vigor. The labor that created property converted resources into the "comforts of life." Savage lands—the America of Locke's time—have great resources, but since they are not improved, "a king of a large, fruitful territory there feeds, lodges, and is clad a lot worse than a day labourer in England."[46] It is this positive view, rather than any absolute right to property, that justifies what Strauss called the emancipation of acquisitiveness, and that adds support to the idea that economic development helps to circumvent the natural law "sufficiency limitation" on the accumulation of property. "Far from being straitened by the emancipation of acquisitiveness, the poor are enriched by it. For the emancipation of acquisitiveness is not merely compatible with general plenty, but is the cause of it."[47] The interpretation pursued here suggests that the emancipation is rather less complete than Strauss indicated, but his general point is important and useful; it touches on a theme that has powerful resonance through the entire history of capitalism.

Similarly, Strauss was on the right track when he suggested that Locke illustrated the spirit of capitalism, though it would be more accurate to say that what we really see is the Protestant ethic. Locke's Protestant ideas, however unorthodox, and his Calvinist ancestry may be important here. Even John Dunn, who tends to be resistant to any efforts to link Locke to the development of capitalism, somewhat grudgingly concedes the possibility of a Weberian reading of Locke's place in history.[48] Surely Locke's stress on the importance of rationality and industriousness was close to Weber's understanding of the essence of Protestantism. And make no mistake, Locke had no use for the idle, including the idle rich. On one level, Locke offered a biting critique of nonproductive aristocrats who did not contribute to the project of economic development.[49] Thus Locke was "able to contrast the social values of 'sobriety, frugality, and industry' associated with trade with the 'debauchery' and 'expensive vanity' of 'lazy and indigent people' who 'waste' their resources through extravagant living."[50]

The point is not to make Locke into a twentieth-century radical, or to deny that he had harsh views of the poor, or, still less, to suggest that he did not intend to explain and justify the unequal distribution of property. Nor is it necessary to argue that he, any more than the Puritan colonists, consciously intended the rise of capitalism. Thought as well as action may have unintended social consequences. All that need be established is that Locke has an important, if complex, place in the development of liberal capitalism, and that this importance is in no way surprising, given Locke's centrality in the development of such an overwhelmingly capitalist culture as that of the United States.

Locke's position on the economy can now be summarized. The theory of property is of critical importance to his thought. Although it is true that the "extended" definition of property is widely used throughout his work, the material aspect is still highly significant. "Estate" is viewed with a mixture of misgiving, combined with a well-developed sense of the benefits that flow from material comfort. Property must be protected, since it is a natural right, but since there are no absolute rights, it may be regulated by government acting in its capacity as an agent of society. In the end, then, the security of property, in all its senses, turns on the complex relationship between society and government.

Society, Government, and the Theory of Consent

The place to begin analyzing the nexus between society and government is with the standard decisionmaking procedure advanced by Locke—majority rule. On the surface Locke's advocacy appears categorical, so much so that Willmoore Kendall labeled Locke an absolute majoritarian democrat.[51] Unfortunately, as C. B. Macpherson rather tartly responded, this claim overlooked the fact that Locke was not a democrat at all.[52] This divergence of interpretation makes it necessary to look more carefully at Locke's views on democracy and also at the complex set of restraints that Locke sought, perhaps somewhat ineffectually, to place around government.

First, it is important to remember again that, in Locke's view, the obligations of natural law did not cease to apply once the social state had been attained. Mankind continued to have a natural right to the preservation of life, liberty, and estate. This right could be abridged only with the consent of the governed; moreover, there appear to be limits as to what we might rightfully give consent to.

Consent comes in two forms—express and tacit. An explicit statement whereby one consents to be bound when one enters into society is a perfectly clear notion and presents no problem. The concept of tacit consent is much more troubling. The potential reach of tacit consent is very extensive. One gives tacit consent by enjoying the use of any of the services provided by a government. Thus, one becomes obligated even by traveling on a highway; in effect, tacit consent "reaches as far as the very being of anyone within the territories of that government."[53] As Hanna Pitkin pointed out, the form of the argument is closely parallel to the tacit consent by which men agree to the unequal distribution of property generated in the state of nature simply by adopting money as the medium of exchange.[54] But if matters were left here, consent would be a virtually meaningless concept; Locke's statement is startlingly strong. Given such a doctrine, practically speaking, there is almost no way not to consent, except by engaging in revolutionary activity. Of course Locke did have a theory of justifiable revolution, but even short of this, as Hanna Pitkin and John Dunn have both argued, the implications of Locke's theory may not be so destructive of meaningful consent as might first appear.[55] In their view, what one really consents to are the terms of the original contract. It is this contract that establishes the limits of obligation. Further, no one is bound to obey decisions made by government in violation of natural law or the fiduciary relationship between governors and governed. In fact, even express consent to the actions of a tyrannical government would be invalid because pledges that contradict the laws of nature cannot create obligations.[56]

One is likely to find this argument persuasive only to the extent that one accepts the laws of nature as a real determinate force in shaping the destiny of a political system. Nevertheless, this line of interpretation clearly illustrates the central theme of Locke's political theory, that is, the attempt to establish a system of limitations on the actions of government. The avoidance of arbitrary action is at the heart of Locke's theory and is perhaps the very heart of liberal thought itself.

The argument of the *Second Treatise* is structured to establish this point. Consider the clear separation between society and government. Individuals in the state of nature contract among themselves to establish society, not government. Society is prior to government, which is thus a creature of society and holds such powers as it has as a trustee for the individuals who make up society. The separation of state from society and the subordination of the former to the latter are the core of liberal constitutional theory. They represent an inversion of the hierarchy that had prevailed in the tradition of Western political theory from the time of Plato on. Men are no longer seen as essentially political creatures; in fact, individual citizens have come to be seen as the repository of rights that are superior to the claims of government. Whereas once a vital function of government had been seen to be the molding of the character of citizens, it would be closer to the truth to say that in the theory of Locke the citizens mold the character of government.

In many ways that is clearly a salutary development. Under the conditions prevailing in modern nation-states, the sort of pervasive penetration of every aspect of the lives of private citizens characteristic of, for example, the political thought of Plato and Aristotle, would be a prescription for a totalitarian regime.[57] But if much is gained, something is surely lost too. The intent of Locke's theoretical system was the preservation of individual rights, although even on theoretical grounds it can be argued that the attempt was not wholly successful. However, along with the subordination of government, there was also a subtle downgrading of the importance of politics and the political as such.[58] As is also the case in the theory of Hobbes, in Locke's theory the true center of man's activity is private rather than public. The emphasis on citizen participation characteristic of ancient political practice and much theory is simply missing.[59] Moreover, the relatively benign character of Locke's state of nature in contrast to Hobbes's has a dual consequence. On the one hand, the element of fear so central to the *Leviathan* is removed: Men are not driven in their desperation to accept the dictates of an unlimited sovereign. Thus they can impose conditions in the form of a trust relationship when they elect to leave nature and enter the sociopolitical condition. On the other hand, as Sheldon Wolin observed, this very fact tends to reduce the state to something of a superstructural phenomenon. Order is not the creation of politics but rather a mere rediscovery of man's natural sociality.[60] Thus, Locke "reversed the traditional priorities to establish society as the support of the political order rather than the reverse."[61] Further down this road in the history of modern political thought is the usurpation of the traditional place of political theory by economic theory,[62] a development that flows naturally from the privatization of human activity and the growing tendency for liberals to characterize man's main activity as economic. The result is reductionist social science and, curiously, the ultimate, antiliberal reductionism of some forms of Marxism.

The ever-increasing emphasis on economic development—on the "wealth of nations"—also comes to threaten individual rights, the protection of which is so central to liberal constitutionalism. The problem becomes one of making rights secure in the face of the concentrations of large-scale economic power that have historically come to be associated with material advance. Locke was quite clear that economic power would not and should not be equally distributed. The problem that has tormented liberalism ever since is the difficulty—some would say the impossibility—of maintaining a system of equal political rights in the face of substantially unequal economic power, particularly when the protection of that distribution is elevated to the status of a natural right.

This problem is left to later liberals; Locke did not devote any attention to it at all. Locke certainly believed in natural rights, which inhere in individuals. However, perhaps surprisingly, the protection of these rights is simply not the subject of the *Second Treatise*. In this work Locke was not concerned with the protection of individual rights against the state; rather he concentrated on the threat to the rights of the great majority, a threat that he believed emanated from the Crown. Locke hoped to justify revolutionary activity, if necessary, to protect the majority against the monarch.[63]

It is now well established that Locke, for all his proverbial caution, was himself deeply immersed in revolutionary activity. From this perspective the *Second Treatise* is a genuinely radical work. No longer is it possible to accept the old notion—fostered by Locke himself—that he wrote after the fact merely to justify the accession of William and Mary to the English throne, though his work may have had that effect.[64] Locke's book is a justification of revolution in a situation in which he perceived a threat of persistent violation of the majority by a small minority, in this case those who wished to see a Catholic on the throne of England.

The obvious political problem is that revolution is hardly a useful day-to-day source of constitutional limitation, and as I have said, revolution is not a remedy open to the individual whose rights have been violated. The most obvious mechanism through which one might begin to guarantee such rights is the exercise of democratic suffrage. That mechanism alone is not likely to be enough unless one makes the optimistic assumption that the power of individuals will be able to outweigh economic power; however, it is at least a start.

Whether it is a start made by Locke is now a matter of controversy. It is important to recall that liberalism and democracy are not synonymous and may sometimes conflict. Certainly democracy as we know it now was unknown in the seventeenth century. Until recently the received wisdom was that Locke was not a democrat in any meaningful sense and that his many references to majorities and to the people, for all their contemporary resonance, related to only a small fraction of the adult male population of his time. In this view the revolutionary radicalism of Locke was not democratic but was rather advanced on behalf of the Whig aristocracy.[65] Whatever Locke's beliefs, this view is certainly consistent with the history of modern political institutions. Liberal democracy is a hybrid that developed over a long period of time;[66] liberalism in its origins is primarily a theory of limited government. If government can be limited by democratic means, well and good, but democracy in the liberal tradition is often seen as a problem for defenders of constitutional liberties and sometimes as an open threat. Not until the nineteenth century can one find a fully developed democratic theory of liberal politics. Of course, it was not until the twentieth century that democracy in the sense of universal adult suffrage was achieved.

With respect to Locke's contribution, this view of history has been challenged by the studies of Richard Ashcraft. Ashcraft argues that Locke was historically linked to the Levellers—the radical wing of Oliver Cromwell's New

Model Army in the English Civil War earlier in the seventeenth century. Against C. B. Macpherson, Ashcraft contends that the Levellers were in fact advocates of widespread suffrage and that the actual practices of that time allowed for an electorate much larger than Macpherson believed.[67] Ashcraft concludes that when the radical faction with which Locke was politically associated talked about returning power to the people in a revolutionary situation, they meant exactly that.[68] In this view, then, the *Second Treatise* was "primarily addressed not to the aristocracy and the landed class, but rather to the urban merchants, tradesmen, artisans, and independent small gentry who constituted the social foundations for any radical political theory."[69] Ashcraft concedes that Locke's text is not unambiguous on the question of membership in the political society, and he does not want to suggest that Locke was advocating a "democratic commonwealth."[70] However, he says that Locke did hold out the possibility that a "compounded and mixed" form of government might emerge from the constitutive operations of the people and that these same people had the power to keep power in their own hands if they were "unwise" enough to wish to do so.[71]

We cannot hope to resolve here the complex empirical problems surrounding the question of the franchise in seventeenth-century England. Much of Ashcraft's case is compelling, particularly when one considers the limited nature of his claims. His reading of Locke revolves around the power of the people in their capacity as a constitutive group. It is, in effect, an interpretation that focuses on the people as the ultimate holder of sovereign power. It does not require us to believe, even if we accept the idea of Locke as a political radical, that he was equally radical in socioeconomic affairs; in fact, he was a socioeconomic conservative.[72] Clearly, he intended to sanction potentially large inequalities in economic distribution, and he often expressed harsh attitudes toward the poor. In spite of the implications of Locke's views on the subject of the regulation of property, he was certainly no modern social democrat. Nor is his theory of a sovereign people, even on the most radical reading, to be seen as a charter for anything like a participatory democracy. In fact, the major references to a role for the people as a constitutive sovereign are to the highly unusual situation of the aftermath of a revolution, which hardly constitutes a form of normal politics.

Rather, it can be argued that the central value in Locke's system as a whole is toleration, not democratic participation. According to Ian Shapiro, it was this toleration that gave Locke's political ideology its ultimately conservative form. Locke's conception of liberty was essentially negative in the Hobbesian sense—the absence of external restraints. The result was to shift action to the private sphere, so that "genuine" freedom was seen as freedom *from* politics. That was reflected in the growing conservatism of Whig leaders after the

Glorious Revolution and "their opposition, after 1694, to anything that could plausibly be called a democratic politics."[73] This reading is consistent with one of the most persistent themes of liberal thought and action—the idea that government exists to maintain the conditions necessary for private individuals to pursue their own privately defined sense of the good. In the terms of current philosophical debates, it is a theory of the primacy of individual rights over the good of the community.[74]

On this theory, then, democratic politics is a fairly weak reed to rely on as a defense against arbitrary government. That is particularly true if one takes into account Locke's somewhat neglected theory of prerogative. He defined prerogative as the "power to act according to discretion, for the public good, without the prescription of the law, and sometimes even against it."[75] It is essentially an executive power against which, if it is abused, the people have no remedy except an *"appeal to heaven,"* for there is no *"judge on earth"* to adjudicate between their claims and those of the executive.[76]

As Sheldon Wolin pointed out, Locke's claim is astonishing "because it amounts to a criticism of the political system of his own creation, to a deconstruction of his own theory."[77] If the central purpose of Locke's theory is to avoid arbitrary government, then the least one can say is that this is a passage in deep contradiction to his central message. It is hard not to be reminded of the activities and theoretical rationalizations of several recent American presidents. As Wolin observed, the implication of this confused body of thought is that the people are a sovereign "entitled to rebel but not to rule."[78]

Conclusions

The Locke that emerges from this discussion is a complex and by no means entirely clear or consistent thinker. There is no doubt that he is significantly different from the champion of Whig constitutionalism celebrated in the textbooks of a generation ago. He is not yet a capitalist, but perhaps contrary to his intentions, he is a significant precursor of capitalism, or, to be more circumspect, his theory is eminently compatible with emerging capitalist practice. The logic of his position required him to develop a theory of individual rights, but his polemical purpose did not lead him to do so. As a result, the tension between the majority rule he espoused and the minority rights his version of natural rights theory seems to require was not brought fully into the open. Individual property rights in the broadest sense are to be protected, but ample scope is left for the regulation of property, again in the broadest sense. At a highly general level he is committed to political equality, but his acceptance of economic inequalities may well undercut this commitment. Still more generally, his thought "expresses the tension within liberalism as a social theory between its universalistic claims to moral and religious equality—liberty, equality and fraternity—and its instrumentalist treatment of human beings as a part of the process of capital accumulation. His position on the relation of the individual to the community is just as ambiguous."[79] These are serious dilemmas, but one should note the potentially explosive character of the more universalistic side of the various polarities.

There is also something to be said for Laslett's interpretation, which stressed natural political virtue; it is clear that Locke was no Hobbesian atomist. However, he can hardly be said to have had a robust sense of community. Michael Oakeshott's conception of *societas*—an association of men formally related to one another and bound together by a set of legal rules—may come closer to capturing Locke's point.[80] Most generally, Locke was an advocate, contra Hobbes, of limited constitutional government, but as we have seen, he undercut his own argument, so that the theoretically restrained government may accumulate large powers and the specter of "imperial" executives begins to grow in the careful reader's consciousness.

Consent also looms large in Locke's theory. There is no doubt that this doctrine, for all its considerable ambiguity, opens the way for a democratization of the liberal tradition. Certainly it is impossible to conceive any form of democracy in which consent does not play a central role. At the same time, the idea of tacit consent is deeply troubling for two reasons. Theoretically, it is problematic because, even on the most limited reading, it tends to make a mockery of the very notion of *meaningful* consent. As I remarked, under this doctrine it is almost impossible not to consent unless one is prepared to engage in revolutionary action. After all, who has not had the experience of voting for candidates who after election have pursued all manner of policies to which one has the most strenuous objections? More practically, since we cannot remain perpetually assembled to give our active consent to what our government does, is it not virtually necessary that we will be governed by policies to which we have given consent in only the most remote possible way? This is a pressing issue for any large-scale liberal democracy.[81]

A word should also be said about the central metaphor of the contract. First, the idea is deeply ahistorical. It asks us to imagine that free, equal men contract with one another in a hypothetical state of nature, devoid of social institutions or of the sense of the past that does so much to make human beings what they are. In fact, contract theory makes two vital assumptions: "One is that the contracting individuals are equal because they have no prior history, the other that the contract represents a 'beginning' in which society starts afresh like the beginning of a new footrace."[82] These assumptions, in stripping us of our history and of our sociological characteristics, lead to a theory that, particularly in its contemporary manifestations, is often excessively abstract and removed from the sociopolitical reality that political theory must ultimately deal with.

The second point is closely related. Contract theory is an inadequate attempt to deal with man's sociality. It is true that Locke's image of man concedes more to that sociality than does Hobbes's. But as Peter Laslett observed, "*Leviathan* was an influence, a gravitational constant, exercised by a large body though at a great distance."[83] And Hobbes's philosophical anthropology is a description of an atomized, asocial, if not antisocial, man. It has been argued that this "radical contractarianism" is at the heart of liberal ideology.[84] This assertion is perhaps too sweeping; it might be more accurate to suggest that the "gravitational" pull of Hobbes is a great force in the liberal tradition and that much of the history of that tradition is an attempt to escape from its power. Much of the account that follows is the story of the oscillations of American thought and policy between Hobbesian atomism and the dictates of a more social conception of man. As C. B. Macpherson put it, "We do well to be afraid of Hobbes; he knows too much about us."[85]

In a sense then, the tensions and confusions of Locke's political thought prefigured the tensions and confusions of much of American liberal political theory in the next three centuries. In Anglo-American politics Locke's problems are our problems because, as John Dunn has suggested, we live within the framework created by a secularized Lockeanism.[86] Dunn may be correct when he adds that that this is surely not a framework within which we can deal with the problems of the late twentieth century. This proposition is inherent in the frequently raised possibility that liberalism has exhausted itself and thus is no longer a viable principle for American society. That proposition is debatable, but it seems hardly open to doubt that to the extent that we do live in a Lockean world, an understanding of the mysteries of Locke's work is indispensable. And those mysteries, the ambiguities that one encounters in reading Locke, are a source of the possibility of interpretive flexibility that has made Lockean ideas so important in U.S. politics. Thus, they allow for a Lockean politics of interpretation. But more immediately, there is the fact that Locke's ideas were central to the intellectual underpinnings of the American Revolution. I turn now to the Revolution and the complexities of its justification.

⚬ 3 ⚬

Liberalism, Republicanism, and Revolution

COMPARED WITH its great modern counterparts in England, France, Russia, and China, the American Revolution is something of a sport. As revolutions go, it can be seen as a paradoxically conservative event. Until almost the end of the period immediately preceding the upheaval, the great majority of colonial leaders, with the exception of a very few militants, such as Samuel Adams, clung to the hope that a final break could be avoided. Many of the appeals to the Crown were cast, not in terms of new, revolutionary doctrines, but rather in the form of an appeal to the traditional, long-established rights of Englishmen.[1] Moreover, the Revolution was not class based: Although class conflict was present, it was not remotely as salient as in the other major revolutions. Class divisions were real and may even have been increasing, but revolutionary sentiment tended to cut across class lines. Thus the leadership was, for the most part, middle and upper-middle class, and the working class and much of what passed for an aristocracy were split.[2]

The Spirit of '76 thus does not look much like the mighty social upheavals that have followed and have often been inspired by it. On this Louis Hartz was surely correct—the colonists did not have to undergo a social revolution, because feudalism had never really been established in the English colonies.[3] Guillotines were not erected in front of Independence Hall, there were no reigns of either terror or virtue, and no Americans would be likely today to castigate the Revolution as a great historical tragedy. Some might perhaps say it was regrettably limited, but no one longs for the return of the ancien régime, as might a fervent rightist in France. Reactionaries in U.S. politics are of a different sort altogether. Even a historian such as Richard Morris, who especially tried to recover the sense of class conflict that *was* present at the time, was forced to concede that what Hartz dismissed as feudal relics were in fact just that, atavistic throwbacks to practices never really dominant in the colonies. Hartz's consensus theory may well homogenize the Revolution too much for the comfort of a careful historian, but his basic concept is sound on that point. No doubt class conflict is always present in all societies, but it is not a historical constant, and if viewed comparatively, it seems to have been of relatively low salience in the American revolutionary period.

On another level, it is striking how much of the debate leading to the Revolution was over the structure of the British Empire. The resulting discussions were therefore legalistic, a characteristic that has continued to be a significant aspect of much subsequent American political thought.[4] And of course the law tends, on the whole, to be a conservative force.

However, it is important not to exaggerate these "conservative" tendencies. In addition to the centrist sobriety, there was quite another side to the Revolution. Let us leave aside for the moment the nature of specific arguments. Whatever conservative coloration the revolutionary events may have assumed, it must be remembered that the colonists succeeded in subverting a legal government in what was the first of the modern anticolonial rebellions, ousted the Tory supporters of the Crown, confiscated their property, and "set the example of a revolutionary program through mechanisms by which the people were deemed to act as the constituent power." From the perspective of the twentieth century, the Revolution may seem rather tame, but it set in motion a train of events and a wave of cultural change that was radically democratic in implication, regardless of how those forces may have been contained since.[5] It is the last point that is most important both politically and theoretically.

In this perspective the American Revolution fits with some difficulty into the consensus framework. As Richard Hofstadter said, many of the ideas were traditional, but to focus on that alone is to miss some factors of major importance. In spite of its traditional and legalistic aspects, the Revolution drew on some of the most deeply radical ideas and movements in the history of the Western world: the Reformation and the Puritan revolution, the Glorious Revolution of 1688, and the whole broad tradition of English dissent and radicalism. If regicide and strident class conflict are our only standards, then we are in danger of missing an "accelerated redistribution of power among social classes or among various social types, a pragmatic disrespect for vested interests [and] the rapid introduction of profoundly important constitutional changes." And despite the relatively low salience of class and hierarchy in the colonial and revolutionary periods, they were not entirely absent. Gordon Wood charted a clear trajectory from monarchy to republicanism to democracy in the period, beginning with the revolt against colonial authority and through the rapid democratization of American society and politics in the postrevolutionary period.[6] That the society did not experience feudalism does not prove the existence of egalitarianism in the colonies; the Hartz thesis has its limits. Put differently, colonial America looks most equal in comparative perspective.

The ouster of the Loyalists is almost certainly more important for the subsequent development of American politics than is usually recognized. The Tories were a diverse lot; some were even able to embrace John Locke, which may tell us something about Locke too, but intellectually their expulsion drained American thought of a form of organic conservatism. That strain has been absent from the spectrum of American political thought ever since.[7] The most Lockean of the Tories nevertheless found something to fear in the ideas and actions of the revolutionaries. In fact, 60,000 or more of them emigrated either to England or (more of them) to Canada rather than live under the new regime.[8] The size of this migration in proportion to the population was twenty times greater than that of the migration from revolutionary France. That statistic suggests not only that the Loyalist cause was no small minority but also that there were real issues at stake that transcended any existing consensus.[9]

Liberalism and Revolution

A brief overview of the major events may be helpful. Politically, the critical period leading to the Revolution began with the passage of the Stamp Act in 1765. More generally, the crisis was precipitated by the end of the Seven Years' War between France and England—to Americans, the French and Indian War. The Crown was faced with two needs: to finance a massive national debt, and to tighten up the structure of the British Empire, thus to end what, at least from the perspective of the colonies, was a period of "salutary neglect." As a result of colonial protest, the Stamp Act was soon withdrawn, only to be replaced by the Townshend Acts, which again established new taxes. Those too were repealed in 1770, but they were followed in 1773 by the Tea Act, which was designed to bail out the East India Company. The result was the near-legendary Boston Tea Party. After a period of escalating tensions, this last event may well have foreclosed the possibility of a peaceful solution to the tax crisis. In any case, the Coercive Acts, designed to restore order to the colony, followed, and they led to what was, in effect, the military occupation of Boston.[10]

The themes of the colonial response to these events are well known.[11] The theory of virtual representation—the idea of representation as "founded upon a vaguely drawn subjective constituency with little active power"[12]—was decisively rejected in favor of the slogan, No taxation without representation. Only the form of representation was at issue for the rebels, along with a variety of technical issues revolving around the extent to which the power of Parliament might vary, according to the particular form of taxation in question. Soon, however, the demand arose for complete home rule, with the Crown's power to tax being denied completely; this position yielded rapidly to the dominion theory of empire, which held that the sole link between Britain and the colonies was a common allegiance to the king. Of course, from there it was but a step to total independence.[13]

This brings us to the Declaration of Independence and the role of John Locke. Since the pioneering work of Clinton Rossiter, not to mention the important studies of J.G.A. Pocock, Gordon Wood, and Bernard Bailyn, it will no longer do to treat Locke as if he were the sole European source of American revolutionary ideas.[14] The colonial leaders were nothing if not eclectic. Their readings ranged back to ancient Greece and Rome, through English libertarian and republican theorists and publicists of the seventeenth and eighteenth centuries, to conservative jurists such as Sir William Blackstone, and to a variety of continental writers as well. Still, Locke was "in the air," so to speak, and his ideas were near the heart of the contemporary climate of opinion. Locke was, as Rossiter suggested, first among equals, "a famous, almost unassailable English philosopher who had glorified a rebellion of Englishmen against an English king."[15]

In spite of this wide variety of sources, it is immediately clear that the argument of the Declaration is cast in essentially Lockean terms. That is true in spite of the fact that Thomas Jefferson, its principal author, claimed not to have consulted Locke or any other writer during the drafting of the document.[16] Still, we know that Jefferson considered Locke—along with Bacon and Newton—to be one of the three greatest men who ever lived,[17] that he felt the *Second Treatise* to be the finest of all works in political theory,[18] and that that work was one of the few prescribed texts included in Jefferson's plan for the University of Virginia curriculum.[19] As Jefferson saw it, he was merely expressing the common sense of the subject as seen by the leaders of the Revolution; in espousing Lockean ideas, he did not feel himself to be enunciating new principles.[20]

The form of the Declaration is clearly that of a large-scale, Lockean syllogism. The famous second paragraph states the premises of the argument. It begins with the assertion of the self-evident truths that all men are created equal and are possessed of certain unalienable rights, notably "life, liberty, and the pursuit of happiness." Governments are said to be created to secure these rights and to derive their power to do so from the consent of the governed. If a government becomes destructive of these ends, a right inheres in the people to alter or abolish it and to institute a new one in its place.

The body of the Declaration that follows is basically a long list of grievances lodged against King George III. These grievances are said to be violations of natural rights and the doctrine of consent, thus leading inevitably to the conclusion that a severance of the ties linking Crown to colonies is justified.

It could hardly be more obvious that these are among the central themes of Locke's political theory—natural rights, consent, and a doctrine of justified revolution. To be sure, Locke is not the sole source of revolutionary thought. Nevertheless, if it is the case that Jefferson merely summarized the ideas that were common currency when he wrote, then it is striking to what extent they follow the model established by the *Second Treatise.*

However, as Cecilia Kenyon observed, it was "Lockeanism with an American gloss."[21] Locke's complex and often ambiguous ideas were simplified and in some ways radicalized. The concept of a state of nature was widely assumed and in fact antedated the *Second Treatise,* but the revolutionary leaders were much less ready than even Locke to accept the notion that the government justified by the "inconveniences" of the state of nature could be completely impartial. In addition, they were more concerned than Locke with the rights of individual men; it is important to recall that Locke's majoritarianism left these rights in a rather precarious position. Although it could not conceivably be maintained that American revolutionary and constitutional theory has successfully solved this problem, the dilemma of individual rights in the context of a system of majority rule has assumed a central place in American political thought.[22]

In addition, the substitution of the pursuit of happiness for "estate" in the familiar Lockean trinity has important implications. What constitutes happiness is notoriously a matter of individual taste, so its emphasis introduces into American thought a note of relativist individualism that goes beyond the already-individualistic theory of Locke.[23] And "pursuit" itself is an interesting word. It would clearly be supremely difficult to guarantee anyone happiness. But there is something a little grim about the idea of pursuing happiness. If Thomas Hobbes was right about the inevitably fleeting nature of felicity, then a great many people are doomed to disappointment in a society that makes the pursuit of happiness one of its founding principles. One cannot but be reminded of Leo Strauss's remark that the ideas of Locke lead to the "joyless pursuit of joy."[24]

The insertion of the pursuit of happiness is of interest for another reason as well. Morton White shows the existence of an intriguing ambiguity in Jefferson's ideas on the subject. A careful comparison of the rough draft and the Declaration itself suggests that in the course of the drafting process the emphasis shifted from the idea of government as an abettor of men in the achievement of life, liberty, and the pursuit of happiness to a protector of the right to engage in the chase.[25] The difference is a question of whether and to what extent government has a positive role to play in the attainment of human ends or whether its role is merely to protect individual rights to pursue these ends. It is not clear if this was a tension in Jefferson's mind or within the drafting committee,[26] but nevertheless, the ambiguity revealed here is a pregnant one for the future of the American liberal tradition. It is near the heart of a great deal of important political debate to this day.

Finally, it may be useful to point to the obvious and note that the replacement of property in Locke's formula hardly indicates a denial of the importance of property in American thought or politics. However, the change is still noteworthy: It does indicate a demotion of the place of material property in the list of natural rights. Certainly, Jefferson could not have been unaware of the significant alteration of Locke's position. Property is still in some sense seen as a natural right, but not as a primary or primitive right in that it is not directly a gift from God; rather, it is what has been called an adventitious right.[27] The implications of this view seem fairly clear. If property is merely an adventitious right, then it is a matter of contingency and more readily subject to social and political regulation than the primary rights are. Thus the way is open for a political system to claim sanction in its founding ideas for public policies that lean toward regulation, as do twentieth-century reform movements. Thus, Jefferson's Americanization of Locke provides a significant interpretive opportunity to such groups.

Cecilia Kenyon shows that many of these ideas move Lockeanism in a more individualistic, even a radically individualistic, direction, and all point toward an Americanized version of Locke. And this very individualism points to a more democratic and relativistic Lockeanism, more democratic than what Locke himself might have endorsed.[28] These new emphases, combined with the essential, if fruitful, ambiguity of the ideas of life, liberty, and particularly happiness, begin to lend to Lockeanism a flexibility that can lend support to the Hartz thesis. So adaptable, not to say ambiguous, a body of ideas can be made to yield many meanings. The results may not always be attractive in later versions, but they contribute to the centrality of liberalism in the history of American politics.

The Republican Correction

At one time the analysis might well have stopped at this point; certainly Louis Hartz in *The Liberal Tradition in America* went no further. But as already suggested, this will no longer quite do. Matters are more complicated, and a purely Lockean interpretation of the Revolution is insufficient. The most sweeping assessment of the scholarly situation came from J.G.A. Pocock, who argued that the work of Bernard Bailyn and Gordon Wood altogether replaced Hartz, so Locke simply ceases to be relevant. Instead we had to focus on the theory of republicanism.[29] But in the light of the evidence discussed so far, that seems rather hyperbolic. Perhaps it would be more accurate to follow Bailyn and suggest that the liberal Enlightenment ideas with which we have been dealing formed the "deep background and gave a general coloration" to the political beliefs of the period.[30] That much at least seems clear; however, in Bailyn's view, whether these ideas were enough in themselves to precipitate a revolution is more doubtful. There is a less sober side to the period, a frenzied, utopian, almost hysterical mood, which, like the other ideas under discussion, cut across the political spectrum and reflected deep social and psychological tensions. Even such leaders as Jefferson and Adams showed an "enthusiastic and visionary extravagance" that reflected such a mood.[31]

To an extent, this mood arose because the late eighteenth century was an age of neoclassicism. The works of the ancients were widely known, though sometimes at second hand or through Machiavelli, by way of James Harrington, Algernon Sydney, and other English republicans of the seventeenth century.[32] In this way the ideas of the civic humanist tradition of republicanism became an important part of the revolutionary ideology. In terms of British politics, this position was derived from the "Country" opposition that sprang up against the "Court" position represented by the Walpole government earlier in the century. In the most extreme version, as argued by Pocock, Locke was virtually set aside and the Revolution became, not a climactic moment in the history of Anglo-American liberalism, but rather the last act of the Italian Renaissance.[33] More moderate, and doubtlessly more accurate, views suggested that the discontents expressed in the civic humanist vocabulary triggered the final conflict between Crown and colonies.[34]

The republican theory seems to take us well beyond not only the somewhat conservative constitutional arguments already discussed but also the most radical arguments based on Locke. The starting point for the discussion was the inspirational value of the ancient republics, combined with the deeply troubling perception that these republics had been highly unstable. It was this perception of temporal instability that Pocock referred to as the Machiavellian moment. More specifically, the dominant belief was that these ancient regimes had perished owing to decay from within, that they had fallen victim to the twin evils of "corruption" and "faction." Corruption was entailed in the pursuit of self-interest. The antidote to the poison was the "sacrifice of individual interests to the greater good of the whole."[35] Such sacrifice, which was the essence of republican ideology, was the defining characteristic of what was known in its vocabulary as civic virtue. However, there was a widespread perception that civic virtue was in short supply, that the idea constituted a vision so "divorced from the realities of American society, so contrary to the previous century of American experience, that it alone was enough to make the Revolution one of the great utopian moments of American history."[36]

Faction, the organized pursuit of interest in opposition to the common good, was the opposite of civic virtue. Leaders as diverse as Alexander Hamilton and Thomas Paine were united in exhorting the public to a renewal of its commitment to that public good—a Machiavellian return to first principles, as Pocock would have it.[37] The clash of interests simply could not be part of the good political order, except insofar as there was a permanent conflict of interest between the governors and the governed.[38] Faction was a sign of social sickness and corruption that must be rooted out. Despite the wide circulation of liberal contractarian principles, there is in this aspect of the revolutionary ideology clearly a conception of the state understood in terms of a premodern organic unity. That was not a new theme in American history. John Winthrop and the Puritans would have understood perfectly over a century before. Indeed, republicanism could be seen as a more relaxed, secularized version of Puritanism,[39] a fact of some interpretive significance, which has often been insufficiently stressed.

What is striking in colonial politics is the absence of the behavior patterns dictated by civic humanist theory. In fact, of course, people *did* pursue their narrowly defined personal interests. Therefore, corruption in the civic humanist sense was seen as a serious problem, and subordination to the Crown came to be perceived as one of the major sources of that corruption. Similarly, the perception of growing inequality also was felt to be inimical to the survival of a sound republic. In this frame of reference, the establishment of republican rule became a matter of some urgency. It had a deep psychological aspect, with the king and his ministers serving as a scapegoat for the escalating tensions. The question became whether the colonists had the moral fiber to meet the demands of the republican theory of good citizenship. Thomas Paine went to the heart of the problem, asserting that the time for independence was at hand; in fifty years it would be too late—the rot would have gone too deep. Growing size and commercial development were a threat.[40] "Virtue," Paine wrote, "is not hereditary; neither is it perpetual."[41] Gordon Wood argued accordingly that the American Revolution was not simply an anticolonial rebellion; it was much more—an effort at moral regeneration, one having great psychological and sociological significance. Because only special people would make good republicans, the urgent task the colonists set for themselves was to show that they were worthy and fit, in the Puritan vocabulary, to occupy a place in a "city on a hill."

The difficulties of meeting such a standard were enormous, given the sociological conditions that republican theorists argued were at the foundation of a successful society. The political system was supposed to be small, both in number of citizens and in geographical area. It was to be socially and culturally homogeneous so as to maximize consensus, economically self-sufficient, dedicated to the simple, frugal life, characterized by social and economic equality, and distrustful of rapid socioeconomic change.[42] Even at the time of the Revolution, it was obvious that some of these conditions, particularly those relating to population and size, could not be met, and that the remainder were threatened by the rapid emergence of commercial, liberal capitalism. Pocock captured this very well; from the perspective of republican theory there is a tension between virtue and commerce. It is an interesting coincidence that 1776 saw the publication not only of the Declaration of Independence but also of the theoretical foundation of modern capitalism, Adam Smith's *Wealth of Nations,* an irony not lessened by the fact that Smith's modern followers often distort him unmercifully in their attempt to use his work to legitimate their position.

What begins to emerge is that the colonial rebels held to at least two sets of ideas that could not always be reconciled and that were in some cases quite incompatible. Harvey Mansfield, Jr., poses the dilemma sharply, if perhaps overschematically: "Civic humanism," he tells us, "is the republican virtue of citizens participating in rule." It is a body of ideas in many ways distinct from liberalism, which "favors rights over community, liberty over duty, representation over participation, and interest over virtue,"[43] a set of dualisms still at the heart of a great deal of contemporary theoretical debate.

But other important currents of thought were also present. One was the English legal tradition, with its emphasis on rights, which provided a "language of liberty" that was at the root of the colonial appeal to the traditional rights of Englishmen.[44] And though Locke conspicuously eschewed reference to history or law in support of his argument, his emphasis on rights was complementary to the traditional legal view.

The other major pattern of thought to take into account was Puritanism, whose role in the Revolution, though not ignored, has, as we have seen, not been sufficiently stressed. It is true that Gordon Wood called republicanism a more secular version of Puritanism, but little attention has been paid to what is no doubt the major premodern, preliberal current of thought in the colonial years. The major exception is in the work of Edmund Morgan, who argued in a brilliant, but neglected, article that the entire period of the Revolution and the emergence of the Constitution was affected, "not to say guided," by a set of values that he called the Puritan ethic.[45] Much of what has been labeled republicanism was already present in the residue of Puritanism that remained even after the substantial secularization of the Puritan ideal. There is the same concern for the simple, austere life, the distrust of self-interest, the same drive for economic self-sufficiency, and, above all, the same elevated sense of moral purpose combined with a sense of declining moral rectitude.

The republican call for a return to first principles bears a startling similarity to the Puritan jeremiad, which called for a return to lost moral principles. The point is not to argue that the republican ideology was of no importance but rather to suggest that Puritanism was there first, that it provided some of the most persistent ideas and attitudes in American culture in addition to well-fertilized soil for republican ideas to grow in. Since all analysts of revolutionary thought refer to the same texts, the ideas stressed in the republican hypothesis are just as likely to have stemmed from the Puritan heritage as from an Anglicized Machiavellianism. Further, as I have already argued, Puritanism was a system of beliefs mightily conducive to the growth of ideas and practices associated with liberalism, ideas and practices that often were subversive of their society of origin and in conflict with the ideas of civic republicanism.

Many of these ideas and practices are closely related to the rise of liberal capitalism. Some part of the confusion over the meaning of Lockeanism is no doubt associated with the recent scholarly controversies over the real nature and intent of Locke's political thought. It may be true that Locke did not *intend* his ideas to provide a justification of unlimited capitalist appropriation, as C. B. Macpherson contended, or even that his theory properly understood was specifically an obstacle to the development of capitalism, as John Dunn and James Tully argued. Moreover, it is true that in the early part of the eighteenth century Locke's ideas were by no means a dominant force in Anglo-American thought.[46] However, their revival came at an opportune time. As Isaac Kramnick showed, by 1760 Locke's ideas had been caught up in the rise of bourgeois capitalism, they *were* interpreted—whatever his intent—in "possessive individualist" terms, and they were widely influential. Kramnick noted that those men knew their Aristotle, Machiavelli, and their Montesquieu. "But they also knew their Locke."[47] One is reminded of Michael Walzer's observation that it is often useful to look for the meaning of a theory in what it *has meant* in history, leaving aside all questions of authorial intent.[48] In attempting to understand the peculiarities of the founding period of American thought, it is important to remember that a complex set of ideas was at work—ideas not necessarily compatible with one another. Some stressed Puritan or republican virtue; others accepted or even welcomed the liberal pursuit of self-interest. It was the liberal ideas that were best suited to the kind of capitalist economy that was rapidly emerging in the former colonies. The result of this turbulence was a degree of ideological confusion as political leaders sought to adapt their ideas to changing socioeconomic conditions.

The position of the urban artisan class is particularly interesting in this regard. In his book on working-class politics and attitudes, Gary Nash also stressed ideological complexity. He identified three primary groupings, the conservative Whigs, the liberal Whigs, and the Evangelicals.[49] Class was certainly a factor in the divisions, though there was no simple correspondence between socioeconomic position and ideological beliefs. Taken together, the Whigs were the dominant group. The conservative Whigs accepted such principles as balanced government, equal justice under law, and the role of a legislature elected by property holders. In economics they were capitalist modernizers, dedicated to the emerging market system. At the same time, they were deeply committed to hierarchical principles. Politically some were Loyalists, some were neutral, and some emerged after the war as leaders of the attempt to curb what they saw as the leveling excesses of the Revolution.

The more liberal Whigs, who, like the conservative Whigs, tended to be well-to-do, favored a market-oriented policy of open economic opportunity. They were strongly Lockean in their belief that liberty could be defined in terms of the security of property. The leaders of the Revolution came primarily from this group; they attempted to recruit those below them in the social hierarchy to provide a mass base for protest. To sum up the differences between the two branches of Whiggery, Nash wrote, "If social stability, acceptance of capitalistic economic relations, and political stewardship were the identifying marks of the conservative Whigs, then equality of opportunity, enthusiasm for the market economy, and political liberty were those of the liberal Whigs."[50] It hardly needs saying that all these positions were well within the spectrum of liberal thought.

The Evangelicals likewise divided into two groups, though both overlapped with the Whigs at many points, especially on the issues of elections, balanced government, and free speech and press. The radical Evangelicals were made up primarily of elements from the lower strata of the social order. Because they lacked property, they had little interest in the emerging capitalist system. They clung to ideas of fair wages and just prices rather than to those of the new competitive order. Theirs was a consciousness that looked back toward the radical Levellers of Cromwell's New Model Army in seventeenth-century England. At the heart of their thinking was a deep-seated egalitarianism that put them at odds with the conservative Whigs, though they could sometimes make alliances with the liberal Whigs.

The other major group of Evangelicals were ardent, moralistic reformers. They too wished to protect liberty and property, but they had a deep distrust of commerce. With their ideas rooted in the Puritan ethic, they saw historical possibilities in the sort of millennial terms so powerfully described by Gordon Wood. Their vocabulary was that of civic humanist republicanism, though—as I have said—that is something very hard to distinguish from a residual Puritanism.

As Nash showed, the potential for tension between this sort of Puritan republicanism and the Whig position was considerable. There was, as Pocock stressed, an incompatibility between the pursuit of self-interest and dedication to the common good. At the same time, it was difficult to convince many in the urban centers that commerce was a corrupting force. It was also difficult for the dominant urban Whigs to accept the egalitarianism of the Evangelical, republican point of view. For those Whigs, equality and freedom were in opposition to each other.[51]

What can be seen here is a mix of ideas, sometimes conflicting, sometimes overlapping, never systematic, and constantly changing as the political situation changed. Surely Lockean liberalism, even taken in the most broadly symbolic way, cannot explain all the complexities of the revolutionary situation. However, neither can the "republican synthesis." Therefore, it is necessary to move toward a new and better integrated picture of the ideology of the American Revolution than we have had. Even Pocock admitted that when the historical past is reconstructed, Locke will have to be fitted back in, though Pocock's own work has not yet moved far in that direction. As Daniel Walker Howe says, the Hartz thesis has been amended rather than abolished.[52]

The vogue of the republican thesis has clearly reached its zenith. It is striking and indeed incredible that neither Pocock nor Wood discussed the Declaration of Independence, whereas Bailyn noted only the lengthy bill of particulars against the Crown without mentioning the Lockean philosophical foundations. Given the historical importance of the Declaration, this neglect is almost beyond comprehension. If anything, the balance in recent scholarship seems to be tilting back toward Lockean liberalism, focusing on constitutional politics and revolution, not on property. The bourgeois Locke, however important as a symbol for much of the remainder of U.S. history, was not in evidence in the revolutionary tracts, though his thinking on religious toleration was.[53]

The republican writers, who tend, in Pocock's reading, to be set in opposition to Locke were seen by Jefferson and the other revolutionary leaders as being perfectly compatible with him. Not for those leaders were the fine classifications of twentieth-century scholars; they were making a revolution, not writing for a political theory seminar. We need to avoid not only the strained monism of Hartz but also an equally strained dualism of liberalism and republicanism, with the latter's being suddenly ousted by the former.[54] Both were present in the revolutionary era. It is also important to factor in Puritanism as well. Thus, I have argued that the Revolution was more complicated than any simple model. So too is much other ideological conflict in America. In particular, the mix of liberalism and republicanism was still very much in evidence during the drafting and ratification of the Constitution, but Puritanism too lingers on.

This is not to say that the theory of the liberal consensus and the theory of the republican synthesis are not useful or that they do not point to significant truths about American history and politics. Rather, my intention is to restore a greater sense of complexity and conflict to the study of the peculiarities of American exceptionalism, just as recent examinations of English thought in the late seventeenth and in the eighteenth centuries reveal a mix of republican and liberal ideas similar to that discussed here.[55] The mother country seems to have been embroiled in much the same sort of turmoil as the colonies. Although both the Hartz thesis and the republican synthesis may be examples of the sort of gross concepts that Ian Shapiro says distort political analysis, simplification through the use of such ideas nonetheless has genuine value.[56] It is one thing to restore a proper sense of complexity, but without theoretical simplification, there can be no understanding of the often bewildering reality of major historical events. To deny that is virtually to deny the vocation of political theory. The trick, of course, is to be aware of the potential reductionism implicit in all theorizing so as to be on guard against turning useful simplification into willful distortion. Finally, one need not necessarily recoil from the idea that political theory has political uses, that it often is not and perhaps cannot be divorced from the political concerns of the theorist or the contemporary interpreter.[57] Certainly much of the scholarly debate over the foundations of American politics has important contemporary implications, a point that can best be discussed later.

One conclusion that emerges fairly clearly is that the ideological tensions of the revolutionary period tended to be partially submerged in a somewhat transitory wave of nationalist sentiment, which also, at least briefly, mitigated the class differences that were emerging. Again in Hartz's comparative perspective, these conflicts were relatively minor. However, in a domestic perspective, they were real and were to reemerge with heightened clarity in the debates over the ratification of the Constitution of 1787.

It is important to understand the Revolution as only the first phase of a very complex process of nation-building or, perhaps more accurately, placing a new political order on the old colonial foundations. That process can be viewed as part of the continuing dialectic between liberalism and republicanism. We should remember, however, that the ideological distinctions are much more evident to us today than they were to the protagonists of eighteenth-century revolutionary and constitutional politics, and that these simplified distinctions did not preempt the ideological field. Finally, neither liberalism nor republicanism is necessarily linked to what we recognize as democracy. It is therefore important not to lose sight of the democratizing impetus that originated in the Revolution and extended well past the debates over the adoption of the Constitution.[58] I now turn to those momentous discussions and the interpretive politics that surrounded them.

ₒ 4 ₒ

Liberalism,
Republicanism,
and the Constitution

IN THIS CHAPTER I will use rather broad definitions of constitution and constitutionalism, going well beyond a formal legal conception of those terms. Of course, the U.S. Constitution is a legal document of great importance, but it is also much more. In legal terms, a constitution is an outline of the laws and customs, or practices, that define and establish the basic structure of a regime and generally try to impose some set of formal limitations on what that regime may do. But to admit custom is already to stretch the idea of law beyond the concept of a mere legal document. To take only one American example, the party system has something approaching constitutional status, but it rests almost entirely on custom and usage. In fact, the Framers were in principle opposed to the development of parties, even though it must be said that they participated vigorously in their creation.[1] And, of course, the British do without a single written constitutional document at all.

I will deal with the Constitution as a legal instrument, but I am even more concerned with it as something that constitutes and sometimes reconstitutes a political community. To make matters more complicated, that community also shapes the constitution, and thereby itself constitutes the constitution, so to speak. This approach has been inspired, in part, by the work of James Boyd White. White focused on the problems of language and community. Communities are defined by languages, "shared conceptions of the world, shared manners and values, shared resources and expectations and procedures for speech and thought."[2] The similarity of this formulation to Michael Walzer's idea of "shared understandings" and Sheldon Wolin's concept of "collective political identity" is striking. And like Wolin's and Walzer's ideas, this way of establishing community and meaning is not only political but critical as well. The standards of judgment implied, "while deeply rooted in certain strains of our tradition and culture, are very far indeed from defending present power arrangements under the bureaucratic state."[3]

As Terrence Ball says, there is also a real closeness to the view of John Dewey: "Society not only continues to exist . . . *by* communication, but it may be fairly said to exist *in* communication. There is more than a verbal tie between the words common, community, and communication. Men live in a community in virtue of the things they have in common; and communication is the way in which they come to possess things in common."[4] White's approach therefore is rooted in powerful intellectual traditions and makes connection with some of the most important contemporary theoretical work.

My goal is to look at the Constitution historically and critically as a force that both shapes and is shaped by a political culture with certain recognizable continuities, but undergoing constant and sometimes rapid, even explosive, change. In this process of change, the meaning of key political concepts, including *interest, corruption, democracy,* and *republic,* has also changed. Since we tend to view the work of the Framers as if it were immutably carved in stone, this should be a salutary perspective, particularly if we also aspire to criticism of existing arrangements. But the Constitution is clearly not immutable in fact, as any reading of the checkered history of its interpretation makes clear. This situation may trouble those who reject the idea of the fundamental law as a "living document," but it is precisely how the Constitution has been treated historically. As Sheldon Wolin argues, the Constitution is simultaneously a political and an interpretive event; what the Framers agreed to was the text's content, not its meaning.[5]

The Two American Constitutions

It is important to remember that the United States has existed under two constitutions rather than one.[6] We often forget that the first constitution was the Articles of Confederation, in force from the end of the Revolution until the ratification of the document drafted in the Federal Convention of 1787. The Articles provided a very loose organizational structure that reserved sovereignty, independence, and all powers to the individual states except those powers expressly delegated to the United States Congress. In form, then, the structure was more like a league of independent nations than a unified, sovereign nation-state.[7] As a defender of the new Constitution, Alexander Hamilton wrote that the "radical vice" of the Articles was that under their authority the government had no power to legislate on individuals but had to act through the state governments in their corporate capacities. Therefore, although in theory the resolutions of Congress were binding, in practice they constituted mere recommendations.[8] Few at the time felt the system to be entirely satisfactory, though to many its replacement was adopted in a high-handed way, since the process ignored the requirement of the Articles that any amendment had to be unanimously approved. Moreover, the convention procedures ignored the fact that the delegates were authorized only to amend, not to produce an entirely new constitution, as they in fact did. These two factors lend a certain rough credence to the view that the Constitution is, in some sense, an example of a form of counterrevolutionary coup d'état.

Whatever the merits of this charge, the Framers of the Constitution were operating in an extremely difficult political situation. The new nation had held together through the Revolution in a most precarious fashion, and quite probably the ineptitude of George III and his ministers helped to keep the rebels together. Certainly, the former colonies were not ready for a state that would be fully sovereign in the European manner. Stated epigrammatically, what many in the separate states wanted was union rather than unity. As we have seen, many of the conditions for the establishment of a unitary system were absent or in decline. Geography alone worked against such a solution: The population of two to three million people was stretched out in a narrow band along the Atlantic seaboard. Although formal political institutions tended to be similar from one state to another, cultural differences between regions were beginning to emerge, and in the case of the North versus the South, the divisions were already becoming intense. Technology and communication were primitive, and the highly decentralized economy needed greater unity and an orderly system for the regulation of interstate commerce.[9]

Considering that those were the conditions in which the new Constitution was forged, it is small wonder that the results proved intensely controversial. The contest was so hard fought that, as a recent analysis has shown, a change of votes by a handful of delegates in the state ratifying conventions would have defeated the proposed document. For example, the Constitution won by a total of only thirty-two votes in the three crucial states of Massachusetts, Virginia, and New York.[10] Even today the Articles and, more generally, the Anti-Federalist position are again finding defenders. To appreciate what was at stake then, it is necessary to confront the theoretical arguments advanced by both sides in the ratification controversy. These debates lay bare many of the essential characteristics of American political thought.

The Federalist
and the Defense of the Constitution

The Federalist, or *The Federalist Papers,* occupies a unique position in the history of American thought. By no means a systematic treatise, it was a series of eighty-five newspaper articles written to influence voters as they cast their ballots for delegates to the critical ratifying convention in New York. However, since it was widely read in other states, it had an impact well beyond its immediate political purpose. But the ad hoc character of the documents should not obscure their importance. If, as Sheldon Wolin rightly argues, only the text but not the meaning of the Constitution had been agreed upon, then the place of *The Federalist* as the first systematic attempt to elucidate the elusive "intent of the Framers" made it almost uniquely important. Whether or not they captured that intent (or even whether there was a single determinate intent), the papers have been treated as if they did, and it is that perception that has left a deep impression on constitutional theory and development.

The principal authors of *The Federalist* were James Madison and Alexander Hamilton; the contributions of John Jay were few in number and, though by no means negligible, may be left aside here. To begin, the closest attention must be paid to Numbers 10 and 51 by Madison, which perhaps come closer than any other documents to capturing the pluralist conflict near the heart of U.S. politics.

Number 10 opens with a discussion of *faction,* that ancient curse of republican forms of government. The term is defined as "a number of citizens whether amounting to a majority or a minority of the whole, who are united and actuated by some common impulse of passion, or of interest, adverse to the rights of other citizens, or to the permanent and aggregate interests of the community."[11] The "latent" causes of faction are "sown in the nature of man" and are therefore ineradicable. Men will fall into conflict over religion, over government, over political leadership; the potential sources of strife are many. "But the most common and durable source of faction has been the various and unequal sources of property." Here we find creditors and debtors, agricultural, manufacturing, mercantile, and financial interests as well as lesser concerns; their regulation constitutes the principal function of government and leads to the creation of faction.[12] When it comes to the acquisition of property, different men have different faculties, the safeguarding of which is the "first object of government."[13]

It follows that the evil of faction can be countered in either of two ways—by removing its causes or by controlling its effects. The former course can be accomplished only by destroying liberty or by establishing a uniformity of opinion. The latter course is an impossibility: It would require a utopian and deeply non-Madisonian attempt to change human nature. However, the former, though conceivable, is a cure worse than the disease.[14] Therefore, the remedy for the evil must lie in finding ways to control its noxious effects. Madison told us we did not have to worry about minority factions, having made the egregiously optimistic assumption that adherence to the republican principle would always allow the majority to defeat a nefarious minority. The implication is that numbers alone are a source of power; thus the impact of money, social status, education, and the like is overlooked, not to mention that an intense minority may be well able to triumph over an apathetic majority.

For Madison, though, the real problem lay in the danger of majorities. A majority faction may be controlled through the devices of representative government. Pure democracies, in which "a small number of citizens, who assemble and administer the government in person, can admit of no cure for the mischiefs of faction."[15] Representation was said to have several advantages over pure democracy. It "refines and enlarges" public opinion by passing it through a body of presumably wise citizens who will have the common good as their goal, a group of citizens, one supposes, much like the Framers. Even more important is the argument that sheer size is a virtue—a virtue made possible only through modern representative government. In a small society, where there will be few parties and interests in contention, it will be easier for these forces to "concert and execute their plans of oppression." However, "extend the sphere and you take in a greater variety of parties and interests; you make it less probable that a majority of the whole will have a common motive to invade the rights of other citizens; or if such a common motive exists, it will be more difficult for all who feel it to discover their own strength and act in unison with each other."[16]

This argument, so familiar to students of American political thought, constitutes a revolution in the theory of republican government. Whereas in civic republican theory and in the work of "the celebrated Montesquieu," frequently quoted during the Federal Convention, small size was held to be a virtue and the only useful antidote to faction, in Madison's theory—and in Hamilton's less well known version—large size is a blessing.[17] Even more striking, faction, though still an evil, is now a necessary evil. Since the real danger is perceived to be in majority faction, the solution is one of splintering the majority into as many fragments as possible in the hope that they will cancel one another out, so that no single one can become dominant.

This approach is an obvious ancestor of the contemporary theory of interest group liberalism, although there is at least one important and subtle difference. Recall that Madison defined faction in contrast to a presumed public interest, the "permanent and aggregate interests of the community." Today's pluralists, because of their commitment to an idealized vision of science, which requires a sharp separation of fact and value, tend to deny that there is any such thing as a public interest.[18] The presumption of public interest gives Madison, for all the occasional cynicism of his appealing to popular sovereignty while advocating a theory designed to restrict it, a moral position still linked, however tenuously, to the theory of civic humanism. Thus Madison was able to criticize the politics of factions, although many of today's social scientists cannot.

Moreover, following the same line of reasoning about the public interest, the point for Madison was not simply to divide the majority, not simply to multiply factions so that a tyrannical majority would find it difficult to form, but rather to render the majority coalition helpless in the hope that a wiser representative elite would rise to the top and rule in the public interest.[19] This vision may appear disingenuous and even fanciful, but rule by the wise is as old as the hopes of Plato and as recent as the dreams of today's technocratic policy scientists, so it is hardly surprising, even if distressing, for it to reappear in the thinking of America's constitution makers.

However, Madison did not entirely abandon the principle of popular control, but he made it the last rather than the first resort. As understood by Madison, democracy was a form of direct popular rule, what we today would call direct or participatory democracy, and it is transparently clear that Madison's sympathies lay with representation rather than the direct participatory tradition of republicanism. Nevertheless, in the political context of the ratification debate, this distinction is a straw man and more than a little shifty, for the Anti-Federalist opponents of the Constitution were not advocates of direct democracy. Instead, as we shall see, they were populist democrats who sought to establish a system of more direct control over their representatives than they felt Madison's scheme allowed. Representative democracy itself is not really at issue.

Finally, the liberal individualism underlying Madison's formulations must be seen. The subordination of the individual to the community, so central to earlier republican thought, began to recede rapidly into the background. To be sure, there was a lingering commitment to the idea of the general interest and to the idea of control by a disinterested elite, but to adapt a striking phrase, we have seen not only the "emancipation of acquisitiveness," which Leo Strauss attributed to Locke,[20] but also what one might call the emancipation of interest. Doubtless it may not be precisely what Madison intended, but the road from Madison to the more jaded contemporary pluralism of a David Truman may be much shorter than Madison's eighteenth-century mind, with its baggage of self-evident truths, might have been ready to contemplate. But this is not the first time we have had occasion to observe the unintended consequences of ideas. Indeed, two hundred years have amply demonstrated that interest group politics is not necessarily so benign as the Founders anticipated.

The whole of Madison's contribution is by no means to be found in the analytical tour de force of *Federalist* 10. The other foundation of Madison's theory is contained in the almost equally original Number 51. Although the earlier paper draws heavily on the institutional theory of representation, it is primarily an essay in political sociology. In Number 51, the focus turns almost entirely to institutional structure. However, the principles underlying both papers are essentially the same. Fragmentation of power and authority are the essential themes of Number 51, just as fragmentation of interests is at the heart of Number 10. It is evident throughout that Madison was possessed by a strongly liberal distrust of government as such, even as he attempted to legitimate a constitutional form stronger than its predecessor. Rhetorically, he asked, "But what is government but the greatest of all reflections on human nature?" And he answered, "If men were angels no government would be necessary." But men are not angels, and we cannot expect to be governed by angels. The result follows: "You must first enable the government to control the governed; and in the next place oblige it to control itself." It is one thing to rely on the principle of popular control. Nevertheless, experience has taught mankind the necessity of "auxiliary precautions."[21]

The precaution recommended is the well-known principle of separation of powers. Each department of government is to have a will of its own and be kept as separate as possible from the others. Here too, the principle of competition is at work. Different units must have the means to protect themselves against one another. These means are rooted in Madison's bleak view of human nature. Appropriate institutions must make up for the higher motives one might hope for, in case they are absent. "Ambition must be made to counteract ambition. The interest of the man must be connected to the constitutional rights of the place."[22] This institutional attachment could be a problem in a republican form of government, where one expects the natural dominance of the legislative body. However, the difficulty can be surmounted by establishing a bicameral legislature whose members are subject to different modes of election and thus to different popular forces. All this diversity is added to an areal division of power established in the federal system. What we have then is a "compound republic" in which power is divided between nation and state and then further subdivided among the various governmental departments.[23] Finally, Madison recurred to the great theme of *Federalist* 10 to argue, again with excessive optimism, the virtues of the extended republic, reaching the conclusion that "a coalition of the majority of the whole society could seldom take place on any other principles than those of justice and the general good"—a wonderful dream to be sure—but one with built-in difficulties, since, though the Framers fully recognized the dangers of factional self-interest, "they necessarily underwrote it in trying to control it."[24]

The two papers I have highlighted by no means exhaust Madison's contribution to *The Federalist*. However, they do spell out the essentials of Madisonianism, and a preliminary assessment is possible. The idea underlying the system as a whole is to make decisionmaking very difficult so as to protect minorities against frivolous or malicious majorities. Authority is fragmented, hemmed in, counterbalanced, separated, and divided, not only at the national level, but also geographically. To be sure, the minority Madison was particularly concerned about protecting was the propertied few. Still, the solution extends in principle to the protection of other minorities as well. Of course, only the most rudimentary knowledge of American history is required to reveal that all too often the scheme has failed in this regard. Nor is this the only shortcoming. The Madisonian ideal is that of policy in the public interest emerging out of a factional struggle and compromise, policy that takes due account of the legitimate interests engaged in conflict. A general consensus guided by a representative but detached elite would then lead to policy based on the "cool and deliberate sense of the community."[25] This happens all too infrequently. More common is that a system designed to make decisionmaking difficult results in stalemate, and the outcome is often an irrational compromise that may appease the interests involved but that has precious little to do with anything so rational as the cool and deliberate sense of the community.

Alexander Hamilton's contributions to *The Federalist,* though enormously important, are, on the surface, somewhat less striking theoretically than Madison's. Hamilton's essays deal extensively with the defects of the Articles of Confederation, economic issues such as taxation, and, above all, the compelling need for strong, "energetic government." The locus of energy was to be in the executive branch of the national government.[26] If it is true, as many contend, that we live under a Hamiltonian rather than a Madisonian Constitution, then it is the emergence of a strong executive that justifies that reading.

However, at this point, I would rather dwell on Hamilton's contribution to the theory of judicial review and to the emergence of a new theory of popular sovereignty as vital elements in his interpretation of the disputed meaning of the Constitution. His immense contribution to political economy can best be considered in the context of the next chapter.

The argument for judicial review is trenchant and disarming by turns. Those opposed to the new Constitution, Hamilton claimed, need not fear the judiciary, because it is essentially a passive body with "no influence over either the sword or the purse."[27] Courts, he continued, have no force or will, but only judgment, so they are the weakest branch of government. The fact that judgment, in the context of the proposed system, might possibly assume enormous proportions is simply ignored. What seems to be implied is an utterly fallacious interpretive theory that holds that constitutional meaning is essentially transparent, an assumption belied by two hundred years of interpretive contention over the meaning of the provisions of the document. Turning to the issue of judicial review itself, Hamilton argued rather disingenuously that it did not imply the superiority of the judicial over the legislative branch. At the same time, however, because no act of a delegated authority can run counter to the commission under which it is exercised, it follows that "no legislative act . . . contrary to the Constitution, can be valid."[28] No matter what that may seem to mean, it is not a theory of ultimate judicial supremacy. Rather, it implies that the "power of the people" is superior to both legislative and judicial branches and that in case of conflict the will of the people as expressed in the Constitution ought to prevail.[29] The fact that this will is to be interpreted by judges who, for all practical purposes, hold life tenure is revealing about Hamilton's deepest attitudes regarding the form and substance of popular control.

More subtle still is the sense that Hamilton, like Madison—and conservatives to this day—placed great stress on the sources of popular control embedded in the new system.[30] As Sheldon Wolin suggests, it might appear that this was a mere rhetorical ploy indulged in for political effect by a notorious anti-democrat in the effort to secure ratification of the new Constitution. That no doubt was part of the approach, but as Wolin says, there was more at stake.[31] The underlying point was made many years ago by the dean of constitutional lawyers, Edward S. Corwin. Corwin told us that the Constitution was both a symbol of restraint and an instrument of power.[32] Although Madison too was concerned with the creation of new governmental powers, his primary focus, which was to become more central in later years, was on the problem of restraints. Hamilton, for his part, was more concerned with the creation of power. In that respect the "people" and the theory of popular sovereignty play a vital part. As far back as Thomas Hobbes, English theorists had attempted to ground absolute governmental power in the contractual consent of a presumably rational set of atomized, competitive individuals.[33] Thus, as modified by Locke's theory of an elected parliament, the people, perhaps unwittingly, become the ultimate source of a power with a high potential to be inimical to their rights and interests. As Wolin has shrewdly observed, the fragmentation of Madisonian politics makes inevitable the emergence of a strong state capable of reintegrating the factionalized fragments celebrated in *Federalist* 10 and *Federalist* 51.[34]

We have tended to lose sight of this important theoretical development because of a "persistent privileging of Madison over Hamilton" in discussing *The Federalist.*[35] The problem is more complex because Hamilton was never fully able to articulate his theory of the state in the context of his effort to legitimate the new Constitution, with its carefully constructed mechanical devices that masked the potential for the development of state power, feared by the Anti-Federalists.[36] In *Federalist* 51 Madison had assumed the natural dominance of the legislative branch in a republican government, but for Hamilton the true test of sound political institutions lay in their "aptitude and tendency to produce a good administration."[37] That is what the new theory of popular sovereignty—as well as Hamilton's policies while in office as the first secretary of the treasury—was designed to secure. With respect to the theory, its most striking aspect was that it ascribed "all power to a mythical entity that could never meet, never deliberate, never take action."[38] This observation may not have quite the dramatic force that Joshua Miller intended it to have, given the lack of a real alternative to large-scale and inevitably remote representative institutions; the Greek polis can never be restored. Remember that the opponents of the Constitution were also supporters of representative government. Still it is salutary to be reminded of how far we are from the direct control over our destinies that is implied in the etymological meaning of democracy. The specter of the contemporary "megastate," whose outlines are sketched in Wolin's *The Presence of the Past,* can be seen in the beginning of our national existence. Alexander Hamilton would be pleased.

Hamilton, Madison, and the Ambiguities of *The Federalist*

Enough has been said already to belie the facade of unanimity that is suggested by the adoption of the single pen name Publius to stand for the authors of *The Federalist.* Further, the idea that all that was secured in the Federal Convention was agreement on a text rather than on its meaning raises the possibility that the Constitution was a bundle of political compromises rather than the entirely coherent architectonic structure that is presented in textbook discussions of separation of powers, checks and balances, federalism, judicial review, and all the rest of the familiar provisions. Although there is no doubt that the Framers were highly informed theoretically, when one examines the complex politics of constitution making, one can easily say that *The Federalist* was written with "a genius for retroactive symmetry."[39] The Constitution is not a document of crystalline clarity based on generally accepted principles. It is no accident that shortly after the publication of the papers, Hamilton and Madison were to find themselves in bitterly opposed camps. Neither found the Constitution ideal, and Hamilton, in particular, was defending a document he felt to be grievously flawed when set beside his own deeply felt political ideas. If one looks beneath the surface agreements of the papers, one can see many of the conflicts that were to dominate American politics in the formative years. Indeed, one can go as far as to argue—with Alpheus T. Mason—that *The Federalist* suffers from a split personality.[40]

Of course, as Mason accepted, there were certain basic principles held in common by Hamilton and Madison. Both had an unsparing—some say dark, others say realistic—view of human nature. Men were not to be trusted and had to be restrained; there was no reason to hold out utopian hopes that the new order would alter this fact. At the same time, whatever misgivings the two men may have shared about the new Constitution, they agreed on the total inadequacy of the Articles of Confederation. Finally, both took it as a given that the unequal distribution of property had to continue to exist as long as liberty was to be preserved.

However, the areas of disagreement are at least as striking. Both were concerned with the problem of faction, but Hamilton was much more inclined to see the roots of the evil exclusively in the soil of economic differences. In addition, Madison's remedy was more consistently pluralistic in character. As a result, he had more faith in fragmentation as the somewhat paradoxical solution to the problem of faction, whereas the more authoritarian Hamilton was inclined to favor a system with an unconfined coercive power at the center. Thus, Hamilton saw in the new Constitution the possibility of creating precisely the sort of centralized order feared by the Anti-Federalist opposition. Therefore, as Mason showed, the two principal theoretical defenders of the document did not agree in the end on the nature and scope of the powers granted to the national government. In the terms of later debates, Hamilton was a "loose constructionist" and Madison was a "strict constructionist." As Madison saw it, the powers granted under the basic law were "few and defined,"[41] whereas for Hamilton something like the opposite was true. In any case, both can be seen as engaged in an attempt to institutionalize the Lockean theory of limited constitutional government, though one may be permitted to doubt the depth of Hamilton's sincerity.

To repeat, the outlines of future conflict are embryonically present in *The Federalist*. The party system that began to emerge in the first decade under the new system was to some extent the result of Hamilton's view that the potential for a strong state was inherent in the Constitution. He attempted to implement that view while he was in a position of power as George Washington's secretary of the treasury.

The Response
of the Anti-Federalist Opposition

The opposition position has rarely received adequate treatment from scholars. As usual, history has been written by the winners; only recently have scholars looked at Anti-Federalist ideas with serious attention to the actual arguments rather than simply dismissing them as the notions of reactionary cranks. The earlier tendency was no doubt aggravated by the absence of a single Anti-Federalist writer or text having the representative, authoritative standing of *The Federalist.* Instead, we are left with an enormous quantity of fragmentary literature, which, when collected by the late Herbert Storing, ran to seven volumes.[42] Included are the writings of leaders of the Revolution Samuel Adams and Patrick Henry, as well as Richard Henry Lee, Richard Yates, and Dewitt Clinton. To some extent, then, a collective portrait is appropriate, though the *Letters of a Federal Farmer,* often attributed— with uncertainty—to Lee, and the "Essays of Brutus," usually credited to Yates, stand out enough to receive special attention. The Brutus papers take on additional interest because, like *The Federalist,* they were initially published in newspapers in the state of New York. Since they ran contemporaneously with their more famous counterparts, they sometimes drew direct responses from Alexander Hamilton.[43]

The standard clichés stemming from the Progressive movement do not go very far to explain the debates between Federalists and Anti-Federalists. Although there was a good deal of rumbling about the perils of aristocracy,[44] the Anti-Federalists were not disturbed by the attempt to frustrate the democratic masses through the complex mechanisms of checks and balances, separation of powers, or even the specter of judicial review. Even though Hamilton's argument on behalf of judicial review had appeared before the meetings were held in such important states as Virginia, New York, and North Carolina, it was not made an issue in the state ratifying conventions; thus, Cecilia Kenyon suggested that it was not a matter of fundamental concern.[45] Similarly, the Anti-Federalists wanted more separation of powers, more checks and balances, than the Constitution called for.[46] Again, however, her suggestion was that, contrary to the views of the Progressives, those were not central issues. Much more to the point was discontent over the lack of a Bill of Rights: The Federalists rapidly conceded on that issue, although the Anti-Federalists were not entirely happy with the result.[47]

A more helpful approach to understanding the opposition is to focus on the debate over the nature of republican government. As Russell Hanson says, that is what the discussion of ratification was essentially about.[48]

All parties agreed that a republican form of government was called for; what was at stake was the ultimate shape that the republic would take. Even if not definitive, Gordon Wood's formulation of the problem is suggestive. "Like Puritanism, of which it was a more relaxed, secularized version, republicanism was essentially anti-capitalistic, a final attempt to come to terms with the emergent society that threatened to destroy once and for all the communion and benevolence that civilized men had always considered to be the ideal of human behavior."[49] Thus, the Anti-Federalists became "fervent defenders of the traditional assumption that the state was a cohesive, organic entity with a single homogeneous interest."[50] The continuity with the Puritan and civic humanist elements of the Revolution is unmistakable. So is a marked similarity to the thought of Rousseau.[51] Like Rousseau, the Anti-Federalists had an aversion to large size. It is important to see that the single interest they fought to defend was local rather than national, a tendency that has frequently recurred in the history of American politics.[52] They had a lingering belief in the ideas of civic virtue and an opposition to the "emancipation of interests" so central to Madisonianism. Even if we concede the possibility that for the Anti-Federalists, "virtue and the common good are instrumental to liberty," it is not clear that those men were liberal or that the "resemblance to pre-liberal thought is superficial."[53]

Instead, I think two things are indicated. First, history does not often, if ever, arrange itself into a conflict between simple, dichotomous alternatives such as republicanism and liberalism.[54] The focus on such a dichotomy has stimulated a great deal of very useful research, as it did in the study of the Revolution, but it has done little justice to the complexity of history. On closer examination, it emerges that the debates over ratification were conducted in a mixture of theoretical vocabularies, including not just liberalism and civic humanism, but also the much secularized residue of Puritanism and, lest we forget, a modernist, state-building theory as well.[55]

This complexity raises a second point. The mix of often seemingly incompatible ideological positions reflects the ambiguities inherent in a period of rapid social, economic, and political change. Thus, the Anti-Federalists clung to a defense of individual liberties that may seem entirely liberal, but that may have stemmed from their awareness that their communities were seriously threatened by the centralizing tendencies of the proposed constitutional system.[56] Similarly, the Federalists, although recognizing that virtue would be in short supply in the system they sponsored, at the same time hoped that their complex institutional mechanisms would permit the genuinely virtuous to rise to the top and enable decisions to be made by an enlightened elite acting in the public interest. As in the case of the Revolution, the participants in the discussion were ready to use whatever arguments were helpful to their cause. In addition, they simply saw no incompatibility among the finely distinguished schools of thought we perceive today. This tendency to mix genres of political thought, ignoring their compatibility or lack of it, was undoubtedly heightened by the rapid advance of commercial society, which arose in the early years of the century. That development was to undermine the values of the premodern system; a certain amount of ideological confusion is a likely result of a period of important socioeconomic change.

Under these conditions even some of the Anti-Federalists began to give ground. Certainly they were well aware that people were capable of self-interested behavior, particularly in the economic arena. Some Anti-Federalists began to challenge the idea that disinterested behavior was likely or even possible. Gordon Wood argued, in a paper that sharply revised his earlier conclusions, that in fact it was the Anti-Federalists who were the real modernists, the ones who pioneered interest group politics.[57] Wood's case is not entirely persuasive, and the documentation is thin: His case rests heavily on the career of a Pennsylvania farmer named William Findley. Still, it is clear that in the course of a debate with Richard Morris, Findley refuted the Federalists' claim to a position above the political fray and advanced something very much like a twentieth-century theory of interest group conflict, sans any commitment to a set of "permanent and aggregate interests of the community" that leaders could be expected to follow. Thus, the suggestion that the Anti-Federalist world of egalitarian democracy was the wave of the future is provocative and worthy of further reflection.[58] At the least, these debates show, once again, the limitations of a dichotomous view of the theoretical debates of the founding period.

Another aspect of the question of the representation of interests in the ratification debate is worth pursuing. Anti-Federalists believed that representation should be a mirror of the complexities of the existing society so that all interests would be represented, a position that once again sounds something like liberal interest group politics,[59] but that also might be said to resemble twentieth-century corporatism. "A fair representation, therefore, should be so regulated, that every order of men in the community, according to the common course of elections, can have a share in it—in order to allow professional men, merchants, traders, farmers, mechanics, etc. to bring a just proportion of their best informed men respectively into the legislature."[60] This view was explicitly rejected by Hamilton in *Federalist* 35. To him, the idea was "wholly visionary." No free election would normally produce such a result. Mechanics and manufacturers would naturally vote deferentially, that is, they would choose landholders, merchants, and professional men. These men, who were apparently believed to be endowed by nature with noblesse oblige, would vote for the benefit of all and avoid the "momentary humors" of the other members of the society.[61] And Madison, usually thought to be more moderate on issues relating to democracy, was even more damning. In *Federalist* 55 he wrote, "Had every Athenian citizen been a Socrates, every Athenian assembly would still have been a mob."[62] At that point, for an instant, the Federalists' mask of popular sovereignty drops and we can observe the instinctive elitism at the heart of their theory of representation.

One other facet of the problem of a proper republican scheme of representation is even more important: the question of the size of legislative districts in the House of Representatives relative to the number of members. Though conceding the need for representation, the Anti-Federalists feared that the institutions proposed would distort the popular will. As they saw it, the Constitution provided for too few representatives for too many people spread over too large a territory.[63] Although the ratification battle was not fought using the standard vocabulary of modern democratic theory, both Brutus and the Federal Farmer used the term *democratic* in reference to the lower house. The nature of the debate makes it quite clear that although the analysis of the Progressive historians, with its image of a deeply divided class system, was not on the mark, it was not entirely wrong either. There was at stake a real issue, which lends at least some credence to the notion of the Constitution as a counterrevolutionary coup d'état, as does the fact that even after ratification the document was by no means universally popular.[64] The language of counterrevolution is probably excessive, but it does suggest the flaw in the simple Hartzian consensus model. There can be a felt need to limit the power of government that is consistent with a wide range of interpretations of the meaning of liberalism. Russell Hanson neatly captured the issue: The Federalists desired a limited popular government, whereas the Anti-Federalists wanted a popular limited government.[65] This difference is subtle but nonetheless real.

Thus, this change in emphasis is *not* insignificant. The Constitution is not designed to foster either close popular control or a high level of citizen participation. We are all too familiar with this fact today. Massive evidence suggests that citizens see the state as distant, out of control, and so strangely and dangerously remote from their concerns that even the minimal participation of voting in elections seems increasingly pointless to many U.S. citizens. That has not always been true—consider Jacksonian America—but the Constitution clearly opens up that possibility, and the fears of the Anti-Federalists have taken on a relevance that they did not seem to have had in the more sanguine times of twenty-five years ago. Frequently, theoretical positions wax and wane in their apparent relevance as conditions change.

The Anti-Federalist position surely does not have all the answers, least of all for our own time. I merely want to redress the balance of the discussion that has so strongly tilted to the Federalist position. But antifederalism is not a politically viable alternative for us today and is by no means free of its own difficulties. Contemporary communitarians who hope to revive the republican components of antifederalism as an antidote to the excesses of interest-oriented liberalism have their hands full. Antifederalism would require a reduction of conflict and a level of social and cultural homogeneity that are well past any hope of attainment today. In any case, such homogeneity would demand an unattractive form of ethnocentricity and a commitment, perhaps, to a religious orthodoxy that would be stifling and, under present conditions, profoundly undemocratic.[66] The homogeneity that gives unity to a small-scale society can come at a great price.

And yet the Anti-Federalists have much to teach us. They understood the dynamics of the proposed new system and realized that those dynamics would move the new Constitution much further along the road to Hamiltonian centralization than their Federalist opponents would have dared to admit. The Anti-Federalists feared that at the end of the road lay a consolidated republic whose sheer scale would make difficult the close popular control over the new state that they desired. Like many modern critics, they saw large size as the enemy of democracy.[67] They also clearly understood that the states were the locus of the only genuine political cultures in the former colonies; there simply was no single *national* culture. One of the triumphs of federalism was to begin the creation of such a culture, even though it had the attributes of a hothouse plant.[68]

It was more than a sham battle within an overwhelmingly liberal consensus that was being fought, which Hartz's theory of an overwhelmingly liberal consensus misses. The great triumph of the Federalists was to clothe their views in the rhetorical garb of popular sovereignty, thus gaining control over the use of one of the most powerful symbolic terms in modern politics.[69] As a result, the Anti-Federalists have had a "bad press," so to speak, in the history books. But, in spite of this, something has lingered on, perhaps in the persistent strand of localism in American politics and perhaps in the deep distrust of politics and politicians, although this attitude is also a part of the liberal tradition.[70]

All these conflicts were sharp enough to undermine, at least partially, the consensus theory of American history. Liberalism was a powerful force from the start, and the ratification of the Constitution was a large step toward consolidating liberalism's hold. However, the dual heritage of Puritanism and civic humanist republicanism was rich and qualitatively different. The existence of this history forces a modification of the Hartz thesis. Moreover, the complex mix of ideas described here also undermines the republican synthesis. It certainly will not do to write Locke or Lockeanism out of American history, as Pocock attempted. The republican theory has been a useful stimulant, but the concept of republicanism simply cannot replace liberalism as an organizational theme for the interpretation of American thought and history.[71]

The ambiguities of the founding period are those of a complex transition in which an older body of thought began to give way to a newer set of ideas, which may have been more suitable to the geographic and cultural characteristics of the new nation. It is very important to call attention once again to the rapid emergence of entrepreneurial capitalism. The growing concern with the pursuit of interests surely was related to that central aspect of capitalism.[72] In this context, it is important to take note of antifederalism as a pointer to the world we have lost, a world that had real virtues; seldom is a major historical change unequivocally for the better. Perhaps above all, the Anti-Federalists raised the most serious questions about what J.G.A. Pocock called the "tension between virtue and commerce," that is, about the quality of political life in a regime based on the pursuit of self-interest.[73] A great deal of the politics of the new regime revolved around trying to resolve these issues. This new politics generated an interpretive struggle over the meaning of the Constitution.

· 5 ·

Defining the
Constitutional Text
and the Emergence
of Party Politics

So far in this study, I have stressed the indeterminateness of the constitutional text and the intellectual turmoil, not to say confusion, generated by the rapidly changing social and economic conditions of the new regime. The power of Gordon Wood's analysis of the founding era rests to a great extent on his sense of the emergence of individualistic, interest-oriented liberal capitalism. Although I have argued that his opposition between liberalism and republicanism was too sharp, owing to the unsystematic mix of those positions in the thought of the Founders, I also argued that this mix reflected the rapid socioeconomic transition that took place in the last quarter of the eighteenth century. To illustrate this change, let us consider the thought of several major revolutionary figures in the transition period. This will help to establish the context in which the debate over the meaning of the Constitution took place.

Franklin, Adams, Paine,
and the Ambiguities of Transition

The intellectual peculiarities brought on by the swift transition to a commercial liberal society can be seen in the thought of such diverse thinkers and actors as Benjamin Franklin, John Adams, and Tom Paine. Let us look at Franklin. Max Weber was certainly not wrong to identify the author of *Poor Richard's Almanac* as an example of the "spirit of capitalism."[1] Familiar maxims, such as Time is money and A penny saved is a penny earned, are those of the petit bourgeois capitalist. Indeed, Franklin, along with his multitudinous other attainments, was a successful, well-to-do businessman. A strong supporter of the new Constitution, he was excited by the possibilities for rapid growth in size, population, and economic output that were inherent in the system. These positions clearly separate him from the Anti-Federalist opposition.

However, there are simultaneous echoes of older traditions in his thinking. Whether the intellectual mixture is stable is another question, but it is there. Franklin distrusted luxury and believed in a life of "happy mediocrity," which called, not for an absolute equality of wealth, but certainly for a widespread distribution of property that would avoid the extremes of rich and poor and lead to a comfortable standard of living for all. Consistent with his nickname "Plain Ben," he called for a life of republican simplicity in a generally egalitarian social order. That position also led him to ideas on economics far removed from those of the rising bourgeoisie. He showed considerable distrust of men of great property, firmly opposed granting special status to the propertied, and decisively viewed property as a social creation rather than a natural right in the manner of Locke. Finally, he saw taxation as a necessary extension of governmental authority if the harmonious social order he sought were ever to be achieved.[2]

The mix of liberal capitalist ideas with the older, premodern conception of a virtuous social order is intriguing. But an Anti-Federalist might well have argued that such a mix, however attractive, was nevertheless incoherent because the sheer size of the proposed regime alone would be fatal to the republican components of the ideal. Once again, it may be suggested that only a period of rapid social transition could have led to such an ill-assorted amalgam of ideas.

The case of John Adams illustrates the same phenomenon even more clealy. Between the 1770s and the 1790s, Adams's thoughts underwent a marked change—a change formulated precisely by John R. Howe, Jr. Howe writes that Adams's "assumptions about the moral condition of the American people and the make-up of American society altered quite significantly between the two periods—essentially from an emphasis on moral virtue and social cohesion to notions of moral declension and social conflict."[3] Adams wrote widely and often more systematically than many of his revolutionary colleagues, though much of his changing position can be gleaned from his voluminous letters. For all his reputation as a somewhat dour conservative, Adams was very much caught up in the optimistic outburst of near utopian neoclassicism during the revolutionary period.[4] He believed in the virtue of the American people; that virtue was a secularized descendant of the Puritanism in his ancestry, combined with the influence of his wide learning in classical studies. Industry, frugality, prudence, and a willingness to subordinate private to public interest were the hallmarks of this conception. And like many others, he believed that independence was needed in order to prevent the corruption of American virtue by the decadent motherland. Again, like others, for Adams the Revolution was a proving ground that would show that Americans possessed the requisite virtue to make republicanism possible.

Following James Harrington, Adams also believed that property entailed power and that the wide distribution of property in America made popular government a necessity.[5] Such a government was made possible by the virtue of the people. Even so, good government had to be balanced government, and above all, as he argued in the *Thoughts on Government,* it had to be government under law—"an Empire of laws and not of men."[6]

By the 1790s, however, disillusionment had begun to set in. Again Howe gives an adept summary: Personal gain rather than disinterested concern for society had become the American way. The earlier cohesion of the colonial system, fostering an egalitarian social order, had given way to the growth of special interests bent solely on their own gratification.[7] The changes that upset Adams were many: Shays's Rebellion was a disquieting factor. In general, he saw an alarming degree of what he termed "disaggregation." The expanding economy was something Adams could not oppose, but the rapid creation of wealth tended to undermine republican virtue, dependent, as it was, on a simple, austere life. He came increasingly to recognize what he felt to be the inevitability of a "natural aristocracy," which could originate from many sources, including, for example, wealth, family status, and intelligence. Of these perhaps the most significant was wealth, which threatened to subvert the broad distribution of property necessary for the success of American republicanism. That led, in turn, to an intensification of social conflict.

These observations convinced Adams of the need for a greater degree of social control. Order had to be preserved; that required a balance between the emerging social forces. On the surface there might appear to be a certain similarity of Adams's position to that of Madison. Certainly, Adams embraced Madison's Constitution. But, as Gordon Wood argues, Adams failed to understand the system, for he saw in it a version of the ancient ideal of the mixed regime. Thus he hoped to isolate the "aristocracy" in the Senate and thereby constrain its influence. But Madison's separation of powers was based on the emancipation of interests rather than on the direct representation of classes. Madison too had seen the emergence of interests in politics and sought to design a wholly new republican order that would make a virtue of this new necessity. Adams saw the same phenomenon but clung to his pre-modern ideals even while endorsing Madison's scheme. As Wood points out, Adams failed to see that the end of classical politics had come and that his elaborate constitutional theories were, in one sense, irrelevant to the new conditions. Yet, they were not entirely irrelevant, for like the Anti-Federalists he opposed, he sensed the problem inherent in a republic without civic virtue and thus hinted at profound problems that were to emerge with great force later in American history.[8]

Thomas Paine similarly reflected the emergence of the new bourgeois liberalism. Paine is an atypical—even deviant—figure in the revolutionary pantheon. Of working-class background, he arrived in the colonies only shortly before hostilities broke out. Motivated by lifelong antimonarchical sentiments, he spent his entire career as an itinerant revolutionary searching for causes to support. No established colonial surpassed him in revolutionary zeal or the messianic fervor with which he pursued the establishment of the virtuous republic. More than any other leader of the rebellion, he was an ardent democrat in something like the modern sense of the word. There were also social democratic overtones in the policies he supported, anticipating the modern system of social security as well as a system of children's allowances.[9] How these innovations were to be carried out is somewhat mysterious, given Paine's deep hostility to government and to taxes. "Society," he wrote, "in every state is a blessing, but government, even in its best state is but a necessary evil; in its worst state an intolerable one. . . . Government, like dress, is the badge of lost innocence."[10] And that is among his more restrained utterances on government, for in *The Rights of Man* he argued that poverty itself was a result of a disturbance of the natural order by the depredations of the state.

But for all his democratic radicalism and all his talk of republican virtue, Paine was tied to the emerging bourgeois, laissez-faire order, a fact that emerged with some clarity after the Revolution. In spite of his reputation as a man of the left, on economic matters the distance from Paine to such contemporary apostles of unlimited capitalism as Milton Friedman is not so great as one might expect.[11] Paine's virtuous republicanism emerged in the form of a highly individualistic liberal radicalism, but not a leftist radicalism in a contemporary sense. To understand Paine, one must remember that he wrote at a time when capitalism was a powerful, antiaristocratic, liberating force. It was a rallying point around which segments of the working class rallied.[12] Paine put aside his earlier worries about the impact of commercialism on virtue. In so doing he captured the evolving American spirit as well as, if not better than, any of his contemporaries.

Hamilton, Jefferson,
and the Emergence of Party Politics

With the successful conclusion of the Revolution and the fundamental restructuring of political institutions brought about by the new Constitution, a different order of problems emerged. The new system had to be made to work, and in particular, the form of the political economy of the new regime had to be thrashed out. This process led to a momentous political debate on the proper interpretation of the Constitution. The argument was not quickly resolved, but the fundamental contours of the issues were set out in the early years in the disputes between Hamilton and Jefferson and their respective followers. The contest led to the emergence of the first modern system of political parties: The Jeffersonians in the Washington administration organized to oppose the dominant Federalists on questions ranging from the problem of how to handle the debts incurred in fighting the Revolution to foreign policy toward England and France, the two great powers with which the new nation was closely linked.

The triumph of Jefferson and his Democratic Republicans in the presidential election of 1800 was a momentous event; not many new nations have been able to transfer power peacefully from one faction to another. Jefferson as always was somewhat enigmatic. He declared in his Inaugural Address that we were all federalists and all republicans, thus lending support to the consensus theory, but in private he suggested that his election was a true revolution. Once again the Hartz theory has its value; all parties to the discussion endorsed some form of capitalism, but the details of the form remained to be worked out, and as always, details count. The struggles between the two factional leaders were real and they mattered. What was at stake was the meaning of an inherently ambiguous Constitution and its relation to a changing economy.

The Hamiltonian Theory

We should remember once again that it was the text and not the meaning of the Constitution that had been agreed to. Understanding this, Alexander Hamilton, from his position as secretary of the treasury during the Washington administration, saw an opportunity. We know that the Constitution hardly matched Hamilton's ideal. Speaking in the guarded privacy of the Philadelphia convention, Hamilton made it abundantly clear that his preferences were for a system involving even less popular control than provided for under the document that was produced, however attenuated that control may appear to contemporary critics. The people, he insisted, were divided into the few and the many, the rich and wellborn as against the mass.[13] "The people," he continued, "are turbulent and changing; they seldom judge or determine right." And, at a private dinner party, he referred to the people as "a great beast."[14] The few and the many should have the power to check each other, but it was the few who had to have a permanent share in government. A democratic assembly could not be trusted to pursue the public good. The institutional consequence of Hamilton's view would be a highly centralized government under the leadership of a powerful chief executive. Hamilton further stated that he saw no reason for the continued existence of the individual states, but in deference to the fact that such a proposal was made impossible by public opinion, Hamilton suggested that the state governors be appointed by the national government so as to render them subservient and so as to decrease the likelihood that state laws contrary to the national Constitution would be passed.[15] Of course, any such laws would be void.

The national government was to consist of a popularly elected lower house, whose members would serve three-year terms, and a Senate made up of members elected indirectly "during good behavior"—that is, for life terms—a plan explicitly patterned after the British House of Lords. The president would also be indirectly elected for a life term and would have veto power over all laws passed; he would be, in effect, an elective monarch. The plan adopted in the end was far removed from Hamilton's secret proposals; after his marathon speech he played a rather small role in the deliberations of the convention.

Aside from a palpable contempt for democracy, what lay behind Hamilton's proposals and policies? A good starting point is Cecilia Kenyon's suggestion that he was a "Rousseau of the Right," with strong leanings toward a version of civic republicanism.[16] To use a different vocabulary, he was that rare American phenomenon, a right-wing statist. *Conservative* is a term often used, but Hamilton's commitment to economic modernization precluded that designation—if conservatism indicates an adherence to the tried and true. Economic modernization is too disruptive to count as conservative in that sense of the term. He hoped, like Rousseau, to foster a sense of identity between the individual and the state or at least to secure a willingness on the part of citizens to subordinate their interests to a higher good. In that he came closer to the conceptions of the civic republicans than the other leading figures of the new nation did, though he surely lacked the republicans' distaste for commerce and their fear of government.

It must be remembered that the country was, in modern terms, an underdeveloped nation.[17] The remedy for this lamentable condition was, in Hamilton's view, a powerful centralized state. A nation without such a government was "an awful spectacle."[18] "We have neither troops, nor treasury, nor government." This was "almost the last stage of humiliation."[19] But with strong government, America could fulfill a great national destiny. The theme of state-building has all too often been neglected in discussions of early American political development because of a tendency to focus on the system of constitutional restraints on power, but it was an important aspect of early American politics nonetheless. Indeed, one can argue that a strong state was a necessary corrective to the antidemocratic fragmentation of the Madisonian system.[20] To neglect this problem is to neglect Hamilton's vision. A strong government dedicated to economic growth would "baffle all the combinations of European jealousy" and create "one great American system superior to the control of all transatlantic force or influence and able to dictate the terms of the connection between the old and the new world!"[21] Notice the order of priorities here. "The difference between Hamilton's conceptions and those of later politicians was that, while he never faltered in his conviction that the economy was an instrument of state power, his successors tended to view the state as an instrument of private economic purposes."[22] It is true that his policies favored business interests, but not to the exclusion of agriculture. The latter had a "strong claim to pre-eminence," he said, perhaps somewhat disingenuously, but that claim should not be an "exclusive predilection."[23] He strongly believed that both these interests would subordinate themselves to a rightist conception of the general will, yet in this, not surprisingly, he was disappointed, since his policies appealed, not to the altruistic impulses of economic elites, but to their economic self-interest.[24] When the agents of his vision did not meet his standards, he was deeply disillusioned, and in 1802 he remarked that the Constitution he had fought to adopt was a "frail and worthless fabric." He concluded that "every day proves to me more and more that this American world was not made for me."[25]

And yet, from Hamilton's own perspective, he yielded to pessimism much too soon. To a significant extent because of his efforts, the United States did indeed become a great world power, one whose strength was based on its economy. Here the unformed nature of the Constitution becomes critical. It is a mistake to argue that because private property was sacrosanct, the Framers intended a capitalist economy, as we understand the term. The essence of capitalism is the employment of capital goods to create more property.[26] The complex preconditions for such a system did not yet exist. As secretary of the treasury, Hamilton worked to establish those factors. The constitutional key was Article 1, Section 10, which banned laws impairing the obligation of contracts. Precisely what that meant seems to have been unclear even to the convention's Drafting Committee.[27] Hamilton's economic program, particularly in its fiscal dimensions, was an attempt to take advantage of this ambiguity. The foundation of Hamilton's system was the sanctity of contracts.

Forrest McDonald goes as far as to claim, "The enactment of Hamilton's fiscal program may justly be regarded as the completion of the Constitution and as the means by which life was breathed into the document."[28] It is not necessary here to pursue the details of the program. Hamilton saw the existence of a public debt as providing the basis for a social revolution. The institutional key was the establishment of the Bank of the United States, whose constitutionality was to be hotly contested by the followers of Thomas Jefferson.[29]

The heart of Hamilton's argument, later picked up by Chief Justice John Marshall in *McCulloch v. Maryland,* was that the power to create such instruments did not have to be spelled out in the Constitution but rather was implied by the very nature of sovereign power itself.[30] The implications of this interpretive position for the expansion of governmental power cannot be overemphasized. Combined with the Hamiltonian theory of the executive, they led inexorably to the constitutional system of the present century. The results of Hamilton's daring were clear. "Although most Americans probably would have chosen otherwise, Congress chose the Hamiltonian way. The United States would be built under a government-channeled, government-encouraged, and sometimes government-subsidized system of private enterprise for personal profit."[31]

All that points clearly toward capitalism as we know it, but it strains at the limits of Louis Hartz's consensus theory. Hamilton's theory was not one of "atomistic social freedom," nor was it economic liberalism on the model of Adam Smith. In fact, Hamilton sneered at the very idea "that trade will regulate itself." He wrote, "This is one of those wild speculative paradoxes, which have grown up among us, contrary to the uniform practice and sense of the most enlightened nations."[32] Further, the assertions of executive power and the drive for centralization did not comport well with the liberal ideal of limited government or, for that matter, with republican fears of abuse of governmental power. However, his shattered hope that business leaders would subordinate self-interest to the public good was much more closely related to civic republicanism than to any version of liberalism. The result was a mix of ideas perhaps unique in American thought, certainly in the thought of Hamilton's time. Still, it is entirely plausible to argue that the movement of American history, particularly in this century, has been toward an essentially Hamiltonian Constitution.[33] The president, though by no means an elected monarch, is normally the dominant figure in the political system. Moreover, in spite of a certain historical ebb and flow, the tendency has been for power to gravitate from the states to Washington; and economically, the sort of symbiotic relationship between state and economy that is so clear today would have gladdened Hamilton's heart.[34]

The Jeffersonian Theory

How Thomas Jefferson would have responded to contemporary conditions is subject to a good deal more dispute. Jefferson is one of the most enigmatic figures in American history. He left a wealth of ideas but no systematic political theory at all. Only one real book exists—the *Notes on the State of Virginia*—and much of that dealt with nonpolitical questions. Aside from that, there is a brief, fragmentary, early autobiography. For the most part, Jefferson's views must be gleaned from his state papers and, perhaps most revealing, from his startlingly voluminous body of letters. In addition to the lack of system, Jefferson's career was shot through with remarkable conflicts between his ideas and his actions. His was a "life of paradox. . . . A Virginia nationalist, a slave-holding *philosophe,* an aristocratic democrat, a provincial cosmopolitan, a pacific imperialist—the paradoxes, it seems clear, are of no ordinary variety, reaching beyond the life of one man. They are as large in meaning and as portentous in significance as America itself." There is much to be said for the view of the great Henry Adams that Jefferson provides the key to the mystery of America. As Adams put it, Jefferson's critics saw him as a visionary, "but if this view of his character was right, the same visionary qualities seemed also to be a national trait, for everyone admitted that Jefferson's opinions, in one form or another, were shared by a majority of the American people."[35]

The result of this confusion and lack of system is an endless debate over the meaning of Jefferson's legacy for succeeding generations. Martin Diamond remarked that U.S. political history "is the story of the American heritage and the fight among the heirs."[36] Jefferson's contribution to this tradition is probably the most disputed of them all, to the extent that a study of his reception in American thought after his death is, in itself, a significant study in the development of the American mind. This fact, however, is not without irony, since, as Joyce Appleby comments, Jefferson opposed the transfer of ideas from one generation to another, and thus, "the true Jeffersonian legacy is to be hostile to legacies."[37] Appleby's comment is a nice instance of the politics of interpretation central to the argument of this book.

In brief, the American Left has often seized on Jefferson's opposition to the commercial, financial, and industrial interests supported by Hamilton and has concluded that, were Jefferson alive today, his commitments to those who were neither rich nor wellborn would lead him into the reformist liberal camp that runs from Jacksonian democracy to populism, through the Progressive Movement to the New Deal, and on to the programs of the New Frontier and the Great Society. The Right has often responded by focusing on Jefferson's means rather than his ends and has held that his belief in a strict, narrow construction of the terms of the Constitution, his localism and fear of centralized government, and his belief in individual natural rights would place him on the side of the libertarian conservatives. Of course we shall never know, but clearly, in one way or another, Jefferson provides aid and comfort to the entire ideological spectrum of American politics, a situation that could hardly arise in the case of a more systematic thinker.

In spite of all that, certain themes do appear with some consistency. First among them is the individualistic idea of natural rights conceived in an essentially Lockean sense. As I argued in the discussion of the American Revolution, recent scholarly amendments to the understanding of Jefferson have not destroyed this basic contention. So strong is this belief that Joyce Appleby might have exaggerated but little when she wrote that Jefferson was less concerned with democracy than with a definition of freedom as "liberation from all social authority, especially that of government."[38] To Henry Adams, Jefferson was not at all a real democrat, but rather a southern republican who saw the real enemy as a Federalist tendency toward monarchy. Thus he was not in a social sense a democrat.[39] Surely it is true that in his own time Jefferson's theory of democracy did little to encourage the use of government as a positive force.

Another frequently recurring theme is no doubt related to Jefferson's abiding distrust of government. Again and again he wrote that "the earth belongs to the living," and thus decisions of earlier generations had no binding claim on those who came later.[40] As Richard Matthews insists, that is a position with important implications, of which Jefferson himself was fully aware.[41]

For instance, in the same letter to Madison, Jefferson was extensively concerned with quite technical considerations governing the law of property. It is important to recall here that Jefferson, in writing the Declaration of Independence, deleted estate, that is, material property, from the list derived from Locke of natural rights and substituted for it the pursuit of happiness. Property, then, is not a natural right and is subject to potentially significant regulation. Locke himself reached a similar conclusion, but the "demotion" of property's status by Jefferson is still important.[42] He was proud of his role in ending the feudal practices of entail and primogeniture and was an advocate of measures to widen the distribution of property. Writing to Madison, Jefferson echoed Locke in claiming that the earth was given to man as a common stock. When there was uncultivated land and there were unemployed poor, it was clear to him that natural rights were being violated. He conceded that "an equal division of property is impracticable," but he stressed the misery that the enormous inequality in property visited upon mankind. "Legislatures" he said, "cannot invent too many devices for subdividing property, only taking care to let their subdivisions go hand in hand with the natural affections of the human mind." The powerful social democratic, if not socialist, implications of this position are striking.[43] It is no wonder that in spite of his lack of system and the resulting inconsistencies, American radicals have always had a soft spot for Jefferson.[44]

The idea that the earth belongs to the living has other important implications as well. In his famous letter to Madison, Jefferson wrote that no society "can make a perpetual constitution, or even a perpetual law." Since a generation lasted approximately nineteen years, every constitution expired at the end of that time. "If it be enforced longer, it is an act of force and not of right."[45]

As might be expected, Madison's response to this "daft" proposal, as Judith Shklar called it, was distinctly cool.[46] Perhaps somewhat disingenuously, Madison conceded that the argument might apply in theory but went on to argue that it was subject to weighty practical difficulties. Would not such a government be "too mutable"? Would the public mind not be excessively agitated? In the nature of things, some obligations did descend from one generation to the next. The instability of the law would simply be too great. There was no relief from such problems other than in "the received doctrine that a *tacit* assent may be given to established Governments and laws." One could not escape this idea "without subverting the very foundation of Civil Society." It would be pleasurable, Madison suggested, to be able to announce to the world such a "salutary restraint on living generations from *unjust* and *unnecessary* burdens on their successors." However, that was a pleasure he had no hope of enjoying. The scheme was simply too theoretical for the American culture. "Further light must be added to the Councils of our Country before many truths which are seen through the medium of Philosophy become visible to the naked eye of the ordinary politician."[47] Interestingly, here Madison, in his reliance on tacit consent, is more Lockean than his famously Lockean friend. The threat he wished to avoid was that of government in perpetual transition, but as Richard Matthews claimed, that was precisely what Jefferson seemed to want, at least as a theoretical proposition.[48]

This same attitude toward change also underlies Jefferson's remarkable rhetoric about the virtues of rebellion. "I hold it," he claimed, "that a little rebellion, now and then, is a good thing, and as necessary in the political world as storms in the physical."[49] Later in the same year the prose got more flamboyant: "God forbid we should ever be twenty years without such a rebellion." And "what country can preserve its liberties, if their rulers are not warned from time to time that their people preserve the spirit of resistance? . . . The tree of liberty must be refreshed from time to time with the blood of patriots and tyrants."[50]

Still, even with this persistent attitude toward change, there is not complete consistency. One must suspect that these statements were made partly for rhetorical effect, for in his letter to Madison endorsing, though with reservations, the new Constitution, he wrote, "The instability of our laws is really an immense evil."[51] Jefferson as president surely did nothing to encourage constitutional dissolution or to promote his statutory equivalent to today's sunset laws or still less to incite rebellion. The same Jefferson who swore "eternal hostility against every form of tyranny over the mind of man" made use of the seditious-libel laws while in office, was notably intolerant of opposition, and in general compiled a weak record as a civil libertarian.[52] Henry Adams was probably not far off the mark in his characteristically cynical assessment: "Jefferson resembled all rulers in one peculiarity of mind. Even Bonaparte thought that a respectable minority might be useful as censors; but neither Bonaparte nor Jefferson was willing to agree that any particular minority was respectable."[53]

The evidence for Jefferson's radicalism, while real, is in conflict with his acceptance of a Constitution frequently denounced as an undemocratic instrument and created to support the commercial and financial forces that he opposed. This tension is significant, as is Jefferson's view of the *Federalist Papers* as "the best commentary on the principles of government which ever was written."[54] As he saw it, the Constitution was not perfect; it omitted a Bill of Rights and it did not insist on the principle of rotation in office. Yet Jefferson, contending that the will of the majority should prevail, was prepared to go along cheerfully with the results.[55]

Jefferson had reason to be satisfied. The election of 1800, which brought his administration to power in place of his more conservative Federalist predecessors, led to an extended period of dominance by his Democratic Republican Party and was, in his view, a genuine revolution in the principles of American government. Furthermore, it successfully met the difficult postrevolutionary challenge of a peaceful transfer of power from one party to another; indeed, the fact that a competitive party system had been established, in spite of the wishes of the protagonists, was in itself a major event in the history of Western democratic politics.[56] The Louisiana Purchase, though of doubtful constitutionality, seemed to secure the Jeffersonian dream of an agrarian republic, and the Federalist Party was soon to disappear altogether. The acquisition of the huge Louisiana Territory was particularly important; here was a Madisonian extension of the sphere with a vengeance.

Jefferson's attachment to agrarian values was one of his most deeply held beliefs. "Those who labor in the earth are the chosen people of God," he wrote. "Corruption of morals in the mass of cultivators," he continued, "is a phenomenon of which no age nor nation has furnished an example." Those who desert the soil were apt to become dependent and "dependence breeds subservience and venality. . . . The mobs of great cities add just so much to the support of pure government, as sores do to the strength of the human body." The proportion of the total of classes of citizens other than farmers "is the proportion of its unsound to its healthy parts."[57] The point is hammered home in a letter to Madison: "I think our governments will remain virtuous for many centuries; as long as they are chiefly agricultural; and this will be as long as there shall be vacant lands in any part of America. When they get piled upon one another in large cities, as in Europe, they will become corrupt as in Europe."[58] The conclusion was obvious: "Let our workshops remain in Europe."[59]

Therefore, for a democratic republic to be secure, it had to be agrarian. But what were the characteristics of democracy and republicanism for Jefferson? Here the absence of any systematic treatment is particularly troubling. At times Jefferson wrote as a convinced theorist of participatory democracy, in spite of his endorsement of a Constitution that hardly fit that model. Admitting that republic was a vague concept, he attempted a definition by saying, "It means a government by its citizens in mass, acting directly and personally, according to rules established by the majority; and that every other government is more or less republican, in proportion as it has in its composition more or less of this ingredient of the direct action of the citizens." But such a scheme, he admitted, could hardly be practiced beyond the limits of a New England township, so that the closest alternative was representative government carried out, if possible, by constituency-instructed delegates chosen for short terms.[60] The similarity to Anti-Federalist critiques of the Constitution, with their emphasis on close popular control, is striking.

It should be noted that this definition appears in a letter written late in life when Jefferson, having left the presidency and in spite of the apparent triumph of his own principles, was becoming increasingly discontented with the Constitution he had endorsed almost thirty years before. In his old age, Jefferson turned more and more to schemes for radical decentralization. Government, he wrote to John Taylor, was turning out to be less republican, in his sense, than he had hoped and expected. The judiciary had become an entrenched power, with a pronounced tendency to be in the control of judges holding office for life; even the jury system, which in 1787 Jefferson had seen as the "only anchor . . . by which a government can be held to the principles of its constitution," seemed to him a weak reed, because of its control by the highly defective courts.[61] Worse still, Hamilton's bank was still in place while Jefferson continued to believe that "banking establishments are more dangerous than standing armies and that the principle of spending money to be paid by posterity, under the name of funding, is but swindling futurity on a large scale."[62] Finally, Jefferson wrote, "Experience has taught me that manufactures are now as necessary to our independence as to our comfort."[63] This must have been a bitter conclusion to draw, but the Sage of Monticello conceded that conditions had changed in important ways since his denunciation of manufacturing in the *Notes on the State of Virginia* in 1785. As Mason

Drukman shrewdly observes, reality kept intruding on Jefferson's hopes. But this new reality called into question the very foundations of his understanding of the needs of a democratic republic.[64]

The solution to this threat of decay was in accord with Jefferson's definition of republicanism.[65] In a series of letters, mostly written in the spring and summer of 1816, Jefferson proposed to amend the Madisonian Constitution by increasing its already substantial degree of fragmentation. The core of his idea was the division of counties into smaller units called wards, which would then be invested with a great deal of potential power. This is a provocative idea, which has probably had more influence on contemporary theorists of participatory government than it ever had in Jefferson's lifetime.[66] The notion first appeared in 1810 in a letter to John Tyler: "These little republics would be the main strength of the great one. We owe to them the vigor given to our revolution."[67] He returned to the theme in his 1816 letters:

> Divide the counties into wards of such size as that every citizen can attend, when called on, and act in person. Ascribe to them the government of their wards in all things relating to themselves exclusively. A justice, chosen by themselves, in each, a constable, a military company, a patrol, a school, the care of their own poor, their own portion of the public roads, the choice of one or more jurors to serve in some court, and the delivery, within their own wards, of their own votes for all elective officers of higher sphere, will relieve the county administration of nearly all its business, will have it better done, and by making every citizen an acting member of the government, and in the offices nearest and most interesting to him, will attach him by his strongest feelings to the independence of his country, and its republican constitution.[68]

Earlier in the year he wrote, "The elementary republics of the wards, the county republics, the States republics, and the republic of the Union, would form a gradation of authorities, standing each on the basis of law, holding everyone its delegated share of powers, and constituting truly a system of fundamental balances and checks for the government." Then, each citizen "feels that he is a participator in the government of affairs, not merely at an election one day in the year, but every day."[69]

As stated above, the purpose of establishing these small republics was clear to Jefferson. To him, the point of the system was the institutional stimulus to the creation of an active citizenry and, even more important, the preservation of the revolutionary spirit, which makes possible the life of political action. This is a theory that anticipates by more than twenty years Alexis de Tocqueville's treatment of the virtues of participatory citizenship in *Democracy in America* and, even more strikingly, Hannah Arendt's theory of council democracy in her brilliant and controversial *On Revolution*. There Arendt argued that the appearance of a highly decentralized, ward-like system of organization has been a central feature of postrevolutionary politics ever since the French Revolution—in the Paris Commune, in the Soviets following the overthrow of the czar, the *räte* in post-Wilhelminian Germany, and the Hungarian workers' councils in 1956.[70]

What is notable about these systems is that they proved to be highly unstable; they simply did not last. And at least for the United States, the reason is quite clear, as Jefferson himself well knew. He fully recognized that representative democracy would largely have to replace direct forms in a country of large size or population. As he himself said, "I doubt if it [the ward system] would be practicable beyond the extent of a New England township."[71] From this point of view the United States had already passed the point of no return; thus, although local self-government might be encouraged, the administration of Jefferson itself showed that power had already begun its steady, though not uninterrupted, drift to the center.

But Jefferson's somewhat surprising earlier reservations about the capacity of the people for self-government are noteworthy in this context. He thought that the people were not qualified to administer government, but only to select those who did. Nor were they qualified to legislate; once again, they had to be restricted to selecting those who did. And of course the lawyer in Jefferson decided that juries were incapable of judging matters of law but were restricted to questions of fact.[72] Also, remember that the geographic scope of any real, direct democracy was extremely limited. Finally, keep in mind Jefferson's intense distrust of all governments. As he said: "I am not a friend to a very energetic government. It is always oppressive."[73] In spite of his frequent claims of support for majority rule, he still feared the concentration of power even when exercised by the many. He feared the executive, but he felt that concentrating power in the legislative branch was also dangerous. As he observed, "One hundred and seventy-three despots would surely be as oppressive as one."[74]

Thus, when even the wards are conceived as affording a heightened Madisonianism in the form of more checks and balances, Jefferson's concern for participation can be seen as less positive than negative, less a matter of self-development in the ancient Aristotelian sense than one of self-defense.[75] Also lacking was a sense of government as a positive force; the state, weak though it was at the time, was to be feared rather than used. This conception of democratic politics is at bottom nonpolitical—if not antipolitical. Defensive in character, like so much of the liberal tradition, this view tends to depoliticize democracy. Happiness and human development are to be found, not in political action, but rather in pursuing the delights of private life.[76] Jefferson would have much preferred to stay at Monticello, pursuing his scientific interests, tinkering with his inventions, working on his project for the University of Virginia, designing buildings, and, in general, indulging his restless intellectual curiosity. This behavior does not reflect the spirit of active citizenship extolled in the tradition of civic republicanism.

Conclusions

Where does this leave us then? Is it possible to generalize about the ideas of the Framers' generation? It is hardly credible to expect that a single paradigm, a single point of view that outlines for an entire nation a view of the basic problems of politics and what to do about them, can achieve dominance.[77] One point of view may be more widely held than others, but if it is sufficiently capacious to do the job, the odds are high that its meaning will be subject to serious dispute. This is particularly likely to be true in a period of rapid social, political, and economic change.

The sketch of the ideas of Franklin, Paine, and Adams illustrates this point. There is in all three a mix of republican ideas about civic virtue, a sense of American destiny that may be republican, but that also is much like Puritan messianism, and a dawning understanding, sometimes perhaps a little bewildered, of the dynamism of the rapidly emerging liberal capitalist economy.

With Hamilton, the picture is even more complex. Hamilton was neither a liberal nor a democrat; popular sovereignty, rather than a commitment to democratic politics, was for him an expedient designed to provide a base of support for a stronger state. Lacking the liberal concern for individual rights, he was open in his scorn for laissez-faire economics. He hoped that business elites would exhibit sufficient civic virtue to further his dreams of national power. In that he was disappointed, but he should not have been, given his own awareness that his economic system would necessarily be built on the foundation of self-interest. He himself had "warned his countrymen against their obsession with classical republicanism." In *The Continentalist,* Number 6, he wrote: "We may preach till we are tired of the theme, without making a single proselyte. The virtuous declaimer will neither persuade himself nor any other person." Nor would it help to search for models in simple ages long gone by.[78] Hamilton, unlike the ideal type of the civic republican, did not look back to the past for support but to the utopian future that he envisaged. Both republicans and liberals feared the strong central government that was at the heart of Hamilton's policies. In truth, he fits no mold. He is the odd man out among the major figures in the American tradition. His approach to political economy was vital to American development, and yet, in spite of his central historical position, he seems alien and detached, particularly in his own time. Perhaps only now can we really understand him as our institutions come to approximate those he championed.

Jefferson lacked Hamilton's single-mindedness and was thus even more complex than his great antagonist. There were traces of the idea of civic virtue, which he located on the farm rather than in the city. He also had an ideal of the active citizen, but as I have argued, this was defensive rather than self-developmental, as it would have been in classical republicanism. He also spoke constantly of republicanism, but its antithesis was not the liberalism of the modern theorist but instead monarchy, with which Jefferson had a life-long obsession. Nor could we find much guidance from history, as civic republicans were wont to do, since "history, in general, only tells us what bad government is."[79] In fact, like Hamilton, Jefferson had his sights set firmly on the future. John Adams understood his friend when he wrote that Jefferson liked better "the dreams of the future, than the history of the past."[80] That is not the thought of a backward-looking republican, fearful of the future.

Was Jefferson then *simply* a Lockean liberal, as Louis Hartz would have us believe? Certainly not simply. Jefferson was not satisfied with the idea of tacit consent, though it must be said that he, like the others, was not able to devise a viable alternative. Nor did he accept the notion of a presocial state of nature. "Man was destined for society," he wrote to Peter Carr. "His morality therefore was to be formed to this object. He was endowed with a sense of right and wrong merely relative to this. This sense is as much a part of his nature as the sense of hearing, seeing, feeling; it is the true foundation of morality."[81] One might call that a theory of individuality instead of individualism; the distinction is intended to convey that the issue of rights can arise only in a social setting. Otherwise the whole question of rights is meaningless, since the very idea implies contacts with others.

Jefferson surely was a theorist of rights, and in spite of his deviations from Locke, there is no doubt of the latter's influence.[82] As Judith Shklar said, that is what he will be remembered for and what he would have wanted to be remembered for: "He remains an icon. This is the man who put human rights on the map forever."[83] In this perspective he appears as something like a Hegelian "world historical figure."

Yet none of that solves the problem of Jefferson. Civic republican elements remain, but the tilt is toward the emerging liberalism of the time, even though that term was not yet in use. Then, there is always the gap between theory and practice to be dealt with. It is true that Jefferson, who saw the tension between virtue and commerce, detested strong political executives, centralization, and the institutions of urban commerce, finance, and industry. And yet he made his peace with all of them. His Federalist opponents feared he would be a dogmatic ideologue. But we must remember that his most dramatic statements on behalf of the virtues of rebellion and his schemes for radical decentralization, for instance, were made in private correspondence and were not for public consumption. They may well have represented deeply held beliefs, but he was much too cautious to act on them in public. Both Hamilton and John Adams understood him. When the election of 1800 was thrown into the House of Representatives, Hamilton supported Jefferson over Aaron Burr, who was preferred by most Federalists. To him, Burr was an unprincipled adventurer, whereas Jefferson was at least incapable of being corrupted. Hamilton made it entirely clear that he despised Jefferson but went on to add that the latter was not "zealot enough to do anything in pursuance to his principles which will contravene his popularity, or his interest. . . . A true estimate of Mr. J's character warrants the expectation of a temporizing rather than a violent system."[84]

And so it proved to be: The revolution of 1800 was less than its supporters hoped and its opponents feared. The thesis of Henry Adams's great study was that, in effect, Jefferson out-federalized the Federalists. He wielded executive authority with vigor, he accepted the necessity of manufacturing, and he left Hamilton's hated financial system in place.[85] In spite of sharp theoretical differences between the two parties, Jefferson's presidency lends support to the consensus thesis about the outline of American history. In practice, apparently radical, intractable differences narrowed considerably.

Still, it is important not to push this point too far. Jefferson did enact much of his program. His administration retired the debt, repealed direct taxes, began a program of internal improvements, reduced the size of government, and vigorously pursued foreign trade.[86] True to his individualism, Jefferson looked to Adam Smith as a mentor in economics.[87] In spite of republican misgivings about a threat to virtue, his program was a form of commercial agrarian capitalism. He promoted farming for profit, not merely as an attempt to achieve the vaunted self-sufficiency of the legendary yeoman farmer.[88] As Joyce Appleby says, this motivation casts early American politics into a contest between two forms of capitalism. The conflicts were real, but one could easily conclude that the commitment to capitalism overrode the differing modes of pursuing profit; in particular, both sides were devoted to economic growth. In the short run, the Jeffersonians won, but in the long term, the triumph of Hamilton's manufacturing system seems to have been inevitable. The sheer dynamism of the economy has been the great force for change in U.S. history; virtually all major social groups have endorsed it to a degree unusual in the Western world. Here the Hartz thesis is powerful. Some form of liberal capitalism has been a constant throughout American history.

As I have been arguing in this and the two preceding chapters, a new view of the American consensus is emerging; whether there is yet agreement among historians is another thing. Hartz's single-factor analysis is clearly too simple, but so too is the republican hypothesis. The new emphasis is on a multiplicity of voices and factions. Isaac Kramnick writes of republicans and liberals, state builders and work-ethic Protestants. James T. Kloppenberg tries to mediate between the claims of liberals, republicans, and the heirs to the Puritan tradition. He concludes that they are not mutually exclusive, least of all to the participants.[89] That is not surprising, since, as I have already suggested, the nation's Founders were too busy to worry about the sort of ideological consistency that would satisfy political theory professors. In my view, the Puritan elements in the American consensus should be stressed more strongly than they have been. In the late eighteenth and early nineteenth centuries, liberalism, particularly liberal capitalism, began to emerge as the clearly dominant element in the amalgam that made up the consensus.

For Dorothy Ross, this heady and complex mixture was the form taken by a new version of American exceptionalism.[90] The consensus, which was loose and provided plenty of room for conflict, quickly proved too weak to ward off the Civil War. Here sadly we can return to Jefferson as an exemplar for the whole nation. For Jefferson, the apostle of human rights, was—like so many of his followers—a slave owner. The poignancy of his predicament was intensified because he was fully aware of the contradiction between his thoughts and actions. He knew that, sooner or later, catastrophe would occur: His own dilemma was reflective of the nation's as a whole. Not until slavery was destroyed would it be even minimally possible to speak of a liberal consensus. However, before turning to the controversy over abolition that plunged the nation into civil war, we need a brief analysis of Jacksonian democracy.

· 6 ·

Some Notes
on Jacksonian Democracy

T HE ADMINISTRATION of Andrew Jackson (1829–1837) is more important politically than intellectually. The period featured a considerable expansion of presidential power at the expense of the states and the Congress. Jackson as president claimed the role of the "tribune of the People," the only officer of government with a national constituency. The political basis of Jackson's claim was the emergence of the first mass electoral coalitions, which followed on the removal in the various states of the remaining restrictions on universal manhood suffrage. The convention system for the nomination of presidential candidates was developed as a democratic antidote to the earlier device of choice by party congressional caucuses, an ironic event, since today conventions are themselves seen as antidemocratic devices designed to ensure control by party bosses. The spoils system for the allocation of administrative positions, which gave the president greater control over the executive branch, was also created. In general, then, it was a period of rapid democratization.

The Jacksonian Ideology

Aside from these political developments, the question of the meaning of the Jacksonian movement is contested territory. The starting point for any consideration of the intellectual history of the period must be the magisterial *Age of Jackson,* by Arthur Schlesinger, Jr., perhaps the last great work to be written squarely in the tradition of progressive historiography.[1] Schlesinger took as his text a passage from George Bancroft: "The feud between the capitalist and the laborer, the house of Have and the house of Want, is as old as social union, and can never be entirely quieted."[2] And elsewhere: "Show me one instance where popular institutions have violated the rights of property, and

I will show you a hundred, nay a thousand instances, where the people have been pillaged by the greedy cupidity of a privileged class."[3] Published well before the *Communist Manifesto,* these images seem strikingly "Marxist" in their militance. Yet they were extreme sentiments in Andrew Jackson's America; even Bancroft did not call for the abolition of capitalism.

For the Jacksonians, the great enemy was not capitalism as such, but monopoly and the "moneyed interests." Jackson, a hard-money man, saw paper money as naturally associated with monopoly and exclusive privileges. Against the monopoly and moneyed interests were arrayed the people—the agricultural, mechanical, and laboring classes—the planters, farmers, mechanics, and laborers.[4] Those people deserved a fair chance to compete.

Consider the great economic issue of the age—the question of whether to recharter the Second Bank of the United States. A careful reading of Jackson's Veto Message suggests that the real aim of the veto was less an attack on capitalism than an attempt to restore a competitive order.[5] The Jacksonian movement was classically liberal in that it sought to split government from business; it was a laissez-faire crusade on behalf of the ambitions of the small capitalist.[6] Like many reform movements in nineteenth-century America, it tended to see progress as the recapture of a past golden age.[7] This insight complements Tocqueville's contemporary observations of the restless egalitarianism of the Americans and their love of change combined with fear of revolution; this is the model of the Jacksonian democrat's life, simultaneously agitated and monotonous, that Marvin Meyers aptly calls the "venturous conservative."[8] As Meyers says, there was clearly some animus against the rich as such, but Jackson's basic occupational classes also allowed for a considerable range of income.[9]

The Jacksonians were caught up in a market revolution being fostered by their National Republican opponents and then their Whig successors. Jackson's coalition was made up of "those petty producers and workers threatened by commercialization, as well as voters in outlying areas not yet integrated into the market revolution." This by no means suggests that the wealthy were excluded—Jackson himself was a wealthy man—nor that some of the Jacksonians did nothing to further the market revolution. The move toward a market economy encompassed both parties; the issues revolved around who was to be advantaged by the developing system. There is a profound difference between a society that has markets—which are, after all, as old as human history—and a society in which markets and market values are dominant. Moreover, the effects of the market revolution were disruptive, the value of markets as a system of exchange notwithstanding.[10]

Insofar as it is true that Jackson's movement was backward looking, it is also true that it contained powerful echoes of prerevolutionary republicanism. As

Meyers shrewdly remarked: "Laissez-faire notions were embedded in a half-remembered, half-imagined way of life. When government governed least, society—made of the right republican materials—would realize its own natural moral discipline."[11] Today we can see that liberalism and civic republicanism conflict in important particulars, that there is, to repeat J.G.A. Pocock's formula, a tension between civic virtue and commerce. But the Jacksonians saw no such conflict. More explicitly, as Sean Wilentz put it, "They did not reject republicanism in favor of liberalism; they associated one with the other."[12] The result was an ideology that combined "republican rhetoric with a post-Madisonian liberalism," in which virtue became the "virtues of merchants." The party system that developed was one in which liberal values were widely shared, but in which there was real room for difference over "party interest, political economy, and republican political morality."[13] Once again, the ideological mix characteristic of the founding period emerges. But insofar as there was a contest between civic virtue and the liberal pursuit of interest, it was the liberal values that proved stronger in the not so very long run. Neither the rhetorical garb of the debates nor the fierce political conflict of the time can obscure what Hofstadter saw a generation ago—the fact that the history of Jacksonian America is an episode in the development of the liberal capitalism at the heart of American culture.

A key document in understanding the Jacksonian passion for competition is the decision in the case of *Charles River Bridge v. Warren Bridge,* written by Chief Justice Roger Taney, Jackson's choice to succeed the great John Marshall. The facts are simple. In 1785 the state of Massachusetts issued a charter to build a toll bridge across the Charles River to the Charles River Bridge Company, an enterprise that proved highly profitable. Some years later the state issued a similar charter to the Warren Bridge Company to build another bridge nearby. Charles River Bridge sued, claiming a violation of contractual rights. The court, speaking through Taney, ruled in favor of Warren Bridge. There was no indication in the first charter that an exclusive privilege had been conferred, nor were such provisions usual in similar situations. The policy implications Taney drew from the situation are particularly important as an indicator of Jacksonian thought: To allow the monopoly to stand would be to hinder progress. Taney articulated the consequence: "We shall be thrown back to the improvements of the last century."[14]

Thus, the Jacksonians saw that Adam Smith could be an ally in the reform project; they understood what all too few understand today, that properly read, *The Wealth of Nations* is not simply a brief against all government intervention in the economy. Judicious intervention of government may be allowable to break the hold of monopoly power. And as again is often the case, business interests frequently did not perceive their long-run interests when confronted by a challenge to their conventional wisdom. I suspect that Schlesinger was right when he suggested that, propaganda aside, those in business often do not really want free competition.[15]

What this points to is a form of Jeffersonian revisionism. The Jacksonians "moderated that side of Jeffersonianism which talked of agricultural virtue, independent proprietors, 'natural' property, abolition of industrialism, and expanded immensely that side which talked of economic equality, the laboring classes, human rights , and the control of industrialism." This new realism, as Schlesinger saw it, stemmed from the fact that the fears of Jefferson, particularly the fear of banks, were now the realities that had to be dealt with. In particular, it was necessary to move beyond a concern for political equality and begin to consider the relationship between political and economic power.[16] And this relationship, of course, accounts for the class tension that is so marked in the Age of Jackson.

Industrialism and the Ideology of Work

But the conversion to the market and the less often noticed development of an industrial system came at a price. Alexis de Tocqueville was more than usually prescient when he predicted the emergence of a class of harsh manufacturers.[17] The discipline of both market and industry was hard indeed. It entailed a Weberian rationalization of labor, a systematic and often exploitative pursuit of profit. At the foundation of the political culture of the North lay the tradition of the Puritan work ethic.[18] In the evocative phrase of Anne Norton, the new industrial discipline began to convert "man into machine."[19] We tend to think of the emergence of industrialism as a post–Civil War phenomenon, but the process was already advancing in the 1830s. The stress on the consensual nature of capitalism, which, in general, I accept, has led to a tendency to obscure the extent of class conflict as the new economic order took root. The terms *capital* and *labor* first began to be used during that time.[20] It is important to stress once again that considerable conflict between capital and labor is possible *within* a capitalist consensus, thus validating the continued importance of classics such as *The Age of Jackson,* as well as newer work on class consciousness, such as Sean Wilentz's *Chants Democratic* and Charles Sellers's *Market Revolution.* It is also worth remarking that much of the labor in the New England textile mills was provided by women, who were among the "first and fiercest critics of the exploitation of labor."[21]

Not surprisingly, given the working conditions, there was a good deal of urban violence from 1830 to 1850. As Norton sums up the feeling, "Affirmations of natural equality confirmed suspicions that increasingly evident social distinctions were arbitrary and unnatural."[22] Thus, "northern political culture . . . retained not only the Puritan covenantal and familial paradigms, which demanded selflessness, temperance, and submission to authority, but also elements of that Revolutionary tradition which affirmed the primacy of popular authority and invested men with a conviction of their natural rights and independent worth."[23]

Under the prevailing circumstances, it is hardly surprising that an ideology celebrating work and labor developed in the Jacksonian era. The work ethic had long been a staple of American culture, but it began to emerge as a specific doctrine at that time. As Judith Shklar brilliantly perceived, it was the "ideology of citizens caught between racist slavery and aristocratic pretensions"; moreover, as she said, it has continued relevance because the conditions that generated it have not altogether disappeared, though I would add that the form of the problem has been substantially altered.[24] The need to work for pay, perhaps even a right to such a status, was a pressing reality, as was the feeling of contempt for the idle rich. The basic conflict was between those who produced and those who did not, resulting in what is often called a "producerist" ideology. The roots lie deep in Anglo-American culture; recall Locke's similar discontent with the idle rich and also that, as Shklar pointed out, in his scheme for the education of a gentleman, Locke prescribed manual labor and accounting because they were useful to the "rational."[25] Max Weber on the importance of the Protestant ethic and the importance attributed to the maxims of Benjamin Franklin should also be kept in mind. However, as Shklar rightly argues, Weber was so obsessed with the relation of Puritanism to work that he failed to note other connections such as "democracy and personal independence."[26]

The stress on work was a radically new way to look at the world: "The sheer novelty of the notion of the dignity of labor in general, and as an element of citizenship can scarcely be exaggerated." Not only work, but the money work brings was important too. Following Tocqueville, Shklar notes that, for Americans, "to have money [has] taken the place that honor occupied in aristocratic societies." The idea that one *is* what one does in the world is an Enlightenment idea that has succeeded more in the United States than it ever could have in Europe.[27] These ideas about money and work have had great resonance in American politics. They were to inform the political struggle against slavery, the Populist battles late in the century, and, even more notably, the mind of Abraham Lincoln, though he, of course, was a Whig and not a Jacksonian—a point that suggests the consensual force of the new ideology.

Reflections on the Whig Opposition

The Whigs were not very successful at presidential politics; since we tend to measure political time—and success—in presidential terms, not so much attention has been paid to their thought as it deserves. Moreover, of course, the party no longer exists, so their ideas have tended to recede from view.[28] Still, a brief review of some of their leading ideas can shed some light on the consensus theory.

There were important cultural differences between Whigs and Democrats, but here I want to focus on politics and economics. Daniel Walker Howe spelled out the essential differences with great clarity. First, as advocates of economic change, the Whigs were much more willing than the Democrats to provide "conscious direction" to these changes. Second, the Jacksonians emphasized equality of opportunity, at least for white males, whereas the Whigs tended to stress morals or duties over individual rights. Third, the Jacksonians spoke of conflict between producers and nonproducers, but the Whigs were more likely to play down conflict and stress what they saw as the organic unity of society.[29] Marvin Meyers summed it up formulaically: "The Whig party spoke to the explicit hopes of Americans as Jacksonians addressed their diffuse fears and resentments."[30]

That is why the "monster bank" was so important. Howe writes, "The Bank issue brought into sharp focus the conflict between two views of the nation's destiny: Clay's vision of economic development planned centrally by a capitalist elite and the Democratic vision of a land of equal opportunity."[31] The premodern, precapitalist Puritan merchant was becoming a capitalist industrialist. The shift from commerce to industry required a higher level of technology as well as of means of transportation and communication. In this view, industry was a democratizing force because it catered to a mass market. The new society was less placid and more dynamic than before, which surely was part of what captured Tocqueville's attention. And, as Howe pointed out, the new industrial entrepreneur was celebrated in a way his commercial forebear was not: "Everyone had always known that the trader owed a lot to luck; the industrialist, in the prime of his glory, was thought to have attained his wealth through merit. Industrialism, in fact, became the focal point of a whole reorientation of values and life-styles for a civilization."[32]

Despite all the differences between Whigs and Democrats, there were still some points in common, though of course with different emphases. One was the contested legacy of Puritanism. The Jacksonian poet William Cullen Bryant declared, "Our civil and religious liberty exist, not in consequence, but in spite of the spirit and genius of Puritanism," whereas the Whigs celebrated "Puritan courage, self-discipline, and resistance to tyranny."[33] Nevertheless, both sides had a belief in the virtue of hard work that transcended party differences. The common source of that belief was in the Protestant ethic of disciplined work and its descendant, the spirit of capitalism. On that there was consensus, though one so broad as to allow a great deal of harsh partisan conflict.

On the question of conflict and consensus, three more observations may be made. The first is an interesting note on the vagaries of electoral politics. In 1824, Jefferson, then in his old age, disapproved of Jackson's candidacy for president. Perhaps more striking still, in 1832, Jefferson's still-surviving secretary of the treasury, Albert Gallatin, and, even more startling, the aged James Madison both supported Henry Clay for election over Jackson.[34] Since Jackson claimed to be Jefferson's heir, there must have been a certain degree of consensual overlap. Indeed, some of the partisan noise may have been largely a matter of electoral rhetoric.

The final point is the most important. Abraham Lincoln, though a Whig before he became a Republican, absorbed much of the producerist ideology of the Jacksonians. In so doing he forged a new, if tragically short-lived, consensus that reconstituted the national sense of self on a level probably not attained since.

Coda: Tocqueville on American Democracy

I have said that the Jacksonian era was more important politically than intellectually, though it should be noted that the great flourishing of classic American literature began during that time, the time in which Emerson and Whitman, for example, began to write. But the United States in that era did inspire one great masterpiece—*Democracy in America,* by a foreign visitor, the aristocratic Frenchman Alexis de Tocqueville. By any standard one of the great works on the theory and practice of egalitarian democracy, and a foundational document of political sociology, Tocqueville's two volumes, whatever their defects may be, are virtually without doubt the finest, most penetrating commentary ever written on American society and politics.

Tocqueville came to the United States possessed by the idea that democracy, which for him was essentially equivalent to egalitarianism, was the wave of the future, a wave that had reached its greatest height in America, and from it the French should learn how to ride the democratic tides that were sweeping over them too. Tocqueville wrote as one in the grip of a theory of historical necessity; the book, he told us, was written under the spell of a kind of "religious dread." For seven hundred years virtually every important event had moved the European nations toward greater equality. The progress could not be halted, though there was hope of directing it. To accomplish this, "a new political science is needed for a world itself quite new."[35]

Tocqueville professed complete neutrality in his sweeping observations; his stance was that of a neutral scientific observer. But his rhetorical strategy was much more complex than this suggests. Although Tocqueville was by no means uncritical of democracy, it seems that his claim to a neutral position and his picture of forces at work that were almost beyond human control was a cover to make his essentially democratic views palatable to his French countrymen, for whom the work was written. As his teacher the historian François Guizot, remarked to him, "You judge 'democracy' like an aristocrat who has been vanquished, and is convinced that his conqueror is right."[36] There is no doubt at all that in Tocqueville's mind aristocratic feudalism had certain advantages for which one must find functional substitutes in democracies, but he had no little difficulty maintaining his pose of scientific detachment. Late in Volume 1 the mask slipped completely away: "An aristocracy cannot last unless it is founded on an accepted principle of inequality, legalized in advance, and introduced into the family as well as the rest of society—all things so violently repugnant to natural equity that only constraint will make men submit to them."[37]

Tocqueville's new science of politics, as he called it, centered on the mores of society, the "habits of the heart" shared by the members of a culture, as well as the various current opinions and "the sum of the ideas that shape mental habits." In short, the term covers the "whole moral and intellectual state of a people."[38] It is the mores that ultimately condition the social and political institutions of a society, through "the slow and quiet action of society upon itself."[39] His work can therefore be seen as a form of interpretive social science and political theory.

I cannot begin to recount here the full rich tapestry of Tocqueville's analysis; the best that can be done is to call attention to a number of points central to the concerns of this study and briefly to point to some of the problems of contemporary politics in the light of the theory presented in *Democracy in America*. His central insight is the one seized on by Louis Hartz as the starting point for his theory of the liberal consensus: "The Americans have this great advantage, that they attained democracy without the sufferings of a democratic revolution and that they were born equal instead of becoming so."[40] The point is not that the Americans had a classless society or that there were no rich and no poor; Tocqueville was too acute a sociologist to have imagined a totally egalitarian society without a system of social stratification. Instead, he saw that the class structure was not hereditary and that *compared to Europe*, American society was amazingly egalitarian and blessed with a hierarchy that was relatively open and in which even the rich worked. Looking at his subject from the viewpoint of a French aristocrat, Tocqueville may have exaggerated what he observed, but from a contemporary perspective, Jacksonian America certainly looks a great deal more egalitarian than what we see today, as long, of course, as attention is confined to white males.

The result of these conditions was a society more just than an aristocracy, one in which the citizens would be contented, though democracies were unlikely to aspire to the greatness that was created by feudal Europe. Democracy was a society of happy mediocrity. But there were serious potential problems, the most notable of which was the tyranny of the majority so much feared by James Madison. The danger lay in the obsession with equality characteristic of democracy. Tocqueville wrote: "I think democratic peoples have a natural taste for liberty; left to themselves they will seek it, cherish it, and be sad if it is taken from them. But their passion for equality is ardent, insatiable, eternal, and invincible. They want equality in freedom, and if they cannot have that, they still want equality in slavery. They will put up with poverty, servitude and barbarism, but they will not endure aristocracy."[41]

However, it was a social and an intellectual tyranny which was Tocqueville's primary fear. He was much less focused on the danger posed to the rich by the poor than was Madison. Instead, he claimed, "I know of no country in which, speaking generally, there is less independence of mind and true freedom of discussion than in America."[42] The passion for equality turns into a hostility to difference and a pressure to conform to the manners, mores, and thoughts of an omnipotent majority. Here is the source of Hartz's fear of the ever-present danger of unanimity in the potentially stifling context of a liberal consensus.

But, fortunately for Americans, there are countertendencies, and Tocqueville was not without hope, though he was surely fully aware of the dangers. Some of the factors at work were matters of pure luck, for instance, the sheer size of the country, which acted as what Frederick Jackson Turner was later to call a safety valve for the discontented, who could always move farther out on the frontier. The isolation of the country from the mainstream of world politics was also important. And the lack of powerful neighbors meant there was no need to fear conquest.

It is also clear that Tocqueville had carefully studied *The Federalist Papers* and that he was sympathetic to the Constitution. He heartily approved of the federal system, which promoted the growth of local communal institutions, and he also favored the unique role of the judiciary in tempering the excesses of the majority. He also saw religion as a powerful force, making for a strong sense of popular morality, and the well-educated citizenry as vital. Moreover, the history that the new nation had was democratic, and there was widespread freedom of the press.

But those are not his most striking ideas. The great theorist of a society without an aristocratic past looked to aristocratic relics as an antidote to the dangers of a leveling egalitarianism. Tocqueville's search was for social features that could serve as functional substitutes for institutions that no longer existed and that could not be resurrected. Lawyers and the judiciary filled such a role for Tocqueville and were thus powerful bulwarks protecting democracy against itself. That position no doubt seems strange to many contemporary Americans, given the widespread disrespect for the legal profession.

However, two other factors are much more important—the absence of a strong centralized state, whose emergence Tocqueville feared, and the great American propensity to join together in voluntary associations. Government was local and decentralized, and the citizens were political activists. How different today is American politics![43]

Here lies the great difference between Madison and Tocqueville. The former's fear of democracy was much greater—at least when the Constitution was written—and he did not come near to sharing Tocqueville's positive attitude toward political participation. The latter thought of "political associations as great free schools to which all citizens come to be taught the general theory of association."[44] In them, in other words, men learn to *be* citizens. Democratic political activity may have its dangers, but the dangers of apathy are far worse, and participation is the antidote to the social stifling of opinion that is the special danger of democracy. Tocqueville may have called for a new science of politics, but there are strong traces of civic republicanism in his theory, an old, rather than a new, source of wisdom.[45]

In fact, with some exaggeration, given Tocqueville's appreciation of *The Federalist,* his work can be seen as a refinement and restatement of the Anti-Federalist position.[46] There is the same fear of the large, centralized modern state and the same willingness to consider a degree of political disorder a sign of a free democracy in action. The greatest danger is apathy, an excessive readiness to obey, whether the controlling force is an administrative despotism or the democratic majority. The great antidote to majority tyranny is politics itself. As Sheldon Wolin says, Tocqueville "was possibly the last great modern writer to believe passionately in the dignity and intrinsic value of political life."[47]

When he wrote, Tocqueville was relatively optimistic about the chances for the United States to avoid the dangers he saw as a threat to egalitarian democracies. In addition to the forces already discussed, he saw at work in the new nation a conception of the pursuit of self-interest subtly different from the vision of James Madison. Madison had hoped that conflicting interests would simply cancel one another out so that a disinterested elite could rise to the top and rule in behalf of the "permanent and aggregate interests of the community." But Tocqueville thought that ordinary citizens, working in their voluntary associations—those schools of citizenship—would develop a conception of "self-interest properly understood." Too coolheaded to be a utopian, he did not hope that civic virtue would be practiced for its own sake. Instead, Americans combine their interests with those of their fellows. They achieve a sort of virtue because they see it as useful. Thus "enlightened self-love eventually leads them to help one another and disposes them freely to give part of their time and wealth for the good of the state." Disinterested action could be seen, but Americans preferred to credit their utilitarian philosophy rather than themselves. The result is "not at all a sublime doctrine, but it is clear and definite. It does not attempt to reach great aims, but it does, without too much trouble, achieve all it sets out to do." This is not a doctrine conducive to great sacrifices, but "its discipline shapes a lot of orderly, temperate, moderate, careful, and self-controlled citizens."[48]

But self-interest properly understood, Tocqueville argued, was not sufficient by itself. It must be supported by religion, and in an essentially utilitarian argument, Tocqueville, who had lost his faith as a young man, argued that moderating self-interest was one of the functions of religion in American culture. Thus, what he saw as one of the functional substitutes for the characteristic structures of an aristocratic society was, somewhat ironically, a religion based not so much on feeling as on sociological necessity.[49]

In spite of the strengths Tocqueville saw in American democracy, he also saw signs of potential trouble with alarming clarity. Like Hamilton and Madison, Tocqueville believed that the United States would become a great commercial nation, not primarily because of its size and resources, but because of the prevailing cultural and moral preoccupations. The American is "enterprising, adventurous, and, above all, an innovator." The American mind is constantly in a "sort of feverish agitation." And to an extent, Tocqueville admired those qualities, particularly when contrasted with the timidity of Europeans, but there were problems.[50]

As noted before, Tocqueville saw Americans as agitated, restless, and averse to change.[51] They were serious and even sad in their pursuit of well-being, and complete satisfaction always eludes them. Nothing seemed permanent: "They clutch everything but hold nothing fast, and so lose grip as they hurry after some new delight." And later, "death steps in in the end and stops [the American] before he has grown tired of this futile pursuit of that complete felicity which always escapes him."[52] The whole analysis calls to mind the remarks of Thomas Hobbes on the fleeting nature of felicity and Leo Strauss's critique of Lockean liberalism as the "joyless pursuit of joy."

These observations temper whatever admiration Tocqueville felt for the commercial spirit of his subjects. From his aristocratic standpoint, it was clear that "the American will describe as noble and estimable ambition that which our medieval ancestors would have called base cupidity." No stigma attaches to the love of money.[53] Thus, Americans become materialistic; they develop a middle-class passion for physical comfort. This, he admitted, was a "decent materialism," but one that nevertheless makes many Americans embrace forms of "religious madness" in penance for the guilt their materialism visits upon them.[54]

This decent materialism made Americans consider all honest occupations honorable, but they gave pride of place to industrial callings. And here arose a great danger. Industrialism lowered the status of the working class and raised that of their masters. Links between rich and poor were broken, and the industrial aristocracy that Tocqueville foresaw would impoverish and brutalize the men it used. "I think," he wrote, "that, generally speaking, the manufacturing aristocracy which we see rising before our eyes is one of the hardest that have appeared on earth."[55]

Though he did not develop the connection as fully as he might, the analysis is prescient and the danger he described turned out to be all too real. Drawing more on European experience than American, Tocqueville saw the development of industry as a great force making for the centralization of power that he dreaded.

> Industry generally brings together a multitude of men in the same place and creates new and complex relations among them. These men are exposed to sudden great alternations of plenty and want, which threaten public peace. Work of this sort may endanger the health, even the life, of those who make money out of it or who are employed therein. Therefore the industrial classes, more than other classes, need rules, supervision, and restraint, and it naturally follows that the functions of government multiply as they multiply.[56]

Moreover, the new aristocrats "bring despotism along with them."[57] But it was a new despotism, much different from the forms practiced in aristocratic European societies. It would be soft and mild; men would be degraded rather than tormented. The state would become centralized and an "immense, protective power" watching over its subjects. Sounding much like Rousseau, in his scornful remarks about English elections, Tocqueville commented that the mere fact that men from time to time were allowed to vote for their masters would not lessen their dependency.[58]

Therefore the great danger was the conversion of the active citizens Tocqueville saw and admired in the United States into an apathetic mass. At the root of this apathy was individualism.[59] Earlier in *Democracy in America*, Tocqueville had identified individualism as one of the greatest dangers in an egalitarian democracy. Individualism was a new idea, going beyond the "passionate and exaggerated love of self" characteristic of egoism. Rather, "it is a calm and considered feeling which disposes each citizen to isolate himself from the mass of his fellows and withdraw into the circle of family and friends; with this little society formed to his taste, he gladly leaves the greater society to look after itself." Men imagined themselves in isolation from one another. Individualism destroyed the vital sense of tradition and made "men forget their ancestors," while at the same time setting them apart from their contemporaries.[60] Such feelings were more pronounced at the end of a democratic revolution. It was for this reason that he thought Americans so fortunate to have been "born equal" and thus so far to have escaped this danger. But individualism and the accompanying apathy and loss of civic virtue were ever-present dangers.

Tocqueville provided here deep insights into the present condition of American politics. Apathy as measured by voter-turnout figures is at a dismayingly high level, and interest groups have taken on many of the characteristics of the "individual" in their pursuit of self-interest, powered by huge sums of money. And many, on both the right and the left, see the welfare state as a form of soft despotism, though it is hard to discern a humane alternative to the present system that does not require the efforts of a state that would certainly seem large by Tocquevillian standards. Size, complexity, and the systems of private power created by the process of economic development he foresaw appear to make the modern centralized state a necessity. The roots of local democracy have withered, as Tocqueville feared, but it is difficult to see how modern American society can decentralize so as to reconstruct anything remotely like the United States of Jackson's time without surrendering power to forces that cannot be controlled by local power. A capitalist industrial economy is clearly deeply involved in these developments, but it is also certain that the problems go beyond what Marxists call the means of production. The problems associated with size, complexity, and industry remain, regardless of who owns the means of production. As always, the problem for Tocqueville is ultimately rooted in the mores, whose corruption threatens the survival of democracy.[61] These are among the deep dilemmas of contemporary American politics to which it will be necessary to return in the concluding chapters.

Beyond those issues, Tocqueville was also dismayingly prescient in his analysis of the terrible problems of race relations in the United States, which seem little closer to solution than they were in the 1830s. In what amounts to an extended appendix to his first volume, Tocqueville discussed the relations between whites, Indians, and slaves—a topic in a sense so clearly not democratic as to be tangential to his main subject. Indians and slaves suffered nothing less than tyranny, and they had only whites to blame for their condition.[62]

Tragically, the fate of the Indians can be passed by briefly because the destruction was so thorough that the victims are no longer a significant force in American society. He painted a grim picture of Native Americans being driven from their lands by greedy settlers and duplicitous governments. And ironically, for one who so admired the law, he stressed how carefully the native lands were acquired by contractual arrangement. "It is impossible," he bitterly remarked, "to destroy men with more respect to the laws of humanity."[63] The result was clearly a form of genocide.

The discussion of slaves and slavery is much more extended. Tocqueville, with his customary acuity, perceived that slavery and its associated practices and mores were the "most formidable evil threatening the future of the United States."[64] His moral condemnation of the system was uncompromising: "All my hatred is concentrated against those who, after a thousand years of equality, introduced slavery into the world again."[65] His condemnation of the prejudice, degradation, and cruelty that marked the "peculiar institution" was equally unsparing, but it was also very subtle. If slavery was fatal to the slave, it was also "fatal to the master." It was like a cancer that attacked the nation indirectly by corrupting the mores.[66] Though Tocqueville believed that the Union would probably survive and that if war came over slavery, it would be between the slaves and their masters, his analysis remains an indispensable prelude to understanding the tragedy of the Civil War. The commercial links between north, south, and west favored continued union, but as he ominously noted, regions founded on differing styles of civilization rooted in different systems of production were unlikely to coexist harmoniously.[67] This proved to be even more true than he realized.[68]

· 7 ·

Abolition and the Crisis of Liberalism

As even a cursory survey of the literature indicates, the American Civil War is one of the most complex and disputed problems in all modern historiography. It has been seen both as an "irrepressible conflict" and as the mere result of the political blundering of inept politicians. It has been interpreted both as a clash over high ideals and as a war fought over essentially material questions. However, no one can doubt that slavery was somehow at the heart of the matter. Here it is not possible to go into the relative weight to be assigned to ideological and material factors. Certainly, the latter were not unimportant; however, the view I adopt here is that profound intellectual, cultural, and psychological motives also divided the adversaries. To argue otherwise threatens to trivialize the central event in the history of the United States, an event that raises questions about the nature of liberal democratic societies that have yet to be satisfactorily answered in this country. It is on this level that the analysis must be carried out.

Slavery in the Constitution

Though the word *slave* is very assiduously avoided in the text of the Constitution and though defenders of the Constitution have tried to deny the central place of the slavery question, the abolitionist argument that slavery is part of the very fabric of the original Constitution is hard to deny. Slavery is alluded to in three places: namely, in the provision giving extra representation to the South in the House of Representatives by counting three-fifths of the slaves in the population base for the apportionment of seats, in the twenty-year ban on the abolition of the slave trade, and in the provision for the return of fugitive slaves.

It was James Madison himself who testified to the crucial significance of the "peculiar institution," stating that "the States were divided into different interests not by their difference of size, but by other circumstances; the most material of which resulted partly from climate, but principally from their having or not having slaves."[1] This view was central to the abolitionist critique of the Constitution as well as to modern reconstructions of the argument.[2] The tragedy lies in the fact that many of the delegates to the Federal Convention saw the horrible dilemma posed by slavery and felt slavery to be wrong. The difficulty was that the delegates, "inhibited by a concern to keep the Union together, by a predisposition to see property rights as sacred, and by an inability to imagine a society in which Negroes and whites could live together as citizens and brothers, . . . failed to grasp the nettle."[3]

In this respect, Thomas Jefferson, though not a delegate to the Federal Convention, illustrates the tragedy in all its dimensions. Fully aware that slavery was in tension with his Lockean theories of natural rights, Jefferson saw the institution as a disaster, not only for the slaves, but perhaps even more for their masters.[4] Slavery would render whites lazy and indeed call into question the security of their own liberties. Jefferson therefore hoped for abolition followed by colonization, the return of the freed slaves to Africa, a widely discussed option right on through the Civil War. Sadly, much of this discussion was buttressed by a catalog of presumed black inferiorities that one might find in contemporary right-wing hate literature.[5]

On the subject of slavery, Jefferson's usual optimism deserted him. An air of impending doom hung over his thinking on the slave question. In the *Notes on the State of Virginia,* he remarked, apropos slavery, "I tremble for my country when I reflect that God is just; that his justice cannot sleep forever."[6] But Jefferson, like so many of his generation and, it might be said, so many since, was simply paralyzed; his principles were one thing and his sense of what might be realized quite something else. Late in life, referring to the revived controversy over slavery that led to the Missouri Compromise, he likened events to a "fire bell in the night" that filled him with terror. It was the "knell of the system. . . . We have a wolf by the ears, and we can neither hold him, nor safely let him go." He even went on to express the fear that the sacrifices of 1776 were in vain; his consolation was that he would not live to see the final catastrophe.[7]

But Jefferson, after all, was not an ogre, nor was he simply a hypocrite. He was a man of his time who shared the prejudices of his age. The really interesting question is not why sensitive men should have felt disquiet over the barbarism of slavery, but rather why so many of them adopted liberal, natural rights theories so widely at variance with one of the basic social institutions of their society. Not surprisingly, that contradiction did not go unremarked. In London, at the time of the Revolution, Samuel Johnson asked, with his customary pungency, "How is it that we hear the loudest yelps for liberty from the drivers of Negroes?"[8]

Historian Edmund Morgan offers an interesting hypothesis to explain the paradox between thought and action about slavery and freedom. Morgan argues that the American settlers, following Locke and other British writers, viewed an undisciplined working class as a source of potential social disorder; importing slaves spared whites the problem of such a class. In the absence of a free group of workers of uncertain behavioral patterns, it became possible for members of the white race to adopt liberal attitudes. Morgan writes, "The development of slavery is perhaps the key to the consensus that prevailed in colonial America, for slavery meant the substitution of a helpless, closely guarded lower class for a dangerous, armed lower class that might fight if exploited too ruthlessly."[9] The result impressed a British diplomat: "Owners of slaves among themselves, are all for keeping down every kind of superiority." This he thought was because of "their being rivals in their own states for the voice of the people, whom they court by dressing and looking like them as much as they can."[10]

Viewed in this way, the contradiction between slavery and freedom was no accident. David Brion Davis drives home the idea: The colonists' "rhetoric of freedom was functionally related to the existence—and in many areas to the continuation—of Negro slavery. In a sense, then, demands for consistency between principles and practice, no matter how sincere, were rather beside the point. Practice was what made the principles possible."[11] Even if people had the best will in the world, the hold of such a system was naturally hard to break. A whole civilization was at stake.

Calhoun, Fitzhugh, and the Attempt to Legitimate Slavery

As the midcentury crisis of secession neared, it became clear that the South deeply needed a fuller ideological defense of slavery. In that region it was widely assumed that slavery was a "positive good" for all concerned—the slaves had been rescued from barbarism and introduced to Christianity, and in return the slaveholders received a steady supply of labor, which was to provide the material foundation for a brilliant new civilization.[12] In the language of today we might say it was a win-win situation.

More complex and systematic—though equally self-serving—arguments were also advanced. The best known, though not the most cogent or provocative, was offered by the powerful senator from South Carolina, John C. Calhoun. For a generation Calhoun was one of the most important figures in American political life. Though famous for his attempt to reason from first principles to a systematic body of political theory, in reality, Calhoun's thought ended in something close to incoherence. Therefore, it provides a telling illustration of how difficult it is for American thinkers to extricate themselves from the confines of liberal individualism.

Calhoun attempted to ground his theory in the essentially nonliberal assumptions of an organic theory of society. He avoided Lockean state of nature arguments and instead started from the position that man was by nature a social being. But this social state could not exist without government.[13] At the same time, however, our individual feelings were stronger than our social feelings. The danger was that government would be conducted by men who would also be moved by selfish forces, the result being "a strong tendency to disorder and abuse of its powers."[14] Suddenly we are face to face with the classic liberal dilemma of preventing governmental violations of the principle of rights. Searching for a way out, Calhoun echoed Madison and concluded that "power can only be resisted by power."[15] In part, this problem can be met by exercising the right of suffrage, but by itself this is an insufficient guarantee. The danger of majority abuse of power still remains.

This danger led Calhoun to draw a vital distinction between what he called the numerical and the concurrent majorities.[16] The definition of the numerical majority was simply the literal meaning of the term. The concurrent majority, however, was rather more complex, since it "regards interests as well as numbers—considering the community as made up of different and conflicting interests, as far as the action of the government is concerned—and takes the sense of each through its majority or appropriate organ, and the united sense of all as the entire community." To obscure this distinction was to court fatal error.[17] Calhoun contended that the numerical majority did not truly represent the people, and that sound, nonrepressive politics required government by the concurrent majority. Under a proper system of rule, each "interest, or portion, or order," had to hold veto power. Only that could avoid the greatest evil, which was anarchy.[18] In the *Discourse on the Constitution,* Calhoun pushed his argument to a still further extreme, going as far as to suggest the need for a dual executive branch, with each section of the country controlling one, and with the assent of both required for any action to be taken.[19] There the abstract language of the *Disquisition* was translated into the language of American constitutionalism.[20]

Calhoun professed to believe that this complex mechanism would increase the likelihood of compromise, but it seems more probable that the consequence would have been complete stalemate or consensus so devoid of content as to be meaningless or worse, wholly irrational—the worst-case scenario of Madisonianism raised to the nth degree. Earlier in his career, Calhoun had argued that since the Constitution was a pact between sovereign states—at best a debatable assumption—the states had the right to "nullify" national legislation. Now he proposed to extend the same power to organized sectional interests as well. As Louis Hartz noted, this was a "profoundly disintegrated" political theory, for it made no sense to abolish the Lockean state of nature only to put in its place a conception of minority rights even more individualistic in its implications. After all, there were minorities within minorities, and why should they too not have veto rights? From the level of the section, the argument retreated to the state, to the county, to the individual plantation.[21] The result is a political absurdity.

The moral peculiarity, not to say obtuseness, of Calhoun's theory should not escape attention either. Nowhere in the theory was slavery even mentioned. The whole elaborate structure was advanced in the form of a defense of minority rights, but the major "right" that concerned Calhoun was the right of a sectional majority to enslave an often large minority within its territory.[22] With Calhoun, we have descended into a Hobbesian view of the world, in which there can probably be no stable order. As George Kateb put it, "A continuous and extensive fear of injustice is incompatible with the life of a society that means to remain one society."[23] Civil war is an expectable outcome of such a system.

Much more interesting, though even more bizarre, was the thought of George Fitzhugh, the leading figure in what Louis Hartz called "the reactionary Enlightenment." For Hartz, that was the great imaginative moment in American political thought—the one attempt to break clear from the confines of the all-pervasive liberal tradition.[24] But Hartz believed that not even the reactionary defense of slavery subverted his theory, since when we get below the surface of southern thought, we find slavery, not feudalism. The revival of nonliberal continental theorists in the antebellum South, he wrote, was simple fraud.[25] Hartz's rediscovery of Fitzhugh led to one of the most brilliant sections of a brilliant book, but it was not quite enough to save his thesis. Hartz did not quite take the full measure of Fitzhugh, who was more than a mere aberration.

I will argue, following historian Eugene Genovese, that Fitzhugh, unlike Calhoun, fully understood the logic of a slave society. The conclusions Fitzhugh reached were often repellent, but at least they have the virtues of consistency and of revealing the fundamental ideological and philosophical conflict underlying the Civil War.

Hartz was right and so are the Genoveses, in spite of the misunderstandings of Eugene Genovese's critics, who believe he claims the contrary; the old slave South was not a feudal society. However, it did display tendencies that were not those of a middle-class capitalist society, tendencies that were, in a somewhat controversial term, *prebourgeois*. Much hinges on the definition of capitalism. The fact that merchants bought and sold goods in markets in the search for profit was not enough to make an economy capitalist; if it were, capitalism would have been a more widespread phenomenon throughout history than it has been. In fact, there would hardly be a problem worthy of investigation.[26] Instead, the defining characteristic of capitalism was "the separation of the laborers from the means of production and the attendant transformation of labor-power into a commodity."[27] From this highly sophisticated Marxist point of view, the key was not merely the sale of goods for profit, but rather the existence of a market for free labor. That was a condition the South conspicuously failed to meet. Its position was unique: "In this essential respect, the Old South emerged as a bastard child of merchant capital and developed as a noncapitalist society increasingly antagonistic to, but inseparable from, the bourgeois world that sired it."[28]

In his theoretical defense of this world, Fitzhugh was rigidly consistent in his repudiation of any form of natural rights theory.[29] In Aristotelian terms he repeatedly argued that man was by nature a social animal. It was nonsense, as he saw it, to say that government rested on consent; instead, its only foundation was force. Harking back to arguments as old as Plato's, he pointed out: "Captains of ships are not appointed by consent of the crew, and never take their vote. . . . If they did, the crew would generally vote to get drunk."[30] For his strongly patriarchal point of view, he was indebted to Locke's antagonist, Sir Robert Filmer, against whom the *Second Treatise* was aimed.[31] Fitzhugh told us that the world was too little governed. If men had any inalienable right, it was a right to servitude. Nineteen out of twenty had a right "to be taken care of and protected, to have guardians, trustees, husbands, or masters; in other words, they have a natural and inalienable right to be slaves." (The same point was made with even more brutality, if that is possible, by Senator James Henry Hammond, who argued that in every society there had to be a class to perform menial duties, a class needing only small intellect and low skills. This class "constitutes the very mud-sill of society.")[32]

According to Fitzhugh, the source of villainy in free society was laissez-faire capitalism, whose methods were "at war with all kinds of slavery."[33] What proponents of free society did not recognize was that the northern laborer was already a slave without knowing it and that his employers—his "oppressors"—were "cannibals all."[34] The superiority of the southern system lay in the fact that it recognized the essential needs of the great majority of mankind and moved to meet those needs in more humane ways than those of the capitalist North.

Going beyond these points, Fitzhugh argued that the two systems were incompatible and could not coexist indefinitely. "One set of ideas," he wrote, "will govern and control after a while the civilized world. Slavery will every where be abolished or every where be re-instituted."[35]

This is the critical point, for it is the logic *of the situation as northern anti-slavery forces saw it.* It is not that northern workers literally feared enslavement, but they did fear competition with slave labor if it were to spread. It was this logical point that Lincoln grasped in his famous "House Divided" speech. He proclaimed:

> I believe this government cannot endure, permanently half slave and half free. . . . It will become all one thing or all the other. Either the opponents of slavery, will arrest the further spread of it, and place it where the public mind shall rest in the belief that it is in course of ultimate extinction; or its advocates will push it forward till it shall become alike lawful in all the states, old as well as new—North as well as South.[36]

Here is the issue. The most profound observers on each side of the sectional dispute realized that more was at stake than a quarrel between capitalist factions. Economic factors were certainly in dispute, but equally in contention were two fundamentally different ways of life. Opposed intellectual commitments were associated with these systems. An economy based on free labor was naturally felt to be more compatible with ideologies that were essentially liberal. The South, for all its Jeffersonian heritage, was powerfully pulled toward a point of view with pronounced antiliberal, incompletely bourgeois, anticapitalist values.[37] The region came to exhibit "a special social, economic, political, ideological, and psychological content."[38] Eugene Genovese argues that the slaveholder was not just another farmer, but one whose basic character was shaped by his relation to his bondsmen. "He had the habit of command, but there was more than despotic authority in this master-slave relationship. The slave stood interposed between his master and the object his master desired. . . . The slaveholder commanded the products of another's labor, but by the same process was forced into dependence upon this other."[39] In this view, the system of slavery was not merely a mode of production but had deep psychological and ideological consequences as well. To Genovese, it was Fitzhugh's merit to have understood this relationship, however ugly his ideas were, in a way that few of his fellow planters did.[40]

I suspect that this complex relationship has real resonance, particularly in its psychological dimension, for this day. How many Americans are there whose sense of well-being is precariously balanced on the foundation of feelings of superiority to a despised other? In any event, no theory of the history of American politics, however persuasive on other grounds, can rest on the assumption that a monolithic liberal consensus existed until after the institution of slavery was excised. Judith Shklar has it exactly right: "Until the Civil War amendments, America was neither a liberal nor a democratic country, whatever its citizens might have believed."[41]

Ideas and Tactics
in the Antislavery Movement

We now must consider the crusade for abolition. For all its enormous political importance, the abolitionist cause did not generate a correspondingly important body of original political theory. The literature is as large and impassioned as one might expect, but little of it went beyond attacks on the abuses of slavery by cruel masters. Perhaps the best example is *American Slavery As It Is,* by Theodore Dwight Weld, which was a best-seller in its time and had a great influence on Harriet Beecher Stowe, the author of *Uncle Tom's Cabin.*[42] Such documents were of enormous importance in shaping public opinion, but they added little to the political theory concerning the slave issue.

However, there was a frequent reassertion of basic theories of natural rights. In its most fully developed form, that culminated in the "higher law doctrine," which held that the natural rights principles incorporated in the Declaration of Independence should be interpreted as a binding part of the Constitution. For instance, Frederick Douglass, an ex-slave who was the most important black abolitionist, while excoriating the brutality of slavery, often ridiculed the hypocrisy of whites who refused to live by the principles of the Declaration.[43] The higher law doctrine is historically entirely specious and has never come close to acceptance by the Supreme Court. It should be noted in passing that this very fact lent some support to the abolitionist contention that the Constitution was a proslavery document.

The most vital immediate issue in the prewar period was the question of extending slavery to the territories as the nation expanded westward. Many leaders on both sides felt that unless slavery could expand, it would not survive. Whether they were correct is immaterial from a political point of view, since many acted on the presumption that in fact they were. Therefore, the place of slavery in the territories was the subject of frequently violent controversy. The Missouri Compromise of 1820 had temporarily settled the question whether new states would enter the Union as slave or free. But in the complex politics of westward expansion, the compromise began to dissolve. It was repealed in the Kansas-Nebraska Act of 1854. The goal of Abraham Lincoln and the emerging Republican Party was the restoration of Henry Clay's resolution of the controversy in Missouri.

The intellectual high point of the discussion was the series of debates between Lincoln and Stephen A. Douglas in their campaign for the Illinois Senate seat in the summer of 1858. Although both did their fair share of pandering to the audience, the arguments were carried on at a remarkably high theoretical and constitutional level.

The outlines of the argument were clear and fairly simple. Douglas, though not an advocate of slavery as such, held to a doctrine of popular sovereignty, which led him to conclude that if the people of a territory wished to allow slavery, it was their right to do so and a matter of indifference to him. Lincoln's position was considerably more complex. He was by no means free of the common racial attitudes of his time, though he was not burdened by the harsh prejudices of his hero Jefferson. Still, it was difficult for him to imagine life in society with freed slaves. He was constantly taunted by Douglas with the charge that he wanted to introduce complete social and political equality between the races, and he regularly denied it, but with qualifications. He softened the message somewhat by regularly insisting that Jefferson's Declaration applied to slaves as well as whites. Thus, in the First Debate, he said, "I agree with Judge Douglas that [the Negro] is not my equal in many respects—certainly not in color, perhaps not in moral or intellectual endowment. But in the right to eat the bread, without leave of anybody else, which his own hand earns, *he is my equal and the equal of Judge Douglas, and the equal of every living man.*" In Springfield, a little earlier, he had claimed that Negroes were "equal in their right to 'life, liberty, and the pursuit of happiness.'"[44]

Still, he admitted that his own feelings would not allow equal political and social treatment. In his great speech at Peoria in 1854, he offered a grimly realistic assessment of the status quo. Even if his own feelings were to allow such treatment, he said: "We well know that those of the great mass of white people will not. Whether this feeling accords with justice and sound judgement, is not the sole question, if indeed, it is any part of it. A universal feeling, whether well or ill-founded, can not be safely disregarded."[45] It makes for harsh reading, but it is not clear that the American people today have advanced far beyond this point.[46]

In any case, for Lincoln, as for so many of his contemporaries, the best answer seemed to lie in colonization, either in Liberia or Central America. In August 1862 he spoke in the White House to a group of free blacks. He was nothing if not direct and should be quoted at some length.

> We have between us a broader difference than exists between almost any other two races. Whether it is right or wrong I need not discuss, but this physical difference is a great disadvantage to us both, as I think your race suffer very greatly, many of them by living among us, while ours suffer from your presence. In a word we suffer on each side. If this is admitted, it affords a reason at least why we should be separated. . . .
>
> Your race are suffering, in my judgement, the greatest wrong inflicted on any people. But even when you cease to be slaves, you are yet far removed from being placed on an equality with the white race. You are cut off from many of the advantages which the other race enjoy.[47]

The answer then was separation, which, we know, was clearly a nonstarter. And yet there was an appropriate note of realism in the clear recognition that freed slaves would be at an acute disadvantage. What then? Did Lincoln show significant signs of growth in his last years in office? Had he lived to preside over Reconstruction, would the subsequent history of race relations in the United States have been any less disastrous?

Unfortunately, the evidence is scanty. We know that Lincoln, in his last speech, three days before his assassination, while discussing Reconstruction measures for Louisiana, indicated that he would be willing to confer suffrage rights on freed blacks who were "very intelligent, and on those who serve our cause as soldiers." He added that his general remarks on Louisianans would apply to other rebellious states as well.[48] George Fredrickson is perhaps right in stating that we know too little to conclude that Lincoln had reversed the thought of a lifetime and become a partisan of black political equality. Perhaps, but who knows? One member of the audience who listened to Lincoln was John Wilkes Booth, who took what Lincoln said at face value. "This means nigger citizenship," he snarled. "That is the last speech he will ever make."[49]

It is true that there was an inherent tension between Lincoln's attachment to the principles of the Declaration of Independence and his reluctance to concede full and equal rights to Negroes. There was, as Richard Hofstadter noted, a rather dubious distinction between slavery and white supremacy: Slavery contradicted the Declaration and white supremacy did not. And yet, in fairness, in his time Lincoln was by no stretch of the imagination a radical white supremacist; if anything, George Fredrickson is right—for him the Negro was a man but not a brother.[50]

At the same time, it is important to remember that Lincoln opposed, on both moral and political grounds, slavery and its extension. Though, like Jefferson, he had no formal political theory, he did hold to a clear-cut constitutional and political position with absolute consistency. Nevertheless, during the war he demonstrated considerable capacity for change. That point is difficult to comprehend today. Lincoln has become so much a figure of myth, the face on the penny or a gigantic marble statue, that we find it difficult to see the man of high principle who had meditated deeply on the theory of constitutional democracy, while simultaneously being a master of everyday coalition politics. Even more exceptional, he was able to express his ideas in some of the greatest prose in American literature. Sadly, we are no longer used to political leaders who talk to us in this way, so Lincoln is further distanced from us. And even the words themselves stand in our way. They are too familiar; we all have heard them time and again; they have even been surrounded by music in Aaron Copland's *Lincoln Portrait*. We need to find ways to read them as if they were new in order to experience their true force.

There was a coherent body of thought in Lincoln's speeches and writings, and the foundation on which it rested was the Declaration of Independence. "All honor to Jefferson," he wrote, for basing the document on an "abstract truth, applicable to all men and all times, and so to embalm it there, that today, and in all coming days, it shall be a rebuke and a stumbling block to the very harbingers of reappearing tyranny and oppression."[51]

Perhaps Lincoln's most extended statement on the Declaration theme was in his address attacking the Kansas-Nebraska Act, four years before his debates with Douglas, who had been the prime mover behind the bill.

> The doctrine of self-government is right—absolutely and eternally right. . . . [Its] just application depends upon whether a negro is *not* or *is* a man. . . . If the negro is a man, is it not to that extent, a total destruction of self-government, to say that he too shall not govern *himself?* When the white man governs himself, that is self-government; but when he governs himself, and also governs *another* man, that is *more* than self-government—that is despotism. . . .
>
> Judge Douglas frequently, with bitter irony and sarcasm, paraphrases our argument by saying, "The white people of Nebraska are good enough to govern themselves, *but they are not good enough to govern a few miserable negroes!!*" . . .
>
> What I do say is, that no man is good enough to govern another man, *without that other's consent.* I say this is the leading principle—the sheet anchor of American republicanism.

After quoting the opening of the Declaration in full, Lincoln added that the relation of masters and slaves was "a total violation of this principle," and concluded that to allow "ALL the governed an equal voice in the government" means that "that, and that only is self-government."[52]

A constitutionalist, Lincoln believed deeply in the document so much that he argued, rather dubiously I think, that the refusal of the Framers to use the word *slavery* and the political positions of a majority of them after ratification indicated, contrary to the views of many abolitionists, that the Constitution was an antislavery instrument.[53] But deep down, he also knew that the Constitution was flawed: "Thus the thing is hid away, in the Constitution," said Lincoln, "just as an afflicted man hides away a wen or a cancer, which he dares not cut out at once, lest he bleed to death; with the promise, nevertheless, that the cutting may begin at the end of a given time."[54]

The solution was to return to the principles of the Declaration of Independence. The famous opening words of the Gettysburg Address are no mere rhetorical striving for effect. They suggest that the nation's true beginning was not in 1787 but in 1776 or even in 1774. The point was driven home in the First Inaugural Address: "The Union is much older than the Constitution. It was formed, in fact, by the Articles of Association in 1774. It was matured and continued by the Declaration of Independence in 1776." It was furthered by the Articles of Confederation. "And finally, in 1787, one of the declared objects for ordaining and establishing the Constitution, was *"to form a more perfect union."*[55]

By 1854, the situation had become grim: "Our republican robe is soiled, and trailed in the dust. Let us repurify it. Let us turn and wash it white, in the spirit, if not the blood, of the Revolution. . . . Let us re-adopt the Declaration of Independence, and with it, the practices, and policy, which harmonize with it."[56]

The roots of this argument in Lockean consent theory, by way of Jefferson, are obvious, as is the fact that Lincoln saw with absolute clarity the truth in Fitzhugh's argument that slave and free labor were incompatible, that no argument for the enslavement of blacks could not also justify the enslavement of whites, and that sooner or later one system or the other had to prevail. He said that neither color, nor intelligence, nor self-interest could justify slavery; any argument open to whites was also open to blacks.[57]

The rallying cry of the antislavery forces became "free soil, free labor, free men."[58] Lincoln's views on the subject of labor are of great interest. In his Wisconsin State Fair speech in 1859, Lincoln stated that all agreed that labor was the source from which human wants were supplied. Some assumed that labor existed only because capital hired or bought laborers. This was an obvious reference to the mud-sill theory espoused by Senator Hammond. But, he went on, others held that there was another theory according to which, "labor is prior to, and independent of, capital; that, in fact, capital is the fruit of labor. . . . Hence they hold that labor is the superior—greatly the superior—of capital."[59] This was Lincoln's own position, and he pushed it hard. In a letter earlier in 1859, Lincoln alluded to the potential for a conflict between personal and property rights and said, "Republicans . . . are for both the *man* and the *dollar;* but in cases of conflict, the man *before* the dollar."[60]

Lincoln liked to dwell on his humble beginnings; in a speech to an Ohio Regiment late in the war, he said:

> I happen temporarily to occupy this big White House. I am a living witness that any one of your children may look to come here as my father's child has. It is in order that each of you may have through this free government which we have enjoyed, an open field and a fair chance for your industry, enterprise, and intelligence; that you may all have equal privileges in the race of life. . . . The nation is worth fighting for, to secure such an inestimable jewel.[61]

That is the language of the Free Soilers, which today may sound quite hopelessly naïve; it surely is the language of the ideological consensus described by Hartz and Hofstadter. It echoes Locke's labor theory of property, the Protestant work ethic, the "race of life" ideal of the early working-class capitalists, described by Isaac Kramnick, and, even though Lincoln had once been a Whig, the producerist ideology of the Jacksonian Democrats.[62] If Lincoln's language is in the consensus, it surely is in its far-left wing, at least as originally stated. The implications of these arguments, if taken with full seriousness, in their original meaning, are oddly radical, coming as they do from the patron saint of the Republican Party; in fact, few Democrats today would be ready to face up fully to their implications. But it was for this sense of the role of labor, certainly not out of any very common sense of fellow feeling with the slaves, that the Civil War was fought.

But once it was granted that slavery had to be destroyed, given existing political conditions, what means were most effective to the end? This means/ends argument added a significant theoretical and ideological dimension to the debate.

On one level, the most provocative contribution to the debate was Henry David Thoreau's classic essay "On Civil Disobedience." The essay is a defense of Thoreau's own civil disobedience, which took the form of refusing to pay his poll tax in protest against the proslavery policies of the government. His case rested on a thoroughly radical individualism. He took the standard liberal argument to the effect that that government is best that governs least and extended it to the edge of anarchism by saying, "That government is best which governs not at all." He did not ask at once for no government, but for "*at once* a better government." The present government cannot be associated with without disgrace. Ordinary political participation was merely a form of "gaming. . . . Even voting *for the right* is *doing* nothing for it." If abolitionists were to withdraw their support from the government of Massachusetts, if even "*one* HONEST man" did so, it would mean the end of slavery. The only place for a just man was in prison. It was not a duty to work for the end of even so monstrous a wrong as slavery; it was a man's duty to "wash his hands of it."[63]

Thoreau's essay is powerfully argued and eloquently written. It is hard to escape the conclusion that there may be some laws that a decent human being is morally bound to disobey, though a very extensive application of this theory is hardly the basis for stable government. The essay has had a major effect in our time as one of the sources of the ideas on nonviolent civil disobedience of Martin Luther King, Jr. But in Thoreau's version, the argument is profoundly nonpolitical and even antipolitical. Politics is a collective activity; major social institutions do not collapse because of the actions of one man. Further, to say that the only absolute duty is to wash one's hands of an evil can lead to a self-serving withdrawal from conflict. Such a withdrawal salves the individual conscience but avoids the possibility that political action will raise the problem of "dirty hands," that is, that politics may require the compromise of high principle in order for any progress toward what may itself be a moral goal to take place.[64]

Regardless of these considerations, it was—tragically—not a movement of nonviolent civil disobedience but a bloody civil war that crushed slavery. The testimony of individual consciences was not enough. Therefore, the question of appropriate means to the desired end must be examined further.

The political situation was extremely complex. There were antislavery leaders who cared nothing for the blacks and were indeed racists; their only concern was protecting the ideal of free labor. There were others, like Lincoln, whose fundamental goal was preservation of the Union, and still others believed with William Lloyd Garrison that the Constitution was "a covenant with Death and an agreement with Hell."[65] For them, disunion was preferable to continued association with slavery. Perhaps the most fundamental division was between those who saw abolition as the reform of a set of basically sound institutions and those who saw it as a near revolutionary change that should uproot not only slavery but also racism, as well as shatter the existing Constitution and begin virtually anew.[66]

The radicals, of whom Garrison was typical, believed that slavery was a great moral wrong—a sin, to be precise—and that the only remedy was the immediate cessation of that sin.[67] Theirs was a doctrine of moral perfectionism, which is hard for contemporaries to accept or to identify with.[68] For the radicals, reform was not enough. They believed the basic institutional structure to have been invaded by slavery and that only the most fundamental reconstruction could repair the damage.

But the movement that ended slavery was not radical in that sense; it was led by Lincoln, one of the great masters of coalition politics. The key to Lincoln's strategy was his belief, first announced in the Peoria speech of 1854, that a slavery that could not expand was "in the course of ultimate extinction."[69] If the Union could be held together and slavery could be kept from expanding, then it would die a natural, if perhaps slow, death.[70]

This inevitability often seems not to have been quite fully understood. It is necessary to understand the complexity of Lincoln's political position. Lincoln reached the White House after one of the more bizarre elections in U.S. history. There were four candidates: Lincoln, for the still new Republican Party; Senator Douglas, for the Northern Democrats; Vice President John C. Breckinridge, for the Southern Democrats; and John C. Bell of Tennessee, for the Constitutional Union Party, a strange residue of the defunct Whig Party. The division of the Democratic Party was especially significant, since it had been one of the few remaining truly national institutions. This distribution of party strength was a major symptom of the sectional crisis. In ten southern states the Republicans were not even on the ballot. In the upper South, Lincoln received only 4 percent of the vote. Although he won a majority of the electoral vote, Lincoln received only 40 percent of the national popular vote. Thus, he was a completely sectional president at the head of a weak coalition.[71] To hold this band of supporters together was a difficult exercise indeed.

It is important to understand that Lincoln believed and tirelessly stated that though he could work against the expansion of slavery, he had no constitutional authority to end slavery itself: That was a state responsibility. Further, it is clear that the necessary two-thirds vote to amend the Constitution and put an end to the practice was not available at that time. It is also quite possible that Emancipation, had it been possible, might have driven the border state Unionists out of the coalition.[72]

At the same time, constitutional government was at stake, "a fundamental idea, going down about as deep as anything."[73] In this framework, secession was wrong. Its central idea

> is the essence of anarchy. A majority, held in restraint by constitutional checks, and limitations, and always changing easily, with deliberate changes of popular opinions and sentiments, is the only true sovereign of a free people. Whoever rejects it, does, of necessity, fly to anarchy or to despotism. Unanimity is impossible; the rule of a minority, as a permanent arrangement, is wholly inadmissible; so that, rejecting the majority principle, anarchy, or despotism in some form, is all that is left.[74]

Therefore, secession was wrong in terms of democratic theory, and the first order of business was to save the Union. In a letter to Horace Greeley, Lincoln stated, "If I could save the Union without freeing *any* slave I would do it, and if I could save it by freeing *all* the slaves I would do it; and if I could save it by freeing some and leaving others alone, I would also do that."[75] The point is not that slavery is not a wrong. It was perfectly clear to Lincoln that it was a great evil; he was outraged by Douglas's professed indifference to whether it was voted up or down during the debates of the 1850s. "I hate it," he said, "because of the monstrous injustice of slavery itself. I hate it because it deprives our republican example of its just influence in the world . . . and especially because it forces so many good men amongst ourselves into an open war with the very fundamental principles of civil liberty—criticizing the Declaration of Independence, and insisting that there is no right principle of action but *self-interest.*"[76]

What Lincoln's strategy in the war shows is that high principle can sometimes be furthered by "low" practical politics. The two are not antithetical, as even Garrison came to see when Lincoln was finally in a position to commit himself fully and issue the Emancipation Proclamation. This was a great moment because a second war aim was added to the cause of preserving the Union. Lincoln's constitutional patience finally ran out. Those who did not like the proclamation "must understand," he said, "that they cannot experiment for ten years trying to destroy the government, and if they fail still come back into the Union unhurt."[77] It is sometimes argued that the proclamation freed no slaves because it applied only in the Confederate states, but that, writes James McPherson, is a mere cliché. The new war aim made it clear that slavery would be destroyed by force if the Union were to win the war. Moreover, the most revolutionary aspect of the policy was the decision to enlist former slaves to fight their old masters.[78]

But if old-fashioned coalition politics played a large part in bringing the end of slavery, there is still a profound sense in which the Garrisonian radicals were right after all. As C. Vann Woodward said, it took "revolution, a civil war, and a repudiation of the old Constitution" to achieve the goal. Moreover, "history supports Garrisonian dogma . . . that to be effective the eradication of slavery had to be root-and-branch, that the racist ideology supporting it permeated the country, and that abolishing slavery in alliance with racists and without eradicating their ideology would be largely an empty victory."[79] The tragedy, as Woodward saw, was that Lincoln knew that the war had to be fought with the support of racists or the cause would be lost.[80] And the present is dismayingly like the past; such is the difficulty of true reform. Politics very rarely offers the opportunity to pit pure good against pure evil.

Perhaps the supreme irony in all this is that the man who led this revolutionary transformation had deeply conservative instincts. Lincoln's first great speech, the Lyceum Address of 1838, was a penetrating attack on the mob violence that was a product of the burgeoning sectional crisis—and by implication an attack on civil disobedience as well. In this speech he proposed that reverence for the Constitution and the law be inculcated as a civil religion to temper the American penchant for the pursuit of self-interest, often advanced as it was in violent ways. A moving and prophetic speech, it may well have provided, as some contemporary political theorists insist, an important corrective to some of the defects of the Constitution, as seen by many of the Anti-Federalists.[81] A political system so dependent on self-interest may prove to rest on very unstable foundations.

The Lyceum speech was pervaded by a concern for continuity and stability. Yet the changes set in motion by the war were fundamental. The most obvious was the destruction of slavery, but that was by no means all. The carefully calibrated system of Madisonian politics broke down in the crisis. Madison argued that under his system no one interest could gain control of the government, but Calhoun recognized the contrary possibility, hence the theory of the concurrent majority. In spite of the ultimate incoherence of that notion, Calhoun proved to be right about the possibility of sectional division; the antislavery forces won in the total absence of *any* support from the region that defended the status quo.[82] The conflict that followed led to the completion of an American nation: The house divided was united by force. As Eric Foner puts it: "We can paraphrase John Adams's famous comment on the American Revolution and apply it to the coming of the Civil War—the separation was complete, in the minds of the people, before the war began. In a sense, the Constitution and national political system had failed in the difficult task of creating a nation—only the Civil War would accomplish it."[83]

James McPherson shows that the change could be seen in the very language used to describe the political system. Before the war the words *United States* were treated as a plural noun; after the war they were used in the singular. *Union* was displaced in the political vocabulary by *nation*. In his First Inaugural Address, Lincoln referred to the Union twenty times and to the nation not at all. In the Gettysburg Address, he did not refer to the Union at all, but did use nation five times in a very short speech. And in the Second Inaugural Address, Lincoln spoke of the southern attempt to destroy the Union and of the North's resolve to preserve the nation.[84]

However, the change cut much more deeply than these important linguistic symbols. The newly formed nation was conceptualized in northern terms. As Alexander Stephens, the vice president of the Confederacy, had realized, Lincoln raised the idea of Union to the level of religious mysticism; it might be added that Walt Whitman turned it into poetry.[85] The words of Lincoln's Second Inaugural Address were the words of a Puritan jeremiad, one elevated to heights of rhetorical and moral force never before seen or equaled since in American political culture. The war is seen as a punishment from God—for both sides. We may hope and pray, Lincoln proclaimed, that "the mighty scourge of war may speedily pass away. Yet, if God wills that it continue, until all the wealth piled by the bondsman's two hundred and fifty years of unrequited toil shall be sunk, and until every drop of blood drawn with the lash, shall be paid by another drawn by the sword, as was said three thousand years ago, so still it must be said, 'the judgments of the Lord, are true and righteous altogether.'"[86]

There *is* a good deal of Jefferson and Locke in Lincoln, but such utterances go far beyond the conventions of liberal theory. Liberty is more than negative liberty—the absence of restraint. Liberty entails not only the removal of restraints but also the creation of the capacity to act. Negative liberty and positive liberty are distinct, though they are not necessarily incompatible. By taking action against slavery, Lincoln used his positive liberty to create the potential for both negative *and* positive liberty for the former slaves.

Thus, the return to Puritanism also encompassed a new—or quite old—sense of liberty. Lincoln's conception of liberty, like that of his contemporary, Daniel Webster, seems related to John Winthrop's idea that there was liberty to do "that only which is good, just, and honest." It was positive in the sense that true liberty is restricted in content. The jeremiad was a call to conscience of a sort that, as I argued earlier, had roots outside the liberal tradition. Lincoln's was also an opportunity concept in the sense that it was intended to free persons so that they could develop their capacities to the fullest extent.[87] It was a politics of conscience, and its loss led into a wilderness of self-interest, which John Patrick Diggins lamented when he wrote of the lost soul of American politics.[88] Lincoln's transcendentally beautiful language constitutes a monument to what we have lost. It certainly is not only the rhetorical but also the moral and intellectual high point of the American tradition.

At the outset, I tried to show that Calvinism unintentionally fed into the liberal tradition. Lincoln's thought is a powerful, though difficult to maintain, synthesis of the two, along with a significant component drawn from his Whig political roots. Locke is there, by way of Jefferson, but it is a subtly transformed Locke. Locke postulated a move away from the state of nature in which, at the beginning, men are actually equal but depart from that condition. For Lincoln, society "is constituted by the movement *toward* a condition in which the equality of men is actual."[89] Finally, the Protestant work ethic, transmuted into the producerist ideology of the Jacksonian Democrats, is also central to Lincoln's reconceptualization of the American tradition.[90] This is a politics of interpretation on the highest possible level.

But more than national unification flowed from the Civil War. The new state that emerged was decisively a large-scale liberal capitalist state. There is a deep irony here, for the Union Lincoln fought to preserve was the world of Jacksonian America—"the world of the small shop, the independent farm, and the village artisan." As for the South, the war fought to preserve slavery created a tragically thwarted opportunity for poor whites and ex-slaves to show their opposition to planter control. "Here indeed," Eric Foner wrote, "is the tragic irony of that conflict. Each side fought to defend a vision of the good society, but each vision was destroyed by the very struggle to preserve it."[91] And, of course, capitalism was to become a new form of what we now call conservatism. Moreover, to heighten the tragedy, Reconstruction would fail to deal successfully with the racial discrimination at the heart of slavery.

The liberalism that Louis Hartz saw as dominant from the start of American history finally emerged triumphant with the destruction of the most fundamentally antiliberal institution and the emergence of full-scale industrial capitalism. But it was to prove a bitter victory for many: Practice fell far short of liberal theory. The focus of politics shifted to the question of the relation of the liberal state to the large corporation, and the concerns of the freed slaves gradually faded into the background of American politics, only to return a century later as the nation was forced to take up the unfinished business of the Civil War, a project that is still tragically far from completion.

· 8 ·

Laissez-Faire Conservatism and the Legitimation of Corporate Capitalism

Every social order requires a legitimating theory. This principle may be particularly true when the social order has undergone a profound upheaval, as was the case in American society in the years following the Civil War. America had always been a system given to rapid change, but the transformation in the period from 1865 to 1900 was especially dramatic. An agrarian society moved quickly toward increasing urbanization; there was an enormous wave of immigration that changed the demographic makeup of the country; moreover, the war and Reconstruction transformed the essential nature of the constitutional structure. And notoriously, it was a period of monumental political corruption, which was often directly related to the momentous economic changes that were sweeping across the reconstituted nation.[1]

The most dramatic of these developments were perhaps the ones that transformed the economy. A few statistics can give some sense of the dimensions of the change. At the start of the war, manufacturing capital was about $1 billion; at the turn of the twentieth century, it was ten times greater. In the same period wage earners increased in number from 1,300,000 to 5,300,000. In 1900 the value of manufactured products was nearly two and one-half times the value of agricultural produce. And the number of inhabitants of cities in excess of 8,000 in population increased during this time from about 16 percent of the U.S. population to almost 33 percent.[2] There were also profound transformations in the organizational structure of business and finance. Though competition reigned supreme at the level of theory and ideology, in fact corporate leaders were endlessly inventive in discovering ways to try to suppress it. Gentlemen's agreements, pools, trusts, and holding companies all were employed. There was also a growing concentration of finance capital in the hands of a relative few.[3] Finally, the system of labor relations in both North and South was radically altered. As Russell Hanson put it, "Reconstruction and the Gilded Age were but two aspects of the more general process by which the capitalist mode of production was reproduced in America on an extended scale."[4] In the end, a striking irony emerged when the North was forced to recognize the conflict between capital and labor, which had been a standard part of the ideology of such southern apologists as George Fitzhugh.[5]

This was an age that saw the full triumph of what Louis Hartz called American Whiggery, the property-oriented right wing of the liberal tradition, as well as what he called democratic capitalism. It was a triumph that lasted: "Unfurling the golden banner of Horatio Alger, American Whiggery marched into the promised land after the Civil War and did not really leave it until the crash of 1929."[6] But *democratic capitalism* is perhaps not the best term to describe the phenomenon, since, as John Diggins argued, the most important change precipitated by the war was the emergence of large-scale corporate capitalism, an economic form in serious tension with democracy.[7] As I noted, this development had prewar roots; Tocqueville had, with his customary prescience, predicted the emergence of a harsh new industrial aristocracy.[8] However, even with his formidable powers, he could not have anticipated the magnitude of the change. Earlier social theories had been based on the predominance of agriculture and the legitimating ideal of the Jeffersonian republic of yeoman farmers. But the new forms of economic organization did not remotely resemble the old order or the ideas that justified it. As John Blum wrote, "Man became economic man, democracy was identified with capitalism, liberty with property and the use of it, equality with opportunity for gain, and progress with economic change and the accumulation of capital."[9]

The resulting social changes were profound, and the nation had to learn to live its life anew. Sidney Fine summed up well the resulting social and intellectual problems:

> The American people had to decide what to do about slums and tenements, public health, the wages, hours, and working conditions of standard and substandard labor, unemployment, and increased inequalities in the distribution of wealth, railroads, and industrial combinations. Although, for the most part, the intervention of government was required for the solution of these issues, existing theories with respect to the role of the state constituted an intellectual barrier to the development of any realistic program of state action. Jeffersonian-Jacksonian liberalism was already an anachronism in the America of the years after the Civil War.[10]

It was not, of course, that the idea of an activist government was entirely new. To be sure, the Jeffersonian/Jacksonian tradition in American thought and politics had been largely devoted to the principles of laissez-faire. However, starting with Hamilton and the Federalists and continuing through the American Plan of the Whig Party, so closely associated with the likes of Henry Clay, there had also been substantial support for an alliance between business and government. As Sidney Fine put it in assessing Hamilton's position, the essence of the Federalist-Whig position was "government aid to business, but no embarrassing government regulation."[11] Under the influence of this point of view, the national government was engaged in the promotion of a considerable number of economic activities, although by the time of the Civil War government intervention had begun to decline, partly because in the 1850s the Democratic Party descendants of Jefferson were in control.[12] State governments were also active from the founding until the war, both as promoters of economic activity and as regulators, though at the state level too governmental economic activity was declining.[13] In general, then, it can be said that laissez-faire, though an important intellectual and political force prior to the great industrial expansion in the latter part of the nineteenth century, was not the completely dominant theory that prevailing myths held it to be. Nevertheless, it became a central part of the legitimating ideology of the newly emergent corporate capitalism.

Laissez-Faire, Conservative Darwinism, and the New Legitimacy

The first infusion of intellectual support for the new economic system was imported from England in the works of sociologist and philosopher Herbert Spencer.[14] Spencer's system was nothing less than grandiose. It was an attempt at a theory that would unite the entire physical, biological, and human universe in one sweeping embrace. Life processes were characterized by a movement from the incoherent simplicity of the protozoa to the coherent complexity of man and the higher animals. The end result of this evolutionary process was a state of perfect equilibrium, reached when differentiation and complexity could go no further. For a biological organism, that would mean death, but for human societies, it led to the establishment of "a stable, harmonious, completely adapted state," which would see the realization of perfect and complete happiness.[15] This evolutionary theory was published six years before Darwin and Wallace brought out the first sketches of the principle of natural selection. In fact, it was Spencer who coined the phrase "survival of the fittest."

That idea is near the core of Spencer's theory. The perfect equilibrium he foresaw could not be achieved without struggle. For Spencer, nature was indeed red in tooth and claw. Taking his cue from the classical economist Thomas Malthus, Spencer argued that the pressure of human needs in a context of limited resources and expanding population would lead to the progress of mankind as a whole. However, for such progress to occur, we must not violate the law of conduct and consequence, which holds that there must be no action that prevents the individual from reaping the benefits or suffering the costs that stem from his actions. When this principle is upheld, progress is the inevitable result: The fit will survive because of their superior intelligence, discipline, energy, and strength, and the unfit will deservedly fall by the wayside.

To Spencer, the social application of this biological law was clear. In a series of works starting with *Social Statics* in 1851 and continuing through *The Man Versus the State* in 1885, he argued that the functions of government had to be limited to the administration of justice and protection against external and internal attack, essentially the same functions sanctioned by classical liberal economic theory dating back to Adam Smith. And that was all. Spencer was opposed to poor laws, state support for education, tariffs, state banking, sanitary supervision, government postal systems, and even protection against medical quacks.[16] His theory was a categorical repudiation of all types of reform that were designed to come to terms with the new realities of industrial capitalism.

The impact of Spencer's ideas in the United States is hard to overestimate. Richard Hofstadter observed that in the thirty years after the Civil War it was impossible to be active in any intellectual pursuit without coming to grips with his work. Philosophers of the stature of Josiah Royce, William James, and John Dewey each felt his influence, as did such pioneering sociologists as William Graham Sumner and Lester Frank Ward. Moreover, sales of his books were exceptionally high, so he was apparently read by the general public as well.[17] Not surprisingly, he was lionized by the rich and powerful, who tended to see themselves at the top of the evolutionary ladder Spencer had depicted. Andrew Carnegie was only somewhat more effusive than most when he raved that as he read Darwin and Spencer, he had an epiphany: "Light came as in a flood and all was clear. . . . I had found the truth of evolution. 'All is well since all grows better' became my motto, my true source of comfort. [Man's] face is turned to the light, he stands in the sun and looks upward." And none other than John D. Rockefeller argued that the growth of a large business entailed merely the survival of the fittest, likening it to the American Beauty rose, which could be produced in all its glory "only by sacrificing the early buds which grow up around it. This is not an evil tendency in business. It is merely the working-out of a law of nature and a law of God."[18]

Spencer's fame reached its greatest height in America in 1882 when, in spite of his dislike of travel, he made a triumphant U.S. tour, climaxing in a legendary dinner held at Delmonico's in New York, with the rich, the famous, and their intellectual acolytes attending. Surprisingly, Spencer chided his audience for the excessive speed and hard work characteristic of American life, yet his listeners responded with effulgent tributes, topped off by evangelist Henry Ward Beecher, who proclaimed that he and Spencer would meet again in eternity among those who had demonstrated their "fitness for immortality."[19]

Among the celebrants at Delmonico's was William Graham Sumner, by any standard the most important of Spencer's American intellectual disciples. Sumner was a pioneering sociologist who, after leaving the ministry, taught for many years at Yale University. An exceptionally prolific writer, particularly of essays, Sumner developed a reasonably systematic and rigidly consistent, if not notably original, statement of conservative Darwinism.[20] In today's terms, Sumner *was* a conservative, though as Robert McCloskey rightly said, he would have vigorously denied the label.[21] Both McCloskey and Sumner were correct in some sense, which opens up an important aspect of the American Right that it is necessary to deal with. Sumner was certainly conservative in the sense that his theory lent itself to the defense of the political and economic status quo of his time, a position well captured by the title of one of his more famous essays, "The Absurd Attempt to Make the World Over."[22] At the same time Sumner would have seen traditional European conservatism as an obscurantist attachment to the past; his thought just as easily can be seen as a transformed version of Hartz's Whiggery, the property-oriented right wing of the liberal tradition, a classification reinforced by Sumner's attachment to an ultraliberal version of laissez-faire, free market economics of a purity perhaps unmatched even by Adam Smith.

Leaving aside the conceptual foundations of Sumner's sociological theory,[23] the basis of his socioeconomic doctrine was a thoroughgoing materialism. He defined "social good" in *Folkways* in terms of *"economic power, material prosperity, and group strength for war,"* and in the same work he claimed that social value conformed to "worldly success and to income from work contributed to the industrial organization."[24] Thus socialists, when they attacked capital, "are simply attacking the foundations of civilization, and every socialistic scheme which has ever been proposed, so far as it has lessened the motives for saving or the security of capital, is anti-social and anti-civilizing."[25] So important was the accumulation of capital that "the savings bank depositor is a hero of civilization."[26]

In good Darwinian style, it is the fittest who will survive and survive well in the struggle to accumulate. Capital *will* become concentrated; there *will* be both monopolies and millionaires. But it is madness to move against those who succeed in the economic conflicts that are so central to the growth of civilization. To set limits to accumulation "would be like killing off our generals in war."[27] However, as I will argue below, that is ambiguous. In fact,

Sumner's preferences are not altogether consistent with the projected outcome of the evolutionary process.

Sumner's true hero was the "Forgotten Man," a character type who appeared again and again in his essays. The Forgotten Man was "the clean, quiet, virtuous, domestic citizen who pays his debts and his taxes and is never to be heard of out of his little circle."[28] This was a man beset on all sides. There were those who forgot that "every man and woman in society has one big duty. That is, to take care of his or her own self."[29] Those who failed to raise themselves from poverty tended to turn to the state as the "protector and guardian of certain classes." The schemes that reformers hatched took the form, "A and B put their heads together to decide what C shall be made to do for D." It was C who was the Forgotten Man.[30] But to Sumner, "It is not the function of the State to make men happy. They must make themselves happy in their own way, and at their own risk."[31] To forget that was to assume that rights pertained to results, when, in fact, they pertained only to chances. Moreover, there were no natural rights, least of all to subsistence. The very notion was "destitute of sense."[32] Rights have to do only with the right to compete, that is, with opportunity. It is the competitive struggle that will determine who are the fittest and therefore who will survive and prosper.

In effect, then, the Forgotten Man is menaced by democracy. Sumner, who claimed to be a democrat, argued that no other form of government was suited to the particular conditions of the United States. But democracy was a new form of government, and it might not yet have found appropriate forms.[33] Furthermore, "history is only a tiresome repetition of one story. Persons and classes have sought to win possession of the power of the State in order to live luxuriously out of the earnings of others."[34] The danger that loomed in democratic systems was that government would be pressured to develop a policy of "favoring a new privileged class of the many and the poor."[35]

However, the ordinary, hard-working middle-class citizen was menaced not only by the derangements of democratic politics and the threats stemming from those below him in the social order but also by the plutocracy above him. Remember that in spite of everything, Sumner still considered himself, with whatever reservations, a democrat. And the greatest enemy of democracy was the plutocracy.[36] Plutocracy was "the most sordid and debasing form of political energy known to us. In its motive, its processes, its code, and its sanctions it is infinitely corrupting to all the institutions which ought to preserve and protect society."[37] The great vice of plutocracy was "jobbery." Jobbery was any scheme to gain financially by illegitimate means, and the United States was "deeply afflicted" by it.[38] Given his views on the supreme virtue of accumulating capital, one might expect such a view to have given

Sumner pause. However, he was at pains to point out that all capitalists were not plutocrats. Still, he felt that all civilized governments tended toward plutocracy; nowhere was this more true than in the United States. In the past the principal limits on plutocracy had been set by the aristocracy, but in America out of necessity they had to come from democracy.[39]

Sumner freely admitted that on his own principles this struggle between democracy and plutocracy was a "lamentable contest."[40] But we had to fall back on laissez-faire and competition because of the incompetence of government. Thus his opposition to government intervention extended even to issues dear to the hearts of business leaders, such as the protective tariff. However enthusiastic Sumner might have been about the achievements of unfettered capitalism, he was never a mere apologist for his heroes. Still, the problem remained: "How can we get bad legislators to pass a law which shall hinder bad legislators from passing a bad law?"[41] After all, "so far as yet appears, Americans cannot yet govern a city of one hundred thousand inhabitants so as to get comfort and convenience in it at a low cost and without jobbery."[42] Given the level of corruption endemic in American politics at the time, it is possible to have a certain sympathy with Sumner's view. However, historical experience with later reform movements, with all their manifest imperfections, suggests that government is not totally helpless before social and economic problems.[43]

But those are the least of Sumner's difficulties and—by extension—of Darwinian, laissez-faire conservatism in general. Perhaps the most obvious problem is that if any slight departure from the straight and narrow of noninterference could derail the whole, presumably inevitable, train of progress, then, "by imputing such power to a few errant men, the theorists mocked the grandeur of their own fundamental laws."[44] Like most determinists, Sumner lacked the courage of his convictions.

There is another, still more fundamental, incoherence in Sumner's theory. The whole ideology is rooted in a competitive struggle between individuals for the rewards of success that prove one to be among the fittest. But as Jeffrey Lustig pointed out, the movement of events was running against the individual. In fact, "the natural drift of events in his era was leading toward concentration, which threatened individualism. Faced with what could have been a crippling contradiction, Sumner hardly paused. He chose for the drift of events."[45] And in so doing, if more recent critics of corporate behavior are correct, he also undermined his already weak claims to be a genuine democrat.

Finally, although more remains to be said about the place of Sumner in the development of American thought, it is possible to see that he fits in a meaningful way into the liberal tradition, in the broad sense of the term. He embraced the economic, laissez-faire variant of liberalism with an unmatched enthusiasm. John Locke too, insofar as he is an ancestor of capitalism and limited government, is clearly in the background. But behind Locke there is also the specter of Thomas Hobbes. Gone is the relatively tame, relatively social, image of Lockean man. In his place is the vicious, no-holds-barred competitor of the Hobbesian state of nature. In fact, McCloskey was quite right to argue that in Sumner's work, "selfishness is raised to the status of an absolute good; the Hobbesian man becomes the moral ideal."[46]

The Impact
of Laissez-Faire Conservatism

One might expect so obviously flawed a theory as conservative Darwinism to have a rather short life, and indeed opposition was not long in forming. Nonetheless, the impact of this dramatic revision of American Whiggery was large and long lasting. It must be borne in mind that it was a mixture of three intellectually powerful currents of Western thought: the Protestant ethic; classical laissez-faire economics; and the principle of natural selection.[47] It is not hard to see the difficulty in transposing Darwin's biological theory into a social system, or to observe that the laissez-faire theory of the market is an empirical fantasy, simply a mirage that has never been seen in the real world, or to notice that the Protestant work ethic is transformed into a twisted parody of itself with all traces of the Puritan distrust of wealth discarded. Still, however odd and even heartless the amalgam, these are not trivial forces in our culture. Their convergence led to a situation in which the laissez-faire associated with Jefferson became a weapon of Hamiltonian capitalists at a time when—with the major exceptions of the tariff and subsidies for railroad development—they were able to dispense with the governmental aid that earlier had been central to Whiggery. As Louis Hartz so trenchantly put it, what happened was that in this climax of American Whiggery, "Hamilton absorbed Jefferson and Horatio Alger emerged."[48]

Businessmen took this new ideology to their hearts, though with an understandable degree of selectivity. Competition was all very well for the working class, but as the rise of the trusts showed, it recommended itself less clearly to business elites. And, of course, laissez-faire reached its limits when it came to the tariff. Still, consistency is not always the most obvious element in the use of an ideology. Thus business was able to legitimate its new organizational forms with the doctrines of what can be called "laissez-faire conservatism." The idea may be an oxymoron, but as Clinton Rossiter put it, the doctrine "rose to prominence between 1865 and 1885, to ascendancy between 1885 and 1920, to domination—to virtual identification with 'the American Way'—in the 1920's."[49]

In government the laissez-faire/Darwinian creed reached its greatest heights in the courts. While former slaves languished, the due process clause of the Fourteenth Amendment was turned into a powerful device for the protection of corporate interests. In his pursuit of laissez-faire, Mr. Justice Field strove mightily to read even the rights enshrined in the Declaration of Independence into the Constitution as part of the defense of corporate property. And it should be remembered that in the *Lochner* case, when Mr. Justice Holmes protested that "the Fourteenth Amendment does not enact Mr. Herbert Spencer's Social Statics," he was writing in dissent. There is little doubt that the courts became perhaps the most powerful line of defense for the new economic order.[50]

But it was not only in the courts, academia, and the boardrooms that laissez-faire conservatism was an influential force. It sank deep roots into popular culture as well. It will surely not have escaped notice that the ideas discussed here are a significant part of what we today call conservatism. Certainly they have penetrated deep into the ideology of the Republican Party, notably under the leadership of Ronald Reagan and his successors.[51] As Richard Hofstadter put it in a period when Darwinism seemed dormant in comparison with today, "One of the keys to the controversy of our time over the merits or defects of the 'welfare state' is the fact that the very idea affronts the traditions of a great many men and women who were raised, if not upon the specific tenets of social Darwinism, at least upon the moral imperatives that it expressed."[52]

All this suggests that the ideas Americans call conservative are a very unusual intellectual phenomenon. If we think of Edmund Burke as the prototypical conservative, then the differences become readily apparent. Whereas European conservatives such as Burke tended to be religious, to rely on intuition, tradition, and the collective historical wisdom of the community, Sumner, Richard Hofstadter pointed out, adopted almost the opposite position. He was a secularist, a rationalist, and a thoroughgoing individualist, and he scorned tradition as a form of sentimentality. A conservatism that focuses on change and innovation is strange. And as Hofstadter continued, it has often been the Right in American politics, the propertied side, less devoted to professions of democracy—Hartz's Whigs, in other words—that has been devoted to innovation, particularly in economic matters.[53] These competitive, individualistic, laissez-faire assumptions, which are so close to the heart of a major current of American conservatism, are, it is clear, deeply liberal in their origins. When we consider the breadth of the liberal tradition, the force of the Hartz thesis is clear.

In the late nineteenth century, then, possessive individualism became the national creed, rapidly eclipsing the Tocquevillian vision of a nation of cooperative voluntary associations, with strong traces of the ideas of civic humanist republicanism, not to mention the Puritan sense of discipline and guilt. Earlier American liberal ideology, the creation of Jefferson, Madison, and their followers, was the product of an agrarian society in which it made some sense to believe in an unregulated economy as long as free land was widely available. The great triumph of the new laissez-faire conservatism was its success in carrying this theory over into the age of corporate capitalism and in persuading the courts, in particular, to treat corporations as if they were simply ordinary individuals. "Thus," as Robert Dahl puts it, "an economic order that spontaneously produced inequality in the distribution of economic and political resources acquired legitimacy, at least in part, by clothing itself in the recut garments of an outmoded ideology in which private ownership was justified on the ground that a wide diffusion of property would support political equality." The result, Dahl concludes, was that Americans have never seriously asked themselves whether there is an alternative to corporate capitalism.[54] But whatever the virtues of corporate capitalism, promoting equality is not one of them. Nor, as many contemporary critics would argue, is it clear that democracy and the large corporation are not at least in serious tension, if they are not altogether incompatible with each other.

In any case, as I have suggested, the perpetuation of an outmoded precapitalist ideological justification for private property must be seen as one of the intellectual triumphs of laissez-faire conservatism. A sometimes heady brew of thought, it continues to be an influential part of the ideological armory of the American Right, right up to the Reagan and Bush administrations and the Republican congressional leadership elected in 1994. That is understandable, if somewhat paradoxical. The preservation of the economic order is a natural function for conservatives, but because to preserve capitalism is to preserve a system dedicated to change, there is a certain often remarked irony here. But that, as Louis Hartz knew well, is the natural fate of "conservatism" in a society in which so much of what is to be conserved is liberal in origin. This has been the basic dilemma of American conservatism: the preservation of the status quo in a society dedicated in principle to a dynamism that is bound to upset the established order and, more subtly perhaps, the support of hedonistic consumption in a system putatively based on the austerities of the Protestant ethic. The question that begins to emerge is whether corporate capitalism is contradictory on the level of its cultural tensions rather than on the basis of the economic contradictions theorized by Marx.[55] These problems bedevil the "conservative" movement to this day.

∘ 9 ∘

The Dilemmas of Populist Reform

Not surprisingly, the new conservative Darwinian ideology soon enough began to meet theoretical opposition. First of all, the principles of Darwinism began to be turned against the Sumnerian/Spencerian version of the theory. The theory of natural selection was designed, the critics pointed out, to explain the survival of species. Why then assume that the struggle is between members of the same species rather than a contest of the species as a collectivity to adapt to the vicissitudes of nature? As E. S. Corwin summed it up, "Instead of the creature being adapted to the environment, the *environment had to be adapted to the creature.*"[1] To assess the situation in this way is to see the problem in an entirely different light.

The implications of the new perception did not lead to a laissez-faire conservative defense of the status quo. Indeed, the "reform Darwinists," as they have come to be called, laid much of the intellectual groundwork for the twentieth-century social and political movements that have taken the liberal label in the ordinary language of political discussion.[2] Theoretically, as Corwin said, this new perception provided the base for new developments in philosophy and social theory: pragmatism, instrumentalism, experimentalism, and functionalism.[3]

In sociology, such figures as Lester Frank Ward and Charles Horton Cooley emerged to challenge the Darwinian orthodoxy. Ward committed what was perhaps the ultimate heresy by arguing that competition actually prevented the fit from surviving, and although he rejected socialism, he called for the planned control of the social system as a whole.[4] Cooley, for his part, moved sharply away from the atomistic individualism characteristic of the writings of Spencer and Sumner. He attacked the materialistic determinism of the conservative evolutionists. A truly ethical life, he thought, required the reform of the social environment, since the individual could not be understood except in "living unity with social wholes." It is in this sense that Cooley can be considered one of the founders of social psychology.[5]

But it was not only conservative Darwinism that came under attack in the last two decades of the nineteenth century. There was also a major assault on the foundations of laissez-faire economics. Among the most important and representative figures in the attack were Richard Ely, Henry Carter Adams, Simon Nelson Patten, and John Bates Clark. To Ely, as to John Stuart Mill, ethics and economics were inseparable. Wages and hours, which reduced the chance for the working man to reap the benefits of civilization, were inherently unjust. Adams's position was similar; both proposed programs designed to elevate the moral plane of competition as well as to look after "the education, health, and general well-being of the citizenry." Patten called for a system of national economic planning. In the 1890s, Clark argued for a neoclassical revival of laissez-faire, but with the difference that the state would assume the role of enforcing genuine competition. All saw themselves as offering alternatives to the Darwinian struggle of laissez-faire conservatism, and all were influential on the movements for change that were to follow, from populism to the New Deal.[6] It was, of course, those movements that were destined to alter the face of twentieth-century American politics.

The Enigma of Populism

Populism was a response to the prolonged agricultural depression of the final two decades of the nineteenth century. For good reason, farmers felt they were the victims of discriminatory banking practices when they did their annual spring borrowing so as to be able to plant their crops and of unfair pricing policies by the railroads when the time came to ship their produce to market. Beyond this consensus on basic concerns, there is little common ground on the place of the populist movement in American history. As James Turner notes, "Even the historian's infinite capacity for disagreement has barely accommodated the quarrels over the Populists."[7]

A part of this problem, I believe, has been due to a failure to observe certain distinctions. First, one must consider the People's, or Populist, Party, which ran James B. Weaver for president in 1892 and then fused—disastrously—with the Democratic Party to support William Jennings Bryan in the election of 1896. A second level of analysis must deal with the broad movement of agrarian discontent that swept through large parts of the South and Midwest during the last third of the nineteenth century. The discontent arose when farmers were confronted with the changing structure of the new economic system, falling prices for agricultural commodities, and a transformed international market. Many who lived in agricultural areas were deeply discontented and accepted parts of the Populist program, but by no means all of these "populists" were members of the People's Party or chose to vote for its candidates.[8] Finally, most subtly, and perhaps most controversially, there is the question of populism as a style of thought and a way of looking at politics that in important ways may transcend agrarian discontent in late-nineteenth-century America.

At that level, populism is at its most elusive. For one thing, it is an international phenomenon; in principle, one could construct an ideal type, which would encompass all varieties. However, the difficulties are formidable. The only two movements that explicitly took the name *Populist* in the nineteenth century were the Russians' and Americans'. However, as C. Vann Woodward pointed out, the populism of the Americans was a mass movement with a few intellectuals attached, whereas that of the Russians was essentially an intellectual movement with a small mass following. Although the comparative perspective is useful, it seems best to follow Woodward's lead and focus on the American experience.[9]

Populism as a style of thought is an enigma that is difficult to capture. On the simplest level, one might say that its guiding principle is that all politics tends to come down to a conflict between "the people and the interests." To say this is to indicate that populists see politics not so much in terms of class, but as a matter of relations between the overwhelming mass of the people as a whole and a small number of vested interests marked by a strong tendency toward conspiratorial action. Such a formulation, it should be noted, can lead to a politics of either the left or the right. That style of politics has been a persistent tendency in America perhaps from the time of the Anti-Federalists and certainly since Andrew Jackson through the ascendancy of Ronald Reagan and his contemporary followers, such as Newt Gingrich.[10]

Another way of approaching the place of populism in U.S. history is somewhat more formal and perhaps more complex. In this view, populism is based on the concept of majority rule, a belief in the beneficence and capability of the common man, and a theory of participatory democracy. Its opposite is committed to an elaborate system of constitutional limitations designed to frustrate the easy triumph of popular majorities and a degree of legalism and perhaps elitism.[11] Like any such dichotomy, this one is no doubt overly schematic, but as a pair of ideal types it is still analytically useful. Again the roots of this paradigm and its alternate are, as I have argued, deep in the very fiber of American politics. It can be added that populism in the sense suggested is an inevitable, though certainly not the sole, component of any theory of democratic politics.

In considering the nineteenth-century populists, it is appropriate to begin with the party and the movement. The People's Party was an outgrowth of the Farmers' Alliance, which was founded in Texas in the mid-1870s and had become a powerful force in the southern states by the middle of the 1880s. In 1889 the southern group merged with the smaller Northwest Alliance to form the National Alliance. It was the latter group that provided the basis for the new party, which ran James B. Weaver for president in 1892. The Omaha Platform, which the party produced for its campaign, is perhaps, for all its brevity, the most basic statement of Populist belief, at least in its more radical form.

The platform opened with a preamble stating a set of general beliefs, and then went on to detail a short, but specific, list of policy demands. Corruption, it said, dominated both state and national legislative bodies, the electoral process, and even touched the judiciary itself. The people were demoralized by economic oppression, and the free press hardly functioned as such. The fruits of the labor of millions were "boldly stolen," and two great classes were emerging—paupers and millionaires. The monetary system was thoroughly corrupt. According to the platform: "A vast conspiracy against mankind has been organized on two continents, and it is rapidly taking possession of the world. If not met and overthrown at once, it forebodes terrible social convulsions, the destruction of civilization, or the establishment of an absolute despotism." In the face of this crisis, the politics of the main parties were a mere sham; it was time to restore government to the "plain people."[12]

The purposes of the movement were identical with the purposes spelled out in the Preamble to the U.S. Constitution. Those, the authors claimed, could be achieved only by a brotherhood of free men, not in a society held together by bayonets. However, the powers of government, which were identical with those of the people, had to be expanded to deal with the conditions of the time.

Declarations and demands then followed. Dimly echoing Locke and directly and clearly echoing the producerist ideology of the Jacksonian Democrats, the platform declared, "Wealth belongs to him who creates it." Those who would not work would not eat. Moreover, the interests of urban and rural labor were identical, as were their enemies. The text throughout is replete with statements of sympathy and support for the cause of urban labor.

More specifically, "The time has come when the railroad corporations will either own the people or the people must own the railroads." Should the latter occur, a constitutional amendment would be necessary to place the expanded new bureaucracy under strict civil service regulations.

Next came a series of monetary demands designed to address the question of farm credit, perhaps the most vexing single issue to the Populists. Those included the famous call for the free coinage of silver; an expansion of the money supply in circulation; the adoption of a graduated income tax, with the revenue to be used to reduce the burden of taxation on domestic industries; a restriction of government spending to the necessary minimum; the creation of postal savings banks and the adoption of the Farmers' Alliance's subtreasury plan, a rather sophisticated device for governmental assistance in increasing the money supply by advancing low-interest loans on the security of crops deposited in government warehouses.[13]

Besides support for the nationalization of the railroads, there was also a call for public ownership of the telephone and telegraph systems, reflecting the same interest in communication. More radical still was a demand for government reclamation of lands held by railroads in excess of their real needs, as well as of land owned by aliens. The distrust of the influx of new populations in the late nineteenth century was also evident in support for the restriction of "undesirable" immigration.

Finally, there was a call for a "free ballot and a fair count in all elections" as well as for a series of specific reforms of political institutions. The platform recommended the devices of the initiative and referendum, the limitation of the president and vice president to one term, and the direct election of U.S. senators.

In short, the Omaha Platform reflected the principal discontents of the Populists, suggested the most comprehensive statement of the proposed remedies of the movement, and at least hinted at the underlying theoretical ideas that shaped their responses to the crisis of the late nineteenth century, as they perceived it.

To this assessment might be added a discussion of *Wealth Against Commonwealth,* by Henry Demarest Lloyd, who was, in the opinion of Norman Pollack, the leading intellectual of the populists. Lloyd was by no means a typical populist and might better be labeled an ardent sympathizer rather than a member of the movement. A graduate of Columbia University, Lloyd was editor of the *Chicago Tribune* until his views became too radical for his father-in-law, who happened to own the newspaper. Deeply impressed by British Fabian socialism and closely allied with such urban radicals as the Socialist Labor leader Eugene V. Debs and the brilliant trial lawyer Clarence Darrow, he supported the radical wing of populism until its final collapse in the election of 1896.

In a movement not notable for general theorizing, *Wealth Against Commonwealth* stands out as a large-scale analysis of monopoly and a statement of principle. The bulk of Lloyd's long study was an analysis of the Standard Oil Corporation, enlivened by four sketches of ordinary people whose lives had been blighted by its actions. This discussion was framed by an ethical critique of the new corporate economy. We were controlled, Lloyd said, by new corporate caesars. Our liberties were at stake: "Liberty produces wealth, and wealth destroys liberty."[14] The ethics of the conservative Darwinists would not do. Anyone who applied the doctrine of the survival of the fittest in his family relations or in his capacity as a citizen "would be a monster and would be speedily made extinct, as we do with monsters."[15] Why then did we not recognize this simple proposition in economic affairs? But Lloyd cut deeper than that and attacked Adam Smith's doctrine of self-interest, calling it a violation of fundamental principles of human nature. Even the most perfect self-interest was still individual and overlooked the fact that the world was social. If we were to transfer this idea to politics, we would call the result anarchy. What we called free competition was only more free than what had gone before. "The true laissez faire is, let the individual do what the individual can do best, and let the community do what the community can do best." This true freedom was still to come.[16]

> We have overworked the self-interest of the individual. The line of conflict between individual and social is a progressive one of the discovery of point after point in which the two are identical. Society thus passes from conflict to harmony, and on to another conflict. Civilization is the unceasing accretion of these social solutions.[17]

That harmony would never occur unless we stopped and thought about what we were doing. Our civilization would not be destroyed by the barbarians from below, as the English historian Thomas Macaulay had predicted, but by those from above. Lloyd wrote, "Without restraints of culture, experience, the pride, or even the inherited caution of class or rank, these men, intoxicated, think they are the wave instead of the float, and that they have created the business which has created them."[18] The danger was in the underlying beliefs of the system. "Believing wealth to be good, the people believed the wealthy to be good." Believing this, we were breeding pharaohs, Lloyd claimed.[19]

This old conception of self-interest had to give way to a new one. Its outlines were prefigured in the critique of the old theory. The question was not whether monopoly would continue, but rather if it would be destroyed through "ruin or reform."[20] For Lloyd, much more consistently than for the populists he supported, this meant socialism. "There must be no Private use of public power or public property."[21] But that should not be seen, as it so often was by critics of socialism, as a threat to individuality. Social isolation did not make an individual. Isolation produced instead the "mere rudiment of an individual." It was relations, ties, and duties that made a man an individual. Therefore, "he who has become citizen, neighbor, friend, brother, son, husband, father, fellow-member, in one, is just by so many times individualized."[22] In striking ways, then, the critique of the old self-interest represents an attempt to transcend the "atomistic individual freedom" that Hartz saw as central to the American political tradition. This is an analysis that carried the populist critique of laissez-faire capitalism to its logical end and threatened to escape altogether from the confines of the liberal tradition, in spite of Lloyd's insistence that he was calling merely for reform.

In the writings of Lloyd and in the Omaha Platform can be seen the outlines of what is arguably the last major critique of industrial capitalism to come from within the mainstream of liberalism. Although many of the populists were not themselves sophisticated men, this response to the dilemmas of late-nineteenth-century America was rather sophisticated. In striking ways it anticipated the contemporary left communitarian answer to liberal individualism. It was not, as Richard Hofstadter tended to argue, simply a nostalgic, backward-looking attempt to escape into a mythical past, nor did it involve either a repudiation of industrialism itself or a refusal to adapt Jeffersonian-Jacksonian theories to a new reality.[23]

Although there were populist anti-Semites, racists, and nativists, they were no more common in the movement than in other parts of American society, so there is little warrant for Hofstadter's argument that the populists were the principal popular source of anti-Semitism, and still less for the assertion, not made by Hofstadter, that the populists were forebears of a kind of native American fascism. Indeed, in the South, populists and ex-slaves briefly joined hands in a movement powerful enough to frighten conservative elite groups, although many white populist leaders, such as Tom Watson, were unwilling in the long run to give up their dominant position. Tragically, they eventually chose sides along racial rather than class lines.[24]

It is clear, then, that the populist movement was not simply a reactionary or a retrogressive phenomenon. Still, it nonetheless had its nostalgic side, and the character of its ideological stance limited its accomplishments as a reform movement. After all, it is worth noting that a majority of farmers did not become populists and that in spite of their sincere rhetoric, the populists simply did not know what to say to urban workers.[25] A good deal of Hofstadter's critique of agrarian radicalism was rooted in his eastern urban outlook, which led him to see much of the movement, in spite of its contributions and its often well justified complaints, as rather provincial. Recent studies of Populist voting behavior have suggested that there was a real measure of truth in that view. Scholars, whether critics or defenders, have tended to assume that Populist supporters were the most economically distressed farmers, but as James Turner pointed out, this glosses over the awkward fact that the worst-off agrarians never joined the cause. Turner compared the vote for Democrats and Populists in Texas, the state Lawrence Goodwyn saw as the heart of the populist movement, and found that it was not economic depression but isolation on the frontier that correlated most strongly with the Populist vote. It was this isolation, Turner argued, that explained the power of the "movement culture" that Goodwyn uncovered and that he saw as the foundation of the populist radicalism. It was the need for social contact that explained its spread, but its quick collapse also illustrated the limits of sociability as a political force.[26] There is evidence that the Texas Populists were bewildered in the face of an alien world, one that they did not fully comprehend.

What this reflects is one of the basic facts of U.S. history, aphoristically captured by Hofstadter: "The United States was born in the country and has moved to the city."[27] As Turner says, "Populists were not so much pulling away from their society as their society was from them."[28] That produced a decline in the wealth and status of the farming population.[29] Populist ideology was rooted in the Jeffersonian-Jacksonian ideology, which, as we have seen, tended to divide the world into producers and nonproducers. The southern and western farmers, for all their sometime sympathy, had little feel for the world of the urban working class. Southern populist rhetoric is replete with attacks on the city, rooted in the ideals of Thomas Jefferson.[30] That was compounded by fundamentalist religious beliefs not well calculated to find deep sympathy among urban workers.[31] It is also not clear that the Populists realized the full radical implications of their critique of capitalism or their program. After all, the socialist elements of the Omaha Platform were abandoned in 1896 when the movement decided to endorse William Jennings Bryan and his free silver panacea.

Once again a major portion of Hofstadter's controversial and much criticized consensus interpretation has been substantially vindicated. The romantic image of the self-sufficient yeoman farmer had some reality in the early period of American history, but very quickly farming became a commercial operation with profit as a goal. This is the hard side of American agrarianism. The soft side, which looks longingly back to an earlier, simpler golden age, tends to come to the fore during hard times such as those that prevailed in so much of the post–Civil War period. Thus the populist utopia bears a striking resemblance to the model of the "simple market society," a society in which goods and services are sold in a market, but in which labor is not itself a marketable commodity.[32]

Much of the motive force behind the intellectual outlook of the populists stemmed from the Jeffersonian tradition, and this reliance on Jefferson too was a source of theoretical tension. There was a clear disjunction between the more radical planks of the Populist program and the ideas of strict construction, states rights, and small-scale government that were at the core of Jefferson's position. And yet Populist leaders such as James "Cyclone" Davis toured the South with the master's writings in hand in an attempt to reconcile the apparent contradictions between program and theory.[33] From a Jeffersonian point of view, some startling arguments were made. Davis based his ideas on the highly general Preamble to the Constitution and, even more heretically, on the doctrine of implied powers. He attempted to avoid the obvious theoretical difficulty by rooting his claims on a somewhat ambiguous letter by Jefferson in which the Virginian argued that the law should not favor constructions that would defeat the principal object of the law in question. As applied to the commerce clause, this view justified government ownership of the railroads, for instance, on the ground that it would promote justice and ensure domestic tranquillity. The key phrase in Jefferson's letter held that a loose construction of the law was to be favored "where no private right stands in the way, and the public object is in the interest of all." As Palmer points out, Davis tended to overlook the first clause in favor of the second.[34] Most southern populists would not have identified this formulation as truly Jeffersonian, and yet the ritual references had to be made. The problem, Palmer notes, was that few populists seriously engaged the notion that such policies as the nationalization of the railroads might necessitate a basic reconstruction of the formal structure of government.[35]

The basic difficulty was that the reformers did not clearly distinguish between Jefferson's still-valid goals as the standard for the good society and the more contingent theories of constitutional form rooted in the simpler political economy of an earlier time, theories that were already dated by the 1830s.[36] One need only add that subtly, but ironically and surely, this understanding pointed the way to the view, often attributed to Herbert Croly, that advocated the pursuit of Jeffersonian ends by Hamiltonian means. That view was to become the common currency of the Progressive movement and of the transformed liberalism of the twentieth century.

Clearly, the economic views of the populist movement were not more consistent than their constitutional thinking, though it can be suggested that the populists were groping their way toward a program designed to meet the stresses created for them by the new corporate order. Henry Demarest Lloyd seemed to have best grasped the socialist implications of the populist position. As Palmer says, the southern populists moved with some ease toward socialism but seemed on occasion almost to make a conscious decision to avoid it. At times this seems to have been a matter of political expediency born of a sense that socialist rhetoric would be unpalatable. At other times, however, the hesitancy reflected the economic heritage of liberalism and the position of the populists as "landowners, or aspiring landowners." Moreover, there was a deep commitment to the teachings of the Protestant ethic and, amazingly, given its associations, a hankering after the middle-class ideology of the conservative Darwinists with its celebration of such unlikely heroes as Ragged Dick and Andrew Carnegie.[37] And finally, in spite of a deep concern with the palpably unequal distribution of wealth, there was not, even in the

Omaha Platform, a call for economic redistribution. Instead, the emphasis fell on the tried and true liberal formulation of equal opportunity.[38]

Still, in general terms, the Populist program had its attractions and may provide a useful benchmark even today. The basic idea underlying the populist position was a two-tier economy, combining a simple market society for those segments of the economy that could be controlled by independent producers with public ownership of the large concentrations of economic power that could not be democratically controlled through the market mechanism. The naïveté of the agrarian radicals prevented them from seeing the enormity of the problems inherent in bringing about such a system or the difficulty in making it work in an urban, industrial social order.[39]

The portrait of populism that emerges here is one of a confused and sometimes backward-looking social movement trying to make sense of a world in a state of rapid flux. The once secure place of the farmer had been severely eroded in that world, and agrarian radicals had many justified complaints against it. Palmer's sympathetic account sums up the situation very well:

> [The] inability to understand the extent to which industrial development had changed the nature of American society gave the antimonopoly greenback analysis in particular and Southern Populism in general a peculiar tone. On the one hand it harked back to an earlier, almost Jeffersonian ideal, a simple market society. On the other it accepted and desired a modern industrial society. The southern reformers understood as well as anyone in America the suffering and injustice which the organization of an industrial society on a capitalist basis brought; they failed to appreciate the fundamental economic and social changes on which this organization was based. This failure . . . must be attributed in great part to the Southern Populists' lack of experience with America's urban and industrial society and the general incapacity of the American intellectual heritage to compensate for this deficiency.[40]

The point is not that populism was a retrogressive movement, although it often did look toward the past for sustenance. Rather, it is that the southern populists were unable or unwilling to abandon the basic premises of the capitalist economy of which they were a part, even when they were bitterly critical of its workings.[41] It was a reform movement working essentially within the confines of the liberal tradition, though surely at times straining at its theoretical and institutional boundaries. The last truly fundamental critique to come from within liberalism, its political failure had momentous consequences.

The populists were caught up in a phase of the process of modernization and rationalization, which has been perhaps the dominant force in the Western world since the sixteenth century. Traditional patterns of communal life were disrupted by the requirements of industry, capitalism, and bureaucratic forms of social organization. The populist response was an attempt to create an ideology fusing Jefferson, the Protestant tradition, and the producerist ideas of Jacksonian democracy. One scholar assessed the response as follows: "A dominant social philosophy in 1850, the belief in a middle way had been placed on the defensive by 1880 and its spokesmen forced to assume an adversarial posture in the face of rapid political and economic consolidation."[42] For all the poignancy of the populist predicament, this stance was too little and too late.

Conclusion

A climax of sorts was reached in the election of 1896. The Democratic Party nominated William Jennings Bryan, who, though not a member of the Populist Party, exemplified the Populist style and embraced at least part of the Populist program by calling for free coinage of silver. After a bitter battle, the Populists endorsed Bryan, and fusion was complete. The result was an electoral disaster for the reform forces. A new majority—"the system of 1896"—emerged under the leadership of William McKinley.[43] An electoral system that had been the world's most democratic measured by voting participation became highly sectionalized, participation declined, party competition was sharply reduced, and the way was paved for the direct primary system and a new flowering of antimajoritarian theory and practice. The Democratic-Populist "coalition of the dispossessed" was a total failure and gave way to the domination of a conservative electoral alignment that was to last for a generation.[44] In spite of the very real sympathy one may have for the grievances of the populists, it is hard to escape the conclusion that the ambiguities of their ideology bear some considerable responsibility for the outcome. However, the populist style and the perception of a clash between the people and the interests have lived on to this day, and at least some of the populist reforms found fruition in the more successful Progressive movement after the turn of the century.

· 10 ·

The Problem
of Progressivism

T HE ORIGINS of the modern American state lie in the ideas and institutional changes of the Progressives. The state that the Progressive movement fostered, which began an attempt to make peace with modernity, produced results that can hardly have been what the populists had in mind. Nevertheless, the incipient modern state did introduce into American politics a conception of activist government, which the populists had previously championed, and it also adopted some of their institutional remedies. As with populism, the historiography of progressivism is extremely complex, so much so that some historians have proposed discarding the very term as conceptually useless.[1] This solution has not taken hold, so it is necessary to try to sort out at least some of the conflicting viewpoints. Part of the difficulty no doubt lies in the fact that progressivism, unlike populism, was a national movement, which manifested itself at the federal, state, and local levels of government and which was subject to considerable ideological debate and political infighting. Moreover, there was often a gap between the fierce moral rhetoric of the movement and its actual accomplishments. Therefore, some observers have been moved, perhaps not entirely without reason, to question the motives of the reformers. One might add that the moral rhetoric of the political leaders often contrasted with the relativism of the Progressive philosophers.

Progressivism, though heir to a good deal of populist rhetoric and ideology, was primarily an urban, middle-class phenomenon; it lasted for a considerable period of time—conventionally, from 1900 to 1920. However, perhaps more important than who the Progressives were and where they were located was the fact that they, unlike the populists, produced a great deal of social and political theory. Further, to a great extent, those ideas continue to be of great importance in shaping contemporary liberal thought. To some extent, reform liberals today might be said to be living still on the intellectual capital of progressivism.

Although the essence of the Progressive movement remains a matter for debate, certain themes seem to be fairly well established as central to its origins, if not to its ultimate historical impact. In spite of some cynicism about the motives of some of the movement's leaders, there can be little doubt that much of the initial impetus came from a genuine revulsion against the widespread corruption of the urban political machines and, more generally, of the political system as a whole by rapacious business interests.[2] This revulsion was no doubt also related to the emergence of the concept of interest as one of the basic categories of political analysis.[3] In fact, a caricature of progressivism as being, like populism, a kind of morality play, with the people pitted against corrupt interests, has a certain limited plausibility,[4] as long as one remembers that the corruption was indeed quite real and the interests often quite genuinely malign. This reality accounted for the power and influence of the muckraking journalists of the time. And the muckraking impulse reached back into American history, as scholars such as Charles Beard attempted to undermine the often mindless veneration of the Constitution so characteristic of conservative thought in the Progressive period by showing the allegedly base and venal motives of the Framers.[5] It was the conflict-oriented image of the history of American politics in the work of Beard and his contemporaries that Louis Hartz and Richard Hofstadter rebelled against. From the beginning, in the Beardian view, U.S. history was a battle between the haves and the have-nots, the democrats and the antidemocrats. Although Beard and his contemporaries were often wrong in detail, it is still not clear whether they were entirely mistaken in the broad general outlines of their historical thought. In any event, the current neo-Beardian revival, stressing the conflicts in the founding period, suggests that the consensus theory has not put those concerns to rest.[6]

Underlying all this ferment were a number of powerful and widely held feelings and aspirations. There was a sense that social forces that threatened to unloose political and economic chaos were at work and that some sort of collective response had to be made to the new order that had emerged with such dazzling rapidity in the four decades following the Civil War. As David Price aptly suggests, among the major themes of progressivism were community and control. The liberal image of the isolated individual began to be revised in favor of a new social psychology; a newly energized community sought to assert some real measure of social control over forces that, in their rapid development, threatened to destroy the established socioeconomic order.[7] A similar synthesis has been advanced by Daniel Rodgers. For Rodgers, one key element is the rhetoric against monopoly, surely one of the most disruptive forces over which control was sought, along with a new emphasis on social bonds, that is, community, and the language of social efficiency, which was to be a primary device for asserting social control.[8] This last manifested itself not only in the new scientific management techniques of Frederick Taylor but also in the deep commitment to science, including social science, linked to pragmatic philosophy.

There was also a great deal of concern with the corruption of urban politics, which, for many reformers, was intensified by the alliance of the big city machines with new waves of immigrants. The result was a number of measures that set in motion the long-term decline of the party system—the rise of the direct primary and the resort to devices such as the initiative, referendum, and recall that had their roots in populism.

A full-scale treatment of the Progressives would also have to deal with a number of other topics. The drive for women's suffrage, which had been gathering momentum through much of the nineteenth century, continued and finally won out when the Nineteenth Amendment was passed in 1920. Less happily, the temperance movement achieved success with the enactment of the "great experiment" of prohibition in 1918. Urban problems also contributed to the emergence of social welfare agencies and, indeed, the development of social work as a profession. There was also a ferment of experimentation at the state and local level, as illustrated by the "gas and water socialism" that led to the municipal ownership of public utilities in a number of cities. And muckraking journalism, dedicated to the exposure of corruption and the abuse of power, emerged and became an important force.

But of all the problems crying out for the imposition of some form of social control, by far the most important, the most controversial, and arguably the most confusing was the rapid growth of industrial and financial power in the form of the trusts. Deep down, the nation was being forced to come to grips with the dynamics of modernization, that constellation of bureaucratic, rationalizing forces that had increasingly dominated the Western world since at least the seventeenth century. In brief, the United States was enmeshed in the world described with incomparable theoretical power by the great German sociologist Max Weber. That world of organizational structures was so threatening to people raised in an earlier, less complex, social system that Weber referred to life in an "iron cage." The United States was caught up in adjusting to the imperatives of this new organizational society.[9]

The best way into the maze of Progressive attempts to deal with the revolution in organizational form is through an examination of the New Nationalism and the New Freedom. Those two political movements, under the leadership of Theodore Roosevelt and Woodrow Wilson respectively, dominated the debates of the period, particularly on the trust question.

The New Nationalism

In spite of his reputation as an insurgent trustbuster, Theodore Roosevelt was a deeply conservative, Republican politician.[10] Roosevelt's rhetoric often obscured his true position, so symbolic actions, however important, were often mistaken for the whole of his position.[11] (That is also a general problem in interpreting the politics of progressivism.) In addition, his well-deserved reputation for flamboyance tended to obscure his intellectual capacities, even though he, along with Woodrow Wilson, made the presidential campaign of 1912 the last one in which basic issues of public policy were debated on anything approaching a high intellectual level by two book-reading, book-writing candidates.

The heart of the New Nationalism had been in place during Roosevelt's presidency; only the rhetoric was radicalized in order to highlight his differences with William Howard Taft and Robert LaFollette in his struggle for control of the Republican Party.[12] The essence of the New Nationalism was not trust-busting but trust regulation. Roosevelt's fame as an antitrust crusader stemmed largely from events like his prosecution of the Morgan interests in the famous Northern Securities case. That was largely a symbolic act, designed to demonstrate the neutrality of the state even as against solidly entrenched business interests.[13] I do not mean to denigrate Roosevelt's actions, for symbolism is of great importance. Moreover, there is no reason to doubt the sincerity of the president in trying to establish the fact that he did not intend to deal with a banker like J. P. Morgan as a coequal potentate. At the same time, Roosevelt's actions were not in any sense part of an assault on the concentrated power of big business as such. In the 1910 speech at Ossowatamie in which he began his insurgency against the Republican establishment, Roosevelt made it clear, saying, "Combinations in industry are the result of an imperative economic law which cannot be repealed by political legislation." Prohibition of combinations had failed; the only hope was to control them in the public interest.[14] Rather too easily wrapping himself in the mantle of Abraham Lincoln, Roosevelt argued that although labor was prior to and independent of capital, nevertheless capital too had its rights.[15] America had to free itself from special interests, work for genuine equality of opportunity, and accept a legitimate role for the state in regulating the economy. That was the path to the "Square Deal."

That speech gave the essence of the New Nationalism, which Roosevelt pursued, in and out of office, throughout his career in national politics. For a more fully developed version of his ideas, we can turn to the influential 1909 book by the journalist Herbert Croly, *The Promise of American Life.*[16] Croly, who, along with Walter Weyl and Walter Lippmann, founded an influential weekly journal of opinion, the *New Republic,* in 1914, was the product of a somewhat prolonged and checkered career at Harvard, where he studied in the golden age of American philosophy under Josiah Royce, George Santayana, and William James. From Royce he absorbed a belief in the need for the individual to be loyal to something higher than himself; from Santayana, a certain elitism tempered perhaps by a belief, derived from Montesquieu, that "democracy is virtue"; and from James, an understanding of pragmatism's experimentalist theory of truth.[17] And always hovering in the background were the technocratic theories of French sociologist Auguste Comte, whose disciple Croly's father had been.[18] But more important than any of those was the political presence of Theodore Roosevelt; among contemporaneous statesmen he was Croly's hero. The book itself reads like a theoretical generalization of Roosevelt's position, fitted into a somewhat schematic—and rather tendentious—interpretation of U.S. history.

It was clear to Croly that the promise of American life—economic well-being, democratic politics, and an improved spiritual condition—could no longer be counted on to appear automatically. The traditional American mixture of "optimism, fatalism, and conservatism" would not serve as a guide to the future. Rather, to fulfill the promise, the future would have to be "planned and constructed."[19]

How we had to proceed was revealed in his analysis of U.S. history. The old struggle between Jefferson and Hamilton was rehearsed again, but with a new twist in that Hamilton emerged as the hero. Hamilton understood that liberty was not to be preserved merely by the enunciation of constitutional rights but also required "an energetic and clear-sighted central government," which "could be fertilized only by the efficient national organization of American activities."[20] His basic theory of government required that the state not just maintain the Constitution but also actively promote the national interest. "All this implied an active interference with the natural course of American economic and political business and its regulation and guidance in the national direction."[21] It must also be understood that, for Croly, nationalism indicated more than mere centralization of the government, though it certainly entailed that too. Rather, nationalism was a "formative and enlightening political transformation." It meant the vanquishing of the special interests, and it is particularly required at the national level of American institutions that at one time in one way or another have been "perverted to the service of special interests."[22]

Generally speaking, Jefferson stood in opposition to those healthy views, according to Croly. He saw at the heart of the Jeffersonian system a tendency to equate democracy with an extreme individualism. This individualistic approach sought egalitarian and, strangely, even "socialistic" goals.

Meanwhile, Croly continued, in the case of conflict between liberty and equality, the tendency among the Jeffersonians was for liberty to give way.[23] Jefferson's triumph over Hamilton unleashed the full force of American individualism, and politics became "a species of vigorous, licenced, and purified selfishness."[24] It was this untrammeled individualism that in the end did the greatest damage to genuine individuality, for it was "the popular enjoyment of practically unrestricted economic opportunities [that was] precisely the condition which makes for individual bondage." Moreover, almost echoing Hegel on the master/slave relationship, Croly explained that it was a bondage that bound the conquerors as much as it did the victims.[25]

The new industrial system, in Croly's view, seemed to echo the slavery of the old South. His conclusions on this theme were strongly negative: Jefferson had much to answer for. Jefferson's was a tradition of national irresponsibility rooted in a still deeper tradition of intellectual insincerity that feared consistent and radical political theory. He offered to his willing followers "a seductive example of triumphant intellectual dishonesty, and of the sacrifice of theory to practice, whenever such a sacrifice was convenient."[26]

To Croly, Hamilton's vision was clearly superior, but it was marred by one major flaw. Hamilton was a finer thinker and statesman than Jefferson, and more candid and honorable to boot. On the whole, Jefferson excelled Hamilton only in understanding his countrymen and therefore being more successful as a popular leader. But Croly's hero had one massive flaw that even seemed to approach the tragic: "He perverted the American national idea almost as much as Jefferson perverted the American democratic idea, and the proper relation of the two fundamental conceptions cannot be completely understood until this double perversion is corrected."[27] According to Croly, Hamilton was right to make the Federalist Party the vehicle of the national idea. His "fatal error" was to make the Federalists "a bulwark against the rising tide of democracy." It was the historical mission of Theodore Roosevelt to mend this flaw by giving a "democratic meaning and purpose to the Hamiltonian tradition and method."[28]

At that point, therefore, a great, if sometimes misunderstood, transformation in the history of American thought occurred. As the Federalists appropriated the vocabulary of popular control from the Anti-Federalists, so Croly proposed to appropriate the rhetoric of democracy in order to preserve the new corporate order. He would preserve that order by taming its worst excesses through a program of regulation. It has often been said—even by Roosevelt, in fact—that the aim was to pursue Jeffersonian ends by Hamiltonian means.[29] But given Croly's sweeping repudiation of everything about the Jeffersonian tradition except its commitment to democracy, that is more a cliché than a reality.[30] What Croly really proposed was the democratization of the Hamiltonian tradition, a feat not easily accomplished. However, a break with the idea of a stringently limited role for government was an idea whose time had come—an idea that influenced even the inheritors of the Jeffersonian heritage.

The New Freedom

Although it is easy to exaggerate the true differences that separated Woodrow Wilson's New Freedom movement from Theodore Roosevelt's New Nationalism, they were nonetheless real. There were also significant similarities: Both programs required a more activist national government, and both called for and acted upon the need for a new era of strong presidential leadership. Roosevelt was famous for his characterization of the presidential office as a bully pulpit, but Wilson was no mean preacher himself. Both men engaged in the practice of appealing directly to the people on behalf of the causes they supported, to an extent undreamed of by even the strongest of nineteenth-century presidential leaders. Their actions amounted to what has been called a basic change in constitutional structure.[31] At the least, the modern presidency began to emerge in the thought and practice of the two Progressive presidents.[32] It might be added that, in spite of Wilson's Jeffersonian roots, the New Freedom, like the New Nationalism, implied a substantial alteration in the structure of the federal system in favor of the national government.

Still, the differences, particularly on the level of theory, continued to divide, even to haunt, the reform liberal movement to this day. The heart of the conflict was over the question of how to approach the trust problem. The backers of the New Nationalism argued that the trusts had to be viewed, on the whole, as a positive development, but one subject to abuse, so it was necessary to use the power of government to regulate them. Wilson hewed closer to the Jeffersonian line. Sounding almost like a populist, Wilson argued that a small number of men controlled raw materials; water power, which was needed to produce energy; the railroads; prices; and credit. Without damaging any of the separate interests involved, it would be possible to "dissect" this peculiar amalgam, and indeed the very "integrity" of business required precisely that.[33] The answer then was antitrust legislative activity, but that answer depended on a distinction that was less than clear. "I am for big business," Wilson proclaimed, "and I am against the trusts." He explained that nonmonopolistic big business had survived by intelligence, economy, and efficiency.[34] In contrast, Wilson argued, Roosevelt had preached a doctrine of the inevitability of monopoly.[35] But how really helpful was Wilson's distinction? As Richard Hofstadter pointed out, there were a host of problems. How should we define efficiency, and how large must a business be before it starts to lose efficiency? Was there a feasible way to dissolve businesses that were already too big as a result of corrupt practices? Was there really an operational definition that allowed for a distinction between the big business Wilson liked and the trusts he didn't? Moreover, in the end, was there a real difference between Wilson's distinction between good and bad trusts and that drawn by his rival?[36]

If there was a difference, it was probably spelled out by Louis D. Brandeis, who filled a role for Wilson similar to that of Herbert Croly in the Roosevelt entourage, though Brandeis was probably more genuinely influential than his Republican counterpart. Brandeis's lifelong project was to update Jefferson for the needs of a modern industrial economy.[37] Until meeting Brandeis, Wilson had been a fairly standard Rooseveltian Progressive. However, as Philippa Strum shows, Brandeis was able to convince Wilson that government could act to restore competition and maintain a competitive economy without itself growing too big to control.[38] This idea was a major key to Brandeis's thinking. Bigness was itself a problem, as witnessed by the publication in 1934 of a collection of his essays under the title *The Curse of Bigness*. Underlying this idea was a pair of concerns as to how to deal with the problems of size, scale, and the alienation that accompanied them in the increasingly "rationalized" economy that Max Weber discussed. How could people prevent the "iron cage," which Weber so heartrendingly described, from destroying their freedom and individuality?[39] Brandeis was also concerned with the extent to which economic democracy or worker's participation could reduce alienation and dependency while making workers creative partners in the operation of the economy and whether such schemes could overcome voter apathy.[40] In effect, he was raising again the Tocquevillian questions about the possibility that localized participation could provide "schools for citizenship" to counter the imbalances inherent in large-scale corporate capitalism.

The intellectual roots of Brandeis's concerns were in his deep interest in Zionism, with its emphasis on smallness and participation, and his knowledge of the ancient Greek polis, an interest inspired by his reading of Alfred Zimmern's *The Greek Commonwealth*.[41] His thinking led ultimately to a theory of workplace democracy. But there were two not entirely compatible streams in his thought. One was Madisonian: Interests were to be arrayed against interests through the power of unions so that the workers could be strong enough to hold their own against management. The other approach moved away from this conflict-oriented position toward the view that the relationship between employers and employed could be cooperative. This second strand of thought was implicitly more radical than the first and moved beyond standard Progressive thinking.[42]

The second position pointed back to an idea broached in the liberal tradition at least as early as John Stuart Mill's *Principles of Political Economy*, first published in 1848. It seemed to imply a system of what we today would call worker management, or economic democracy, though Brandeis made no specific plan. That was, at least in part, because Brandeis knew how far away the American political economy was from making such a proposal politically viable or, one might add, even worth discussing as a serious policy. As Brandeis told an interviewer in 1913: "We already have had industrial despotism. With the recognition of the unions, this is changing into a constitutional monarchy. . . . Next comes profit sharing. This, however, is to be only a transitional, half-way stage. Following upon it will come the sharing of responsibility, as well as of profits. The eventual outcome promises to be a full-grown industrial democracy." He went on to add that here there was something to learn from the socialists.[43]

This thinking clearly looked toward economic democracy as a desirable organizational form for the future. Still, he was unclear, as many advocates of workers' control have been to this day, about the pattern of ownership the new scheme implied. The logic of the position was radical and went far beyond orthodox progressivism, but the public formulation was much more cautious. Not even when Brandeis advised President Franklin Roosevelt in the 1930s did he push for legislation to enact what was at the time still a highly experimental system even in England. In any case, public speculation along these lines came to an end when President Wilson named Brandeis to the Supreme Court in 1916.[44]

On the worker-management level Brandeis remained a visionary whose ideas might still have real contemporary importance but in their time were far ahead of the rest of the Progressive movement. His contributions to the New Freedom movement were much more orthodox; in fact, it can be said that Brandeis was the chief architect of Wilson's program. He wrote the Clayton Antitrust Act and was a designer of much of the rest of the program of Wilson's first term. He was involved in the creation of the Federal Reserve Board, an institution consistent with his long opposition to the "money trust." He was also instrumental in designing the Federal Trade Commission, a departure from his general opposition to Rooseveltian regulation. That opposition was based on a belief that no antitrust law could ever be so specific as to obviate the need for a regulatory body with the flexibility to apply more general statutes. Thus, Brandeis offered neither pure competition nor managerialism, but a theory of regulated competition.[45]

Some Preliminary Conclusions

My discussion has focused on two seemingly different, but in fact closely related, programs. A good deal of the action of the first two decades of the twentieth century, as well as much of its ideological support, was obscured by the rhetoric of the two sides. Thus, to Richard McCormick, "Roosevelt . . . for all the excitement he brought to the presidency in 1901, veered wildly in his approach to the problems of big business in his first term—from 'publicity' to trust-busting, to jawboning to conspiring with the House of Morgan."[46] For his part, Wilson was surprisingly frank. In his 1916 speech accepting renomination by the Democratic Party, he announced, "We have in four years come very near to carrying out the platform of the Progressive Party, as well as our own; for we are all progressives."[47]

Perhaps this statement should not be surprising to anyone who is familiar with the organizational interpretation of the Progressive movement. It should also not be surprising to anyone who has studied Weber on the seemingly inexorable power of the organizational revolution that has characterized modernity—the closing in of the proverbial iron cage of the large-scale institutions that accompany modernization. This view would lead us to expect that a rhetorical attack on corporations could not amount to much. In this view, the large corporation was the model institution for the whole society.[48] Sophisticated business leaders fully understood that and saw that they could profit from the regulations presumably designed to control them. Richard Olney came to this realization as early as 1892. In a letter to a railroad president who had asked him to help abolish the Interstate Commerce Commission, Olney replied: "Looking at the matter from a railroad point of view exclusively, [this] would not be a wise thing to undertake. . . . The Commission . . . is, or can be made, of great use to railroads. It satisfies the popular clamor for a government supervision of railroads, at the same time that the supervision is almost entirely nominal. . . . The part of wisdom is not to destroy the Commission, but to utilize it."[49]

For some, the very attempt to regulate apparently seemed quixotic. Brandeis insisted, "I have considered and do consider, that the proposition that mere bigness can not be an offense against society is false, because I believe that our society, which rests upon democracy, can not endure under such conditions." But, Thomas McGraw argues, this opinion not only flew in the face of the fact that history was moving in a direction counter to Brandeis's wishes but also ignored the economic advantages of large corporations. The trouble with Brandeis was that for him, political considerations dominated economic ones. His complaint was an "aesthetic/political argument and not an economic one."[50] To that, the political theorist concerned with the health of democracy can only reply: "Precisely. That is the point of the exercise." One can well argue that one of the major problems of contemporary American democracy is that McGraw is quite right about the general movement of American economic development. (It is perhaps appropriate to wonder about the advantages of large scale, when the floundering of the American economy in the decade since McGraw wrote is taken into account.)

Whatever the motives of American leaders, there is no doubt at all that the period from 1900 to 1920 witnessed the emergence of the modern American state. It may seem ironic that the trend for large organizations to beget large counterorganizations appeared under Woodrow Wilson, the heir of Thomas Jefferson. But one must remember that Wilson had a major academic career in the thirty-five years before he became governor of New Jersey in 1910 and began his meteoric ascent to the presidency. An examination of his writings in that academic period lessens the irony. As a political theorist, Wilson was not a disciple of Jefferson. He wrote in 1893 that the Sage of Monticello's speculations were "exotic . . . false and artificial" as well as "abstract, sentimental, rationalistic, rather than practical. . . . The very aerated quality of Jefferson's principles gives them an air of insincerity."[51] Instead, a properly organized democracy would be a government of the few. It seems that Wilson, in his academic phase, saw his own theories as a renewal of the Federalist tradition.[52] With leadership as the key, he surely would have agreed with his rival, Roosevelt, that the presidency made a bully pulpit. Again violating Jeffersonian theory, if not practice, he wrote in 1908, "The President is at liberty, both in law and conscience, to be as big a man as he can." The president was the party leader and the only one who could speak for a national constituency.[53] Finally, there was World War I, which greatly expanded the power of government in general and the presidency in particular. As Randolph Bourne, the most corrosive social critic of the time, correctly remarked, "War is the health of the state."[54]

The Progressive movement set the United States well along the road toward the modern, centralized, bureaucratic state. It would be hard to claim that Richard Olney was entirely wrong in his assessment of the probable winner in an economic struggle played out in the context of this state. Thomas McGraw should be able to rest content in the knowledge that the economic motives he hoped to see elevated above the political concerns of Brandeis were indeed the controlling forces in American policy toward the political economy. To a great extent Americans are living in a world of institutions and ideas that are a product of the period from 1900 to 1920. I do not mean to say that the Progressive reformers, insofar as they are to be taken at face value, had no successes to their credit. We are all probably better off in the regulated world the Progressives created than in what went before; still, one need only scan a newspaper frequently to know that the regulatory state has not tamed the giant corporation or brought full security to all. Nor can anyone claim that democracy is more secure than it was seventy years ago. By many standards it is weaker.

All the same, progressivism remains a very important phenomenon; the twin themes of community and control are still with us, sometimes waxing, sometimes waning. The excesses of conservative social Darwinism have been brought under control, although the experiences of the 1980s and 1990s show that they are far from being eliminated. (Gordon Gecko, in the film *Wall Street*, may well have provided the ideal for that decade with his credo, "Greed is good.") We still debate about means and ends, but few will argue that government can or should simply stand aside and let "nature" take its course. Nor do many claim that the individual can or should stand completely alone; our understanding of human nature is, leaving aside a few notable exceptions, an image of the human animal as essentially social. There is, of course, considerable debate about the relation between the individual and the community, but not many will deny that the social individual has both rights and duties in relation to the community. The precise relationship is one of the central debates in contemporary social theory.

In a very general way, Louis Hartz was right; the Progressive debates were carried on within a liberal framework. Historically, liberalism has been concerned with the fate of putatively equal, rights-bearing individuals. The Progressives shifted the ground of the debate somewhat. Following the lead of the populists, they began to argue that the aims of such individuals could be furthered by the action of the positive state. Reform liberalism was born. It has succeeded much less often than the supporters of the Progressives believe, but it is still the case that the basic framework of public discussion is the one laid out in the early years of the twentieth century.[55] This was true even of the 1980s, when, though the Reagan administration shifted the debate far to the right and political discussion revolved around the need to roll back the alleged excessive extensions of programs carried out in the spirit of the Progressives, the president still (rhetorically) accepted the "safety net" provided by the New Deal. (The new Republican congressional leadership threatens that too.)

Even though Hartz was right in a general way, in the details, as is often the case, his analysis was weak. He saw the reform movement as an attempt "to adapt classical liberalism to the purposes of small propertied interests and the laboring class," while at the same time the movement was rejecting socialism.[56] Of course, he was right about socialism, but his interpretation took the antimonopoly wing of the Progressive reformers for the whole of the movement.[57] Certainly it did scant justice to the New Nationalism and exaggerated Roosevelt's record as a trustbuster. However, as usual, Hartz was very subtle even in pursuit of his single-factor thesis. He understood that despite all the rhetoric, the differences in practice between the branches of the movement were much smaller than the campaign oratory suggested. The allegiance to capitalism overrode everything else; whereas other capitalist societies developed socialist parties, in the United States that was out of the question politically. The consensual framework was too confining to make any such approach viable. Surely Hartz was on the mark when he remarked, "We say of the Progressive era that it was a time of tumult, but in our own age we know what tumult is, and few of us would be willing to date Armageddon at 1912."[58]

Although the pattern of policies has tended to develop along New Nationalist lines, the debate has never been fully resolved. Much of the New Deal featured a quarrel between the two schools of thought as they fought for the ear of the president. Even though Franklin Roosevelt may have felt that he worked out an adequate synthesis of the two, it is not easy to say that his judgment was correct. Clinton administration Secretary of Labor Robert Reich, one of the most acute analysts of the issues surrounding current industrial policy, argues that even today the basic policy alternatives are descended from those laid down by Theodore Roosevelt and Woodrow Wilson. The proper terms for our contemporaries, he claims, are the "planners," descended from the New Nationalism, and the "atomizers," descended from the New Freedom. The problem with the former was the arrogance in their belief that they knew what to do for the economy; the problem with the latter is a sentimental belief in small scale and in the existence of really free markets.[59] The debate goes on, and we shall have occasion to return to it. However, for the moment it is important to turn to the most important philosophical statement to come from the Progressives.

Coda: John Dewey
and the Philosophy of Progressivism

To turn to the work of John Dewey is to raise the study to an altogether different level of analysis. We leave far behind party programs and policy proposals. Nevertheless, Dewey was the quintessential Progressive philosopher. This is true in spite of the fact that much of his work fell outside the conventional—1900–1920—time boundaries of the movement. Dewey, who published his first article in 1882, continued to write until the end of his very long life in the middle of the twentieth century. *The Public and its Problems,* his major work in political theory, was not published until 1927. Still, he was much concerned with the themes of community and control and elevated their analysis to the plane of philosophy. Leaving aside the great philosopher-statesmen such as Madison, Jefferson, and Lincoln, he may be the best political theorist produced in the United States and is one of the few of world-class rank. Today, his reputation is ascendant, though he has not always been so highly appraised. James Kloppenberg, somewhat hyperbolically, put him on a level with Max Weber, and Jürgen Habermas, the great contemporary German social philosopher, suggests that he supplied the democratic theory missing in Marx.[60]

Dewey's philosophical work can best be understood as part of what Morton White called "the revolt against formalism." That was an early-twentieth-century movement that embraced not only philosophy but also law, economics, history, and political science. Perhaps the best introduction to its approach is the famous maxim of Oliver Wendell Holmes: "The life of the law is not logic; it has been experience." Thus, to understand the origin of legal rules, we must realize that "the felt necessities of the time, the prevalent moral and political theories, institutions of public policy, avowed or unconscious, even the prejudices which judges share with their fellow men, have a good deal more to do than the syllogism in determining the rules by which men should be governed."[61]

The "revolt against formalism" in the disciplines affected fostered the historical analysis of social phenomena and a broad concern with the embeddedness of those phenomena in the entire culture surrounding them. There was a "concern with change, process, history, and culture."[62] For Dewey, this concern meant that philosophy was not a search for true "reality" in the manner of Plato. Rather, it was a matter of seeing that "*knowledge is always a matter of the use that is made of experienced natural events,* a use in which given things are treated as indications of what will be experienced under different conditions."[63] We have achieved knowledge when we arrive at accurate expectations of what the consequences of our actions will be.

The result of this approach to knowledge was a continual testing of our environment. The world was constantly changing; therefore so was our knowledge of it. We had to learn to live with a degree of uncertainty, but to say that truth was whatever "worked," or to repeat the notorious maxim of William James that truth was to be found in the "cash value" of an idea, was not to succumb to a mindless relativism. As Robert Westbrook puts it: "This working was not in itself the truth of the idea. Truth was antecedent to its verification: ideas were true not because they worked, they worked because they were true."[64] Nor was Dewey a positivist who denied the scientific value of normative statements. As White, withholding his own agreement, said,

Dewey held that "a judgement that something is desireable is just as scientific as a judgement that something is desired, if not more scientific."[65]

This approach does lead to a great deal of emphasis on social science as a vital component of intelligent social policy. For Morton White, that could be troubling; he was bothered, rightly I think, by Dewey's disdain for formal logic and found his "methodolatry" and his "scientific cheer-leading" to be a cause for impatience.[66] The contemporary political theorist, looking at the same ideas, is also likely to feel some unease. There is a danger, in a complex society, that expert social scientists will come to usurp the role of the democratic citizen and impose their solutions to social problems on the presumably far less expert "man in the street." But Dewey was aware of this threat of technocracy. He saw the problem as analogous to the idea of the Platonic philosopher king. "Rule by an economic class," he wrote, "may be disguised from the masses; rule by experts could not be covered up. It could be made to work only if the intellectuals became the willing tools of big economic interests."[67]

Dewey was not too worried about the threat, though if he lived in the present era of policy scientists ready to act as hired guns, he might well have thought again. In fact, his next point suggested why. The difficulty was that expertness was most likely to attach to specialized questions, where the assumption was that the general direction of policy had already been determined. But suppose it was not? "A class of experts is inevitably so removed from common interests as to become a class with private interests and private knowledge, which in social matters is not knowledge at all."[68] But the problem was not what the public did not know; it was easy to exaggerate the expertise needed to make basic decisions about the general direction of society. What was needed to avoid the dominance of experts was education, which, as Tocqueville had observed, could be gained by participation in democratic politics. Beyond that, the essential problem was to improve the "conditions of debate, discussion, and persuasion."[69]

The branch of social science with which Dewey was most closely associated was social psychology. He completely banished such liberal analytical devices as the notion of the atomistic individual existing in a state of nature. He said that men were by nature social but that existing arrangements did not recognize that fact. "Not only the state but the society itself has been pulverized into an aggregate of unrelated wants and wills." "Individualism, as an ism, as a philosophy" rested on a fallacy.[70] This ideology could be traced back to Locke, but it was hopelessly outdated since the work of Thomas Hill Green, an English philosopher in the 1880s.[71] The role of the state, according to Dewey, was to remove obstacles that stood in the way of individual self-development. Making a frontal assault on the theory of conservative

Darwinism, Dewey commented that he would like to see more genuine "rugged individualists." But under current conditions, mere individual initiative was not enough. The present system produced, not independence, but "parasitical dependence on a wide scale."[72] Dewey shrewdly remarked in this connection that "to see the propertyless man in the saddle under such conditions requires a peculiarly exuberant imagination."[73]

The individual, then, is a social being and not an atomized particle. Individuals can and should be in a position to develop their capacities in society; they really have no other choice. All of us are ineluctably social. Dewey felt that in his time the problem was that necessary free choice was being frustrated by plutocratic control. It was in this context that he developed his theory of the democratic state.

Much of Dewey's writing in the 1920s was done in response to his younger colleague in the Progressive movement, Walter Lippmann, who, as we have seen, was a cofounder of the *New Republic*. Lippmann was one of the twentieth-century pioneers of what has come to be called the realist or elitist theory of democracy. Significantly, the epigraph to his book *Public Opinion* is a long passage from Plato's *Republic* in which Socrates develops the myth of the cave. The denizens of the cave are in the dark, bound hand and foot, and able to perceive reality only as the flickering shadows cast on the wall before them by a fire at their backs. The only way to acquire knowledge of reality is to escape from the cave into a world of abstract, absolute truths, which can be discovered only by the philosophically trained mind. That is precisely the sort of formalism against which Dewey had rebelled.

For Lippmann, the myth of the cave was a perfect parable for the condition of modern politics: We were governed by fictions, by the pictures in our heads. The fictions were not lies and in fact were useful to us: "The fiction is taken for truth because the fiction is badly needed."[74] The political world was "out of reach, out of sight, out of mind." We necessarily operated with those pictures in our heads; stereotypes guided our lives: "In the great blooming, buzzing confusion of the outer world we tend to pick out what our culture has already defined for us, and we tend to perceive that which we have picked out in the form stereotyped for us by our culture."[75] The result was that for Lippmann, as for Plato, democracy was at best a hazardous business. But if things seemed bad for Plato, he, at least, did not have to deal with the modern mass media, which do so much to put the pictures into the heads of the members of the public.[76]

In spite of the fact that Dewey was an instinctive democrat in a way that Lippmann could never be, he took Lippmann's strictures very seriously, as well he might.[77] He understood that the world of the Framers of the Constitution had been irrevocably altered with the passage of time. There had been an enormous transformation in scale since the localist origins of America. Americans lived in a continental state, and their political institutions were stretched in an improvised way to do their jobs. "Railways, travel and transportation, commerce, the mails, telegraph and telephone, newspapers, create enough similarity of ideas and sentiments to keep the thing going as a whole, for they create interaction and interdependence."[78] For their part, the mass media could collect a quantity of information that far outran the capacity of the public to process and absorb it in any useful way. Dewey noted that news was whatever had just happened, but it was of little meaning until it had been interpreted; until then "events are not events, but mere occurrences, intrusions." This accounted for the triviality of so much of what passed as news.[79] In this view, the public, just as today, seemed simply bewildered much of the time. Dewey's prescience on these matters is remarkable.

His democratic theory was an attempt to deal with all this; as part of the effort he was led to develop a conception of the state. He began with an analysis of the relation of the private and the public that in many ways was reminiscent of John Stuart Mill. For instance, if A and B conversed, the exchange was private. If the conversation began to affect others, it took on a public dimension.[80] This was essentially the distinction Mill drew between self-regarding and other-regarding acts, though Dewey would no doubt see fewer purely self-regarding acts than his great predecessor. In any case, just because an act was private does not mean that it was nonsocial or antisocial. And very important from the liberal viewpoint, Dewey wrote, "Just as behavor is not antisocial or nonsocial because privately undertaken, it is not necessarily socially valuable because carried on in the name of the public by public agents. The argument has not carried us far, but at least it has warned us against identifying the community and its interests with the state or the politically organized community."[81]

This pointed toward the definition of the state. *Private* was defined in opposition to official, and thus we could say: "The public consists of all those who are affected by the indirect consequences of transactions to such an extent that it is deemed necessary to have those consequences systematically cared for. Officials are those who look out for and take care of the interests thus affected."[82] There was no particular mystery about any of this for those who avoided abstract formalism; presumably here he had thinkers such as Locke and Hobbes in mind. What remained was to distinguish the state from other modes of organized life. The characteristic of the public as a state was that its behavior had consequences beyond those directly involved. "The obvious external mark of the organization of a public or of a state is thus the existence of officials. Government is not the state, for that includes the public as well as the rulers charged with special duties and powers. The public . . . is organized in and through those officers who act in behalf of its interests. Thus the state represents an important although distinctive and restricted social interest." In Westbrook's words, Dewey's was a "conception of the organization of one key group, the public."[83]

Continuing Dewey's reasoning, the state had to be thought of as fluid and changing: "Almost as soon as its form is stabilized, it needs to be re-made." We also must not absorb all associations into a state monopoly or make all social values into political ones. As Robert Westbrook writes, in this theory "democratic politics is in fundamental respects a never ending politics of discourse."[84] In part, that was the meaning of the revolt against formalism in politics. It was also well within the liberal tradition.

However, Dewey was deeply dissatisfied with the status quo. Our institutions were obsolete, and the public had lost its way. It is this, as Westbrook says, that Dewey saw as the explanation for the rise of democratic realism such as Walter Lippmann's. As Westbrook also observes, the way out was not something Dewey discussed very effectively.[85] Climbing to a still higher level of abstraction, Dewey proclaimed, "Till the Great Society is converted into a Great Community, the Public will remain in eclipse."[86] Social science could help in the necessary process of education, but it was not enough and there was danger of control by an elite of experts, as we have already seen. This was where he began to differ sharply with Lippmann. The basic answer lay in an increase in democratic participation at the local level. "Democracy must begin at home, and its home is the neighborly community."[87] Democracy and community were one and the same: "Regarded as an idea, democracy is not an alternative to other principles of associated life. It is the idea of community life itself."[88] This pointed the way back to Jefferson, the Anti-Federalists, and even to the Puritan communities. In such settings, we could improve "the methods and conditions of debate, discussion, and persuasion."[89]

But this is all very abstract, and though it may be appealing, Dewey offered no program. There was a hint that he had hope for a movement away from territorial organization toward occupational groupings, but he deliberately eschewed detailed proposals.[90] This is troubling because Dewey was very much aware of the odds against him. He saw clearly that "disparity, not equality, was the actual consequence of *laissez faire* liberalism"; the result was that "our institutions, democratic in form, tend to favor in substance a privileged plutocracy."[91] There was a movement away from free market economics in the direction of reformist social legislation, but "the cause of liberalism will be lost for a considerable period if it is not prepared to go further and socialize the forces of production now at hand, so that the liberty of individuals will be supported by the very structure of economic organization."[92]

The themes of community and control are very much in evidence here, but in the call for decentralized participatory democracy and the advocacy of socialism, Dewey strained at the bounds of not only progressivism but of the American liberal tradition itself. His achievement was to show, like John Stuart Mill before him, that liberalism was not bound to an atomized image of man and to suggest the possibility that there could be liberal politics without liberal economics. How this transformation was to take place, given the inroads of large-scale capitalism on local community democracy, was unclear, as was the problem of preserving democracy in tightly organized localities, which, as we know, are often the loci of serious antidemocratic abuses.[93] With these problems still unsolved, Dewey might well leave us, very much unwittingly, with a theory of a large state dominated by technocratic elites.

Still, Dewey remains valuable; his problems remain our problems; and it is not clear that our contemporaries have done better. At the least, his work showed that there was more to American liberalism than Hartz's "atomistic freedom."[94] For all its flaws, liberalism has more resources than suggested by that narrow formula. Once again, the tradition turned out to be more complex than sometimes implied by the consensus, a point reinforced by the fact that Dewey, the most important Progressive intellectual, emerged as a sharp critic of the climax of the movement, the New Deal of Franklin D. Roosevelt.

• 11 •

The New Deal and the Apotheosis of Reform

N̲o movement is more important in twentieth-century American politics than the New Deal, nor is there any political leader whose significance surpasses that of Franklin Delano Roosevelt. Nevertheless, the New Deal produced virtually nothing in the way of serious political thought. The contrast with other great upheavals, such as the period of the founding or the Civil War, is striking. Even the Progressives, working in relatively tranquil times, produced a legacy that still fuels much of the discussion in our politics. The point is not that there were no ideas associated with the New Deal, but that there was no single, coherent intellectual position that could be passed on to later generations of reform leadership. This lack of theory is not without consequence, as we shall see. But for the moment it is necessary to focus on theories *about* the Roosevelt administration.[1]

Of course, the New Deal is a response to the Great Depression, which was touched off by the stock market crash in 1929, and which led in turn to what was close to a total breakdown of the economic system: industrial collapse, massive unemployment, and financial chaos. So desperate were the conditions when Roosevelt took office in March 1933 that the normally cumbersome decisionmaking procedures of the legislative process were effectively suspended. That anomaly made possible a flood of legislation in the next three months, which became the benchmark for presidential success—a mark extremely unlikely ever to be met again by an occupant of the presidential office. By the time the reform impulse was exhausted in the early days of Roosevelt's second term, the relation of U.S. government to the society and the economy had been transformed. A welfare program that emphasized work over the dole was established. There were extensive new regulations covering the banking and securities industries. In one way or another, industry was also widely regulated. Unemployment compensation and wages-and-hours legislation were passed, and the social security system was established. And this is only a partial list. The question to consider here is, what were the ideas that led to this remarkable outpouring?

Richard Hofstadter suggested that at the heart of the New Deal was not a philosophy so much as a personal style. As Justice Oliver Wendell Holmes, Jr., put it, Roosevelt had a second-class intellect but a first-class temperament.[2] By any standard, the president was a brilliant political leader, not only within the government, but also of mass opinion. The first great master of media politics, Roosevelt was truly charismatic. That does not mean that there were no ideas in the New Deal, but the man at the center was neither an intellectual nor an ideologue. His early program did not develop according to some predetermined plan. In the short run at least, that may have been just as well, given the unprecedented conditions that faced him when he took office in the worst days of the Great Depression. Roosevelt captured the spirit of his own administration very well when he likened himself to a quarterback in a football game calling one play at a time according to what had happened in the previous effort. Bold, persistent experimentation was what was called for: "It is common sense to take a method and try it: if it fails, admit it frankly and try another. But above all, try something."[3] It is clear that on the whole, his flexibility served him well.

Labels are always potentially deceiving, but they may offer a clue to the mystery that was Franklin Roosevelt. One of the labels most commonly used for him is *pragmatic*, and he probably was, in the vulgar sense of the term. But the fact that John Dewey, the greatest political theorist of pragmatism, was a severe critic of the New Deal should give us pause. Dewey surely had the New Deal in mind when he wrote in 1935: "Liberalism must now become radical. . . . But 'reforms' that deal now with this abuse and now with that without having a social goal based upon an inclusive plan, differ entirely from effort at re-forming, in its literal sense, the institutional scheme of things. . . . Any liberalism which is not also radicalism is irrelevant and doomed."[4]

If pragmatic will not quite do, then *liberal* may come closer to the mark. In fact, the New Deal marks a significant shift in the vocabulary of American politics. *Liberal* was a term Roosevelt applied to himself. In 1941 he said:

> The liberal party is a party which believes that, as new conditions and problems arise beyond the power of men and women to meet as individuals, it becomes

the duty of the Government itself to find new remedies with which to meet them. . . . The conservative party in government honestly and conscientiously believes the contrary. . . . It believes that, in the long run, individual initiative and private philanthropy can take care of all situations.[5]

This understanding of what I have called "reform liberalism" is now commonplace in American political discussion, but in the 1930s it was new. In fact, Roosevelt's opponents did not easily concede his transformation of the meaning of the term *liberal*.[6] The word already had connotations of generosity, which Roosevelt succeeded in linking to government. Herbert Hoover, for one, had feared that and vigorously contested Roosevelt's use of the label, but Roosevelt insisted because liberal indicated not only generosity but also freedom; such flexibility was very useful in political polemics. And by his second term, when Roosevelt was on the attack, liberal was increasingly used as a positive label, whereas *conservative* and *reactionary* became terms of opprobrium. At the same time he was able to say that his form of liberalism protected private property by "correcting such injustices and inequalities as arise from it. . . . Liberalism becomes the protection for the far-sighted conservative. . . . I am that kind of conservative because I am that kind of liberal."[7]

In the perspective of the New Deal, that does not seem an unreasonable claim; in fact, leftist historians have often complained that the movement was essentially conservative.[8] The historical judgment has merit, though the leftists' criticism is unfair in at least one sense, since Roosevelt never pretended to be in pursuit of radical reform.[9] He saw himself as "a little to the left of center," a self-evaluation that Frances Perkins, his secretary of labor and a person who knew him well, took as accurate.[10] Nevertheless, it was a great rhetorical coup for Roosevelt to succeed in redefining the terms of political debate. Scholars now routinely accept his definition of liberal and see the politicians and thinkers we call conservative as really nineteenth-century, generally free market, liberals.[11] Again, that is not historically incorrect, but it does suggest the extent of Roosevelt's triumph. He redefined the basic ideological vocabulary through which Americans conducted politics. Of course, to define the terms of debate is to win half the battle. Not until less than thirty years ago did liberal cease to be a term of approval and emerge as the dreaded "L word." When that occurred, the basic shape of American politics changed again.

The Two New Deals

The New Deal has a complex relationship to the Progressive movement. There was some continuity of personnel; Franklin Roosevelt, himself a distant cousin of Theodore Roosevelt, had been undersecretary of the navy in the Wilson administration. There was also a real continuity of ideas, since FDR drew on both the New Nationalism and the New Freedom for inspiration. At the same time, many of the old Progressives rejected their descendant, and in many important ways, the New Deal was significantly different from earlier reform movements.[12]

The substantive differences were far more important than those of personnel. Of course the vocabulary of politics was not entirely new and inevitably owed a great deal to the Progressives, but I believe, with Hofstadter, that it is analytically useful to stress the differences. He writes, "Granting that absolute discontinuities do not occur in history, and viewing the history of the New Deal as a whole, what seems outstanding about it is the drastic new departure that it marks in the history of American reformism."[13]

It is this sheer novelty that the single-factor approach of Louis Hartz failed to grasp. Of course the United States under FDR remained within the Lockean liberal framework, broadly considered. In the depths of the depression European countries were able to appeal to socialist traditions and also, alas, to new Fascist idols, whereas in the United States, Roosevelt was able to keep his sights focused on the right. There the only possible real enemy awaited him, whether in the form of the latest version of Hartz's Whiggery or, more menacingly, in rightist populist movements with leanings toward a native American fascism.[14] Yet Hartz missed the originality of the New Deal within the liberal tradition, though he did see the sheer excitement felt by the young New Dealers, who seemed to have all the energy of their Marxist opposites in Europe. But it is precisely because he was so concerned about demonstrating the liberal tradition's hegemony and because of his too narrow understanding of its content that he missed the originality. The liberal tradition was there, and that tradition, in the broad, Hartzian sense, managed, however uneasily, to combine Hamilton and Jefferson; what the New Deal did not include, Garry Wills pointed out, was "Algerism," with its individualist religiosity and its strong feeling that welfare policies were destructive of character. That fact might account for the moral shock Roosevelt's enemies felt in the face of his policies.[15]

Hofstadter shows that it was possible to work within the consensus theory while still remaining alert to innovation. It may be helpful to follow, and occasionally amplify, the outline of his somewhat schematic sketch of the differences between progressivism and the New Deal.

1. When Theodore Roosevelt became president, the economy was in very good condition; when FDR took office, the economy had ground to an almost complete halt and the very existence of capitalism seemed threatened. The idea of a free competitive order could no longer be taken for granted, as it had been even by Progressives who saw the need for regulation of that system.

2. The New Dealers were not really prepared for the situation; orthodox economics had taught them nothing about it. The early New Deal has a reputation for a commitment to planning, but to argue that such a commitment inspired the "flood of Legislation" is to "confuse planning with interventionism." Instead there was a "chaos of experimentation."[16] The centerpiece of the early New Deal was the National Recovery Act, the NRA. This legislation involved the virtual suspension of the antitrust laws, so industries could develop wage and production codes designed to stabilize their particular segments of the economy. It was certainly not centralized planning; at worst it involved government abdication of constitutional responsibility to private concerns. In the event, the system did not last long, because in 1935 it was declared unconstitutional by the Supreme Court in *Schechter v. U.S.*[17]

3. A somewhat accidental by-product of the destruction of the NRA was the emergence of a much stronger labor movement than had been a part of the political economy before. Under the NRA it had been politically necessary to allow organized labor a seat at the table when production codes were drawn up, and there were also concessions in the arena of collective bargaining. When the NRA died, the portions affecting labor were replaced by the Wagner Act, which granted labor the right to organize, particularly in heavy-manufacturing industries such as automobiles and steel. The theory of countervailing power, developed by John Kenneth Galbraith, helps to explain the new approach. His theory, that there was a countervailing power that could be brought to bear against those who wielded "original power," replaced the economic myth that holds that power had no place in the market. Liberalism came to be seen as a way to protect the unorganized who occupied weak positions in the economy; conservatives would be busy protecting positions of original power.[18] The new approach gave the New Deal a social democratic cast, which had been missing from earlier reform efforts. Social security, wages-and-hours legislation, and housing had become part of the government's agenda.

4. There was also a new fiscal role for government, again somewhat accidental. Big governmental spending and unbalanced budgets proved to be a powerful stimulus to the economy, a fact discovered when a reduction in spending triggered the "Roosevelt recession" of 1937. Many thought that FDR had adopted the economics of John Maynard Keynes before 1937, but it was not until later that the Britisher's controversial and unorthodox theories were understood and openly accepted. Only the onset of war, as Keynes himself came to see, seemed to be a motive sufficient to generate spending on the level required.[19]

5. Then there was the question of the big city political machines that had so exercised Progressives. Lacking their political moralism, FDR simply made the machines part of his power base. If they could help to meet his goals, that was sufficient. This pragmatic approach was also symptomatic of the lowered moral temperature of the New Deal. The one striking exception to my statement that the movement produced little theory was provided by Thurman Arnold, a lawyer, legal scholar, and assistant attorney general in charge of antitrust actions. His theoretical writings exhibited a willingness to eschew Progressive moralism in favor of the language of technocratic bureaucracy. In fact, it was the conservative Right that professed moral outrage over the actions of the administration.[20]

6. Finally, what of the trusts, the great issue of political economy that had dominated the Progressive Era? Here the record is complex and inconsistent. The NRA, which was the heart of what has come to be called the First New Deal, was deeply indebted to the New Nationalism of Theodore Roosevelt. It was premised on the idea that a free competitive market was no longer viable; to Arthur Schlesinger, Jr., "The essence of the First New Deal was affirmative national planning." But that seems not quite on the mark; as Hofstadter remarked, intervention was not planning. And although it was true that competition was to be regulated, the regulation was decentralized into the various industries, ostensibly working in cooperation with labor; they were all under the supervision of an administrative body, the National Recovery Administration.[21] The system involved an extensive delegation of legislative power; it was this delegation that the Supreme Court found unconstitutional in the *Schechter* case. There was no attempt to create or restore a competitive economic order, which made the NRA a dramatic initiative, but one doomed to failure by the court.

But the New Deal did not pursue a consistent policy on antitrust. Of course, that was due in large part to the court's invalidation of the NRA, but it was perhaps also a product of ideological infighting in the administration. Before the court acted, the whole system was in political and administrative trouble. It was replaced by something that was, at least on the surface, quite different.

The Second New Deal was "a coalition between lawyers in the school of Brandeis and economists in the school of Keynes." But, Schlesinger went on, that did not mean the complete triumph of Brandeis. Brandeis's "faith in smallness was too stark and rigorous." He "exalted smallness and localism per se," but the young New Deal lawyers were "trying to make competition work in an economy which would be technologically advanced as well as socially humane."[22] There was a change in tone in the second period; all scholars of the period have agreed that the initial ideological exuberance of the early years had dissipated somewhat. In view of the subsequent development of American politics, Hofstadter's analysis is especially striking. A good deal of the action had shifted to the trust division of the Justice Department, under Thurman Arnold. But there was no Brandeisean zeal to restore some presumably pristine competitive order. As Hofstadter said:

> [The approach was] severely managerial, and distinctly subordinated to those economic considerations that would promote purchasing power and hence recovery. It was, in short, a concerted effort to discipline the pricing policies of business, not with the problem of size in mind, nor out of consideration for smaller competitors, but with the purpose of eliminating that private power to tax which is the prerogative of monopoly, and of leaving in the hands of consumers vital purchasing power.[23]

In this view the New Deal cannot be seen as an ideological movement, in spite of the ideological currents swirling all around. It is important to remember that the New Deal developed in the shadow of fascism and Stalinism. Again Hofstadter: "Roosevelt and his supporters were attempting to deal with the problems of the American economy within the distinctive framework of American political methods," so "in a certain way they were trying to repudiate the European world of ideology."[24] After World War II, this anti-ideological stream came to be the major theme in American political thought. Whether the New Deal provided a satisfactory synthesis of the New Nationalism and the New Freedom is a matter of judgment; Roosevelt seemed to think it was, and interestingly enough, Justice Brandeis seemed to have agreed.[25]

The Legacy of the New Deal

However controversial in its own day, the New Deal has been absorbed into the mainstream political culture; like Jefferson and Lincoln, Roosevelt has entered the pantheon reserved for very few. Even Ronald Reagan professed to honor him and to claim that the problems of contemporary liberalism stemmed from a betrayal of Rooseveltian principles.

What is it that has been so fully absorbed, in spite of the fact that in some sense the New Deal was a failure? As is widely recognized, it was not the domestic programs that ended the depression, but rather the spending for war. "Dr. New Deal" was replaced by "Dr. Win the War," thus validating, in a massive unintended experiment, the Keynesian model of economic growth through governmental stimulation. But in its sincere attempts to cope with the wreckage created by the depression, the New Deal first of all achieved what Irving Howe called the "socialization of concern," in the form of social security, unemployment insurance, wages-and-hours legislation, the right to organize unions—the whole panoply of policies that Ronald Reagan called the "safety net." This was certainly a part of Roosevelt's enormous success. As Frances Perkins said, the president gave off a sense "that the people mattered."[26] The fact that those policies today seem unable to cope with the problems of the new urban "underclass" does not diminish their importance as a starting point.

Second, Roosevelt created the vast New Deal electoral coalition, which was to dominate presidential politics for the next thirty to forty years, depending on when one wants to date the long, slow collapse of the often strained alliance. In the days of the New Deal, this coalition was characterized by a highly personalized mass politics based on the charisma of the president. Roosevelt did make an abortive attempt to reconstruct the Democratic Party along the lines of a European social democratic party. When that failed, he began to appeal over the heads of party and Congress by going directly to the people with the case for his program.[27] This move led to a striking incongruity in New Deal politics. Just as the New Deal abandoned the idealistic fervor of the first phase for the tough-minded managerialism of the second, Roosevelt heated up his personal rhetoric to appeal to his wide constituency. "Economic royalists" became his favorite term of abuse for opponents. He railed against "government by organized money," which was as dangerous as "government by organized mob."[28] In the same speech, at the climax of the 1936 campaign, he said: "Never before in all our history have these forces been so united against one candidate as they stand today. They are unanimous in their hate for me—and I welcome their hatred. I should like to have it said of my first Administration that in it the forces of selfishness and of lust for power met their match. I should like to have it said of my second admin-istration that in it these forces met their master."[29] There may have been a discrepancy between Roosevelt's campaign rhetoric and the actual policies he and his advisers pursued, but the language suggests much about the mood of the 1930s. It is inconceivable to imagine the most radical mainstream polit-ical leader today uttering sentiments remotely like these, even in the context of a heated electoral campaign. To do so would invite political disaster; the more conservative spirit of our time would see extremist demagoguery in the presidential rhetoric.

A third part of the inheritance from the Roosevelt era is a transformed sys-tem of interest group politics. As the political parties began their long, and at first imperceptible, decline, interest groups began to rise in power. James Madison had seen them—factions, he would have said—as evils that had to be lived with and if possible used. In modern liberal theory, they came to be viewed as of positive benefit. Moreover, with parties no longer a power-ful intermediary between interests and government, the groups can now directly approach Congress and the appropriate executive agencies. This is the system commonly referred to, in Theodore Lowi's term, as "interest group liberalism."[30]

The fourth major change to emerge from the 1930s can properly be called the Roosevelt revolution, if by "revolution" we mean discontinuous change. The term *Roosevelt revolution* is, as Lowi says, a useful exaggeration.[31] There was an enormous growth in the functions of government as well as in the sheer size of the permanent civil service. There were basic shifts of power not only away from the states and toward Washington but also within the central government as legislative supremacy gave way to a system of presidential government. This shift was accompanied, as mentioned above, by huge delegations of power from Congress, which was presumably setting basic standards of policy, to adminis-trative agencies, which were presumably filling in the mere details left by the legislation. But, Lowi argues, this limitation was revealed as a fiction when it became clear that the agencies were making coercive decisions on their own.[32]

As always, the growth of the state was accelerated by war, and war led to the development of the national security state. It is important, however, to remember that this development was preceded by the rise of a strong domes-tic state. All these changes involved a profound redefinition of America's "col-lective identity," to use Sheldon Wolin's term. Lowi writes, "A new synthesis of power was being consolidated, one that conjoined three distinct elements: regulation, welfare, and empire."[33] I leave aside the question of whether the acquisition of empire was an act of deliberate policy or an attempt to fill a power vacuum or some combination of the two; the result was the same—a massive increase in the power of the American state. Such a presence was indeed new and revolutionary in the context of U.S. political development.[34]

Here is where the great originality of the New Deal lies. It is true that partly because of the force of circumstance and partly because of Roosevelt's experimental temper, the New Deal never developed a fully consistent set of economic and social policies. But in his 1932 campaign speech to the Commonwealth Club in San Francisco, Roosevelt did lay down a line of analysis he was to pursue throughout his presidency. After rehearsing the history of the conflicts between Hamilton and Jefferson, Wilson and Theodore Roosevelt, FDR turned to the theme of economic development. America had become a mature economy, its industrial plant built, the great age of discovery and expansion over. New needs were at hand,

> the soberer, less dramatic business of administering resources and plants already in hand, of seeking to establish foreign markets for our surplus production, of meeting the problem of under consumption, of adjusting production to consumption, of distributing wealth and products more equitably, of adapting existing economic organizations to the service of the people. The day of enlightened administration has come.[35]

Often this speech has been read in the light of its economic views, views that now seem dated, with the Keynesian revolution and decades of economic growth behind us, but the true key to the Roosevelt presidency lies in the emphasis on administration. Historically, the party system grew out of the Jeffersonian desire to curb executive power. There had been hostility to parties in the Progressive movement, but the Roosevelt campaign was the first transformative movement to call for large-scale exercise of executive power. Although the New Deal built what V. O. Key would have called a strong party-in-the-electorate, though one based more on the charismatic authority of the president than on the party organization, the long-term effect of the New Deal was the weakening of the party system, a process that has continued apace to this day. One should make no mistake: There is a great tension between the politics of the administrative state and the politics of democracy. That tension was intensified in the years after the end of the New Deal.[36]

To sum up: The New Deal built, partly by inadvertence, a new, powerful, and on the whole benign state, a welfare state that also became a warfare state, based on what became an extremely successful mixed economy. It restored stability in a time of enormous crisis, and it created institutions and policies of lasting value. Reform politics is terribly difficult; the Roosevelt administration did well by all but the most demanding ideological standards.

It is not surprising, though surely unfortunate, that some reforms were left undone. Recovery was incomplete, the race problem had not even begun to be seriously addressed, and the conundrum of the large corporation, which had nagged at the nation since the end of the Civil War, was unsolved. And Alan Brinkley argues that liberals' near-total replacement of the early New Deal concern for control of corporate power by a politics of rights and entitlements was a serious mistake.[37]

These dilemmas were left for later reform liberal generations to solve. That has proven difficult. Enlightened administration was not enough. In 1948, at a time of liberal disillusionment with Roosevelt's successor, Harry Truman, Richard Hofstadter wrote: "Bereft of a coherent and plausible body of belief—for the New Deal, if it did little more, went far to undermine the old ways of thought—Americans have become more receptive than ever to dynamic personal leadership as a substitute. This is part of the secret of Roosevelt's popularity, and, since his death, of the rudderless and demoralized state of American liberalism."[38]

Viewed in the history of American reform, the New Deal represented, for a time, the culmination of that tradition in American politics. Suddenly, American reform liberals found that most of the demands that had been basic to their programs for many years had been realized, as illustrated by the startling triumph of Harry Truman in the election of 1948. Eric Goldman noted that this election symbolized acceptance of the belief by most Americans that government was ultimately responsible for the welfare of the economy and, further, the acceptance of a greatly enlarged international role for the United States. The Kennedy and Johnson administrations expanded and extended those commitments, but they did little to change the basic conception of the role of government established in the New Deal. As Goldman wrote, "In an important sense this liberal conquest came as liberalism turned into a form of conservatism." The conservative mood was fostered by a solidification of the New Deal consensus. The process began with Truman's 1948 reelection and was completed when the Republican Party returned to power in 1953 after years in "the wilderness." During those years the party had often threatened—or promised—to repeal the whole liberal edifice, but the Republicans left the Roosevelt legacy substantially in place. That was perhaps the most important impact of the Eisenhower presidency.[39] Only today does the Republican Party show signs of reviving its earlier position.

· 12 ·

Liberalism in Search of New Directions

ERIC GOLDMAN'S COMMENT that the Eisenhower administration will be remembered in history for not dismantling the Roosevelt legacy may seem paradoxical, but there is a great deal to be said for his analysis. Any sense of reform liberal triumph dissipated very quickly after World War II. The alliance with the Soviet Union was shattered, the USSR occupied what had been East Central Europe, and the Maoist revolutionaries won out in China. The cold war was on; this is not the place to probe causes, give credit, or assess blame. The fact is that there was every good reason for liberals to oppose Stalinism and Maoism, even if the dangers from those sources, particularly the dangers of internal subversion, were grotesquely exaggerated and led to the hysterical anti-Communist excesses of Senator Joseph McCarthy and his acolytes. As a result, for the better part of two decades anticommunism was at the center of American politics, often at the expense of adequate attention being paid to other pressing issues, notably civil rights. The other loser was domestic political civility, the sense of comity Richard Hofstadter saw as central to democratic politics.

The political struggle over the anti-Communist label was long, bitter, and complicated.[1] This struggle need not occupy us here; there was, however, an intellectual change in the reform movement that must be sketched. The key figures were the young historian Arthur Schlesinger, Jr., and the theologian Reinhold Niebuhr. Schlesinger's contribution, in effect a manifesto for the new liberal ginger group, Americans for Democratic Action, was an attempt to define the political space to be occupied by liberals as of 1949—*The Vital Center*.[2] Left and Right were both failures: "Western man in the middle of the twentieth century is tense, uncertain, adrift."[3] Totalitarians on both the left and right had nothing to offer; the differences between the two were more apparent than real. We had to beware the Soviets, he wrote, but "I am persuaded that the restoration of business to political power in this country would have the same calamitous results that have generally accompanied business control of the government; that this time we might be delivered through the incompetence of the right into the hands of the totalitarians of the left."[4] The experience under FDR was critical. "Mid-twentieth century liberalism, I believe, has thus been fundamentally reshaped by the hope of the New Deal, by the exposure of the Soviet Union, and by the deepening of our knowledge of man."[5]

The new liberalism, influenced by the grim experiences of the mid–twentieth century, was for many given philosophical voice by Niebuhr. To turn to Niebuhr is to return to the Puritans at the beginning of American history. In a long series of books, Niebuhr laid out a theory of human nature rooted in the idea of original sin:[6] We were caught in a moral dilemma that was at least as old as Machiavelli. There was, Niebuhr argued, a sharp distinction to be made between the behavior of individuals and that of social groups, a distinction that "justifies and necessitates political policies which a purely individualistic ethic must always find embarrassing. [As a result], politics will, to the end of history, be an area where conscience and power meet, where the ethical and coercive factors of human life will interpenetrate and work out their tentative and uneasy compromises."[7] This position might have been expected to lead to endorsement of the New Deal programs, but in the 1930s Niebuhr sided with Dewey in criticizing the administration in spite of his philosophical antipathy to the latter. However, by the end of the 1930s, as the New Deal policies had begun to hit home, Niebuhr resigned from the Socialist Party and became a confirmed Rooseveltian experimentalist.

The problem of sin remained. For Niebuhr, we could not expect to create Utopia; we would not have our "city on a hill." The conclusions were grim: "Nothing that is worth doing can be achieved in our lifetime; therefore we must be saved by hope."[8] Democracy was no panacea, for there were no final answers; at best, it was "a method of finding proximate solutions for insoluble problems."[9] And it was this view of man that provided the justification for democracy itself. "Man's capacity for justice makes democracy possible; but man's inclination to injustice makes democracy necessary."[10] Finally, we should never lose sight of the necessity and ubiquity of power. Coercion, Niebuhr wrote, was at the root of all political matters. The only sure protection against the power of others was the exertion of a counterforce. Justice could be achieved only by imposing an order, a balance of power, upon the anarchic conflict of self-interest that characterized human behavior. All schemes of justice had such a balance of power at their foundation. At best, "such a balance, once achieved, can be stabilized, embellished, and even, on occasion, perfected by more purely moral considerations."[11]

The close fit between Niebuhr's analysis of political reality and a limited, cautious approach to political action is obvious. Once this connection is granted, there is little room for idealistic crusades. Moral suasion is a mere embellishment; the essential goals of politics lie in the world of power. This view of domestic politics is not unique; most of us long ago gave up any illusions about the prospects for idealism. Indeed, the idea of confronting power with power is as old as Madison. Nevertheless, Niebuhr's theory had an important, though clearly not conclusive, impact in international relations as an antidote to an American tendency to embark on sometimes quixotic idealistic crusades.[12]

Niebuhr's bleak view fitted well with the chastened liberalism of the 1950s and with the markedly anti-ideological approach to politics that emerged as a dominant force. Consider Schlesinger's defense of democracy: "The people as a whole are not perfect; but no special group of the people is more perfect; that is the moral and rationale of democracy. Consistent pessimism about man, far from promoting authoritarianism, alone can inoculate the democratic faith against it."[13] That may be so, but it is a far cry from the high hopes and spirits of the early New Deal; it is the birth of "skeptical liberalism" and a long step toward the theory of the end of ideology, which was to emerge as a major force by the end of the decade.[14]

Other ideas in the new liberalism attempted to break new ground in the age of skepticism that had followed the exertions of war and depression. In particular, the quality of life in corporate America was questioned. First, many began to worry about the pressure to conform to a rather narrowly defined set of social norms. That conformism had been a concern, off and on, in American social thought since the time of Alexis de Tocqueville, though not all commentators recognized the full extent of Tocqueville's prescience. Three catch phrases of the time—the "age of conformity," the "lonely crowd," and the "organization man"—were intimately related to the question of how to live in the world of the large, bureaucratized corporation. The issue became one of preserving any sense, in that setting, of the individuality so central to the liberal consensus.[15]

To David Riesman, individuality, once the keynote of the American character, had suffered great setbacks. American ideology, Riesman contended, remained competitive, but at the same time there had been a marked shift from what he called "inner-direction" toward an ideological justification for submission to the group, so one's peers became the "measure of all things."[16] It had become an other-directed society.

Although the very term *other-direction* suggests superficiality and lack of a sense of self, Riesman was not exclusively critical. In both types of character formation, direction "comes from the outside and is simply internalized at an early point in the life cycle of the inner-directed."[17] He thought that the political impact of this change was mixed. In politics the inner-directed tended to be "moralizers," whereas the other-directed were inclined to be "inside-dopesters." This change in style was marked by a shift from indignation to tolerance in political psychology and by a shift in the structure of decision-making from a pattern of ruling-class dominance to one in which power was dispersed among a variety of conflicting interest groups, or "veto groups." This shift was a sign of growing sophistication. Nineteenth-century moralizers tended to see politics in confused, ethically limited, and sometimes slightly "paranoid" ways, which made subtlety and tolerance difficult.[18] The inside-dopester, however, though not inclined to political fanaticism, was likely to have a cynical view of politics—something which at best is a kind of spectator sport.[19] Thus, although Riesman did not hope for the return of inner-direction, he could not applaud the ascendancy of the other-directed either. What Riesman sought was neither inner- or other-direction, but rather to build on the present social base to achieve the goal posited by all classical social thought and some forms of liberalism: the fullest development of the individual personality.[20] It is noteworthy that in spite of Riesman's qualms, the "new" American character structure he described was an ideal candidate for a detached, inactive, nonideological politics—precisely the politics of the 1950s.

The other major book in this vein was *The Organization Man*, by William H. Whyte, Jr. Whyte's view was similar to Riesman's, but he forsook the more or less neutral tone of *The Lonely Crowd* for open criticism. Whyte described what he saw as the decline of the Protestant ethic and the rise of what he called a social ethic, as a substitute. The major beliefs of this new ethic were "scientism, belongingness, and togetherness." Whyte summed up his major propositions as "a belief of the group as the source of creativity; a belief in 'belongingness' as the ultimate need of the individual; and a belief in the application of science to achieve the belongingness."[21]

Two points stand out. First, the evidence for a major shift in the character structure of the "typical" American is not entirely solid. As we have seen, Tocqueville noted as far back as the 1830s a lack of personal independence and a tendency to cling to socially determined norms. To this extent, American individuality was something of a myth, though surely worthy of aspiration in the manner of Emerson, Thoreau, and Whitman. In this sense, Riesman and Whyte were measuring their contemporaries by a false standard.[22] Second, in spite of that fault, both books were best-sellers, even though Riesman's, in particular, was by no means easy reading. The talk about conformity clearly struck a nerve in the corporate middle class. Even if the problem was a mere extension of an old behavioral pattern, it was real.

The other aspect of the concern for the quality of American life was less ambiguous and, perhaps, somewhat more influential. In *The Affluent Society* John Kenneth Galbraith argued that the "classical program" of American liberalism had become obsolete. Until the 1930s, the key to liberal thought had been the achievement of economic security through the redistribution of existing income, the strengthening of previously weak groups such as trade unions, the development of stronger government, greater economic security, aid to farmers, and regulation of the corporation.[23] In the late 1930s, with the coming of the Keynesian revolution in economics, there had been an important shift. The liberal program bore the marks of this intellectual revolt. By the 1950s, the emphasis was on production, almost for its own sake. In the depths of the depression, with the almost total breakdown of productive capacity, that had been understandable. Twenty years later, Galbraith claimed, the question of *how* the product was distributed was a secondary matter: "There is almost no concern at all over the *kinds* of private goods and services that are produced. *All* are important and the *total* counts." As Russell Hanson observes, after the New Deal, "American conceptions of democracy came to be associated with a particular kind of government, one whose primary responsibility was to serve the material interests of a consumer community." Consumer economics became the heart of politics, as Hanson observed, and the success of an administration was increasingly seen as a question of whether it could deliver the goods.[24] The result was a profound social imbalance, a community that was characterized by "private affluence and public squalor."[25]

The programmatic results of this imbalance are quite striking. Social imbalance leads to disaster—decaying cities, crime, environmental degradation—a host of problems of which we are presently more aware than when Galbraith first began to inveigh against them. Still, it is clear that even now we are not ready to face up to the full implications of Galbraith's position. To right the balance, much higher levels of taxation would be required. Galbraith was willing to argue that some of these taxes should come in the form of sales taxes, which are always attacked by liberals as regressive. Conservatives, in any case, and many liberals as well, are ideologically or politically uneasy with the very idea of tax increases.

Higher taxes were a price Galbraith was willing to pay, on the assumption that this was a society where the great majority of people were no longer poor. Galbraith did not deny the existence of poverty, as some of his critics seem to believe. The point was that the affluent society was that rare social system in which the poor were a distinct minority. Galbraith's timing was unfortunate; only two years later, Michael Harrington shifted the balance of discussion when he "rediscovered" the problem of poverty. But much of the moral edge of his discussion stemmed from the fact that the poor were then a minority that was easy to ignore, both politically and socially, in an age of "I'm all right, Jack" social values. Galbraith is not now much in fashion, though liberal reformers briefly flirted with an attempt to overcome their abhorrence of taxation in the early stages of the Clinton administration. However, Galbraith still has much to teach, not least in his more general discussion of the structure of capitalist economy, to which we will return later. In today's world of environmental degradation, in which the public squalor he attacked is readily apparent to all, he appears even more prescient than he did in 1958.

The work of social critics like Riesman, Whyte, and Galbraith in the 1950s represented a trend that Arthur Schlesinger named "qualitative liberalism." The new liberalism reflected a variety of conditions: a sense of "anxiety and frustration" about the state of American culture, a vague feeling that somehow things were not right, boredom with materialistic complacency, and a general questioning of the purposes of society. The signs of ferment were everywhere: the Beat Generation, the revival of satire, the growth of religion, and the popularity of books like Riesman's, Whyte's, and Galbraith's. "The final lesson of the affluent society," Schlesinger wrote, "is surely that affluence is not enough—that solving the quantitative problems of living only increases the importance of the quality of the life lived."[26]

Qualitative liberalism did not transform the reform movement, as Schlesinger might have hoped. Cultural improvement is not the banner to unfurl if one wants to start a mass movement, particularly if the program demands more taxes. Besides, as Schlesinger himself knew, "the qualitative aspects of life are only marginally within the reach of government."[27] Still, the ideas did not die; they were early signs of a ferment that assumed forms perhaps not envisaged by Schlesinger—for example, the environmental movement. The ideas did not signal radical reform, but they are not unequivocally consistent with the popular image of the bland 1950s.

Social Science as Liberal Ideology

Much of the social science of the 1950s, however, was bland, implicitly supportive of the status quo, and often simply beside the point. The three key ideas were a new theory of democracy rooted in studies of mass voting behavior, a metamorphosis of Madisonian pluralism into a form the old master would have intensely disliked, and the concept of the end of ideology. They reinforced one another, and by 1960 they had been established as orthodoxy in political science.

The place to start is with the great economist Joseph Schumpeter's revision of what he took to be classical democratic theory. He argued that the classical idea that the people held rational ideas on every public issue and that they gave expression to these views by choosing representatives to carry them out in pursuit of the common good was wrong. Selection of representatives was thus made secondary, in the classic model, to the primary purpose of democracy, which is to vest in the electorate the power of deciding issues.[28] To a great extent this model of democracy was Schumpeter's own concoction; it seems to be a mixture of Mill and Rousseau, but no single thinker ever produced the theory of democracy that he described.[29] However, having created his straw man, Schumpeter subjected it to criticism and proposed an inversion of its basic terms: "And we define: the democratic method is that institutional arrangement for arriving at political decisions in which individuals acquire the power to decide by means of a competitive struggle for the people's vote."[30]

Schumpeter's definition has great strengths. It focuses on the electoral process by which candidates and parties acquire power. For a large representative democracy, that is descriptively valid, since it is centered on a set of institutions and practices whose importance no democrat would deny. One should note though that it was a theory of elite behavior and made no reference to the possibility of direct citizen involvement in self-government. In fact, Schumpeter said explicitly that the only role for the citizen was to vote and then get out of the way so that the chosen elites might govern in peace; voters should not even try to influence their representatives by mail after they are elected.[31] To do so would be to court irrationality, since the paradigm case of rational thinking was economic calculation. When voters entered the world of politics, they descended to an altogether lower level of thought.[32]

As a theory of democratic politics with an extremely limited role for the citizen, it was the Anti-Federalist nightmare come true.[33] Nevertheless, during the 1950s and 1960s, Schumpeter's conception was at the heart of orthodox democratic theory, in part because it seemed to fit so well with what research in voting behavior was discovering. According to *The American Voter,* one of the great monuments of large-scale empirical research, the voter was neither well informed nor particularly rational. Everyone's ideal, the vaunted independent voter, was merely too confused to form partisan attachments; his independence had nothing to do with presumed judiciousness. Finally, the voter's decision had little to do with the issues of the time; he or she was much more likely to choose on the basis of the personal characteristics of the candidates or, even more likely, on the basis of identification with one of the political parties.[34]

Because all that fitted nicely with Schumpeter's political thought, social scientists were quick to draw what seemed to be the appropriate conclusions.

Low rates of political participation were signs, not of democracy in distress, but of political health. After all, if the voters did not know what they were doing, then the less they were involved, the better. Apathy was functional: It cushioned the political system against the shock of conflict.[35] Heinz Eulau outdid everyone in his enthusiasm: Apathy signaled the "politics of happiness."[36] Only the dean of research on political parties, V. O. Key, raised an obvious objection to this revaluation of the citizen's role. He wrote, "The masses do not corrupt themselves; if they are corrupt, they have been corrupted." It was leadership that was at fault. The ideas or, one might wish to add, the lack of ideas, of voters did not stem from themselves: In the main, mass opinion was a response to the cues, the proposals, and the vision propagated by the political activists.[37] As Key put it at the start of his final book, his premise was that voters were not fools.[38]

Pluralism provided its own defense of the status quo. The intellectual roots of pluralism went back to *Federalist* 10, by James Madison, though not without significant change. A more immediate source was in the Progressive period, with its rediscovery of interest groups. The classic statement of pluralism was Arthur Bentley's: "The great task in the study of any form of social life is the analysis of [its] groups. When the groups are adequately stated, everything is stated. When I say everything, I mean everything. The complete description will mean the complete science, in the study of social phenomena, as in any other field."[39]

The modern restatement of this point of view came in David Truman's influential study of interest group politics in the United States, *The Governmental Process*, published in 1951. Three points should be featured. First, Americans, through their membership in interest groups, had great access to the major centers of political power; the multiple group memberships of citizens provided a fairly automatic mechanism for reducing the level of tension in U.S. politics. Second, U.S. politics rested on a latent consensual foundation, which would be defended by a large "potential" interest group if the values imbedded in the consensus were challenged. Conflict thus took place within a quite restricted set of "rules of the game." Third, one did not need to account for such a thing as a public interest, because no such thing existed; it was what Bentley would have dismissed as a metaphysical spook. This idea, of course, signaled a major break with Madison, whose definition of faction—today's interest group—precisely stated that its existence was in opposition to the "permanent and aggregate interests of the whole."[40]

Truman's descriptive account of interest group politics remains of great value; his theory has faired much less well. The theory of a potential interest in the rules of the game sounds suspiciously like a theory of the public interest of precisely the sort he was at pains to deny. As Charles Frankel pointed out, a politics without such a concept had little chance of rising above the level of a cat fight in an alley.[41] Contrary to Truman's belief, most Americans were not represented by an organized interest; as Elmer Schattschneider elegantly showed, the bottom levels of society were not at all well represented, and thus, "the flaw in the pluralist heaven is that the heavenly chorus sings with a strong upper-class accent."[42] Finally, Stanley Rothman notes that most of the groups described in Truman's study represent economic interests. The roots of group theory lie deep in the possessive liberal tradition that goes back to the individualism of Hobbes and Locke. Groups pursue rationally calculated interests, as in the capitalist theories of economic man.[43] One can begin to see the emergence of the more overtly economic models that in the 1980s became what Sheldon Wolin calls the "new public philosophy."[44]

The other major discussion of pluralism was more self-consciously theoretical, not only empirically, but also normatively. Robert Dahl's contribution to constitutional theory was, in effect, an attempt to render it superfluous. "Insofar," he wrote, "as there is any general protection in human society against the deprivation by one group of the freedom desired by another it is probably not to be found in constitutional forms. It is to be discovered, if at all, in extra-constitutional factors."[45] The success of the Constitution rested on social prerequisites; Dahl, although he was critical of Madisonianism, acknowledged that in a sense the latter's theory of fragmentation worked. The problem we faced was not the tension between majority rule and minority rights, because the majority never ruled—we were governed by a constantly shifting coalition. It was thus more accurate to say that we lived under a system of "minorities rule."[46] Though Dahl sees the Constitution as undemocratic, that is of little consequence, since constitutional forms count for so little.[47]

Dahl's theory is close to pluralism, though Dahl and his close colleague, Charles Lindblom, preferred the term *polyarchy* and saw their theory as more comprehensive than Truman's. Polyarchy was a system of bargaining and compromise, with the participants subject to the discipline of electoral competition among elites of the sort theorized by Schumpeter. Pluralist liberals were often charged—I have charged them here—with a more or less unconscious slippage from empirical description to normative prescription. However, as Robert Booth Fowler points out, the significance of Dahl's *Preface to Democratic Theory* was that he was quite self-conscious in this enterprise.[48] That is what makes Dahl's work so important as an indicator of the intellectual currents of the 1950s. If we take into account only the denial of rights built into segregation, we can see that to be so delighted by the condition of the political system, one would have to be quite blinded by the American success story. But that was the norm for the period in much political science theory. It was an age of the politics of contentment.

The capstone of liberal social science in the period was the theory of the end of ideology, which was common currency in both Europe and the United States from the mid-1950s on. The most sophisticated statement in the United States came from Daniel Bell, whose book *The End of Ideology* carried the evocative subtitle *The Exhaustion of Political Ideas in the Fifties.*[49] Bell argued that the radical ideologies of the nineteenth century had been discredited by the catastrophes of the twentieth. Therefore, in the Western world, these ideas had lost their former potency, their capacity to appeal to intellectuals. The reasons were not hard to find. The Moscow trials, the Nazi-Soviet Pact, the concentration camps, the failure of the Hungarian rebellion in 1956, and other sobering events made the sort of chiliasm that Bell associated with ideology difficult, if not impossible, to maintain. In addition, the transformation of the predatory capitalism of the nineteenth century into the modern welfare state also lessened the zeal of reformers.[50] The intellectuals of the 1930s, who had been infected with the virus of messianism, had paid a price in lost innocence; they had tasted power and become corrupt. The end of ideology was the reaction to this situation.[51]

The anti-ideological politics of the 1940s and 1950s was the result. There was a skepticism toward the rationalistic claims of socialists that an alteration of the economic base of society would solve all the pressing American social problems. Bell saw a kind of antirationalism linked to the vogue of thinkers such as Freud and Niebuhr. No longer did the liberal intellectual feel compelled to make the world over; instead, the feeling seemed to be that the task was too great even to contemplate. Revolution had been replaced by acquiescence.

Much of this judgment rings true; the 1930s certainly were a more ideological decade than the 1950s. However, at the center of the swirl of ideas in the earlier decade was Franklin Roosevelt, presiding over a period of change, without commitment to any of the more flamboyant ideologies of the time. And insofar as Bell tended to equate messianic socialism with the concept of ideology itself, he exaggerated the impact of such ideas on the American scene, a fact fully understood at the time by despairing Marxists.

However, Bell was correct in assessing the general mood of satisfaction and the sort of politics that accompanied it. A more interesting question was whether the new mood was really desirable. Certainly the complacent form stated by sociologist Seymour Martin Lipset was not. In *Political Man*, his widely read synthesis of the sociological literature on democratic politics, Lipset wrote that democracy was "the good society itself in operation."[52] It was clear in context that American liberal democracy was his paradigm case. But as some critics argued, that could lead to a denial of the role of the intellectual as social critic; in such a case "the intellectual has no other function than to describe and to celebrate the arrival of a Lipsetian utopia."⁵³ For Lipset to have written that way about American society while race relations were in turmoil, poverty was being rediscovered, and the cold war was on in full force meant that indeed he had simply entered into what C. Wright Mills would call the "new American celebration." The good society had not yet come; indeed, one might think that the deep-seated skepticism of the liberal intellectuals would have inoculated them against the idea that it ever would. In a Niebuhrian world, it would have been more plausible to argue that there was always more to be done, and of course Bell and Lipset, in their more sober moments, knew that to be the case.

Part of the problem with the Bell-Lipset thesis of the end of ideology was the extremely pejorative definition of the central term, *ideology*. In the aftermath of World War II, a degree of preoccupation with totalitarian ideologies was understandable. But not all ideologies are totalitarian. If a more neutral definition of ideology is used, it is possible to evaluate the consequences of a particular set of ideas as they work out in practice. Is the choice really between ideologically motivated extremism and piecemeal adjustment in the absence of an overall vision? According to Carl Friedrich, there was a very important distinction to be made between an ideology defined as "a system of ideas concerning the existing social order, and at the same time concerning actions to be taken regarding it," and a totalitarian ideology defined as "a total rejection of an existent society and a program of total reconstruction."⁵⁴

Ideology in the second sense is surely a problem, but the absence of ideology in the first sense may doom a society to frustration. A healthy political system must have some sense of values, some long-range goals that can function as a conception of the public interest, some general idea of welfare. Consider the following: "'Liberals such as Lipset are proud of the progress which has been made in the Western world, but it is curious that they never acknowledge the fact that we have gotten as far as we have precisely because of the ideologies which stirred men to action.' And if the end of ideology is, in fact, the case, 'then we have the best explanation of why we in the West are standing still.'"⁵⁵

To his credit, Bell, always a complex figure, conceded something to this case. In response to a critique by sociologist Dennis Wrong, Bell stated that "the end of ideology must not mean the end of utopia as well." The intellectual still had a role to play, even in a world devoid of ideology. Noting the fear of the masses and, indeed, the fear of almost any purposive social action at all, which characterized so much of what in the 1950s was called "the new conservatism," Bell admitted to sharing some of those fears. However, he insisted that one had to maintain a detached and even alienated position so as to avoid the acceptance of "any particular embodiment of the community as final."⁵⁶

Thus, not everyone leaped to applaud at the time the now clearly ephemeral triumphs of the 1950s or the social science that did so much to legitimate them. The most important dissidents tended to be political theorists, of whom the otherwise widely divergent Sheldon Wolin and Leo Strauss can serve as examples, though not as typical cases. Both will be considered more fully in later chapters, but a few words are appropriate here. Wolin was troubled by the reductionism and fragmentation of much pluralist liberal theory —and by much else in addition, it must be said. Here it is sufficient to show his position on the need for a larger vision than the social sciences could hope to provide:

> Political theory must once again be viewed as that form of knowledge which deals with what is general and integrative to men, a life of common involvements. The urgency of these tasks is obvious, for human existence is not going to be decided at the lesser level of small associations; it is the political order that is making fateful decisions about man's survival in an age haunted by the possibility of unlimited destruction.[57]

Leo Strauss was even more blunt and, as it happened, prophetic: "Only a great fool would call the new social science diabolic: it has no attributes peculiar to fallen angels. It is not even Machiavellian, for Machiavelli's teaching was graceful, subtle, and colorful. Nor is it Neronian. Nevertheless one may say that it fiddles while Rome burns. It is excused by two facts; it does not know that it fiddles, and it does not know that Rome burns."[58]

Stirrings of Discontent

The explosion was soon to come, and hints were present even in the supposedly somnolent 1950s. First, of course, was the civil rights movement, which was to revitalize the reformist tradition and also to challenge it and test its limits. But that is a subject for later.

More to the immediate point was the emergence of the new Student Left. It was not accidental that the student movement was strongest at three universities: the University of Michigan; the University of California, Berkeley; and the University of Wisconsin. They were all very large, bureaucratically organized, seemingly impersonal, dedicated to research—often at the expense of teaching, it seemed to some—and all were varied enough intellectually to support a group of dissident students, both on campus and on its fringes. The complaints of the student leftists notwithstanding, they were places of great intellectual vitality. However, the size, complexity, bureaucratic organization, and involvement with big science, often under government sponsorship, made them seem to their critics perfect microcosms of American society.[59]

The Student Left was not particularly theoretical in its orientation. However, its leaders did adopt the ideas of two older scholars—sociologist C. Wright Mills and German-Jewish émigré political theorist, Herbert Marcuse—as their own.

Mills was an American original: colorful, larger than life, and armed not only with Marx, as one might expect, but also with the theories of Max Weber and the early-twentieth-century Italian theorists of the role of elites: Gaetano Mosca, Roberto Michels, and Wilfredo Pareto. In a series of studies, he outlined a picture of American class structure, culminating in his theory of the *power elite*, a term that has entered the language of many who have never read Mills.[60]

Seldom does a social scientific work demonstrate or generate such passion. Deviating sharply from the reigning pluralist school, Mills contended that all the really important decisions—particularly those relating to war and peace—were in the province of a relatively small, well-defined, triadic elite composed of the corporate rich, the upper echelons of the military, and a group dubbed the "political directorate." The picture he painted was grim: decisionmaking by an unrepresentative, irresponsible elite, dedicated above all to cold war values. The seemingly high level of consensus said to pervade U.S. politics was the product of elite manipulation. America was a mass society dominated by the values of a corporate economy propagated through the mass media. The pluralists' depiction of free political competition was a highly romanticized distortion of reality. Only on more or less minor issues did anything like pluralistic competition exist. For Mills the elite was an elite only in terms of its power; from the point of view of a radical democrat, it was morally and intellectually inferior.

Mills saw liberalism itself as in crisis: Liberal ideals were "viable" and "compelling" but divorced from the realities of a large-scale, bureaucratized corporate order. The sociological assumptions on which the latter rested had to be reformulated, and the ideals themselves given up, substantially revised, or rearticulated so that they would recover their force in the new conditions of modern America.[61] This conviction led him to offer a scathing critique of the "end of ideology" thesis, insisting that any serious theory had to have an ideological, critical component; it was this insistence that led him to call for a New Left, adopting a phrase already in use in Britain.[62]

Mills's analysis in *The Power Elite* was not without flaws. Robert Dahl argued that although Mills had described an elite with a great potential for power, he did not demonstrate through an analysis of specific decisions that it had actually utilized that power. Journalist Richard Rovere had no trouble showing that for several important issues of foreign-policy making, not the power elite, but the constitutionally appropriate decisionmakers, had been responsible. Thus, for instance, President Truman was the one who chose, almost single-handedly, to use atomic weapons against Hiroshima and Nagasaki.[63]

However, these challenges to Mills's theory were less damaging than they might appear. Pluralist and elite theorists shared certain perceptions of the nature of American politics. They agreed that ordinary citizens were little involved in politics beyond the act of voting; we know that this tendency has since intensified. Both—rightly or wrongly—accepted the position that it was the social system rather than formal-legal constitutional rules that gave shape to politics. They agreed that the presidency was the dominant force in the national government and that Congress had, for the most part, been relegated to a secondary role. Finally, both argued that it was the prevailing consensus, whatever its source, that tended to define the political issues that would be raised.

At that point significant differences began to emerge. Pluralists tended to see the consensus as in some sense a collective product of society, as a more or less spontaneously generated body of ideas. Elite theorists tended to believe that the consensus was produced by elite manipulation, particularly through the mass media. From this belief it was an easy step to the idea that the power elite distorted the political system by refusing to make some theoretically *possible* proposals for public actions into legitimate public issues; that is, they were not presented as suitable subjects for debate, let alone public action. (Thus, until recently, the idea of a national health system was beyond the scope of polite discussion, and even now, to utter the dreaded words "socialized medicine" is beyond the pale.) Following that insight, elite theorists came to focus on the somewhat elusive politics of nondecision making in an attempt to understand how consensual constraints related to the universe of possible policies,[64] whereas pluralists tended to stress the actions of official government institutions. The concept of a nondecision is a horror for those committed to a positivist philosophy of social science, since it is obviously impossible to observe a nondecision being taken; nonetheless, the idea is a compelling one simply because any political observer can list potential policies obviously precluded by the current consensus.[65] It was the great merit of Mills's somewhat crude study to have raised these issues.[66] Like Herbert Marcuse a few years later, Mills developed a sense of the "system" as a unity, with government, business, and the culture industry as an interlocking set of supposedly separate institutions.

Marcuse was a theorist of quite another sort. As with Mills, a first reading of his work tends to be overwhelming, but on reflection one might begin to have doubts. Much of what he said was common currency at the time, though it was recast in a Germanic philosophical idiom that lent it an unwarranted impression of originality. Marcuse drew heavily on Mills as well as on a number of more journalistic writers. He wrote about "one dimensionality," which is like the "end of ideology" thesis and the consensus theory rolled into one. It signified a loss of the capacity for negative thinking, of the possibility of mounting a viable critique of the society. Instead, according to Marcuse, the system had an amazing ability to absorb and neutralize dissent. The dominant philosophical schools had abandoned criticism in favor of the mindless analysis of the meaning of concepts. Similarly, social science was given over to the investigation of narrowly defined problems. It produced a body of work whose effect was justification of the status quo. The working class, captivated by the delights of the consumer culture, had given up its historical place as an agent of socioeconomic and political change. Television had become a cultural menace that spread the values of the dominant elites.[67] The indictment was so sweeping that there seemed to be no way out of the political impasse. Marcuse was driven to the hope that the "substratum of the outcasts and outsiders, the exploited and persecuted of other races and other colors, the unemployed and the unemployable" would be the needed source for change; "their opposition is revolutionary even if their consciousness is not."[68]

The political conclusions drawn from this analysis, unfortunately, were menacing. One-dimensional society, Marcuse thought, was an instance of totalitarian democracy. Under these conditions, the liberal theory of toleration was repressive. "Apparently undemocratic means" might be required to unleash the forces of true democracy. True freedom of thought did not exist, and its restoration might "necessitate new and rigid restrictions on teaching and practices in the educational institutions which, by their very methods and concepts, serve to enclose the mind within the established universe of discourse and behavior—thereby precluding a priori a rational evaluation of the alternatives." (Here, twenty-five years ahead of its time, was the pure theory of political correctness raised to the highest level.) What was needed was a "liberating tolerance," that is, toleration of movements from the left and intolerance of movements from the right. The answer was a new version of Plato's educational dictatorship: In a distortion of John Stuart Mill that, as David Spitz noted, rose almost to the sublime, Marcuse called for rule by everyone in the "maturity of his faculties"—"the democratic educational dictatorship of free men."[69]

This idea obviously moved well beyond the boundaries of any form of liberal theory and, indeed, beyond any plausible conception of democracy. And by the late 1960s, many of the new leftists had already embraced both Marcuse's theory and the implied practice.

Some of Marcuse's indictment of U.S. politics and culture was support-able, but his political views were disastrous and his vision too claustrophobic, too exaggerated to ring true.[70] Many others, from Strauss on the right to Wolin on the left, had attacked the deficiencies of analytical philosophy and had done it with more skill. Nor was the critique of the social sciences any-thing new; Strauss and Wolin had weighed in from the point of view of tra-ditional political thought and Mills had advanced a powerful case against the "abstract empiricism" and "grand theory" that diverted the various disciplines from their traditional role as critics of the social system as a whole. Of course the mass media have always been fair game. Though the individual points in Marcuse's indictment were not without merit, it was the totality that would not hold up. Marcuse's great failing was a wild imagination, which led him to see the United States as already a totalitarian society and therefore ripe for desperate remedies. The democratic educational dictatorship of free men is simply oxymoronic nonsense. Though he wrote after the new Student Left had begun to form, and thus cannot be said to have been a direct influence on its inception, his desperation eerily foreshadowed the radical distancing of the students from their own society. That was a major source of their down-fall. Marcuse's work illustrated the pitfalls awaiting the critic who so dis-tanced himself from the society he hoped to change that he lost all hope of effectiveness. Without endorsing here the full range of Michael Walzer's the-ory of connected criticism, I ask his question: Who really can be expected to pay attention to the critic who is so clearly disconnected from his surround-ings as to reveal a fundamental misunderstanding of his subject? Such dis-tancing, as Walzer says, "is the enemy of critical penetration," not to men-tion political effectiveness.[71]

Yet to leave matters there would be unfair to Marcuse. One source of Marcuse's appeal to the Student Left was, I think, his sense, which was their sense, of "the system" as a totality. Marcuse exaggerated wildly, but the interre-latedness of politics, the economy, the educational system, the military, and the mass media was not totally imaginary. He was trying to deal with the structure of the rationalized, bureaucratized, large-scale industrial society, which had led Max Weber early in the century to characterize our life as enclosed in an "iron cage." This is indeed a major problem, but once again Marcuse's judgment failed him, for he could not see that the infinitely more sober Weber was on the same side of this question. With the 1960s long passed, Weber's tragic pages seem to speak to us more directly than do Marcuse's. Those who hope to deal with industrial society must return to Weber to find an appropriate starting point.[72]

The New Left: Corporate Liberalism
and Participatory Democracy

The student movement of the 1960s was not particularly given to theoretical analysis; the young rebels were more interested in action than in abstraction, and many hoped to avoid the sterile ideological infighting that had marked the "Old Left" of the 1930s. However, there were two major exceptions. At the University of Wisconsin, a group of graduate students and their mentors in the History Department founded a journal called *Studies on the Left*, which covered a wide range of subjects but was particularly notable for developing a reinterpretation of the emergence of large-scale corporate capitalism and its relation to the Progressive movement—a theory that has deeply influenced subsequent thinking on the subject.[73] And a group of students, primarily from the University of Michigan, founded the Students for a Democratic Society (SDS). That organization was dedicated above all to the idea of participatory democracy, which was destined to become a catchword of the decade and which also made a major imprint on the academic political theory of a generation.

The work of the dissenting students at Wisconsin was an early harbinger of the discontent with the reform liberal tradition. The discontent was to turn into deep conflict by the end of the 1960s. Particularly at issue was the interpretation of the Progressive movement. The standard liberal view held that the Progressives were to be taken at face value; they were indeed seriously interested in Progressive reform, using the agencies of the modern state. The term *corporate liberalism,* coined by Martin Sklar, was used in a work published in 1960, before it could be said that there was a New Left in the United States. The theorists of corporate liberalism saw reform as a sham intended to preserve corporate interests and ensure their continued dominance. The reforms, moreover, were closely tied to the expansion of U.S. power throughout the world.[74] And yet, Sklar admitted—somewhat grudgingly, I think—that the reforms were indeed reforms.[75] Still, it was very much in the spirit of the 1960s, particularly as the war in Vietnam moved to the center stage of political conflict, to view liberals as hypocrites and liberalism itself as "nothing but a fundamentally dishonest conservatism."[76] This view, rooted in the work of Wisconsin historian William Appleman Williams, even though controversial, is by no means entirely without validity and continues to inform much of the current thinking on progressivism. Writing on Williams, Christopher Lasch summed up his contribution:

> If we now take for granted that American liberalism cannot be understood as an antibusiness creed, if we take for granted that the twentieth-century liberalism has been shaped at least in part by the interests of the great business cor-

porations, and if we now argue not about whether progressivism and the New Deal had a stabilizing rather than a "revolutionary" effect on American capitalism but about the degree to which they were deliberately designed to have that effect, then we owe this to the influence of Williams.[77]

The idea of corporate liberalism, therefore, has entered the mainstream of American historical interpretation. Indeed, it has been raised to new levels of sophistication by the more-recent work of Martin Sklar.[78] Sklar correctly saw that the Progressive movement was part of an attempt to come to grips with the dramatically transformed world that had emerged, with the modern corporation as its central institution, after the Civil War. This new world of highly organized, bureaucratically controlled institutions was clearly not compatible with the dominant nineteenth-century liberal individualism that had reached its peak in the synthesis of Abraham Lincoln. If liberalism was to survive, it had to be reconstructed to meet the demands of the new organizational society Max Weber was theorizing about during the heyday of the Progressive movement. At that point, as Alan Brinkley observes, the organizational synthesis associated with Robert Wiebe and other historians began to merge with the findings of the corporate liberal school (this statement is valid as long as one ignores the ideological cutting edge of the latter).[79] Thus it is no accident that both schools were steeped in the literature of classical social science theory and of its turn-of-the-century acolytes, who created theories of modernization and development.

The Progressive movement has provided much of the intellectual framework within which we attempt to grapple with the problems of bureaucratization, corporate capitalism, and modernization and its discontents. They have yet to be satisfactorily resolved, but we still live on the intellectual capital of the reform movements of the early part of the twentieth century. The corporate liberal theorists should be given credit for having raised these issues in a new critical light. Still, that the historians' turn to modernization theory has occurred at the same time as political scientists and sociologists have begun to raise serious questions about it, particularly in its modern, as opposed to classical, guise, is ironic. We need to think seriously about whether progress and modernization are one and the same.[80]

Although the distinction should not be drawn too sharply, the Wisconsin group was more theoretically oriented than the SDS, the Michigan group.[81] It is not possible to trace here the brief, but dismaying, trajectory of the SDS and the New Left in the 1960s. Even those sympathetic to the movement, who see real achievements in it, also recognize that it came to a bad end. What started as an outburst of genuine youthful idealism ended in sectarian squabbling, a repudiation of any meaningful politics, violence, and, for many, a descent into a countercultural or political underground. At its (early) best, the Student Left injected a much-needed voice of morality into American politics. Politically, the theory of participatory democracy led to an emphasis on community organization; as Michael Walzer put it, it was "an effort to teach participatory democracy to the poor . . . to persuade them that they have a great deal to gain through a particular sort, and less to gain through any other sort, of political activity." But for all the virtues of participatory democracy, it revealed a serious weakness in the young rebels' understanding of American reform politics, for as Walzer observed, community was likely to be of value only when it "plays into or leads toward the creation of larger organizations—trade unions and political machines—of a sort that New Leftists generally do not regard with favor."[82] One can begin to see here a split that contributed to the ultimate demise of the Student Left.

But worse was to come. From the Berkeley rebellion in 1964 to the killings at Kent State in 1970 there was repression. Of that there can be no doubt; still, the movement had its own self-destructive tendencies. As it moved from a critique of the deficiencies of American democracy, to an increasingly strident campaign against the repugnant war in Vietnam, to an embrace of deeply antidemocratic leftist factions, to terrorism, to an adoption of countercultural styles that could only alienate the working and lower-middle classes, without which they could not hope to succeed, SDS tore itself apart. In May 1970, Sheldon Wolin and John Schaar, among the most sympathetic of contemporaneous observers, wrote, "The New Left is now dead, partly crushed by the weight of an increasingly oppressive system, partly wrecked by its own inability to develop a new radical theory beyond both liberalism and socialism or a conception of action coherent enough to sustain its members in a political vocation."[83] Walzer was even harsher, referring to "years of sectarian in-fighting, ideological debauch, and pseudorevolutionary violence."[84] Had the Student Left remained true to the thought of Albert Camus, whose writings influenced the SDS manifesto, the Port Huron Statement, those students would not have severed themselves from the only political base they had outside the elite universities. Theirs, like Marcuse's, was an example of the political fecklessness of criticism that took a stance so far away from its target that it lost all leverage.[85]

What was missing here was good theory or even a willingness to take seriously the theory that was available. If the Left had taken Mills and Marcuse truly to heart, they would have realized that the system of power portrayed in their works would not collapse easily in the face of an outburst of democratic idealism. The students seemed deaf to the wisdom that politics generally takes a long period of hard work to achieve even the most worthy goals; seldom, probably never, does it provide instant gratification.

Nevertheless, by advocating participatory democracy, the rebellious students did introduce into the theoretical discussions of the next generation a stimulating, if vague, notion. The idea of participatory democracy was the central concept in the Port Huron Statement. Tom Hayden, the principal author of the statement, borrowed the term itself from his Michigan philosophy teacher Arnold Kaufman.[86] The document was loose, rambling, and much too long. Yet it was clearly based on wide reading and had a genuine appeal for anyone aware of the problems of American democracy. Some influences were obvious—Mills and John Dewey in particular. Camus was there and also Jean-Paul Sartre; so too were Dahl, Wolin, Erich Fromm, Bell, and Lipset, as well as Fidel Castro and statements from the very conservative Young Americans for Freedom. Those and others appeared on a reading list prepared for the SDS by Hayden; it was typical graduate student reading of the period.[87]

The statement was a product of the affluent society, the work of a generation "bred in at least modest comfort."[88] Its members claimed, perhaps too melodramatically, to be haunted by the bomb—"by the sense that we may be the last generation in the experiment with living."[89] The students viewed themselves—arrogantly, but perhaps not incorrectly—as a vanguard minority. The majority saw the temporary equilibria of society as fixed and permanent.[90] Echoing Dewey and Mills, Hayden pointed to a politics without publics; instead there was a mass society satiated with consumer goods, manipulated by corporate-controlled media, engaged in a senseless cold war, dominated by the military-industrial complex, and beset by racial discrimination.

The answer—if there was one—was participatory democracy. According to the statement, "As a social system we seek the establishment of a democracy of individual participation, governed by two central aims: that the individual share in those social decisions determining the quality and direction of his life; that society be organized to encourage independence on men and provide the media for their common participation."[91]

What exactly all that meant was not clear; however, the basic idea that people should have some direct say in making decisions central to their lives could hardly be controversial to any democrat. James Miller explains that the delegates to the Port Huron meeting were by no means in agreement about their central commitment to participatory democracy. To Hayden it meant action, to Paul Booth a perfect Student Nonviolent Coordinating Committee (SNCC) project, to Sharon Jeffrey a way to find authenticity in life, to Bob Ross some not very well-defined form of socialism, and to Richard Flacks a transformation of the meaning of socialism to emphasize its democratic characteristics; to Steve Max it was simply a slogan that sounded good but didn't really matter.[92] To its authors, the statement seems to have meant everything and hence nothing. Participatory democracy was not, as some have thought, intended to substitute for representative democracy; instead, it was a supplement to it.[93] The statement was also a challenge to the social democratic alliance with government; it was distrustful of capitalism, but also of governmental bureaucracy.[94]

In one of the most thoughtful assessments of SDS, James Miller claims to see a statement of the main themes of civic republicanism, a tradition in which he also placed John Dewey and Aristotle, a classification that would probably annoy both.[95] In the SDS's emphasis on a public, as opposed to an individual, interest, one can see Miller's point, but the intellectual history to support this contention is just not there. It was not until later in the decade that the republican tradition was rediscovered. As Miller himself showed, there was also an existentialist commitment to the authenticity of action. That could not necessarily be reconciled with the spirit of sober public discussion of the issues of the day. As the manifesto put it, the goal was to order politics so as to "provide outlets for the expression of personal grievance and aspiration . . . to relate men to knowledge and power so that private problems—from bad recreation facilities to personal alienation—are formulated as general issues." This seems to have been the origin of the slogan, The personal is political, which was to become important in the women's movement.[96]

But participatory democracy is hard work, and the trajectory of SDS through the 1960s suggests that its members did not have the patience for it. This was not necessarily a fault, nor was it surprising, though it surely reflected a degree of ideological innocence and incoherence. As Michael Walzer remarks, the commitment to a Rousseauian level of citizenship implies a systematic denigration of the private life, an ideal that cuts deeply against the American grain.[97] Moreover, although there surely can be satisfaction in political activity, it is probably a very bad way to deal with personal angst. Certainly, it is possible that the out-of-control spin of the activists in the late 1960s may reflect this truth. The descent into the absurdities of the counterculture proved disastrous, a high price to pay for the pursuit of the authentic self, whatever that may mean.

What started as a genuinely appealing instance of youthful idealism turned sour with this loss of control. The adoption of the countercultural style and the capitulation to hard-line Marxist groups, such as Progressive Labor, cut the students off from any conceivable base of popular support. The lurch to the hard-core Left might also have been predicted; surely its roots were obvious in hindsight. The SDS members, sensibly enough, were anxious to avoid the sectarian ideological infighting that had characterized leftist movements in the 1930s. There was also an understandable reaction against the hysterical anticommunism associated with Senator Joseph McCarthy in the 1950s. Anticommunism had a bad name and anti-anticommunism became ideologically fashionable. Under the prodding of Michael Harrington, the representative of the League for Industrial Democracy, a militantly anti-Stalinist, anti-Communist, social democratic group, Hayden's original draft was rewritten to make it more clearly critical of Communist systems around the world. Still, the effort was a bit halfhearted. It appears that many of the young delegates were little interested in, and basically uninformed about, the doctrinal niceties involved. An anecdote that made the rounds at the time was telling: A visitor to SDS headquarters in Chicago noted portraits of both Jefferson and Lenin on the wall and suggested that sooner or later, one would have to come down.[98]

But the leftward lurch went too far beyond the confines of the American consensus, however defined. Essentially the SDS abandoned democracy and adopted a style of protest that cut it off from any possible following. The consequences for reform were momentous, since the reaction against the Left was to become an important factor in the conservative realignment of U.S. politics that began in 1968 with the election of Richard Nixon. The civil rights movement and the rapidly emerging women's movement were additional factors. In effect, the ideological contours of contemporary thought grew out of the drive for racial and gender justice, the government programs that were designed to serve them, the increasing sense on both left and right that democratic institutions were not working well, and the series of economic crises that shook the nation after the prosperity of the 1960s. Thus the 1960s mark the beginning of a period of political and social upheaval that is still going on. During the decade there appeared the first shoots of a rich flowering of political theory, which touched off a debate over the past quarter century about the nature of American society and the meaning of the liberal tradition. It is striking and more than a little ironic that just as the fortunes of the reform liberal tradition began a precipitous decline, the theory and practice of rights-based liberalism began to flourish. In fact, with the publication in 1971 of *A Theory of Justice,* by John Rawls, rights moved to the center of international debate. But before turning to the debate about rights, it is necessary to discuss the controversies over race and gender that grew out of the 1960s.

• 13 •

Race, Gender,
Difference, and Equality

T HE FAILURE to deal in any satisfactory way with race has been the primal curse of American politics, a curse that still has the potential to destroy both liberalism and democracy. Conflict over gender is also of long standing, though it does not cut so deeply into the national soul and psyche. Politically and theoretically, race and gender have had close connections. In the nineteenth century, many abolitionists were women and many male abolitionists such as William Lloyd Garrison were feminists; today, many on the left seem to hope that an alliance between blacks and feminists will lead to a revival of reform politics.[1]

Theoretically, the relation of race and gender issues to liberal theories of rights is interesting and complex. Activists on both issues, historically, have been drawn to liberal ideals, but at the same time they have often been highly critical of them. The universalism in which the liberal language of rights is cast appeals to women and minorities, whereas the manifest gap between liberal theory and liberal practice appalls people. That raises the question whether the shortfall is inherent in the theory. At the same time, the manifest differences between, and sometimes within, races and genders suggest to some activists that theory and policy should be based on the particular rather than the general—and often highly abstract—universals of the liberal tradition. Of course, those are not the only issues, but they do provide a framework for much of the discussion in this chapter.

The Problem of Racial Equality

In 1944, in his monumental study of what he called the "American dilemma," Gunnar Myrdal argued that "the American Negro problem is a problem in the heart of the American."[2] By that he meant that the conflict was fundamentally a clash between the generally egalitarian tenets of the "American Creed" and a set of lower-order values that sanctioned the wide range of discriminatory behavior common then and, all too often, today.

Twenty years later, in a now unduly neglected book, Charles Silverman was moved to challenge Myrdal's formulation. Myrdal was too optimistic, Silverman concluded. Although it was true that for more than a thousand pages Myrdal and his colleagues had meticulously documented the miseries of the American Negro, his basic contention was wrong in that there was no American dilemma. Whites in the United States, Silverman argued, were not in a state of internal conflict because of the gap between their ideals and their behavior. At most they were upset because the domestic tranquillity had been shattered, rather than because justice was not being done.[3]

Another twenty years later, it was possible for Jennifer Hochschild to argue that, in effect, Silverman was closer to the truth than Myrdal—racial discrimination existed because there was a symbiotic relationship between it and the perceived needs of whites.[4] In other words, whites believed themselves to benefit from the existence of a despised Other.

In 1992, it was still plausible for Andrew Hacker to conclude that the warning of the Kerner Commission of 1968 was correct. We are, Hacker proclaims in the title of his study, *Two Nations: Black and White, Separate, Hostile, and Unequal*.[5] Nor are these insights new. Hacker is able to trace the genealogy of his position to the characteristically prescient warnings of Alexis de Tocqueville in his classic *Democracy in America*.[6]

It is true that one can document social and economic progress on the part of American blacks. But in spite of forty years of Supreme Court decisions, in spite of the achievements of the civil rights movement, in spite of a spate of government programs, even in spite of the emergence of a significant black middle class, the problem of race continues to gnaw at the vitals of American society.

Many explanations have been advanced for the tragedy of American race relations, but before turning directly to them, we should consider at least a part of the wide range of reactions of blacks to the conditions that beset them. America has always been a polyglot nation, especially since the middle of the nineteenth century, but blacks have not followed—or maybe one should say, have not been allowed to follow—the usual pattern of ethnic assimilation.[7] Perhaps the most profound of black thinkers was W.E.B. Du Bois. The Negro, he told us in 1903, was

> born with a veil, and gifted with second-sight in this American world, a world which yields him no true self-consciousness, but only lets him see himself through the revelation of the other world. It is a peculiar sensation, this double consciousness, this sense of always looking at one's self through the eyes of oth-

ers. . . . One ever feels his two-ness,—an American, a Negro; two souls, two thoughts, two unreconciled strivings; two warring ideals in one dark body, whose dogged strength keeps it from being torn asunder.

The history of the American Negro, Du Bois went on, was the history of this strife. The Negro wanted neither to Africanize America nor to bleach his skin. "He simply wishes to make it possible for a man to be both a Negro and an American without being cursed and spit upon by his fellows, without having the doors of Opportunity closed roughly in his face. This, then, is the end of his striving: to be a co-worker in the kingdom of culture, to escape both death and isolation."[8]

This double consciousness could lead in at least two directions. Du Bois, at that stage of his long career, clearly hoped for what we today might call a multicultural fusion, an acceptance of blacks into American culture that would not require a denial of African ancestry, or in other terms, an integration on the basis of a meaningful equality. The alternative was a move toward some form of black nationalism. At their core, those are questions of identity; they have been of deep concern to countless black intellectuals.

To make that statement opens up complex psychological questions that can only be touched on briefly. Arguably, blacks have experienced a prolonged "identity crisis," to borrow Erik Erikson's well-known term. The problem is a persistent one in much black literature. In his great novel, *Invisible Man*, Ralph Ellison made the seemingly paradoxical claim that although the Negro, by reason of his color, stood out in American society, he was invisible in the sense that he was unseen as a person, that, as many others had noted, he existed in the minds of whites largely as a "problem."

The early essays of James Baldwin also explored this territory with rare sensitivity and eloquence.[9] Leaving aside his often murky psychosexual theorizing, Baldwin's thinking was rich with historical, sociological, and personal insight.[10] Early on, he took himself, like so many other American writers, into exile in France, only to discover that

> I was a kind of bastard in the west; when I followed the line of my past I did not find myself in Europe but in Africa. [The creations of European civilization] were not my creations, they did not contain my history. . . . I was an interloper; this was not my heritage. At the same time I had no other heritage which I could hope to use—I had certainly been unfitted for the jungle or the tribe. I would have to appropriate these white centuries, I would have to make them mine.

And, Baldwin went on, he had to face what he had, like all other Negroes, hidden from himself, the fact that he "hated and feared white people."[11]

But the duality is more complex than that. Black intellectuals came to accept their "hybrid" status and to forge an identity out of the extremity of their situation. For Baldwin the moment of self-discovery came during his European exile. To his surprise, he discovered that white Americans were no more at home in Europe than he, for the simple reason that both were Americans and therefore set apart from Europe by a common background. At the same time he came to see that color "operates to hide the graver questions of the self."[12] America, then, was so enmeshed in questions of race that they went to the very core of what it meant to be an American.

Since the days of slavery, the identity of many whites has been defined in relation to a black Other. In effect, what Baldwin did was to rediscover the Hegelian Master/Slave relationship I alluded to in my discussion of the theory of slavery. If Baldwin was right and whites do, in significant numbers, define themselves in contrast to blacks, then the social and political implications are potentially immense. In Baldwin's view, "Our dehumanization of the Negro then is indivisible from our dehumanization of ourselves; the loss of our own identity is the price we pay for the annulment of his." He went on, "This creates an impossible, a fruitless tension between the traditional master and slave."[13] "Walk through the streets of Harlem and see what we, this nation, have become."[14]

Division by color was useless and obsolescent, said Baldwin. America was the country best placed to see this, but it had failed to seize the opportunity. If Americans could bring themselves to see that they were barely a white nation and accepted themselves as what they were, then they might bring new life to the achievements of the West. "The price of this transformation is the unconditional freedom of the Negro." As Baldwin wrote in an open letter to his nephew, "You and I know that the country is celebrating one hundred years of freedom one hundred years too soon. We cannot be free until they are free."[15]

On a theoretical level, this seems to point clearly in the direction of liberal principles of universal equality. In *Notes of a Native Son,* Baldwin wrote, "I don't like people who like me because I'm a Negro; neither do I like people who find in the same accident grounds for contempt." And in another of the essays, "The black man insists, by whatever means he finds at his disposal, that the white man cease to regard him as an exotic rarity and recognize him as a human being."[16]

But things are not so simple as these statements suggest. And whatever the principles involved, Baldwin had little respect for white liberals, who were guilty of "incredible, abysmal, and really cowardly obtuseness." Typically, they could see blacks only as symbols or victims, but never as men.[17] White liberals lacked authenticity; they were not sincere.

Baldwin saw the situation as desperate: "A bill is coming that I fear America is not prepared to pay."[18] Things were so grim that they forced

Baldwin to raise a question that shook white liberals to the core: "Do I really *want* to be integrated into a burning house?"[19] And the available alternatives seemed stark. "At one pole," he wrote, "there is the Negro student movement. This movement, I believe, will prove to be the very last attempt made by American Negroes to achieve acceptance in the republic, to force the country to honor its own ideals." At the other pole was the separatist ideology of the Black Muslims, today more commonly known as the Nation of Islam.[20]

The black student movement made fantastic demands on its followers. Led by Martin Luther King, Jr., and steeped in the theory of nonviolence derived from Thoreau, Tolstoy, and Gandhi, these young people were asked not only to abstain from physical retaliation when attacked but even to refuse to hate the attacker.[21] As Baldwin wrote: "The student movement depends, at bottom, on an act of faith, an ability to see, beneath the cruelty and hysteria and apathy of white people, their bafflement and pain and essential decency. This is superbly difficult. It demands a perpetually cultivated spiritual resilience, for the bulk of the evidence contradicts the vision." But it was the Muslims, Baldwin thought, who seemed to have the evidence on their side.[22]

King's movement was deeply rooted in the universalist principles of the liberal theory of rights. He asked, in effect, what Lincoln had asked—the reenactment of the Declaration of Independence. That partly accounts for the resonance of the civil rights movement, not only among liberal reformers, but in much of the nation. The principles at stake were too deeply ingrained in America to be denied with any degree of intellectual respectability, though, of course, the gap between rhetoric and practice remained large. Voting rights and equal access to public places, nevertheless, were ideas whose time had to come—once they were pressed by a serious political movement, especially one so gratifyingly nonthreatening in its deep commitment to abstention from violence. The passage of the Voting Rights Act of 1965 was perhaps the high point of principled liberalism in the twentieth century.

But King's primary base of support, which was in the moderate, southern, black middle class, was rooted in a demand for the most elemental rights, which were hard to deny without the most transparent hypocrisy. As the campaign spread to the North, it began to collide with the intractable realities of the urban ghettos. Those realities could not be addressed by legislation to reverse the overt denial of civil rights that legalized segregation had fostered. As George Fredrickson remarked, nonviolent protest could easily be seen by ghetto blacks as a way of making white liberals feel comfortable; it was to those ghetto blacks that Malcolm X gave voice.[23] Surely this concern for the opinion of whites is what fed Baldwin's animosity, as a resident of Harlem, to what he saw as the weakness of those same liberals. And it was that tension between liberal theory and liberal practice that created the tremendous conflict in his mind between his universalist ideals and the racial particularity and separatism of Malcolm X and the Black Muslims—the conflict that gave *The Fire Next Time* much of its power. Fredrickson said of Malcolm, "In exposing whites to the real feelings of many blacks he revealed the dimensions of the American racial problem to an extent that the King of the early 1960s was unable to do."[24] But it was probably Baldwin, because of his easy access to the liberal journals of opinion, who shook white intellectuals first. For many of them, it was Baldwin who introduced the world of black separatist thought.

The Autobiography of Malcolm X was the saga of the pimp, street hustler, and common criminal who gave up his ways when he discovered the teachings of Elijah Muhammad's Black Muslim movement. Malcolm's early position was rooted in an ideology that can only be called racist. A basic Muslim teaching was that whites were "devils," that white society was beyond redemption, and that separation of the races was the only way out. (Today, of course, the antiwhite sentiments have often taken on a deeply anti-Semitic overtone.) Separation, however, according to the Black Muslims, had to be accompanied by giving up crime, alcohol, drugs, and developing a set of behaviors that had an eerie similarity to the ascetic discipline of the Puritan communities of the seventeenth century. Oddly, the program was a segregationist's dream; in fact, George Lincoln Rockwell, the leader of the American Nazi Party, was said to have expressed his approval.[25] But at the same time, the Muslims, with their emphasis on character, which sounds so much like the contemporary conservative emphasis on the importance of behavioral change as an antidote to the social pathologies of the ghetto, were able, as Baldwin observed, to accomplish

> what generations of welfare workers and committees and resolutions and reports and housing projects and playgrounds have failed to do: to heal and redeem drunkards and junkies, to convert people who have come out of prison and to keep them out, to make men chaste and women virtuous, and to invest both the male and the female with a pride and a serenity that hang about them like an unfailing light.[26]

The attractions as well as the problems were obvious. The social achievements were indeed impressive, but the idea of black nationalism all too easily slid into a fantasy world. Baldwin understood that: "The glorification of one race and the consequent debasement of another—or others—always has been and always will be a recipe for murder."[27]

But in the conflict between Martin Luther King and Malcolm X, the more immediately practical issue was their disagreement over violence as a weapon of protest. To the end, King rejected violence, whereas Malcolm was prepared to endorse it, at least as a matter of self-defense.[28] These stark alternatives still remain in the minds of some black leaders.[29]

Yet, in certain ways, as they neared their untimely deaths, King and Malcolm did move somewhat closer together. King was responding to the sheer intractability of the problems of the ghetto, and Malcolm was softening in his attitude toward whites after his break with Elijah Muhammad and his embrace of orthodox Islam. King began to make concessions, not so much to black nationalism, as to some form of the emerging ideology of "black power." This idea sounded menacing to many whites—and perhaps was in certain of its forms—but it entailed a recognition of the fact that to compete successfully in American group politics, it was necessary to organize and achieve a degree of cohesion.[30] As conservative political theorist Herbert Storing suggested, there was tension built into the idea: "Revolutionary rejection of America and conventional ethnic politics—as American as apple pie—can both be found here." The shift from Malcolm's rhetoric of black nationalism to that of black power was, as he said, worth noting.[31] It opened up the possibility of working within the system, though it was a system transformed by the newly found power of blacks.

The extent to which the politics of race can be discussed in terms of ideas laid out in the 1960s is distressing because it indicates how much remains to be done and also because so few significant black leaders have arisen to replace the murdered Martin Luther King and Malcolm X. King seems to have receded into the background as a force in the black communities, and Malcolm is as much a figure of myth as a reality.

King has had no real successor. At the time of his death he was moving in an increasingly radical direction—if we define radicalism in the American context. He had come increasingly to believe that his struggle was not only for basic civil rights. He felt that it had to be associated with the movement against the Vietnam War and that it was necessary to make an assault on urban poverty as well as employment and housing discrimination. In brief, he was beginning to turn into a militant social democrat.[32]

On that score, King's most notable successor is University of Chicago sociologist William Julius Wilson. A number of years ago, Wilson won notoriety and no little argument with a book titled *The Declining Significance of Race*.[33] He does not say that race was an insignificant factor, but rather that social class is also an important part of the dilemma of U.S. race relations. He notes the emergence of a black middle class as well as the growth of an urban underclass.[34] Some have argued that this position worked to the advantage of conservatives, but that was not Wilson's intent. Instead, the theme of his more recent book, *The Truly Disadvantaged*, is that the change of the American worker from industrial to service occupations has been detrimental to blacks.[35] In a defense of his work, Wilson has spelled out the policy implications of his position:

> Any significant reduction of the problem of joblessness and related social dislocations in the inner-city ghetto will call for a far more comprehensive program of economic and social reform than what Americans have usually regarded as appropriate or desireable. . . . I therefore proposed a liberal-left social democratic policy agenda that highlights macroeconomic policies to promote more balanced economic growth and create a tight labor market, public sector employment programs for those who have difficulty finding jobs in the private sector, manpower training and education programs, a child support assurance program, a child-care strategy, and a family allowance program.[36]

The great advantage is that much of Wilson's program can be race-neutral. The U.S. economy is unhealthy, and many whites are disadvantaged by that too, though by no means in the same proportions as blacks. This program therefore has the merit of appealing to the mutual interests of both blacks and whites, and at the same time having the theoretical advantage of drawing implicitly on universal norms deeply rooted in American liberal culture.[37]

But this is not an age dominated by the memory of Martin Luther King, and race-conscious remedies are still with us and are probably necessary. Affirmative action programs are the leading example of such remedies; given the long history of discrimination against women and racial minorities, they still have a role to play, particularly if the fine distinction between affirmative action and a quota system can be maintained. That is not easy, even though it was the original intent of the relevant legislation, because once there is a commitment to make positive efforts to recruit the disadvantaged, there is also a powerful temptation to demand measurable results. Of course, in a just society, quotas would be unjust on their face.[38] But in a society that is manifestly not just, the problem is much more difficult. The very idea of quotas strains against the principles of the system, but a white male must be terribly clear that he has never benefited from discrimination before he can oppose any and all affirmative action or quota programs.[39]

At the same time, a number of people who are now viewed as conservatives because of their opposition to affirmative action, such as sociologist Nathan Glazer, started out as liberal activists fighting for civil liberties in a color-blind society. To them, many of whom are Jewish and remember when quotas were devices for exclusion rather than inclusion, affirmative action is really just another form of discrimination, however well meaning in intent. A deviation from the intent of the Civil Rights Act, affirmative action began in the early 1970s.[40] The difficulties are numerous.

The problems affirmative action was designed to deal with have been only marginally affected. Moreover, benefits for nonwhites have come at the cost of increased tensions with whites. Not surprisingly, conservatives have attacked the programs. In addition to Glazer, prominent conservative political theorist Harvey Mansfield has articulated some interesting ideas. He concedes that affirmative action programs have some advantages: There is revenge, his rather unkind label for the attempt to make up for the unquestioned historical wrongs done to blacks; there is the opportunity for blacks to learn on the job, even if they are not very well qualified; and, perhaps most important, there is the chance for blacks to earn respect by having their share of good jobs. "When blacks are respected, America can then respect itself and no longer suffer guilt for the American dilemma. The gap between America's ideals and the American reality is essentially revealed in its treatment of blacks."[41]

But for Mansfield, the disadvantages easily outweigh the advantages. The programs are contradictory, he says, because they assert both that blacks are equal and that they need special help because they are unequal. Mansfield's argument is clever but not very convincing: It collapses two senses of equality into one; clearly it is possible to say that blacks are, or should be, equal before the law and in their human dignity, while at the same time saying that they are unequal in the distribution of social goods. The real problem, then, is whether we can or should guarantee equality of result as well as equality of opportunity. That is a question for serious debate.

Second, Mansfield argues, accusations of racism, particularly institutional racism, tend to become routine and run the risk of offending Americans who are not racist, which can only generate further racial tension. "It [affirmative action] wants to make us less conscious of race by the route of making us more conscious. On the face of it, to reach that goal by this route is not likely."

Third, affirmative action tends to make blacks irresponsible by making them blame others for their problems. It is condescending to give excuses to blacks, says Mansfield, and they have to learn to fend for themselves. The real practical problem is that affirmative action "makes blacks conspicuously dependent on the rest of America by becoming dependent on government."[42]

However, the deepest theoretical issue is that affirmative action has been advanced as a matter of justice, when the real problem should be seen as a matter of pride. But justice, says Mansfield, should not be the only consideration. The real question is "whether it is good for blacks and other beneficiaries of affirmative action to regard themselves and to be regarded as victims."[43] An interesting point, particularly if seen in the context of the dependency argument. But one does not have to be on the right politically to lament dependency and the decline of an active citizenry that may accompany it. And in fact, justice is at issue, since no one can really dispute that blacks have historically been the victims of injustice. Further, Mansfield makes a striking admission that seriously undercuts his own arguments.

Blacks do have a significant contribution to make, he tells us: "They have been the victims of democratic injustice and have seen freedom from underneath, and in consequence they know what most other Americans can hardly imagine, that democratic majorities can do terrible wrong. This is a valuable gift for a free people."[44] Yes indeed, but the teachers of this lesson have paid a heavy price to be in a position to educate the rest of us, which suggests that justice as well as pride is very much at stake.

Arguments like Mansfield's have also been made by a significant number of black intellectual leaders, and they cannot be easily dismissed. The contentions are similar and need not be rehearsed at length. Some of those intellectuals accept the label *conservative*; others do not. One who did was political economist Glenn Loury. Loury focused on the relative success of the civil rights movement in laying the legal foundation for a society that could square the promise of American constitutionalism with the practice. To him, "the moral victory of the civil rights movement is virtually complete." And constitutionally, he believed, the movement was a complete success.[45] The new American dilemma was what to do about the urban underclass described by Wilson. Given the dimensions of this problem, the state of the law, and the failure of special actions on behalf of blacks, Loury concluded that problems had to lie elsewhere than in discrimination. Blacks had to learn that equality of opportunity did not guarantee equality of result. What was at stake was a matter of character, what Mansfield would call pride.[46] To succeed, blacks would have to adopt the character and work habits of the white middle class.

Yale law professor Stephen Carter is also skeptical of affirmative action, largely on the basis of what is essentially the pride argument, though he admits without shame that he is a beneficiary of affirmative action. However, unlike Loury, he refuses the conservative label: He says that it is oversimplified and fails to recognize his support for other civil rights programs generally opposed by conservatives and that he believes the conservative movement has become a haven for racists.[47] Shelby Steele also denies being a conservative but, nevertheless, echoing Martin Luther King, focuses on issues of character rather than color.[48]

These arguments have their appeal, but the positions of Loury and Steele are also troubling. They are too sanguine about the triumph of equality before the law; one should consider, for example, the well-known discriminatory pattern in the administration of the death penalty. There is real progress in the development of legal remedies, but surely no legal utopia.[49] More disturbing still is the absence of an economic context. Without that, the emphasis on character alone, admirable though it may be, looks too much like a bootstrap stunt. It would be good if inner-city blacks developed better work habits, stayed away from drugs, stayed in school, and had many fewer teenage pregnancies. (The same can be said of suburban white children.) But it would also be good if ghetto schools were better, if there were more jobs for black teenagers, and, in general, if Wilson's action program were adopted. It seems likely that the two developments, if they occur at all, would occur hand in hand; that is, it seems likely there would be a reciprocal relation between good work habits and the probability of finding a good job.[50]

These arguments also tell us something about the black conservative minority within a minority.[51] The first thing to notice is the shift in the terms of discourse that defined conservative and liberal. Some black conservatives, such as Thomas Sowell, are true blue, free market, Chicago school types, which is to say that they are nineteenth-century economic liberals. They believe in the virtues of competitive individualism governed by the natural laws of Adam Smith's invisible hand. Others are unreconstructed 1950s liberals dedicated to a color-blind society, that is, to the values of universalist liberal equality. Many, like Carter and Steele, simply do not fill the established ideological categories into which black liberals were supposed to fit. (It should be added that according to survey evidence, often the black rank and file have been more conventionally conservative than their intellectual and political leaders.)[52]

But the classic values of liberal rights theory, with all their strengths and weaknesses, are not at the heart of current discussion in the black community. Martin Luther King, to repeat, does not cut much of a figure, and Malcolm X has become, in death, the focus of attention—a myth as much as a man. Not only that, he has become a marketable commodity.[53] That is not all, of course. Myths and symbols are important, and as Cornell West suggested, Malcolm provides an outlet for black rage. The rage is not hard to understand; the question is its social and political usefulness.

The emergence of Malcolm seems to be a response to the deficiencies of contemporary black leadership; it is also related to a deepening concern with the problem of black identity and its relation to American political culture as a whole. Adolphe Reed speculates that it was the decline of Jesse Jackson as a political force that allowed Malcolm to emerge to fill the gap, just as Jackson, without conspicuous success, had attempted to fill the void left by the death of Martin Luther King. But, Reed points out, harshly but accurately, King and Malcolm had the great advantage, as icons, that they were dead and thus could literally do no wrong.[54] Thus, Malcolm can exist as almost a pure symbol who can be made to represent whatever his followers wish.

It is also important that Malcolm was a product of the underclass, the plight of which became more conspicuous during the Reagan-Bush years, which were qualitatively different from the Nixon era in their utter lack of interest in the problems of the urban poor.[55] But, as Reed says, "not even the growing threat of the Reagan/Bush assault on black Americans could rekindle an assertive, popular political movement." Instead we have seen the rise of cultural politics: "This discourse avoids the problem of black demobilization by redefining the sphere of political action to settle on everyday practices of self-presentation and popular cultural expression."[56]

For anyone who understands that the idea of the melting pot is a myth in the sense that even well-assimilated groups often maintain a sense of collective identity, this focus on cultural politics is not necessarily a bad sign. Racial and ethnic groups have every reason to be proud of their cultural heritage; the rich variety of American hyphenates can be an antidote to the enormous pressures toward homogenization that are so great a force in the culture. Besides, Stokely Carmichael and Charles Hamilton were probably right to argue in *Black Power* that some degree of racial unity was a prerequisite to successful participation in interest group politics. That kind of politics may be distasteful and is in desperate need of reform, but in a sense, it is the only game in town. Those who cannot play at all are likely to receive short shrift when the distribution of social goods is made.

But too often, cultural politics, or identity politics, as it is sometimes called, has frequently not been aimed at the political arena; instead it has been an escape from politics or from the intractable realities of a grim existence.[57] Some of the manifestations are deeply worrying; others are merely annoying; and still others may be genuine puzzles. Whatever hope blacks maintain for a separate cultural identity, reports that some young blacks consider it a mark of "acting white" to study hard, use the library, or speak standard English are very disturbing. This, I think, is a manifestation of what Cornell West refers to when he writes of the nihilism rampant in the ghetto: "*the lived experience of coping with a life of horrifying meaninglessness, hopelessness, and (most important) lovelessness.*"[58] One of the prerequisites of liberation from the underclass is entry into the economy, and the key to that is precisely the skills being rejected in what can only seem a cry of despair.

The sometimes zany claims for Afrocentricity that call for a wholesale rewriting of world history are largely on the order of an annoyance, though one that must be debated if it threatens the quality of education. All such nationalist movements are likely to produce some quackery. It is important, however, to keep our eyes fixed on the more important issues. At the same time, to the extent that such exaggerated claims intensify already existing racial divisions or divert us from the deeper problems, they cannot simply be shrugged off.[59]

Questions sometimes arise when the members of a group begin to debate what the "real" racial or ethnic identity requires. But the very idea that one's cultural identity "requires" anything at all is an affront to some. Thus the always iconoclastic Julius Lester says, "Having been involved in the civil rights movement, I didn't fight against whites trying to limit and define me to turn around and have blacks try to limit and define me."[60] But this seems to be precisely what much of the cultural debate is about. It reached a symbolic climax of sorts during the confrontation between Clarence Thomas and Anita Hill at the time of the confirmation hearings after Thomas's nomination to the Supreme Court. I have no particular interest here in who was telling the truth; I am more concerned with the way the issue was turned into a debate over who spoke for blacks—who was "typical"?

To put the question in this way reveals its absurdity. Of course neither was, and Julius Lester's point was borne out. One had only to look at the parade of black witnesses on both sides to see the fact that the idea of a single, representative "black" borders on the ridiculous. More generally, the search itself maintains the age-old pattern of stereotypical thinking. In fact, as the work of Orlando Patterson, the great comparative sociologist of slavery, shows, there has been great diversity among blacks, going back to slave times, and the underclass, the middle-class, and the working-class blacks all have their ancestors in the slave system. Patterson goes on to say that it is the silent, working-class blacks, a plurality of the black population, that are neglected and badly need attention. The black community is complex, not simple, and has to be thought of as such.[61]

As Cornell West says, the urge to simplify and reduce all the complexities of existence to race, making it the sole determinant of politics, illustrates the peril of race thinking. Even for a group that had suffered the most severe discrimination, the tendency of black leaders to line up behind Clarence Thomas and ignore the obvious fact that he was an unqualified token signaled, in West's view, a crisis, a failure of nerve.[62]

In deliberately oversimplified terms, the issue comes down to whether blacks should be treated as equals operating under a color-blind constitution, as the leaders of the civil rights revolution had argued, or whether racial difference and the undoubted discrimination associated with it must be taken explicitly into account to achieve the goal of equal treatment under law.

The answer cannot be as simple as the question. Moreover, since this is not a public policy study, I have no formula to offer. Some special treatment will no doubt be necessary, but in the context of a basically liberal culture, policies that aim at a universal egalitarianism are more consistent with the putatively "shared values" of the society than is special treatment. Egalitarian policies are also more likely to win support from other racial and ethnic groups that have their own problems to cope with and—rightly or wrongly—see programs aimed at blacks as a form of reverse discrimination. Policies that stress the distinctiveness of a racial group fly in the face of the individualistic heritage of the liberal tradition in America. To the extent that they prevail, they represent a significant deviation from the pattern discerned by Louis Hartz in his analysis of that tradition. Given the existing hostilities, it is extremely difficult to come up with a politics that reaches across racial lines in universalist terms. But such a politics is theoretically justifiable and has the best chance, even if slim, to succeed. This is where rights-based, social democratic liberalism appears in its best light.

The Feminist Challenge to Liberalism

Since Betty Friedan published *The Feminine Mystique* in 1963, a vast and often impressive body of feminist theory has appeared. It is impossible to begin to cover all its variety here, so I will limit myself to a discussion of the relation of these theories to the liberal tradition. I hope also to show that the problems that concern the women's movement are theoretically analogous to those involving race. Therefore, although I do not deny the importance of much feminist thought or the claims of the women's movement, I will discuss them more briefly than I did the race-related issues.[63]

From the start, liberalism has been near the center of American feminism, either as an intellectual force or, sometimes, as an object for attack. The central demand was for women to be treated as free and equal to men, which, of course, had allowed the movement and its thinkers to draw heavily on the liberal tradition, with its language of universal human rights. But fairly quickly, the rhetorical advantages of liberalism seemed to some to be a mask for the various forms of male privilege. The result was that there were many feminist doctrines, so many that one leading feminist thinker concluded that feminism was an essentially contested concept, that is, not only was there no general agreement on its meaning but in principle there could be no such agreement.[64]

In the face of this, Sondra Farganis has developed an ideal type, sketching the general outlines of the feminist position as she sees it.

> By feminism, I mean an ideology or belief system, an integrated set of theoretical assumptions that taken together structure a world-view which its adherents take to be true. It is grounded in a moral premise that assumes the injustice of treating men and women inequitably. Women are now seen to be oppressed by men through long-standing historical structural arrangements that initiate, support and legitimate that oppression (patriarchy). The objective of feminism is

to constitute itself as a political movement to undo this gendered domination. While the movement need not be governed by a spiteful hostility towards men, and could constitute itself as a vanguard for the improvement of human relationships, its governing animus is grounded in a valuation of gender differentiation that has power implications.[65]

This is a valuable analytical device, though my own reading of feminist literature has suggested that there might be significant dissent from some aspects of it. It is also by no means clear that Farganis herself subscribes to it. No feminist would deny the existence of significant inequalities in the treatment of men and women, and the emergence of gender as a concept is of major importance. No longer is gender a mere synonym for one's sex. Instead, gender is a social category that refers to the "*deeply entrenched institutionalization of sexual difference.*" Gendered relationships, thus defined, are widely said to permeate our society.[66] However, *domination* is a very strong term that might not be accepted by all feminists, nor, I think, would all accept the vanguardist implications of the model. Nevertheless, few would deny the world would be a better place for all if most feminist reforms were widely accepted. A few feminists do seem to be governed by a spiteful hostility to men, though I think they too are in a minority. There are also signs that some feminists would like to see the establishment of a "party line," which would define membership. That "party line" would probably look something like the Farganis model.[67]

Since the mid-1960s, there have been significant changes in emphasis in feminist theory. The opening wave of feminism in the 1960s was in the tradition of rights-based, individualist liberalism. It was, in fact, partly a dissident outgrowth of the civil rights movement, one that emerged when the young women in the movement began to perceive the subordinate position they occupied in what was ostensibly a crusade for equal rights.[68] But almost simultaneously, the women's movement began to erode its liberal foundations. The new slogan, The personal is political, implied a critique of the traditional liberal separation between the public and the private and of the liberal claim to a universalism that was really particular, a theory about men but masquerading as a theory about all human beings.[69] In this view, what appeared in John Locke to be an attack on patriarchy was in fact undermined almost immediately by women's being restored to a place in the private sphere so they would be excluded from participating in the activities of the public sphere. Even liberals distinguished between public man and private woman in spite of the sweeping vocabulary that suggested "the people" constituted a universal category; for Locke, the subordination of women was "natural" simply because men were stronger.[70]

A tension thus emerged between the commitment to a potentially radical liberal claim to individual rights and the performance of liberalism in theory and practice. As Anne Philips asks, given the natural affinity of liberalism and feminism, how did liberalism "end up so badly"?[71] (I assume for the moment that it did end up badly.) Not only have women been relegated to the private sphere, but the unique contribution that women are said to be able to make to the public sphere has been stifled.[72] And the construction of a private sphere for the family is potentially dangerous. It is one thing to wall off an area into which the arm of the state might not reach—the idea encapsulated in the slogan that a man's home is his castle—but quite another to use this valuable concept to protect wife beaters and child abusers.

And yet there is a significant downside to the equation of personal with political affairs. Jean Elshtain's argument on this point is of particular value, since she herself is critical of liberalism. As she says, the claim is not that the personal and the political are related in interesting ways previously obscured from us by a smoke screen of sexist ideas nor that personal and political concerns may be analogous. Instead, there is an equation—the personal *is* political. There is a "collapse of the one into the other." The private sphere is completely politicized; we are left with nothing but a set of power relations.[73]

But the obliteration of the public/private distinction has always been a goal of authoritarian movements, and the radical wing of feminism has not been immune to that charge. The early radical feminists such as Susan Brownmiller saw the male drive for power as a product of biology; Brownmiller's answer was to respond in kind, to learn to fight dirty. As Elshtain says, Brownmiller's answer to the male lust for power was simply to invert it—her argument had a machismo cast: It featured "raw power, brute force, martial discipline, uniforms, militaristic law and order with a feminist face."[74] But whatever the limits of liberalism may be, feminist fascism is not the way out. It is this sort of thinking that puts off not only many men but also, I would speculate, many women who might otherwise be feminists but who cannot share in the hostilities of a Susan Brownmiller or the other radicals of the movement of the 1970s, or for that matter of more recent times.[75]

Sondra Farganis sums up the feminist critique of liberalism by saying, "The feminist critique of liberalism, while appreciating the protections afforded rights, choices, and privacy, rests on four grounds: that 'individual' really means 'male individual': that it [liberalism] fails to live up to its radical potential for equitable treatment; that it obfuscates the relationship between the private and the public by speaking of them as distinct rather than intertwined spheres; and that by failing to concern itself with the concrete experiences of everyday life, it ignores certain social needs and communal responsibilities."[76]

A more recent phase of feminism has focused on the particular rather than the general, on what differentiates women from men. In psychologist Carol Gilligan's words, women speak in a different voice.[77] The claim to rights has not been abandoned, but the emphasis has shifted from the political and the economic to the needs of community. There is new concern for what is said to be a superior female capacity for care and nurturing. "As opposed to saying that men and women are equal in ability or potential, a woman-centered approach argues that men and women have different attributes and abilities but that society does not value them in the same way." The special qualities of women are then assigned a high positive value.[78]

Plainly, this is an argument that can cut more than one way, and it raises the question whether one wants to emphasize or play down gender differences. Anne Philips captures the dilemma very well. Those who stress care and nurturing are resistant to the idea that women should attempt to fit themselves into a world that was made by men for men; that world can be changed and men can adapt. At the same time, there is no need for predominantly female activities to be devalued or pushed into the background. However, there is a counterview: "Advocates of stricter equality have argued—with considerable force—that once feminists admit the mildest degree of sexual difference, they open up a gap through which the currents of reaction will flow."[79] The danger is that once difference is brought to the fore, it will be taken to be a sign of inferiority or weakness that can be exploited by those who oppose the restructuring of society that feminists demand. The risk is that the reform impulse behind feminism will be blunted and outworn stereotypes will be validated.

This problem has led to a countermove from first-wave feminists, such as Susan Moller Okin and Mary Dietz, who espouse a kind of "humanist liberalism." Drawing, somewhat paradoxically, on the work of Catharine MacKinnon, a theorist militantly opposed to liberalism, Okin concludes that few of the discriminatory patterns of behavior and institutional structure really have their roots in biological difference—they are gendered rather than sexual. The goal for such feminists is a gender-free society, a society in which social institutions, starting with the family, have to be democratized and liberalized to remove discrimination. To "feminize" politics, to try to build on the "different voice" of women, without such an ambitious reconstruction would be a fruitless undertaking. And even an antiliberal like Elizabeth Fox-Genovese states the case in what seemed to be universalist liberal language: The "delightful difference" between boys and girls "has few necessary consequences for political roles in a world of adult women and men—a world that will never realize the dreams of radical egalitarianism but that can meet the tests of equity and justice."[80]

As a case in point, consider the issue of comparable worth. Once again, Fox-Genovese is on the mark when she points out that, on average, women earn about 60 percent of what men earn. That, she says, is explained in substantial part by the tendency of women to be "segregated" into women's professions such as nursing, social work, librarianship, elementary and secondary education, and the like.[81] The idea of comparable worth goes well beyond the hardly debatable concept of equal pay for equal work. Comparable worth accepts the stereotyping of jobs according to gender and simply insists that women receive pay for "female jobs" equal to wages for comparable male jobs. Surely the work of nurses is as valuable as that of sanitation workers, though it would be a serious mistake to undervalue the work of the latter.[82] But as a society we claim to value the caring professions. Comparable worth forces us to face up to the fact that we are unwilling to pay for what we allegedly value. The job market clearly does not provide economic justice for women. As Fox-Genovese says, "The proponents of comparable worth are in effect arguing that we specifically reward those who contribute to our self-image as a moral and humane society."[83] But to intervene in the job market is to tamper with the primacy of economic liberalism in American political culture. That is a radical idea, and it needs to be taken seriously in a way that the early wave of radical feminism did not require. Such intervention could only come about through a rethinking of the relation of the economy to the general society as well as to the political system.

But once the principle of difference is admitted, then it quickly becomes apparent that there are differences among women too—all women are not exactly alike. This leads to a new emphasis on difference, closely associated with fashionable schools of postmodernism. In this view, as Okin points out, gender becomes a problematic category "unless qualified by race, class, ethnicity, religion, and other such differences."[84] Black, working-class, and lesbian feminists have demanded attention. Okin rejects that view, insisting that sex oppression is a discrete form of discrimination that exists independently of race or class; still, she admits that feminism is a movement that has been dominated by white, middle-class heterosexuals. Although otherwise disagreeing with Okin, Elizabeth Fox-Genovese also stresses the class bias of the movement, rather more strongly than Okin, in fact.[85]

But once all that has been stated, it then becomes even more clear than before that gender is not the only source of identity; important as gender undoubtedly is, human beings are infinitely complicated. As Anne Philips writes:

There is no "core" self behind all our differences, but neither is there *one* difference that essentially constitutes our self. Thus, important as sexual/bodily identity is, it is not the only or defining characteristic of a person, for what will seem to be the most essential feature will change (and should change) with the issue at stake. . . . When universality has been conceptualized that suppresses all individual and group difference, this is what needs to be changed: but not into an unmitigated celebration of "the" difference.

It is here that Philips "parts company" with the radical theorists of difference.[86]

Almost as soon as the idea of women as a unitary bloc took hold, fragmentation set in. Postmodernists are suspicious of the idea of "gender" as a form of "essentialism." In this view people do not have essences; they are socially constructed—that is, alleged essences are fabrications that all too often serve the purposes of the status quo. And surely the postmodern theorists are right to argue that there is no single female viewpoint; to use Sondra Farganis's list, there are disagreements over "reproductive technologies, abortion, pornography, sexual harassment, and the ERA." Many women remain uninterested in feminism or at least do not subscribe to the full list of typical feminist positions.[87]

The sheer variety of feminist, not to mention feminine, positions, seems logically to push the analysis back toward the level of the individual woman, her views, and her choices and hence toward liberal perceptions and arguments. That is because once the variety of characteristics covered by the category of gender is recognized, then the thought begins to emerge that women (and men) are shaped, as Philips suggests, by so many separate and distinct factors that to concentrate on only one of them does violence to social reality. However, theorists of difference might well rebel at these conclusions.

They have some good arguments on their side. The very fact that all people have views shaped by their personal circumstances suggests that there may be an important place in political theory for an emphasis on the particular, which cannot be subsumed under a form of universalism. Since Marx—or perhaps before—the liberal claim to treat all people equally has been greeted with suspicion. But although the promise of valuing all people equally may often be unfulfilled, the problem may lie more in the difficulty of meeting the goal than in liberal theory itself.[88] Surely for problems of gender as well as for problems of race, there may be justifiable reasons to violate universal norms on behalf of groups that have experienced discrimination.[89] Nevertheless, the Enlightenment ideal of respect for the personhood of all on the basis of common standards is not ignoble; it can provide a powerful standard for social criticism. That ideal has the further advantage of being deeply embedded in the American cultural fabric, even though its principles are frequently violated. Therefore, those who espouse it have certain inherent rhetorical advantages that are of real value in political debate. It is important to consider the foregoing arguments in light of current challenges to these principles by postmodernism, feminism, and multiculturalism.

Liberalism, Postmodernism, and Multiculturalism

The theoretical and sometimes tactical alliance between some forms of feminism, some of the advocates of multiculturalism, and the postmodernist movement in philosophy, literary criticism, and political theory poses a profound challenge to the theory of the liberal consensus. Philosophically, postmodernism is a repudiation of virtually all that liberalism stands for. Perhaps not since George Fitzhugh and the other members of the reactionary Enlightenment has there been a challenge of such force, though it should be said that, so far, the force has been largely confined to academic circles. The extent to which the idea can be said to reflect practice, so that we may speak of a postmodern world as well as a postmodern theory, is difficult to say. As a first approximation, we can consider what Stephen White calls the "postmodern problematic."[90]

The first point in the problematic is what French theorist Jean-François Lyotard calls the "incredulity" toward the grand "metanarratives" that have justified the scientific and political projects of the modern world. This, according to Lyotard, is not so much a new historical period as a new state of mind, though one, White says, that is widespread in the post–World War II world.[91] Because of its assumption of universality, the postmodernists reject the revival of liberal theory on the grand scale, which began with the 1971 publication of John Rawls's *A Theory of Justice*. So too they reject Marxism, the grandest of the metanarratives and the most prominent modern critique of liberalism, on the ground that it is fatally compromised by its commitment to modern technology and methods of production.[92] One might add that this critique, like postmodern feminism, raises questions about the public/private distinction that have been central to the debate between liberals and socialists; where one leaves off and the other begins in the political economy is not an easy question, but it must be faced.

A second source of postmodernist concern is the attempt to rationalize the problems of the modern political economy through the institutions of the welfare state. However well intentioned the welfare state may be, it still has a tendency to produce a group of powerless clients. But lest confusion arise, the Marxist critique, which runs along similar lines, has also been rejected by postmodernists, since it posits the possibility of a better society, a comfort they are unable to countenance.[93]

A third aspect of the postmodern problematic is an awareness that new information technology is politically ambivalent; it may foster a greater democratization of the polity by making more and better information available to the public, but it is just as likely, given the control of the media by large corporate organizations, that the result will be a powerful force working toward cultural manipulation and political control.[94]

Fourth, there is the explosion of "new social movements," which are concerned less with problems of economic distribution than with questions of identity and status. Examples include the women's movement, antinuclearism, gay rights organizations, many ethnic movements, and the lingering countercultural opposition to mainstream, middle-class life. Social theorists who want to resist the bureaucratic power of the capitalist welfare state have been powerfully drawn to these potentially disruptive forces.[95]

Moving beyond White's list, there has also been so much emphasis on the interpretation of culture that claims to truth have been undermined by the stress on the way in which social context shapes our social understanding; there is no foothold outside the system in which we live that can give us a neutral perspective.[96] We are what we think we are. It is as if there were no "reality" but rather just a set of personalized interpretations, with none of them having any warrant to be more accurate than any other.

Those are serious problems. Though it seems unlikely that Marxism will simply disappear, it was dealt a heavy blow by the demise of the Soviet Union and its satellites in Eastern Europe. However, it must be said that since Marxism is a critique of capitalism rather than a theory of socialism, it is probably premature to predict its demise—or that of socialism, for that matter; still, both are in need of extensive repair. Likewise, the apparent triumph of liberalism will no doubt be less permanent than it may appear, given the economic distress that afflicts so many capitalist economies. It is also by no means clear that contemporary political systems are capable of dealing with the multinational corporation, but again, one need not be a postmodernist to reach that conclusion.

It is also true that the welfare state is not by any means a complete success, and that the new information technologies are as full of danger as they are of promise. Moreover, the new social movements are a palpable fact of everyday politics. Finally, only the most naïve social scientists, of whom there are surprisingly many, cling to the idea that the study of politics can be a purely scientific, value-free enterprise, independent of the social context of the investigator. Once again, it is not necessary to be a postmodernist to see that.

In general then, for the postmodernists, there is a widespread sense that the world is in flux, that there are no foundations, that the ground is shifting under our feet, and that the entire world is undergoing a profound transformation with no clear end, combined with a sense that our established institutions are ill equipped to deal with the changes that are under way. But these forces have been seen and discussed for a generation or more by modernists ranging from Marxists to Weberians, to critical theorists, to liberals, to figures difficult to classify such as Daniel Bell. The question arises, What do we have to gain and to lose by adopting postmodern perspectives?

Many contemporary feminists have said a great deal is to be gained.[97] Second-stage feminism stressed differences and intimated that women had essences, whether genetically or socially determined; postmodernism pushes the idea of difference much further, rejecting essentialism by arguing that there is "no stable or consistent self," since race, class, and ethnicity shape identities in diverse ways.[98] Instead, postmodernism stresses the earlier idea that the personal is political and raises grave doubts about the possibility of any approximation of objectivity in the social sciences. The once-promising principles of Enlightenment universalism that are at the heart of liberalism are challenged on the ground that they have never been achieved, or that when they have, they have worked to the advantage of men, or that the principles are basically faulty. If such ideas were to take root, as Farganis suggests they have, they would strike at the founding principles of the American regime and raise the possibility of a systemic legitimation crisis.[99]

As should by now be obvious, liberalism is a broad umbrella term under which can be grouped movements and ideas of very different tendencies. Consequently, charges made against liberalism in general may apply, at best, only to a subdivision of liberal theory. Thus the postmodernist feminist complaint, shared generally by the communitarian critics (to be discussed later), that liberals stressed the abstract individual divorced from her social setting, is relatively easy to refute. It may apply to John Locke, though just barely, but it certainly does not apply to John Stuart Mill, or to return to the United States, to John Dewey. As Ronald Beiner, himself a critic of liberalism, says, "But of course the best versions of liberalism have never been guilty of the atomistic fallacy"; in fact, many classic liberals "were no less distressed than contemporary communitarians by the prospect of modern atomism."[100]

More troubling, because it is so widespread in academic circles, is the notion that there is no objective reality, that, as Ann Scales puts it, "feminist analysis begins with the principle that objective reality is a myth. . . . Male and female perceptions of value are not shared, and are perhaps not even perceptible to each other."[101] As I have said, there is a glimmer of truth here. We all know that objectivity is hard to achieve, that our perceptions are affected by our social conditioning, and that facts have no meaning until they are placed in an interpretive framework. These are now commonplaces of good social science. But to perceive difficulty is not to insist that the difficulties cannot be overcome, so that nothing is left but a set of personalized and ultimately indefensible beliefs. Jean Elshtain makes the point with great force:

"To go beyond the reality of perspectives to the claim that there are only perspectives, that facts themselves are arbitrary inventions and that there is only 'my reality' and 'your reality' is to embrace nonsense. And to go still further and argue that the conditions of knowledge change with a change of gender, that men and women inhabit disparate epistemological universes, is to embrace not only nonsense, but dangerous nonsense." Or as another critic, echoing Jeremy Bentham on natural rights, puts it, "Despite its initial emphasis on groups, 'perspectivism' turns out to be individualism on stilts," illustrating Tocqueville's "direst predictions."[102]

To argue that is simply to subvert the possibility of effective, or even intelligible, social and political criticism. If we all live in our own reality and thus all our interpretations or perspectives are purely subjective, then why should anyone accept anyone else's claims about the facts, the demands of justice, or the requirements of morality?[103] The foundations of postmodernism are built of sand.

As to the undoubted fact that the social environment does have an important role in shaping the individual self, there is one more significant point to be made. Farganis raises an important issue but is somewhat off the mark in her formulation of it. This is the problem of "how to value the idea of human agency without incorporating liberal notions of individualism which de-emphasize the sociality of personhood."[104] She is right to worry about the need to retain a sense of human agency, but if the argument presented here is correct, liberal individualism need not deny the social character of the self. The fact that some under the liberal umbrella—many libertarians for example—have come close to doing that does not count as a general attack on liberal thought. Liberalism is not unflawed theory: One of its occasional flaws is a lack of attention to sociality. But Enlightenment liberalism is still an enormous resource for those who care about the fate of the individual in the modern megastate. It is difficult to see how we can do without liberalism, and to use it we must gain a surer, less-stereotyped feel for a very complex body of ideas. Liberalism as commonly understood does not have all the answers, but a politics in American culture that does not draw on its strengths can be of little use as an instrument of change.

A closely related problem is how to preserve some form of the classic liberal distinction between state and society, public and private. That the distinction needs to be rethought in domestic affairs is undoubtedly true; it needs to be reconceptualized perhaps even more in the economic arena. Many, though probably not all, feminists view the public/private division as a central concern, and well they may if the above arguments are correct. However, the attack on that distinction, coupled with the critique of liberal universalism as a mere disguise for male domination, threatens to turn dissent from illegitimate authority into a general revolt against all forms of authority and leads to "the triumph of new and more sinister" forms of control.[105]

In fact, the refusal of postmodernist feminists to confront the power relations between state and economy and to offer an alternative has led to a misidentification of the enemy. If it is generally agreed that there is a connection between modernism and capitalism, then it behooves us to identify the forces behind postmodernism. Is anyone so blind, asks Elizabeth Fox-Genovese, "as not to recognize those economic forces precisely in the international conglomerates that are propelling the revolution in technology as well as tolerating, when not financing, the destruction of family, church, and every other institution that aspires to a measure of autonomy? . . . Thus," she continues, "my own candidate for the primary beneficiary of postmodernism triumphant is the new global economic order, notably the multinational corporations, the largest twenty-five of which have annual products that exceed the GNPs of the United States and Western Europe combined."[106] The recognition of this new international order and its relation to domestic politics has scarcely begun; postmodernism has been largely silent on the subject.

That failure to offer an alternative is bound up to the aimless relativism that has been characteristic of postmodern thought. Once again, it is true that we all are encumbered by our cultural biases. Let us grant for the sake of argument what many feminists insist, that the possessive individualism that affects much of American culture is somehow rooted in the male psyche. But, asks Elizabeth Fox-Genovese, are those ideas only "self-serving autobiography?" The creators of liberal theory no doubt assumed that property holders would be men, "but they did not tie their theory to that assumption." Instead, they "fashioned the political subject or individual as a category to which very different kinds of people might lay claim." It is true that they did not expect women to be added to the category. Nor, "in time and place, did they expect propertyless men or black slaves to do so. But their failures of imagination did not inherently compromise the theory to which countless people whom, in practice, it initially excluded have subsequently laid claim."[107] This judgment is striking because it came from a cultural conservative and socioeconomic radical who is sharply critical of liberal individualism. Fox-Genovese's argument suggests not that liberalism is in any way beyond criticism but rather that the basic ideas of liberal theory have an inherent flexibility that opens opportunities for reform, and further that postmodernists who have nothing to put in liberalism's place after their nihilistic attacks have little to offer politically and may well play into the hands of their enemies.

The problem of multiculturalism is even more troubling because it spills outside the hothouse of academic theory. A part of the American reality that cannot be interpreted away is the simple, indisputable fact that we are a multicultural society. That is nothing new; the question is how we respond to its current manifestations. At least in the universities, it is also true that an alliance, or marriage of convenience, exists between feminists and multiculturalists. But as so often when postmodern theory appears, there is a decided political irrelevance. A joke that has been making the rounds captures the point: "Well," said the postmodernist, "we can't change society, but at least we can capture the English Department."

But that simply circumvents a real social problem. The standard liberal model of ethnic assimilation was well depicted by the image of the melting pot. By now it has been accepted that the melting pot did not melt—at least not completely. Ethnic groups have often assimilated to U.S. political and economic institutions but at the same time have retained a marked sense of cultural particularity. As a result, American identity is amazingly complex. The United States is a nation of immigrants, of hyphenated Americans, whose identities may emphasize either side of the hyphen; sometimes they may choose to emphasize neither.[108] U.S. history is a "tale of peoples trying to be a People, a tale of diversity and plurality in search of unity."[109] It should not have escaped notice that in this book "race" has been used only in references to African-Americans, even though we are witnessing a tide of Asian and Hispanic immigration. There are, of course, serious conflicts among those groups, not just between blacks and whites. But liberal universalism, however much distorted by excess piety and however far from being an empirically accurate account, is nevertheless an important force: "Molded by the Enlightenment and forged in the Revolution, American universalism has been simultaneously a civic credo, a social vision, and a definition of nationhood."[110]

This vision has been challenged by the recent upsurge of multiculturalism. A long list of "endowment groups" has come to press a range of claims based on race, ethnicity, gender, physical condition,[111] and, one might add, sexual identity. What the groups ask is some form of public recognition of these identities. Charles Taylor writes, "The thesis is that our identity is partly shaped by recognition or its absence, often by the misrecognition of others, and so a person or group of people can suffer real damage, real distortion, if the people or society around them mirror back to them a confining or demeaning or contemptible picture of themselves." A claim to dignity is made by those who are often seen as "others."[112] No one can escape the pressures of personal and collective or cultural identity; the danger is that the politics of identity will "convert differences into otherness and otherness into scapegoats."[113]

A tension is generated here by people's claim to rights as members of specific groups in a society that has been dominated by individualistic, putatively universal liberal values. The claims are often, though perhaps not always, legitimate; the question is whether liberal thought and politics have the flexibility to do justice to them when they are. William Connolly fears that liberalism does not, that in one of its common forms, it easily slips into a form of thought that leads to a "normalization" of the individual that is hostile to genuine individuality and that tends to reduce politics to no more than a defense of rights.[114]

Although one might add that a defense of rights is not a negligible thing, other theories of the individual go further than Connolly suggests. George Kateb has tried to develop a theory of the individual who is resistant to the conformist pressures of "normalization." By no means a devotee of the New Left, Kateb nevertheless insists that the movement was not just a "lightweight response to minor and short-lived complaints." And in spite of the scorn of the student radicals for the liberal tradition, the liberation movements beginning in the 1960s that had the will to "stop being ashamed of one's arbitrary or unchosen characteristics" were rooted in rights-based individualism; there was no need to turn to the dubious arguments of the postmodernists. "Feminism, gay rights, certain racial assertions, and other social movements are faithful to the spirit of rights-based individualism, precisely because the will to end shame is more important than any further ideal aspiration."[115]

But Kateb is also aware of limits, which set the boundaries of much of the current debate:

> Democratic diversity is therefore not, in principle, infinitely permissive, nor is it in practice. . . . The point of special relevance is that if ever greater numbers of individuals stop thinking of themselves as individuals and, instead, retribalize in ethnic or other fixed-identity groups, the normal level of democratic individuality may grow weaker. The heart of rights-based individualism would also sicken. Fixed pluralism, rather than limited and temporary associations, is foreign to the culture of democracy.[116]

The best-principled defense that endowment groups have is precisely the liberalism that multiculturalists and postmodernists scorn.

Once again, a critical defender of liberalism, or one who hopes to revitalize the tradition, must face the often large shortfall between theory and practice. On one level that is politics as usual in the United States, but the stakes have been raised. Sheldon Wolin writes, "Notions of difference that emphasize ethnic, racial, religious, or gender singularity are radical extensions rather than rejections of pluralism."[117] A distinction can be made between diversity and difference. Diversity merely recognizes unlikeness and is therefore easier to incorporate into pluralist politics. Difference, in contrast, "possesses a certain inner coherence that may indicate the presence of a hard core of nonnegotiability, some element that is too intimately connected with identity to allow for easy compromise."[118]

The deepest dilemmas of pluralist liberal America are connected with difference and equality. In spite of strenuous efforts to end discrimination against women, minorities, and ethnic groups, and in spite of the fact that the large protest movements that fought for equality often were supported by citizens who were not themselves victims of discrimination or might even benefit from it, the programs designed to achieve equality were either "discontinued, severely limited, or sabotaged bureaucratically."[119] In principle, says Sheldon Wolin, "liberal pluralism grants rights that are supposed to enable differences to be expressed as diversities, and defended and hence to be recognized, right down to the smallest and most privileged element, the individual."[120]

Here Wolin appears to be describing a view that is something like a synthesis of the arguments of Charles Taylor and George Kateb, but the results of the synthesis are deeply unsettling. Liberal principles have led to a toleration of difference, but also to a belief in merit and unequal reward. The best liberalism can offer is an amelioration of the differences Higham would call endowments; thus, in theory, a society could be rendered color-blind or sex blind.[121] But the results of such efforts have been dismally unencouraging. Tocqueville was unable to imagine an inegalitarian America; today, Wolin argues, it is difficult to imagine it becoming egalitarian. Almost turning Louis Hartz on his head, Wolin observes: "Because Americans are born unequal they must now learn equality. For some, it will mean rejecting dependence and inferiority; for others it will mean rejecting superiority."[122]

Empirically it is easy to agree with Wolin and with regard not just to race and gender, but also to political power more generally. Still, it is hard, in the absence of a counterproposal, to dismiss liberalism on principle, at least on the arguments of Wolin outlined here. Instead, the massive shortcomings of ameliorative strategies testify to the magnitude of the difficulties. These difficulties are not merely the result of race and gender discrimination but are part of a more general maldistribution of political and economic power. In particular, and in spite of the repeated mantra "race, gender, and class," the last category tends to get short shrift from the currently fashionable Left that is so potent a force in academic circles.[123] Not for the first time in U.S. history there is the chance—the likelihood in fact—that natural political alliances will be aborted as race cuts across class lines. Representatives of endowment groups who stake everything on a repudiation of liberal politics and its theoretical foundations are playing a dangerous game in this particular political culture.

Often the question of multiculturalism has been posed in relation to education. The demand for recognition extends to the curriculum; sometimes it starts there, perhaps to the detriment of more immediately pressing social, political, and economic concerns. Michael Walzer offers an answer to the curricular question that may be of more general import. He says that education in politics needs to focus on the history and contemporary forms of democracy. This part of education will necessarily be "Eurocentric," since democracy as we know it is largely a European phenomenon.[124]

Thus, to be genuinely multicultural, it would be necessary to recognize the specifically Anglo-American roots of American democracy. The U.S. Constitution, rather than being the product of a long evolution, as in England, was constructed, but it was made out of the material of an ethnic tradition. Unlike the French, the Framers did not claim to work from first principles that transcended particularism and approached universality. However, they did intend that the principles be more than ethnic and have implications for other nations. Thus, John Burt points out, the Constitution was not intended to be an ethnic property, but rather "the origin of a new kind of ethnicity in which political values stand in place of cultural traditions." And beyond that, "only the United States presents itself as a *culture*— as opposed to a state—which can be joined as an act of will, and only the United States would be ashamed of its failure to be such a culture."[125] This shame can cut very deep, both among new immigrants about to be assimilated and by the hegemonic culture when it takes its ideals seriously.

Clearly, will is a property of the individual. Burt's powerful argument underlines the extent to which U.S. constitutional forms and political culture are permeated by liberal individualism. It is true that there are other traditions, such as civic republicanism and Puritanism, that we must take into account, and it is also true that there are darker currents of racism, nativism, and misogyny running below the surface and indeed coming into full view with dismaying frequency. But the "official" shared beliefs on which the polity, if not the culture, rests are by now primarily liberal and individualist. The result is that those who argue on behalf of endowment groups rather than individuals fly in the face of deeply embedded patterns of thought. This by no means necessarily invalidates such arguments, but it does greatly increase the political problems of those who make them. That can be seen even if, for the sake of argument, we agree that the appeal to tradition is often largely hypocritical. However, even hypocrisy does not by itself invalidate the liberal arguments. They give force to the position of those like William Julius Wilson who push for race-neutral social programs as a partial antidote to the problems of the urban ghettos. Finally, it is dangerous for those who criticize the deficiencies of American democracy to indulge in charges of Eurocentrism when it is clear that democracy might well not exist anywhere without the example of European ideas and institutions.[126]

A second point on multiculturalism is also important. We need to tell the rich and complex story of the contributions of a huge range of races, ethnic groups, and religions to American culture, as well as to give due weight to the place of women in that history. But as Walzer writes, the history must be honest: "The story that needs telling is not only about how different ethnic and religious cultures are in fact *different* but also about how they have been commonly transformed by their new American home—Americanized without being melted down or assimilated."[127]

But the call for honesty leads to some very tricky problems. As Canadian philosopher Charles Taylor has argued, a culture has a right to be recognized, to be taken seriously and not just to be dismissed because it diverges from the mainstream of a society. But it cannot demand as a matter of right a favorable final judgment. Such a judgment threatens to be not only condescending but also ethnocentric, unless the judge has immersed himself in long study of the minority. Then his evaluation will not merely be a form of congratulation for being like the mainstream.[128] And as many have pointed out, the demand for recognition in the curriculum, regardless of quality, is an assertion of power rather than a defensible scholarly or literary judgment.

This debate over education has important implications for the larger culture. Whether it is a strength or a weakness, an individualistic orientation has characterized that culture, so claims made on the basis of group identity are inevitably a source of tension and disturbance that pose a challenge to the theory that the United States is a liberal society. That is especially true where liberal principles of freedom of speech are at stake. At this juncture, basic civil rights to equality and free speech appear, tragically, to be on a collision course, or so we have been told by feminist legal theorist Catharine MacKinnon, though she by no means perceives this conflict as a tragedy.[129]

MacKinnon's long crusade against sexual harassment and pornography has taken a new twist, providing much of the theoretical underpinning of a new challenge to First Amendment freedoms. What is involved is a massive extension of the "harm principle" developed by John Stuart Mill in his great essay *On Liberty.* When Mill argued that the sole justification for interference with the freedom of individuals was to prevent harm to others, he surely intended the principle to apply to physical harm. The harm principle is notoriously ambiguous, but in the context of Mill's larger argument on free speech, he surely did not intend to include a category of "words that wound."[130]

But to construct such a category is the goal of many feminist, racial, and ethnic leaders. In her analysis of pornography, MacKinnon completely obliterates any distinction between an act and a representation of an act. "Social inequality," she writes, "is substantially created and enforced—that is, *done*— through words and pictures."[131] Thus inequality becomes the issue, and free speech, rather than being in a preferred constitutional position, is subordinated. But racial and gender discrimination are real phenomena; they are not by any stretch of the imagination a product of mere words. If they were, we could easily make them disappear by verbal sleight of hand, by declaring, for example, that poverty is beautiful.[132] Obviously this will not do.

MacKinnon and the critical race theorists, such as Mari Matsuda and her colleagues, are on very dangerous ground. They operate on the basis of the best humanitarian motives; they wish to end racial, ethnic, and gender discrimination and degradation. But in the event, the means may easily subvert the ends. Hate speech, for example, is obviously repugnant and offensive. But simple epithets, though painful, are relatively easy to dismiss. What of more complex messages of racial inferiority couched in social science jargon that would not be actionable, but that might be much more wounding? Or what if, as has often happened, speech codes designed to protect minorities against "assaultive speech" that is racist in intent are turned against the minorities?[133] And what if women or members of minority groups feel that the most dispassionate analysis of their difficulties reflects badly on them? Consider a relatively noncontroversial example. In the University of Michigan speech code, subsequently thrown out by the courts, an example of prohibited speech was to claim that "in this subject, men do better than women." But in the case of mathematics, that is true; it is also something women mathematicians worry about, as is the small number of women who choose to become mathematicians. Presumably male success in math is a socially determined condition, but under the Michigan rules it would be forbidden to discuss the topic. It is difficult to see how the problem can be addressed if it cannot be talked about. On a larger and more controversial scale, the same difficulty could easily arise in an attempt to discuss the social disorganization of the inner city, which is so clearly linked to the problems of racial minorities.[134]

This line of argument aimed at the restriction of free speech for fear of giving offense is to attack liberalism at what is perhaps its strongest point. Liberalism is not flawless. With respect to women and racial or ethnic minorities, its focus on the individual may make it difficult for many to understand that some groups are systematically mistreated and thus individuals may sometimes not be able to cope with their plight without group-oriented remedies. Still, racial, ethnic, and gender policy that transcends those groupings is likely to be more politically palatable than are group-specific actions. Besides, such policies take into account that, in spite of the fact that it is clearly easier to be a white male in U.S. society than not, there are large numbers of whites who are also victims of the status quo. The tension between treating people equally as individuals and trying to address issues of inequality by focusing on the differences between groups is real and points to serious issues. To strike at free speech is to strike at the possibility that these problems can be responsibly addressed.

The classic liberal response to defamatory speech is to attack the speech. It is true that free speech has never been recognized as an absolute. Libel is actionable, as is false commercial speech. The old rule that we may not claim First Amendment protection if we falsely cry fire in a crowded theater still holds. However, the life of liberalism and, I think, the life of democracy depend on the widest latitude for free, critical speech.[135] Free speech may not be an absolute: Few want to base its defense on the legal rights of pornographers and hate mongers. But even pornography may have some social value, and where it does not, it may be regulable by means other than speech restriction,[136] although control of even the most deplorable hate speech presents the sort of difficulties indicated above. And it can be shown that the defense of racist speech in the Terminiello case of 1949 was turned to good advantage to defend the rights of civil rights protesters in the 1960s.[137] Thus, First Amendment absolutism may often appear to be extreme and wrongheaded—perhaps sometimes it is—but one should depart from it under only the most compelling circumstances and with a full awareness that the course of action is inherently dangerous.

The current assault on free speech in the name of feminism and racial minorities is also an assault on a significant component of the liberal consensus. The attack is not confined to writers who may be said to occupy a fringe position, but MacKinnon's extremism may well weaken her case.[138] Postmodernist literary critic Stanley Fish has weighed in with an insouciantly titled book, *There's No Such Thing as Free Speech: And It's a Good Thing Too,* and even Cass Sunstein, a moderate liberal legal theorist with communitarian leanings, has offered a book-length defense of speech restriction.[139] If there is a liberal consensus, to the extent that free speech guarantees are part of it, its continued viability has been called into question. The concern about limiting speech is a product of the attempt to achieve what Richard Hofstadter called "comity." There is no longer a consensus around the old civilities. But this collapse is closely related to the postmodernist critique, with its "principled" reduction of truth to power claims.[140] Thus the irony is that the attack on this front comes not from the Right but from the Left fighting under the flag of feminism and racial justice. The irony is doubled by the fact that much of the conservative reaction that has reshaped American politics in the past twenty-five years has been powered by reaction to precisely those forces. The liberal consensus as it has developed in this century is caught in a gigantic pincers movement. To understand the full dimensions and rather peculiar nature of the liberal crisis, it is necessary to turn to the efflorescence of conservative theory in recent decades.

· 14 ·

Liberalism in Retreat: The Conservative Critique

To discuss American conservatism is to enter into a semantic bog because the word has many definitions. Indeed, the question whether American conservatism even exists has been asked, but since there are Americans who call themselves conservative or who are called so by others—the two groups do not entirely coincide—I will use the term and dispense with surrounding the word by any question-raising quotation marks. Ambiguous though it is, the word *conservatism* is so deeply embedded in the American vocabulary that there is no escaping it by choosing another with fewer potentially confusing connotations.

At least three general meanings can be attached to conservatism.[1] First, it is often seen as the ideology of the aristocratic reaction to the French Revolution, the liberal values of the Enlightenment, and the rise of the bourgeoisie.

Second, there have been attempts to spell out a list of basic ideas shared by all conservatives, the approach that Samuel Huntington refers to as the "autonomous definition of conservatism." The classic statement is in Edmund Burke's denunciation of the French Revolution, but the most recent general American exposition is to be found in Russell Kirk's six canons of conservatism. These include belief that "a divine intent rules society" and all political problems are fundamentally "religious and moral"; the conservative society feels "affection for the proliferating variety and mystery of traditional life"; "civilized society requires order and classes"; there is a close connection between freedom and property and "economic levelling and progress" should not be equated; a "faith in prescription" is necessary; and, finally, not only "change and reform are not identical" but also innovation carries with it great dangers.[2]

The third form of conservatism is what Huntington refers to as "situational conservatism," simply a set of ideas designed to justify any particular status quo. Normally, this takes the form of protecting a particular distribution of power and influence. Although conceding that most conservatives draw on all of these elements, Huntington argues that the situational definition is the most useful.[3] If this is true, it poses a problem. The status quo that American conservatives are concerned to protect is deeply involved with liberal capitalism. My argument is that American conservatism, for all its occasional insights, has never quite succeeded in escaping the problems inherent in preserving a social and political order with such a high liberal content. In particular, the warm embrace of capitalism, one of the most powerful agents for change in the modern world, constantly threatens conservatism with intellectual incoherence. It is difficult to build an autonomous conservatism on the basis of a theory in which change is an essential part of the social order. Put differently, it has been hard for American conservatives to escape from the consensus described by Louis Hartz, particularly its economic component. That is the peculiar fate of traditionalist conservatism in a predominantly liberal culture.

Conservatism as a Movement

It is widely recognized that much of the content of what Americans call conservative is deeply grounded in the liberal tradition. From the social Darwinists to Ronald Reagan and George Bush, and on to Newt Gingrich, it is clear that classical laissez-faire economics is central to the ideology of conservatism. It is equally clear that much, though certainly not all, of libertarian theory is put to use by people commonly called conservative. Much conservative thought is also clearly not traditional in anything like the European sense. Thus, a good deal of the Reagan-Bush program was devoted to an attempt to create the conditions for a dynamic economic expansion that would inevitably lead to more of the "creative destruction" that Joseph Schumpeter claimed was central to capitalism.[4]

The first politically salient eruption of contemporary American conservatism came in the 1950s.[5] Russell Kirk's *Conservative Mind* was probably the leading philosophical statement, but the most prominent figure was certainly the enfant terrible of the movement, William F. Buckley. Immediately upon graduation, Buckley achieved notoriety with *God and Man at Yale*, a biting assault on the education he had received there. He quickly followed this by publishing *McCarthy and His Enemies*, a ringing endorsement of the anti-Communist ideas and practices of the junior senator from Wisconsin, Joseph R. McCarthy, and by the creation of his magazine, the *National Review*, which became a rallying point for the expression of conservative ideology and programs.

While liberals were celebrating the end of ideology, Buckley and his colleagues at the *National Review* were engaged in what they saw as a life and death struggle against communism for the soul of Western civilization.[6] But their ideology was eclectic. Buckley was by no means a systematic thinker and often espoused causes that other conservatives had to have seen as quixotic or worse. Thus he endorsed voting for blacks on the basis of race alone, supported the Panama Canal Treaty, and spoke on behalf of legalizing homosexual acts.[7] Nor has he ever produced a serious, comprehensive statement of his idea of conservatism.

National Review provided an ecumenical meeting place for a wide range of conservative thinkers. What emerged was a "fusionist" consensus—highly unstable—but a consensus nonetheless. Some contributors were utilitarian free marketeers, and others stood for "virtue," tradition, and an "objective moral order." A Reagan staffer was quoted as saying that fusionism meant "utilizing libertarian means in a conservative society for traditionalist ends." A neat stunt, one might add, if only one could bring it off. What held this strange amalgam together was anticommunism.[8] They also shared, I think, a certain romanticism, in the sense of a revolt against the prevailing tendencies of American life and politics in favor of a return to a simpler golden age.

But the most cursory inspection of this consensus reveals its potential incoherence—an incoherence that has plagued American conservative thought from the start. The fact that there was total agreement on anticommunism might account for the visible shock of disbelief that many conservatives displayed as the inevitability of a Soviet collapse became clear.[9] E. J. Dionne summed up the problem: "Postwar conservatism was thus conceived in contradiction. Virtue and freedom are not necessarily in conflict, but they are radically different starting points for political philosophy and are destined to create different creeds."[10] Ironically, fusionist conservatism recapitulated a great deal of the ideological conflict of the American tradition. Nevertheless, however unstable, the consensus held long enough to be part of a winning political movement that changed the face of U.S. politics.

By 1964, hard work at the grass roots had brought the Republican Party into the control of movement conservatives who had no use for the Eastern, more or less liberal, establishment that had long held power. And Barry Goldwater, though he was ahead of his time, was, as Dionne said, the model fusionist candidate.[11] However, more work was needed to bring the conservative movement to power. Richard Nixon helped pave the way through his southern strategy, which successfully exploited the discontent many Democrats in the South felt over the direction of the national party. But Nixon was never a movement conservative in the sense that Ronald Reagan was to be; moreover, it is obvious that the Watergate Affair temporarily derailed the drift toward conservatism presaged by Nixon's election in 1968.

It must also be clear that the vagaries of leftist politics, the prominence of the counterculture, the sexual revolution, the abortion issue, the surging strength of fundamentalist religion, crime, drugs, and the perceived inadequacies of the Carter administration did as much to bring about the conservative triumph in 1980 as did the efforts of the conservatives themselves. With characteristic concision and acerbity, conservative political theorist Harvey Mansfield has summarized the issues as they appeared to conservatives in 1980. What he saw was a repudiation of the values of the 1960s. To those who held them they were

> the Third World, human rights, liberation, freedom of choice, equal rights for women, freedom for irreligion, rights of defendants, gay rights, consumerism, school desegregation, affirmative action, free expression, and welfare rights. To those who oppose them, they [were], respectively: lack of patriotism, abandoning one's friends, lack of self-restraint, easy abortion, interchangeability of the sexes, atheism in schools, increased rights for criminals, respectability for homosexuals, contempt for producers, forced busing, reverse discrimination, license to pornographers, and living off others.[12]

The list is obviously tendentious but is no doubt a fair appraisal of the issues as seen by many conservatives and by many voters.

A Typology of Conservatives

The fusionist movement that coalesced around William Buckley and the *National Review* in the 1950s finally achieved power with the election of Ronald Reagan, though ironically Buckley had less influence in the Reagan administration than might have been expected.[13] The coalition, like all broad ones, was loosely strung together, with many of the components potentially at odds. Some of the difficulties inherent in the very idea of an American conservatism can be seen through an analysis of the individual groups that made up the conservative coalition. I have here followed a classification used by Harvey Mansfield.[14]

The Responsible Conservatives

The "responsible Conservatives" are politically important, but not very interesting intellectually. The prototype is Senator Robert Dole; most others are also officeholders, though Mansfield notes that a number of economists "give this position an intellectual tinge, but no more than that." Their goal is not to generate ideas, Mansfield tells us, but rather to clean up the mess left by the ideas of others. Distrusting the more fervent conservatives, they are not ideologues. As Mansfield prophetically notes, because their stance is essentially reactive, they are better situated to be in the minority than in the majority, a proposition being tested by the elevation of Dole to majority leader after the election of 1994.[15]

A note on reason, intellect, and intellectuals is important here. Some might think that Mansfield's remarks about intellect are meant to be a rebuke, but that is not the case. Instead, they reflect a distrust of intellectualism, which makes conservative intellectuals a bit uneasy about their status. Conservatives doubt that the intellect can "grasp society as a whole." Reason must be kept in its place and might better be called prudence in the sense of Edmund Burke. "Conservatives believed that reason was necessary and useful in things up close to us, in front of our noses, but farther away things in the big picture have to be understood as in the domain of nature, when *nature* is understood as beyond human control." There are two political consequences of this argument: The first is a distrust of ideologues, even conservative ideologues, and the second, "a doubt about the extent and even the possibility of self-government."[16] Any rebuke here is aimed at liberal intellectuals and their conservative counterparts; in Mansfield's school of thought, *intellectual* is a term of opprobrium—*philosopher* is the appropriate term of praise.

Libertarianism

The second stream of the modern fusionist consensus is libertarianism. Mansfield has aptly characterized this current and in doing so has identified its crippling flaw: "The libertarian," Mansfield writes, "cannot conceive the sociability of man."[17] Philosophically the line of descent is from Thomas Hobbes, with his image of atomized individuals rattling around in a terrifyingly violent state of nature, by way of Jeremy Bentham, with his egregious notions of the calculability of interests and the fictional nature of the very idea of community. It is no accident that many economists fall into this group, particularly members of the Chicago school, such as Friedrich Hayek and Milton Friedman, since reason for Hobbes and Bentham was essentially a process of weighing desires and aversions against each other in a series of economistic cost/benefit analyses. The free marketeers have found their philosophical counterpart in Robert Nozick's *Anarchy, State, and Utopia*.

Consider first Hayek, probably the most powerful intellect of the group. A Nobel laureate in economics, Hayek turned to political and social theory for most of his work after the 1944 publication of his most famous book, *The Road to Serfdom*. What Hayek feared was that the rationalistic hubris of social tinkerers would lead them to try to impose an economic blueprint that featured "central direction of all economic activity according to a single plan, laying down how the resources of a society should be 'consciously directed' to serve particular ends in a definite way."[18] The likely consequence of such an attempt would be going down the road to serfdom forecast in his title. The only answer was a resort to the automatic equilibrating mechanisms of the competitive free market.

Still worse, Hayek believed, a planning system presupposes the existence of a complete ethical code, seemingly analogous to the plan itself, in which all human values have an assigned place. Since there is no hierarchical ordering of values on which all can agree, these questions will be left in the hands of the planners, thus leading to an excessive reliance on administrative discretion. But that undermines the moral system of a planned society; it is the very negation of libertarian individualist morals. An act cannot be moral unless the actor is responsible for his action: "Only when we ourselves are responsible for our own interests and are free to sacrifice them has our decision moral value. . . . A movement whose main premise is the relief from responsibility cannot but be antimoral in its effect, however lofty the ideals to which it owes its birth."[19]

This is powerful and deeply felt, but it will not withstand analysis. We have ample historical evidence that planning as Hayek defined it has not and probably cannot work and that it can have horrible political consequences. But planning need not be so comprehensively defined. We also have ample historical evidence to show that less-extensive governmental intervention in the economy can have positive effects and still not lead to serfdom, though there is still much room for debate on the exact nature of the appropriate proportions in the mixed economy. But the free market is something that has probably never existed except in the theoretical constructs of economists. We also know that even though planned economies have their difficulties, so too do those that most closely approximate the free market. Ironically, in the same year that Hayek published *The Road to Serfdom*, Karl Polanyi, another refugee from Hitler's Europe, published an important work that showed that the free market was not a natural phenomenon, that an attempt was made to create one as a specific act of public policy in the early nineteenth century, and that the disorder it induced was a powerful incentive to the growth of the socialist movement as it sought to impose social control over the destructive new system.[20] Further, it should be insisted that although there are no cases of fully socialist democratic systems, many times democratic socialist or social democratic parties have come to power without the noxious consequences feared by Hayek. Finally, even if we provisionally concede, for the sake of argument, that capitalism is a necessary condition for democracy to be possible, it is certainly not a sufficient condition. Nazi Germany alone destroys that hypothesis.

Still, the moral critique Hayek offered is potentially powerful. But it too is weak. It is true that moral action requires free choice, but Hayek ignored the denial of choice inflicted on, for example, the impoverished. They are so lacking in resources that it is not possible for them to become part of the exceedingly narrow moral universe of the libertarian economist. One purpose of government involvement in the economy is to increase the number of those who benefit from having genuine choice. What the nature of that involvement should be is a matter of legitimate debate, but there is little reason to believe that the free market fantasy is a particularly viable option. Mansfield is quite right; libertarians have difficulty in conceiving the sociability of man, but because of this failing they also have trouble imagining a role for politics. That is particularly true of economists, whose entire discipline rests on a view of man as a rational calculator in hot pursuit of his interests in a setting in which the market is abstracted from all other social institutions. However, this failing is not limited to economists. One of the characteristics of contemporary social theory is the prominence, if not dominance, of economistic modes of thought. This trend can be seen in the philosophy of Robert Nozick and in some of the principal analytical approaches of contemporary political science, in the latter case often carried out by scholars who do not realize the conservative implications of their work.

The libertarian philosophy has been generalized by Nozick in *Anarchy, State, and Utopia*. His argument begins with a notably sweeping statement of individual rights: "Individuals have rights, and there are things no person or group may do to them (without violating their rights). So strong and far-reaching are these rights that they raise the question of what, if anything, the state and its officials may do."[21] But this formulation, although it seems to provide a secure foundation for rights, is undermined from the start because the commitment to a general theory of rights is more apparent than real. The rights in question are quickly reduced to the right to private property, surely an important consideration, but hardly the whole universe of rights. Nozick's only real concern seems to be the protection of "capitalist acts between consenting adults."[22] Judging from the arguments made in his book, Nozick is unconcerned with rights, for example, to free speech, religion, assembly, or against unreasonable searches and seizures or self-incrimination, or of privacy, or to vote. One could go on, but the point is obvious.

In a passage strongly influenced by Hayek's sweeping conception, Nozick proclaims that no "end-state principle or distributional patterned principle of justice can be continuously realized without continuous interference with people's lives." But government is dangerous well short of this situation; even "taxation of earnings from labor is on a par with forced labor."[23] On the basis of such an absurd principle, government would indeed be limited; in fact it would be impossible. And that would truly be tragic for those who could not survive without the help of the state.

In addition, the connection of property rights to politics is highly problematic. For Nozick, the fundamental question of political philosophy is not the question of the meaning of justice or the nature of the best political system, nor does it relate to political institutions. The real question is whether there should be a state at all.[24] The answer is a guarded yes, since anarchy is not a possibility. However, only a minimalist state is required, or indeed allowable, for the protection of property rights. But this flirtation with anarchy had a heavy price.

An air of unreality surrounds Nozick's argument. He wished to explain politics in terms of the nonpolitical and this led him back, in good American fashion, to a version of Locke's state of nature.[25] Why he chose Locke for a model is not altogether clear; Hobbes might have done just as well, given the potential for a social Darwinian war of all against all that was built into Nozick's theory. But Nozick's is a strange state of nature. It is difficult to imagine its members as representative of the range of human types that might be useful if one wanted to explore the need for a state. As George Kateb remarks, Nozick's men are "unlike most people to the point of bizarre eccentricity. There is nothing natural about them; they are only lopsidedly social. . . . The state of nature is a meeting of highly intelligent American economists."[26]

Like Hayek, Nozick seems unable to imagine the limits placed on freedom to exercise rights by a life of abject poverty. And like Hayek's theory, Nozick's is profoundly apolitical.[27] Nozick's book, a brilliantly written, brilliantly argued tour de force, fitted out with wonderful "man from Mars" examples, is altogether out of touch with the mundane life of the day-to-day world. One of the characteristics of economics seminars is that they typically deal with an imaginary, purely theoretical setting. All too often in contemporary moral and political philosophy, this situation is reproduced. Benjamin Barber's remark about Nozick can be extended to an unfortunately large list of others: "If reality defies the philosophical criteria by which it is judged, all the worse for reality."[28] In particular, the institutional reality ignored by Nozick is the world of the large corporation.[29] A political theory that cannot see that reality is of little use, except, of course, for corporate propagandists, and for that reason the theory may be dangerous for others. A final irony is that, as George Kateb points out, even the minimalist state cannot be guaranteed on Nozick's principles, since, as a result of the unbounded importance attached to the right to property, there can be no real limits on the efforts of the state to secure that right.[30] It appears that what Nozick offers is a new version of social Darwinian struggle, tricked out in the very latest fashions in philosophical technique.

In doing so, Nozick is in step with the fashion in political "scientific" analysis. The current "hot" approach in political science is the public choice, or rational actor, approach. Shrewdly, if uncomfortably, Harvey Mansfield has lumped these theorists together with the libertarian conservatives.[31] Some advocates of the rational choice position, such as William Riker, would identify themselves as conservative; others, such as Jon Elster, see themselves as on the left—even as a socialist, in Elster's case.[32] In either case, one can see what is sometimes referred to as "economic imperialism"—like Nozick's philosophy, yet another attempt to reduce the political to the nonpolitical. But as with Nozick and the Chicago school economists, the price of this abstraction from the political is high. Governmental and economic institutions are swept away, and we are left once again with rational calculators playing economic games.

For some, the games may be entertaining enough, but the result may be a conservative bias not intended by some of the players. Slowly but subtly, according to Theodore Lowi, *"economics has replaced law as the language of the state."*[33] It is no accident that this penetration of political science by economics occurred during the market-oriented Reagan-Bush years. Lowi asks, why economics? He gives two answers. One comes from British economist Joan Robinson: "Economics has always been partly a vehicle for the ruling ideology of each period as well as partly a method of scientific investigation."[34] The second answer is that economic modes of analysis, with their air of precision and certainty, make it easier to close off debate. Political leaders in both parties know full well that they are using these ideas as weapons; the oddity, says Lowi, is that political scientists take them seriously as science.[35]

What can be seen here is part of a massive sea change that began with the emergence of large-scale capitalism in the late nineteenth century and that accelerated rapidly through the twentieth. One might expect reform liberals to have been skeptical of this development, given their willingness to interfere with the market. But conservatives of Mansfield's stripe are also distinctly uncomfortable. The economizing mode, as Daniel Bell calls it, does not allow people to come to grips with the most basic problems of society, for example, the appropriate size and scope of social units, the changing meanings of the public and the private, the meaning of democracy, and the need to subordinate economic technocrats to ends unknown to the arcane world of microeconomics. Bell writes that economics is a utilitarian study; it deals with maximization, optimization, and least cost. It is a means to given ends, but it cannot help to determine what those ends should be. In a rather ugly neologism, Bell suggests that theorists need to resort to a *sociologizing* mode of analysis that attempts consciously to determine social needs in line with a conception of the public interest. For example, the corporation is an economizing institution at the center of the private enterprise system. No one votes in the market economy, Bell says, but now as one sees "the creation of more private goods at the expense of other social values," one has to examine such large-scale questions.[36] Questions such as those are the essence of politics. They are therefore questions, not of economics, but of political philosophy. As Bell reminds us, we are being driven "back to the classical questions of the polis. And this is as it should be."[37]

Bell is a little hard to classify ideologically, but he can probably best be thought of as a social democrat. As such, Mansfield might view his notion of the sociologizing mode with a certain suspicion—as a representative of the sort of global rationalism conservatives distrust. Still, Mansfield is by no means happy with economic imperialism or libertarianism in general. This is not his brand of conservatism. In the end, libertarians tend to be rationalists of the wrong kind. They must remind Mansfield of Edmund Burke's warning about the reign of "sophisters, economists, and calculators," and Mansfield, a distinguished Burke scholar, can tell us from his own experience that Burke "does not sell well in Reagan's America."[38] It is doubtful that Bell and Mansfield would be in full agreement about the classical questions of the polis, but Mansfield surely would agree on the need to return to them. In this effort, the libertarians could be of little use. Mansfield rightly says of them, "They surely believe in *limited* government, but it is doubtful they believe in government. . . . They believe in the sovereignty of the self but not in the self-government of the self; so they are liberal on the social issues or on the general question of permissiveness, while conservative on economic issues."[39]

The remark on the resistance to self-government of the self is more than a little tendentious, but Mansfield's basic point is well taken. The libertarians are a notably unstable part of the conservative coalition, and in party terms they can hardly be classified as reliably Republican.

The Neoconservatives

In some respects the neoconservatives are a more interesting group, if only because they are much less likely than the libertarians to dwell in a world of economic abstractions. A snide joke has it that the neoconservatives are simply liberals who have been mugged. That may have some truth in it, but it is closer to the mark to say that they are "nervous liberals" and that what they are nervous about is the triumph of liberalism and its consequences.[40] It is true that many of them are ex-liberals, and more than a few were members of one or another Communist sect in the 1930s.

Their principal journal is the *Public Interest,* founded in 1964 by Daniel Bell and Irving Kristol. It began as a moderately liberal, anti-ideological outlet for studies of public policy issues that could span the gap between the general public and the hard social science of the professional journals. Under the pressures of the 1960s and 1970s, there was a slow but steady move to the right, which was paralleled in the formerly liberal monthly *Commentary.*[41] The idea behind the *Public Interest* was to temper the alleged ideological excesses of liberals with a good dose of social science reality, or as Mansfield wryly puts it, to combine social science with common sense—"a mix of oil and water if there ever was one."[42]

Several neoconservative positions stand out. The first is a strong sense of "the limits of public policy." Nathan Glazer has argued that public policy is attempting to deal with the collapse of traditional ways of handling "distress," that U.S. policies make these problems worse, that the attempt to do too much has led to a crisis of rising expectations, that this revolution has been fueled by the wave of equality that has been the dominant force in the West throughout the modern period, that the very existence of social policy has created new demands, and that a "new class" has risen to deal with them but has itself become part of the problem. Charles Murray followed Glazer's critique with a more detailed analysis that purported to show the same thing.[43]

Because it is useful to be reminded of the deficiencies of contemporary social science, not all of Glazer's critique can be summarily dismissed. In particular, the pretensions of economics to hegemonic status are bogus. And social science certainly does have unintended consequences. Still, Glazer's critique is almost a paradigm case of what Albert Hirschman calls the "rhetoric of reaction" and an example of the perversity thesis, the idea that the attempt to remedy a social problem has the perverse effect of making things worse than they were.[44] Nevertheless, Glazer bases his case largely on the obvious inadequacies of the welfare system and the war on poverty. It is conventional wisdom that there was a war on poverty and that poverty won, but to repeat the aphorism is to ignore the successes of other social programs.[45] It is not even clear that the war on poverty was a total failure, though it is certain that the war in Vietnam prevented it from being fought to a conclusion. The antipoverty forces abandoned the field, but some of the work they left behind was of real value.[46] To be aware that social policies are unlikely to be panaceas is only good sense; still, it is potentially disastrous simply to assume failure in advance.

A second theme that runs throughout the thinking of the neoconservatives is a stress on character, an idea most commonly associated with James Q. Wilson. Wilson writes that when the *Public Interest* began publication in

1965, economics was just starting to assume its central place as a guide for public policy. But it became clear that what economists called tastes and what others called values or beliefs are not always responsive to economic incentives. "They do not respond, it seems, because the people whose behavior we wish to change do not have the right tastes or discount the future too heavily. To put it plainly, they lack character."[47] Good character, Wilson continues, consists in at least two things, empathy and self-control, which include the capacity to take into account the consequences of one's actions. Or in a somewhat broader formulation, the "moral virtues include courage, moderation, fidelity, and good temper."[48] And this moral sense is not a product of intellect or calculation; it is inherent in human nature, as Aristotle would have argued.[49]

This is very impressive, and the move away from the infatuation with economic modes of thought is pure gain. It is also refreshing to see a clear-cut defense of middle-class values. Further, there is no doubt we could all benefit if we had better character. But we have encountered this argument before in the discussion of the social disorganization of the inner cities. Surely, as Cornell West, who is no neoconservative, says, black leaders need to turn their attention to character formation. But this attention is not likely to be very fruitful if it is not combined with programs addressed to the structure of modern capitalism and the role of the large corporation.

Here is where Wilson is weak; he is not insensitive to the problem of the moral character of the large corporation, and he is aware that many of what we have come to call the "social issues" have their roots in the hedonistic culture of capitalism and the rapacious energy with which some corporations pursue profit. But all he has to offer us on this score is a discussion of Adam Smith that shows quite nicely that Smith was not the buccaneer that many of his followers have been.[50] The "system of natural liberty" Smith defended was far removed from the contemporary capitalist world system; this system was not what he theorized, and I doubt it would have been much to his liking. As evidence, we only have to remember the jaundiced view he took of the businessmen of his own time. Thus capitalism remains the Achilles heal of American conservatism.

For a more direct attempt to confront the problem, it is interesting to turn to Irving Kristol, often called the Godfather of the neoconservatives because of his extensive contacts in the worlds of foundations, journalism, publishing, and the universities.[51] Kristol did not forget, at least not until recently, what he had learned as a young socialist—that capitalism was not based on virtue and that therefore it posed moral problems. Economically capitalism works, says Kristol, and although it may not be a sufficient condition for a regime of personal liberty, it does seem to be a necessary condition. But it raises difficulties; it breeds an adversary intellectual culture. It is no longer clear that "it is possible for the individual, alone or in purely voluntary association with others, to cope with the eternal dilemmas of the human condition." And the large bureaucratic structures characteristic of capitalism are very different from what Adam Smith had in mind.[52] Capitalism is spiritually thin and may not provide enough support for the contentment that traditional societies offer.

Capitalism promised material plenty, individual freedom, and the possibility that the individual could perfect his self, so there would be a virtuous society made up of virtuous men. It was the failure of the third promise, undermined by the dynamics of capitalism itself, that raised questions about the legitimacy of capitalism.[53] Friedrich Hayek's argument in *The Constitution of Liberty* that the free society might not be the just society and that freedom was preferable to justice troubled Kristol. He even granted partial acceptance to George Fitzhugh's remark that "in such a society virtue loses all her loveliness." Kristol doubts that the charge was true when Fitzhugh wrote, but with the passage of time, it has gained validity.[54] But in the end, Kristol does not believe that people can live with the dilemma Hayek proposed. In fact, he dismisses Hayek's rationale for capitalism as academic. Instead, he says that modern capitalism is legitimated by a belief in the Protestant ethic at the lower socioeconomic level, by the Darwinian ethic among small businessmen, and, most important, by a standard of technocratic competence for elites. But sooner or later, elites will fail the performance test and technocrats cannot create a "beautiful, refined, gracious, and tranquil civilization."[55] Thus, the libertarian justification for capitalism will not do, and the more acceptable alternatives are not quite enough. In fact, modernity itself is not enough; we must turn to premodern political thought to find appropriate answers.[56]

In this connection, Kristol makes a quite startling, though atypical, argument. He tells us: "The most important political event of the twentieth century is not the crisis of capitalism, but the death of socialism. . . . For with the passing of the socialist ideal there is removed from the political horizon the one alternative that was rooted in the Judeo-Christian tradition and in the Western civilization which emerged from that tradition." He says that anticapitalism is now associated with barbarism; thus dissent is liberated from the socialist tradition, which had been a civilizing force because it shared so many values with its opponent.[57] One should make no mistake; Kristol is not going soft on socialism. What he sees is that the original sources of socialist dissent predated scientific Marxism. It is the utopian socialists Marx scorned that Kristol is drawn to because he sees them as more dissatisfied with modernity itself than with liberal capitalism.[58] If only, he wishes, the contemporary critics of capitalism were so civilized.

From the neoconservative point of view, it is culture that is the central flaw in capitalism. But Kristol provides only interesting suggestions. For a full-scale theory on this subject it is important to turn to his close friend and colleague Daniel Bell. Bell points out that in sociological theory it is normally assumed that societies are best seen as more or less well integrated wholes. Politics, economics, and culture tend to be all of a piece; they constitute a unified system. But Bell thinks this cohesion has been lost in modern capitalism. We are now confronted with what he calls the "disjunction of realms."[59] The relations among the three parts of society have become uneasy. The technoeconomic system does not determine the other two realms. If anything dominates, is the true "control center" of modern society, it is the polity. The culture stood to one side, so to speak, and is dominated by the desire for individual self-realization or self-gratification.[60] Historically society has moved "from the Protestant ethic to the psychedelic bazaar."[61] "The Protestant ethic and the Puritan temper were the world-view of an agrarian, small-town, mercantile and artisan way of life."[62] Those ideas did not just succumb to the 1960s counterculture; they were the victims of a long, slow decline fostered by capitalist economics, "by the free market to be precise."[63] It was this loss that led to the cultural contradictions of capitalism. "What this abandonment of Puritanism and the Protestant ethic does, of course, is to leave capitalism with no moral or transcendental ethic." It lost its source of legitimation.[64] We are left with a hedonistic pop culture of self-gratification. The main hope Bell sees is a religious revival.

If in fact Bell is a neoconservative, then *The Cultural Contradictions of Capitalism* stands as the movement's finest monument. But Bell refuses the label and insists that although he is a cultural conservative, in economics he is a socialist, and in politics, a liberal.[65] This oddly appealing amalgam is made possible by the disjunction of realms that he theorizes. It is not very profitable to argue over labels for long. Bell surely earned his reputation as a cultural conservative. Still, his economic and political commitments have made him rather an odd man out among his presumed colleagues. Someone on the left can find quite as much ammunition in Bell's book as can a conservative. It is probably not accidental that these days Bell is more likely to publish in *Dissent* than in the *Public Interest* and that he is no longer an editor of the latter.

But this blurring of ideological lines is to some extent a characteristic of the neoconservatives. Bell was not the only one queasy about the label. Only Irving Kristol fully embraced it, at least for a time; at this writing it seems that he has moved out of the neoconservative camp altogether to stake out a position much further to the right. However, it is helpful to look at his codification of the basic principles of the group.

1. It is distrustful of modern liberalism but has a "loose, uneasy, though not necessarily unfriendly" relation with business.
2. It is strongly anti-utopian.
3. It is not opposed to the welfare state, but it is opposed to the paternalistic state that hopes to "solve" social problems.
4. It is not opposed to equality of opportunity, but it is opposed to equality of condition (and hence, by implication, to a redistributive state).
5. It supports a market economy, which it sees as conducive to economic growth, but it does not support the libertarian antipathy to welfare.
6. It supports traditional culture and despises the counterculture. Its view is that the individual liberated from traditional culture will soon be a nihilist.
7. Its philosophical roots are in "premodern, preideological" political theory. Aristotle is admired, Locke is respected, and Rousseau is distrusted.
8. Family and religion are indispensable supports for a decent society.[66]

And in the end, Kristol told us, if the political winds should shift, he might wind up a neoliberal. But not yet! Although admitting that he had been a cold warrior, he now says that the post–cold war enemy is not communism but "the fundamental assumptions of contemporary liberalism."[67] If conservatism has anything at all to do with the preservation of tradition, one can only comment that this is an amazing comment for a conservative in a liberal, democratic society.

My discussion so far has mainly focused on economics and culture. However, there is a theory of democracy closely tied to the neoconservatives, one that is fearful of the democratic masses, emphasizes the limits of governmental power, and laments the alleged weakness of government, particularly in the executive branch, and the resulting dangerous decline in the authority of the state. Its most significant proponent has been Samuel Huntington.[68]

The immediate source of concern for Huntington is the "dramatic upsurge of democratic fervor in America" in the 1960s. This "apparent vitality" of democracy raises questions "about the governability of democracy."[69] Government activity has expanded, but the shift toward defense expenditures has been replaced by one toward welfare. This democratic surge is "a general challenge to existing systems of authority, public and private."[70] The balance of power between forces of government and opposition has changed, favoring Congress and the increasingly powerful mass media over the presidency.[71] According to Huntington, Americans are faced with an excess of democracy, which has to be met by a moderation of the democratic impulses of the society. They need to recall the voting studies of the 1950s that noted, "The effective operation of a democratic political system requires some measure of apathy and non-involvement on the part of some individuals and groups."[72]

This democratic disorder is part of a deeper dynamic in U.S. history. Americans have a deep consensual commitment to a creed that encompassed liberty, equality, individualism, democracy, and constitutionalism. This is, in Huntington's words, the "only country in the world in which a majority of the population has belonged to dissenting Protestant sects." The origins of American politics date back to the Puritan revolution in seventeenth-century England. "That revolution is, in fact, the single most important formative event of American political history."[73] The values of the American Creed are in opposition to the legitimacy of all government: "No government can exist without some measure of hierarchy, inequality, arbitrary power, secrecy, deception, and established patterns of superordination and subordination."[74]

Thus there is a persistent gap between the ideal and the actual working of the institutions of American politics. Huntington refers to it as the IvI gap, the distance between the ideals of the system and the performance of its institutions. He says that Americans have responded to the gap in four ways: by being hypocritical and denying the gap; by being complacent and ignoring it; by being cynical and tolerating the shortfall; or by being moralistic and attempting to remove it.[75] In a note, Huntington admits the obvious; those labels are all pejorative. One could instead talk about morality, realism, satisfaction, and patriotism, but these more pleasing labels ignore the important point, which is that each response is in some way unsatisfactory.[76] Perhaps, but the substitution of moralism for morality, I will argue, is especially troubling.

Huntington applies his schema to an analysis of American history and discerns four periods of what he calls creedal passion: the revolutionary era, Jacksonian democracy, progressivism, and the 1960s and 1970s—the S&S years, in his designation. The periods were characterized by widespread discontent, political ideas were taken seriously, the traditional values of the creed were reasserted and moral passion ran high, participation expanded, and major institutional reforms were attempted.[77]

Much of what Huntington says about those periods is interesting, learned, and sometimes insightful. But, as Samuel Beer, Huntington's teacher and Harvard colleague, suggests, it is a very strange periodization of American history.[78] Huntington is surely right to trace the moral strain in American politics to the Puritans—this is, once again, the heritage of the jeremiad. But if this is so, why was not the Civil War, when the great rhetoric of Lincoln took the jeremiad to unparalleled heights, a period of creedal passion? Does Huntington shrink, as well he might, from calling Lincoln a mere moralizer? And why was not the New Deal era, in which moral passion rose so high, particularly in Franklin Roosevelt's second term, not also a time of creedal passion? Also, as Beer points out, Huntington simply ignores the momentous social and economic programs of the Johnson administration in the 1960s. Huntington's rather weak answer is that those periods focus on economic and social forces; they do not affect the basic structure of institutions. But applied to the Civil War, that is simply ridiculous. At that time, in effect, a new nation was created; it was institutional change with a vengeance. And, as Beer notes, the drive for voter rights was driven by great passion, a passion deeply rooted in the creed, as the great speeches of Martin Luther King, Jr., showed. And that too was an institutional, not merely a social, change.

Huntington's real worry is all too clear. He is opposed to the politics of creedal passion when it threatens a significant democratization of the political system. His great fear is a weakening of presidential power; moreover, writing in the midst of the cold war, he feared any restraint on U.S. ability to compete in that contest.[79] Truly, reading Huntington, one can see that war, even if cold, is a threat to democracy. He seems simply unable to conceive the possibility that the revulsion from authority in the S&S years might have been fully warranted, a perfectly reasonable response to the depredations of successive governments against the basic principles of constitutional rule.

Aside from the problems with his historical analysis, there are two great difficulties with Huntington's theory. The first, as is already abundantly clear, is his hostility to democracy, for which, deep down, he has something approaching contempt. Though he has no real-world, nondemocratic alternative in mind,[80] Huntington's model society is nicely captured in an image from his first book, where he contrasts the pristine order of West Point with the disorderly sprawl of the small town outside the gates.[81] Even for those who are aware that democracies sometimes do terrible things, this is an exceedingly unattractive image.

Huntington's other great flaw is his contempt for "moralism," or political morality, as I prefer. Even he admits that without creedal passion, the American system cannot avoid "stagnation and decay." Thus, "in this sense, a creedal passion period is American politics' finest—and most dangerous—hour."[82] But to be fearful of what is best in the American tradition will not do as a theory—not even, perhaps especially not—as a conservative theory.

What then can we make of the neoconservatives? Peter Steinfels in his fine book *The Neo-Conservatives: The Men Who Are Changing American Politics* takes them with great seriousness, as they deserve, and concludes that they may provide the authentic conservatism the Left has always said is needed in American politics. But the influence of this group in the Reagan-Bush years does not appear to have been as great as might have been expected in the 1970s. Perhaps, though Huntington and the later Kristol are exceptions, the neoconservatives were too moderate for the movement conservatives. Probably so, though I think the flaw lies deeper. The neoconservatives represent in microcosm the difficulties of American conservatism as a whole, though they are perhaps more conscious of the contradictory nature of their enterprise than others. These writers are basically highly intelligent technocrats who worry about the problems of modern capitalism and think they can manage them better than reform liberals or social democrats. But to manage those problems, they would have to detach themselves from the system in a way that, as conservatives, they are unable to do. There will not be a viable conservatism in this country until its adherents figure out what to do about capitalism. Until they do, the Left may have more to say about the preservation of traditional values than the conservatives do, a fact surprisingly, if fleetingly, grasped by Irving Kristol in his nostalgic lament for socialism.

The Fundamentalist Right

The fourth major group in the conservative coalition consists of the Christian and sometimes non-Christian fundamentalists. If conservatives tend to worry about the excesses of reason, they may rest easy here because the animating force of the fundamentalists is faith, not reason. I do not mean to be snide. As E. J. Dionne points out, there is a considerable body of sophisticated theology behind fundamentalist religion, though it is not much in evidence among its contemporary leaders.[83] Dionne notes that fundamentalism began as an attack on modernity and in that fight fundamentalists had many secular companions. But there is much to be worried about in fundamentalism: Examples include the claim of prominent minister Baily Smith that God does not hear the prayers of Jews,[84] the deep intolerance in speeches like those of Pat Buchanan at the 1992 Republican National Convention, and the statement of Randall Terry of Operation Rescue that he wanted the government out of the lives of citizens, except, of course, those of sinners.

But pathological conditions often lead to pathological responses; the fact that the responses are pathological does not dispose of the precipitating conditions. We must deal with two pathologies rather than one. There is more than enough social pathology in modern America, though we may disagree on both its nature and its cause. This is why a highly sophisticated conservative like Harvey Mansfield can endorse part of the list of fundamentalist dislikes—pornography and easy abortion for example—and welcome their support for "family values" and opposition to "godless communism,"[85] though he might very well deplore the manner of their responses.

In any event, fundamentalism, whatever its intellectual power, remains a force to be reckoned with, a force that may trouble the Republican Party just as much as the Democrats, since it is so clearly incompatible with the libertarian segment of the conservative coalition. We need not linger long over the ideas of the Religious Right; theories about the place of fundamentalism are more important here than the thought of the leaders.

We should recall Samuel Huntington's argument about the enormous importance of the Protestant background of American culture. This is an aspect of American traditionalism, one might say its most, and virtually only, truly conservative aspect. Daniel Bell tells us, "The history of American politics and culture, one might say, is the recurrent tension between traditionalism and modernity."[86] It is the product of the rapid industrialization and urbanization of a rural, agrarian society. The tensions do not necessarily follow conventional left/right distinctions. Whereas traditionalists now tend to be on the right, during the populist movement they were on the "left." And a significant part, though certainly not all, of the political conflict deals as much with questions of culture as with immediate economic interests. A split is quite possible, so that culturally conservative forces can be politically and economically to the left. The point is that there is a useful, but very slippery, distinction to be made between the politics of interest and the politics of culture.[87] When originally developed, what came to be called the theory of cultural politics was an attempt to interpret the radical right movements of the 1950s and 1960s as products of anxiety over declining social status, and often to link the bases of support for those movements with the geographic bases of the populism of the 1890s. Although there was undoubtedly a very sour downside to the populist movement, the theory did not withstand careful examination, and what had appeared to be status politics often turned out to be old-fashioned, economically oriented Republican politics.[88]

However, the distinction between economically determined interest politics and cultural politics has proved too valuable to discard. It helps explain the presence of the "culture wars" that do so much to define U.S. politics today. What is at stake are issues of the nature of the family, the difference between art and pornography, the purpose of education, the place of law, and the nature of politics and what can and what cannot be accomplished by political means in a liberal democracy.[89] For James Davison Hunter, author of the leading study of the culture wars, these issues seem to be *the* cutting edge of contemporary politics. Even so astute an observer as sociologist and political scientist Alan Wolfe took him at his word.[90] This proved not to be true for the 1992 election: The basic issue was in fact defined by the famous slogan, "It's the economy, stupid." Still, no one can doubt that these issues continue to be issues of great force and that we have not heard the last of them.

Debate on these questions is highly polarized, so that centrist positions are virtually eclipsed. Discussion on both sides, secular and fundamentalist, is conducted in deeply moralistic terms. For many of the disputants it is the very meaning of America and its history that is at stake.[91] Even the usual patterns of class alignment characteristic of U.S. politics are blurred. As Hunter says, "The progressive alliances tend to draw popular support from among the highly educated, professionally committed, *upper* middle classes, while the orthodox alliances tend to draw from the *lower* middle and working classes."[92]

Good scholar that he is, Hunter tries to be evenhanded and goes as far as to suggest that in their common shrillness, it is hard to distinguish the two sides, if one can ignore the specific messages. But, Wolfe insists, it is possible. It is true that liberals can be arrogant and intolerant, but their language *can* be distinguished from that of the fundamentalists. In the clear gulf of incomprehension that separates Randall Terry of Operation Rescue from Faye Wattleton of Planned Parenthood,[93] there is a discernible difference: "Liberals discovered tolerance for a reason; fundamentalists have yet to learn what it is."[94] This is to say that liberals have learned the great historic lesson that toleration is the price of religious freedom and the Right has not.

What is at stake here is the very definition of what is public and what is private. Although it is true that the line has shifted over time, the existence of such a distinction is at the heart of American constitutionalism. Alan Wolfe exaggerates, but he is correct about the general nature of the struggle: "The great political and economic forces that are usually understood to shape public policy are viewed as clashes between private interests. At the same time, matters of religious belief, aesthetic taste, and cultural preference—once thought to be private and individualistic—assume center-stage in the large public dramas enacted in the media."[95]

These are momentous shifts in perspective; though the level of debate is often exceedingly, depressingly low, the issues are not trivial. The liberal Left has made a serious mistake in allowing the fundamentalist Right to define the issues in a way that makes it appear that liberals care nothing for "family values." As none other than Irving Kristol suggested in his lament for the lost cause of socialism, the Left has often made its case by defending tradition against the destructive forces of capitalism. And Wolfe writes, "When rock music turns sexist, movies glorify violence, television sells junk to children, and pornographic comic books appeal to teenagers, liberals ought not to be too smug about holding the moral high ground."[96] This then is not territory that the Left ought or needs to concede. Even the issue of family values, which became the stuff of low farce when Vice President Dan Quayle chose to invoke it to attack a television character, is really no laughing matter, as black thinkers such as Cornell West readily admit. Liberals, in their response to Quayle, as Russell Baker pointed out, sounded as if they were opposed to love, marriage, and the family. But this failure to grasp the importance of family ignores the fact that single-parent families may need assistance. As Carey McWilliams puts it, "Paradoxically, the liberal inclination to denounce as repressive any idea that the two-parent family is a standard leaves liberals only a limited, economic justification for aiding single-parent households, while conservatives, who accept the standard, are too niggardly to offer help."[97] Those who need help the most get caught in the middle.

What then is the state of the conservative movement? Politically, in spite of the setback in 1992, it is still powerful, as the 1994 congressional elections show. Intellectually, however, it is not an impressive structure; in a word, it is incoherent. Many of its thinkers make interesting points. Even the fundamentalists seem to be groping toward the idea advanced by many more-moderate critics of liberalism—the notion advanced by communitarians and others that the focus on individual rights, the alleged lack of concern for the legitimate claims of community, the seeming emphasis on procedure over content, and the affinity with moral relativism all combine to make liberalism a thin and unsatisfying body of ideas. But the conservative coalition does not make theoretical sense. The libertarians and fundamentalists cannot abide each other. The neoconservatives distrust the laissez-faire economists. Many prefer a strong state for the regulation of what were once thought to be private affairs, while repudiating such a state in the economic arena. All positions, even those that exhibit reservations, fully endorse capitalism.

But if conservatism has anything to do with preservation at all, then this endorsement is a dangerous liaison, because capitalism is the greatest force for change in the modern world. One should recall Schumpeter's claim that the essence of capitalism is "creative destruction."[98] Reasonable people can differ over whether the destruction is creative or not. But until conservatives can develop a theory that successfully accounts for and integrates the force of capitalist enterprise, conservatism cannot be intellectually viable in this most capitalist of countries. If there is any body of ideas that is capable of providing a solid basis for a genuine American conservatism, it stems from the thought of the German-Jewish émigré political theorist Leo Strauss and his large number of students and intellectual descendants.

Straussian Conservatism and American Politics

Strauss was by all odds the single most influential teacher of political theory in the United States in the past fifty years. In the 1950s no one would have predicted such an outcome. He was dismissed by many political theorists as the author of interesting, but often eccentric, studies of figures in the history of political thought, and by social scientists as a hopelessly backward critic of the foundations of the new fashions in scholarly research on politics.

But Strauss was much more than a historian of political thought. He was, in fact, an original, if highly convoluted, theoretical critic of modernity. He wrote but little on American politics, though much of what he did write about modernity has important implications for it; his students, in contrast, have written a great deal on the United States, and they have become both politically and intellectually influential. Ralph Goldwin was a White House aide to President Gerald Ford; William Kristol, a student of Harvey Mansfield at Harvard, was chief of staff for Vice President Quayle and continues to be active in an attempt to reshape the intellectual foundations of the Republican Party; others have been on the staff of the National Security Council; the American Enterprise Institute for Public Policy Research provides a home for many; and eclectic Irving Kristol, the father of William Kristol, has shown marked Straussian influence, as has the equally eclectic and even more influential columnist and television commentator George Will.

Strauss's theory of modernity is difficult to approach, since it must, for the most part, be gleaned from his criticisms of the major political thinkers.[99] The secondary literature is sometimes useful, but often problematic, because Strauss tended to polarize his readers; there are few neutrals in this discussion—Strauss is venerated by his followers and thoroughly detested by many of his critics as antiliberal, antimodernist, and antidemocratic.[100] Here I will try, as briefly as possible, to outline the essentials of Strauss's critique of modernity and then consider the application of his teachings to the American political and constitutional system.

Strauss began his intellectual life as a student of Martin Heidegger in Weimar Germany. In Strauss's mind, Heidegger was the great philosophical mind of the century. Next to him, we were told by Strauss, so great a figure as Max Weber appeared as a mere child. But Heidegger was a historicist who looked down on the permanent, objective things. As Strauss somewhat obliquely put it:

> It was the contempt for these permanencies which permitted the most radical historicist in 1933 to submit to, or rather to welcome, as a dispensation of fate, the verdict of the least wise, and least moderate part of the nation while it was in its least wise and least moderate mood and at the same time to speak of wisdom and moderation. The biggest event of 1933 would rather seem to have proved, if such proof was necessary, that man cannot abandon the question of the good society, and he cannot free himself from the responsibility for answering it by deferring to History or to any other power different from his own reason.[101]

In other words, Strauss alluded to the fact that Hitler came to power and Heidegger became a Nazi; if that could befall the greatest mind of the time, then there had to be something wrong with modern philosophy. That is what set Strauss on his lifelong search for the source of modernity's defects and eventually sent him back to the ancient world as the appropriate starting point for more adequate political reflections.

According to Strauss, modernity was in a state of crisis. The crisis had washed over humanity in three waves. The first was the work of Machiavelli followed by Hobbes. For Strauss, Machiavelli's main point was that "there is something fundamentally wrong with an approach to politics which culminates in a utopia, in the description of a best regime whose realization is impossible." Instead of following the ancients such as Plato, people must be guided by the objectives that real-world societies pursue. "Machiavelli consciously lowers the standards of social action. His lowering of the standards is meant to lead to a higher probability of actualization of that scheme which is constructed in accordance with the lowered standards."[102] Hobbes too lowered the standards; he too was oriented by success. Fear of violent death drove men to accept government, which then turned to fear of government.[103]

Hobbes based his theory on a right rather than a law—the right of self-preservation. "Modern and classical political philosophy are fundamentally distinguished in that modern political philosophy takes 'right' as its starting point, whereas classical political philosophy has 'law.'"[104] But the teaching of Hobbes was too harsh and required mitigation; that mitigation was the work of Locke. Locke, in Strauss's view, accepted the Hobbesian emphasis on self-preservation—Locke was essentially Hobbes in sheep's clothing—but what men needed for preservation was less a gun than food, in other words, property.[105] Thus Hobbes, followed by Locke, introduced into political theory a radical rights-based individualistic liberalism and began to lay some of the groundwork for capitalism. What early modernity offered was a change in the basic problem of political theory. No longer were the basic questions the nature of virtue and the best regime, but rather the material comfort of man and the problem of political obligation—the question of why we should obey the laws of the state.[106] This is what it means to lower the standards.

The United States, according to Strauss, is essentially a product of the first wave of modernity. Therefore, it is possible to treat the second and third waves more briefly, though it is important that to the Straussians, they remain significant threats to the American regime. The second wave began with Rousseau. The great Genevan, dissatisfied with Hobbes and Locke, began with an attempt to return to the premodern world, to the world of the classical city, but in the end he arrived at a still more radical version of modernity. Hobbes and Locke had held out the possibility of an appeal from the positive law to a higher law, or at least to the law of self-preservation. But Rousseau appealed to the general will, "the will of a society, in which everyone subject to the law must have had a say in the making of the law," a will that could not err.[107] This replaced a "transcendent natural right" as the standard of justice. Though Rousseau would have despised modern totalitarianism, the consequence of his position was horrifying: "If the ultimate criterion of justice becomes the general will, i.e., the will of a free society, cannibalism is as just as its opposite." But this involved making the highest human values into merely historical doctrines; they lost the transcendent status they had in the ancient world. This historicization of philosophical truth first by Kant and then Hegel already contained the "delusions of communism."[108]

The third wave of modernity was inaugurated by Nietzsche. This stage involved a further radicalization, for whereas Hegel had seen history as having a rational end, Nietzsche faced up to the fact that history could warrant no faith in rationality or progress. Ideals were simply human creations. Values were created by an act of will or power.[109] The political implications of this thinking were menacing. In spite of the fact that any political use of Nietzsche involved a perversion of his teaching, he was read by and inspired political men. Strauss then remarked, in his typically gnomic way: "He is as little responsible for fascism as Rousseau is responsible for Jacobinism. This means, however, that he is as much responsible for fascism as Rousseau was for Jacobinism."[110]

From these observations Strauss drew political conclusions. We could not ignore Nietzsche and simply return to earlier modes of thought. That was why liberal democracy was in crisis, a crisis that was theoretical but nonetheless real. "The theory of liberal democracy, as well as of communism, originated in the first and second waves of modernity; the political implication of the third wave proved to be fascism." The proximity of liberal democracy to communism might appear disconcerting, but there was hope because liberal democracy, unlike communism and fascism, "derives powerful support from a way of thinking which cannot be called modern at all; the pre-modern thought of our western tradition."[111]

Therefore, it is the crisis of the West that "induces us to turn with passionate interest, with unqualified willingness to learn, toward the political thought of classical antiquity."[112] Strauss said not to look there for "recipes for today's use," because the "relative" success of modern political philosophy had created a form of society radically different from that known to the classical theorists.[113] Still, if one could return to the original form of political science, one might obtain help in meeting the crisis of the modern era, which "consists in the West's having become uncertain of its purpose."[114] He pointed out that people had come to doubt the modern project. What they had to do was come to an understanding of classic as opposed to modern natural right and to grasp the ancient understanding of democracy and liberalism.

Classic natural right must be distinguished from conventionalism, which holds that law and justice are purely human creations with no roots in nature. Thus, in Plato's *Republic*, when Thrasymachus claimed that justice was merely the interest of the stronger, he was making a conventionalist claim. Strauss said that modern theories of natural right or justice were egalitarian—all men equally hold certain inalienable rights. But egalitarian natural rights were rejected by the classics. "Since men are unequal in regard to human perfection, i.e., in the decisive respect, equal rights for all appeared to the classics as most unjust."[115] The political implication of this was that "the simply best regime would be the absolute rule of the wise; the practically best regime is the rule, under law, of gentlemen, or the mixed regime."[116] The gentleman would be a man of moderate wealth derived from the land, but who lived the life of an urban patrician. The best practical regime, then, would be one in which this patriciate, "well-bred and public spirited, obeying the laws and completing them, ruling and being ruled in turn, predominates and gives society its character."[117] The mixed regime, as Shadia Drury noted, is "an aristocracy that is strengthened by the admixture of monarchical and democratic institutions," after the manner of Plato's *Laws* and Aristotle's *Politics*.[118]

Again to follow Drury's argument, we need more detail, so we turn to Strauss's brief but important discussion of Aristotle's conception of natural right. The implications of the analysis are somewhat startling. For Aristotle, natural right was most fully developed among fellow citizens; only there did the relations of justice reach their full growth. In addition, Aristotle asserted something even Strauss admitted to be surprising—that natural right was changeable.[119] This is what was startling to Strauss, given his insistence on the importance of the permanent things. In all societies, he said, there had to be universally recognized principles, but at the same time, "civil society is incompatible with any immutable rules," because in some circumstances it might be necessary to disregard them in the interest of preservation. However, "for pedagogic reasons, society must present as universally valid certain rules which are generally valid." These rules, rather than the exceptions, had to be taught, and they had to be taught without qualification.[120] In other words, we have to be prepared for extreme and dangerous situations and ready to lie to the people. This "variability of the demands of justice" was seen by both Plato and Aristotle, both of whom avoided the dangers of absolutism and relativism. For both, the rule was "There is a universally valid hierarchy of ends, but there are no universally valid rules for action."[121] A striking doctrine, perhaps even valid, but certainly not without problems. We can all probably agree that there is more than one means to a given end, but those means are debatable, and means, as is widely recognized, have a way of becoming ends. Even more seriously, this argument leaves open the possibility that a given end might justify means we might all reject. Thus, Strauss seemed to leave us in a quandary every bit as complex as the modern theorists he decried. Moreover, this seeming casualness about means opens the way to certain difficulties in the Straussian doctrine of constitutionalism.

It is clear then that in his standards of judgment, Strauss was less absolutist than is commonly thought and that his political standard was by no means democratic. What then was his understanding of modern liberalism? Here a distinction must be drawn between the ancient and the modern. To the ancients, a liberal was a man who behaved in a way becoming to a free man rather than a slave. He preferred the "goods of the soul to the goods of the body." Liberality, for Strauss, was a name for human excellence. And finally, "the liberal man cannot be a subject to a tyrant or to a master, and for almost all practical purposes he will be a republican." What we call conservatism today is essentially the same as classical liberalism.[122] *In that sense*, classical political philosophy was liberal, though it must be said that that is not the meaning of liberalism in ordinary speech about American politics today.

Here liberal education enters. Prior to the modern world, democracy was a regime in which all, or almost all, men were men of virtue who had developed their rational capacities to a high level. "Democracy, in a word, is meant to be an aristocracy which has broadened into a universal aristocracy."[123] It was once thought that such perfection was beyond human capacities. "This still and small voice has by now become a high-powered loudspeaker."[124] Strauss said that modern democracy had become mass democracy, but the classical ideal was seen by the social sciences as a delusion. We needed liberal education to counter this development, but only the few could be truly liberally educated.[125] That may seem to be a harsh teaching, "but we are not permitted to be flatterers of democracy precisely because we are friends and allies of democracy."[126]

To Strauss, by contrast, modern liberalism is a paltry thing.[127] Liberalism stressed liberty rather than authority; authority derived from society. There are no fixed norms, since norms respond to changes in needs; these changes reflected historical progress. It is optimistic and radical, democratic and egalitarian. It focuses on groups rather than the deeds of great men. Finally, it is deeply sympathetic to science, technology, and to the international system of commerce. This is a poor teaching: "True liberals today have no more pressing duty than to counteract the perverted liberalism which contends 'that just to live, securely and happily, and protected but otherwise unregulated, is man's simple but supreme goal' and which forgets quality, excellence, or virtue."[128]

That, in the most general possible way, is Strauss's view of the great struggle between ancients and moderns. How did Strauss, his students, and his followers, apply these ideas to American politics? Joseph Cropsey offers the most general answer in a brilliant, though grandiose, theory of the place of the United States in world history. He notes that modernity has been relentlessly self-critical. This is implicit in the idea of the three waves of modernity: "Modernity has grown by consuming itself." That is to say, modernity, "through thinking about itself has more or less continually modified itself." The modifications have not been for the better and have moved Americans in the direction of nihilism, a condition in which their deepest beliefs have no grounding, so that they are intellectually unprepared to defend themselves in a time of crisis. "The United States is an arena in which modernity is working itself out."[129] The hope for the United States is that it is rooted in the first stage of modernity, that is, the hope that "our moral resources will incline to fortify themselves at the spirited wells of modernity."[130] In this connection, it is worth pointing out that in the historiographical struggle between the partisans of the "republican synthesis" and those who hold to a view of American origins as essentially liberal, the Straussians side decisively with the liberal interpretation.[131]

This support reflects Strauss's belief that liberal democracy can draw support from the premodern tradition. Locke could give us hope because of his concern for the education of gentlemen, who were roughly equivalent to the citizens of the ancient republic, and because of his commitment to a theory of natural right reflected in the concern of the Declaration of Independence for the self-evident rights—life, liberty, and the pursuit of happiness.[132] And Strauss viewed Alexander Hamilton's stress in *Federalist* 35 on deferential voting, which Hamilton expected to lead to the domination of educated professional men, as a good sign. Strauss also suggested that liberal education might help, but his accompanying discussion of John Stuart Mill can only be described as pessimistic on that score.[133]

In the total context of Strauss's work, those ideas based on early liberalism must be seen as very weak reeds to offer support; those intellectual commitments appear to be either desperate or insincere. One should remember that Strauss's treatment of Locke in *Natural Right and History* was essentially a denunciation: Locke had placed right ahead of law and duty, he had emancipated our acquisitive instincts, thus paving the way for capitalism and turning life into a "joyless quest for joy."[134] Here as elsewhere, Strauss relied on doctrines he did not really accept; he was willing to do so only because he saw the other modern alternatives as so much worse and because he knew that a return to the polis was impossible.

Strauss's strictures on Locke and capitalism brought him and his followers face to face with the issue that had so often undermined American conservatism. Joseph Cropsey writes brilliantly, if enigmatically and very abstractly, on this topic, as well as on the relation of politics to economics. For Cropsey, the domination of politics by economics is based on a great mistake. For two thousand years the sole social science was political philosophy. Only an act of abdication by political philosophy made possible the autonomy of economics. But as soon as we consider the relation of economics to politics we are compelled to engage in political philosophy. "Our inquiry into the autonomy of economics leads us to discover the unalienable hegemony of political philosophy."[135]

Economics, and, one might add, the American regime are based on "the axiom of the irreducibility of the individual and hence the sovereignty of his passions. The short title of this idea is Individualism."[136] But this cannot be satisfying; thus people are dissatisfied. Cropsey's statement on this point is quite startling:

> We are dissatisfied with ourselves because our regime and life are marked by private striving for the satisfaction of individual goals rather than seeking to attain our individual ends through the mediation of a perfectly social act of provision. Alienated from one another, we are alienated from ourselves, for it is contrary to the nature of humanity to live in a state of even latent uncooperativeness with the others.[137]

This terse statement is striking; it is hard to say what its policy implications are. It does not sound very conservative, in any of the conventional senses, though it no doubt reflects the reaction of a premodern sensibility to modern capitalist economics. Still, it could very well come from a left communitarian critic of capitalist liberalism. Cropsey's hostility to communism was deep and undeniable; however, for a moment, there is a glimpse of the possibility of a conservative welfare state. What would such a state look like? Is that Cropsey's intent? I do not know; the text does not tell us; the questions are tantalizing.

Martin Diamond speaks in more-orthodox Straussian terms. Like the others, he sees a lowering of the standards, though not necessarily for the worse. For Diamond, the American regime is a system founded on the pursuit of interest, a foundation that was "low but solid."[138] This interest-oriented politics is at the heart of the theory of the constitutional system discussed in *The Federalist Papers*. Diamond recognizes a risk that the system will magnify and multiply "the selfish, the interested, the narrow, and the crassly economic."[139] However, Americans should compare modern U.S. practice, not with ancient and medieval theory, but with ancient and medieval practice. Here

Americans look better because the system has raised to unprecedented heights the benefits, freedom, and dignity enjoyed by the many.[140]

But that is not all, according to Diamond. The American system aspires to the bourgeois virtues. It reaches not toward ancient heights, "but toward positive human decencies and excellences." People have to distinguish, as discussed in Chapter 4, between greed, or avarice, and acquisitiveness. The latter is generated in commercial society and is to be preferred because it aims more at getting than at having. That is said to be a more moderate desire.[141] But that seems a distinction without a difference; no one who observes the economic scene in America can fail to see the abuses associated with the process of getting. This foundation may be low, but it does not seem very solid.

There is also another problem, associated, I think, with the Straussian insistence on timeless, unchanging principles, even though the structure of the economy has changed since the commercial republic was theorized. Madison could not have imagined, even Hamilton probably could not have imagined, the qualitative change that took place following the Civil War and the emergence of the modern large-scale corporation. The dominant institutions in a large corporate economy are capable of damage unimaginable at the time of the eighteenth-century origins of the commercial republic. More than most American conservatives, the Straussians have thought about the drawbacks of the contemporary political economy; they cannot be said to have arrived at a solution that promises an escape from the great fault line of conservatism in this country. They accept the principles of the commercial republic, but that republic is an artifact of the eighteenth century. It bears little relation to the economy based on the modern corporation.

What then of democracy? It is obvious that Strauss, while recognizing that modern liberal democracy was the best we could hope for, still had some trouble concealing his contempt for it. Others reveal a similar skepticism; Harvey Mansfield complains of "the galloping informality or increasing democratism of our politics." And Walter Berns could not be more blunt: "The Constitution is more democratic today than in the past and promising (or threatening) to become still more democratic."[142] It is Martin Diamond who gave the standard and most persuasive Straussian defense of the democratic character of the Constitution and who is perhaps the most committed democrat among the Straussians. Even Diamond expresses his reserve: American politics is "decent, even *though* democratic."[143]

Still, he is anxious to defend the Constitution against Charles Beard and his contemporary descendants. Diamond admits that the Framers made invidious comparisons between democracies and republics. But both were part of the same genus, popular government.[144] He denies, perhaps somewhat implausibly, that the Declaration of Independence was an exceptionally democratic document, the better to skewer the Beardian notion that the Constitution was an antidemocratic text. In any case, it is an easy task to dispose of Beard's now discredited arguments, though not quite so easy to attack an argument such as Gordon Wood's that reaches neo-Beardian conclusions on the basis of other evidence. After all, there was a real difference between Federalists and Anti-Federalists on the nature of the democracy provided for in the Constitution. Diamond then rehearses Madison's familiar arguments about the multiplication of interests so as to give "a beforehand answer to Marx," an answer that promotes interest politics rather than class politics.[145] The complexity of the Constitution and the instances in which special majorities were called for are not antidemocratic, but rather devices that ensure the triumph of a calm, carefully considered majority; in the long run, a persistent majority can win victory.

Nor is this system contemptible: "It never denies the unequal existence of human virtues or excellences; it only denied the ancient claim of excellence to *rule* as *a matter of right.*"[146] This is as good a conservative defense of democracy as one is likely to get; it lacks the openly grudging character of the position of Strauss himself, as well as some of his followers. Still, there remains a question whether, given the political connections of the Straussians and their understanding of the Constitution as a whole, it is a conservatism that is compatible with democracy.

Here I think the leading figure is Harvey Mansfield, whose recent writings are perhaps the most comprehensive Straussian treatment of U.S. politics, ranging from the elections of the past dozen years, through a number of significant policy issues, to a theory, albeit not a comprehensive one, of the Constitution as a whole. Perhaps one could say of the Straussians in general what Carey McWilliams has said of Mansfield's *America's Constitutional Soul* in particular: "If American conservatives listened to Mansfield, one would have to take them seriously, and such a conservatism may be the only way to evoke a liberalism that one can take seriously."[147] In any case, the dialogue that might result could only raise the level of political discourse.

Much of Mansfield's book is of great value even for those who disagree with the author's politics. We have already encountered his sharp, if not entirely convincing, critique of affirmative action. More important, he stresses the dignity of institutional and constitutional analysis against the intrusions of behavioral scientists and rational choice theorists. He casts a skeptical eye over recent conservative politics and shows a clear awareness of the serious intellectual failings on evidence there. Surely, he has no illusions. As

McWilliams suggests, the logic of Mansfield's position leads to the conclusion that "Reaganism was hollow, without a soul, constitutional or otherwise."[148]

More than most Straussians, Mansfield seems dubious about the reliance on the pursuit of interest at the heart of American constitutionalism. He believes that Americans have subordinated pride to interest and that the pursuit of interest might lead to a loss of freedom, particularly in the form of dependency. Perhaps, but dependency is an issue best left until later. Certainly he is right to say that dependency is a problem in American politics and policy, though that is not an insight unique to the Right.

Finally, his major theoretical contribution is an insistence on the importance of constitutional form. In Mansfield's view, we have lost sight of this and in doing so display a "willful disillusionment with a government that works." Much too casually confusing liberalism with postmodernism, he claims, "Postmoderns do not as a rule recommend more democracy, claiming it to be a good even in unlimited amount; rather, they attack every obstacle standing in the way of popular will."[149] Of course, the truth of this observation is subject to endless debate, and many liberals might well agree on the importance of form. Many of the most ardent defenders of proceduralism are political liberals, after all.

However, there is a tendency for Straussians to become constitutional fundamentalists. It has been reported, for example, that a Straussian lawyer in the Reagan Justice Department was the author of Attorney General Edwin Meese's speech on original intent. But this doctrine, as Sheldon Wolin remarks, can lead to a "misplaced biblicism."[150] At the same time, there seems to be a huge contradiction at the heart of Mansfield's theory of forms and formalities. For example, his book on the theory of the executive, *Taming the Prince*, emerges as, among other things, a convoluted theoretical apologia for a strong president on the model of Ronald Reagan, who was hardly notable for his constitutional purism.

Machiavelli is the great villain for Straussians, a "teacher of evil," who first opened the floodgates of modernity. One would think that his teaching has to be avoided, but no, according to Mansfield, he needs only to be tamed.[151] We must be realistic about the true nature of modern politics. This politics claims to represent the people, but some are better represented than others; it claims democratic credentials but is actually oligarchic; it is run by extra-constitutional institutions such as parties; it aims, not at the freely chosen pursuit of happiness, but at a particular notion of happiness; its people claim to be citizens, but they are only voters, and sometimes not even that; the leaders pretend to be executives, but they are really rulers. This, a deliberate contrivance, is the reality of all modern government.[152]

Americans' idea of constitutionalism causes them to focus on the restraints on government. In doing so, "it is doubtful whether, . . . we are faithful to the capabilities of the American constitution, for the forms of that Constitution show what free government aspires to as much as they check its ambition."[153] Lockean constitutionalism teaches that the legislature was to make laws the people thought right, but Machiavellian realism teaches that "the constitution must keep the people secure."[154] What we need from the people is that they display "an active forbearance from governing."[155]

We need, Mansfield writes, principled leadership, which in turn is the basis for responsible rule. "Periods of executive leadership such as the Reagan Revolution show what American government means."[156] It is upsetting to say so, but that may be empirically true. Still, the disdain for constitutional form this analysis displays is astonishing, coming, as it does, from a leading exponent of this honorable principle. Mansfield's "realism," however, permits him to ignore some of the major events of our time. "Mansfield constructs his prince for America," Sheldon Wolin tells us, "but he does it without reference to the three constitutional crises, occurring within the short span of two decades, provoked by executives defying recognized limits on their power: Vietnam, Watergate, and Irangate."[157] Wolin does not exaggerate when he refers to the contempt for democracy shown here.

Perhaps, in the end, this is where Straussian principles lead us; the danger is surely real, even if the conclusion is not inevitable. What Mansfield seems to be doing here is what Strauss said was sometimes necessary. The people are to be led to believe certain salutary myths about their government, but the wise will understand that these myths are just that and that they may be ignored with impunity. But that is not principle; it is pure opportunistic deceit. It is a poor foundation for liberal democratic politics or for a truly responsible conservatism.

What then can be said of the curious amalgam that is contemporary American conservatism? Much of what is covered by the label is conservative only in what Huntington calls the situational sense; it is dedicated to the preservation of a particular distribution of economic and political power at the heart of which is the large corporation. The group most truly devoted to the preservation of traditional values is the fundamentalist Right. They are the only members of the coalition who reject liberalism almost in toto, but they too embrace liberal capitalism with considerable fervor. Though some of the problems they address are real and pressing, their image of a Christian nation is deeply incompatible with American constitutionalism and with the social organization of an increasingly pluralistic social order. The libertarians can agree with them on almost nothing, and the neoconservatives cannot find much common ground with them either. The only thing they all share is a commitment to capitalism, but that, as I have repeatedly remarked, entails an attachment to a form of economic organization whose basic principle is change, which subverts many of the deepest values of both fundamentalists and neoconservatives. Whatever the virtues of capitalism as a way to produce goods, its roots lie deep in the liberal tradition and provide little support for a stable tradition. This dilemma is part of what it means to be conservative in an essentially liberal culture.[158] The theory of Louis Hartz is on the mark here. Intellectually coherent conservatism is hard to come by in such a society. The Straussians might appear to offer some hope, but they too have embraced capitalism, if only for reasons of political expediency. For the same reason they also accept liberal constitutionalism, though Mansfield's work shows they are ready to subvert it.

But if my reading of the Straussians is correct, the problems cut much deeper than this. A careful examination of many of their writings reveals a deep aversion, not only to liberalism, but to democracy itself. We can learn much about the history of political thought from the Straussians, though what we learn is often somewhat eccentric. One can only admire the seriousness with which they attend to the classics of political theory and their willingness to learn from them. But in the end, much of the Straussian teaching represents a serious threat to democratic legitimacy.[159]

This will not do! It is necessary to see if contemporary liberalism and its radical democratic and communitarian critics can offer something of value to help us regain our bearings at this dismal time in American politics.

• 15 •

Rights-Based Liberalism

ONE OF THE IRONIES in the recent history of liberalism is that during the past twenty-five years, when the electoral collapse of the reform liberal consensus became obvious, there has been a revival of liberal political philosophy, driven particularly by a concern for individual rights. Also noteworthy is that this revival developed in the face of the corrosive skepticism about the foundations of rights that stems from postmodernist political and social thought.[1] The revival has also come at a time when the claim to a variety of rights has been increasingly prominent in American life and, simultaneously, perhaps the most common source of intense political conflict. In somewhat schematic form, one might say that the first period in American constitutional law dealt with the basic structures and powers of the government and reached a climax in the Civil War, the second period dealt with the attempt to come to grips with the new corporate economy that emerged after the war, and the third focused with growing intensity on individual rights, particularly after the 1954 school desegregation decision in *Brown v. Board of Education.*

There is irony here too because the Bill of Rights, which provides the legal foundation for the politics of rights, was something of an afterthought of the constitutional framers. It was produced largely to placate the Anti-Federalists and thus to help secure the passage of the main document itself. The original argument of Hamilton and Madison was that the Constitution alone was adequate to secure rights and that, in fact, rights might be threatened by explicit listing, since to do so might seem implicitly to leave unlisted rights without protection. Besides, Alexander Hamilton blandly observed, how could powers not granted to the new government possibly be abused?[2] Moreover, for Madison, amending the Constitution was a "nauseous project."[3]

The pressures for such a bill, however, were very strong, not least because of a British tradition of guaranteed rights, reaching as far back as the Magna Carta in 1215. The contemporary political pressures were also very strong. Not only was the Anti-Federalist opposition in favor of a formal declaration of rights, but also, his general support for the new Constitution notwithstanding, was Madison's friend Thomas Jefferson. Moreover, Madison's own political position was somewhat precarious, and partly to bolster it, he committed himself to introducing a series of amendments in the First Congress.

But the Anti-Federalists were not happy with the result. They had hoped for a new convention that would undertake a more thorough revision. It was partly to forestall such a move and to preserve the basic features of the document he had done so much to shape that Madison entered into the amending process. Rather than making basic structural changes, he shifted the focus toward the rights of individuals and fought hard for the new provisions. Gordon Wood claims that although there might have been a new Constitution without Madison, there certainly would have been no Bill of Rights. Whereas Federalists were satisfied, thinking that the amendments were innocuous, the Anti-Federalists went into opposition. No one, not even Jefferson and Madison, could have imagined the extent to which individual rights guaranteed by the Bill of Rights and reinforced by the Fourteenth Amendment would be at the heart of twentieth-century politics.[4]

In fact, the results have been strangely mixed. Without the Constitution, the democratic momentum of U.S. politics might have been stronger, and without the force of constitutional sanction, the attachment to the idea that material property was an untouchable right might not have taken hold. At the same time, it is striking that the William Lloyd Garrisons who wish to burn the Constitution have been a minority among reformers, no doubt at least in part because the document, particularly as amended, offers recourse to the "disinherited."[5] This is a fact that may have important implications for the "political identity" and "shared understandings" of Americans.

Rights in Contemporary Liberalism

The explosive politics of rights generated by the Supreme Court decisions of recent decades has been accompanied by a flourishing debate among political theorists that goes to the heart of the American experience. This debate was sparked by the appearance in 1971 of *A Theory of Justice* by philosopher John Rawls, a work that almost single-handedly revitalized the virtually moribund discipline of political philosophy in the Anglo-American world. It is certainly the most discussed political theory written in English since the days of John Stuart Mill.[6] *A Theory of Justice* is a work of vast scope and philosophical ingenuity, rooted in the tradition of analytic philosophy, which may be a source of some of its weaknesses. It is also in the tradition of reformist, welfare-state liberalism, of which it is perhaps the fullest, though most abstract, expression.

If not a school, the book can at least be said to have founded a style that pervades much of political theory in the English-speaking world.

The defining characteristics of this style include a resistance to principles drawn from natural law, self-evident truths, or the word of God. There is also an unwillingness to draw on social conventions, history or a theory of history, or any sense of communal as opposed to individual rights. It is a form of political theory whose formulations are derived from a very abstract hypothetical situation—unfortunately bearing no relation to political or social reality.[7] More attractive, there is an attempt to create a theory of justice that rejects utilitarianism, always a possible source of abuse in the area of rights.

The hypothetical opening move of Rawls's argument was to posit the closely related conceptions that he labeled the "original position" and the "veil of ignorance." This strategy takes us back to what looks somewhat like a social contract theory, though no formal contract is actually posited. However, together, these two ideas are roughly analogous to the state-of-nature hypothesis in classic social contract theory.[8]

Though elaborated to great complexity, the basic argument of *A Theory of Justice* is simplicity itself. The essential features of the original position are "that no one knows his place in society, his class position or social status, nor does anyone know his fortune in the distribution of natural assets and abilities, his intelligence, strength, and the like. I shall even assume that the parties do not know their conceptions of the good or their special psychological propensities. The principles of justice are chosen behind a veil of ignorance."[9]

According to Rawls, those who occupy the original position are not altruists. They are rational calculators who wish to further their own interests, but because they are ignorant of their own special circumstances, they lay down rules for a just society that are fair, since it is potentially to their benefit to do so. In this sense, justice is equivalent to fairness. "The choice which rational men would make in this hypothetical situation of equal liberty . . . determines the principles of justice."[10] The two essential principles deal with the basic liberties that a just society requires and with social and economic inequality. Rawls's first statement of his rules announces: "First: each person is to have an equal right to the most extensive basic liberty compatible with a similar liberty for others. Second: social and economic inequalities are to be arranged so that they are both (a) reasonably expected to be to everyone's advantage, and (b) attached to positions and offices open to all."[11]

The basic liberties, for Rawls, include political liberty—the right to vote and to be eligible for public office, free speech and assembly, liberty of conscience and freedom of thought, the right to hold personal property, and freedom from arbitrary arrest, all working under the rule of law. The second principle, the difference principle, applies to the distribution of wealth and income as well as to hierarchical organizations. The first principle is prior to the second; thus departures from equal liberty cannot be justified by greater social and economic advantage. The emphasis is squarely on equality. All social values must be distributed equally "unless an unequal distribution of any, or all, of these values is to everyone's advantage." Or, in a later, more explicit, formulation of the difference principle, social and economic inequalities must be "to the greatest benefit of the least advantaged." Thus injustice is defined as "simply inequalities that are not to the benefit of all."[12]

The priority of liberty places Rawls squarely in the liberal tradition, though the implications of the difference principle clearly lead him away from the old canard that liberty and equality are inevitably in conflict.[13] But the level of abstraction of the analysis leaves some ambiguity as to the extent that greater equality would be provided for under Rawls's system. It is easy to see that the needs of society for managers and doctors, for instance, might lead to a good deal of inequality of reward, that is, if differential incentives were required to meet demands for such specialists. However, a careful reading of widely scattered suggestions in *A Theory of Justice* suggests a stronger egalitarian impulse than a bald statement of the difference principle might suggest. Thus, "the fair value of liberty" might require public financing of elections and the use of public money to further free discussion, as well as substantial economic redistribution and a redefinition of property rights. "Fair equality of opportunity" might require an equalization of life chances. So too might the value of self-respect, though Rawls often makes the rather strained simplifying assumption that relative levels of wealth and income have no moral significance. If we take all these factors into account, "it is virtually inconceivable that a society as inegalitarian as our own could be just or nearly just by Rawlsian standards."[14] Rawls's liberalism appears to be one that draws on socialist criticisms. Liberals can support the theory because of the priority it gives to liberty over economic redistribution, and socialists can support it because the redistributive implications of the difference principle seem to ensure that those freedoms will not be mere formalities.[15]

In many respects, it is a very appealing theory. Its solicitude for the least well off is salutary in a society frequently distinguished by a social Darwinian distrust or even contempt for the working and nonworking poor or, more generally, for the disadvantaged. Rawls's book provides a needed theoretical foundation for a welfare state, in fact, for a welfare state that goes well beyond the limited commitment to social provision characteristic of American society. Indeed, that may account for part of its impact outside the limited sphere of political philosophers.[16]

Nevertheless, there are serious problems in Rawls's theory. The strongly redistributive implications that can be derived from or read into the difference principle are, seen from the left, a best-case scenario. In spite of them, Rawls is strikingly indifferent to questions of political economy: The choice between socialism and a system of private property is "left open."[17] As Benjamin Barber says, under present circumstances, that is a little like a geometer's leaving open the question of whether parallel lines meet.[18] Besides, capitalist assumptions are deeply embedded in the original position. Those rational calculators thinking away behind the veil of ignorance are deeply imbued with a capitalist conception of rationality; once they leave the hypothetical world, they will turn their rationality toward the pursuit of interest in the manner we are all familiar with. After Rawls poured a good deal of liberal economics and psychology into the original position, it was no great trick, John Schaar remarked, for him to pour it out again. The result is that "the world presented looks distressingly like the one we have, but with a little more equalization of income and welfare." What Rawls did was to commit the fundamental error of universalizing his own time and place.[19] (As anyone who teaches political theory knows, it is very hard at times to convince American students that there can be any form of behavior that is not "rational," calculating, and self-interested. However attractive the alternative, it is likely to be dismissed as unrealistic.)

In this Rawls is simply representative of his time. Economic modes of thought have penetrated deep into moral philosophy, political theory, the social sciences generally, the management of the arms race, and on and on. This economistic vogue may be related to the desperate attempt to tame an economy seemingly so complex and distended, so internationalized as to defy control by the modern state. That theme provides a grim counterpoint to the progressive theme of community and control, which has characterized reform liberalism since the Progressive movement.[20]

Furthermore, Rawls is tied to the economy in another way. Whatever the virtues of liberal capitalist political economies, and they are considerable, since their first stirrings in Locke it has been clear that they are associated with great inequalities of wealth and power and that these inequalities increasingly threaten social stability. The welfare state is a partially successful attempt to deal with these problems. But this solution is dependent on high levels of economic growth, and the recent performance of the economy and the looming constraints of environmental degradation threaten to impose limits to growth. A political system that has hitherto paid little attention to redistribution may be faced with new stresses. Thus Schaar: "If the ethos of equality, or envy, prevails while the promise of growth and abundance is threatened, the liberal states will come to a day of reckoning when other principles of justice than those presented in this book will be needed."[21] Less ominously, one could suggest that the Rawlsian position is inextricably linked to a Keynesian economics of growth.[22] This is not necessarily a bad thing, but it has its political perils at a time when the success or even the legitimacy of a political system is so often measured by the success of the economy. A polity that assesses its legitimacy in that way can find itself in deep trouble in an extended period of economic weakness.

The economic implications of Rawls's theory are therefore somewhat ambiguous. But the political implications are even less clear. In fact, strange though it may seem to political scientists, his theory of justice is not a political theory at all, though, in fairness, it does have political implications. This problem is an obvious consequence of the logic that grows out of the concept of the original position or, more generally, out of the basic form of social contract theory that Rawls's work approximates. By imagining away class, social position, wealth, income, or any sense of the self save as an abstract calculator, Rawls has imagined away the very stuff of politics. Conflicts over these things are a large part of what politics is about.

Rawls's theory may be a theory of justice in some highly abstract sense, and such theories may have their uses, but it is explicitly not a theory of the political system.[23] Rawls's rational, calculating men are not citizens. They have no interest in a politics of participation. "In a well-governed state," he writes, "only a small fraction of persons may devote much of their time to politics. There are many other forms of human good." That is probably true enough, but the conclusion he draws is excessively optimistic: "But this fraction, whatever its size, will most likely be drawn more or less equally from all sectors of society."[24] And we should remember also that politics was banished only in the original position and only long enough to decide on what turns out to be some rather ambiguous rules of the game. Once we lift the veil of ignorance and leave the original position for what Barber called the "historical position," the congruence of the concern for self and the concern for justice upon which Rawls's theory depends will quickly divide and self-interested behavior will become the norm.[25]

There is nothing wrong with self-interested behavior as such; one reason for political participation, John Stuart Mill told us, is self-protection, since we cannot count on others to look out for our interests. But Mill, and Alexis de Tocqueville too, hoped that participation would further a concern for others as well, a concern all too often missing from the interest group liberalism central to American politics today. But why not start a theoretical analysis of the basic problems in the real world rather than in a theoretical construct whose analytical utility is suspect once an attempt is made to study politics as it exists? The price Rawls pays for the elegance of his formulations is high, for he "abolishes human complexity in the interests of quasi-mathematical theory."[26]

This problem would be less troubling if it were characteristic of Rawls only; instead, it plagues his whole school. The problem is simply an excessively high level of philosophical abstraction closely associated with an economic mode of reasoning whose central weakness, as well as its strength, is its frequently extreme simplification of reality. That reasoning, like Rawls's, abstracts from politics, race, gender, class, and indeed from anything that cannot easily be subjected to the cost-benefit calculations of a rational utility maximizer. Rawls himself makes a truly amazing contrast: Although admitting that constitutional democracy faces a real challenge in disparities of property and wealth that are incompatible with political equality, he goes to add, "The fault lies in the fact that the democratic political process is at best regulated rivalry; it does not even in theory have the desirable properties that price theory ascribes to truly competitive markets."[27] Economic modes of thought become the measure.

Rawls's goal was to rise above the hurly-burly of particularistic interests in search of an untainted standard that would be of use in all cultures and polities. But his is not the world we live in. For starters, this approach cannot "begin to grapple with the political dilemmas of an age in which political life is dominated by renascent particularisms, militant religions and resurgent ethnicities."[28] To this list it is important to add the modern corporation, particularly in its multinational forms.

The last point is particularly ironic. A style of thought so closely related to economic theory shows itself unable to deal with the central economic institution of the century. Rawls is clearly in the reform tradition of American liberalism, but he does not even attempt to tackle questions such as the role of the corporation or the relation of government to the economy or the difficult problem of the border between public and private, questions that have been central to reformers since the populist movement of a century ago. Perhaps no one else can claim real success in this effort, but the topic will not go away through philosophical sleight of hand.

This failure of Rawls does not mean there has been no liberal thought on the subject since the New Deal. John Kenneth Galbraith, always popular with the public and always distrusted by economists because of his iconoclastic disdain for professional norms, has provided a suitably large-scale frame of analysis for the modern political economy in *The New Industrial State*.[29] Several themes stand out in Galbraith's work. Modern corporate capitalism requires a great emphasis on planning. The substantial use of heavy capital and advanced technology cannot be subjected to the vagaries of the market. The risks are too great, so the market must be brought under control. The techniques by which the market may be controlled, suspended, or superseded are complex and need not be discussed here.[30]

What is important is Galbraith's incisive discussion of the relation of government to the economy. In the new industrial system, true to the predictions of the more astute corporate executives during the Progressive Era, the economy has won extensive influence over the polity. Indeed, for many purposes the state has been reduced to providing services for industry. The state attempts to regulate aggregate demand, maintain the public sector of the economy on which this regulation depends, and provide an increasing volume of skilled manpower.[31] What has emerged is a close union of state and economy, which leads Galbraith to assert, "Men will look back in amusement at the pretense that once caused people to refer to General Dynamics and North American Aviation and A.T.&T. as *private* businesses."[32]

Thus the contemporary mixed economy is a planned economy in which the planning is the result of an informal, but nonetheless firm, alliance between government and the industrial system. This analysis involves a partial repudiation of Galbraith's earlier concept of countervailing power insofar as that theory provided an image of a semiautomatic balance. Automaticity became less important—in spite of the ritual claims of corporate elites to be under the control of markets—because such balancing of economic forces as existed had to be the result of conscious action. This analysis is powerful; it is also very much in the New Nationalist tradition of Theodore Roosevelt and the NRA of Franklin Roosevelt. For Galbraith much of this concentration of economic power was socially useful. It is certainly not that he is uncritical of the corporation or the system of which it is a part. The semiprivate planning arrangements he describes leave important lacunae in transportation, housing, environmental degradation, and the like. Today Galbraith would no doubt add medical care. If we can bring such problems under control, "the industrial system will fall into its place as a detached and autonomous arm of the state, but responsive to the larger purposes of the society."[33]

Much of this rings true. It is useful to be reminded that the idea of the free competitive market is largely a myth. The loose sort of planning Galbraith describes is the norm in major industrial societies. The problem is that the United States, perhaps because of its attachment to the myth of the market, has often played the game less well than its competitors. However, Galbraith's relatively benign view of the new industrialism is overly optimistic. It was his hope that a new elite of technocratic planners, the "educational and scientific estate," emboldened by its strategic position as the source of management expertise, would influence the system on behalf of genuinely public concerns. This is an elite in a strategic place, analogous to the great financiers in the heroic period of industrial expansion. But there is little sign that managerial elites are proving to be as enlightened as Galbraith hoped. Instead, as their support for educational change suggests, they have remained narrowly technical in their approach.[34] It is not likely that democracy or a more humane society is very secure in the hands of corporate managers, nor deep down do I think Galbraith thinks so. Even his hopes for the technostructure are shadowed by his knowledge that it is out of public control.[35]

This conclusion about the structure of the political economy and the business-government relationship is underlined by the recent work of Robert Dahl and Charles Lindblom, who have significantly modified the theory of pluralism, developed in the 1950s, which, for many, made them the examplars of the complacency of mainstream political science at that time.[36] Their studies fill in some of the details of the broad framework spelled out by Galbraith. For those familiar with their earlier work, the new edition of *Politics, Economics, and Welfare* is startling and often illuminating. Dahl and Lindblom show themselves to be as convinced as Galbraith of the close linkages of business and government and considerably less optimistic about the prognosis. In this system, business leaders play a qualitatively different role than other actors; theirs is a privileged position. They function like public officials, even though they hold no government position.[37] Political and economic inequality is substantial and destructive of the possibility of genuine democracy.[38] Moreover, the problems are structural and cannot be alleviated by "more thoughtful, better informed, or more scientific problem solving."[39] There is a fundamental institutional derangement, so that "in Vietnam, in Watergate, and in the corruption in business and government . . . the overwhelming evidence suggests [that these events are] more central than peripheral to the system."[40]

At the heart of the problem, according to Dahl and Lindblom, is corporate capitalism, the inequality it fosters, and its capacity to manipulate public opinion. The privileged position of business means that it has control over "jobs, prices, production, growth, the standard of living, and the economic security of everyone."[41] Given the importance of these functions and the extent to which since the New Deal the success of a government has been measured in economic terms, it follows that "government needs a strong economy just as much as business does, and the people need it and demand it even more." Thus the government has to induce business to perform.[42] One can easily see this motivation in the competition between states in the Union to induce business to operate within their boundaries, as well as in the increasing international competition to entice business to locate in nations all around the globe. That is nothing very new, though the problem may have intensified; as early as 1912 Woodrow Wilson proclaimed: "The government of the United States at present is a foster-child of the special interests. It is not allowed to have a will of its own. It is told at every move, 'Don't do that, you will interfere with our prosperity.'"[43]

That business elites have great power has been widely accepted across a wide ideological spectrum. The question is whether they are subject to adequate public control. Business, Lindblom says, is privileged. It has disproportionate influence in interest groups, political parties, and electoral politics. But the power of business goes beyond this. Corporations have been able to persuade the public to accept their special position and, beyond that, to exercise substantial control over the agenda of politics, so that some major potential issues never receive sustained public attention or are buried altogether. One should recall the discussion in Chapter 12 of Bachrach and Baratz on the concept of the nondecision—the easily conceivable policy alternative that gets a poor hearing or no hearing at all.[44] For example, it took health policy so long to achieve a prominent place in the political process and then there was an extremely limited range of alternatives that could be seriously considered. Some form of managed care, which would have been a bonanza to the largest insurance companies, seemed to be the only politically viable option, whereas a single-payer system, which could be plastered with the dread label *socialized medicine*, could just barely rise to the level of a discussible possibility.

Dahl adds to the indictment. We are bogged down, he argues, in an ideology of agrarian democratic republicanism. This ideology is deeply indebted to Locke's theory of property; it was developed in a context in which one of the major facts of life was an abundance of land. As long as there was equal opportunity to acquire property, political equality would be easy to achieve. Along with this perception went a sharp distinction between public and private, according to which the public sector should clearly be democratic, but in which private enterprise, that is, farms, could be run as their owners pleased. The largely agricultural economy was just not seen as a matter of public concern.[45] This is at the heart of what Richard Hofstadter called the "agrarian myth"—the compellingly seductive image of the independent yeoman farmer as the model citizen; for all the ambiguity of Jefferson's ideas, this image was at the center of his thinking. But by the end of the nineteenth century and the failure of populism, the gap between this ideology and the real structure of the corporate economy had become immense.[46]

The large corporations, Dahl argues, should be seen as analogous to the state, yet they are by no stretch of the imagination democratically controlled, in spite of the enormous impact they have on the lives of all of us. The decisions of corporate managers are not widely seen as public matters, because they are perceived to stem from the rights attached to privately owned property. "But," Dahl argues, "the justification of private property as a natural, inalienable, or fundamental right provides scant justification for the existing ownership and control of large corporations."[47] Here the Jeffersonian heritage is woefully inadequate.

This level of corporate power and its theoretically weak, though politically powerful, defense is a major feature of the problem of rights in the contemporary setting and cannot be ignored. The modern corporation is at the heart of a great deal of the economic and political inequality that must be dealt with by a theory of justice. It is deeply involved with individual rights, the well-being of communities, and the problems of distributive justice. A theory of rights or justice that cannot encompass the role of the corporation is likely to be of limited use. Since the present book is not a study in public policy, it is not the place to explore alternative patterns of ownership that might be more just and more conducive to democracy. But the work of Galbraith, Lindblom, and Dahl has made clear the need to rethink the relation of the public to the private in the economic sphere even more than in family relations. In this era we have seen that centrally controlled bureaucratic socialism is inadequate economically and politically, but this understanding does not lead automatically to the conclusion that there is no alternative to corporate capitalism. The latter has been misleadingly presented as part of a pattern of transactions among free individuals in a competitive market setting.[48] That we know to be a fantasy. But for now we can leave that question aside.

If this portrait of corporate America is the setting for which a theory of justice must be created, one might have been encouraged that John Rawls was about to descend from the heights of abstraction when he argued that justice as fairness was a political rather than a metaphysical concept.[49] As Rawls now sees it: "Justice as fairness is a political conception in part because it starts from within a certain political tradition. We hope that this political conception of justice may at least be supported by what we may call an 'over-lapping consensus,' that is, by a consensus that includes all the philosophical and religious doctrines likely to persist and to gain adherents in a more or less just constitutional democratic society."[50] Tolerance becomes the key virtue, the only alternative to which is an autocratic state. Thus, "philosophy as the search for truth about an independent metaphysical and moral order cannot, I believe, provide a workable and shared basis for a political conception of justice in a democratic society."[51]

This move might appear to link Rawls to theorists such as Michael Walzer, who argues that justice rests on an interpretation of the "shared understandings" that underpin a society. But that is not the case. Rawls, in his recent book, *Political Liberalism*, which offers a revision and restatement of the ideas proposed in *A Theory of Justice,* specifically rejects that position. In fact, he argues, we turn to political philosophy when our shared understandings break down.[52] The unfortunate result is that Rawls's revised position is of as little use as a guide to justice in the "historical world" as was his first effort. We look in vain for an engagement with the central political issues of the twentieth century. It is a disappointing work; John Gray may be excessively harsh, but he is not completely wrong when he refers to its "complete political irrelevance" even for the United States, indeed, its "utter political emptiness."[53]

Rights Theory After Rawls

The failure of Rawls to make his moral philosophy politically relevant does not leave liberals silent on the theory of rights. The work of Judith Shklar, though unsystematic and disarmingly unpretentious, is based on a deep understanding of American politics and culture.[54] Hers is a "liberalism of fear," based on a deep desire to avoid cruelty. She argues that cruelty was the first of the "ordinary vices," a vice that philosophers have ignored, but that preoccupies historians and dramatists. We would do well to pay attention to it because of the unique cruelty so pervasive in the twentieth century. It is not in the least unreasonable for sensible people to be motivated by fear, given the history of the world since 1914.[55] "We fear a society of fearful people," because constant fear makes freedom impossible.[56] It is not by accident that she chooses to theorize about injustice rather than justice. We are more likely to talk of the former than of the latter, she writes,[57] perhaps, I suppose, because we see more of it.

Shklar is not satisfied with the "normal" or legal form of justice, and *Faces of Injustice* has no particular bearing on it; her real concern is with the victims of injustice and cruelty.[58] Not for her are the system-building ambitions of a Rawls; she is fiercely "anti-academic" in her "hostility to general principles, universal truths, moral and political laws."[59] There are times when she seems surer of what is to be avoided than of the outlines of the good society. One is reminded of the sociology of Barrington Moore, who made few positive claims, but who knew full well the sources of basic human misery. They are not hard to name: war, cruelty, hunger, toil, injustice, oppression, and general human nastiness. Moore offered a form of negative utilitarianism that could tell us what to avoid. Without deluding himself that anyone had discovered lawlike patterns of human behavior or suggesting any misplaced optimism, he hoped that social science in the classical tradition of Marx and Weber could suggest some of their causes and explore proposals to eliminate them. Shklar's is a "negative" or a "dystopic" liberalism that is similar to Moore's in spirit, though without his social scientific commitments.[60]

Shklar's unassuming but penetrating effort to move beyond negative liberalism and to outline the good society leads her to a consideration of the idea of citizenship in the United States. Hers is a modest conception, not remotely like the high ideal of republican citizenship. She says that citizenship is a mark of social standing, and its "two great emblems" are the right to vote and the opportunity to earn.[61] This is not a theory about the politics of virtue, nor is it much related to nationality; it is rather about two ideas deeply grounded in the problems of American history and culture. They are vitally necessary if one is to have self-respect in this society. Citizenship as standing is so important because the vote and the opportunity to earn were so long denied to so many in a republic ostensibly committed to political equality.[62]

The right to earn is based on Locke and Puritanism, more than she may have realized in the case of the latter, and it continues through the Jacksonian Democrats up to the populists and on to the labor movement of the twentieth century. And as I argued earlier, part of the energy of the antislavery movement came from workers' fear of being treated like slaves; of course, the vote was denied for decades to former slaves and women alike. The drive to secure these basic rights helps to explain great stretches of U.S. history. Though the right to vote is formally secure, the right, and sometimes the obligation, to earn are still at the heart of current debates on welfare and employment policy. Shklar's brilliant though modest book does much to illuminate these matters. In it she moves past a negative liberalism of fear and toward a social democratic political system, though I suspect she might have shrunk from that label. Still, it is hard to say what else to call a theory that posits the government as the employer of last resort if needed to secure the opportunity to earn. Also, though the theory *is* modest, its implications are staggering to one who considers the transformation that the information revolution is making in the labor market. What will these changes imply for the right to earn?

But the deepest theory of rights-based liberalism is offered by George Kateb. Though not a system builder like Rawls, he is more in touch with American thought and politics and he cares about institutions, particularly the institutions of representative democracy, while looking more deeply into the philosophical foundation of rights than Shklar. Nevertheless, the philosophical foundation is deliberately modest. The very implication that rights need an elaborate defense causes him to worry that this alone would weaken them.[63] Like Shklar and Moore, he has a keen sense of what is to be avoided, but there is a foundational commitment to the value of human dignity—"the equal dignity of every individual"—at the base of his thought.[64]

Kateb admires Rawls's "war on utilitarianism," but he rejects his belief that respect for the dignity or the inherent worth of persons is not a suitable basis for a theory of justice. For Kateb, the foundation for rights is the basic fact that each person is a creature "capable of being a free agent and a moral agent."[65] This foundation is resolutely, almost defiantly, secular; in principle, we could reject the standard of dignity in favor of the "superior dignity of the more-than-human," but in spite of the admittedly Protestant origins of the theory of rights, Kateb believes that if we introduce religion into the discussion, debate becomes impossible. Rights are the only way to protect human dignity, and to Kateb there is simply no credible external foundation for a critique of the theory.[66] Thus, the argument for rights is based essentially on self-evidence.

But in the United States, rights are deeply rooted in the culture of constitutional law. In the Bill of Rights, rights against government were the norm; the two centuries of judicial interpretation of those rights has produced a body of thought on the subject that is incomparable in "richness, subtlety, and ingenuity." These ideas and their realization are a "unique contribution to the meaning of human dignity."[67] Still, these rights are fragile—it is the Warren Court, not the Rehnquist Court, that Kateb admires—but the constitutional setting provides an anchor that the more abstract theory of Rawls cannot offer.[68] Kateb's work is also grounded in the tradition of American political thought, particularly Emerson's and Whitman's, but also Thoreau's and Lincoln's, though Lincoln's deserves more attention than it receives. Those four men constituted the "second generation of intellect, the true inheritors of the founding of the American polity. They disclose the fuller meaning of the founding." He adds, "I do not think there has been a third generation."[69]

Consistent with his focus on rights, Kateb's is a deeply individualistic theory, but it is individualistic with a difference. His is a theory of *democratic individuality*, and though it might pass almost unnoticed, he chides other defenses of the individual for not meeting the adjectival standard or for being antisocial. As he sees it, "individualism redefines human bonds; it does not foolishly try to eliminate them."[70] Even so, we have to be wary of social conventions; we cannot live without conventions, but we are more than their totality. The democratic individual would stand to one side of them; thus Kateb is drawn to the civil disobedience of Thoreau and he loves to quote Emerson's maxims: "The law is only a memorandum" and "Good men must not obey the laws too well."[71] Social conformity thus counts for very little.

Democratic individuality, for Kateb, has three components: the negative, a willingness to disobey bad laws or conventions on the basis of a careful consideration of the requirements of one's own moral character; the positive, the capacity of a person to create or choose his own self; and, rather more vaguely, the impersonal, an ability to transcend one's self so as to achieve a new relation to experience, lying beyond mere self-interest.[72] It was these ideas that the Emersonians raised to new heights and that made them into major figures in the history of democratic theory. There is a positive exaltation of the potential of the individual and of democracy as well; the Emersonians—and Kateb too—are examples of what Nancy Rosenblum calls heroic individualism, a romantic, almost rhapsodic, assertion of liberal individualism "at its most militant and self-assertive. Its resources for reconstruction are the revolutionary elements of liberalism—self-government, consent, and independence." Here is an instance of what has been called the "individualism of the strong."[73]

The focus on rights leads Kateb to a deep distrust of government and, even more, of the state; he carefully distinguishes between the two. Democracy ends when society is ruled. A society may be said to be ruled when "important decisions are made by self-chosen or hereditary or appointed officials rather than by elected ones, or when elected officials make important decisions in secret or on their own unchecked initiative or in such a way as to evade accountability." When these traits appear, a government becomes a state. Rights are eroded when government begins to act like a state. This condition is not caused "solely or even substantially" by socioeconomic inequality. Its principal cause lies in the preeminence of foreign policy, and from this perspective Kateb believes that "a strong case could be made for saying that the United States is not a democracy." In fact, genuine democracy is impossible when foreign policy issues become central to a nation's politics.[74] This is a powerful indictment, but when one considers the conduct of the war in Southeast Asia or the Iran-Contra affair, the charge implied does not seem exaggerated.

For Kateb, the best form of government is representative democracy because it is conducive to the development of a morally distinctive human type. Political authority is chastened—"demystified or desacralized"—when it is subjected to regular contestation in elections.[75] The temporary character of authority stimulates "independence of spirit," an "incitement to claim the status of citizen." Authority arises from partisan contestation. It creates a healthy aura of moral indeterminacy, since it makes clear that there are alternative answers to questions that have a moral side, a condition not to be confused with mere relativism or skepticism.[76] Good democrats must learn to live with a degree of uncertainty.

Authority is further chastened by constitutionalism, which, Kateb writes, reached its highest theoretical development in American thought and experience, not only in the Bill of Rights, but also in the structural principles of separation of powers, checks and balances, and federalism. These features aim to lessen discretionary exercise of power, which, in turn, leads to a healthy weakening of inhibitions against challenging authority.[77]

This, as Kateb knows, is not a theory without problems. The "readiness to say no" might turn to obstinacy, moral indeterminacy might turn into "mindless skepticism," and the system could degenerate into a "mechanical formalism." Perhaps worst of all, the democratization of small matters might become a "substitution for real democracy."[78]

Beyond this, Kateb sees the allure, the sheer power, of the idea of direct democracy. Only in a direct democracy do the people really rule. He even concedes that the moral phenomena associated with direct democracy are superior to those associated with representative democracy. The trouble, in his view, is that the moral costs are even greater. The radical flaw in direct democracy is its communitarianism. The idea of community contains a great egalitarian moral vision, but the potential for loss is "unspeakably great." The individual is submerged, the sense of self lost.[79] And community is essentially a conservative idea. Communitarians "reject conflict, tension, ill-definition, uncertainty, partisanship, deviance, rebellion. They reject disorder in all its forms."[80] The ancient idea of participatory democracy is flawed. "The modern self is larger and therefore better than the classical self." None of the theorists of direct democracy from Aristotle to Hannah Arendt were able to show otherwise. Athens is the dream, but it is the exception. "Sparta is the horror."[81]

More troublingly, though perhaps understandably at present, Kateb, with Ralph Waldo Emerson and Walt Whitman, considers politics a rather low form of activity, though it is not to be eschewed altogether. "Always vote," Whitman told us, but stay aloof and detached from the parties. Kateb celebrates a politics of "episodic citizenship," a temporary association of citizens that aims to protest great atrocities, to end violations of the Constitution and the Bill of Rights, and to fight executive excess and lawlessness. The civil disobedience campaigns of the 1960s are a case in point.[82] What Kateb offers is rather like a political version of the idea of the Minuteman, the readiness of an aroused citizenry to rise up against the usurpations of power by an irresponsible state.

It is important to distinguish Kateb's vision of democratic individuality from other forms of individualism, particularly the economically oriented version often called *possessive individualism*, closely associated with capitalism. Democratic individuality, to Kateb, is more than that; it is more than atomism; more than money is at stake. Rights-based individualism is based on human dignity and is hostile to or critical of other forms of individualism.[83] This is not the "every man for himself" individualism of libertarians or social Darwinists. The rights of property are not absolute and are clearly inferior to human dignity. Society has a positive obligation of Samaritanism, and individuals have a right to be "spared from utter degradation or to be saved from material misery." This is basic if one is to live a life. Kateb says that these social democratic rights, as well as the Fourteenth Amendment claims to equal protection, go beyond mere governmental abstention from action or a commitment to mere proceduralism, as do freedom of speech, press, religion, assembly, association, and privacy.[84]

Because he thinks relief of material misery is a basic right vis-à-vis society and government, Kateb is willing to allow a "welfarist" attempt to improve the condition of the poor, disadvantaged, and disabled. But these claims do not extend to any attempt to impose socioeconomic equality. Rights-based individualism is not radical egalitarianism; inequality will continue to exist.[85] With Whitman, Kateb is willing to condemn the life of mere "moneymaking," but the solution would be a wider ownership of property, which up to a point guarantees democratic individuality; after that point property rights can become dangerous because they might inspire "redemptive collectivist proposals."[86]

This is a powerful and in many ways attractive vision. However, two problems are evident. There is little sign that contemporary elections in the United States, surely a representative democracy, are of sufficient quality to produce the beneficial effects on character Kateb hopes for. The idealism of the civil rights movement and the early days of the new student Left, though not its final decadent phase, are fine examples of the episodic citizenship Kateb admires, but they come all too seldom. One can hardly look at the passion for the death penalty, "three strikes and you're out," mistreatment of minorities, and the common demands for censorship, even on university campuses, to feel much hope that citizens will rise up in episodic wrath to protect constitutional rights. And Kateb concedes that if large numbers of people come to believe that the system does not work, "the game is up."[87] But today we are in the world of Schumpeter's democracy, in which the psychotechnics of party management triumph over serious discussion of issues and many people already believe that democracy is what the first of its great economic theorists claimed it was—"a sham."[88] We can wish that the American representative democracy displayed the merits that Kateb claims it makes possible, but it is far from clear that it does. Direct democracy is no solution to this problem, but the current institutional framework does not seem to meet his high standards.

Finally, there is a tension within Kateb's remarks on the relation of politics to economics. He is surely right to argue that human dignity generates a right to protection against material misery and to an alleviation of the plight of the disadvantaged, especially in a society as rich as that of the United States. But under present conditions, such alleviation would require a large government, if not a large state, bearing in mind Kateb's careful distinction between the two. That is particularly true in a context dominated by corporate capitalism. Kateb's strictures against Robert Nozick's theory of rights, to which he was otherwise sympathetic, make clear his awareness of the institutional setting, but his theory of rights, as developed in *The Inner Ocean*, would be strengthened if he explicitly acknowledged the problem posed by corporate power.[89]

The dilemma is a serious one, and not just for Kateb's theory. A large powerful government is a potentially dangerous force, difficult, some say impossible, to subject to democratic control, but it is hard to see by what other means the modern corporation can be brought to heel. We need to bear in mind the dramatic conclusion to Charles Lindblom's analysis of corporate power: "The large private corporation fits oddly into democratic theory and vision. Indeed, it does not fit."[90] Surely only government is remotely capable of righting the balance; at the moment the odds seem to favor the corporation. Kateb's theory does not seem to offer an answer to this problem, though that is not really his subject, and it must be said, it is not clear that anyone else has a solution either. If there is one, it probably lies somewhere in the theoretical territory between the radical democratic populism of a Sheldon Wolin and a revivified social democratic reform liberalism. But for either of these approaches to be of use, there must be a secure foundation in individual rights, a foundation to which Kateb has made an important contribution. However, before we can turn to those schools of thought, it is necessary to consider the extensive communitarian critique of liberalism, which has been at the heart of debate in American political thought for the past twenty years.

· 16 ·

Problems of Liberalism:
Rights, Economy,
Community, and the State

By THE LATE 1960s, the deficiencies of liberal pluralism were becoming clear and were codified, so to speak, in Theodore Lowi's seminal book, *The End of Liberalism*, in which he claimed to show, through an analysis of several public policy arenas, that interest group liberalism could not plan, achieve justice, or end poverty. Moreover, he said that because of the tendency of Congress to delegate excessive discretionary power to administrative agencies, interest group liberalism was systematically implicated in a subversion of the rule of law.[1] This indictment was particularly disturbing, since Lowi was not a reactionary critic of the reform tradition and, in fact, had been associated politically with Robert Kennedy.

Lowi's book was an analysis of a pluralism out of control, a situation in which government tended to be the captive of interests it ostensibly regulated. Though not part of Lowi's argument, the theory of civic republicanism, with its emphasis on the subordination of self-interest to the common good, had clear attractions in this context. If such an attitude had once prevailed, perhaps it could be resurrected.

The Communitarian Critique
of Liberalism

It is no accident that the communitarian critique and the historical rediscovery of republicanism arose at essentially the same time. Regardless of the motives of Bernard Bailyn, Gordon Wood, and J.G.A. Pocock when they rediscovered the republican past of the United States, there is little doubt that

287

some theorists have seized on the presumably deep if obscure embeddedness of the republican tradition as a weapon with which to attack the current forms of liberalism. Others have responded with a vigorous defense of liberalism or with the consensus theory of the liberal tradition, apparently also for political reasons. Much of the dispute is over the founding—or perhaps the founding myths—of American society. That is not surprising; the founding of a society has always been deeply stirring to its members. The very beginnings of political theory are involved with the emergence of democracy in ancient Athens, and as Peter Euben says, "Stories about or analyses of origins are political projections as much as they are accurate accounts of the past."[2] Put differently, they involve questions of meaning and interpretation. That may explain some of the intensity of the debate over the relationship of liberalism and republicanism in early American history. By now, as I have shown in the early chapters of this study, a consensus has begun to emerge, admitting that liberalism and republicanism were never posed as clear-cut alternatives in the minds of the Founders, that Puritanism must be given its due place, and that at some point in the early national period, republicanism rapidly gave ground to the forces of liberalism.

But it may be that for contemporary thought this scholarly problem is less important than the interpretive politics surrounding it. Some supporters of the republican synthesis, such as Michael Sandel, are clearly drawn to the interpretation because they see in it an alternative to what they consider the defects of liberalism; some defenders of the theory of liberal dominance use it to isolate the source of what they claim to be the malaise of American politics. It is striking that the criticisms of liberalism offered by these two schools often seem rather close in substance.[3] J.G.A. Pocock seems anxious to demolish both Marxian and Straussian accounts of the centrality of liberalism in the development of capitalism, a view shared by those otherwise opposed schools of thought. The result is to downplay liberalism as a dominant force in modern politics, an interesting argument, but one pressed much too far.[4] For their part, the Straussians wish to preserve the liberalism they distrusted as the best realistically possible modern alternative on which to build their conservative theory. They dislike liberalism, but they see no better position; liberalism is bad, but the other contenders are worse.[5] And, finally, some defenders of the liberal thesis and critics of the republican synthesis find the former attractive because it confirms the historical foundations of their own liberalism.[6]

Communitarianism, however, goes much deeper than an affinity between its advocates and certain schools of historical interpretation. To communitarians, liberalism is undermined by a weak conception of the human self, an impoverished notion of what it means to be a person. Though Michael

Sandel is not the only powerful advocate of this view, I will focus on him particularly because he raises other issues especially important in this study.[7] The problem he sees in contemporary, rights-based liberalism lies in Rawls's conception of rational calculators operating in the original position behind the veil of ignorance. The question they ask is not, "Who am I?" but "What shall I choose?"[8] However, they ask this question in a vacuum. The self that reasons toward a theory of the just society is a self stripped of all particularity, of all the characteristics that make a human being more than a disembodied abstraction. This self, Sandel says, is "unencumbered" by history, tradition, community, social structure, or any other of the conditioning factors that make us what we are. This is an atomistic individualism too abstract to be credible. What we need is a theory, not of the unencumbered self, but of the "situated" self.[9]

Rawls's rational actors insist on the priority of the right over the good. However, Sandel claims, the absence of a theory of the good leads us into a relativistic abyss. Without such a theory, liberals commonly argue that tolerance, freedom, and fairness are needed. But of course, Sandel is correct to argue that those values cannot be defended by the claim that no values could be defended.[10]

This is good social-psychological theory and an apt criticism of Rawls and of libertarian versions of liberalism, but it will not do as a critique of liberalism *tout court*. Once again, we should recall Dewey, with his deeply social conception of human nature, or even so intense a rights-oriented liberal as George Kateb, who, explicitly though briefly, insists on man's sociality. Without this foundation, his argument for a general duty to Samaritanism would make no sense.

However, it is clear that the politics of rights has been increasingly central for the past generation or more. Rawls's doctrine of the priority of the right over the good is troubling to Sandel. Descended from Kant, Rawls's conception denied that justice was grounded in any conception of human ends or purposes. Moral laws are laws we give to ourselves.[11] It is that which necessitated the stress on rational choosers in a modernized analogue to the state of nature. But here the difference principle raises a problem. The assets to be shared according to the principle are common assets. The principle is intended to be a guide to sharing. "As such, it must presuppose some prior moral tie among those whose assets it would deploy and whose efforts it would enlist in a common endeavor."[12] There must be a conception of community, a conception that Rawls lacked in *A Theory of Justice*. And the community has legitimate claims that may be undercut by an undue emphasis on rights.

Other communitarian thinkers have taken up this theme; Mary Ann Glendon's analysis of the increasingly rights-oriented character of American law is particularly striking. Glendon is not engaged in a foolish attack on basic constitutional rights, but she does believe that the claims to rights are often excessively individualistic, oblivious to civic or social duties, and stridently absolutist in their formulation; the debate over abortion is a clear case in point. The result, she says, has been an impoverishment of American political discussion.[13] Some of her case makes good sense, for example, her amusing discussion of the extravagant rhetoric of the debate over flag burning. When the Supreme Court upheld such actions as a part of the right of free speech, one critic of the decision, when asked what the flag symbolized, answered that it stood for our right to do whatever we want, thus reducing his position to nonsense, since that argument obviously embraced flag burning.[14] And no doubt there are many claims to legal rights that might better be made as arguments for specific public policies, thus reducing the notorious litigiousness of American culture. Because American politics rests on compromise, to frame issues in terms of rights tends to undercut that possibility. Abortion is only the most conspicuous example.

Still, there are serious problems with Glendon's analysis. The relation between rights and duties is complex. An established right imposes duties on others, and as Cass Sunstein says, when Glendon speculates that we may have a duty to help others—to rescue them in some circumstances, for instance—she comes close to arguing for a new right. How different really is her position from Kateb's general right to Samaritanism? Furthermore, some rights, such as that to free speech, are best thought of as *both* social and individual, given their intimate connection to democratic debate. Finally, Glendon is surely right to lament the impoverishment of democratic discourse, but Sunstein is equally right to claim that this condition predated the rights explosion. Clearly, for instance, the impact on democracy of the mass media and sound bite analysis of complex problems is greater and more dangerous than any excessive rights talk, strange though some claims to rights might sometimes seem to be.[15]

Moreover, the relation between rights and community is exceedingly complex; liberals and communitarians may sometimes reach the same conclusion by different routes. Thus, "the civil rights movement of the 1960s might be justified by liberals in the name of human dignity and respect for persons, and by communitarians in the name of recognizing the full membership of fellow citizens wrongly excluded from the common life of the nation."[16] However, those laudable goals are obviously not mutually exclusive, and one could well argue for both without fear of inconsistency.

In other cases there might be greater divergences, but Sandel's examples tend to understate the complexity and variety of what can be called liberal.

Thus some rights-oriented thinkers may be less willing, for example, in a fit of libertarian zeal, to regulate pornography or plant closings than communitarians may be, but this attitude is not likely to be true across the board, and even reformist liberals may worry about the concentration of power generated by the strong state.[17] For all the subtlety of Sandel and other communitarians, they sometimes display a tendency to oversimplify liberalism, an oversimplification that borders on caricature, or, put differently, a tendency to treat Rawls as the sum total of liberal possibilities.

More generally, as I have suggested, a theory of rights need not necessarily serve only the purposes of individuals. As Michael Walzer writes, the unencumbered selves described by Sandel originally were burdened by the encumbrances of divinity; the sense of rights that Americans consider theirs owes much of its force to its Puritan origins in the English Civil War in the seventeenth century.[18] Many have shaken off these encumbrances, but it is still true that rights have a subversive logic—that is part of their power—which also gives them important social and political functions, according to Walzer. The claim to rights can enlist the government in support of purely individual freedoms, to be sure, but the rights to protest and to privacy facilitate "the collective and cooperative forms of social action." They make possible the politics of difference, subject to abuse, but also so necessary in a society as pluralist as this.[19] This is a nation of multiple communities. The purpose of the Bill of Rights is not so much to privatize as to "make the constituent elements of the society inaccessible to the state"; its purpose is not to create "a single all-encompassing solidar-ity."[20] As the preconditions of a decent democratic politics, these ideas point the way toward a reconciliation of liberalism and communitarianism.

But, Walzer continues, the reconciliation can be pressed only so far. The two ideals cannot be collapsed into one. Therefore, liberal societies need periodic correction in the form of a communitarian critique.[21] Communitarians are at least partly right; liberalism put into practice is capable of generating unsettling forms of social behavior. Citizens of liberal societies are subjected to what Walzer calls the Four Mobilities—social, marital, geographic, and political. In this perspective, liberalism is, most simply, the theoretical endorsement of these phenomena. But in spite of these disruptions, we can still speak to one another, and even when we disagree, our differences are argued out in the same language. The civil rights movement was the paradigm case. Martin Luther King, Jr., spoke the language of a tradition we all understand. This was a liberal tradition, modified, primarily, though not exclusively, by Protestantism and republicanism. The language was "the language of individual rights—voluntary association, pluralism, toleration, separation, privacy, the career open to talents, and so on." The language is inescapable, but "who among us seriously attempts to escape?" Certainly none of the communitarians.

Still, the unceasing restlessness of liberal society is self-subverting; this is why we periodically need the communitarian correction. Walzer notes that liberalism is not a theory designed to make people comfortable. Nonetheless, in American society, communitarians have to face the fact that there is no one out there but liberal selves. "It would be a good thing, though, if we could teach those selves to know themselves as social beings, the historical products of, and in part the embodiments of, liberal values."[22] And, of course, when we do that, we are plunged back into questions of race, gender, class, and ethnicity because these are among the factors that shape the self.

Much of the critique of Rawls's liberalism has dealt with his argument for a neutral state, given that there can be no communal definition of the good in a liberal society. What Walzer offers in "The Communitarian Critique of Liberalism" is a brief sketch of a nonneutral state that he believes to be compatible with liberal principles. This is part of the communitarian correction. The more manifest the Four Mobilities, the more likely that the state will be the one good shared by all, an apt observation, one might add, but not without its dangers. Still, citing Walzer's short list of examples designed to enhance group ties, the state could work to enhance communal organizations such as the trade unions, fostered by the Wagner Act, encourage religious groups through tax exemptions and other subsidies, and pass laws to regulate plant closings. A good reform liberal or social democratic state could thus "enhance the possibilities for cooperative coping," the sort of state John Dewey seemed to have had in mind in *The Public and Its Problems*. (It is also worth noting in the historical context of this study that, in Walzer's view, the theory of a nonneutral state owes nothing, contrary to what is often claimed, to the civic republican revival, which he dismisses as essentially an academic phenomenon; unlike Dewey's communitarianism, the theory of a nonneutral state had no external reference.[23])

But Sandel makes one more argument that is powerful and must be considered. In a very short space he offers a sweeping interpretation of much of twentieth-century political history. That is occasioned by his felt need to reply to the charge that however great the attractions of community, they mask a darker politics, which is likely to emerge in the large nation-state. That is Kateb's position, for example; thus the priority of rights, whatever its defects, Kateb says, is a safer form of politics.[24] It is therefore important to look also at the darker consequences alleged to result from the implementation of liberal theory.

We stand, Sandel tells us, at the end of the great liberal projects of this century. We now have what he calls a procedural republic, a political system that has a "tendency to crowd out democratic possibilities" and "to undercut the kind of community on which it nonetheless depends." The terrible tensions through which we live are a result of the working out in practice of liberal theory. We are beset by a sense that in spite of the expansion of suffrage, rights, and entitlements, we have lost control of the forces that dominate our lives. The process of nationalization begun by Theodore Roosevelt and theorized by Herbert Croly, that sense of national purpose that went beyond mere centralization, has failed. The synthesis of Jefferson and Hamilton consummated in the New Deal no longer sustains us.[25] "Liberalism has made its peace with concentrated power," but the project is a failure because, short of great emergencies such as war, no community on the national scale is possible. We therefore shift from a "politics of common purposes to one of fair procedures." Rights expand and override local preferences. The scale of politics is enlarged and moves from the more democratic sites such as legislatures and parties to courts and the executive bureaucracy.

The conclusion is grim:

> We find ourselves implicated willy-nilly in a formidable array of dependencies and expectations we did not choose and increasingly reject.
>
> In our public life, we are more entangled, but less attached, than ever before. It is as though the unencumbered self presupposed by the liberal ethic had begun to come true—less liberated than disempowered. . . . As the scale of social and political organization has become more comprehensive, the terms of our collective identity have become more fragmented, and the forms of political life have outrun the common purpose needed to sustain them.[26]

If all liberals are not Rawlsian theorists of the unencumbered self, then we cannot lay all the blame for these conditions at their feet. However, there are asocial currents in the broad liberal tradition, so liberalism cannot be let off scot-free either. But the fact that we have allowed rights to override local preferences and that many have turned to the courts or executive bureaucracies can often be explained by the egregious violations of the most basic rights at the level of the local community. Further, some of the conditions described can be traced to those parts of the liberal tradition we have learned to call conservative. So it is not clear that Sandel has fixed the blame as clearly as he might, though the general outlines of the degradation of American politics he so eloquently describes are widely, if not generally, felt by large numbers of American citizens. To date, however, Sandel has offered only a brief sketch of his critique. For a fuller discussion along the same lines, we can turn to a group of populist democrats who share some of his positions, but who arrive at their conclusions through an independent line of analysis.

Democratic Populism
as a Critique of Liberalism

Populist movements such as the Jacksonians or the agrarian radicals of the late nineteenth century have not always been very sophisticated intellectually, but in recent decades a body of thought has been developed that offers a powerful alternative to the liberal tradition—moreover, an alternative that is more detached from liberalism than its predecessors. This comes from a group of theorists that emerged in the Berkeley of the 1960s, though its members are now widely dispersed.[27] The leading thinkers of that group were Sheldon Wolin, John Schaar, and Norman Jacobson, who were followed by a large number of students; the most important of them for present purposes are Wilson Carey McWilliams, Hanna Pitkin, and J. Peter Euben.

Among these latter-day populists, there are theoretical elements that suggest an affinity with the communitarians, though this connection is not uppermost among their concerns, and they have displayed little interest in, and sometimes hostility to, civic republicanism. Wolin contends that republicanism muted the tension between what he sees as their elitist tendencies and the irreducibly populist character of democracy, whereas Schaar and McWilliams find much more to admire in the Puritan tradition than in civic republicanism, to which they have paid much less attention. They offer a politics of interpretation, or rather, a reinterpretation of the American tradition.[28]

Though Sheldon Wolin is the most important of these theorists, Carey McWilliams offers the fullest and most general statement of their position relative to the whole history of American political thought. McWilliams concedes that Louis Hartz is essentially correct about the nature of American politics, that he has "demonstrated beyond the need for further argument the degree to which conscious and formal thought about politics has shaped itself in terms of the categories of enlightenment liberalism."[29] But there is another tradition, a current of fraternal politics rooted in Puritanism, which generations of thinkers had struggled to keep alive in the face of the overweening power of Enlightenment ideas.

What McWilliams offers is a tentative natural law theory of fraternity: Man has a fraternal nature that is based on "interpersonal affection" and that is therefore limited in the number of persons it can encompass and the size of the territory in which the achievement of fraternal relationships is possible. The idea of fraternity contains within itself a set of standards that can measure the failure to attain ultimate values, and it suggests "a necessary tension with loyalty to society at large."[30] In discerning this tradition, McWilliams contributes to the restoration of a sense of the complexity of

American politics and history, a sense largely missing in Hartz's brilliant single-factor analysis.

For McWilliams, the much-touted American pragmatism, the seeming unwillingness to come to terms with so many of the great problems posed in Western political theory, raises the suspicion that we have been avoiding the tensions not only within American thought, but within the individual American as well. "There may exist an American creed, but it is a compendium of convictions hardly consistent with one another."[31] He says that the liberal idea of fraternity is based on a misunderstanding of the nature of man and that misunderstanding leads to the liberal utopia, blind to the need for communion, in which "a world of total private liberty and the ability to gratify desires" somehow allows an "instinct" for brotherhood to emerge.[32] The Judeo-Christian tradition counters this delusion and also avoids the trap of succumbing to the myth of some medieval fraternal paradise. That tradition preserves an understanding of man's social nature and holds to the ancient belief that he is "critically dependent on society and politics" for the achievement of his ends.[33] The two bodies of thought differ in their view of man; in the Puritan view fraternity is a "means to human perfection and a norm in everyday political and social life," whereas for liberals man is no longer by nature a political animal whose potential can be fully realized only through participation in the life of the polity.[34] In the latter view, humans have become essentially private creatures.

The dominant liberal tradition has focused on mechanistic formal institutions and organizations. This is a substitute for the ancient view that politics has to be centrally concerned with education, or, more precisely, with character building. The Madisonian institutional structure is based on interest rather than affection. The stress is on procedure rather than substance and leaves the "development of man's justly fearful spirit to others than the state."[35] The Framers' goal was the liberal dream of a self-regulating pluralism, and the bias of the system has led to the encouragement of Tocquevillian individualism, the hedonistic pursuit of material well-being and technological progress, and the downgrading of community.[36] And, as will become clear, it also has led to a weakening of democracy itself.

This brings us to the contribution of Sheldon Wolin. Wolin's position in contemporary American thought is virtually unique, so much so that he is difficult to classify ideologically, a sign of great originality in its own right. Wolin has sought to apply his broad learning in the entire tradition of Western political theory to the contemporary crisis in American politics.[37] His approach is simultaneously conservative and radical—conservative in his concern to preserve the past and honor the complexity of politics and the human condition and in his distrust of contemporary social science, not to mention the entire modern technological project. It is radical in the classic sense of going to the root while at the same time rejecting ideological frameworks that merely reflect the politics and ideas of the contemporary status quo.[38]

Wolin would, I think, accept the analysis given by McWilliams, though he does not seem to share the latter's deep interest in Puritanism. His deepest concern is with democracy; his radicalism appears in his contention that there is no single institution in America today that is democratic in character. Quite the contrary, in fact:

> Every one of the country's primary institutions—the business corporation, the government bureaucracy, the trade union, the research and education industries, the mass propaganda and entertainment media, and the health and welfare system—is antidemocratic in spirit, design, and operation. Each is hierarchical in structure, authority oriented, opposed in principle to equal participation, unaccountable to the citizenry, elitist and managerial, and disposed to concentrate increasing power in the hands of the few and to reduce political life to administration.[39]

This is a harsh indictment; Wolin offers an interpretation of American thought, the origins of which he traces back to the beginnings of American political development. He entirely rejects the tradition of social contract theory ranging from Hobbes and Locke to Rawls. As we saw in the discussion of Locke, the problem with contract theory is its implication that a society and its members have no history. Social contract theory rests on two mythical assumptions: that the contracting individuals are equal because they have no history and that the contract represents a fresh start, as in a footrace. But even granting the hypothetical nature of the contract, the symbolism is profoundly misleading. "The contract depends upon collective amnesia."[40] No modern society starts with its members on an even footing, so contract theory, regardless of its utility as an analytical abstraction, bears little relation to the realities with which contemporary citizens and their leaders must deal.

But contract theory was not the only false start. The basic problem of American politics lies in a contest over its collective identity that goes back to the debates among the Framers. Wolin notes that in the eighteenth century political theorists began to refer to the body of the people. In the colonies there were two such conceptions, with different ideas on collective identity and power. One was conceived as active, political, and democratic: It was a "body politic." The other was seen as a group of private people who were essentially passive: They were members of a deliberately antidemocratic system, a political economy. The classic statement of the body politic was the Declaration of Independence; the political economy was embodied in the

Constitution, *The Federalist Papers*, and the major papers of Alexander Hamilton on money, credit, debt, and his interpretation of the powers of the national government.[41] Wolin's formulation suggests that, contrary to Louis Hartz, and in spite of his own general emphasis on the centrality of liberalism in America, there has been no unanimity; the very notion of collective identity has been a contested one.[42]

The ideas of the Declaration were not mere abstractions. They reached back to the seventeenth century and to the idea of political and religious associations founded on voluntary choice. Politically, by the time of the Revolution, those ideas were institutionalized in the highly decentralized, locally based system of the Articles of Confederation; the politics was democratic, participatory, and egalitarian. Those who made up the body politic and opposed the Constitution tended to be small farmers, who took it for granted that it was perfectly natural to tinker with the economy in their interest; the economy had not yet become a sacred object.[43] That was the project of the advocates of a political economy.

The Constitution, in Wolin's view, was designed to break the power of the states and curb the participatory democratic politics established there. The goal was to create a new national economy supported by a strong national state. Hobbes and Locke might not have been democrats, but their theories were not deliberately aimed against democracy, as were the ideas of the American Framers. "The development of an avowedly antidemocratic science of politics was the contribution of Americans." The basis for this interpretation is, of course, a literal acceptance of Madison's distinction between democracy and representative government in *Federalist* 10. If we accept this move, then Wolin is clearly right, but as we will see, he is not completely consistent in his rejection of representative in favor of direct democracy.[44] Still, in support of Wolin's reading, one must say that there were times, as shown in the discussion of constitutional theory, when even the cautious Madison let down his guard and revealed a contempt for democracy as deep as that of his more open collaborator, Hamilton.

The Madisonian solution to the problem of authority in the eighteenth century was a version of the theory of pluralism. What Wolin sees in Madisonian theory is not a generally noble attempt to restrict the power of the state so much as an effort to save the state from democratization. The supreme irony is that in making it extremely difficult for majorities to form, Madison made it virtually necessary to create a strong Hamiltonian state in order to overcome the incoherence of pluralist politics. At the same time he made it very hard for such a state to achieve legitimacy in a political culture with a deeply inbred distrust for authority. Wolin reminds us that pluralist theory, which sees society as nothing but a congeries of groups, subverts the very idea of "the people" as a body politic, an idea that further undercuts the legitimacy of a democratic political system.[45] Finally, in contemporary tech-nological society, pluralism pits the need for group participation and repre-sentation against the need for technically sound solutions that can be admin-istered by hierarchical, rigid bureaucracies. "Now the evolution of pluralism has placed it on a collision course with technical rationality."[46] Democracy is the clear loser and pluralism threatens to become a politics with no legitimate foundation, a system with no real basis for the exercise of authority.[47]

The modern state is the Anti-Federalist nightmare come to pass; the fears of the opponents of the Constitution turned out to be on the mark, though they did not eventuate as quickly as the Anti-Federalists no doubt feared. The triumph of the Constitution and the consecration of the *Federalist Papers* as *the* interpretation of the document involved what was essentially a theoretical coup, the imposition of a nationalist culture and political system in place of an organically developed, highly decentralized form of govern-ment. According to Wolin, we are so used to the Constitution that it appears conservative to us, but in the context of the eighteenth century it was, in fact, deeply radical in its displacement of the existing forms of gov-ernment.[48]

By their setting in motion the development of a large state dedicated to working in tandem with the economy, the Framers abandoned democracy, conceived as "committed to the claim that experience with, and access to, power is essential to the development of the capacities of ordinary persons because power is crucial to human dignity and realization. Power is not something to be shared, but something to be used collaboratively in order to initiate, to invent, to bring about."[49] Democracy is a form open to the pos-sibility of what Hannah Arendt would call action, which entails the capacity to bring something new to the world.[50]

For those concerned with the survival of such a politics, the Anti-Federalists had the better of the argument, though they were unable to meet the challenge of developing a coherent, overarching theory of politics to match the Federalists' theory. Their idea of democracy was closer to the ancient ideal than the modern one, though they recognized that a larger regime was necessary for their time. No doubt representative government was necessary, but the representatives should be close to the people and not act as a government of strangers. They believed that mass electorates were easily manipulable by elites. Small districts were a requirement of democratic poli-tics. Only they could achieve an adequate level of popular control. Elections were more like what we today would call caucuses. Of course, rights were of interest, but they were necessary primarily to protect the localities from the potential for abuse by the new state that was looming up.[51] The emphasis of all the Berkeley school theorists is on small-scale political units, citizen participation, close popular control of government, and the priority of politics over economics.

Wolin, in spite of his misgivings about the Constitution, concedes that throughout the nineteenth century the two bodies, the body politic and the political economy, coexisted. Democratic participatory politics remained in good health at the local level as Americans moved west and founded communities with political forms designed to meet their needs; the great popular movements of farmers and workers also contributed to that health. But the political economy was stronger still. Particularly in the years following the Civil War, the state and its economic base grew larger and more bureaucratized, creating, in spite of sham struggles, an ever tighter union between state and economy. Meanwhile, citizens became progressively more depoliticized. Wolin bitterly quotes Bertolt Brecht:

> *Wouldn't it*
> *be simpler in that case if the government*
> *Dissolved the people and*
> *Elected another?*[52]

Historical agents of democratic politics such as parties declined, and we have reached, in Wolin's words, a "level of political deliberation somewhere between idiocy and prolonged adolescence." Life has been depoliticized by trivializing the commonality of politics and "then claiming that it is represented by the public opinion poll and mass elections dominated by the powers big money can buy."[53] Once again, the image of democracy celebrated by Joseph Schumpeter comes into view.

Accompanying the rise to dominance of the political economy has been a new public philosophy. We have ceased to rely on religious, moral, or ethical terms in evaluating the legitimacy or performance of our political system. The new standard, which is based on economic theory, is common to liberals and conservatives alike—further evidence of the penetration of liberal economics through the entire range of the consensus. (In fact, this might be one of the few genuinely stable parts of the liberal ideological hegemony.) Before social problems can be dealt with, the reigning public philosophy requires that they be cast into a form that makes them discussible in terms of costs and benefits, the tests of economic rationality. In contemporary parlance this position has been identified as conservative, but in fact, it is radically antitraditional. Moreover, the claim that economic analysis is a neutral product of purely rational considerations cannot be sustained. Instead, it is

deeply embedded in the power relationships established by large corporations. Finally, the assumptions on which economic theory rests are profoundly antipolitical. Starting with Adam Smith, economic thinkers have
doubted the competence of political leaders, as well as the very possibility of
altruistic, community-oriented behavior. Words like *citizen* and *community*
became subversive in the economic polity. The result is that "when a notion
of human motives and potentialities that was originally conceived to explain
private behavior is pressed into public service, its limitations become serious.
In the ordinary course of political events—as well as in the extraordinary
occasions of war, natural disaster, and even economic crisis—the constant
assumption cannot be that most citizens are egoistic and insatiable."[54]

The economic polity is committed to change, which is treated as synonymous with progress. But the idea of progress has undergone a subtle alteration; it has been transformed into the social scientific concept of modern-
ization. Where once the Left endorsed progress and change, it is now the
Right that embraces modernization and that is caught up in the presumably
"creative destruction" of capitalism. The Left, such as it is in the United
States, is dedicated, according to Wolin, to outworn New Deal, Fair Deal,
New Frontier, and Great Society programs. It is the party of "consolation."[55]
Writing today, Wolin would no doubt want to add the programs of the
Clinton administration to this list.

Thus progress has become an economic notion and is closely bound up,
not only with economic theory, but also with modes of scientific, instrumental rationality that are necessary for the development of technology. Both
the technology and the modes of thought are destructive. The environmental degradation caused by technology is not hard to find. Generations yet to
come face the possibility of a depleted planet, and as Schaar says, "The arche-
ologists of the future who dig around in our dumping grounds are in for
some fatal surprises."[56] The commitment to technology is the product of a
mad, Faustian dream of total control over nature, a dream that seemingly
knows no limits. Schaar notes that there are some signs that people have
begun to see this, but the need is for a true revolution in thought. In this
view, a mere redistribution of the costs of the system of the sort tradition
ally sought by the Left is totally inadequate.[57]

Economic theory is a mere instrument of calculation, self-interest, and
self-preservation. It deals purely with means to given ends; it can tell us nothing about the ends themselves. It is merely an intellectual technology. It is an
abstract thing, torn from any meaningful sense of social context. The result
is a world in which mind of a very peculiar sort is triumphant. But, "the alternative to mind is not mindlessness but reflection grounded in experience."[58]

This is what a concept of politics translated into rational choice theory cannot give us.

None of this should be taken as an assault on modernity as such, though no one could say that Wolin and his colleagues are not fully aware of the defects of modern thought and the commitment to technology. As McWilliams says, "Compassion *alone* would forbid any advocacy of the destruction of modernity." This, after all, is an age that turns laboratories into "temples of hope." Still, technology and technologists often seem to have no sense of limits and the institutions associated with technology are, in fact, frequently hierarchical and antidemocratic. Thus to Schaar: "Process is in command. State, economy, and society are remote, huge, and thoroughly technicized and bureaucratized."[59]

In spite of the benefits of technology and in part because of the institutions created in a technological republic, the system has produced casualties—citizens who, for whatever reason, are unable to function successfully. But the institutions designed to deal with such problems are failures for the most part. John Schaar has repeated the conventional wisdom to the effect that in the war on poverty, poverty won a decisive victory. Thus, the welfare state, rather than providing the completion of liberalism by providing the material basis for citizenship, has been a failure even at that most basic level. Worse, the interests of the welfare state are not separable from other state concerns; the welfare state and the warfare state are blood relatives. Instead of citizens, what the welfare state has produced is a class of dependents.[60]

Finally, according to Wolin, the stresses inherent in American society are producing another of the periodic crises in collective identity so characteristic of our system. The ties that hold us together are wearing thin as racial and ethnic groups tear at each other in a newly distended pluralist system.[61] And this crisis is surely made worse by the economic difficulties so readily seen in the political economy.

However, to Wolin, the heart of the present crisis is political more than economic. But this is true in a special way. Politics in the usual sense, "the legitimized and public contestation, primarily by organized and unequal social powers, over access to the resources available to the public authorities of the collectivity," is endless. What has concerned Wolin for a lifetime has been the *political*, "an expression of the idea that a free society composed of diversities can nonetheless enjoy moments of commonality when, through public deliberations, collective power is used to promote or protect the well-being of the collectivity."[62] Only democracy is compatible with "the political," and the modern state—the megastate, as Wolin calls it—is antithetical to both. The state has co-opted the politics of elections and political parties. New forms are needed.[63]

Democratic politics cannot hope to be permanently established; it is necessarily evanescent. It can succeed only temporarily and has to be constantly recreated. It is best not even to think of it as a form of government; its closest analogue is perhaps Kateb's concept of episodic citizenship, though given Wolin's distrust of constitutional forms, it has nothing to do with the citizen rising to defend constitutional rights in times of grave crisis. It is a moment rather than a form.[64] And it is a moment to be treasured.

The new politics that is required will be revolutionary, though definitely nonviolent. The model for revolutionary politics is, surprisingly, in the theory of John Locke. For Locke, revolution was justified after "a long train of abuses." And he was remarkably open to a democratic revolution that would generate new forms of power.[65] But a new citizen's politics will not be the creation of abstract, rights-bearing individualists. It must come from a revitalization of the local sources of power, from the family to the workplace, to the towns and cities, to name only a few possibilities. The new grassroots politics can take the form of movements for "rent control, utility rates and service, environmental concerns, health care, education, nuclear power, legal aid, worker's ownership of plants, and much more. Their single most important feature is that they have grown up outside the state-corporate structure and have flourished despite repeated efforts to discredit them."[66] For both Wolin and Schaar, there is a need for new political forms, because any attempt to use the state as an aid to solving the problems of modernity has only succeeded in making it part of the problem. We have to move away from statist, centralized, and specialized organizations. Our watchword has to be—at least for Schaar—"All Power to the Fragments."[67]

One assumes that this watchword was a piece of brilliant hyperbole intended to underline the need for a revitalization of local political culture. But Wolin is clear on the limits of such an approach. Localism had inherent limits and is "politically incomplete." There are problems in society that are general rather than parochial. At times it is necessary to seek out "the evanescent homogeneity of a broader political." What this seems to imply is, willynilly, an appeal to the inherently antidemocratic forces of the state. Thus Wolin reaches the grim conclusion that democracy is "doomed to succeed only temporarily"; he is sure that no one really believes that "the people" actually rule in any of the industrialized democracies of the world today.[68] For all that he tries to offer hope, Wolin's disaffection from contemporary politics is so great that his conclusions read like a cry of despair, a lament for the loss of something of unutterable beauty.

Much of this powerful indictment, however painful, is hard for a democrat to deny. Elections frequently are shams. Money all too often *can* buy political power. American citizens show real signs of demoralization; they *are* extensively, though not completely, depoliticized. The interest group system seems out of control, and the party system, which could provide a rallying point for democratic forces, seems at times to have declined to the point of insignificance. The collective identity of Americans seems badly worn. Moreover, it is easy to identify with Wolin's apparent sympathy for the marginalized and the dispossessed. One might think that given his focus on the politics of difference, he is aligning himself with the postmodernists. But that, I think, is a misreading. He approves of neither postmodern theory nor postmodern politics, though it must be said his remarks on the latter are few and scattered. His critique of French philosopher Michel Foucault, the most fashionable of postmodernist thinkers, is scathing and very telling; Foucault simply does not engage the central institutions of our time, and in that omission, he fails to address the truly political.[69]

Furthermore, the welfare state is a problem. No one, least of all its intended beneficiaries, is very satisfied with it. Without conceding the conservative case against it, one must admit that it has not overcome the problem of dependency and may well contribute to it. When we hear proposals for the fingerprinting of all welfare recipients in the State of New York, the Tocquevillian "soft despotism" feared by Wolin does not seem at all remote. Since all these problems have arisen in a predominantly liberal regime, the question must be raised whether they are inherent in the theory.

In addition, the state, to which we so often turn, is a dangerous force. It has tremendous power and a tendency to abuse that power. Still, it is hard to imagine any new form that would succeed it that would be less dangerous; even Wolin concedes that some problems, frequently menacing ones, are beyond the capacities of localities to deal with. At this point Wolin's theory becomes troubling. His faith in the democratic character of our localities is too complete. One of the many reasons for the gravitation of power toward Washington is the need to protect minorities against the abuses of local majorities. Wolin's deep distrust of constitutionalism is problematic in this connection. For him, a constitution and democracy do not go together naturally. "Constitutional democracy is democracy fitted to a constitution. It is not democratic or democratized constitutionalism because it is democracy without the demos as actor."[70] I have no wish to deny that the Constitution was designed with a certain antidemocratic intent, which is subject to serious criticism. But aside from the fact that Wolin's is an exceptionally strict standard, his position overlooks the fact that the demos may do things that violate the necessary requirements of democracy by any conceivable criterion. We can argue about the precise meaning of the Bill of Rights, but a civilized politics that does not include some version of its guarantees is an impossibility. If we value democracies, it may sometimes be necessary to keep them from committing suicide, which is where the abuse of rights can lead. This is the force of the liberal component in liberal democracy. Though unpleasant dilemmas may arise, in general we further democracy by protecting individual rights. This is why we need adequate theories of rights.

Moreover, as George Kateb, who surely rivals Wolin in his distrust of the state, notes, Wolin has a tendency to criticize rights when they have led to bad results. Thus he appears ready to suppress antidemocratic speech by the Ku Klux Klan[71] and, by extension, may be expected to endorse anti–hate speech laws. But, as Kateb suggests, that can lead to a stifling conception of good citizenship. Besides, as I have already argued, there are better ways for liberals to deal with the horrors of hate speech; we might just possibly be able to hypothesize circumstances that justify suppression, but speech restrictions are the last rather than the first resort for coping with the dilemma.

Indeed it is not clear that the state, as seems so commonly believed, automatically bungles whatever it attempts. It would be better to say that the war on poverty was abandoned rather than simply lost. To claim the latter is radically misleading. We know that the programs of the Great Society had a substantial positive effect for blacks and the poor generally and that there was even a modest, if temporary, movement toward redistribution.[72] It is not a criticism of these programs as such, flawed though they no doubt were, that their effects were undermined by the war in Vietnam. In the current climate of sometimes hysterical opposition to government, this point is often lost and bears repetition. More generally, who really would wish the government to abandon the attempt to enforce safety standards on the auto industry or to monitor the marketing of prescription drugs and the activities of the tobacco industry? With respect to the environment, one should remember that the Cuyahoga River is no longer a fire hazard and that life is returning to the Great Lakes as a result of governmental regulation. Of course, the list could be extended, but the facts are clear. For all its problems, the modern state has not been a total loss.

At the opposite end of the scale from the thinking of Wolin and Schaar is the reemergence of the state as a subject for social science research; for a generation it had been dismissed as a nonscientific, essentially metaphysical, concept, rooted in the Western world and better replaced by the supposedly more neutral and scientific concept of the political system. And beyond that looms the possibility of a full-scale revival of a normative theory of authority and the state, perhaps even inspired by Hegel, the grand master of metaphysics. One major theorist, writing in the aftermath of the Watergate scandal, noted that there were "injuries against state-mindedness by the highest state authorities themselves." Neither liberals nor Marxists have developed adequate conceptions of authority. The classic liberal image of the patrolman merely directing the flow of free transactions is questionable. Marxist and elitist theories of domination lead either to cynicism or Armageddon. In such conditions, it can be argued, the Hegelian view that "political authority is there to amplify and sustain the solidarity of a people by acting as a focal point of reverence and by suspending particular wills and interests" holds its attractions.[73] This too is a troubling formulation, especially in its reference to the state as an object of reverence, and it is doubtful that anyone believes that a Hegelian state is about to emerge in the United States or that it would provide a miraculous solution to problems of the United States were it to do so. Nevertheless, that sober thinkers are driven to something so far outside the American political culture is an indicator of present conditions.

The state is not going to disappear; Sheldon Wolin and his colleagues clearly understand that. It is difficult to imagine what forces short of thermonuclear holocaust would bring about its final destruction. We need the large state. The suffering that would be brought about by its demise is frightening to contemplate. That, I think, is the source of the anguish in Wolin's recent writing. He is right to be concerned, though his concerns have not allowed him to offer enough in the search for a way out. But Wolin is right that the costs associated with the large state are huge. The security it provides is frequently minimal at best; it offers little to anyone imbued with the ideals of truly democratic participation. It has great power, which is subject to abuse and frequently is abused. If it is hard to imagine life without the modern state, it may yet prove to be impossible to live with it. The dilemma was captured by Henry Kariel in a superb aphorism: "Just as small-scale, humanly comprehensible groupings are essential, so are large-scale, humanly incomprehensible ones."[74]

What Wolin expresses is a particularly poignant example of what James Morone calls the democratic wish. Morone says that Americans have a deep distrust of authority and government that periodically leads to a democratic upsurge by the "people." But typically movements for democratization result in a growth in government, so the cycle is endlessly repeated.[75] This seems to me the reality of American politics and the heart of Wolin's dilemma. He may appear to be so disaffected as to be out of touch with American politics, an example of what Michael Walzer would call a disconnected critic. But in truth Wolin is closely connected; the American distrust of the state goes back at least to the Anti-Federalists. Brutus and the Federal Farmer may have lost out to the Federalists, but as Wolin has said, they still have things to teach us.

His radical democratic populism may be stronger on criticism than on construction, but his views are likely to be part of any revivified American democracy.

But Wolin is handicapped in achieving direct influence in U.S. politics because his standard for democracy seems impossibly high. Consider the contrast between his work and that of the Straussian conservatives. In spite of the fact that Wolin has written some notably harsh criticisms of the Straussian position, their seemingly opposed theories share some ideas, though they draw different lessons from them. Wolin, Strauss, and their colleagues are antiliberal; beyond that they are critical of the whole social and natural scientific project that grew out of the Enlightenment. One source of this view seems to be the German philosopher Martin Heidegger, directly in the case of Strauss, who was his student, and indirectly, in the case of Wolin, who was deeply influenced by Hannah Arendt, another of Heidegger's pupils in Weimar Germany. In addition to their opposition to liberalism, both groups are deeply skeptical of any attempt to make the world over according to some rationalistic plan designed to transform either the natural or social environment.

Where they diverge most sharply is in their reaction to the upheavals of the 1960s. The Straussians put aside their distrust of liberalism and decided to cling to the Constitution as the best option in a world gone mad. For his part, Wolin, in some sense radicalized by the student rebellion at Berkeley and the Vietnam War, took a sharp turn to the left and embraced an increasingly strong form of participatory democracy that was anathema to the Straussians. But by embracing a conservative constitutional liberalism, the Straussians were able to find common ground with the Republican Party, which has given them an influence Wolin cannot match. Wolin continues to distrust rationalistic public solutions to policy problems and is as contemptuous of the Democratic Party as he is of the Republicans. The result is a powerful critique, but one that gives him no political leverage, so he can have little direct influence. However, to repeat, a democratic critique of American politics must, almost of necessity, draw on a revived democratic populism, though it must commit itself to something more lasting than the "democratic moment."[76] In the wake of Proposition 187 restricting the rights of immigrants in California, it is clear that such populist surges must pass constitutional tests. Under present conditions, grassroots populist movements seem more likely to spring from the right than from the liberal left.

But before returning to that, it is necessary to consider the prospects for a renewal of the social democratic tradition now being kept marginally alive by the Clinton administration. This too must surely be part of a movement of democratic reform.

Social Democracy
and the Liberal Tradition

What in a less narrowly constrained tradition of political culture would appear as some form of socialism is exemplified in the United States by the line running from Jefferson to Jackson to Lincoln to populism, progressivism, the New Deal, and its numerous successors. I have argued that there have been few new ideas in the reform tradition since the days of Theodore Roosevelt, Croly, Brandeis, and Wilson. The New Deal, though of enormous historical importance, provided rather little that was intellectually new, and the Fair Deal, New Frontier, and New Society programs were extensions of the logic of their predecessors. A more vital reformist thrust may have to move outside the frame established by this string of programs and reach toward a moderate democratic socialism, though doubtless, it would be just as well if its proponents do not use that unpopular label.

For more than forty years, the principal voice of American democratic socialism has been the quarterly magazine *Dissent*. Founded in 1954 by literary critic Irving Howe and sociologist Lewis Coser, *Dissent* has been a basically friendly critical voice, scrutinizing liberalism and the Democratic Party from the left and pointing out their foibles, while maintaining a strongly anti-Communist, anti-Soviet stance. Predominantly, though not exclusively, socialist, and influenced by Marx without ever seeming sectarian, it has maintained a critical position on U.S. politics, while staying within the limits of the American tradition, even if at times near the outer edge.

Many important writers have appeared in *Dissent*'s pages over the years. Until their deaths, Howe's was an ever-present voice, as was Michael Harrington's. In recent years Robert Dahl and Daniel Bell have contributed often, which says a lot about their ideological movement since the 1950s, and perhaps something about *Dissent* as well. However, from the point of view of political theory, its most important contributor has been its current coeditor, Michael Walzer. In a series of books and articles over a period of thirty years or more, Walzer has slowly pieced together an increasingly comprehensive, though not very systematic, body of theory, ranging from domestic politics, to the theory of political obligation and distributive justice, to some important explorations in international relations.[77] The interrelatedness of his work is important, I think; some of his critics are misled because they approach him piecemeal and do not attend to the connections.[78]

I will approach Walzer contextually and politically, that is, in relation to the liberal tradition, rather than by focusing on the philosophical underpinnings of his work, which is the tack most often taken by his critics. Walzer has been attacked from the left as a "mere" liberal and from the right as a radical socialist. He himself, in one place or another, has used a variety of terms to define his position: *democratic socialist, social democrat, principled radical, and unreconstructed democrat*—by which he presumably meant to reject Joseph Schumpeter's democratic revisionism. But Walzer's critics, concentrating on labels, have paid too little attention to the content of his arguments and too much to their foundations—or lack thereof. My strategy is to reverse that priority.

Walzer's relation to liberalism is suggested by a remark he made about the essays collected in *Radical Principles:* "At times I have thought it important to defend liberalism against liberals in rapid retreat from some of its principles; at other times I have criticized those tendencies within liberalism that make for dissociation and weaken the structures of self-government."[79]

Walzer sees liberalism historically as a way of drawing a map of the world, a map that moved in the direction of the just society Walzer sketched in *Spheres of Justice.* The preliberal world was an undifferentiated mass, with society conceived as an "organic and integrated whole." Over time liberals began to separate what had been integrated—church from state, society from political community, which led in turn to the creation of a separate sphere for economics and the market, the severing of the family from the state, a result of the end of dynastic government, and the clear division of public from private life. Thus, in the classic phrase, a man's home becomes his castle. The Left, particularly the Marxist Left, has never been too impressed by these efforts, viewing them alternatively as an ideological pretense to cover the truly destructive connections that remained, or conversely, as so successful that they created a world of isolated individuals.[80] But Walzer's work involves another critique of liberalism, a critical extension, in fact, that builds on the liberal "art of separation" in an attempt to turn it into something more.

With liberals, Walzer accepts that "individual agreement is indeed an important source of our institutions, and individual rights of our freedoms." But by itself alone this is bad sociology. "The individual who stands wholly outside institutions and relationships and enters into them only when he or she chooses" does not exist. Thus, "the individual lives within a world he or she did not make."[81] Walzer is a pluralist, but his pluralism is more than the "pleasant illusion" so commonly found in contemporary American thought. He considers the pluralism of David Truman and the early Dahl and Lindblom as "merely an elaborate way of missing the point" about power in American society.[82] Walzer is also a consent theorist, but he is not happy with the thin theory illustrated by Locke's notion of tacit consent: We do not generally incur obligations on the basis of the demands of individual conscience, but instead through participation in the activities of political or social groups of which one is a member. Though he admits that the term *consent* has a wide variety of meanings, he says that the assumption of obligations is not automatic but rather the product of "willful membership." Principled commitments, however, are "usually also commitments to other men, from whom or with whom the principles have been learned and by whom they are enforced."[83]

This led Walzer to a theory of pluralist citizenship in which the claims of the state are valid only when the citizen has a choice between them and those of the groups of which he was a member. Only when such a plurality of choices exists can genuine citizenship extending beyond a mere legal status be said to exist.[84] This is a goal more than a reality, since Walzer clearly recognizes the class bias of the pluralist system in which "group membership and participation climb startlingly as one climbs the social scale."[85]

There are other limits to Walzer's pluralism, though they should not be overstressed. He is more interested in ethnic than racial pluralism, and the claims of feminists have not yet loomed large in his theory, though they have not been ignored. Nor is his a civic republican theory in which political participation is the highest of all values. Instead he has offered what might be called a chastened, rather than a high, theory of citizenship. He wishes to preserve the rights of the "ardent noncitizen" who loves private life and who fears, in Oscar Wilde's phrase, that "socialism would take too many evenings." In a passage somewhat reminiscent of Kateb's episodic citizenship, Walzer defends the "kibitzers," the "laggard citizens," who emerge from time to time to criticize the work of the activists. These citizens too have their place. It is worth remarking that the essay in which these remarks appear was originally subtitled "Two Cheers for Participatory Democracy."[86]

The liberal state that Walzer's citizen inhabits is a welfare state; in fact all states are welfare states. The difference among them is in their conception of what welfare requires, for example, the salvation of souls or the tending of bodies.[87] The welfare state is surely not the last word, but it is perhaps the highest achievement of liberalism. Its deficiencies are manifest, particularly in the United States, which, to its shame, has "one of the shabbier systems of communal provision in the Western world."[88] For a socialist, the welfare state cannot be the final goal, but in spite its problems, including its failure to provide the material base necessary to facilitate meaningful citizenship for all, it has made the lives of many ordinary people more free and secure, though it has done so at a price. The danger is of an administrative state, privatized, free of politics, and made up of voluntarily passive citizens.[89] For these and other reasons, we would probably do well to "end welfare as we know it," but its real achievements must be preserved. Complete destruction would be an act of wanton cruelty.

What lies beyond the welfare state is a form of socialism. But Walzer's socialism is unusual in that it is at least as much political as it is economic. He wants to abolish neither private property nor authority, but rather to make both more widely shared and thus more legitimate. Socialism and democracy are seen as essentially the same, "two forms of procedural justice, focused on a certain conception of human *doing* that expresses the deepest values we associate with human *being*."[90] The leftist critique of liberalism is concerned first with "the critique of private government," the political power that wealth brings. Walzer says that in our political map of the world, we need to redraw the line, so "wrongly drawn for a long time," that separates economics and politics. This is a political job for all of us: "Liberalism passes definitively into democratic socialism when the map of society is socially determined."[91]

"What I tried to do in *Spheres of Justice*," Walzer has said, "was to imagine what it would be like if we had a perfect welfare state."[92] In American society, given the enormous strength of liberalism, the resources needed to bring this about must come out of that tradition. We are back to the interpretive issue raised in my Introduction, where I quoted Walzer: "Justice and equality can conceivably be worked out as philosophical artifacts, but a just or an egalitarian society cannot be. If such a society isn't already here—hidden, as it were, in our concepts and categories—we will never know it concretely or realize it in fact." If a better society is hidden within us, then we must interpret the resources of our political tradition to make its possibility apparent and then work to establish it. This is a "radically particularist" account of justice, which Walzer worked out with no attempt to achieve great social distance from his subject, to situate himself behind a Rawlsian "veil of ignorance," for example.[93] This approach has led to much controversy, but before turning to that, I want to attend to some of the neglected substance of Walzer's argument.

Walzer is a pluralist, but he is also an egalitarian, and the two positions are connected. Egalitarianism, he argues, is complex rather than simple. Simple equality is the idea that there is a single dominant good that must be equally distributed. More often than not, I suspect, people think first of money, but the good could be perceived holiness or political power, or any number of things people value. But that is just the point; people value many different things, and all of those goods must somehow be distributed. Under simple equality, the problem of justice is to keep the single dominant good from being monopolized. Thus if money is that dominant good, egalitarians would seek to equalize it.

But in the theory of complex equality, it is the dominance rather than the monopoly that is said to be the problem. Walzer writes that the possession of one good should not be translatable into control over others. There are many goods: membership, security and welfare, money and commodities, office, both public and private, education, social recognition, political power, and so on. How much a given society values each of these goods will be socially determined and, therefore, will vary widely according to the meaning attached to them by the particular society. There is no reason to expect, as a general rule, that in any complex society a single person or a single group will legitimately monopolize all of these goods. The danger is the illicit conversion of one good into another. Thus the basic principle of just distribution: "No social good x should be distributed to men and women who possess some other good y merely because they possess y and without regard to the meaning of x."

Under this principle, one citizen chosen for office over another will have more political power than his rival, but that is not disturbing so long as the winner does not achieve advantages over the loser in other distributions, such as medical care or education for his or her children.[94] Following the British philosopher Bernard Williams, Walzer argues that each good should be distributed for "relevant reasons." Thus the relevant reason for providing medical care is that someone is sick, not that he or she has money to pay for it. Relevant reasons are historically and socially conditioned, based on the "shared understandings" of the society, hence the notable variation in what different societies call just.[95] In the context of this study, the crucial distributive spheres are security and welfare, wealth and commodities, and political power, though something must also be said about private and public office. I will use them to discuss the substantive core of Walzer's theory, as well as to illustrate his controversial approach to the theory of justice, considered as the major alternative to the work of John Rawls.

Since every state is a welfare state, the sphere of welfare is a good place to begin. In a political community, the first thing the members owe one another is the "communal provision of security." The relevant reason for provision of relief to the poor is need, subject to the limitations of the available resources. Obviously, Walzer writes, poor communities have less to distribute, so the level of provision is necessarily lower. There is a basic right to life; no community can passively allow members to starve while there is food to feed them, an argument not unlike Kateb's duty of Samaritanism.[96] But beyond this basic minimum, what constitutes need is socially determined, though with an important limitation: "In any community, where resources are taken away from the poor and given to the rich, the rights of the poor are being violated." And in democratic systems communal provision will be more extensive because of the wider participation of the citizens. "If all states are in principle welfare states, democracies are most likely to be welfare states in practice."[97]

But remember that need is socially determined: Beyond what is needed for physical survival, what constitutes welfare varies. It would be hard, Walzer says, to claim that ancient Greeks were wrong to view drama or medieval Jews were wrong to view education as important to welfare. We must therefore ask what sort of welfare state the shared understandings of the United States require.

Clearly there must be social provision of the requisites of life, of physical survival. But beyond this, Walzer uses health care as an example. Longevity is now a recognized social need. Disease is seen as a plague, but one that can be dealt with. In addition, Walzer argues, Americans have made a commitment to communal provision, which, having been made, must be extended equally to all members. This is true in spite of the fact that we know that poverty is a powerful bar to equal medical treatment. Middle- and upper-class Americans consult doctors more often than the poor *and* are less likely to be sick. In such a situation, needed goods cannot be left to the whims of the economic market. One might argue, Walzer says, that the refusal to fund a U.S. national health service means that Americans have made a political decision in favor of a minimal standard for everyone in the form of urban clinics, with free enterprise medicine for anything above minimum. This would be inadequate policy, in his view, but not unjust; however, Americans have *not* made that decision, since federal, state, and local governments now "finance different levels of care for different classes of citizens." But, Walzer goes on, "the poor, the middle class, and the rich make an indefensible triage." He is led to the conclusion that when communal funds are spent for research, hospitals, and the payment of private doctor's fees, these services have to be equally available.[98]

I take up this discussion in some detail, both because of its recent political interest and because it illustrates Walzer's mode of argument. His argument for expanded health care is a prototype of the argument for an expanded welfare system generally, though only a few additional details are given and much of the remainder is devoted to Walzer's legitimate worries about dependency in the welfare state. Without using the term, he too is worried about the potential for "soft despotism" that troubles Sheldon Wolin.[99] The argument is clearly more political than philosophical, and the politics is one of interpreting the shared meanings of American culture. But Walzer's critics argue that the debates over health care show that there are no shared understandings or that, if there are, they do not mean what he claims. Walzer has an answer, which has been much debated. Before looking at it, however, let us consider two other distributive spheres, because they often have drawn the same criticisms and received a similar response.

The most discussed distributional problem, particularly among advocates of simple equality, deals with money and commodities. There are two problems connected with money—how it is distributed and what it can buy. The key feature of money is that it "abuts every other sphere," which is why it is so important to set appropriate limits on its use. We need a list of what Walzer calls "blocked exchanges," things that money cannot buy or that should not be for sale. Walzer lists fourteen such exchanges; a few pertinent examples will suffice here. In particular, we cannot buy and sell human beings or First Amendment rights; criminal sales can be banned; criminal justice cannot be paid for; and political power and influence or political office cannot be auctioned off.[100] Slavery aside, it is clear that these blocked exchanges can often be unblocked, though usually the sale takes place somewhere out of the open market.

But, Walzer goes on to say, "once we have blocked every wrongful exchange and controlled the sheer weight of money itself, we have no reason to worry about the answers the market provides." Thus, we can afford to let economic markets work, as long as they are a "zone of the city, not the whole of the city. . . . It is one thing to clear the Temple of traders, quite another to clear the streets," since there is nothing degraded about buying and selling as such.[101] Thus economic inequality is not by itself a major concern, and it is probably useless to seek to abolish it. We know, Walzer tells us, that "money equally distributed at twelve noon of a Sunday will have been unequally redistributed before the week is out."[102]

I suspect the list of blocked exchanges is part of the shared understandings in American culture; I also suspect that part of the contemporary revulsion against politics stems from the frequency with which the blockages fail. It is also clear that the market is deeply entrenched in American thinking, and thus nonmarket distributions have a hard time winning popular approval. Also, interesting, if inconclusive, evidence suggests popular support for economic inequality—in fact, a fear of equality stemming from the idea that its realization would dash the American dream of climbing the economic ladder.[103] These forces clearly make it more difficult than might be supposed to win support for redrawing the lines between the spheres of economics and politics. Whether it is possible to block inappropriate exchanges without a greater redistribution of wealth and income than will be provided by the market is also open to question, a point to which I will return.

The distribution of political power according to the theory of complex equality is structurally similar to the distribution of money and commodities.

The state is a crucial agency because it guards the boundaries of the other distributive spheres. Political power is a necessity, but it is also necessary to contain it within *its* boundaries. "Political power protects us from tyranny . . . and itself becomes tyrannical." We must have constitutional limitations—in Walzer's terms, blocked uses of power, which complement the blocked exchanges in the sphere of money and commodities.[104]

The limitations that stem from the shared understandings in the United States forbid slavery, and also execution, imprisonment, or compulsory service, except following accepted procedures. There is a realm of personal privacy that cannot be breached, again except in accordance with accepted procedures. There are standards of guilt and innocence, and punishment may not be used as a means of political repression. Political power cannot be sold or auctioned off, nor can it be used to further private interests. Private property is a protected sphere, as is religious life. Similarly, although the state may prescribe a curriculum, it cannot violate academic freedom. Finally, freedom to debate the shared understandings and the boundaries of the distributive spheres must be guaranteed, not only in the arena of politics, but within all the other spheres as well. We are not wrong to think of these limits as guarantees of freedom, but they are also potent egalitarian forces. "Limited government, then, like blocked exchange, is one of the crucial means to complex equality."[105]

Once the blockages are established, how should power be distributed? Historically, there are two standard answers to this question. The first is that it should go to experts in whatever is particularly relevant to the society; the second holds that it should be "possessed or controlled" by those who are subject to it. The first, as old as Plato's philosopher king, is the prototype of all antidemocratic arguments. All such arguments, says Walzer, "if they are serious, are arguments from special knowledge." In an increasingly complex world, dependent on advanced technology that few understand, that first answer provides a potentially dangerous argument against the aspiration to democracy. But, as Walzer says, if we examine the classic Platonic metaphors, we are likely to reject rule by experts. Plato often referred to the ship's captain into whose hands the passengers placed not only their hopes to arrive at their destination, but even their very lives. But it was the passengers, not the captain, who decided where they wished to go.[106] This is the realm of democratic decision. The old maxim from public administration, The expert should be on tap, not on top, seems to apply here.

Therefore we need a rule for the democratic distribution of power. "Once we have located ownership, expertise, religious knowledge, and so on in their proper places and established their autonomy, there is no alternative to democracy in the political sphere." Only in a theocracy or a plutocracy where an undifferentiated conception of goods prevails can undemocratic government be justified. But democracy is not a simple term, and it does not fit well with simple equality. At any time in a government there are leaders and followers, and the latter will have less power than the former. Democracy is a way of allocating that power—it is the *political* way of doing so. To Walzer, "Democracy puts a premium on speech, persuasion, rhetorical skill. Ideally, the citizen who makes the most persuasive argument—that is, the argument that actually persuades the largest number of citizens—gets his way. But he can't use force, or pull rank, or distribute money; he must talk about the issues at hand." Democratic decisions are likely to reflect the wishes of the politically skilled, so democratic politics is the province of politicians.[107]

In spite of what many contemporary Americans seem to hope, politics and politicians are unavoidable. They will not go away. Citizen/voters are needed and are critical to the survival of the system, "but the citizen/politician is crucial to its liveliness and integrity." These stronger forms of participation are aspects of complex equality, because democracy does not require equal power. According to Walzer, that is not troubling if the autonomy of the spheres is maintained so that political distribution is not disrupted by extraneous factors. Nor can the winners of the political debate use their power to exclude the losers from participation. An electoral victory does not include the right to rule in perpetuity.[108] The latter does not happen in American politics, but as Walzer knows, in fact the distributional boundaries are all too often violated; again, this is probably a source of the widespread disgust with politics so apparent today. In the Conclusion (Chapter 17), I will return to a consideration of the specific nature of the violations and some possible remedies.

Assuming for a moment that this general understanding of politics is shared, at least at some high level of abstraction, Walzer's theory seems plausible as a sketch of politics in an electoral democracy. In spite of his socialist aspirations, he is safely within the tradition of individualism that has been characteristic of U.S. political culture, though he could not accept the "atomistic social freedom" that Hartz saw as the "master assumption" of American political thought. This connection to the political culture can be seen in Walzer's views on the controversial subjects of affirmative action and quotas.

Walzer treats that subject under the general heading of office, defined as "any position in which the political community as a whole takes an interest" and regulates how it is filled. The current tendency in politics and political theory is to redefine every job as an office—"for the sake of justice."[109] All citizens with some minimum skills have an equal right to be considered for office, but no one can be said to deserve or have a right to win the competition. As an example, Walzer deals with American blacks, though I think the same arguments apply to other racial and ethnic minorities and to women. He had no difficulty accepting "fair employment practices, open search and selection procedures, extensive recruiting, serious efforts to discover talent even when it isn't conventionally displayed, and so on." These are the practices that usually go under the label of affirmative action.[110]

The "reservation of office," what is commonly called a quota system, is more problematic, he says. We might be able to make an argument in favor of quotas, though that would have to include a description of the current crisis *and* a careful showing of the inadequacy of alternatives. This argument, he suggests, has not yet been made and alternative policies have not yet been tried. He says further that quotas look like the first rather than the last resort, and the last is what they should be. To adopt a quota system is to violate the rights of candidates.[111]

This might seem like a conservative argument, but on the whole, it is quite different from the position of, say, Harvey Mansfield. Quotas, Walzer claims, simply reiterate the established hierarchies and the class structure as a whole. Instead, the hierarchies should be transformed through a substantial redistribution of resources and wealth. One might then just argue, as he does, that this is in line with the social understandings that shape the welfare state, though he admits that the opposition will be strong. It is less clear to me that this position comports well with his willingness to let the market determine the distribution of wealth and income, in spite of the large inequalities that result. Still, his conclusion is politically persuasive and is in line with social democratic policy analysts like William Julius Wilson. "In general, the struggle against a racist past is more likely to be won if it is fought in ways that build on, rather than challenge, understandings of the social world shared by the great majority of Americans, black and white alike."[112] If that is an unworkable politics, then it suggests the limits of reform in the United States today.

Bearing in mind that the foregoing is an extremely abridged sketch of Walzer's theory, it is now possible to see what the outlines of a politics congruent with his theory would look like. Some of the more specific details can best be discussed later, but a general outline is easy to summarize.

> The appropriate arrangements in our society are those, I think, of a decentralized democratic socialism; a strong welfare state run, in part at least, by local and amateur officials; a constrained market; an open and demystified civil service; independent public schools; the sharing of hard work and free time; the protection of religious and familial life; a system of public honoring and dishonoring free from all considerations of rank and class; workers' control of companies and factories; a politics of parties, movements, meetings, and public debate.

All this will require, Walzer goes on, men and women who are at home with these practices and are prepared to defend them. A life devoted to defending complex equality is strenuous, but so too is the defense of liberty. And he concludes with a variation on the old liberal maxim: Eternal vigilance is the price of both.[113]

Walzer's ideal political arrangements will also require an active even if restrained government. He has never indulged in the Marxist fantasy of the withering away of the state, but in an article published in 1993 he concedes that given the difficult problems associated with excluded groups in American society, the state has to play a larger role in the creation of complex equality than he had imagined ten years before when *Spheres of Justice* was published.[114] For instance, justice may require state efforts to bring the excluded into the system, as in the effort to extend voting rights to blacks, or it may be necessary for the state to act to increase the amount of a good to be distributed, such as educational opportunity.[115]

But that is not a statist theory, nor, of course, is it a theory of republican civic virtue. In liberal society, Walzer claims, we are probably less civically virtuous but more civil than we once were—there is more comity, in Richard Hofstadter's sense, than there once was. Depending on the point of view, this can be seen as one of the costs of liberalism, though I think, contra Walzer, that it is questionable whether our politics is as civil as it was in 1974 when Walzer first published the analysis. My own view is that comity, or civility, is under deep pressure, which may pose a threat to important political values. In any case, Walzer sees a need to devolve more state power into the hands of ordinary citizens. That too will not come without conflict, but conflict need not worry us if it forces political leaders to come to grips with questions about the common good. However, we would still not have a politics of civic virtue. To achieve civic virtue, Walzer says, we need a new politics that "must be a socialist and democratic politics [which] must not supersede but stand in constant tension with the liberalism of our society."[116]

The problem of the state is difficult. The state has a necessary role, but since it will not wither away, "it must be hollowed out." That means a renewed emphasis on the major functional organizations of the society such as unions and professional organizations. And it also requires more attention to the "local units of work, education, and culture." These are areas where we might hope for a renewal of democratic politics.[117]

All of this is quite consistent with Walzer's summary description of his ideal welfare state; it has been reinforced by his recent interest in developing the theory of civil society. Surveying four theories of the relation between state and society, he rejects the civic republican ideal of citizenship, the Marxist emphasis on economics, the capitalist attempt to locate the good life in the marketplace, and the idea of the nation tied together by blood and history.[118]

All these theories ignore important areas of social complexity, according to Walzer. In theory building, we must start with social beings, because we are social before we are economic or political. The idea of civil society is a corrective to the four theories just mentioned. It is a liberal version of them all, incorporating them, but insisting that each leave room for the others. In this perspective, liberalism is an anti-ideology, perhaps not an unattractive position today, but also one generating its own problems.[119] The civil society perspective is more receptive to political and economic conflict than either civic republicanism or the Marxist image of a cooperative economy. Within civil society, neither citizenship nor production can absorb all social life. In addition, the two traditional leftist perspectives make the mistake of setting politics and work against each other.[120] In the market solution, there will be great inequalities, but these will be less likely to translate into domination in a civil society with a well-established network of associations, the state included. As Walzer claims, perhaps too optimistically, "Poor people with strong families, churches, unions, political parties, and ethnic alliances are not likely to be dominated or deprived for long." Like so much else, the precise nature of our associational life is a subject for debate, and through those debates, we decide not only about the associations, but also about democratic forms.[121]

Of course, all of this theory of civil society reflects Walzer's form of pluralism, but, he claims, it escapes the liberal vice of assuming that pluralism is "self-sufficient and self-sustaining." To achieve pluralism requires effort and some use of the state. Thus, civil society challenges state power but also uses it. This theory of the state differs from traditional liberalism, because it is more than just a framework for the civil society; Walzer does not see human beings as essentially private creatures, bent on pursuing their own (largely economic) interests, as classical liberals tend to do. In this sense, citizenship has a certain "practical preeminence," but it is more akin to Kateb's episodic citizenship than to the Rousseauian image of people flying to the assemblies to perform their duties.[122]

Walzer has sketched an attractive politics, but one nowhere fully realized. Perhaps it is unrealizable, but it has the advantage of pulling together much of what is valid in rights-based liberalism, radical populism, and social democracy, while still maintaining some connection with the tradition of reform liberalism. If this politics cannot be a useful force for change in this society, then perhaps nothing can. Before exploring this possibility, however, it is necessary to consider Walzer's critics.

Generally, the critics are of two kinds—those who have attacked Walzer's relativism and, sometimes closely related, those who have been concerned with the theory of social criticism implicit in *Spheres of Justice* and developed more fully since. Some of the latter have also been troubled by the politics that flows from these theories, and I will be concerned more fully with those critics but first will consider the debate on relativism.

Though the point has been exaggerated, there is certainly a strong relativist undercurrent in *Spheres of Justice*, in fact, more than an undercurrent; Walzer concedes the radical particularism of his argument. He admits that he cannot tell us whether societies that are just in the terms of his theory are also good societies, nor can he tell us whether one just society, just in its own terms, is better than another. *We* may be appalled by the Indian caste system, for instance, but if the villagers accept the system, an outsider cannot tell them it is unjust, though he can try to convince them of the superiority of an alternative. (Like Kateb, Walzer may believe that when questions of religious faith enter, it is hard to see how a purely rational argument can carry the day.) Nor can he tell us that more differentiated societies are more just than those less differentiated, though he has a clear preference for the added scope for justice in the former.[123]

It is the remarks on caste that seem to have particularly irritated Walzer's critics. Understandably, they want to be able to issue an unambiguous condemnation of such horrific institutions.[124] The common starting point toward this end is to criticize the theory of shared understandings. The very idea that there is political debate and conflict undermines the idea that such commonalities exist. In the worst-case scenario, severe conflict might indicate that no community could be said to exist.[125] And further, suppose the shared understandings of a society are ghastly, as they might have been in the Nazi years in Germany. (I doubt that we really know how widely shared Nazi values were.) Then, to validate *our* highest moral principles, we must abandon particularism, climb out of Plato's cave, and seek higher, universal truths. That is what drives philosophers in Rawls's camp to the "mathematical preference functions, fictitious social contracts, and other paraphernalia" that Schaar complains about.[126]

It is the Rawlsian search for universal truths that Walzer opposes. The reasons are partly philosophical because he believes that few such general truths exist. But the reasons are also political, both because conflict over the meaning of the shared understandings is to be expected and because, as a democrat, he believes philosophy must take second place to politics. Philosophical truth requires a radical detachment from the community; just as democracy can make no special claims on philosophical opinion, "philosophers have no special rights in the political community"; the philosopher is only another "opinion maker."[127] To that one can add that the contribution to democratic debate by philosophers may be very valuable; opinion makers can be very important. Still, since the history of philosophy is a history of disagreement, we ought not to hope for "knockdown arguments" that will settle issues once and for all. That is why politics is a permanent phenomenon.

But Walzer's relativism has been much exaggerated; he does not leave us in a world of endless debate in which every argument is as good as every other. He does not fall into the trap of extremist postmodernism. Even in *Spheres of Justice* he laid down some firm rules. He writes that complex equality provides no help for totalitarianism because, by definition, it overrides the autonomy of the distributional spheres. And slavery is beyond the scope of a theory of distributive justice; there are no shared understandings between slaves and masters—they are at war, and the applicable theory is the theory of just and unjust wars. There are also some human or natural rights that are not just matters of social convention, notably life and liberty. The reason they achieve so little attention in Walzer's theory of distributive justice is that they are of little use outside the spheres of membership and welfare. When Walzer wrote on the theory of the just war, he made extensive use of arguments based on these rights.[128] But what, for example, can natural rights tell us about the choice of elected officials, the distribution of private jobs, or the awarding of public honors? All are important social goods, but surely they are not won as a matter of right without regard to the conventions of society. To look for more secure foundations threatens to run afoul of Aristotle's warning that we should seek no greater precision than the nature of the subject allows.

In recent years, Walzer has devoted more attention to universal, nonparticularist rights, though his argument made only "minimalist" claims. He opens his argument with the example of television coverage of street demonstrations in Prague in late 1989. The marchers carried signs, some saying simply, "Truth or Justice." Seeing the pictures, Walzer says, he knew immediately what they meant, even though he was largely unfamiliar with the culture the marchers shared. These people were not marching on behalf of any particular philosophical doctrine of truth or justice, nor were they marching to defend utilitarianism or the difference principle or any other such position, though some of the marchers may have had views on such matters; they may also have differed on them. But it was clear enough what they meant by justice: "an end to arbitrary arrests, equal and impartial law enforcement, the abolition of the privileges and prerogatives of the party elite—common, garden variety justice."[129]

Moral terms, Walzer reminds us, have minimal and maximal meanings, and we can give thick or thin descriptions of them. The relationship between the two meanings and the descriptions of them is the reverse of what philosophers often claim. We do not start with the more generalized meaning, which is necessarily thin because it applies everywhere. Instead, "morality is thick from the beginning, culturally integrated, fully resonant, and it reveals itself thinly only on special occasions, when moral language is turned to specific purposes." Thus, we can all agree with the prophet Amos when he condemned "grinding the face of the poor," but we will not agree so easily on just what it means to treat the poor with justice. But when we see the poor being ground down we will immediately recognize it and we will react strongly. "Thinness and intensity go together, whereas with thickness comes qualification, compromise, complexity, and disagreement."[130]

The realm of thickly described moral principles is the realm of complex equality and shared understandings. Those who search for greater precision will doubtless be unsatisfied by these arguments, but since twenty-five hundred years of theorizing has not established secure foundational positions, perhaps it is time to look elsewhere for our standards of justice. It is also worth remembering that politics rarely is about ultimate values. The level of abstraction is generally lower than that and revolves around the application of principles in particular cases. That limitation does not obviate the need for theory; we need more theory, but it does lower the level of abstraction and move us in the general direction of Plato's cave.[131]

At this point criticism of Walzer becomes more explicitly political. What if there are no widely shared common understandings? To return to the example of medical care, it is clear that there is great dispute about what good public policy, not to mention distributive justice, requires. Many of Walzer's critics put forth arguments that take this form, but he has an answer. Just as the logic of rights is subversive, so too is the logic of shared understandings. There are "latent and subversive" meanings that underlie the disputes over many policy issues.[132] The classic case is the appeal of racial reformers from Abraham Lincoln to Martin Luther King, Jr., to the principles underlying the Declaration of Independence, the Constitution, or other foundational documents. Although some may privately reject these principles, it is hard to make public arguments against them that meet standards of intellectual or political respectability. These standards change over time. Segregation could pass muster in 1896 but not in 1954. By then, desegregation was an "idea whose time had come." The basic logic of the principles of the regime won out, even though the victory was far from complete.

But sometimes, as the desegregation example shows, the meaning of the shared understandings will be deeply contested. And "when people disagree about the meaning of social goods, when understandings are controversial, then justice requires that the society be faithful to the disagreements, providing institutional channels for their expression, adjudicative mechanisms, and alternative distributions."[133] This points the way to a politics of justice, a politics of parties, movements, court decisions, and possibly locally different attempts to realize justice, though the American experience with the latter is disquieting. Local understandings may conflict with broader ones and lead local minorities to appeal to a more general public. Thus the politics of justice will be complex and without end.

There are two other criticisms of the concept of shared understandings that may cut more deeply. Walzer sees the American consensus as essentially liberal, though subject to periodic communitarian correction. But by staying within the American cave, does Walzer commit himself, in spite of his socialist beliefs, to an implicitly conservative defense of the status quo? Are liberal principles good enough, or must we look to more radical solutions for our problems? Peter Euben insists that we must, that the thin liberal theory of consent is not enough, that we need full-time participatory citizens of a type not encouraged by liberal pluralism, and that, in brief, we have to face up to alternatives Walzer does not endorse. We have to find ways to get greater critical distance from American politics than Walzer's method allows.[134]

Walzer's answer is given in his theory of social criticism, implicit in *Spheres of Justice*, and developed more fully since. He argues that we need both critical distance and critical principles. These principles can be discovered, invented, or derived from a process of interpretation. Discovery is akin to revelation or to finding the principles of utilitarianism, whereas the Rawlsian difference principle is an instance of invention.[135] What Walzer defends is the method of interpretation of shared social understandings. It is true that we need critical distance, but the critic should be "a little to the side, but not outside; critical distance is measured in inches." We are inclined to discount criticism from our enemies.[136] To be politically successful, the critic must retain some connection to us or we may pay no attention to him. Of course the question arises, How do we tell good social criticism from bad, a proper from an improper interpretation? Walzer's answer, or "nonanswer," as some may see it, is that the argument has no end.[137] We will continue to debate the criticisms and the interpretation of the tradition.

Again, this answer will not satisfy Walzer's theoretical opponents, though some may be mollified by his recent moves toward transcultural, if minimalist, standards. Ian Shapiro, one of Walzer's most sympathetic critics, admits that the theory of social criticism is powerful as a set of strategic considerations but claims it cannot tell the critic what to say; it is politically, but not philosophically, useful.[138] But a politically powerful tool is no small thing, and anyone hoping to develop a more secure theory of the basis of criticism will have to develop a stronger view than has yet been discovered or invented. If Walzer does not give us knockdown arguments, then at least he offers a politically plausible, democratically useful contribution to debate. What he does not offer is certainty, but one of the necessities of democracy is the capacity to live with a high degree of uncertainty. That is one reason why democracy is a difficult politics, constantly under threat, and also why liberal theories of free speech are important. They recognize human fallibility and therefore support, indeed require, democratic politics.

John Schaar takes a different tack in his critique of Walzer's relation to liberalism. Once the market is sufficiently constrained so that inappropriate exchanges are blocked, Walzer is willing to accept a good deal of economic inequality. But Schaar, rather surprisingly, sides with the Marxist contention that capitalism is inherently unjust because it takes human labor into the sphere of money and commodities. Thus, for Marx and Schaar, capitalism "is unjust precisely because capital dominates labor *inside* the market." From the point of view of justice, the problem in the United States today is the great inequality in income across race, class, and gender lines. What is needed is something like simple equality, "if not a full equalization of income, something much closer to it than is now the case among us."[139] This is one of the more telling criticisms of *Spheres of Justice*. It may be that proper boundary maintenance would reduce the gross disparities in wealth and income in this country, but I incline to the view that, although complete income equalization is impossible and probably undesirable, greater redistribution may be required by Walzer's theory than he admitted in *Spheres of Justice*. Extreme poverty marginalizes its victims, whose exclusion from the affairs of society cannot be justified. Perhaps Walzer later agreed, since he recently wrote of the excluded that he "cannot imagine a just society in which there were large numbers of such people."[140] Of course, given prevailing conditions, to say that is to say that American society is grossly unjust.

A final word from Schaar on liberal shared understandings. He applauds Walzer's avoidance of the "sterilities and abstract generalities" of the Rawlsian approach to justice, but he sees Walzer as so "entrapped" within his spheres that he cannot establish priorities among them or defend any principle that applies across the board other than the prohibition against boundary crossing. Walzer's recent work cuts against this, but in general, I think he would contend that the prohibition is enough for most purposes. But Schaar then goes on to offer a corrective. He argues that the greatest American debate on equality and justice, perhaps the greatest debate anywhere, was carried on by Lincoln and Douglas. In particular, Schaar encourages us to think as deeply as Lincoln on the ideas of liberty and equality expressed in the Declaration of Independence.[141] Having argued in this book that Lincoln represented the high point of American political thought, a synthesis of Puritan, liberal, Jacksonian, and Whig thought, of matchless nobility and grandeur, I can only agree.

But with the exception of the Puritan ideas, these are all well within the liberal tradition; what Lincoln took from the Puritans was the style of the jeremiad and the emphasis on the work ethic, which are also completely compatible with liberalism. What Lincoln gave us was a beautiful lamentation over the traduced ideals of Jefferson's Declaration. If these ideals are not part of the everyday shared understandings of Americans, then they are surely part of the "subversive logic" of those understandings. For an antiliberal like Schaar, this is a massive concession to the vitality and importance of the liberal tradition in U.S. politics. In spite of its limitations, perhaps that tradition does represent a good deal of what is best in us.

However, suppose finally that the shared understandings we have been discussing no longer hold. Suppose, in Wolin's terms, that our collective identity is being shattered, that Hartz's liberal consensus is no more. Peter Euben has raised this question, which is at the heart of the problem of this book. Euben tries to turn Walzer against himself by quoting his essay on the disintegration of English political culture in the seventeenth century. In such a crisis, Walzer had written, old symbols eroded, political ideas became disjointed and inconsistent, old ideas were clung to with something like desperation, and then they were so extravagantly manipulated that they lost all meaning.[142] That, Euben suggests, is akin to our situation today, a situation demanding a more radical rethinking than Walzer has offered.

Perhaps this call for a more radical critique than Walzer offers is valid, though of course, radicalism is partly a matter of perception. Compared to some, Walzer's ambitions are modest. He does start from within the liberal tradition, but I think he moves away from it without entirely repudiating it. French theorist Chantal Mouffe was probably right to call Walzer's project a radicalization of liberal democracy.[143] It may be that such a radicalization is not enough, that Walzer needs to achieve greater critical distance from the tradition he criticizes and hopes to change. To some critics, this will seem excessively limiting, so that change on these terms is impossible. However, Walzer's position has the advantage of being a plausible extension of the reformist politics of the twentieth century. To paraphrase Samuel Huntington, himself no reformer, *genuine* reform is the most difficult of all politics.[144] Those who seek firmer foundational arguments should remember the strategic leverage Ian Shapiro concedes that connected criticism offers.

And, as I have tried to show, the gap between Walzer and some of his critics, notably the Berkeley school populists, is smaller than it might seem. In the final chapter, I will try to give a brief sketch of a possible synthesis of the various schools of reform theory. For reform to have any hope of success, it is necessary to keep in mind the present, not very healthy, condition of U.S. politics. That is the sometimes grim reality with which we must start. If I may paraphrase John Stuart Mill, we must make policies for people and situations as they are or are capable of speedily becoming.[145] Utopia is not possible; a move toward basic decency would be welcome.

· 17 ·

Conclusion

Once we leave the historical evidence behind, these times of great political and intellectual uncertainty in which we live do not allow for very many firm conclusions. Here I will present a historical summary of the strengths and weaknesses of the theory of the liberal consensus, suggesting how we reached our present condition. I will then briefly sketch the current challenges to the central liberal tradition and offer some political and institutional conclusions.

The consensus theory, as developed most fully by Richard Hofstadter and Louis Hartz, suffers because their work largely ignores the vital force of Puritanism in American life.[1] Indeed, much of the attention Puritanism has received from others has been excessively negative; for some it is simply a term of abuse. But that is a gross simplification of a complex, somewhat ambiguous movement. The Puritans surely were not liberals in any sense, but they laid the groundwork for a frequently constructive tradition of political morality—not moralism in the negative sense—which has been the driving force for many important reform movements. Though the Puritans were not democrats as we understand the term, theirs was still a vital experiment in participatory democracy. If Max Weber was right, they also provided, however unintentionally, a base for the development of capitalism. Moreover, the work ethic that grew out of the theological complexities of their religious beliefs was at the heart of the reformist politics of Jacksonians and populists, and it was of real significance for the abolition movement as well; it continues today as a vital part of the American orthodoxy.

I also think the best current history shows that the Puritans anticipated much of the civic republican attempt to subordinate private to public interest. This contributes to the general weakening of the fashionable republican synthesis. It is now clear that early American political thinkers did not see the same sharp distinctions between liberalism and republicanism that contemporary analysts claim to find. Those earlier men were revolutionaries and constitution writers. Many were acute thinkers—we would be lucky to have their equals today in places of power—but they were truly *political* theorists, whose efforts were not designed to satisfy scholars in graduate seminars. Puritan, republican, and liberal ideas were thoroughly mixed together, though with the rapid and early emergence of capitalism, liberal ideas of self-interested individualism became increasingly functional to the developing society. In this sense, liberalism is a broad umbrella term. At its heart is the image of the self-interested, rights-bearing, more or less equal individual. The strength of the consensus theory is that so much of American politics can be accounted for in its terms, notably the absence of any strong socialist tradition or any traditionalist conservatism in the European style.

But the consensus theory cannot adequately account for the Civil War. The parties may have prayed to the same God and read the same Bible, but surely, at the very least, there was a breakdown of the collective identity, of any shared understanding of the meaning of the Constitution. As long as slavery existed, the United States could be called neither liberal nor democratic. The Civil War amendments opened the way to an imperfect realization of both. And Lincoln provided a theory of unrivaled grandeur that is *the* great synthesis of American political thought—combining a Puritan jeremiad lamenting the betrayal of the liberal theory of rights as expressed in the Declaration of Independence, the work ethic as filtered through Jacksonian democracy, a belief in the priority of labor over capital, and a Whig commitment to a role for government in economic development. What is more, Lincoln created that theory while he was picking his way through a political minefield of unbelievable complexity.

However, Lincoln's synthesis did not last. Among the consequences of the Civil War was the emergence of large-scale, corporate, industrial capitalism in place of the existing small-scale, primarily agrarian capitalism. The new system was defended, rather implausibly, in classical, liberal individualist terms, drawing on a selective version of the Protestant ethic, laissez-faire economics, and Darwinian natural selection. The liberal tradition was maintained, but in a mutant form. From the time of the populists until quite recently, much of the energy of reform liberalism was devoted to efforts, partially successful at best, to tame the corporation. These post-Reconstruction movements reshaped the political landscape, culminated in the emergence of the modern regulatory state, and collapsed in ruins with the triumph of Ronald Reagan in the election of 1980.

Politics today is carried out within the general framework of the state created by the New Deal and its successors, but the discussion takes place on turf now defined by the loosely integrated Reagan coalition. With the defeat of George Bush, that coalition too seemed in parlous condition, though it revived significantly in the Republican victory in the congressional election of 1994.[2] The new congressional majority may be in a position to dismantle much of the New Deal; there are signs that at least some members of the coalition wish to do so. For its part, the Clinton administration is devoted to a much chastened version of big government liberalism, but it is not clear what its true commitments are. The weakness of President Clinton has left conservatives in a position to control the terms of debate, though their coalition has been rendered intellectually incoherent by the range of opinion it tries to represent, stretching from libertarians to fundamentalists. The first response to the congressional victory was to give pride of place to the anti-government agenda of lower taxes, deregulation, program termination, Draconian welfare reform, crime, and the drive for a balanced budget amendment. The Religious Right supported this approach, though, sooner or later, they will press their own claims on issues such as abortion, gay rights, and school prayer. But in the early months of 1995, the proposals of the anti-rationalist, libertarian wings of the movement were in the ascendance, along with some neoconservative ideas. Still, though Republican Party discipline in 1995 was remarkably strong, the intellectual incoherence of the conservative movement was beginning to be apparent.[3] The enactment of that program would mean a rejection of the major tendencies of twentieth-century government—tendencies that have prevailed regardless of which party has been in power.

At the heart of the conservative dilemma is the commitment to capitalism, which, whatever its considerable merits as a productive system may be, is necessarily dedicated to ceaseless, destabilizing change. The key to capitalism, as Joseph Schumpeter said, is "creative destruction." That is what makes the Hartz thesis so powerful; much of what passes for American conservatism is really a form of liberal, possessive individualist, competitive, economic thought, leavened with a Darwinian theory of social survival. Even the traditionalist religious conservatives do not escape. Only the followers of Leo Strauss have come close to developing an intellectually coherent conservative philosophy, but in the end they too fail because, although they despise the status quo, they see no viable alternative that would not be worse. They embrace an economic system that subverts their highest ideals.

Thus, the conservative triumph is a serious challenge to the reform movements of the twentieth century, but not to the liberal tradition more broadly considered. Competitive, individualistic, ostensibly free market liberalism is dominant. So too is a version of conservative Darwinism that threatens to jettison even the "safety net" grudgingly accepted by Reagan. The branch of the liberal tradition that celebrates what Hartz called "atomistic social freedom" is now in control. In language that is odd coming from a self-defined conservative, Speaker of the House Newt Gingrich announced that he was a "revolutionary," whereas his Democratic opponents were "reactionaries." Strange times! A responsible conservatism will have to find a way to come to terms with the forces of destruction they now embrace. That will require more than science fiction fantasies about the wonders of technology. Unless these concerns are addressed, the level of debate in American politics is inevitably lowered.[4]

It is also lowered by the inability of reform liberal political leaders to articulate a serious defense of their position. The reaction to the Republican offensive in early 1995 was almost entirely defensive, as reform liberals seemed panicked by the unexpected loss of Congress and ready, in spite of themselves, to join the speaker's revolution. As Chapters 15 and 16 make abundantly clear, the ideas for a genuine debate on the role of government are there, but in a politics driven by opinion surveys, they are unlikely to receive much discussion. The ideological initiative lies with the conservative branch of the liberal tradition, reversing the situation that has prevailed since the days of the Progressives. In Hartz's terms, the Whigs are back.

Of less immediate political concern, though in the long run perhaps equally troubling for the liberal consensus and for political theory generally, are some contemporary tendencies in political and social thought that come from the left. These include some forms of feminism and multiculturalism. That there is discrimination against women and members of racial, ethnic, and sexual minorities is not open to question. However, the liberal constitutional tradition is focused on individuals; an attempt at group-based solutions goes against the grain of American culture. If Michael Walzer's idea of connected criticism has any unquestioned validity, it is as a theory of strategic action. Aside from the inherent power of the liberal theory of rights, an approach that turns liberal values against the performance of liberal society is more likely to succeed than one that seems to so many an outrage to traditional values. Liberal practice is often hypocritical; why not, in the spirit of self-criticism, turn liberal theory against it?

However, those are contentious points. Sometimes group-based remedies may be necessary, though usually, I think, as a last resort. Much more troubling is the alliance of feminists and multiculturalists with postmodern theorists. Although it is true that none of the claims of traditional philosophers to have discovered secure foundations for their ideas seem acceptable, the sweeping relativism of the postmodernists leaves them no ground on which to stand. As I argued in discussing postmodernist feminism, if everything is a matter of interpretation, if all claims to authority are merely power grabs, then why should we pay attention to such postmodernist arguments? Why are they exempt from their own corrosive skepticism?

That is not to say that there is nothing of any value in postmodernist theory. Postmodernists may help sensitize us to the terrible trials of the outcasts of society and to some politically relevant questions of personal identity. There has also been an interesting attempt to relate postmodernism to such traditional concerns of political theory as the theory of justice.[5] But Michel Foucault, the fashionable French postmodernist so influential in the United States, devoted much of his writing to sexuality and the inmates of prisons and asylums. In doing that, he systematically avoided the major political and economic institutions of our time, the large multinational corporation, and the centralized state, particularly in its war-making activities. Although it is true that prisons and asylums are state institutions that are sometimes put to political use and that sexuality has become a political issue, it is also true, as Michael Walzer observes, that most of us do not live in carceral institutions.

Moreover, Foucault's thinking on the difficulty of achieving objective knowledge about the operation of society has already been fully probed by Sheldon Wolin, Charles Taylor, and many others; beyond Foucault's flamboyant verbiage there is not much new there on this subject. In spite of his apparent interest in politics, it is difficult to take him completely seriously as a political theorist, given the near irrelevance of his work to the central political and economic issues. His denial of the possibility of a theory of political legitimacy underscores this point. Nor can it be said that his American acolytes have, as yet, produced critiques of U.S. society and politics on the level of Walzer and Wolin on the left, Kateb and Shklar in the liberal center, or the best of the Straussians or neo-conservatives on the right. And, in an ironic twist, the effort of many postmodernists has been undercut by their working on an excessively high level of abstraction, in much the same way as the school of Rawlsian liberals has done. Postmodernists will have to come down from the rhetorical heights and engage in a more direct encounter with American society than they have up to now.[6]

Among postmodern American theorists, Richard Rorty has made an effort to engage concrete issues that Foucault did not, but Rorty's political writings, though closer to the concerns of this book than those of other postmodernists, have not been very successful.[7] He has contributed to the current revival of interest in the political theory of John Dewey, though many of the participants in the revival have disowned his reading of Dewey. Rorty's dismissal of traditional epistemology is inconsistent with Dewey's faith in social science, misplaced though it may have been.[8] At least Rorty has avoided the trap of feckless, baseless political radicalism that is so common among postmodernists. But he pays a high price: His liberalism appears to many to be complacent and heavily dependent on obsolete and controversial cold war assumptions. His belief in the viability of widespread "shared understandings" far exceeds anything suggested by Michael Walzer. And his paper on human rights demonstrates the impossibility of developing such a theory without *some* minimal philosophical basis. The best that can be said about Rorty's postmodernism is that it is harmless.[9]

So far, postmodernism seems to be largely an academic phenomenon. Were these ideas to become a significant part of the American collective identity or shared understandings, it would be a fundamental alteration of the liberal political culture that would have profound, if unpredictable, consequences. But though there are identifiable postmodernist styles in the fine arts and in literary theory and philosophy, it is not clear that there are corresponding phenomena in society. It seems possible that postmodernism is really just a heightened form, or the latest phase, of modernity. To suggest otherwise is to suggest a change of millennial proportions. Perhaps there is one, but caution seems warranted.

The most interesting postmodernist suggestion is Jean-François Lyotard's that both liberalism and Marxism, indeed all the modern "metanarratives," have exhausted themselves. Again, that is possibly true; certainly both liberalism and Marxism need rethinking. But Marxism is a theory about capitalism, not socialism, and the collapse of the Soviet Union does not by itself invalidate the theory. Similarly, liberal capitalism seems a very lively corpse, though the liberal triumphalism of Francis Fukuyama and his followers is decidedly premature; the New World Order proclaimed after the Gulf War was obviously a fantasy—New World Disorder is so much more to the point that it has become a cliché.[10]

But there are observable developments that challenge liberal assumptions. America was a nation slow to develop a modern state, in spite of the best efforts of Alexander Hamilton. In his *Philosophy of History*, Hegel argued that there was no such thing as an American state. A state would arise only when class distinctions appeared, when there were great distinctions between the rich and the poor, when it became difficult for people to satisfy their felt needs in the accustomed way, and when, in effect, the frontier closed, so that people begin to feel pressed together.[11] For Hegel, America's formlessness and sparse population set it apart from the mainstream of European history, whereas, for Locke, those conditions were what made a weak state possible. They are also among the forces that made for American exceptionalism, the sense that the United States has represented something historically unique. Perhaps what is happening is the Europeanization of American politics, whereby the United States rejoins the mainstream of history; that is, we may be seeing the end of exceptionalism.[12] Of course, this is a perilous juncture; as Sheldon Wolin and George Kateb insist, the state is dangerous, but they also know, with Michael Walzer, that it is not going to wither away, in the old Marxist phrase.

However, the "megastate," as Sheldon Wolin calls it, does not perform at the level expected by the public. The built-in stalemate mechanism so carefully crafted by James Madison works all too well, especially because of the ceaseless multiplication of interest groups. The result is a politics seemingly devoid of anything remotely like civic virtue, a politics that Madison would have deplored. In the eyes of the electorate, the system of interest group liberalism that grew out of the New Deal failed, but so too did the capital-oriented substitute offered by Presidents Reagan and Bush. The Clinton administration has an opportunity to pick up the pieces; should Clinton fail, as seems likely to many, some see the threat of a genuine legitimacy crisis.[13] The results of the 1994 election suggest a perception in the electorate that Clinton has indeed failed. It is not clear whether the results indicate merely a revolt against the Democratic Party's version of reform liberalism, or whether something much more epochal has occurred—a genuine reversion to nineteenth-century ideas of localism and individualism and a rejection of the twentieth-century state. The view I have developed here suggests that the latter is unlikely, but it is certain that we will see important experiments along those lines.

But it is not easy to bring about massive change in political structure or policy in the United States. James Madison did his work well—some say all too well. A number of seasoned observers argue that in spite of the dramatic rhetoric of the Republican congressional majority elected in 1994, the odds still favor incremental change. Even the Contract with America, the Republican blueprint for "revolution," appears to Theodore Lowi and Benjamin Ginsberg to be largely incremental. Further, it is important to bear in mind that, as Carey McWilliams asserts, "the anger of Americans at government, however, is a mark of their need for it. Less government would not 'empower' citizens, it would only leave them subject to the domination and powers of the market, technology, and international society."[14] These speculations may turn out to be incorrect, but it is clear that it may take years of intense politics to discover if they are. Of course, a Republican presidential victory in the 1996 election could have an enormous impact.

This situation is occurring in a context in which seasoned, experienced foreign observers note that U.S. politics is so opaque as to defy understanding. As a former British ambassador put it, anyone who claims to know how a particular decision came to be made in Washington is either "a fool or a liar."[15] The American system, then, is one in which democratic responsibility is almost impossible to affix. At the same time Americans expect miracles from presidents, who are simply not able to deliver.[16] Some people now seem to expect similar miracles from Congress. They too seem likely to be disappointed. The voter malaise that is an almost inevitable result could all too easily descend into something worse.

Fundamental political issues are at stake. At the deepest level, there is a crisis in the liberal theory of consent and in the electoral system related to it.[17] In the Lockean liberal theory celebrated by the consensus theory, the consent of the governed legitimates the power of government. But consent is notoriously easy to come by. More often than not it is tacit rather than expressed by some conscious act, a fact especially troubling for participatory democrats, since consent in a representative democracy is really consent to *be* governed.

In modern representative systems, the standard mechanism for ascertaining consent is through elections. Joseph Schumpeter's theory of competition for office among alternative sets of elites established the norm and, sadly, describes the practice. Political activities other than voting are discouraged. The result is a very thin theory of legitimacy. If the central event of democratic politics is the election, then the quality of electoral politics is vital. We can assess that quality by looking at the turnout rate, the voter's sense of political efficacy, the extent of meaningful deliberation on the issues, the evenness of competition in the mass media, and the extent to which debate is not solely controlled by those same media.[18]

Leaving aside nonpresidential elections for simplicity's sake, it would take a willfully optimistic student of presidential politics to contend that these criteria are met on any remotely satisfactory level. Turnout is poor, the media are dominant, the level of debate is astonishingly low, and the financial costs of entry into the game are even more astonishingly high. The last factor is of particular importance, a source of deep systemic corruption, a sign of the breakdown of the all important barriers between the sphere of political power and that of money and commodities.

The money stems from interest groups and political action committees (PACs). The importance of PAC money is a sign of a fundamental derangement in the relationships between the interest group system and the party system. In a no longer fashionable jargon, Americans have developed an amazing capacity to articulate interests but very little capacity to aggregate them. Aggregation is the work of political parties, whose role is to choose candidates and organize large numbers of voters out of the fragments created by the pluralist system.

The weakness of parties is one of the regrettable legacies of the Progressive movement, which introduced primary elections, civil service reform, limitations on patronage, and the like, in an effort to curb corruption by removing opportunities for graft and taking the essential nominating process out of the hands of the party bosses. The weakening was continued by the New Deal and the growing tendency to appeal directly to the people through the mass media, over the heads of governmental officials. Probably the growth of the welfare system also contributed to the decline of parties, as some of the welfare activities of the machines were taken over by the state. The old saying that all politics is local is still valid to some extent, but its force has been attenuated by national-level campaigning, particularly in primaries, being limited to a brief airport appearance scheduled in time to make a sound bite for the evening news. The candidates, backed by "make-up artists for the face and mind," touch down and are quickly off again. As Michael Walzer points out, campaigns in this style are like quick commando raids, whereas campaigns fought by parties are long-term struggles.[19]

It is not true that caucuses and conventions are necessarily less democratic than primaries. The former can be run by volunteers, whereas the latter increase the demand for big money. At their worst, caucuses and conventions are a politics of local bosses rather than of national celebrities. At their best, they are a politics of organizers, activists, and militants,[20] though it must be said that those on the left cannot be sure that they will be the beneficiaries of such activities. Consider, for example, the success of the fundamentalist Right in a growing number of states. The lesson is that all politics is about organization. The virtue of local party politics is that it features direct citizen involvement, whereas media-dominated politics is more passive and distant. But those who do not enter the competition cannot succeed.

Walzer's preference for the old days of locally based, participatory political parties is consistent with his recent emphasis on civil society and his long-standing pluralist concern with the revitalization of local centers of power—that is part of the politics of "hollowing out." It is also consistent with the emphases of the radical populists of the Berkeley school. For Sheldon Wolin and John Schaar, democratic politics is local politics or nothing. They too worry about the decline of parties, but it is no longer possible to disperse all power to the fragments, which limits the political force of their arguments in the world of the modern American state.[21] However, Wilson Carey McWilliams has reflected extensively on the theory of the political party in the context of American political culture; his theory opens up the possibility of a synthesis between Berkeleyite populism and social democracy.

In a series of essays, McWilliams has laid out the intellectual genealogy of the theory of political parties in the United States.[22] Only a brief sketch is possible here, but that is sufficient for present purposes. McWilliams writes that intellectually, if not through direct historical causation, the roots of party lie in the Anti-Federalist concern for localized politics and close control over representatives. Tocqueville systematized that argument with his famous theory that local voluntary associations were the heart of American democracy, schools of good citizenship in something like the civic republican sense. But, McWilliams says, as American life "grows more specialized, more mobile, and more pervaded by the media, local communities and personal bonds of all kinds are becoming increasingly fragile." One result is that "contemporary political parties are less and less effective as representatives and civic educators."[23] Though it is not a panacea, party revival is necessary for the health of American politics. And party revival may require a new way of thinking about democracy, well within the liberal tradition, but far removed from the current orthodoxy. Donald Robinson was surely right when he wrote, "Unless the yearning of John Stuart Mill for human development replaces the stoic realism of Schumpeter, parties will not be able to tap the idealism of a democratic citizenry."[24]

However, it is easier to say that we need to revive parties than it is to do it. The most obvious approach is through drastic campaign finance reform, preferably through public financing of elections. Also, perhaps the level of financing should be low so as to reduce the amount spent on television. Deprived of such financing, candidates might actually have to confront voters face to face. If the moneys were in the hands of the party leaders, that would automatically strengthen their position. But it would be at the price of centralization. However, to give the funds directly to the candidates would free them from domination by interests, but at the price of turning them into local barons.[25] Once the roots of local democracy wither, it is not easy to bring them to life. And it must be said, Congress is very resistant to campaign reform.

A second set of proposals that should get a fair hearing came from Lani Guinier. Guinier's nomination to be assistant attorney general for civil rights was hastily withdrawn by President Clinton when her ideas proved controversial. It is clear that the label "quota queen" hung on her by the *Wall Street Journal* was terribly unfair. Her system of cumulative voting involves creating new districts with multiple members. Each voter would have a number of votes equal to the number of members and would be free to cast them all for one candidate or to split them among two or more. Cumulative voting does not violate the one-person-one-vote rule, and it is not in principle a race-based system. It has theoretical problems related to the nature of majority rule, raising the question of what groups in a nation filled with minorities need special protection. Moreover, no one really knows how her ideas would work in practice.[26] Conceivably, they could lead to interesting new coalitions and might contribute to the revitalization of local politics; they might also be disastrous. The point is that at a time when there is a desperate need for new ways of thinking about politics, the public interest was not served by the premature stifling of debate on Guinier's ideas.

While proposals for institutional reform are on the table, it may be useful to consider the term limits fad. That is no doubt most interesting as a symbol of popular disgust with government. However, it has been advocated by columnist George Will, so it does not lack frequent and very conspicuous theoretical support. Still, the support is a little surprising, coming from one who reveres *The Federalist Papers,* whose authors explicitly rejected the idea. Its origins are in populist antifederalism, which saw frequent rotation in office as a way to further popular control, but Will claims to believe that it would foster civic virtue. Perhaps, but under present conditions, there are obvious problems. First, there already are term limits—two years for members of the House and six for senators and, of course, eight years constitutionally ordained for presidents. But voters frequently, if inconsistently, fail to seize this opportunity to dismiss incumbents, perhaps because, though they believe Congress in general to be a hopeless mess, they tend to be satisfied with their own representatives. Further, although democracy in some sense might be served by giving more people a chance at office, term limits are still a restriction of the democratic suffrage, one that has the potential to deprive citizens of honest, dedicated, and frequently expert public officials. The inevitable effect would be to transfer considerable power to the unelected, but more permanent, congressional staff system.[27] It remains to be seen whether the dramatic cutback in congressional staffing by the Republican majority elected in 1994 will affect this prediction. In any case, in 1995 the Supreme Court ruled state term limits on U.S. representatives unconstitutional, though it is doubtful that the last word has been heard on this subject.

But the most dramatic and perhaps most interesting reform entails an assault on one of the very nearly sacred doctrines of political science, the superiority of the two-party system. Leading the attack is Theodore Lowi, who has even made some organizational efforts in support of his idea. Certainly when a multibillionaire pseudopopulist like Ross Perot can win almost 19 percent of the presidential vote, in spite of the absence of any real program, it is a strong signal of significant voter alienation.[28] His showing suggests that if Walter Dean Burnham is right about the party system, a failed Clinton administration may be the catalyst to provide the force needed for a new party.

Lowi believes that the consensus that has held American politics together for the past hundred years for those on the right and the past fifty years for those on the left is in shambles. With considerable exaggeration of the radicalism of the Democratic Party, he contends that it committed suicide through the constant expansion of big government—hence what he called the end of liberalism. But the new Republican majority quickly bogged down, though not, as I have said, without reshaping the contours of political debate. In any case, their apparent failure to deal successfully with the economy precipitated their resounding defeat in 1992. The two parties are intellectually and structurally exhausted. The two-party system is "braindead." A third party could be an honest broker and hold the balance of power. Lowi argues that this would end "gridlock," though it might just as well intensify it. But it might also provide alienated voters with new democratic outlets for the expression of their discontents and needs.[29] The question is open, and the problem is worth exploring.

Alterations in the structure of political institutions are open to discussion, though the possible results are shadowed by the law of unintended consequences. But without structural economic changes, political alterations are likely to be of no avail. Walzer is right: The lines between economic and political power must be redrawn. Though those on the populist left do not use his vocabulary, they seem to agree. Of course, not all corporations are guilty, but the list of abuses of law and ethics leading up to the savings and loan debacle and the amazingly brazen behavior of the leaders of the tobacco industry are too well known to require recounting here.[30] However, we are brought back to Aesop's *Fables* and the problem of belling the cat. Under current conditions, it is hard to see the politics that would lead to real control over the corporation. A strong political party might be able to tap the deep well of discontent with elites, economic as well as political ones, but no such party now exists. The Democratic Party is essentially as beholden to corporate America as are the Republicans.

Given the international nature of capitalism, the political problem is of staggering dimensions. In general, nationalization of industry has not been very successful, and there is no political support for it even if it had been. Walzer notes that corporations are like nation-states with imperial ambitions, and he rightly suggests that they may need to be dealt with through some collective security system.[31] But collective security is a difficult politics to pursue; nations will surely have differing interests in economic affairs, just as they do in the area of military security. The time for this idea may come, but I doubt it is here yet.

The idea of workplace democracy holds more promise. It has impeccable liberal credentials going back to John Stuart Mill's *Principles of Political Economy*, as well as to Louis Brandeis, and it is endorsed by Wolin, Schaar, and, more extensively, by Walzer. However, the most developed contemporary theory comes from Robert Dahl. The reasoning is simplicity itself: If democracy is justified in the state, it is also justified in governing economic enterprises.[32] Given the centrality of work in the lives of most people, this argument is compelling, and although it would be a dramatic change in the pattern of corporate ownership and control, it obviously does not violate liberal democratic principles. In addition, there has been some experience with economic democracy, in the United States and Europe. As recently as summer 1994, the employees of United Airlines, after a long struggle, took control of the company they worked for. Dahl does not advance his theory as a panacea; the record of this form of ownership is mixed, and of course, it would require a major consciousness change in American attitudes toward property.[33] Moreover, there is no organized movement advocating this reform. Finally, worker-run corporations might be as viciously competitive as are their current counterparts. Still, it is an approach with some potential to rein in the corporation as we know it, and it would increase democratic control over daily life for many.

But even if we assume the utility of some or all of these reforms, they are likely to be of little effect if the liberal consensus is shattered, if the collective identity no longer holds, if the shared understandings underpinning the political system no longer maintain their force. At a very high level of abstraction, Americans appear deeply attached to the Constitution; it is very difficult for them to imagine any other form of democratic government. Below the surface, however, all is not well. There is massive, and often justified, discontent with the operation of the political system. The fundamentalist Right is in open revolt against basic liberal principles; Pat Robertson, for example, simply denies that the First Amendment requires the separation of church and state; moreover, he is propagating an anti-Semitic, hate-filled conspiracy theory of international and domestic politics.[34] There is constant speculation among well-informed observers that the Bill of Rights would not be readopted in a popular referendum today. The gulf between the races seems to grow greater almost daily; opinion surveys show that whites see great progress, whereas blacks perceive deepening racism and discrimination.[35] Everyone sees the condition of the inner cities as appalling. Elites across the board are distrusted. Elementary political civility is at a lower level than anyone now living can remember.

And all these tensions are at work during a time when the economic future is uncertain. The United States is struggling to ascertain its place in the international economic order as American workers watch helplessly from the sidelines. Central to that is the emergence of what Daniel Bell presciently called the "postindustrial society," a society increasingly geared toward service industries and high technology, while older manufacturing industries are in decline.[36] The result is a society not only in which technical expertise is of great importance but also in which those without that expertise, and sometimes even those who have it, are deeply insecure because of the rapidly changing job market. Nothing today better illustrates the unsettling qualities of capitalist dynamism. Whether the "destruction" will prove to be "creative," as Joseph Schumpeter believed it would, remains to be seen. Reactions to these developments include varying degrees of anticipation, delight, dread, awe, and horror. What seems clear to many is that a fundamental change is taking place, that things will never be the same again.

The United States is at a precarious point in its history. All political systems have some form of consensus. The resilience of a regime is limited by the logic of its worldview. The organizational principles of a society limit its capacity to "learn without losing its identity." And "a system loses its identity when later generations do not recognize themselves within the tradition."[37] When that happens, the very legitimacy of a regime may be called into question. It would be premature to assert that the United States has reached such a condition. But given the discontent with the liberalism so central in both theory and practice in the United States, the threat cannot be dismissed. If there is not a legitimacy crisis, then surely there is a condition in which legitimacy is threatened. A legitimate state "deserves the obedience and support of a good person." Such a state must rest on consent and promote justice. No state ever meets its own standards; however, as George Kateb says, it is "transparent" that "the legitimacy of the democratic state in America is imperfect."[38]

American liberalism has displayed great resilience. I have tried to show that Americans have a richer legacy to draw on in the liberal tradition than Hartz thought. His contention was that the central notion in American political culture is "atomistic social freedom." The fuller tradition I have tried to demonstrate may show us a path beyond the present impasse. The way out, if there is one, will require an interpretive politics of a very high order to show the connections between the best in the American past and a better future. In the early months of 1995, the conservative movement played interpretive politics with great brilliance, successfully appealing to the localism and distrust of government that are part of the heritage of liberalism. My own interpretation calls for a synthesis of three elements: the theory of a rights-based democratic individuality developed by George Kateb; the version of a locally based populist democracy theorized by Sheldon Wolin and the Berkeley school; and the social democratic tradition exemplified by Michael Walzer, with his recognition of the need for state action on a broad front tempered by a concern for local participation.

Some may say this trio is a mismatch, an attempt to square the theoretical circle. Perhaps, but I think I have shown a greater kinship among these points of view than is commonly recognized. In any case, it is difficult for me to conceive a revived reform tradition that does not build on these elements. All three are troubled by the domination of American politics by economic interests. Only a strong state can begin to counter the huge concentrations of economic power generated by corporate capitalism; moreover, the state also must necessarily play the major role in healing the casualties inflicted by that system. However, the state itself is potentially dangerous. One way to counter the dangers is through the action of vigorous voluntary associations of citizens, operating at the local level. However, not only the state but also the local authorities may abuse power. Therefore, it is necessary to protect the individual and minority rights so vital to healthy democracy. Though often praised in theory but ignored in practice, these traditions still have deep roots in the political culture. This foundation makes possible a powerful body of connected criticism.

Thus, though there is little basis for optimism, one can hope that an alliance between rights-based liberalism, the populist Left, and the tradition of social democracy is possible as a countermovement to the current return to conservative Darwinism. The first order of business, I think, is to break the alliance between the corporation and the political system. That would be a massive step toward democratization and could give people a new sense of power, which might in turn stimulate democratic forces. There is no convincing evidence that the frequently asserted relation between democracy and capitalism is necessary rather than contingent. As Michael Walzer suggests, if the marriage between the two need not necessarily end in divorce, there is at least reason to consider a trial separation.[39] It would be too much to say that if this were to occur, all else would fall into place. But if the greatest threat to democracy is the intrusion of economic power into the political sphere, that is where we should start. If this position were well argued, it might unite some of the fragments of the culture that are otherwise seriously at odds.

This is a hard politics to achieve. But combined with a racially neutral, social democratic policy aimed at poverty, discrimination, and job creation, and with an attempt to revitalize the local roots of democracy, it is based on the reinterpretation of the liberal idea consistent with American traditions. Lincoln provides the best text: "The dogmas of the quiet past are inadequate to the stormy present. The occasion is piled high with difficulty, and we must rise with the occasion. As our case is new, so must we think anew, and act anew. We must disenthrall ourselves and then we shall save our country."[40]

Notes

Introduction

1. Quoted in Michael Walzer, *The Revolution of the Saints: A Study in the Origins of Radical Politics* (Cambridge: Harvard University Press, 1965), 207.

2. Sheldon Wolin, "Contract and Birthright," *Political Theory* (May 1986), 182. This study also appears in S. Wolin, *The Presence of the Past* (Baltimore: Johns Hopkins Press, 1989), 137–150.

3. Ibid., 183.

4. Ibid., 182.

5. Michael Walzer, *Spheres of Justice: A Defense of Pluralism and Equality* (New York: Basic Books, 1983), xiv. The connection between Wolin and Walzer that I have suggested should not blind the reader to the fact that there are significant differences between them. These will be discussed in the concluding chapter.

6. Louis Hartz, *The Liberal Tradition in America* (New York: Harcourt Brace, 1955). Hartz further developed his ideas in collaboration with several others in L. Hartz et al., *The Founding of New Societies* (New York: Harcourt Brace, 1964). A group of Hartz's students succeeded in producing a posthumous book by piecing together their notes from his renowned course on nineteenth-century European thought. See *The Necessity for Choice: Nineteenth-Century Political Thought,* ed. Paul Roazen (New Brunswick, N.J.: Transaction Books, 1990). Roazen and Benjamin Barber contributed excellent essays on Hartz. It is noteworthy that Hartz did not include a discussion of Tocqueville.

7. Richard Hofstadter, *The American Political Tradition,* 25th anniversary ed. (New York: Knopf, 1973), xxix–xxx. For an extensive review of the literature on the consensus-conflict controversy, see Bernard Sternsher, *Consensus, Conflict, and American Historians* (Bloomington: Indiana University Press, 1974).

8. Samuel Huntington, *American Politics: The Promise of Disharmony* (Cambridge: Harvard University Press, 1981), 7.

9. Hartz, *Liberal Tradition,* 6. For a similar analysis by Richard Hofstadter, see *The Age of Reform* (New York: Knopf, 1955), 9. Long before the Marxists, Europeans began to see that something unusual was happening in the American colonies. See Jack P. Greene, *The Intellectual Construction of America: Exceptionalism and Identity from 1648 to 1800* (Baltimore: Johns Hopkins University Press, 1993). See also *Is America Different? A New Look at American Exceptionalism,* ed. Byron E. Shafer (New York: Oxford University Press, 1991). This analysis may make the consensus theory appear to be a celebration of the unique virtues of American democracy. However, Hofstadter clearly wrote *The American Political Tradition* from a position well to the left of the ideas he described, and Hartz, who was, like Hofstadter, influenced by Marx, clearly managed to achieve enough critical distance from the dominant liberalism to be troubled by its narrowness. Not all consensus theorists managed this detachment. See Daniel Boorstin, *The Genius of American Politics* (Chicago: University of Chicago Press, 1953). Boorstin rejoiced in what he took to be the absence of serious ideological conflict in American history. For a discussion of some of the possible conservative implications of consensus see John Higham, "The Cult of the 'American Consensus': Homogenizing American History," *Commentary* (February 1959), 93–100, and "Beyond Consensus: The Historian as Moral Critic," *American Historical Review* (April 1962), 609–625.

10. Hartz, *Liberal Tradition,* 140, 62.

11. J. David Greenstone, "Political Culture and American Political Development: Liberty, Union, and the Liberal Bipolarity," *Studies in American Political Development,* vol. 1 (New Haven: Yale University Press, 1987), 1–49. This is perhaps the most important critical study of the Hartz thesis. I cannot here go into the discussion Greenstone offers of the distinction between the liberal tradition as a limiting versus a causal factor. The article now appears in a fine book, J. D. Greenstone, *The Lincoln Persuasion: Remaking American Liberalism* (Princeton: Princeton University Press, 1993). Without denying the importance of Hartz or the centrality of liberalism in U.S. politics, Greenstone significantly amends the Hartz thesis. He reaches conclusions, particularly on Lincoln, that are complementary to mine, though by following a quite different analytical path. For another significant discussion, see John P. Diggins, "Knowledge and Sorrow: Louis Hartz's Quarrel with American History," *Political Theory* (August 1988), 355–376. Diggins's *The Lost Soul of American Politics* (New York: Basic Books, 1984) is the most extended attempt to restate the central importance of the liberal ideology at length and in depth. For other discussions, see the Symposium on Hartz in *Comparative Studies in Society and History* (1963), 261–284. Hartz made a further contribution to this debate in the same issue of that journal: "American Historiography and Comparative Analysis: Further Reflections," 365–378.

12. Robert A. Dahl, "The American Oppositions: Affirmation and Denial," in *Political Oppositions in Western Democracies,* ed. Dahl (New Haven: Yale University Press, 1966), 51–53.

13. Richard Hofstadter, *The Progressive Historians* (New York: Knopf, 1968), 457.

14. Wolin, "Contract and Birthright," 182.

15. Russell Hanson, *The Democratic Imagination in America* (Princeton: Princeton University Press, 1985), 13. In many ways Hanson's book is parallel to this one, though in writing of liberal democracy, he focused on the democratic component, whereas I am more concerned with the liberal side. However, in a discussion of U.S. politics, the two can never be entirely separated. For a my review of Hanson's book, see *Political Theory* (May 1987), 265—269. On the relationship between democracy and liberalism, see also Amy Gutmann, "How Liberal Is Democracy?" in Douglas MacClean and Claudia Mills, eds., *Liberalism Reconsidered* (Totowa, N.J.: Rowman and Allanheld, 1983), 25–50; and Don Herzog, "Up Toward Liberalism," *Dissent* (Summer 1989), 356–357.

16. Jennifer Hochschild, *The New American Dilemma* (New Haven: Yale University Press, 1984).

17. On the idea of essential contestability, see also William Connolly, *The Terms of Political Discourse,* 2d ed. (Princeton: Princeton University Press, 1982).

18. Hartz, *Liberal Tradition,* 10. This observation provided the theme of Rogers Smith, *Liberalism and American Constitutional Law* (Cambridge: Harvard University Press, 1985). More recently, H. Jefferson Powell argued a similar point, extending it by saying that not only do political issues get transformed into legal questions, but they also become moral issues, so that the law defines the American identity. This may overstate the case, but the insight is important. See Powell, *The Moral Tradition of American Constitutionalism* (Durham, N.C.: Duke University Press, 1993), 3–4. Note also George Kateb's remark that the two centuries of judicial interpretation of the Bill of Rights constitute the richest, most subtle, and ingenious body of thinking on rights—"a unique contribution to the meaning of human dignity." See Kateb, *The Inner Ocean: Individualism and Democratic Culture* (Ithaca: Cornell University Press, 1992), 3. In this perspective there may be more important American thought than Hartz recognized.

19. Samuel H. Huntington, *American Politics: The Promise of Disharmony* (Cambridge: Harvard University Press, 1980). The recent work of Michael Walzer, which will be discussed in Chapter 16, has drawn extensively on this conflict between ideals and social reality as a major factor in the development of social criticism.

20. Rogers Smith, "The 'American Creed' and Constitutional Theory," *Harvard Law Review* (May 1982), 1696–1700, 1697. Smith develops his reservations on the Hartz thesis in

"Beyond Tocqueville, Myrdal, and Hartz: The Multiple Traditions in America," *American Political Science Review* (September 1993), 549–566. My disagreements with this important article appear in Chapter 13.

21. Michael Walzer, "In Defense of Equality," in *Radical Principles* (New York: Basic Books, 1980), 256.

22. I have drawn here on my introduction to J. P. Young, *Consensus and Conflict: Readings in American Politics* (New York: Dodd, Mead, 1972), 2–3. See also the literature cited therein.

23. Hofstadter, *Progressive Historians*, 451, 452. I have been helped in these reflections on consensus history by Andrew Delbanco, *The Puritan Ordeal* (Cambridge: Harvard University Press, 1989), 3–7. The concluding chapter of *Progressive Historians* is one of the most brilliant explorations of the consensus question. See 437–466. The most extended treatment is Sternsher, *Consensus, Conflict, and American Historians*.

24. Hartz, *Liberal Tradition*, 20.

25. Lionel Trilling, *The Liberal Imagination* (Garden City, N.Y.: Anchor Books, 1957), 7. Trilling added that some writers carry within themselves a large part of that dialectic. I suggest that this may be particularly true of certain seminal figures, such as Jefferson and Lincoln. Daniel Joseph Singal suggested that an almost dialectical synthesis of Progressive and consensus historiography might be emerging, one that allows for both conflict and consensus. See Singal, "Beyond Consensus: Richard Hofstadter and American Historiography," *American Historical Review* (October 1984), 1002.

26. Trilling, *Liberal Imagination*, xiii.

27. Ibid., viii. Much of Richard Hofstadter's work was conceived in a similar spirit. See *Age of Reform*, 15–22.

28. Hofstadter, *Progressive Historians*, 454–455. My analysis of the levels of consensus draws in general on Hofstadter.

29. Michael Walzer, "On the Role of Symbolism in Political Thought," *Political Science Quarterly* (June 1967), 198. Walzer also notes that there can be an arbitrary reassertion of the old symbols of consensus that may offer sustenance for a time. One may speculate that some of the resurgence of constitutional fundamentalism in recent years may be related to this sort of tension. I was reminded of this passage in Walzer's essay by J. Peter Euben's sympathetic but critical discussion of Walzer's *The Company of Critics* (New York: Basic Books, 1988). See Euben, "Fanfare for the Common Complaints," *New York Times Book Review* (January 8, 1989), 18.

30. I see Greenstone's *Lincoln Persuasion* as engaged in a similar project, though under the influence of a quite different background. Though his book is much more narrowly focused on a single period than mine, I believe our studies complement each other. It is a great loss that Greenstone's premature death prevented completion of his book as he had planned and of the larger project of which it was to be a part. For an extremely rich study written very much under Greenstone's influence, see David F. Ericson, *The Shaping of American Liberalism: Debates over Ratification, Nullification, and Slavery* (Chicago: University of Chicago Press, 1993). Like Greenstone, Ericson supports a theory of a liberal consensus, but one more complex than Hartz's pioneering work.

Chapter 1

1. Ralph Barton Perry, *Puritanism and Democracy* (New York: Vanguard Press, 1944), 82. In what follows, I have drawn heavily on Perry, 82–116.

2. Ibid., 91.

3. Ibid. Sheldon S. Wolin, *Politics and Vision* (Boston: Little, Brown, 1960), 192–194; and Michael Walzer, *The Revolution of the Saints: A Study in the Origins of Radical Politics* (Cambridge: Harvard University Press, 1965). Wolin at 165–194 and Walzer at 22–65 and passim present important discussions of the interplay between Calvinist theology and politics.

4. Perry, *Puritanism and Democracy,* 104–106.

5. Perry Miller, *Errand into the Wilderness* (Cambridge: Harvard University Press, 1956), 141. My interpretation throughout has been deeply influenced by Miller's work. See especially 141–152. See also P. Miller, *Nature's Nation* (Cambridge: Harvard University Press, 1967), 1–120. Miller is no longer particularly in scholarly fashion; his work was almost pure intellectual history and paid little attention to social context. Many are skeptical as to the weight he attached to Puritanism in the formation of American culture. Still, his work remains a scholarly monument, and all serious study of the Puritans must begin there. For a survey of the historiography of the subject, see Gordon Wood, "Struggle over the Puritans," *New York Review of Books* (November 9, 1989), 26–34.

6. Samuel Willard, quoted in Miller, *Errand into the Wilderness,* 145.

7. Sacvan Bercovitch, *The American Jeremiad* (Madison: University of Wisconsin Press, 1978), 3; and Miller, *Errand into the Wilderness,* 142. On the question of terminology, I follow Bercovitch. For a contrasting point of view, see George Armstrong Kelly, *Politics and Religious Consciousness in America* (New Brunswick, N.J.: Transaction Books, 1984), 27.

8. John Winthrop, "Speech to the General Court," in *The Puritans,* ed. Perry Miller and Thomas H. Johnson, vol. 1 (New York: Harper Torchbooks, 1963), 207. Here and elsewhere I have modernized spelling and punctuation. For a brilliant discussion of Winthrop, see John H. Schaar, "Liberty/Authority/Community in the Political Thought of John Winthrop," *Political Theory* (November 1991), 493–518. Schaar's article is an important contribution to the contemporary debate over the relation between liberal individualism and the claims of community (see Chapter 16). See also Wilson Carey McWilliams, *The Idea of Fraternity in America* (Berkeley: University of California Press, 1973), 133–149.

9. Jean-Jacques Rousseau, *The Social Contract,* trans. Maurice Cranston (Baltimore: Penguin Books, 1988), 64. The distinction between positive and negative liberty is drawn from Isaiah Berlin, "Two Concepts of Liberty," in *Four Essays on Liberty* (New York: Oxford University Press, 1969), 118–172. For a defense of the idea of positive liberty, see Charles Taylor, "What's Wrong with Negative Liberty," in *Philosophy and the Human Sciences* (Cambridge: Cambridge University Press, 1985), 211–229. Taylor was right to warn that both views slip easily into caricature. This is probably true of no formulation more than Rousseau's, which when read in context and with due attention to his assumptions, seems much less menacing than when taken out of its textual setting.

10. On this idea, see McWilliams, *Idea of Fraternity in America,* esp. 123–126.

11. John Winthrop, "A Model of Christian Charity," in Miller and Johnson, *Puritans,* 197.

12. Walzer, *Revolution of the Saints.*

13. Miller, *Errand into the Wilderness,* 143.

14. Winthrop, "Model of Christian Charity," 195.

15. Winthrop, "Speech to the General Court," 207.

16. Miller, *Errand into the Wilderness,* 146.

17. Ibid., 143.

18. Ibid., 147–150.

19. George Armstrong Kelly, "Faith, Freedom, and Disenchantment," *Daedalus* (Winter 1982), 132; and Joshua Miller, *The Rise and Fall of Democracy in Early America: 1630–1789* (University Park: Pennsylvania State University Press, 1991), 21–50. J. Miller confirms, with much more detail, the suggestion made here, even though I am not able to concur with all of the implications he draws in his conclusion.

20. Kelly, "Faith, Freedom, and Disenchantment," 132.

21. Edmund Morgan, Review of Kurt Samuelsson, *Religion and Economic Action, William and Mary Quarterly* 20 (1963), 135–140.

22. Max Weber, *The Protestant Ethic and the Spirit of Capitalism,* trans. Talcott Parsons (New York: Scribner's, 1958), 21.

23. Ibid., 52–53.

24. Ibid., 48–53. Franklin, of course, was not a Calvinist, but a Quaker. Remember that his sayings illustrated the spirit of capitalism, not the Calvinist Protestant ethic.

25. Ibid., 104.

26. Ibid., 115.

27. Morgan, Review of *Religion and Economic Action*, 137.

28. Weber, *Protestant Ethic*, 172. Michael Walzer is among those who have contended that Weber overstated his case by suggesting that Puritanism encouraged not only asceticism but also "continuous or unrestrained accumulation." Walzer, *Revolution of the Saints*, 304. It seems to me that this criticism misses the force of the first sentence quoted above and also that it overlooks the careful differentiation of the terms of Weber's theory spelled out by Morgan. Some support is given to Walzer by some of John Wesley's views and Weber's use of them. See *Protestant Ethic*, 175. For a useful survey of the literature on the Weber thesis, see David Little, Religion, Order, and Law (New York: Harper and Row, 1969), 226–237. For a study that supports in general the interpretation given here, see Stephen Innes, *Creating the Commonwealth: The Economic Culture of Puritan New England* (New York: Norton, 1995).

29. On this topic see C. Vann Woodward, *American Counterpoint* (Boston: Little, Brown, 1971), 13–46.

30. Weber, Protestant Ethic, 173–174.

31. Alan Simpson, *Puritanism in Old and New England* (Chicago: University of Chicago Press, 1955), 35.

32. Winthrop, "A Model of Christian Charity," 199.

33. Miller, *Errand into the Wilderness*, 2.

34. Bercovitch, *American Jeremiad;* and Miller, *Errand into the Wilderness*, esp. 1–15.

35. Loren Baritz, City on a Hill (New York: Wiley, 1964), 31.

36. Miller, *Errand into the Wilderness*, 8–9.

37. David E. Shi, *The Simple Life* (New York: Oxford University Press, 1985), 20. More generally, see 8–27; and Perry Miller, *The New England Mind: From Colony to Province* (Boston: Beacon Press, 1961), 40–52.

38. Miller, *From Colony to Province*, 51. For a very subtle discussion of the tensions within eighteenth-century economic and social thought, see J. E. Crowley, *This Sheba, Self: The Conceptualization of Economic Life in Eighteenth-Century America* (Baltimore: Johns Hopkins University Press, 1974).

39. Arthur M. Schlesinger, Jr., *The Cycles of American History* (Boston: Houghton Mifflin, 1986), 12.

40. Ibid., 13, 12–14. These themes are explored in Ernest L. Tuvesen, *Redeemer Nation* (Chicago: University of Chicago Press, 1968).

41. Samuel P. Huntington, *American Politics: The Promise of Disharmony* (Cambridge: Harvard University Press, 1981), 14, 154.

42. Ibid, 129.

43. McWilliams, *Idea of Fraternity in America*, 149.

Chapter 2

1. See John Locke, *Two Treatises of Government*, ed. Peter Laslett (New York: Mentor Books, 1965); John Dunn, *The Political Thought of John Locke: An Historical Account of the "Two Treatises of Government"* (Cambridge: Cambridge University Press, 1969); Leo Strauss, *Natural Right and History* (Chicago: University of Chicago Press, 1953), 201–251; and C. B. Macpherson, *The Political Theory of Possessive Individualism: Hobbes to Locke* (Oxford: Oxford University Press, 1962), 194–262. A useful summary of the interpretive situation to that point is Alan Ryan, "The 'New' Locke," *New York Review of Books* (November 20, 1969), 36–40. Since that time, important additions to the literature are James Tully, *A Discourse on Property: John Locke and His Adversaries* (Cambridge: Cambridge University Press, 1980); Richard Ashcraft, *Revolutionary Politics and Locke's Two Treatises of Government* (Princeton: Princeton University Press, 1986), and *Locke's Two Treatises of Government* (London: Allen and Unwin, 1987); Ruth W. Grant, *John Locke's Liberalism* (Chicago: University of Chicago Press,

1987); and Edward J. Harpham, ed., *John Locke's Two Treatises of Government: New Interpretations* (Lawrence: University Press of Kansas, 1992). Harpham's introductory chapter is an outstanding survey of the complexity of the current interpretive situation in the literature on Locke.

2. Citations of the *Two Treatises* are to the section numbers of the Laslett edition cited in Note 1. Thus, in this case, Locke, II, 19. Spelling will be modernized.

3. Ibid., II, 21.

4. Ibid., II, 13, 90, 136, 124–126.

5. Ibid., II, 123–124.

6. Ibid., II, 149.

7. Ibid., II, 222.

8. Ibid., II, 95.

9. The importance of Locke's Calvinism is particularly stressed by Dunn in *Political Thought of John Locke.* The comment on Hobbes and Locke is from Ralph C. Hancock, *Calvin and the Foundations of Modern Politics* (Ithaca: Cornell University Press, 1989), 20. On the "theistic" Locke, see Stephen M. Dworetz, *The Unvarnished Doctrine: Locke, Liberalism, and the American Revolution* (Durham, N.C.: Duke University Press, 1990), esp. 118–123. Carey McWilliams cautioned me on the complexities of Locke's theology. On this topic see "Civil Religion in the Age of Reason: Thomas Paine on Liberalism, Redemption, and Revolution," *Social Research* (Autumn 1987), 452–458.

10. John Dunn, "The Politics of Locke in England and America," in *Political Obligation in Its Historical Context* (Cambridge: Cambridge University Press, 1980), 59.

11. Locke, II, 6.

12. Ibid.

13. Ibid.

14. For the most important attempt to reduce Locke to Hobbes, see Strauss, *Natural Right and History,* 224–225. See also Richard Cox, *Locke on War and Peace* (New York: Oxford University Press, 1960). For a devastating critique of this point of view, see Richard Ashcraft, "Locke's State of Nature: Historical Fact or Moral Fiction," *American Political Science Review* (September 1968), 900–902. See also Hans Aarsleff, "Some Observations on Recent Locke Scholarship," in *John Locke: Problems and Perspectives,* ed. John W. Yolton (Cambridge: Cambridge University Press, 1969), 262–271; and Charles Monson, "Locke and His Interpreters," *Political Studies* 6 (1958), 120–126.

15. Ashcraft, "Locke's State of Nature," 902.

16. Laslett, "Introduction," *Two Treatises,* 122.

17. Ibid., 130.

18. Locke, II, 172.

19. Ibid., I, 92. I was led to this passage by Nathan Tarcov's discussion in "A 'Non-Lockean' Locke and the Character of Liberalism," in *Liberalism Reconsidered,* ed. Douglas MacLean and Claudia Mills (Totowa, N.J.: Rowman and Allanheld, 1983), 134.

20. Laslett, "Introduction," 129.

21. On the relations between Locke and Hobbes, see Dunn, *Political Thought of John Locke,* 77–83; and Laslett, "Introduction," 80–105.

22. Locke, II, 193.

23. Karen Iverson Vaughn, *John Locke: Economist and Social Scientist* (Chicago: University of Chicago Press, 1980), 97.

24. Karl Marx, *Theories of Surplus Value,* vol. 1 (Moscow, 1963), 367, quoted in Harvey Mansfield, Jr., "On the Political Character of Property in Locke," in *Powers, Possessions, and Freedom: Essays in Honour of C. B. Macpherson,* ed. Alkis Kontos (Toronto: University of Toronto Press, 1980), 23.

25. Macpherson, *Political Theory of Possessive Individualism,* 194–221; and Strauss, *Natural Right and History,* 234–251. Quote at 246. Criticism of capitalism sometimes produces strange bedfellows. For the extent of Strauss's agreement with Macpherson, see Strauss's

review of Macpherson's study, now conveniently available in Leo Strauss, *Studies in Platonic Political Philosophy* (Chicago: University of Chicago Press, 1983), 229–231.

26. Alan Ryan, "Locke and the Dictatorship of the Bourgeoisie," *Political Studies* 13 (1965), 229.

27. Mansfield, "On the Political Character of Property in Locke," 36–37.

28. Locke, II, 25.

29. This is a central theme of James Tully's stimulating and controversial study, *Discourse on Property.*

30. Locke, II, 26.

31. Ibid., II, 34.

32. Ibid., II, 27. This passage often leads commentators to attribute to Locke a labor theory of value that is an ancestor of Marx's. It would be more accurate to refer to a labor theory of property. See Ramon Lemos, "Locke's Theory of Property," *Interpretation* (Winter 1975), 231.

33. Locke, II, 28.

34. Macpherson, *Political Theory of Possessive Individualism,* 215.

35. Locke, II, 31.

36. Ibid., II, 33.

37. Ibid., II, 47.

38. Ibid., II, 48.

39. Ibid., II, 135.

40. Ibid., II, 111.

41. Dunn, *Political Thought of John Locke,* 248.

42. Tully, *Discourse on Property,* 154.

43. Locke, II, 50.

44. Laslett, "Introduction," 118. See also Lemos, "Locke's Theory of Property," 226–244.

45. Karl Polanyi, *The Great Transformation* (Boston: Beacon Press, 1957), 55. Cf. Macpherson, *Political Theory of Possessive Individualism,* passim.

46. Locke, II, 41. In connection with the history of capitalist theory, it is interesting to note that Adam Smith cited this passage in the *Wealth of Nations.*

47. Strauss, *Natural Right and History,* 242–243. On the removal of the sufficiency limitation, see Macpherson, *Political Theory of Possessive Individualism,* 211–220. For a good discussion of the literature on Locke's theory of property see Ian Shapiro, *The Evolution of Rights in Liberal Theory* (Cambridge: Cambridge University Press, 1986), 90–97.

48. Dunn, *Political Thought of John Locke,* 213. Note, however, Dunn's wry remark that something "historically astonishing has taken place when the conception of the calling has become assimilated to the duty of a member of a contemporary capitalist society to yearn ceaselessly for consumption" (262).

49. Ashcraft, *Revolutionary Politics and Locke's Two Treatises,* 273.

50. Ibid., 268.

51. Willmoore Kendall, *John Locke and the Doctrine of Majority Rule* (Urbana: University of Illinois Press, 1965).

52. Macpherson, *Political Theory of Possessive Individualism,* 196.

53. Locke, II, 119.

54. Hanna Pitkin, "Obligation and Consent," *American Political Science Review* (December 1965), 995.

55. Ibid., 995–997; and Dunn, "Consent in the *Political Theory of John Locke,*" in *Political Obligation in Its Historical Context,* 29–52, esp. 35–37. Dunn expresses agreement with Pitkin's conclusion, if not her mode of analysis, on 52.

56. Pitkin, "Obligation and Consent," 996.

57. It is perhaps necessary to add that since these conditions did *not* exist in ancient Athens, I do not subscribe to the once popular cliché that the ancients were themselves totalitarian.

58. The following discussion is heavily influenced by Sheldon S. Wolin, *Politics and Vision* (Boston: Little, Brown, 1960), 286–351.

59. On this point, in addition to Wolin, see Shapiro, *Evolution of Rights*, 128.

60. Wolin, *Politics and Vision*, 306.

61. Ibid., 309.

62. Ibid., 302. See also Joseph Cropsey, "On the Relation of Political Science and Economics," in *Political Philosophy and the Issues of Politics* (Chicago: University of Chicago Press, 1977), 32–43.

63. Dunn, "Consent in the Political Theory of John Locke," 44. If anything, Hobbes, not generally included among the great champions of human rights, offered a better defense of the individual than Locke in that Hobbes insisted on the natural right of the individual to resist when his existence is threatened by some action of the sovereign. On this subject see George Kateb, "Hobbes and the Irrationality of Politics," *Political Theory* (August 1989), 355–391.

64. Richard Ashcraft, "Revolutionary Politics and Locke's *Two Treatises of Civil Government:* Radicalism and Locke's Political Theory," *Political Theory* (November 1980), 429–486.

65. With his characteristic acerbity, John Dunn has summed up Locke's view of democracy by saying, "There is no doubt that he would have regarded voting on all issues by a whole population as a grotesquely dangerous and practically absurd political structure." See *Political Thought of John Locke*, 128–129.

66. C. B. Macpherson, *The Real World of Democracy* (Oxford: Oxford University Press, 1966), 5–11.

67. Ashcraft, *Revolutionary Politics and Locke's Two Treatises*, 148–149.

68. Ibid., 560.

69. Ibid., 578–579.

70. Ibid., 583.

71. Ibid., 584. Ashcraft is unclear here as to whether the word *unwise* referred to Locke's own thinking or to the perception of Locke's ideas held by his ideological adversaries. For a concise account of the complex political setting in which this whole argument took place, see Shapiro, *Evolution of Rights*, 113–114.

72. Shapiro, *Evolution of Rights*, 80–81, 108 n. 38.

73. Ibid., 128. See also 117.

74. For a good collection summarizing the current state of this debate, see Michael Sandel, ed., *Liberalism and Its Critics* (New York: New York University Press, 1984).

75. Locke, II, 160.

76. Ibid., II, 168.

77. Sheldon Wolin, "Democracy and the Welfare State: Staatsräson and Wohlfahrs-staaträson, *Political Theory* (November 1987), 487. See also Shapiro, *Evolution of Rights*, 115. Note that Locke distinguished an executive power that dealt with domestic concerns and a federative power that was involved in foreign relations. However, in practice the two "are always almost united" (Locke, II, 147). For a more benign reading of Locke on prerogative, see Grant, *John Locke's Liberalism*, 72–73ff.

78. Wolin, "Democracy and the Welfare State," 485.

79. Ashcraft, *Revolutionary Politics and Locke's Two Treatises*, 265.

80. Shapiro, *Evolution of Rights*, 122.

81. For a series of contemporary essays that attempt to deal with the problem of making consent more meaningful in specific circumstances, see Michael Walzer, *Obligations: Essays on Civil Disobedience, War, and Citizenship* (Cambridge: Harvard University Press, 1970).

82. Sheldon S. Wolin, "Contract and Birthright," in *The Presence of the Past: Essays on the State and the Constitution* (Baltimore: Johns Hopkins University Press, 1989), 141.

83. Laslett, "Introduction," 88.

84. David Gauthier, "The Social Contract as Ideology," *Philosophy and Public Affairs* (Winter 1977), 135.

85. C. B. Macpherson, *Democratic Theory: Essays in Retrieval* (New York: Oxford University Press, 1973), 239. For an attempt to analyze American thought and politics from a Hobbesian perspective, see Frank M. Coleman, *Hobbes and America* (Toronto: University of Toronto Press, 1977). For a critique, see Terry Heinrichs, "Hobbes and the Coleman Thesis," *Polity* (Summer 1984), 647–666. For the pull toward Hobbes, see also William Sullivan, *Reconstructing Public Philosophy* (Berkeley: University of California Press, 1982), 79–80.

86. Dunn, *Political Thought of John Locke,* 267. Although Dunn is skeptical of some aspects of the Hartz thesis, this conclusion is certainly consistent with Hartz's general view. In more recent work, Dunn has repented of his harsh earlier judgment of Locke. See "What Is Living and What Is Dead in the Political Theory of John Locke," in Dunn, *Interpreting Political Responsibility* (Princeton: Princeton University Press, 1990), 9–25. Unfortunately, what he finds most viable is the contractarian theory of legitimacy, which, although of historical importance and still of some analytical use, seems to me to be one of the weakest parts of the theory, as I have suggested above.

Chapter 3

1. Clinton Rossiter, *Seedtime of the Republic* (New York: Harcourt Brace, 1953), 315.

2. Ibid., 314; Edmund Morgan, "Conflict and Consensus in the American Revolution," in *Essays on the American Revolution,* ed. Stephen G. Kurtz and James H. Hutson (Chapel Hill: University of North Carolina Press, 1973), 314; Richard B. Morris, *The American Revolution Reconsidered* (New York: Harper and Row, 1967), 60, 69; Patrice Higonnet, *Sister Republics: The Origins of French and American Republicanism* (Cambridge: Harvard University Press, 1988), 183. Higonnet's book, though not uncontroversial, is a rich synthesis of recent literature and is explicitly concerned with comparing the American and French Revolutions.

3. Louis Hartz, *The Liberal Tradition in America* (New York: Harcourt Brace, 1955), 3, 71ff.

4. Rossiter, *Seedtime of the Republic,* 333–342.

5. Robert R. Palmer, *The Age of Democratic Revolutions,* vol. 1 (Princeton: Princeton University Press, 1959), 232, 213–235; and Gordon Wood, *The Radicalism of the American Revolution* (New York: Knopf, 1992). See also Judith N. Shklar's subtle commentary on Wood's book: "Pictures of America," *Yale Journal of Law and Humanities* (Winter 1993), 191–200.

6. Richard Hofstadter, *The Progressive Historians* (New York: Knopf, 1968), 459–460; Wood, *Radicalism of the American Revolution;* and Richard J. Ellis, *American Political Cultures* (New York: Oxford University Press, 1993), 95–119. For the special case of the South, see Eugene Genovese, *The Southern Tradition* (Cambridge: Harvard University Press, 1995). Ellis, while recognizing the importance of liberalism in American history, sees a much more varied society than Hartz did.

7. William H. Nelson, *The American Tory* (Oxford: Oxford University Press, 1961), 189–190.

8. Hofstadter, *Progressive Historians,* 460.

9. Higonnet, *Sister Republics,* 193. Interestingly, as Higonnet pointed out, most of the Loyalists were also poor, which seems to do significant damage to the idea of the Revolution as primarily a class conflict.

10. Rossiter, *Seedtime of the Republic,* 317–325; Higonnet, *Sister Republics,* 172–173. In view of his special relation to the Declaration of Independence, the thoughts of Thomas Jefferson on these events may be of particular interest. See "A Summary View of the Rights of British America," in Jefferson, *Writings,* ed. Merrill Peterson (New York: Library of America, 1984), 105–122.

11. Selections from the vast literature may be found in *Pamphlets of the American Revolution,* ed. Bernard Bailyn (Cambridge: Harvard University Press, 1965); and *Tracts of the American Revolution, 1763–1776,* Merrill Jenson (Indianapolis: Bobbs-Merrill, 1967).

12. Alfred De Grazia, *Public and Republic* (New York: Knopf, 1951), 14.

13. Rossiter, *Seedtime of the Republic*, 333–342.

14. Ibid.; J.G.A. Pocock, *The Machiavellian Moment* (Princeton: Princeton University Press, 1975). Gordon Wood, *The Creation of the American Republic* (Chapel Hill: University of North Carolina Press, 1969); and Bernard Bailyn, *The Ideological Origins of the American Revolution* (Cambridge: Harvard University Press, 1967).

15. Rossiter, *Seedtime of the Republic*, 356–361, quote at 358–359.

16. It should be noted that the Continental Congress voted independence, not on July 4, but on July 2. The Declaration was intended as a justification to the world of this action. A committee consisting of Jefferson, John Adams, Benjamin Franklin, Roger Sherman, and Robert Livingston had started work on June 10. A draft was submitted to the congress on June 28 and was approved, with revisions, on July 4. See Carl Becker, *The Declaration of Independence* (New York: Vintage Books, 1958), 1–2. Though it dates back to 1922, Becker's book remains the best introduction to the subject. For a depth of philosophical analysis that Becker lacks, see Morton White, *The Philosophy of the American Revolution* (New York: Oxford University Press, 1978). Jefferson's draft is of considerable interest. See Jefferson, *Autobiography*, in *Writings*, 19–24.

17. Letter to Benjamin Rush, January 16, 1811, *Writings*, 1236.

18. Letter to Thomas Mann Randolph, May 30, 1790, in *The Life and Selected Writings of Thomas Jefferson*, ed. Adrienne Koch and William Peden (New York: Modern Library, 1944), 609.

19. Charles Wiltse, *The Jeffersonian Tradition in American Democracy* (New York: Hill and Wang, 1960), 143.

20. Becker, *Declaration of Independence*, 24–79, esp. 24–27.

21. Cecilia Kenyon, "Republicanism and Radicalism in the American Revolution: An Old-Fashioned Interpretation," *William and Mary Quarterly* (April 1962), 168. This very important article has been unduly neglected in the recent literature.

22. The preceding discussion draws much from ibid., 168–178.

23. Ibid., 171–175.

24. Leo Strauss, *Natural Right and History* (Chicago: University of Chicago Press, 1953), 251. On the problem of happiness, see also the brilliant article by John Schaar, ". . . And the Pursuit of Happiness," in *Legitimacy and the Modern State* (New Brunswick, N.J.: Transaction Books, 1981), 231–250.

25. White, *Philosophy of the American Revolution*, 244–256. Cf. Jefferson's draft, *Writings*, 19.

26. White, *Philosophy of the American Revolution*, 252.

27. Ibid., 213–228; see esp. 225. Here, and also with respect to the idea of the pursuit of happiness, White showed the importance of the now largely forgotten Swiss theorist Jean-Jacques Burlamaqui in the shaping of Jefferson's thought.

28. Kenyon, "Republicanism and Radicalism in the American Revolution," 168–173.

29. Pocock, *Machiavellian Moment*, 509. For a survey of the large literature dealing with the "republican synthesis" in early American history, see Robert Shalhope, "Toward a Republican Synthesis: The Emergence of an Understanding of Republicanism in Early American Historiography," *William and Mary Quarterly* (January 1972), 49–80, and "Republicanism and Early American Historiography," *William and Mary Quarterly* (April 1982), 335–356. Briefer, but more up-to-date and reflective of the current state of discussion, is Jesse Lienesch, *New Order for the Ages* (Princeton: Princeton University Press, 1988), 4–9.

30. Bernard Bailyn, "The Central Themes of the American Revolution," in *Essays on the American Revolution*, ed. Stephen G. Kurtz and James H. Hutson (Chapel Hill: University of North Carolina Press, 1973), 7.

31. Wood, *Creation of the American Republic*, 121, 46–125. See also Bailyn, *Ideological Origins of the American Revolution* and "Central Themes of the American Revolution."

32. Pocock, *Machiavellian Moment*, and "Virtue and Commerce in the Eighteenth Century," *Journal of Interdisciplinary History* (Summer 1972), 119–134. See also Richard

Gummere, *The American Mind and the Classical Tradition* (Cambridge: Harvard University Press, 1963).

33. Pocock, "Virtue and Commerce in the Eighteenth Century," 120.

34. Bailyn, "Central Themes of the American Revolution," 10–14; and John Murrin, "The Great Inversion, or Court Versus Country: A Comparison of the Revolution Settlements in England (1688–1721) and America (1776–1816)," in *Three British Revolutions: 1641, 1688, 1776*, ed. J.G.A. Pocock (Princeton: Princeton University Press, 1980), 391.

35. Wood, *Creation of the American Republic*, 53.

36. Ibid., 54.

37. Pocock, "Virtue and Commerce in the Eighteenth Century," 121.

38. Wood, *Creation of the American Republic*, 58.

39. Ibid., 59, 418.

40. Ibid., 94–95.

41. Thomas Paine, *Common Sense*, ed. Isaac Kramnick (Baltimore: Penguin Books, 1976), 107–108, 120.

42. Benjamin Barber, "The Compromised Republic: Public Purposelessness in America," in *The Moral Foundations of the American Republic*, ed. Robert H. Horwitz (Charlottesville: University Press of Virginia, 1977), 21.

43. Harvey Mansfield, Jr., Review of *The Machiavellian Moment*, *American Political Science Review* 71 (1974), 1151.

44. J. H. Hexter, "Republic, Virtue, Liberty and the Political Universe of J.G.A. Pocock," in *On Historians* (Cambridge: Harvard University Press, 1979), 255–303.

45. Edmund S. Morgan, "The Puritan Ethic and the American Revolution," *William and Mary Quarterly* (January 1967), 3, 3–43. An important book, which appeared too late for me to consult fully, also stresses the Protestant dimensions of eighteenth-century American thought. See Barry Alan Shain, *The Myth of American Individualism* (Princeton: Princeton University Press, 1994). Shain indicated (see 195) that fully 75 percent and perhaps as much as 85 or 90 percent of the revolutionaries had Puritanism in their moral and religious background. Only 15 percent of church congregations in 1775 were Anglican. See also literature cited by Shain. In general, Shain supports the interpretation I give here, though we have our differences; certainly I see individualism as more than a myth. However, his book is important. Garrett Ward Sheldon sometimes also found Puritanism where others found republicanism. See *The Political Philosophy of Thomas Jefferson* (Baltimore: Johns Hopkins University Press, 1991), 148, 152. It is interesting to note that in his standard text on the founding, Morgan gives no more than a passing glance to the republican synthesis. See *The Birth of the Republic*, 3d ed. (Chicago: University of Chicago Press, 1992). This appears to refute the contention of Daniel Rodgers that Morgan's study is a brilliant but isolated work in search of the republican paradigm. See Rodgers, "Republicanism: The Career of a Concept," *Journal of American History* (June 1992), 15.

46. John Dunn, "The Politics of Locke in England and America," in *John Locke: Problems and Perspectives*, ed. John Yolton (Cambridge: Cambridge University Press, 1969), 41–80; and Isaac Kramnick, "Republican Revisionism Revisited," *American Historical Review* (June 1982), 629–664.

47. Kramnick, "Republican Revisionism Revisited," 664.

48. Michael Walzer, *Exodus and Revolution* (New York: Basic Books, 1985), 7.

49. The following five paragraphs rely heavily on Gary B. Nash, *The Urban Crucible* (Cambridge: Harvard University Press, 1986), 217–224.

50. Ibid., 220.

51. Ibid., 223.

52. See Daniel Walker Howe, "European Sources of Political Ideas in Jeffersonian America," in *The Promise of American History*, ed. Stanley I. Kutler and Stanley N. Katz (Baltimore: Johns Hopkins University Press, 1982), 42. On Pocock's recent work in relation to Locke, see Lance Banning, "Jeffersonian Ideology Revisited: Liberal and Classical Ideas in the New American Republic," *William and Mary Quarterly* (January 1986), 3ff.

53. Scott D. Gerber, "Whatever Happened to the Declaration of Independence? A Commentary on Republican Revisionism in the Political Thought of the American Revolution," *Polity* (Winter 1993), 214. For the fullest statement on the latest view of the place of Locke, see Stephen Dworetz, *The Unvarnished Doctrine* (Durham, N.C.: Duke University Press, 1990), passim and 201, 93, and 239, for the points made here. For a book that appeared too late for me to use but that also argues for the centrality of Locke, see Jerome Huyler, *Locke in America* (Lawrence: University of Kansas, 1995). Locke's revolt against patriarchy was also central to American revolutionary thought. See Jay Fliegelman, *Prodigals and Pilgrims: The American Revolution Against Patriarchal Authority: 1750–1800* (Cambridge: Cambridge University Press), 1–29 and passim.

54. Daniel T. Rodgers, *Contested Truths* (New York: Basic Books, 1987), 9.

55. See, for example, Alan Craig Houston, *Algernon Sidney and the Republican Heritage in England and America* (Princeton: Princeton University Press, 1991). See 1–11 and 268–278 for a discussion of the arguments especially relevant to this study. See also Shelley Burtt, *Virtue Transformed: Political Argument in England, 1688–1740* (Cambridge: Cambridge University Press, 1992); Jeffrey Isaac, "Republicanism vs. Liberalism: A Reinterpretation," *History of Political Thought* (Summer 1988), 349–377; and John Wettergreen, "James Harrington's Liberal Republicanism," *Polity* (Summer 1988), 665–687.

56. Ian Shapiro, "Gross Concepts in Political Argument," *Political Theory* (February 1989), 51–76.

57. On the dangers of political abuse, see ibid., 70. Shapiro develops his ideas much more fully in *Political Criticism* (Berkeley: University of California Press, 1990).

58. See, in general, Wood, *Radicalism of the American Revolution.*

Chapter 4

1. On the party system as the unwritten eighth article of the Constitution, see Austin Ranney, "Political Parties and Article VIII of the Constitution," in *Crisis and Innovation,* ed. Fred Krinsky (New York: Basil Blackwell, 1988), 47–63.

2. James Boyd White, *When Words Lose Their Meaning: Constitutions and Reconstitutions of Language, Character, and Community* (Chicago: University of Chicago Press, 1984), 193, and *Heracles' Bow: Essays on the Rhetoric and Poetics of the Law* (Madison: University of Wisconsin Press, 1985), 78. A similar, more recent, formulation is offered by Anne Norton: "The Constitution is at once text and nation. It is the act that founds the nation and the sign that marks it. It is the expression and annunciation of collective identity, at once the people's advent and their epiphany. It is an effort to represent what the people are and to record what they have been. It reconstructs, as all such representations do, the present and the past that it records. It reveals, as all such representations do, that those who represent remake themselves." See Norton, *Republic of Signs: Liberal Theory and American Popular Culture* (Chicago: University of Chicago Press, 1993), 123. I am less convinced by some of the postmodernist analysis that follows.

3. White, *Heracles' Bow,* 78. For Wolin and Walzer see my Introduction.

4. John Dewey, quoted in Terrence Ball, "When Words Lose Their Meaning," *Ethics* (April 1986), 621. It was Ball's article that first brought the importance of White's work to my attention. For Ball's own, more historically rooted, approach to questions of constitutional law, see Terrence Ball and J.G.A. Pocock, eds., *Conceptual Change and the Constitution* (Lawrence: University Press of Kansas, 1988).

5. The recent work of Sheldon Wolin, although I may dissent from some of its conclusions, express or implied, is a model of the sort of constitutional commentary we need. See Wolin, *The Presence of the Past* (Baltimore: Johns Hopkins University Press, 1989). For the discussion of the Constitution as an interpretive event, see 3 and 84–85.

6. Norman Jacobson, "Parable and Paradox: In Response to Arendt's *On Revolution,*" *Salmagundi* (Spring-Summer 1983), 123–139. I write here in only the most formal terms.

One can certainly argue that the post–Civil War Constitution was so fundamentally changed that it became a different document altogether or that less-formal changes have been equally important; thus Theodore Lowi can write meaningfully of our being in the third American republic. See Lowi, *The End of Liberalism: The Second Republic of the United States,* 2d ed. (New York: Norton, 1979). See also Bruce Ackerman, *We the People,* vol. 1 of *Foundations* (Cambridge: Harvard University Press, 1991).

7. For the text of the Articles, see Michael Kammen, ed., *The Origins of the American Constitution: A Documentary History* (New York: Penguin Books, 1986), 10–18.

8. Alexander Hamilton, John Jay, and James Madison, *The Federalist Papers,* ed. Clinton Rossiter (New York: Mentor Books, 1961), 108. Further citations to this source will be given by author, paper number, and page in Rossiter's edition. Thus, in this case, Hamilton, *Federalist* 15, 108. There are many useful editions of *The Federalist.* Rossiter's offers a useful annotated table of contents and the text of the Constitution collated with the relevant papers. Jacob Cooke, The Federalist (Middletown, Conn.: Wesleyan University Press, 1961) has provided a scholarly, critical edition of the text, which is widely cited. Isaac Kramnick, *The Federalist Papers* (Baltimore: Penguin Books, 1987) offers an outstanding introduction, which surveys the current interpretive positions. In citing the essays, I modernize spelling.

9. David Minar, *Ideas and Politics: The American Experience* (Homewood, Ill.: Dorsey Press, 1964), 111–112.

10. Jacobson, "Parable and Paradox," 135.

11. Madison, *Federalist* 10, 78.

12. Ibid., 79.

13. Ibid., 78.

14. Ibid., 79.

15. Ibid., 81.

16. Ibid., 83. The problem of majority tyranny is real, but as I suggested above, it is at least as likely that powerful minorities may deprive minorities of their rights. For a similar speculation see Robert A. Dahl, *A Preface to Economic Democracy* (Berkeley: University of California Press, 1985), 27.

17. Hamilton, *Federalist* 9, 71–76.

18. David Truman, *The Governmental Process* (New York: Knopf, 1951), 51. On the emergence of the twentieth-century concept of interest, see Daniel Rodgers, *Contested Truths* (New York: Basic Books, 1987), 177–211.

19. Garry Wills, *Explaining America: The Federalist* (Garden City, N.Y.: Doubleday, 1981), 179–264. This is an extended treatment of Number 10, with some of which I disagree. I do accept his discussion of the role of a disinterested elite.

20. Leo Strauss, *Natural Right and History* (Chicago: University of Chicago Press, 1953), 245. Martin Diamond made an attempt to distinguish between acquisitiveness and mere greed or avarice. In the latter the emphasis is on having, whereas in the former the emphasis is on the getting. That (the getting) is held to be a more benign activity, which in its moderation allows America to reach up to the republican virtues. That seems to me a dubious distinction: It overlooks the depredations that may accompany the activity of getting. See Diamond, "Ethics and Politics: The American Way," in *The Moral Foundations of the American Republic,* ed. Robert H. Horwitz, 3d ed. (Charlottesville: University Press of Virginia, 1986), 99–102. It is an interesting paradox that Americans, having underwritten the pursuit of interest in the Constitution and having thereafter pursued such a politics with great vigor, frequently display a hearty contempt for politics and politicians. See Cecilia Kenyon, "Republicanism and Radicalism in the American Revolution: An Old-Fashioned Interpretation," *William and Mary Quarterly* (April 1962), 178.

21. Madison, *Federalist* 51, 322.

22. Ibid.

23. Ibid., 322–323. Cf. Madison, *Federalist* 39, 240–246.

24. Madison, *Federalist* 51, 325; and Richard Hofstadter, *The American Political Tradition,* 25th anniversary ed. (New York: Knopf, 1973), 16.

25. Madison, *Federalist* 63, 384. Hamilton also used the "deliberate sense of the community" phrase in Number 71, 432. For an extended argument that the Madisonian ideal actually works, see Joseph M. Bessette, "Deliberative Democracy: The Majority Principle in Republican Government," in *How Democratic Is the Constitution?* ed. Robert A. Goldwin and William A. Schambra (Washington, D.C.: American Enterprise Institute, 1980), 102–116.

26. See esp. Hamilton, *Federalist* 23, 152–157. For Hamilton on the executive power, see the series *Federalist 67–Federalist 77*, 407–464.

27. Hamilton, *Federalist* 78, 465.

28. Ibid., 467.

29. Ibid., 468.

30. For a contemporary example see Martin Diamond, "Democracy and *The Federalist:* A Reconsideration of the Framers' Intent," *American Political Science Review* (March 1959), 52–68.

31. Wolin, *Presence of the Past*, 12. Joshua Miller develops a more detailed analysis of the emerging doctrine of popular sovereignty in "The Ghostly Body Politic: *The Federalist Papers* and Popular Sovereignty," *Political Theory* (February 1988), 99–119. I have been greatly assisted by Miller's article, though I cannot accept all his conclusions.

32. Edward S. Corwin, "The Constitution as Instrument and as Symbol," in *Corwin on the Constitution*, ed. Richard Loss, vol. 1 (Ithaca: Cornell University Press, 1981), 168–179.

33. Miller, "Ghostly Body Politic," 103, 107. See also Wolin, "The Idea of the State in America," in *The Problem of Authority in America*, ed. John P. Diggins and Mark E. Kann (Philadelphia: Temple University Press, 1981), 45. This essay is an important supplement to the ideas developed in Wolin, *Presence of the Past*.

34. Wolin, "Idea of the State," 48.

35. Isaac Kramnick, "The 'Great National Discussion': The Discourse of Politics in 1787," *William and Mary Quarterly* (January 1988), 23. Kramnick is very helpful on the development of Hamilton's theory of the state. See 23–29. This brilliant article has implications for the debate over liberal versus republican interpretations of the Constitution, to which we will return. It is now included in Kramnick's important book *Republicanism and Bourgeois Radicalism* (Ithaca: Cornell University Press, 1990).

36. Wolin, "Idea of the State," 50. Of course, sheer political discretion may have prevented Hamilton from spelling out his full vision.

37. Hamilton, *Federalist* 68, 414.

38. Miller, "Ghostly Body Politic," 104. Edmund Morgan traces the development of what he also sees as the fiction of popular sovereignty in *Inventing the People: The Rise of Popular Sovereignty in England and America* (New York: Norton, 1988). Although he insists throughout that the idea of popular sovereignty is a fiction, Morgan also claims that his argument is not pejorative. See 13–15. I pass here on whether his claim is plausible.

39. John P. Roche, "The Founding Fathers: A Reform Caucus in Action," *American Political Science Review* (December 1961), 804, 799–816, passim.

40. Alpheus T. Mason, "*The Federalist:* A Split Personality," *American Historical Review* 57 (1951), 625–643. Sheldon Wolin also pointed to the differing positions of Hamilton and Madison in *Presence of the Past*, 114–117. So too did Stanley Elkins and Eric McKitrick, though they did not agree with the Mason thesis as it applies to *The Federalist*. See *The Age of Federalism: The Early American Republic, 1788–1800* (New York: Oxford University Press, 1993), esp. 79–114. This is an indispensable study of the early national period.

41. Madison, *Federalist* 45, 292.

42. Herbert A. Storing, ed., *The Complete Anti-Federalist* (Chicago: University of Chicago Press, 1981). Storing's introduction to the papers has been published separately as *What the Anti-Federalists Were For* (Chicago: University of Chicago Press, 1981).

43. See the account of the interplay between Yates and Hamilton in Terrence Ball, "'A Republic—If You Can Keep It,'" in Ball and Pocock, *Conceptual Change and the Constitution*, 137–164.

44. On the dangers of aristocracy see George Mason, "Objections to the Constitution of Government Framed by the Convention," "Letters from the Federal Farmer," and "Essays of Brutus," in Kammen, *Origins of the American Constitution,* 258, 267, and 303 respectively.

45. Cecilia Kenyon, "Men of Little Faith: The Anti-Federalists on the Nature of Representative Government," *William and Mary Quarterly* (January 1955), 29–30. But see Brutus on the problem of judicial review, "Essays of Brutus," 338, 360, and on the judiciary in general, 331–360.

46. Kenyon, "Men of Little Faith," 23.

47. Richard E. Ellis, "The Persistence of Anti-Federalism After 1789," in *Beyond Confederation: Origins of the Constitution and American National Identity,* ed. Richard Beeman, Stephen Botein, and Edward C. Carter II (Chapel Hill: University of North Carolina Press, 1987), 298–299. Of amendments proposed by Anti-Federalists, one that would have increased the number of representatives was rejected and the text of what was to become the Tenth Amendment did not refer to powers *expressly* delegated to the national government, thus implicitly increasing the potential power of the national government. For a fuller discussion of these points, see Chapter 15.

48. Russell Hanson, *The Democratic Imagination in America* (Princeton: Princeton University Press, 1985), 64ff. See also Hanson, "'Commons' and 'Commonwealth' at the American Founding," and Terrence Ball, "'A Republic—If You Can Keep It,'" in Ball and Pocock, *Conceptual Change and the Constitution,* 165–193 and 137–164 respectively.

49. Gordon Wood, *The Creation of the American Republic* (Chapel Hill: University of North Carolina Press, 1969), 418.

50. Ibid., 499.

51. Kenyon, "Men of Little Faith," 9, 38–39.

52. Ibid., 38.

53. Storing, *What the Anti-Federalists Were For,* 83.

54. Rodgers, *Contested Truths,* 9–10.

55. Kramnick, "'Great National Discussion,'" passim; James T. Kloppenberg, "The Virtues of Liberalism: Christianity, Republicanism and Ethics," *Journal of American History* (June 1987), 9–33; and Mark Kann, "Individualism, Civic Virtue, and Gender in America," in *Studies in American Political Development,* vol. 4 (New Haven: Yale University Press, 1990), 46–51. For a different view that also rejects the republican synthesis, see Richard C. Sinopoli, "Liberalism, Republicanism, and the Constitution," Polity (Spring 1987), 331–352. Sinopoli developed his views more fully in *The Foundations of American Citizenship: Liberalism, The Constitution, and Civic Virtue* (New York: Oxford University Press, 1992). This study is filled with interesting and useful comments on the literature, particularly in the extensive notes.

56. Kramnick, "'Great National Discussion,'" 12. As Wilson Carey McWilliams sees it, the language of individual rights does not really capture the spirit of the Anti-Federalists. See "Democracy and the Citizen: Community, Dignity, and the Crisis of Contemporary Politics in America," in Goldwin and Schambra, *How Democratic Is the Constitution?* 92.

57. Gordon Wood, "Interests and Disinterestedness in the Making of the Constitution," in Beeman et al., *Beyond Confederation,* 102–103 and 69–109, passim; and G. Wood, *The Radicalism of the American Revolution* (New York: Knopf, 1992), esp. 257–261.

58. Interestingly, however, Findley does not appear in either of the standard one-volume collections of Anti-Federalist materials.

59. See Kramnick, "'Great National Discussion,'" 14.

60. "Letters from a Federal Farmer," in Kammen, *Origins of the American Constitution,* 270. Kammen accepts the standard attribution of these papers to Richard Henry Lee, but Kramnick adopts a later view that they are the work of Melancton Smith, the great antagonist of Hamilton in New York.

61. Hamilton, *Federalist* 35, 214–216.

62. Madison, *Federalist* 55, 342.

63. "Letters from the Federal Farmer," 273–274, 282–283, 296; "Essays of Brutus," 309, 323–324. Brutus also mentioned the unmentionable, assaulting the four-fifths clause, which

included slaves in the number of those to be counted in the apportionment. See also Kenyon, "Men of Little Faith," 10–13; and Edmund Morgan, "The Argument for the States," *New Republic* (April 28, 1982), 33.

64. On the unpopularity of the new Constitution, see Ellis, "The Persistence of Anti-Federalism," 297.

65. Hanson, "'Commons' and 'Commonwealth' at the American Founding," 179.

66. Walter Berns, "Does the Constitution 'Secure These Rights'?" in Goldwin and Schambra, How *Democratic Is the Constitution?* 71–73; Diamond, "Ethics and Politics," 81; and Don Herzog, "Some Questions for Republicans," *Political Theory* (August 1986), esp. 481–490.

67. Wolin, *Presence of the Past,* 96.

68. Ibid., 87. See also Michael Allen Gillespie and Michael Lienesch, eds., *Ratifying the Constitution* (Lawrence: University Press of Kansas, 1989), passim. This is a state-by-state analysis of ratification politics, with each discussion organized around a different theoretical controversy. The technique may be slightly artificial, but it is still rich and enlightening. For the standard account of the nationalist position, see Samuel H. Beer's magisterial *To Make a Nation: The Rediscovery of American Federalism* (Cambridge: Harvard University Press, 1993). As Cass Sunstein notes, it is interesting that the question of whether the Framers were liberals or republicans never emerges in Beer's book. See Sunstein, "Founders, Keepers," *New Republic* (May 24, 1993), 39.

69. Gordon Wood, "Democracy and the Constitution," in Goldwin and Schambra, *How Democratic Is the Constitution?* esp. 14–17.

70. For discussions of the residues of antifederalism, see Michael Lienesch, *New Order of the Ages* (Princeton: Princeton University Press, 1988), 204–214; and Ellis, "The Persistence of Anti-Federalism," 295–314.

71. On the vicissitudes of the republican theory, see Daniel Rodgers, "Republicanism: The Career of a Concept," *Journal of American History* (June 1992), 11–38. This is an outstanding survey of the literature on republicanism; it is marred only by the distrust, common among historians, of theoretical generalizations as organizing concepts. David F. Ericson makes the interesting argument that republicanism and pluralism are generically both forms of liberalism. See Ericson, *The Shaping of American Liberalism: The Debates over Ratification, Nullification, and Slavery* (Chicago: University of Chicago Press, 1993), 10–26. Ericson's notes also include a fine survey on the liberal versus republican debate.

72. For a discussion of theories of the relation of politics to economics at the time of the founding that stresses the mix of republican, liberal, and jurisprudential ideas in this period of rapid change, see Cathy D. Matson and Peter S. Onuf, *A Union of Interests: Political and Economic Thought in Revolutionary America* (Lawrence: University Press of Kansas, 1990). Gordon Wood provides a useful survey of recent literature on the emergence of interest-oriented entrepreneurial capitalism in Wood, "Inventing American Capitalism," *New York Review of Books* (June 9, 1994), 44–49.

73. Storing, *What the Anti-Federalists Were For,* 74–76.

Chapter 5

1. Max Weber, *The Protestant Ethic and the Spirit of Capitalism,* trans. Talcott Parson (New York: Scribner's, 1958), esp. 48–56. It should be said that my brief consideration of Franklin, Adams, and Paine by no means does justice to their overall importance, which a comprehensive history would show.

2. My interpretation of Franklin has been deeply influenced by Paul W. Connor, *Poor Richard's Politics: Benjamin Franklin and His New American Order* (New York: Oxford University Press, 1965), passim.

3. John R. Howe, Jr., *The Changing Political Thought of John Adams* (Princeton: Princeton University Press, 1966), xiii. I have drawn heavily on this brilliant study.

4. Ibid., 46; and Gordon Wood, *The Creation of the American Republic* (Chapel Hill: University of North Carolina Press, 1969), 48–49, 53–54, 92.

5. Howe, *Changing Political Thought of John Adams,* 87.

6. George A. Peek, Jr., ed., *The Political Writings of John Adams: Representative Selections* (Indianapolis: Bobbs-Merrill, 1954), 86.

7. Howe, *Changing Political Thought of John Adams,* 102.

8. Wood, *Creation of the American Republic,* 567–592.

9. Thomas Paine, *The Rights of Man,* ed. Henry Collins (Baltimore: Penguin Books, 1969), 265–266.

10. Thomas Paine, *Common Sense,* ed. Isaac Kramnick (Baltimore: Penguin Books, 1976), 65.

11. Isaac Kramnick, "Tom Paine: Radical Democrat," *democracy* (January 1981), 127–139, 133; cf. Kramnick, "Introduction," *Common Sense,* 46–58.

12. See the works by Kranmick cited above, and Eric Foner, *Tom Paine and Revolutionary America* (New York: Oxford University Press, 1976). Isaac Kramnick, *Republicanism and Bourgeois Radicalism* (Ithaca: Cornell University Press, 1990), is now the standard work on the emergence of bourgeois radicalism in England and America.

13. Max Farrand, ed., *Records of the Federal Convention of 1787,* vol. 1 (New Haven: Yale University Press, 1937,1966), 288, 299. The notes covering Hamilton's six-hour speech on June 18 outlining his ideal system are found on 282–293 (Madison) and 294–301 (Yates). Hamilton's own notes are at 304–311.

14. Ibid., 299; and Henry Adams, *History of the United States During the Administrations of Thomas Jefferson* (New York: Library of America, 1986), 60–61.

15. Farrand, *Federal Convention,* vol. 1, 293.

16. Cecilia Kenyon, "Alexander Hamilton: Rousseau of the Right," *Political Science Quarterly* (June 1958), 161–178. See also Gerald Stourzh, *Alexander Hamilton and the Idea of Republican Government* (Stanford: Stanford University Press, 1970).

17. Jacob E. Cooke, ed., *The Reports of Alexander Hamilton* (New York: Harper and Row, 1964), "Introduction," xxi.

18. Alexander Hamilton, John Jay, and James Madison, *The Federalist Papers,* ed. Clinton Rossiter (New York: Mentor Books, 1961), *Federalist* 85, 527.

19. Hamilton, *Federalist* 15, 106.

20. On state-building see Kramnick, *Republicanism and Bourgeois Radicalism,* 279–288; Sheldon S. Wolin, *The Presence of the Past* (Baltimore: Johns Hopkins University Press, 1989), esp. 117–118; and for the point about Madisonianism, see S. Wolin, "The Idea of the State in America," in *Authority on America,* ed. John P. Diggins and Mark Kann (Philadelphia: Temple University Press, 1981), 48–49.

21. Hamilton, *Federalist* 11, 85, 91.

22. Wolin, *Presence of the Past,* 20.

23. Hamilton, *Reports,* 118–119.

24. Kenyon, "Rousseau of the Right," 170.

25. Quoted in Mason Drukman, *Community and Purpose in American Political Thought* (New York: McGraw-Hill, 1971), 119.

26. Forrest McDonald, "The Constitution and Hamiltonian Capitalism," in *How Capitalistic Is the Constitution?* ed. Robert A. Goldwin and William A. Schambra (Washington: American Enterprise Institute, 1982), 49–50.

27. Ibid., 59–61.

28. Ibid., 68.

29. Ibid., 68–70. Hamilton's "Opinion on the Constitutionality of the Bank" may be found in Cooke, *Reports,* 83–114.

30. Cf. *McCulloch v. Maryland.*

31. McDonald, "Constitution and Hamiltonian Capitalism," 71.

32. Alexander Hamilton, *The Continentalist,* no. 5, in *Selected Writings and Speeches of Alexander Hamilton,* ed. Morton J. Frisch (Washington: American Enterprise Institute, 1985), 55.

33. See Clinton Rossiter, *Alexander Hamilton and the Constitution* (New York: Harcourt Brace, 1964). That is not to say that the Madisonian aspects of the constitutional system are of no importance. Jennifer Nedelsky gives us a brilliant analysis of the document as essentially Madisonian, but although she recognizes the contemporary deficiencies of Madison's theory of property, she still does not give proper attention to Hamilton. See Nedelsky, *Private Property and the Limits of American Constitutionalism* (Chicago: University of Chicago Press, 1990). This is still one of the most important studies in recent constitutional theory. On the differences between Hamilton and Madison, see Kramnick, *Republicanism and Bourgeois Radicalism,* 286–288; and Wolin, *Presence of the Past,* 114–117.

34. See John Kenneth Galbraith, *The New Industrial State* (Boston: Houghton Mifflin, 1967); and Charles E. Lindblom, *Politics and Markets* (New York: Basic Books, 1977).

35. Robert W. Tucker and David C. Hendrickson, *Empire of Liberty: The Statecraft of Thomas Jefferson* (New York: Oxford University Press, 1990), 3. The complexities of Jefferson's character and their relation to his thought have been widely explored. The classic treatment is in Henry Adams's masterpiece, *History of the United States During the Administrations of Thomas Jefferson,* where the complexities are at the core of the huge work. See especially the brilliant analysis of Jefferson's First Inaugural Address in H. Adams, History, 126–147. See also 97–102. On the great difficulty of portraying Jefferson, see 188, where Adams insisted on the need to "paint touch by touch with a fine pencil" in the "shifting and uncertain flicker of its semi-transparent shadows." Other studies that emphasize Jefferson's contrarieties are Bernard Bailyn's rather harsh essay "Thomas Jefferson," in his essay collection *Faces of Revolution* (New York: Knopf, 1990), 22–41; Richard Hofstadter, *The American Political Tradition,* 25th anniversary ed. (New York: Knopf, 1973), 18–43; and a critical but balanced treatment, Judith Shklar, "The Renaissance American," *New Republic* (November 3, 1984), 29–35. See also Stanley Elkins and Eric McKitrick, *The Age of Federalism: The Early American Republic, 1788–1800* (New York: Oxford University Press, 1990), 195–208; and the papers by Appleby and by Wood cited in Note 37.

36. Quoted in Joyce Appleby, "Jefferson: A Political Reappraisal," *democracy* (Fall 1983), 140.

37. Merrill Peterson, *The Jefferson Image in the American Mind* (New York: Oxford University Press, 1962); Joyce Appleby, "Jefferson and His Complex Legacy," in *Jeffersonian Legacies,* ed. Peter S. Onuf (Charlottesville: University Press of Virginia, 1993), 2. Appleby's entire essay is one of the best on the ambiguities of Jefferson's career. See 1–16. In the same volume, Gordon Wood's essay also stresses the debate over Jefferson's legacy up to the present. See "The Trials and Tribulations of Thomas Jefferson," 395–417.

38. Appleby, "Jefferson: A Political Reappraisal," 140.

39. H. Adams, *History,* 142.

40. Jefferson, Letter to Madison, September 6, 1789, in *Writings,* ed. Merrill Peterson (New York: Library of America, 1984), 959, 963. See also Jefferson to Samuel Kercheval, July 12, 1816, ibid., 1401–1402; Jefferson to Major John Cartwright, June 5, 1824, ibid., 1493–1494; and Jefferson to John Adams, April 25, 1794, in *The Life and Selected Writings of Thomas Jefferson,* ed. Adrienne Koch and William Peden (New York: Modern Library, 1944), 527.

41. Richard K. Matthews, *The Radical Politics of Thomas Jefferson* (Lawrence: University Press of Kansas, 1984), 19–29. This study is an important attempt to construct a consistent position out of Jefferson's writings. As should already be clear, I do not agree; however, Matthews's book is one of the best recent works on Jefferson and I have learned much from it. One source of difference between us is that Matthews, by remaining strictly on the level of ideas and ignoring Jefferson's actions while in office, slighted the many contradictions between theory and practice that helped to make him such a complex figure. See 128 n. 3. For Jefferson on the "extensive application" of his position that the earth belongs to the living, see Jefferson to Madison, September 6, 1789, *Writings,* 963. Another useful study of Jefferson's political ideas finds, not a unity, but rather a developmental pattern from liberalism to repub-

licanism, thus reversing the now standard interpretation of the movement of American history. See Garrett Ward Sheldon, *The Political Philosophy of Thomas Jefferson* (Baltimore: Johns Hopkins University Press, 1991). Sheldon's book is also very helpful in its discussion of the theories of the liberal consensus and the republican synthesis.

42. See the discussion of Locke in Chapter 2 herein.

43. Jefferson to Madison, October 28, 1785, *Writings*, 841–842. Note that Jefferson wrote this letter from prerevolutionary France, where the inequalities of French society deeply impressed him. Matthews comments on these materials in *Radical Politics of Jefferson*, 26–29.

44. See, for example, Staughton Lynd, *Intellectual Origins of American Radicalism* (New York: Pantheon Books, 1968), 76–86.

45. Jefferson to Madison, September 6, 1789, *Writings*, 963.

46. Judith N. Shklar, "Redeeming American Political Theory," *American Political Science Review* (March 1991), 7.

47. Madison to Jefferson, February 4, 1790, in *The Mind of the Founder: Sources of the Political Thought of James Madison,* ed. Marvin Meyers (Indianapolis: Bobbs-Merrill, 1973), 230–234.

48. Matthews, *Radical Politics of Jefferson,* 23.

49. Jefferson to Madison, January 30, 1787, *Writings,* 882. The utility of rebellion was also endorsed in a letter to Abigail Adams, February 22, 1787, ibid., 889–890.

50. Jefferson to Colonel William Smith, November 13, 1787, ibid., 911. In the same letter Jefferson noted that thirteen states had been independent for eleven years, with only one rebellion (Shays's Rebellion in western Massachusetts); that was an indication that we need not fear instability, since it translated into one rebellion in a century and a half per state.

51. Jefferson to Madison, December 20, 1787, ibid., 918.

52. Jefferson to Dr. Benjamin Rush, September 23, 1800, ibid., 1082. For the somewhat murky evidence on seditious libel, see Leonard Levy, *Freedom of Speech and Press in Early American History: Legacy of Suppression* (New York: Harper Torchbooks, 1963), xiii and 299–306. On Jefferson's civil liberties record, see Leonard Levy, *Jefferson and Civil Liberties: The Darker Side* (Cambridge: Harvard University Press, 1963). A harsh summary of the indictment of Jefferson's record is contained in Hiram Caton, *The Politics of Progress: The Origins and Development of the Commercial Republic, 1600–1835* (Gainesville: University Presses of Florida, 1988), 507.

53. H. Adams, *History,* 210.

54. Jefferson to Madison, November 18, 1788, and Jefferson to Thomas Mann Randolph, May 30, 1790, *Life and Selected Writings,* 452, 497.

55. Jefferson to Madison, December 20, 1787, *Writings,* 914–918; and Jefferson to Madison, July 31, 1788, *Life and Selected Writings,* 450–452. In a letter to John Adams, November 13, 1787, Jefferson was much more deeply reserved: See *Writings,* 913–914. There he likened the presidency to "a bad edition of a Polish king."

56. Jefferson to Judge Spencer Roane, September 6, 1819, *Writings,* 1425. On the emergence of the party system and the importance of the election of 1800, see Richard Hofstadter, *The Idea of a Party System* (Berkeley: University of California Press, 1969), 74–169, esp. 122–128. Note that Hofstadter saw Jefferson's actions regarding seditious libel in a more benign way than did Leonard Levy. See Note 52. Joyce Appleby suggests that the Jeffersonian Democrats were less a political party than a "radical political movement, mobilized to save the American Revolution from . . . its Thermidorean reaction." See Appleby, "Jefferson and His Complex Legacy," 5.

57. Jefferson, *Notes on the State of Virginia, Writings,* 290–291.

58. Jefferson to Madison, December 20, 1787, ibid., 918.

59. Jefferson, *Notes on Virginia,* ibid., 291.

60. Jefferson to John Taylor, May 28, 1816, ibid., 1392.

61. Jefferson to Thomas Paine, July 11, 1789, *Life and Selected Writings,* 480; and Jefferson to Samuel Kercheval, July 12, 1816, *Writings,* 1397.

62. Jefferson to Taylor, May 28, 1816, *Writings*, 1395.

63. Jefferson to Benjamin Austin, January 9, 1816, ibid., 1371.

64. Drukman, *Community and Purpose*, 88, 102–104. In general, I have found Drukman's treatment of Jefferson very helpful.

65. Ibid., 89–93.

66. Hannah Arendt, *On Revolution* (New York: Viking Press, 1965), 252–259; and Matthews, *Radical Politics of Jefferson*, esp. 81–91.

67. Jefferson to John Tyler, May 20, 1810, *Writings*, 1227.

68. Jefferson to Kercheval, July 12, 1816, ibid., 1399.

69. Jefferson to Joseph Cabell, February 2, 1816, ibid., 1380.

70. Arendt, *On Revolution*, 252.

71. Jefferson to Taylor, May 28, 1816, *Writings*, 1392.

72. Jefferson to Abbé Arnoux, July 1789, in *Directions in American Political Thought*, ed. Kenneth Dolbeare (New York: John Wiley, 1969), 62.

73. Jefferson to Madison, December 20, 1787, *Writings*, 917.

74. Jefferson, *Notes on Virginia*, ibid., 245.

75. Drukman, *Community and Purpose*, 92.

76. Schaar, ". . . And the Pursuit of Happiness," in *Legitimacy in the Modern State* (New Brunswick, N.J.: Transaction Books, 1981), 231–250.

77. Daniel Rodgers, *Contested Truths* (New York: Basic Books, 1987), 9.

78. Drew R. McCoy, *The Elusive Republic* (New York: Norton, 1982), 132; and Hamilton, *The Continentalist*, no. 6, July 4, 1782, in *Selected Writings of Hamilton*, 63–64.

79. Jefferson to John Norvell, June 14, 1787, *Writings*, 1176.

80. John Adams to Jefferson, September 3, 1816, in *The Adams-Jefferson Letters*, ed. Lester J. Cappon (Chapel Hill: University of North Carolina Press, 1959), 487.

81. Jefferson to Peter Carr, August 10, 1787, *Writings*, 901. For Jefferson on man's sociality, see Drukman, *Community and Purpose*, 80–81; and Matthews, *Radical Politics of Jefferson*, 53, 64–65. Matthews holds that Jefferson's conception of human nature was influenced by his study of and contact with Indians.

82. To Thomas Mann Randolph, May 30, 1790, Jefferson wrote, "Locke's little book on government is perfect as far as it goes": *Life and Selected Writings*, 496. Elsewhere he counted Locke, along with Bacon and Newton, as one of the three greatest men who ever lived: Jefferson to John Trumbull, February 16, 1789, *Writings*, 939.

83. Shklar, "The Renaissance American," 35.

84. Hamilton to James A. Bayard, January 16, 1801, in *Selected Writings of Hamilton*, 462.

85. For a concise summary of H. Adams's view, see C. Vann Woodward, "Henry Adams," in *The Future of the Past* (New York: Oxford University Press, 1989), 345–347.

86. Joyce Appleby, *Capitalism and a New Social Order: The Republican Vision of the 1790s* (New York: New York University Press, 1984), 103.

87. Jefferson to Thomas Mann Randolph, May 30, 1790, *Life and Selected Writings*, 496.

88. Joyce Appleby, "Commercial Farming and the 'Agrarian Myth' in the Early American Republic," *Journal of American History* (March 1982), 833–849. Appleby was at pains to criticize Richard Hofstadter's theory of the agrarian myth, which she traced back to Jefferson. She was right that his evidence was shaky on this point, but no one who has heard farmers lament their plight in times of agricultural recession and laud the virtues of the self-sufficient family farmer can doubt that the agrarian myth, wherever it began, is real. This is a point of some importance in understanding the populist movement. For Hofstadter, see *The Age of Reform* (New York: Knopf, 1955), 23–24, 30.

89. James T. Kloppenberg, "The Virtues of Liberalism: Christianity, Republicanism, and Ethics in Early American Political Discourse," *Journal of American History* (June 1987), 9–33. For a similar view see Jeffrey C. Isaac, "Republicanism vs. Liberalism: A Reconsideration," *History of Political Thought* (Summer 1988), 349–377. For a view from the law, see Cass Sunstein, "Beyond the Republican Revival," *Yale Law Journal* (July 1988), 1539–1590.

90. Dorothy Ross, *The Origins of American Social Science* (Cambridge: Cambridge University Press, 1991), 22–30.

Chapter 6

1. Arthur M. Schlesinger, Jr., *The Age of Jackson* (Boston: Little, Brown, 1945). I have also drawn heavily on an essay by Schlesinger, "The Ages of Jackson," *New York Review of Books* (December 7, 1989), 48–51. Here Schlesinger defended and updated the argument of his classic book. For an assessment of the current place of the book in the historical literature, see Donald B. Cole, *"The Age of Jackson:* After Forty Years," *Reviews in American History* (March 1986), 149–159. Perhaps no historian since Schlesinger has stressed class and class conflict more than Charles Sellars, *The Market Revolution: Jacksonian America, 1815–1846* (New York: Oxford University Press, 1991).

2. George Bancroft, quoted in Schlesinger, *Age of Jackson*, 163, and "Ages of Jackson," 48. A portion of the passage from Bancroft served as an epigraph for Schlesinger's volume.

3. Bancroft, quoted in Schlesinger, *Age of Jackson*, 162.

4. Andrew Jackson, "A Political Testament," in *Social Theories of Jacksonian Democracy*, ed. Joseph Blau (Indianapolis: Bobbs-Merrill, 1954), 17–18. See also, for example, William Leggett, "Rich and Poor," in ibid., 71.

5. Richard Hofstadter, *The American Political Tradition*, 25th anniversary ed. (New York: Knopf, 1972), 44–66. For the text of the message, see Jackson, "Bank Veto Message," in R. Hofstadter, *Great Issues in American History*, vol. 2 (New York: Vintage Books, 1958), 291–295. For an extended treatment of the veto, see Marvin Meyers, *The Jacksonian Persuasion* (New York: Vintage Books), 16–32.

6. Hofstadter, *American Political Tradition*, 55.

7. Richard Hofstadter, *The Age of Reform* (New York: Knopf, 1955), 9.

8. Meyers, *Jacksonian Persuasion*, 43; and Alexis de Tocqueville, *Democracy in America*, trans. George Lawrence (Garden City, N.Y.: Anchor Books, 1969), 614–616, 634–645.

9. Meyers, *Jacksonian Persuasion*, 23.

10. Sean Wilentz, "Society, Politics, and the Market," in *The New American History*, ed. Eric Foner (Philadelphia: Temple University Press, 1990), 65. Sellars, *Market Revolution*, is the major synthesis of this period with a focus on the market revolution. For the classic theoretical account of the disruptiveness of markets, see Karl Polanyi, *The Great Transformation* (Boston: Beacon Press, 1957).

11. Meyers, *Jacksonian Persuasion*, 31. For Wilentz's interesting work on republican ideology, see his study of working-class politics in New York, Sean Wilentz, *Chants Democratic* (New York: Oxford University Press, 1984), 61–103, esp. 101–103. Robert Remini, in his now standard biography of Jackson, also adopted the republican hypothesis to interpret the movement up to 1832. Interestingly, after that, he sees republicanism being pushed aside in favor, not of liberalism, but of democracy. See the abridged edition: Remini, *The Life of Andrew Jackson* (New York: Harper and Row, 1988). For republicanism see 143–144, 155–156, 247. For commentary see Donald B. Cole, "Honoring Andrew Jackson Before All Other Living Men," *Reviews in American History* (September 1985), 359–366. Sellars, *Market Revolution*, tends to pit republicans against Democrats rather than liberals.

12. Sean Wilentz, "On Class and Politics in Jacksonian America," in *The Promise of American History*, ed. Stanley I. Kutler and Stanley N. Katz (Baltimore: Johns Hopkins University Press, 1982), 55.

13. Ibid., 56.

14. Chief Justice Taney in *Charles River Bridge v. Warren Bridge*, in Hofstadter, *Great Issues in American History*, vol. 2, 301–305, quote at 305. See also Hofstadter's headnote, 301.

15. Schlesinger, *Age of Jackson*, 314–317, 338.

16. Ibid., 312.

17. Tocqueville, *Democracy in America,* 555–558.

18. See the important but controversial study by Anne Norton, *Alternative Americas: A Reading of Antebellum Political Culture* (Chicago: University of Chicago Press, 1986), 19–32, esp. 32. I do not accept Norton's idea that the North was more martial than the South. Nor do I find her forays into psychoanalysis very helpful.

19. Ibid., 33–63.

20. Ibid., 47.

21. Ibid., 49–52, quote at 51–52. As late as 1874, women worked at least twelve hours a day.

22. Ibid., 58. This feeling suggested to Norton that there were survivals of "Jefferson's tentative admiration for anarchy" in urban violence, which seems more doubtful. See 59.

23. Ibid., 62–63. The continued importance of religion was also indicated by the temperance and abolition movements, both of which had evangelical foundations. On the former see 72–77. Abolition will be discussed in Chapter 7.

24. Judith N. Shklar, *American Citizenship: The Quest for Inclusion* (Cambridge: Harvard University Press, 1991), 64. My argument in this section is heavily reliant on 63–79. My citations to Shklar's book cannot begin to convey my indebtedness to her, not only for my understanding of Jackson, but for the whole middle period generally.

25. Ibid., 70.

26. Ibid., 79. I think Shklar blurred Weber's important distinction between the Protestant ethic and the spirit of capitalism, so her brief remarks on Weber are a little unfair. See Chapter 1 herein.

27. Ibid., 68.

28. Daniel Walker Howe, *The Political Culture of the American Whigs* (Chicago: University of Chicago Press, 1979), 11–12. I rely a great deal on Howe's fine study. For Schlesinger on the Whigs, see *Age of Jackson,* 267–283.

29. Howe, *Political Culture of Whigs,* 21.

30. Meyers, *Jacksonian Persuasion,* 13. Howe contended that this argument applied only to the economic area, but since political economy is my primary focus, it will do nicely. See Howe, *Political Culture of Whigs,* 19–20.

31. Howe, *Political Culture of Whigs,* 139.

32. Ibid., 97.

33. Ibid., 89.

34. Ibid., 91. It is also interesting to note that Schlesinger, whose treatment of the Whigs in *Age of Jackson* was far from gentle, later revised his estimate. He by no means withdrew his positive evaluation of Jackson or his view that the policies of Hamilton, Adams, and Clay were designed to further business interests. However, he now concedes that the Whig program was also designed for the benefit of the nation in its pursuit of economic growth. "In retrospect the Hamiltonians had a sounder conception of the role of government and a more constructive policy of economic development than the antistatist Jacksonians": Schlesinger, "Ages of Jackson," 50.

35. Tocqueville, *Democracy in America,* 11–12 and 9–20 passim.

36. Quote in Sheldon Wolin, "Can We Still Hear Tocqueville?" *Atlantic Monthly* (August 1987), 81. I have been much influenced by this article as well as Wolin's discussion of Tocqueville in *The Presence of the Past* (Baltimore: Johns Hopkins University Press, 1989), 66–81. Wolin's praise of Tocqueville is somewhat more guarded here than in his earlier article. My discussion of Tocqueville's analytical strategy is indebted to Marvin Zetterbaum, *Tocqueville and the Problem of Democracy* (Stanford: Stanford University Press, 1967), 1–40.

37. Tocqueville, *Democracy in America,* 399.

38. Ibid., 287. For an outstanding discussion of the centrality of the concept of "mores" in Tocqueville's work, see Roger Boesche, "Why Could Tocqueville Predict So Well?" *Political Theory* (February 1983), 495–524.

39. Tocqueville, *Democracy in America,* 395.

40. Ibid., 509.

41. Ibid., 506. However, note that Tocqueville also saw the possibility of a point at which freedom and equality would "meet and blend," a world in which perfect freedom and equality are both achieved: "Democratic peoples are tending toward that ideal" (see 503).

42. Ibid., 254–255.

43. This discussion is much influenced by the studies of Wolin cited in Note 36, which attempt a subtle correction of the Hartz thesis. However, I think he is stretching a fine point too far in his repeated suggestions that there were archaic relics of feudalism in Jacksonian America. It takes more than decentralization and the absence of a strong state to create feudalism. Still, Wolin's insights are important.

44. Tocqueville, *Democracy in America*, 522. Some contemporary social scientists are deeply concerned by the decline in participation in voluntary associations in the United States. See Robert D. Putnam, "Bowling Alone: America's Declining Social Capital," *Journal of Democracy* (January 1995), 65–78.

45. I have been much influenced here by Richard Krouse, "'Classical' Images of Democracy in America: Madison and Tocqueville," in *Democratic Theory and Practice,* ed. Graeme Duncan (Cambridge: Cambridge University Press, 1983), esp. 67–72, 75–78.

46. Wilson Carey McWilliams, "Democracy and the Citizen: Community, Dignity, and the Crisis of Contemporary Politics in America," in *How Democratic Is America,* ed. Robert A. Goldwin and William A. Schambra (Washington, D.C.: American Enterprise Institute, 1980), 96–101.

47. Wolin, "Can We Still Hear Tocqueville?" 80.

48. Tocqueville, *Democracy in America*, 525–527. Zetterbaum is particularly notable for the stress he places on this doctrine. See *Tocqueville and the Problem of Democracy,* esp. 101–109. Zetterbaum does not believe the doctrine strong enough to bear the weight Tocqueville places on it. Deeply indebted to the work of Leo Strauss, Zetterbaum sees Tocqueville, in spite of his own admiration for him, as a victim of the characteristically modern lowering of the standards set by political theory (see esp. 104–105). For a discussion of the Straussians' place in contemporary American conservatism, see Chapter 14 herein.

49. Tocqueville, *Democracy in America*, 528–530.

50. Ibid., 400–407; quotes at 404. For a fuller treatment of the relation of commerce to American character than is possible here, see Ralph Lerner, *The Thinking Revolutionary: Principle and Practice in the New Republic* (Ithaca: Cornell University Press, 1987), 195–221. Though not overlooking his concerns, Lerner sees Tocqueville as more favorably disposed to commerce than I do, and he himself takes a less dark view of American economic development than argued in this book.

51. See citations in Note 8.

52. Tocqueville, *Democracy in America*, 536.

53. Ibid., 621.

54. Ibid., 530–535; quotes at 532, 534.

55. Ibid., 555–558; quote at 558. Quite inconsistently with the burden of his analysis, Tocqueville goes on to add that this aristocracy will be "one of the more restrained and least dangerous" (558).

56. Ibid., 684.

57. Ibid., 685.

58. Ibid., 690–695.

59. Ibid., 735–736. It seems odd that Tocqueville relegates this central point to a note in an appendix.

60. Ibid., 506, 508.

61. See McWilliams, "Democracy and the Citizen," 99. John Stuart Mill is also very interesting on this point. In his admiring review of *Democracy in America,* he suggested that Tocqueville has confused democracy with civilization, in other words, "the whole of the tendencies of modern commercial society." See Mill, "Tocqueville on Democracy in America

(Vol. II)," in *Essays on Politics and Culture,* ed. Gertrude Himmelfarb (Garden City, N.Y.: Anchor Books, 1963), 257.

62. Tocqueville, *Democracy in America,* 316–317.

63. Ibid., 339 and 316–330 passim.

64. Ibid., 340.

65. Ibid., 363.

66. Ibid., 345, 376. My student Roy Cager has pointed out that though Tocqueville saw the evil of slavery very clearly, he was burdened enough by condescending nineteenth-century racial assumptions that he did not see the slaves as individual people, let alone as social or political actors.

67. Ibid., 376.

68. For a penetrating discussion of the relations of the three races in America that is much more extensive than possible here see the two chapters devoted to the subject in Lerner, *Thinking Revolutionary,* 139–191.

Chapter 7

1. Max Farrand, ed., *Records of the Federal Convention,* rev. ed., vol. 1 (New Haven: Yale University Press, 1966), 486.

2. Staughton Lynd, "The Abolitionist Critique of the United States Constitution," in *The Antislavery Vanguard,* ed. Martin Duberman (Princeton: Princeton University Press, 1965), 209–239.

3. Ibid., 238.

4. John C. Miller, *The Wolf by the Ears: Thomas Jefferson and Slavery* (New York: Free Press, 1977), 41. For a discussion of Locke's own position on slavery, see James Farr, "'So Vile and Miserable an Estate': The Problem of Slavery in Locke's Political Thought," *Political Theory* (May 1986), 263–290. Farr contended that Locke's theory of slavery was "woefully inadequate as an account of Afro-American slavery" and, further, that *Locke knew this.* Locke was therefore guilty of a form of "immoral evasion" (264, 281).

5. Thomas Jefferson, *Notes on the State of Virginia,* in Jefferson, *Writings,* ed. Merrill Peterson (New York: Library of America, 1984), 264–270, 288.

6. Ibid., 298.

7. Jefferson to John Holmes, April 22, 1820, in Jefferson, *Writings,* 1434.

8. Samuel Johnson, quoted in Miller, *The Wolf by the Ears,* 8.

9. Edmund Morgan, "Slavery and Freedom: The American Paradox," *Journal of American History* (June 1972), 5–29, and "Conflict and Consensus in the American Revolution," in *Essays on the American Revolution,* ed. Stephen G. Kurtz and James H. Hutson (Chapel Hill: University of North Carolina Press, 1973), 293–296. Quote at 295. Morgan develops his thesis fully in *American Slavery, American Freedom: The Ordeal of Colonial Virginia* (New York: Norton, 1975).

10. Sir Augustus John Foster, quoted in Morgan, *American Slavery, American Freedom,* 380. Cf. David Brion Davis, *The Problem of Slavery in Western Culture: 1770–1823* (Ithaca: Cornell University Press, 1975), 260–262.

11. Davis, *Problem of Slavery in Western Culture,* 262.

12. For an early example of this rationale, see Thomas R. Dew, "Review of the Debate in the Virginia Legislature of 1831 and 1832," in *Great Issues in American History,* ed. Richard Hofstadter, vol. 2 (New York: Vintage Books, 1958), 314–320. See also Dwight Lowell Dumond, *Antislavery Origins of the Civil War in the United States* (Ann Arbor: University of Michigan Press, 1959), 44.

13. John C. Calhoun, *A Disquisition on Government and Selections from the Discourse* (Indianapolis: Bobbs-Merrill, 1953), 3.

14. Ibid., 7.

15. Ibid., 11.

16. Ibid., 22–31.

17. Ibid., 23.

18. Ibid., 30.

19. Ibid., 100–104.

20. George Kateb, "The Majority Principle: Calhoun and His Antecedents," *Political Science Quarterly* (December 1969), 596–597.

21. Louis Hartz, *The Liberal Tradition in America* (New York: Harcourt Brace, 1955), 159, 161–162.

22. Calhoun did endorse the "positive good" argument in the Senate. Kateb, "The Majority Principle," 596.

23. Ibid., 604.

24. Hartz, *Liberal Tradition,* 147, 145–200.

25. Ibid., 147.

26. Elizabeth Fox-Genovese and Eugene Genovese, *Fruits of Merchant Capital* (New York: Oxford University Press, 1983), 7.

27. Ibid., 4.

28. Ibid., 5. See also Eugene Genovese, *The Political Economy of Slavery* (New York: Vintage Books, 1967) and *The World the Slaveholders Made,* with a new introduction by the author (Middletown, Conn.: Wesleyan University Press, 1988). There is a good deal of controversial literature surrounding the Genoveses' interpretation of the economic position of the slave South. See James B. Oakes, *The Ruling Race* (New York: Knopf, 1982) and *Slavery and Freedom: An Interpretation of the Old South* (New York: Knopf, 1990). Oakes tends to define capitalism in terms of market relations. For reviews of the literature, see Edward L. Ayers, "The World the Liberal Capitalists Made," *Reviews in American History* (June 1991), 194–199; and particularly George R. Fredrickson, "The Challenge of Marxism: The Genoveses on Slavery and Merchant Capital," in *The Arrogance of Race* (Wesleyan: Wesleyan University Press, 1988). However, the debate on the relation of the market to the form of the labor force does not centrally affect the basic incompatibility of slavery and any form of liberal politics. Therefore, although I agree with many of the criticisms of Fredrickson and others, I also agree with Eric Foner that the Genoveses' work has continued to be the basic starting point and thus has set the agenda for work on these questions. See Eric Foner, "The Slaveholder as Factory Owner," *New York Times Book Review* (May 22, 1982), 27, 11ff, passim.

29. George Fitzhugh, *Cannibals All, or Slaves Without Masters,* ed. C. Vann Woodward (Cambridge: Harvard University Press, 1960), and Fitzhugh, *Sociology for the South, in Antebellum,* ed. Harvey Wish (New York: Putnam, 1960), 41–96.

30. Fitzhugh, *Cannibals All,* 243.

31. Ibid. and Woodward's "Introduction," xxxiv–xxxvii.

32. Fitzhugh, *Cannibals All,* 69; and James Henry Hammond, quoted in Fredrickson, *Arrogance of Race,* 23. Lincoln specifically attacked this view of labor in his Wisconsin State Fair speech, September 30, 1859. See Lincoln, *Selected Speeches and Writings: 1859–1865,* ed. Don Fehrenbacher (New York: Library of America, 1989), 96–99 (cited hereafter as Lincoln, *Writings* 2).

33. Fitzhugh, *Sociology for the South,* 47.

34. Fitzhugh, *Cannibals All,* 87.

35. Fitzhugh, *Sociology for the South,* 95.

36. Abraham Lincoln, Speech at Springfield, June 16, 1858, in *Selected Speeches and Writings: 1832–1858,* ed. Don Fehrenbacher (New York: Library of America, 1989), 426 (cited hereafter as Lincoln, *Writings* 1). Note the comma after "endure" in the first sentence. This punctuation mark is not always included. When it is, the shift is toward a more "urgently ominous" view of the prospect for survival, a view considered menacing in the southern states. Without the comma, it is less so. On the punctuation problem and the more general difficulty of accurately transcribing the text of Lincoln's speeches, see Andrew Delbanco,

"To the Gettysburg Station," *New Republic* (November 20, 1989), 33. Delbanco's essay is one of the best recent short pieces on Lincoln. As for Fitzhugh, we know that Lincoln was a "preoccupied" reader of him. See Yehoshua Arieli, *Individualism and Nationalism in American Ideology* (Cambridge: Harvard University Press, 1964), 425–426 n. 40.

37. On the ways in which the slave system retarded capitalist development, see E. Genovese, *Political Economy of Slavery,* 13–39.

38. Ibid., 13.

39. Ibid., 32. See also Davis, *Problem of Slavery in Western Culture,* 557–564. This analysis is rooted in the master-slave dialectic in Hegel's *Phenomenology of Mind.*

40. E. Genovese has come to believe that Fitzhugh was not so alone as Genovese had first thought. See the new "Introduction" to *World the Slaveholders Made,* ix–xi. Nonetheless, Fitzhugh remains a special figure for Genovese. It may be noted in passing that Fitzhugh's attack on capitalism is rare in the annals of American thought and bears a striking resemblance to the Marxist critique.

41. Judith Shklar, "Redeeming American Political Theory," *American Political Science Review* (March 1991), 4.

42. For excerpts, see Theodore Dwight Weld, "Slavery As It Is," in Hofstadter, *Great Issues,* vol. 2, 323–329. For a study based on extensive reading in the vast pamphlet literature, see Dwight Lowell Dumond, *Antislavery* (Ann Arbor: University of Michigan Press, 1961). Dumond's book may be biased and even eccentric, but no one surpassed his knowledge of the often fugitive pamphlet literature, from which he quoted extensively. This is a book that seethes with moral indignation. For a critique of Dumond see C. Vann Woodward, *The Future of the Past* (New York: Oxford University Press, 1989), 272–279.

43. Dumond, *Antislavery Origins of the Civil War,* 70–77; Dumond, *Antislavery,* 228–233. For a classic Douglass speech, see "Fourth of July Oration," in *What Country Have I?* ed. Herbert A. Storing (New York: St. Martin's Press, 1970), 28–38, esp. 31–32. On Douglass see Fredrickson, *Arrogance of Race,* 80–88.

44. First Debate at Ottawa, Illinois, August 21, 1858, in Lincoln, *Writings* 1, 512, and Speech at Springfield, July 17, 1858, in ibid., 478.

45. Speech at Peoria, October 10, 1854, in ibid., 316.

46. Jennifer Hochschild and Monica Herk, "'Yes But . . .': Principles and Caveats in American Racial Attitudes," in *Majorities and Minorities: Nomos XXXII,* ed. John W. Chapman and Alan Wertheimer (New York: New York University Press, 1990), 308–335.

47. "Address on Colonization to a Committee of Colored Men," Washington, D.C., August 14, 1862, in Lincoln, *Writings* 2, 353, 353–357. The quotation is presented as a summary of the president's remarks. Lincoln did believe that colonized blacks would be capable of self-government. See Fredrickson, *Arrogance of Race,* 65–66.

48. Speech on Reconstruction, April 11, 1865, in Lincoln, *Writings* 2, 697, 699.

49. Fredrickson, *Arrogance of Race,* 71–72. In general, Fredrickson's chapter on Lincoln and racial equality (54–72) is very valuable. Fredrickson does concede Lincoln's egalitarian manner and suggested that it "resulted from a depth of self-awareness that made it possible for him to control his prejudices precisely because he acknowledged their existence and recognized their irrational character" (62). John Wilkes Booth is quoted in James M. McPherson, *Battle Cry of Freedom: The Civil War Era* (New York: Oxford University Press, 1988), 852.

50. Richard Hofstadter, *The American Political Tradition,* 25th anniversary ed. (New York: Knopf, 1972), 115–116; and Fredrickson, *Arrogance of Race,* 66–67.

51. Letter to Henry L. Pierce and others, April 6, 1859, in Lincoln, *Writings* 2, 19.

52. Speech on the Kansas-Nebraska Act, Peoria, October 16, 1854, in Lincoln, *Writings* 1, 328.

53. James M. McPherson, *Abraham Lincoln and the Second American Revolution* (New York: Oxford University Press, 1990), 126. For an example of Lincoln's historical efforts, see his address at Cooper Institute, New York, February 27, 1860, in *Writings* 2, 111–116.

54. Lincoln, quoted in McPherson, *Lincoln and the Second Revolution,* 126.

55. "First Inaugural Address," March 4, 1861, in Lincoln, *Writings* 2, 217–218.

56. Speech on the Kansas-Nebraska Act, in Lincoln, *Writings* 1, 339–340.

57. Fragment on Slavery, probably 1854, in ibid., 303.

58. The standard work on this subject is Eric Foner, *Free Soil, Free Labor, Free Men* (New York: Oxford University Press, 1970).

59. Speech at Wisconsin State Fair, September 30, 1859, in Lincoln, *Writings* 2, 96–97.

60. Letter to Henry L. Pierce and others, April 6, 1859, in ibid., 18.

61. Speech to the 166th Ohio Regiment, Washington, August 22, 1864, in ibid., 624.

62. Isaac Kramnick, *Republicanism and Bourgeois Radicalism* (Ithaca: Cornell University Press, 1990), 5–18 and passim.

63. Henry David Thoreau, "On Civil Disobedience," in *Directions in American Political Thought,* ed. Kenneth Dolbeare (New York: John Wiley, 1969), 199–211. Interestingly, the nonviolent Thoreau also wrote passionately in support of the very violent John Brown. See *Walden and Other Writings,* 681–708. George Kateb points out that Thoreau believed violent revolution was justified to end slavery. See Kateb, *The Inner Ocean: Individualism and Democratic Culture* (Ithaca: Cornell University Press, 1992), 103.

64. See Michael Walzer, "Political Action: The Problem of Dirty Hands," in *War and Moral Responsibility,* ed. Marshall Cohen et al. (Princeton: Princeton University Press, 1974), 62–82. George Kateb, a writer deeply sympathetic to Thoreau, writes that it is "unfortunate for him to urge us to wash our hands of such an evil," but notes that the politics of saying no is a healthy democratic impulse. See Kateb, *The Inner Ocean,* 89, 103.

65. William Lloyd Garrison, quoted in Fredrickson, *Arrogance of Race,* 77. On Garrison generally see 73–80.

66. See Aileen Kraditor, *Means and Ends in American Abolitionism* (New York: Pantheon books, 1969), 3–38, 274–277; C. Vann Woodward, *American Counterpoint* (Boston: Little, Brown, 1971), 140–162; and Harry Jaffa, "Abraham Lincoln," in *American Political Thought,* ed. Morton Frisch and Richard Stephens (New York: Scribner's, 1971), 125–144.

67. The Protestant evangelical roots of much of the antislavery movement are worth noting. See Dumond, *Antislavery,* esp. 158–165 and passim.

68. Woodward, *American Counterpoint,* 143.

69. To avoid endless repetition, I will just note that there are fifteen index entries under this idea in Lincoln, *Writings* 1, and five more in *Writings* 2.

70. Although everyone quotes these passages, it was only Harry Jaffa, in *Crisis of the House Divided* (New York: Doubleday, 1959), who captured their full significance. See especially 371. See also Jaffa, *Equality and Liberty* (New York: Oxford University Press, 1965), 147ff.

71. McPherson, *Battle Cry of Freedom,* 213–233.

72. "First Inaugural Address," Lincoln, *Writings* 2, 215; and Jaffa, *Equality and Liberty,* 153–154.

73. "Reply to Chicago Emancipation Memorial," September 13, 1862, in Lincoln, *Writings* 2, 365; and Jaffa, *Equality and Liberty,* 144.

74. "First Inaugural Address," Lincoln, *Writings* 2, 220.

75. Letter to Horace Greeley, August 22, 1862, in Lincoln, *Writings* 2, 358. It is worth noting that Frederick Douglass had a clear understanding of why Lincoln seemed to temporize on the question. In the context of his time, Lincoln was "swift, zealous, radical, and determined." See Douglass, "Oration in Memory of Abraham Lincoln," in Storing, *What Country Have I?* 53 and 46–56 passim.

76. Speech on Kansas-Nebraska Act, in Lincoln, *Writings* 1, 315.

77. Lincoln, quoted in McPherson, *Lincoln and the Second Revolution,* 36.

78. Ibid., 34–35.

79. Woodward, *American Counterpoint,* 143, 161. Woodward's analysis builds on Kraditor, *Means and Ends in American Abolitionism.*

80. Woodward, *American Counterpoint,* 162. Woodward added that Lincoln fought the war in the name of white supremacy, which is not wholly wrong by any means but does

neglect the moderation of Lincoln's racial views in the context of his time, as well as the possibility of change, had he been spared to preside over Reconstruction.

81. Lincoln, Springfield Lyceum Speech, on "The Perpetuation of Our Institutions," in *Writings* 1, 28–36; Herbert J. Storing, *What the Anti-Federalists Were For* (Chicago: University of Chicago Press, 1981), 74–76; and Jaffa, *Crisis of the House Divided*, 183–232.

82. Eric Foner, *Politics and Ideology in the Age of the Civil War* (New York: Oxford University Press, 1980), 52.

83. Ibid., 53.

84. McPherson, *Lincoln and the Second Revolution*, viii.

85. See the classic essay on this theme by Edmund Wilson in *Patriotic Gore: Studies in the Literature of the American Civil War* (New York: Oxford University Press, 1962), 99–130. See also Sacvan Bercovitch, *The American Jeremiad* (Madison: University of Wisconsin Press, 1978), 174. On Whitman see Anne Norton, *Alternative Americas: A Reading of Antebellum Political Culture* (Chicago: University of Chicago Press, 1986), 315–329. I have been stimulated by Norton's book and have learned much from it, though I have some serious reservations about the study (see Chapter 6, Note 18). Her sense of deep cultural differences between North and South is marred by an excessive use of psychoanalytic categories of analysis and a tendency to play down the critical role of slavery in determining the sectional divisions. Her understanding of Lincoln's Puritan antecedents is undermined by her psychoanalytic reduction of Lincoln to a paternalistic figure, which has the effect of unnecessarily diminishing him.

86. Lincoln, "Second Inaugural Address," in *Writings* 2, 687.

87. On Lincoln's conception of liberty as an instance of positive liberty and its relation to Puritanism, see J. David Greenstone, *The Lincoln Persuasion: Remaking American Liberalism* (Princeton: Princeton University Press, 1993), 235–237, 253–285; and McPherson, *Lincoln and the Second Revolution*, 61–64. It is not quite clear that Greenstone, a political theorist, and McPherson, a historian, see the distinction between negative and positive liberty in the same way. Greenstone stresses the Puritan aspect, stemming from Winthrop, whereas McPherson focuses on positive liberty as an enabling concept. The classic source of the distinction is Isaiah Berlin, *Four Essays on Liberty* (New York: Oxford University Press, 1970), 118–172. See also the important paper by Charles Taylor, "What's Wrong with Negative Liberty," in *Philosophy and the Human Sciences* (Cambridge: Cambridge University Press, 1985), 211–229. On Greenstone's use of the concept of negative liberty, see James M. McPherson, "Liberating Lincoln," *New York Review of Books* (April 2, 1994), 7–10.

88. John P. Diggins, *The Lost Soul of American Politics* (New York: Basic Books, 1984), 296–333.

89. Jaffa, *Crisis of the House Divided*, 321.

90. Judith N. Shklar, *American Citizenship: The Quest for Inclusion* (Cambridge: Harvard University Press, 1991), 81–82. Harry Jaffa notes that in 1860 the Republican Party presented itself as being on the left. It achieved (briefly, one might add) what Lincoln's Whig predecessors had failed to accomplish, becoming the party of the independent farmer; thus it inherited the mantle of Jefferson and Jackson while also giving political roots to the economic program of Hamilton. See Jaffa, *Equality and Liberty*, 41. See also McPherson, *Lincoln and the Second Revolution*, 49.

91. Foner, *Politics and Ideology*, 32–33.

Chapter 8

1. On corruption see the classic account by an ironic, biting, bitter contemporary: Henry Adams, *The Education of Henry Adams*, ed. Ernest Samuels (Boston: Houghton Mifflin, 1973), 255–283. See also Richard Hofstadter's treatment in *The American Political Tradition*, 25th anniversary ed. (New York: Knopf, 1973), 162–182.

2. Sidney Fine, *Laissez Faire and the General-Welfare State* (Ann Arbor: University of Michigan Press, 1956), 23–24.

3. Robert Wiebe, *The Search for Order: 1877–1920* (New York: Hill and Wang, 1967), 23–27. For the technical differences between the different forms of industrial organization, see 23–24. On the concentration of capital, see the excerpts on the subject from the sensation-making report of the 1912 Pujo Committee, in *The Progressive Movement: 1900–1915,* ed. Richard Hofstadter (Englewood Cliffs: Prentice-Hall, 1963), 158–160. For a lively account of the development of industry at this time, see James MacGregor Burns, *The American Experiment,* vol. 2: *The Workshop of Democracy* (New York: Knopf, 1985), 73–110.

4. Russell L. Hanson, *The Democratic Imagination in America* (Princeton: Princeton University Press, 1985), 183.

5. Ibid., 186.

6. Louis Hartz, *The Liberal Tradition in America* (New York: Harcourt Brace, 1955), 203 and 203–227 passim. Hartz here accepted the stereotypical view of Alger as the symbol of unbridled pursuit of wealth. Recent work suggested that "Alger was a Tocqueville in very simple dress; home, church, women, they were all the essential moral grounding that made individual economic success possible; liberalism built on conservatism so to say" (quote from private communication by Robert Booth Fowler). For a fascinating reading of the Alger stories, designed to counter the stereotype employed by Hartz, see Carol Nackenoff, *The Fictional Republic: Horatio Alger and American Political Discourse* (New York: Oxford University Press, 1994). Nackenoff made the odd mistake of reading Hartz as seeing the American ideology as forged around 1840, when clearly he saw it as existing from the start. This is a minor mistake in an interesting book.

7. John P. Diggins, *The Lost Soul of American Politics* (New York: Basic Books, 1984), 322.

8. Alexis de Tocqueville, *Democracy in America,* trans. George Lawrence (Garden City, N.Y.: Anchor Books, 1969), 558.

9. John M. Blum, quoted in Robert A. Dahl, *A Preface to Economic Democracy* (Berkeley: University of California Press, 1985), 72.

10. Fine, *Laissez Faire and the General-Welfare State,* 24.

11. Ibid., 15.

12. Ibid., 18–20.

13. Louis Hartz, *Economic Policy and Democratic Thought: Pennsylvania, 1776–1860* (Cambridge: Harvard University Press, 1948); Oscar and Mary Flug Handlin, *Commonwealth: A Study in the Role of Government in the American Economy, 1774–1861* (Cambridge: Harvard University Press, 1948); Fine, *Laissez Faire and the General-Welfare State,* 23.

14. For the following brief account of Spencer and his influence I am deeply indebted to Richard Hofstadter, *Social Darwinism and American Thought* (Boston: Beacon Press, 1955), 31–50; and Fine, *Laissez Faire and the General-Welfare State,* 31–46.

15. Hofstadter, *Social Darwinism,* 37.

16. Ibid., 41; and Fine, *Laissez Faire and the General-Welfare State,* 38.

17. Hofstadter, *Social Darwinism,* 33–35.

18. Andrew Carnegie and John D. Rockefeller, quoted in ibid., 45.

19. On Spencer's tour see ibid., 48–49; and Eric Goldman, *Rendezvous with Destiny* (New York: Vintage Books, 1956), 71.

20. In my treatment of Sumner, I have been influenced by, in addition to the studies by Hofstadter and Fine already cited, Robert Green McCloskey, *American Conservatism in the Age of Enterprise* (Cambridge: Harvard University Press, 1951), 22–71.

21. McCloskey, *American Conservatism,* 31.

22. William Graham Sumner, "The Absurd Attempt to Make the World Over," in *Social Darwinism: Selected Essays,* ed. Stow Persons (Englewood Cliffs, N.J.: Prentice-Hall, 1963), 168–180.

23. On this see McCloskey, *American Conservatism,* 43–46.

24. Quoted in ibid., 46.

25. William Graham Sumner, "The Challenge of Facts," in *Social Darwinism,* 87. This essay was originally entitled "Socialism" and is so listed in the Persons collection, but the title was altered by the editor of Sumner's collected papers. It is cited in that form so often in the literature that I have retained the more common usage.

26. Quoted in McCloskey, *American Conservatism,* 49.

27. W. G. Sumner, "What Social Classes Owe to Each Other," in *Directions in American Political Thought,* ed. Kenneth M. Dolbeare (New York: Wiley, 1969), 235.

28. W. G. Sumner, "The Forgotten Man," in *Social Darwinism,* 123 and 110–135, passim.

29. Sumner, "What Social Classes Owe Each Other," 239.

30. Ibid., 232, 240.

31. Ibid., 234.

32. Ibid., 243; and Sumner, "The Challenge of Facts," in ibid., 83.

33. Sumner, "What Social Classes Owe Each Other," in ibid., 238.

34. Ibid., 233.

35. Sumner, quoted in McCloskey, *American Conservatism,* 58.

36. Sumner, "The Conquest of the United States by Spain," in Dolbeare, *Directions in American Political Thought,* 247.

37. W. G. Sumner, "Democracy and Plutocracy," in *Social Darwinism,* 145.

38. Sumner, "What Social Classes Owe Each Other," in ibid., 241.

39. Ibid., 237–238.

40. Sumner, "Democracy and Plutocracy," in ibid., 149.

41. Sumner, "What Social Classes Owe Each Other," in ibid., 238. Stow Persons suggests that for the tone of his essays, Sumner owed less to his admiration for businessmen than to his contempt for politicians. See Persons, "Introduction," *Social Darwinism,* 6.

42. Sumner, "The Conquest of the United States by Spain," in ibid., 247.

43. It may not be coincidental that laissez-faire seems to flourish in periods of considerable governmental corruption, such as late-eighteenth-century England, late-nineteenth-century America, and the 1980s, once again in the United States.

44. Wiebe, *Search for Order,* 136.

45. R. Jeffrey Lustig, *Corporate Liberalism: The Origins of Modern American Political Theory,* 1890–1920 (Berkeley: University of California Press, 1982), 81.

46. McCloskey, *American Conservatism,* 37, 47.

47. Sumner, *Social Darwinism,* 51.

48. Hartz, *Liberal Tradition,* 215–216.

49. Clinton Rossiter, *Conservatism in America,* 2d ed. (New York: Vintage Books, 1962), 131. It is a useful term because it does not overemphasize the part played by conservative Darwinism. For a not very convincing revisionist attempt to downplay the importance of this current of thought, see Robert C. Bannister, *Social Darwinism: Science and Myth in Anglo-American Social Thought* (Philadelphia: Temple University Press, 1979). See also Edward Chase Kirkland, *Dream and Thought in the Business Community: 1860–1900* (Ithaca: Cornell University Press, 1956), 13–15.

50. On the role of the courts, see Fine, *Laissez Faire and the General-Welfare State,* 126–164; and Daniel T. Rodgers, *Contested Truths: Keywords in American Politics Since Independence* (New York: Basic Books, 1987), 147–156. For Holmes, see *Lochner v. New York,* 198 U.S. 45, 74. For Fields, see McCloskey, *American Conservatism,* 72–126.

51. On this see Robert B. Reich, "Ideologies of Survival," *New Republic* (September 20 and 27, 1982), 32–37. This is a useful article, though I believe it understates the place of Darwinism in the conservative tradition of this country as a whole.

52. Hofstadter, *Social Darwinism,* 11.

53. Ibid., 8–9. Hofstadter's companion argument, that until the time of the New Deal the reform tradition in U.S. politics tended to look backward in the interest of restoring or protecting old values, is more complex and controversial.

54. Robert A. Dahl, *A Preface to Economic Democracy* (Berkeley: University of California Press, 1985), 71–73, and *Dilemmas of Pluralist Democracy: Autonomy vs. Control* (New Haven: Yale University Press, 1982), 176–180.

55. Daniel Bell, *The Cultural Contradictions of Capitalism* (New York: Basic Books, 1978). For a discussion of Bell, see Chapter 14 herein.

Chapter 9

1. Edward S. Corwin, "The Impact of the Idea of Evolution on the American Political and Constitutional Tradition," in *Evolutionary Thought in America,* ed. Stow Persons (New Haven: Yale University Press, 1950), 191.

2. The term *reform Darwinism* was coined by Eric Goldman in *Rendezvous with Destiny* (New York: Vintage Books, 1956), 73ff.

3. Corwin, "Impact of the Idea of Evolution," 191.

4. Richard Hofstadter, *Social Darwinism in American Thought* (Boston: Beacon Press, 1955), 74, 85. On Ward generally, see 67–84; and Sidney Fine, *Laissez Faire and the General-Welfare State* (Ann Arbor: University of Michigan Press, 1956), 253–264.

5. Charles Horton Cooley, quoted in David E. Price, "Community and Control: Critical Democratic Theory in the Progressive Period," *American Political Science Review* (December 1974), 1666. On Cooley see 1665–1667.

6. Fine, *Laissez Faire and the General-Welfare State,* 251, 198–251. On the later influence of these economists, see 379. Fine's magisterial study of the late-nineteenth-century critique of laissez-faire conservatism and the intellectual foundations of the twentieth-century mixed economy can be found on 167–369.

7. James Turner, "Understanding the Populists," *Journal of American History* (September 1980), 354.

8. Turner (in ibid.) is notable for his suggestive, if preliminary, analysis of who actually voted for the Populists.

9. See C. Vann Woodward, "The Ghost of Populism Walks Again," *New York Times Magazine* (June 4, 1972), 64. Among the best comparative efforts are Ghita Ionescu and Ernest Gellner, eds., *Populism: Its Meanings and National Characteristics* (London: Weidenfeld and Nicolson, 1969); "To Define Populism," *Government and Opposition* (Spring 1968), a discussion based on the papers in Ionescu and Gellner; and Margaret Canovan, *Populism* (New York: Harcourt Brace, 1981). For a useful discussion of Canovan, see C. V. Woodward, "Who Are 'the People'?" *New Republic* (May 1, 1981), 32–34.

10. George McKenna, ed., *American Populism* (New York: Capricorn Books, 1974), xii and xi–xxv passim; James A. Nuechterlein, "The People vs. the Interests," *Commentary* (March 1975), 66–75. McKenna's collection provides a useful survey of populist writings from the Revolution to the 1970s. Nuechterlein offered a heuristically valuable analysis, although I differ sharply with his political stance. Richard Hofstadter also used the "people vs. the interests" formulation. See "North America," in Ionescu and Gellner, *Populism,* 17. It is also clear, as Michael Kazin shows, that populism can cover the ideological spectrum from left to right. See Kazin, *The Populist Persuasion: An American History* (New York: Basic Books, 1995). Sean Wilentz suggests that economic grievances are expressed on the populist left and cultural grievances on the right. See Wilentz, "Populism Redux," *Dissent* (Spring 1995), 149–153.

11. I owe the idea for this schema to a personal communication from George Armstrong Kelly. He bears absolutely no responsibility for the use I have made of his suggestion. The attempt here and in the previous paragraph to give some specificity to the idea of populism as a style of thought is important because Richard Hofstadter, in his valuable but controversial book, *The Age of Reform* (New York: Knopf, 1955), had a tendency, as Turner put it, to define populism so broadly that it was converted into a metaphysical category. See Turner, "Understanding the Populists," 355. More generally, the attempt to specify the different "lev-

els" of populism is needed because, at the other end of the scale from Hofstadter, defenders of populism, such as Lawrence Goodwyn, refused to grant movement credentials to anyone who was not a member of the People's Party. See Goodwyn, *Democratic Promise: The Populist Moment in America* (New York: Oxford University Press, 1976). Goodwyn's book is now widely considered the standard overall survey of populism, though I believe his enthusiasm for the movement should be tempered a bit.

12. "The Omaha Platform," in *The Populist Mind*, ed. Norman Pollack (Indianapolis: Bobbs-Merrill, 1967), 60–61. Subsequent quotations are from this document, 59–65.

13. Ibid., 63–65. As Fine pointed out, this plan is suggestive of the crop loan programs developed by the New Deal. See Fine, *Laissez Faire and the General-Welfare State*, 309. For a contemporary economist's analysis of the controversial subtreasury plan, see William P. Yohe, "An Economic Appraisal of the Sub-Treasury Plan," in Goodwyn, *Democratic Promise*, Appendix B, 571–581.

14. Henry Demarest Lloyd, *Wealth Against Commonwealth* (New York: Harper, 1894), 2.

15. Ibid., 495.

16. Ibid., 496–497.

17. Ibid., 506.

18. Ibid., 510.

19. Ibid., 515.

20. Ibid., 517.

21. Ibid., 523.

22. Ibid., 527.

23. Hofstadter, *Age of Reform*, 23–130; Norman Pollack, *The Populist Response to Industrial America* (Cambridge: Harvard University Press, 1962); and Bruce Palmer, *"Man over Money": The Southern Populist Critique of Industrial Capitalism* (Chapel Hill: University of North Carolina Press, 1980). Palmer's study is particularly valuable because it was the first attempt to sort through the mass of fugitive materials in order to make a systematic synthesis of populist thought. The account is warmly sympathetic but not uncritical; I have been much influenced by it. It is a tribute to Palmer's scholarship that his presentation of the evidence is so thorough that it makes possible interpretations such as mine that are sometimes at variance with his conclusions.

24. Hofstadter, *Age of Reform*, 61ff., 76ff.; Walter Nugent, *The Tolerant Populists* (Chicago: University of Chicago Press, 1963); C. Vann Woodward, *Origins of the New South* (Baton Rouge: Louisiana State University, 1951), esp. 251–258, and *The Strange Career of Jim Crow*, 3d ed. (New York: Oxford University Press, 1974), 60–65; Tom Watson, "Jefferson's Creed," in Pollack, *Populist Mind*, 397–399; and Palmer, *"Man over Money,"* 217. See also the symposium in *Agricultural History Review* (April 1965), 59–85, with contributions by Norman Pollack, Oscar Handlin, Irwin Unger, and J. Rogers Hollingsworth. This debate focused on the anti-Semitism and fascism questions, but it raised some more general issues as well and also illustrated the intense heat and contemporary political content of the discussion of populism.

25. Goodwyn, *Democratic Promise*, 4–5, 180, 353.

26. Turner, "Understanding the Populists," 367.

27. Hofstadter, *Age of Reform*, 23. Cf. Turner, "Understanding the Populists," 370.

28. Turner, "Understanding the Populists," 371. Turner linked his analysis to a revival of Frederick Jackson Turner's frontier thesis. He did not stress the support his analysis lends to Hofstadter's analysis, though Alan Brinkley suggests it does in "Richard Hofstadter's *The Age of Reform*: A Reconsideration," *Reviews in American History* (September 1985), 469.

29. Palmer, *"Man over Money,"* 202. Such an interpretation is central to Hofstadter's *Age of Reform*.

30. Palmer, *"Man over Money,"* 200.

31. Ibid., 126–137.

32. Hofstadter, *Age of Reform*, 23–59; Palmer, *"Man over Money,"* 12–13; and for the simple market society, see C. B. Macpherson, *The Political Theory of Possessive Individualism* (New York: Oxford University Press, 1962), 51–53. It should be said that Macpherson's model was developed as an analytical tool rather than as an empirical description of any historically existing society.

33. On Davis, see Palmer, *"Man over Money,"* 44–45; and Goodwyn, *Democratic Promise*, 374–375.

34. Palmer, *"Man over Money,"* 45.

35. Ibid., 46–47.

36. Ibid., 49.

37. Ibid., 31–37.

38. Ibid., 32; and Robert A. Dahl, *Dilemmas of Pluralist Democracy* (New Haven: Yale University Press, 1982), 180. Dahl points out that the farmers' goal was not to put a ceiling on the accumulation of wealth but to put a low floor under income.

39. Palmer, *"Man over Money,"* 121. One is reminded of John Kenneth Galbraith's conceptualization of the contemporary economy in *The New Industrial Economy.* See Chapters 12 and 15 herein.

40. Palmer, *"Man over Money,"* 124.

41. Ibid., 220.

42. John L. Thomas, *Alternative America: Henry George, Edward Bellamy, Henry Demarest Lloyd and the Adversary Tradition* (Cambridge: Harvard University Press, 1983), 364–366.

43. The phrase is Elmer Schattschneider's in *The Semi-Sovereign People* (New York: Holt, 1960), 81. See also Walter Dean Burnham, "The Changing Shape of the American Political Universe," *American Political Science Review* (March 1965), esp. 23–28.

44. Burnham, "Changing Shape," 23–28.

Chapter 10

1. Useful surveys of the literature are Daniel T. Rodgers, "In Search of Progressivism," *Reviews in American History* (December 1982), 113–132; Robert Wiebe, "The Progressive Years: 1900–1917," in *The Reinterpretation of American History and Culture,* ed. William Cartwright and Richard Watson (Washington, D.C.: American Historical Association, 1973), 425–442; David M. Kennedy, "Overview: The Progressive Era," *Historian* (May 1975), 453–468; Richard L. McCormick, "Progressivism: A Contemporary Reassessment," in *The Party Period and Public Policy* (New York: Oxford University Press, 1986), 263–288. For an astute commentary by a political theorist that places progressivism in the whole context of American thought, see Eldon J. Eisenach, "Reconstituting the Study of American Political Thought in a Regime-Change Perspective," *Studies in American Political Development* 4 (1990), 201–216. His rich and important book on the period is somewhat tangential to the central concerns of this study. I hope to return to it on another occasion. See Eisenach, *The Lost Promise of Progressivism* (Lawrence: University Press of Kansas, 1994).

2. Richard L. McCormick, "The Discovery That Business Corrupts Politics," in *Party Period and Public Policy,* 311–356.

3. Daniel T. Rodgers, *Contested Truths* (New York: Basic Books), esp. 176–186. See also David G. Smith, "Pragmatism and the Group Theory of Politics," *American Political Science Review* (September 1964), 600–610.

4. James A. Nuechterlein, "The People vs. the Interests," *Commentary* (March 1975), 66–75.

5. Charles A. Beard, *An Economic Interpretation of the Constitution* (New York: Macmillan, 1935). For a pioneering effort in this vein, see J. Allan Smith, *The Spirit of American Government* (New York: Macmillan, 1907).

6. For Beard's critics, see Forrest Mcdonald, *We the People* (Chicago: University of Chicago Press, 1958); and Robert E. Brown, *Charles Beard and the Constitution* (Princeton: Princeton

University Press, 1957). Gordon Wood's *The Creation of the American Republic* (Chapel Hill: University of North Carolina Press, 1969) might be described as neo-Beardian in that Wood saw a genuine struggle over the nature of democracy between supporters and opponents of the new Constitution. For a current appraisal of Beard's status, see John P. Diggins, "Power and Authority in American History: The Case of Charles A. Beard and His Critics," *American Historical Review* (October 1981), 701–730. See also Clyde W. Barrow, "Charles A. Beard's Social Democracy: A Critique of the Populist-Progressive Style in American Political Thought," *Polity* (Winter 1988), 253–276; and "Historical Criticism of the U.S. Constitution in Populist-Progressive Political Theory," *History of Political Thought* (Spring 1988), 111–128.

7. David E. Price, "Community and Control: Critical Democratic Theory in the Progressive Period," *American Political Science Review* (December 1974), 1663–1678.

8. Rodgers, "In Search of Progressivism," 123.

9. The outstanding example of the new "organizational synthesis" of progressivism is Robert Wiebe, *The Search for Order: 1877–1920* (New York: Hill and Wang, 1977). See also Wiebe, "Progressive Years." For Weber see Hans Gerth and C. Wright Mills, eds., *From Max Weber* (New York: Oxford University Press, 1946): "Politics as a Vocation," 77–128, esp. 125–128, "Science as a Vocation," 129–156, "Bureaucracy," 196–244; and Max Weber, *The Protestant Ethic and the Spirit of Capitalism,* trans. Talcott Parsons (New York: Scribner's, 1958), esp. 179–183.

10. Richard Hofstadter, *The American Political Tradition,* 25th anniversary ed. (New York: Knopf, 1973), 203–233; *The Age of Reform* (New York: Knopf, 1955), 237–238; John M. Blum, *The Republican Roosevelt* (Cambridge: Harvard University Press, 1954); and David Green, *Shaping Political Consciousness: The Language of Politics in America from McKinley to Reagan* (Ithaca: Cornell University Press, 1987), 58.

11. Thus, for example, Martin Sklar, in a generally useful book, persisted in calling Roosevelt a leftist, and a statist leftist at that. Sklar, *The Corporate Reconstruction of American Capitalism: 1890–1916* (New York: Cambridge University Press, 1988), 351.

12. Green, *Shaping Political Consciousness,* 54–76.

13. Hofstadter, *Age of Reform,* 233; and John Milton Cooper, *The Warrior and the Priest: Woodrow Wilson and Theodore Roosevelt* (Cambridge: Harvard University Press, 1983), 83.

14. Theodore Roosevelt, *The New Nationalism,* ed. William Leuchtenberg (Englewood Cliffs, N.J.: Prentice-Hall, 1961), 29.

15. Ibid., 24–25.

16. Herbert Croly, *The Promise of American Life,* ed. Arthur M. Schlesinger, Jr. (Cambridge: Harvard University Press, 1965). The most important studies of Croly are Charles P. Forcey, *The Crossroads of Liberalism: Croly, Weyl, Lippmann and the New Republic* (New York: Oxford University Press, 1961); and David W. Levy, *Herbert Croly of the New Republic* (Princeton: Princeton University Press), 1985. Christopher Lasch, "Herbert Croly's America," *New York Review of Books* (July 18, 1965), 18–19, is also an acute, if short, commentary. *Promise of American Life* was Croly's most influential book, but it may be that by ignoring his later *Progressive Democracy,* I do some injustice to the totality of his thought. See Kevin C. O'Leary, "Herbert Croly and *Progressive Democracy,*" *Polity* (Summer 1994), 533–552.

17. Only the influence of Santayana was made explicit. Croly, *Promise of American Life,* 454. For the rest see John William Ward's Introduction to *The Promise of American Life* (Indianapolis: Bobbs-Merrill, 1965), xi–xii.

18. Levy, *Herbert Croly,* is particularly insistent on this point.

19. Croly, *Promise of American Life,* 5, 6, 5–7 passim.

20. Ibid., 44.

21. Ibid., 40.

22. Ibid., 273.

23. Ibid., 43–44.

24. Ibid., 49.

25. Ibid., 409–410.

26. Ibid., 419.

27. Ibid., 29.

28. Ibid., 169.

29. Cooper, *Warrior and the Priest,* 217.

30. Sklar, *Corporate Reconstruction of American Capitalism,* 401. For a major restatement of the Jefferson-Hamilton synthesis, see Samuel H. Beer, *To Make a Nation: The Rediscovery of American Federalism* (Cambridge: Harvard University Press, 1993).

31. Jeffrey Tulis, *The Rhetorical Presidency* (Princeton: Princeton University Press, 1987).

32. Cooper, *Warrior and the Priest;* and Ronald Steel, "Where Modern Politics Began," *New York Review of Books* (February 16, 1984), 30–33.

33. Woodrow Wilson, *The New Freedom,* ed. William Leuchtenburg (Englewood Cliffs, N.J.: Prentice-Hall, 1961), 113–114.

34. Ibid., 109.

35. Ibid., 117.

36. Hofstadter, *Age of Reform,* 248.

37. Philippa Strum, *Louis D. Brandeis: Justice for the People* (Cambridge: Harvard University Press, 1984), x. My account of Brandeis is deeply indebted to Strum's fine book, which combines biography and constitutional law with an extensive treatment of Brandeis's political thought. More recently she published a study even more sharply focused on Brandeis as a political thinker and edited a collection of his contributions to democratic theory. See Strum, *Brandeis: Beyond Progressivism* (Lawrence: University Press of Kansas, 1993), and *Brandeis on Democracy* (Lawrence: University Press of Kansas, 1994). For the legal aspects of Brandeis's career, the standard treatment remains Alpheus T. Mason, *Brandeis: A Free Man's Life* (New York: Viking, 1946). For a view of the relation between Brandeis and Wilson that does not stress the impact of Brandeis, as Strum does, see Cooper, *The Warrior and the Priest,* 194.

38. Strum, *Louis D. Brandeis,* 198, 221.

39. See texts by Weber cited in Note 9, this chapter.

40. Strum, *Louis D. Brandeis,* 152.

41. Ibid., xi.

42. Ibid., 174.

43. Quoted in ibid., 185. It should be noted that, even then, Brandeis exaggerated the impact of the union movement.

44. Ibid., 190–191.

45. This paragraph is based entirely on ibid., esp. 205–215. See also Gerald Berk, "Neither Markets nor Administration: Brandeis and the Antitrust Reforms of 1914," *Studies in American Political Development* (Spring 1994), 24–27 and 24–59 passim.

46. McCormick, *Party Period and Public Policy,* 329–330.

47. Wilson, quoted in Green, *Shaping Political Consciousness,* 79.

48. McCormick, *Party Period and Public Policy,* 313.

49. Richard Olney, quoted in Samuel P. Huntington, *American Politics: The Politics of Disharmony* (Cambridge: Harvard University Press, 1981), 119. See also the documentation on 278 n. 62. I will leave aside for now the contention of some scholars associated with the New Left of the 1960s that the outcome predicted by Olney was the goal sought by the Progressive leaders. Alan Brinkley notes that the conclusions of this "corporate liberal" group and those of the organizational school were compatible if one left aside the ideological edge of the New Left historiography. See Alan Brinkley, "Prosperity, Depression, and War, 1920–1945," in *The New American History,* ed. Eric Foner (Philadelphia: Temple University Press, 1990), 135 n. 5.

50. Thomas K. McGraw, "Rethinking the Trust Question," in *Regulation in Perspective,* ed. McGraw (Cambridge: Harvard University Press, 1981), 37, 41. See also 52–54 for further examples of Brandeis's alleged naïveté.

51. Quoted in Niels Aage Thorsen, *The Political Thought of Woodrow Wilson: 1875–1910* (Princeton: Princeton University Press, 1988), 221.

52. Ibid., 227, 240.

53. Woodrow Wilson, *Constitutional Government in the United States* (New York: Columbia University Press, 1908), 69.

54. Randolph S. Bourne, *War and the Intellectuals* (New York: Harper and Row, 1964), 71.

55. For a contemporary restatement and defense of the Progressive position, as well as a sketch of the history of relations between government and the economy in the United States, see Arthur M. Schlesinger, Jr., "Affirmative Government and the American Economy," in *The Cycles of American History* (Boston: Houghton Mifflin, 1986), 219–255.

56. Louis Hartz, *The Liberal Tradition in America* (New York: Harcourt Brace, 1955), 228.

57. James T. Kloppenberg, *Uncertain Victory: Social Democracy and Progressivism in European and American Thought, 1870–1920* (New York: Oxford University Press, 1986), 487 n 27 and 501 n 15.

58. Hartz, *Liberal Tradition*, 230, 255.

59. Robert Reich, "The Fixer," *New Republic* (March 7, 1988), 33–34.

60. Kloppenberg, *Uncertain Victory*, 350–351, 394; and Jürgen Habermas, *Autonomy and Solidarity*, ed. Peter Dews (London: Verso Books, 1986), 151, 193. Unfortunately, Kloppenberg's time frame did not allow for a full-scale consideration of Dewey's most important political writings. The two major books on Dewey's political theory are Alfonso J. Damico, *Individuality and Community* (Gainesville: University Presses of Florida, 1978); and Robert B. Westbrook, *John Dewey and American Democracy* (Ithaca: Cornell University Press, 1991). Westbrook's is the standard work on the subject. However, Damico approaches Dewey from the position of a political theorist rather than a historian and offers valuable insights. A major study by Alan Ryan is forthcoming.

61. Oliver Wendell Holmes, quoted in Morton White, *Social Thought in America: The Revolt Against Formalism* (Boston: Beacon Press, 1957), 13, 16–17.

62. White, *Social Thought in America*, 11–12.

63. Dewey, quoted in ibid., 138.

64. Westbrook, *Dewey and American Democracy*, 134.

65. White, *Social Thought in America*, 242.

66. Ibid., 241, 253.

67. John Dewey, *The Public and Its Problems* (Denver: Allan Swallow, 1927, 1954), 205–206.

68. Ibid., 207. As Michael Walzer notes, all arguments against democracy are "arguments from special knowledge." See Walzer, *Spheres of Justice* (New York: Basic Books, 1983), 285.

69. Dewey, *Public and Its Problems*, 206–209. Still, Dewey did seem excessively optimistic about science and technology: "I think that interest in technique is precisely the thing which is most promising in our civilization, the thing which in the end will break down devotion to external standardization and the mass-quantity ideal." See John Dewey, *Individualism Old and New* (New York: Capricorn Books, [1930], 1962), 30.

70. Dewey, *Public and Its Problems*, 21–22. As Dewey wrote elsewhere: "It is not an ethical 'ought' that conduct *should* be social. It *is* social, whether bad or good." Quoted in Westbrook, *Dewey and American Democracy*, 287–288. Or again, a formulation from as early as 1888: "The non-social individual is an abstraction arrived at by imagining what man would be if all his human qualities were taken away. Society, as a real whole, is the normal order, and the mass as an aggregate of isolated units is the fiction." Quoted in Kloppenberg, *Uncertain Victory*, 97.

71. John Dewey, *Liberalism and Social Action* (New York: Capricorn Books, 1935, 1963), 24.

72. Ibid., 25, 38.

73. Dewey quoted in Westbrook, *Dewey and American Democracy*, 276.

74. Walter Lippmann, *Public Opinion* (New York: Macmillan, 1922), 19. Lippmann was a very important figure in his own right. He was perhaps the most influential journalist of his time, and his power was international as well as domestic. For a very good, full biography, see Ronald Steel, *Walter Lippmann and the American Century* (Boston: Little, Brown, 1980).

75. Lippmann, *Public Opinion,* 29 and 81. Damico points out that Lippmann adopted the classic Platonic distinction between genuine knowledge and mere opinion but without adopting Plato's theory of a world of ideas in which true reality resides. Damico, *Individuality and Community,* 105.

76. For a fuller discussion of Lippmann's arguments as they relate to Dewey, see Westbrook, *Dewey and American Democracy,* 293–300.

77. Dewey acknowledged his debt to Lippmann in *Public and Its Problems,* 116.

78. Ibid., 113–114.

79. Ibid., 179–180.

80. Ibid., 13.

81. Ibid., 14–15.

82. Ibid., 15–16.

83. Ibid., 27–28; Westbrook, *Dewey and American Democracy,* 304.

84. Dewey, *Public and Its Problems,* 31–32, 72; and Westbrook, *Dewey and American Democracy,* xvii.

85. Westbrook, *Dewey and American Democracy,* 308–309.

86. Dewey, *Public and Its Problems,* 142.

87. Ibid., 213. See also Westbrook, *Dewey and American Democracy,* 310–314.

88. Dewey, *Public and Its Problems,* 148.

89. Ibid., 208.

90. Ibid., 212, 157.

91. Dewey, *Liberalism and Social Action,* 37, 85.

92. Ibid., 88. It is interesting to note that Dewey knew relatively little about Marx and was very much part of the left-wing anti-Communist politics of his time. See Westbrook, *Dewey and American Democracy,* 463–495.

93. Westbrook, *Dewey and American Democracy,* 315–318.

94. Damico, *Individuality and Community,* 126.

Chapter 11

1. In this study I am concerned with the domestic phase of the New Deal, which extended to 1940 at the latest; actually, the reform impulse was pretty much played out by 1937 or 1938. My understanding of the substance of the movement owes much to the three volumes of *The Age of Roosevelt* published to date by Arthur M. Schlesinger, Jr.: *The Crisis of the Old Order, The Coming of the New Deal,* and *The Politics of Upheaval* (Boston: Houghton Mifflin, 1956, 1959, 1960). These volumes take the story only through 1936; the completion of the series will be a major historical event. The work is strongly pro-Roosevelt, but the presentation of the evidence is so thorough that one can draw other conclusions from it than Schlesinger did. I have also been influenced by James MacGregor Burns, *Roosevelt: The Lion and the Fox* (New York: Harcourt, 1958); and William Leuchtenberg, *Franklin D. Roosevelt and the New Deal* (Chicago: University of Chicago Press, 1963), both of which are admiring but by no means uncritical. The collapse of the New Deal is brilliantly explored in *The Decline and Fall of the New Deal Order,* ed. Steve Fraser and Gary Gerstle (Princeton: Princeton University Press, 1989). As in many essay collections, the papers are exploratory and not really cumulative; many are parts of larger studies that were in progress. However, individually they are of high quality, and the editors' introductory and concluding remarks are very useful in forging a coherent whole. The discussion of that collection in James T. Kloppenberg, "'Who's Afraid of the Welfare State?'" *Reviews in American History* (September 1990), 395–405, has been helpful. I have also been much influenced by Richard Hofstadter's two interpretations of the New Deal: *The American Political Tradition,* 25th anniversary ed. (New York: Knopf, 1973), 311–247, and *The Age of Reform* (New York: Knopf, 1955), 300–326. As is often the case with his work, Hofstadter's writings on the New Deal have been controversial. For a defense see Alan Brinkley, "Richard Hofstadter's *The Age of Reform:* A Reconsideration," *Reviews in American History* (September 1985), 474–476.

2. Hofstadter, *American Political Tradition,* 311; and Schlesinger, *Coming of the New Deal,* 14.

3. Schlesinger, *Coming of the New Deal,* 193; and Roosevelt, "Speech at Ogelthorpe University, May 22, 1932," in *New Deal Thought,* ed. Howard Zinn (Indianapolis: Bobbs-Merrill, 1966), 83. Roosevelt gave this speech before he had even been nominated for the presidency.

4. John Dewey, *Liberalism and Social Action* (New York: Capricorn Books, 1935, 1963), 62. For a fuller critique of the New Deal by Dewey, see "The Old Problems Are Unsolved," in *New Deal Thought,* ed. Zinn, 409–416. For Dewey on the collapse of capitalism, see "The Collapse of a Romance," in *The Strenuous Decade,* ed. Daniel Aaron and Robert Bendiner (Garden City, N.Y.: Anchor Books, 1970), 13–17.

5. Roosevelt, quoted in David Green, *Shaping Political Consciousness* (Ithaca: Cornell University Press, 1987), 119.

6. The following discussion is based on ibid., 120–134.

7. Roosevelt, quoted in ibid., 175.

8. See, for example, Barton Bernstein, "The New Deal: The Conservative Achievements of Liberal Reform," in *Towards a New Past: Dissenting Essays in American History,* ed. Bernstein (New York: Vintage Books, 1967), 263–288.

9. Jerold S. Auerbach, "New Deal, Old Deal, or Raw Deal: Some Thoughts on New Left Historiography," *Journal of Southern History* (February 1969), 18–30.

10. Frances Perkins, "A Little Left of Center," in Aaron and Bendiner, *Strenuous Decade,* 112. Looking a little puzzled when asked, the president summed up his philosophy by saying that he was "a Christian and a Democrat—that's all" (108–109). The brief excerpt from Perkins's memoirs (106–112) is one of the best brief character sketches of Roosevelt.

11. Green, *Shaping Political Consciousness,* 126–127. It is worth noting that some writers routinely identified as *conservative* have refused the label and insisted on *liberal* as the proper designation.

12. On the tensions between the New Deal and many of the old Progressives, see Otis Graham, *An Encore for Reform* (New York: Oxford University Press, 1967).

13. Hofstadter, *Age of Reform,* 301. In the discussion that follows, I draw heavily on Hofstadter's treatment, 300–326.

14. Louis Hartz, *The Liberal Tradition in America* (New York: Harcourt Brace, 1955), 269. For a multitude of nonmainstream ideologies, mostly on the far right, see Schlesinger on the "Theology of Ferment," *Politics of Upheaval,* 15–207; and Alan Brinkley, *Voices of Protest* (New York: Knopf, 1982).

15. Garry Wills, *Nixon Agonistes* (Boston: Houghton Mifflin, 1970), 564. I accept Wills's use of the Alger stereotype but call attention to my discussion in Chapter 8 of the newer understanding of the Alger stories. Whether the new interpretation is true to Alger or not, the mythical Alger character has real weight in American culture, however absurd the rags-to-riches claims may be in fact.

16. Hofstadter, *Age of Reform,* 305.

17. See Schlesinger, *Coming of the New Deal,* 87–176. The NRA has often been treated as an abject failure, but Schlesinger tried to rehabilitate it. So too did liberal economist John Kenneth Galbraith in *The Liberal Hour* (Boston: Houghton Mifflin, 1959), 4, 84. Another positive assessment was by political scientist Donald R. Brand in *Corporatism and the Rule of Law* (Ithaca: Cornell University Press, 1988). On the *Schechter* case, see Schlesinger, *Politics of Upheaval,* 277–283. It is interesting that Justice Brandeis joined in this decision, seeing it as an attack on centralization (280).

18. John Kenneth Galbraith, *American Capitalism: The Concept of Countervailing Power* (Boston: Houghton Mifflin, 1956), 151. For a fuller treatment of this aspect of Galbraith, see James P. Young, *The Politics of Affluence* (San Francisco: Chandler, 1968), 50–63.

19. Hofstadter, *Age of Reform,* 307. Keynes met Roosevelt and was disappointed. He told Frances Perkins that he had "supposed the President was more literate, economically speaking," than he was. Quoted in Schlesinger, *Politics of Upheaval,* 406.

20. Hofstadter, *Age of Reform*, 317–322.

21. Schlesinger, *Politics of Upheaval*, 389. For a full treatment of the First New Deal, see Schlesinger, *Coming of the New Deal*, 179–194. For an outstanding brief summary of the NRA, see Alan Brinkley, *The End of Reform: New Deal Liberalism in Depression and War* (New York: Knopf, 1995), 38–39: "The NRA established 'code authorities' (not unlike trade associations) in major industries and allowed manufacturers to agree on common pricing policies without fear of antitrust prosecution. In exchange, firms were required to recognize and bargain with labor unions and submit to a vaguely defined level of government supervision of their agreements."

22. Schlesinger, *Politics of Upheaval*, 387–408. For the ideology of the Second New Deal, see ibid. Schlesinger based his analysis of the two New Deals on interviews or correspondence with many members of the administration. His interpretation has been widely accepted, but see the long dissent quoted in a letter from economist Leon Keyserling in ibid., 690–692 n. 2.

23. Hofstadter, *Age of Reform*, 311–312.

24. Ibid., 325. Russell Hanson sees the New Deal as the beginning of what came to be known in the 1950s as the "end of ideology." Hanson, *The Democratic Imagination in America* (Princeton: Princeton University Press, 1985), 259.

25. Schlesinger, *Coming of the New Deal*, 194; and Philippa Strum, *Louis D. Brandeis: Justice for the People* (Cambridge: Harvard University Press, 1984), 387. Brandeis said in 1940 that FDR was greater than Jefferson and almost as great as Lincoln. Strum suggested that Brandeis's approval transcended his own programmatic concerns, which Roosevelt had abandoned. For Strum, the coherent synthesis of the New Nationalism and the New Freedom is an impossibility (see 394). Strum makes an interesting argument that Brandeis's concerns are as relevant in her lifetime as they were during his and that his fear of concentrated power had been echoed by political leaders and movements as diverse as "Nixon, Carter, Reagan, Common Cause, Ralph Nader, the New Left, and the New Right." She continues, "Perhaps Lerner was right: Brandeis's voice did belong to another era—a later one" (413).

26. Irving Howe, "From Roosevelt to Reagan," *Dissent* (Winter 1983), 46; and Frances Perkins, quoted in Schlesinger, *Politics of Upheaval*, 652. I will leave aside the question of the sincerity of President Reagan's belief in the "safety net." One could argue that even when he said that, all too many people already fell below the net. A colleague of mine remarked, "You can't fall up into the net."

27. Theodore J. Lowi, "The Roosevelt Revolution and the New American State," in *Comparative Theory and Political Experience*, ed. Peter J. Katzenstein et al. (Ithaca: Cornell University Press, 1990), 203.

28. Roosevelt, quoted in Schlesinger, *Politics of Upheaval*, 638.

29. Roosevelt, quoted in ibid., 639.

30. Lowi, "Roosevelt Revolution," 203. This is the major theme of Lowi's important interpretation of contemporary American politics. See Theodore Lowi, *The End of Liberalism*, 2d ed. (New York: Norton, 1979).

31. Lowi, "Roosevelt Revolution," 199.

32. Ibid., 200–202.

33. Ibid., 202; and Sheldon S. Wolin, *The Presence of the Past: Essays on the State and the Constitution* (Baltimore: Johns Hopkins University Press, 1989), 21–22. For a more detailed account of the emergence of the modern American state in the New Deal years, see Alan Brinkley, "The New Deal and the Idea of the State," in Fraser and Gerstle, *The Rise and Fall of the New Deal Order*, 85–121.

34. On this theme see the important essay by Sheldon Wolin, "The Idea of the State in America," in *The Problem of Authority in America*, ed. John P. Diggins and Mark Kann (Philadelphia: Temple University Press, 1981), 41–58.

35. Roosevelt, "Commonwealth Club Address," *Public Papers and Addresses I: 1928–1932* (New York: Random House, 1938), 751–752. For a full treatment of this speech, which has influenced my reading, see Sidney M. Milkis, *The President and the Parties: The Transformation*

of the American Party System Since the New Deal (New York: Oxford University Press, 1993), 38–51. The principal author of this speech was Adolph A. Berle, though the candidate himself was also involved. John Dewey's *Individualism Old and New* appears to have been a major influence. On the drafting see Milkis, *President and Parties,* 38–40, 323–324 n. 72.

36. Milkis, *President and Parties,* 5–13. This is a very important book, though I am not always in agreement with the position the author seems to have taken on specific public policy issues over the last fifty years.

37. See Brinkley, *End of Reform,* 3–14, 265–271. For Brinkley's views on what can be learned from the New Deal today, see "Legacies of the New Deal," *Chronicle of Higher Education* (May 19, 1995), B1–2.

38. Hofstadter, *American Political Tradition,* xxix.

39. Eric Goldman, *Rendezvous with Destiny* (New York: Vintage Books, 1956), 333–334, and *The Crucial Decade—and After* (New York: Vintage Books, 1960), 293.

Chapter 12

1. On the linguistic politics of anticommunism, see David Green, *Shaping Political Consciousness* (Ithaca: Cornell University Press, 1987), 164–206.

2. Arthur M. Schlesinger, Jr., *The Vital Center,* 2d ed. (Boston: Houghton Mifflin, 1962).

3. Ibid., 1.

4. Ibid., xxiv.

5. Ibid., xxiii.

6. Niebuhr's writings were vast. The major items included *Moral Man and Immoral Society* (New York: Scribner's, 1932), *Nature and Destiny of Man,* 1-vol. ed. (New York: Scribner's, 1951), *Christianity and Power Politics* (New York: Scribner's, 1940), *The Children of Light and the Children of Darkness* (New York: Scribner's, 1944), and *The Irony of American History* (New York: Scribner's, 1952).

7. Niebuhr, *Moral Man and Immoral Society,* 4.

8. Niebuhr, *Irony of American History,* 63.

9. Niebuhr, *Children of Light and Children of Darkness,* 118.

10. Ibid., xi.

11. Niebuhr, *Christianity and Power Politics,* 104.

12. For Niebuhr's impact on the theory of international politics, see Kenneth Thompson, *Political Realism and the Crisis of World Politics* (Princeton: Princeton University Press, 1960); and Robert C. Good, "The National Interest and Political Realism: Niebuhr's 'Debate' with Morgenthau and Kennan," *Journal of Politics* (November 1960), 597–619.

13. Schlesinger, *Vital Center,* 170. For Schlesinger on Niebuhr, see "Reinhold Niebuhr's Role in American Political Thought and Life," in Arthur M. Schlesinger, Jr., *The Politics of Hope* (Boston: Houghton Mifflin, 1963), 97–125. It is possible to question how different Niebuhr's thought was from conventional liberalism once we get beyond questions of intellectual style. See Wilson Carey McWilliams, "Reinhold Niebuhr: New Orthodoxy for an Old Liberalism," *American Political Science Review* (December 1962), 874–885.

14. For the idea of skeptical liberalism, see the excellent survey by Robert Booth Fowler, *Believing Skeptics: American Political Intellectuals, 1945–1964* (Westport, Conn.: Greenwood, 1978). Two historical studies of more or less the same period lack the theoretical insight of Fowler but are nonetheless useful. See John P. Diggins, *The Proud Decades: America in War and Peace, 1940–1960* (New York: Norton, 1988); and Richard H. Pells, *The Liberal Mind in a Conservative Age: American Intellectuals in the 1940's and 1950's* (New York: Harper and Row, 1985). The difference between Fowler on the one hand and Diggins and Pells on the other illustrates the differing, and one hopes complementary, range of interests and analytical styles

of political theorists and intellectual historians. See also J. P. Young, *The Politics of Affluence* (San Francisco: Chandler, 1968).

15. Richard Hofstadter, "What Happened to the Antitrust Movement?" in *The Paranoid Style in American Politics* (New York: Knopf, 1965), 223–224.

16. David Riesman, *The Lonely Crowd,* rev. ed. (New Haven: Yale University Press, 1961), 3–36, 82.

17. Ibid., 159.

18. Ibid., 177.

19. Ibid., 182–187.

20. Ibid., 239–261.

21. William H. Whyte, Jr., *The Organization Man* (Garden City, N.Y.: Anchor Books, 1957), 7.

22. Seymour Martin Lipset, "A Changing American Character?" in *Culture and Social Character,* ed. Lipset and Leo Lowenthal (New York: Free Press, 1961), 136–171. There is, however, evidence that supports the notion of a character change in the 1950s in Clyde Kluckhohn, "Have There Been Discernible Shifts in Values in the Past Generation?" in *The American Style,* ed. Elting Morison (New York: Harper, 1958), 136–171.

23. John Kenneth Galbraith, *The Affluent Society* (Boston: Houghton Mifflin, 1958), 187–188.

24. Ibid., 190, emphasis added; and Russell Hanson, *The Democratic Imagination in America* (Princeton: Princeton University Press, 1985), 291.

25. Galbraith, *Affluent Society,* 257.

26. Arthur M. Schlesinger, Jr., "The New Mood in Politics," in *Politics of Hope,* 81–82; and *Vital Center,* xiv.

27. Schlesinger, *Vital Center,* xiv. Cf. Pells, *Liberal Mind in a Conservative Age,* 173.

28. Joseph A. Schumpeter, *Capitalism, Socialism, and Democracy,* 3d ed. (New York: Harper, 1950), 250.

29. Carole Pateman, *Participation and Democratic Theory* (Cambridge: Cambridge University Press, 1970), 17–20.

30. Schumpeter, *Capitalism, Socialism, and Democracy,* 269. Consider the difference for democracy if even so small an alteration in the definition as that of E. E. Schattschneider were substituted: "Democracy is a competitive political system in which competing leaders and organizations define the alternatives of public policy in such a way that the public can participate in the decision-making process." See Schattschneider, *The Semi-Sovereign People* (New York: Holt, Rinehart, Winston, 1960), 141.

31. Schumpeter, *Capitalism, Socialism, and Democracy,* 295.

32. Ibid., 262 and 261–262 passim.

33. I have offered a very narrow discussion of Schumpeter's important theory, though it serves my purposes. For more detailed discussion, see Pateman, *Participation and Democratic Theory,* 1–21; Peter Bachrach, *The Theory of Democratic Elitism* (Boston: Little, Brown, 1967), 17–25; and Nicholas Xenos, "Democracy as Method," *democracy* (October 1981), 110–123.

34. Angus Campbell, Philip Converse, Warren Miller, and Donald Stokes, *The American Voter* (New York: Wiley, 1960).

35. Bernard Berleson et al., *Voting* (Chicago: University of Chicago Press, 1954), 305–323.

36. Heinz Eulau, quoted in Fowler, *Believing Skeptics,* 193. Fowler's book contains a very useful guide (149–214) to the social scientist's revision of the theory of democracy.

37. V. O. Key, Jr., *Public Opinion and American Democracy* (New York: Knopf, 1961), 558. One should note that Key's book was based on a reanalysis of the data collected by the authors of *The American Voter.*

38. V. O. Key, Jr., *The Responsible Electorate* (Cambridge: Harvard University Press, 1966), 7.

39. Arthur Bentley, *The Process of Government* (Bloomington: Indiana University Press, 1908), 208–209.

40. The fullest statement of David Truman's theory of American politics came in the final chapter of *The Governmental Process* (New York: Knopf, 1951), 501–524. On the absence of a need to account for a public interest, see 51.

41. Charles Frankel, *The Democratic Prospect* (New York: Harper and Row, 1962), 200.

42. Schattschneider, *Semi-Sovereign People*, 35.

43. Stanley Rothman, "Systematic Political Theory: Observations on the Group Approach," in *Consensus and Conflict*, ed. J. P. Young (New York: Dodd, Mead, 1972), 219. Rothman's article is the most systematic critique of Truman; I have benefited greatly from it. See 207–226.

44. Sheldon S. Wolin, "The New Public Philosophy," *democracy* (October 1981), 23–36.

45. Robert A. Dahl, *A Preface to Democratic Theory* (Chicago: University of Chicago Press, 1956), 134. Since I am including Dahl here among the complacent liberal ideologists of the 1950s, it is only fair to point out that his work has become much more critical in the past twenty years. Some of that material will be discussed in Chapters 15 and 17.

46. Ibid., 132. For a sharp criticism of Dahl on this point, see Harvey Mansfield, Jr., *America's Constitutional Soul* (Baltimore: Johns Hopkins University Press, 1991), 156. One of the major themes of Mansfield's book is a running defense of "forms and formalities" of constitutionalism, whose importance social scientists tend to deny. His book is a leading example of the Straussian school of political theory, to be discussed in Chapter 14.

47. Mansfield, *America's Constitutional Soul*, 8.

48. Fowler, *Believing Skeptics*, 200–201. I have followed Fowler quite closely in this paragraph.

49. Daniel Bell, *The End of Ideology* (Glencoe, Ill.: Free Press, 1960).

50. Ibid., 373.

51. Ibid., 291–292.

52. Seymour Martin Lipset, *Political Man* (Garden City, N.Y.: Anchor Books, 1963), 439.

53. Stephen W. Rousseas and James Farganis, "American Politics and the End of Ideology," in *The New Sociology*, ed. Irving Louis Horowitz (New York: Oxford University Press, 1964), 272.

54. Carl J. Friedrich, "Political Philosophy and the Science of Politics," in *Approaches to the Study of Politics*, ed. Roland Young (Evanston, Ill.: Northwestern University Press, 1958), 186. For the classic exposition of the need for a neutral concept of ideology, see Clifford Geertz, "Ideology as a Cultural System," in *Ideology and Discontent*, ed. David Apter (New York: Free Press, 1964), 47–76.

55. Andrew Hacker, quoted in Rousseas and Farganis, "American Politics and the End of Ideology," 272–273. On the question of the need for moral criticism, see the harsh exchange between Henry David Aiken and Bell: Aiken, "The Revolt Against Ideology," and Bell and Aiken, "The End of Ideology: A Debate," in Young, *Consensus and Conflict*, 149–185.

56. Daniel Bell, "Ideology and the Beau Geste," *Dissent* (Winter 1961), 75; and *End of Ideology*, 16.

57. Sheldon S. Wolin, *Politics and Vision* (Boston: Little, Brown, 1960), 434. For Wolin's major statement setting out the advantages of "traditional" political theory over social science, see S. Wolin, "Political Theory as a Vocation," *American Political Science Review* (December 1969), 1062–1082.

58. Leo Strauss, "An Epilogue," in Herbert J. Storing et al., *Essays on the Scientific Study of Politics* (New York: Holt, Rinehart, Winston, 1962), 327. It should be said that Strauss and Wolin were far from being in agreement on most issues. See John H. Schaar and Sheldon S. Wolin, "*Essays on the Scientific Study of Politics*: A Critique," *American Political Science Review* (March 1963), 125–150. Responses by Storing et al. are on 151–160. Other discussions of the biases of social science are C. Wright Mills, *The Sociological Imagination* (New York: Oxford University Press, 1959); and Terrence Ball, "The Politics of Social Science," in *Recasting*

America: Culture and Politics in the Age of Cold War, ed. Lary May (Chicago: University of Chicago Press, 1989), 76–92. On political science specifically, see William E. Connolly, *Political Science and Ideology* (New York: Atherton Press, 1967); and Philip Green and Sanford Levinson, eds., *Power and Community: Dissenting Essays in Political Science* (New York: Vintage Books, 1970), especially the essays by J. Peter Euben, Sanford Levinson, Kenneth Dolbeare, John Schaar, Tracy Strong, and Wilson Carey McWilliams.

59. An important series of articles grew out of the Berkeley rebellion of 1965. At first John Schaar and Sheldon Wolin stayed fairly close to descriptive accounts of the events, but as time passed, the essays took on more general significance and evolved into a significant theoretical commentary on some of the central events of the 1960s. See Wolin and Schaar, *The Berkeley Rebellion and Beyond: Essays on Politics and Education in the Technological Society* (New York: New York Review of Books, 1970).

60. C. Wright Mills, *The Power Elite* (New York: Oxford University Press, 1956). In my discussion of Mills, I have drawn in substance and language on my comments in Young, *Consensus and Conflict,* 9–11, 227. For the discussion of Mills I owe much to my teacher James Meisel. Mills's other major works include his study of the middle class, *White Collar* (New York: Oxford University Press, 1953); *The Sociological Imagination* (New York: Oxford University Press, 1959), a slashing and often devastating critique of mainstream social science; and a collection of essays, *Power, Politics, and People,* ed. Irving Louis Horowitz (New York: Oxford University Press, 1963).

61. Mills, "Liberal Values in the Modern World," in Horowitz, *Power, Politics, and People,* 187–195. The similarity to John Dewey should be noted here. Mills wrote his doctoral dissertation on pragmatism. It was published as C. Wright Mills, *Sociology and Pragmatism* (New York: Oxford University Press, 1964). On Dewey see 279–463.

62. Mills, *Power, Politics, and People,* 247–259.

63. Robert A. Dahl, "A Critique of the Ruling Elite Model," and Richard Rovere, "The Interlocking Overlappers—and Some Further Thoughts on the 'Power Situation,'" in Young, *Consensus and Conflict,* 248–267.

64. Peter Bachrach and Morton S. Baratz, "Two Faces of Power," *American Political Science Review* (December 1962), 947–952.

65. The two previous paragraphs rely heavily on Connolly, *Political Science and Ideology,* 27–29. It does not necessarily follow from this discussion that the consensus is consciously manipulated, though studies might show that to some extent it is. It is probably a mix. Thus Americans have a deep belief in capitalism, which is no doubt reinforced by the mass media. Theodore Lowi raises the possibility that there might be different power structures for different areas of policy. See Lowi, "American Business, Public Policy, Case Studies, and Political Theory," in Young, *Consensus and Conflict,* 267–292.

66. For a series of studies inspired by or commenting on Mills, see Horowitz, *New Sociology.* The major reviews of *The Power Elite* have been collected under the title *C. Wright Mills and the Power Elite,* ed. G. William Domhoff and Hoyt Ballard (Boston: Beacon Press, 1968). There is a very interesting essay dealing with Mills's background, personality, and influence on the New Left: Jim Miller, "Democracy and the Intellectual: C. Wright Mills Reconsidered," *Salmagundi* (Spring-Summer 1986), 82–101.

67. Herbert Marcuse, *One Dimensional Man,* 2d ed., intro. Douglas Kellner (Boston: Beacon Press, 1991).

68. Ibid., 256.

69. Marcuse, "Repressive Tolerance," in Robert Paul Wolff, Barrington Moore, Jr., and Herbert Marcuse, *A Critique of Pure Tolerance* (Boston: Beacon Books, 1969), 97, 99–101, 100–101, 109, 106. For a detailed critique see David Spitz, "Pure Tolerance: A Critique of Criticisms," in *Beyond the New Left,* ed. Irving Howe (New York: McCall, 1970), 111–117.

70. For an assortment of critical views, see Allan Graubard, "One Dimensional Pessimism: A Critique of Herbert Marcuse's Theories," in Howe, *Beyond the New Left,* 144–165; Alasdair

MacIntyre, *Marcuse* (London: Fontana/Collins, 1970), 62–86; and Michael Walzer, "Herbert Marcuse's America," in *The Company of Critics* (New York: Basic Books, 1988), 170–190. For more-favorable assessments, see Kellner, "Introduction to the Second Edition," and George Lichtheim, "Forward to Utopia," in *The Concept of Ideology* (New York: Vintage, 1967), 177–189. In "The Political Thought of Herbert Marcuse," *Commentary* (January 1970), 48–63, George Kateb gave a very balanced assessment of the broad range of Marcuse's thinking.

71. Walzer, *Company of Critics,* 190; see, more generally, Michael Walzer, *Interpretation and Social Criticism* (Cambridge: Harvard University Press, 1987). See also Graubard, "One Dimensional Pessimism."

72. For Marcuse on Weber, see "Industrialism and Capitalism in the Work of Max Weber," in Herbert Marcuse, *Negations* (Boston: Beacon Press, 1968), 201–226. Much of the significant work in this area has been done by the German-based Frankfurt School, of which Marcuse was a member. The most important studies are those of Jürgen Habermas. For an outstanding introduction to the critical theory of the Frankfurt School, see James Farganis, "A Preface to Critical Theory," *Theory and Society* (Winter 1975), 483–508.

73. A useful sampling of work from *Studies on the Left* is in *For a New America: Essays in History and Politics from* Studies on the Left, *1959–1987,* ed. James Weinstein and David W. Eakins (New York: Vintage, 1970). There are some interesting memoirs of the Madison New Left in *History and the New Left,* ed. Paul Buhle (Philadelphia: Temple University Press, 1990).

74. Martin Sklar, "Woodrow Wilson and the Political Economy of Modern United States Liberalism," in Weinstein and Eakins, *For a New America,* 46–100. The interpretive issues are complex; and it is not possible to follow the nuances here. Thus, for example, Sklar recommended discarding both the New Nationalism and the New Freedom as tools of analysis. See 92–103, 99. Yet in his conclusion he saw the possible triumph of Crolyism as a disaster that would indeed require a new freedom.

75. Ibid., 86. Sklar is less grudging about the utility of progressive reform in his more recent studies. See further discussion in this chapter.

76. Robin L. Einhorn, "Give Me an 'L,'" *Nation* (January 27, 1992), 99. It should be said that Einhorn is critical of this view of liberalism, which she sees as depriving it of a usable past, thereby undercutting its present political effectiveness.

77. Christopher Lasch, "William Appleman Williams on American History," *Marxist Perspectives* (Fall 1978), 118. For Williams on progressivism, see William Appleman Williams, *The Contours of American History* (Cleveland: World, 1961), 345–412. For Williams's influential and controversial ideas on the expansionist tendencies of U.S. foreign policy, see *The Tragedy Of American Diplomacy,* rev. ed. (New York: Delta Books, 1962).

78. See Martin Sklar, *The Corporate Reconstruction of American Capitalism: 1890–1916* (Cambridge: Cambridge University Press, 1988) and *The United States as a Developing Country: Studies in U.S. History in the Progressive Era and the 1920s* (Cambridge: Cambridge University Press, 1991), esp. 1–77 and 209–218. Actually, Sklar disdains the New Left label, preferring to think of himself as an "extremely old leftist" in the sense that he, in addition to being a socialist, was grounded in "Enlightenment and nineteenth-century rationalism, humanism, and evolutionism" (197).

79. Alan Brinkley, "Prosperity, Depression, and War," in *The New American History,* ed. Eric Foner (Philadelphia: Temple University Press, 1990), 135. Brinkley follows the work of Louis Galambos.

80. For Sklar on modernization theory, see *United States as a Developing Country,* 45–55. Sklar clearly understands that modernization theory added little to classical social thought. Robert Wiebe's important statement of the organizational interpretation of American society is thoughtfully reconsidered in the light of social science theory in Kenneth Cmiel, "Destiny and Amnesia: The Vision of Modernity in Robert Wiebe's *The Search for Order,"* *Reviews in American History* (June 1993), 352–368.

81. The literature on the student politics of the 1960s and the SDS is now huge. I have drawn particularly on James Miller, *"Democracy Is in the Streets": From Port Huron to the Siege of Chicago* (New York: Simon and Schuster, 1987). Broader in focus but also very useful is Todd Gitlin, *The Sixties: Years of Hope, Days of Rage* (New York: Bantam, 1987). Maurice Isserman, *If I Had a Hammer: The Death of the Old Left and the Birth of the New Left* (New York: Basic Books, 1987), is very good on the subject indicated by its title. In spite of the fact that he was the best known of the student activists, Tom Hayden's memoirs are less useful and interesting than one might hope. See *Reunion* (New York: Random House, 1988). The flood of books induced by the twentieth anniversary of the movement's climactic clash with the Chicago police at the 1968 Democratic National Convention drew a number of significant review articles by former movement activists. See Paul Berman, "Don't Follow Leaders," *New Republic* (August 10 and 17, 1987), 28–35; Winifrid Breines, "Whose New Left?" *Journal of American History* (September 1988), 528–545; Murray Hausknecht, "Generational Conflict and Left Politics," *Dissent* (Fall 1988), 497–500; Maurice Isserman, "Spin Control," *Dissent* (Fall 1988), 501–503; Maurice Isserman, "The Not-So-Dark and Bloody Ground: New Works on the 1960's," *American Historical Review* (October 1989), 990–1010. More generally, see Peter Clecak, "'The Movement' and Its Critics," *Social Research* (Autumn 1981), 521–556; and Alan Brinkley, "Dreams of the Sixties," *New York Review of Books* (October 22, 1987), 10–16. There are valuable comments by political theorists who were close to, but not part of, the movement in Wolin and Schaar, *Berkeley Rebellion and Beyond,* and the articles collected in Part 2 of Michael Walzer, *Radical Principles: Reflections of an Unreconstructed Democrat* (New York: Basic Books, 1980), 109–185. See also Hanson, *Democratic Imagination in America,* 203–350, for a general discussion of leftist movements of the 1960s. My understanding of the Student Left was affected by personal experience. From 1952 to the fall of 1961 I was a student at Michigan. I was two to three years ahead of the radical generation, and Tom Hayden was known to me only as the author of rambunctious editorials in the student newspaper. I was part of the left-leaning group that congregated around Marshall's bookstore, and I knew people at the avant-garde artistic fringe of the SDS. I was also involved to some extent with the social democratic wing of the Michigan Democratic Party. Through the 1960s, I was in constant conversation with members of the SDS and other radical groupings.

82. Walzer, *Radical Principles,* 113.

83. Wolin and Schaar, *Berkeley Rebellion and Beyond,* 118.

84. Walzer, *Radical Principles,* 157.

85. Walzer, *Company of Critics.* On Camus as a connected critic, see 136–152.

86. See Arnold Kaufman, "Human Nature and Participatory Democracy" and "Participatory Democracy: Ten Years Later," in William E. Connolly, *The Bias of Pluralism* (New York: Atherton, 1969), 178–212. The full text of the Port Huron Statement is conveniently available in Miller, *"Democracy Is in the Streets,"* 329–374. There is a valuable collection of student Left documents in *The New Student Left: An Anthology,* ed. Mitchell Cohen and Dennis Hale (Boston: Beacon Press, 1966).

87. For the intellectual influences on Hayden, see Miller, *"Democracy Is in the Streets,"* 44, 78, 93–94.

88. Ibid., 329.

89. Ibid., 330.

90. Ibid.

91. Ibid., 333.

92. Ibid., 144–145.

93. Ibid., 141.

94. Richard J. Ellis, "Rival Visions of Equality in American Political Culture," *Review of Politics* (Spring 1992), 270, 270–275.

95. Miller, *"Democracy Is in the Streets,"* 16, 145–146.

96. Ibid., 333. The influence of C. Wright Mills is very clear here. For Mills the problem of social science was to find methods so that "the personal uneasiness of individuals is

focused upon explicit troubles and the indifference of publics is transformed into involvement with public issues." Mills, *The Sociological Imagination,* 5. More generally see 3–24. Oddly, "The personal is political" was first a feminist slogan that originated in female disgust with the subordinate position of women in the New Left. See Sara Evans, *Personal Politics* (New York: Vintage, 1980). On the strong current of individualistic existentialist warmth that suffused the SDS, see Gitlin, Sixties, 105–109.

97. For an essay that gives two cheers for participatory democracy on the basis of these considerations, see Michael Walzer, "A Day in the Life of a Socialist Citizen," in *Radical Principles,* 128–138, 131.

98. On the controversy over communism in Port Huron, see Gitlin, *Sixties,* 109–126; Miller, *"Democracy Is in the Streets,"* 110–140; and Berman, "Don't Follow Leaders," 28–35. Miller's is the best account of the intellectual origins of SDS. Given later developments, it is ironic that the first time Richard Flacks heard Tom Hayden speak, he returned home and told his wife, "I've just seen the next Lenin." See Miller, *"Democracy Is in the Streets,"* 102. Michael Harrington, though he remained critical of the student Left, came to regret the part he had played in what became an almost comically confused attempt to draft language on the Communist issue that all could agree to. See Harrington, *Fragments of a Century: A Social Autobiography* (New York: Saturday Review Press, 1973), 144–150.

Chapter 13

1. On the historical relation between abolition and early feminism, see Jean Fagan Yellin, *Women and Sisters: The Antislavery Feminists in American Culture* (New Haven: Yale University Press, 1989). For a perception of the political possibilities of an alliance between feminists and racial activists, see the account of the 1992 meeting of the Socialist Scholars' Conference in *Chronicle of Higher Education* (May 6, 1992), 19–21. The long search for a substitute for the Marxist proletariat that failed to fulfill its presumed historical mission continues.

2. Gunnar Myrdal, *An American Dilemma,* rev. ed. (New York: Harper, 1962), lxxi.

3. Charles Silverman, *Crisis in Black and White* (New York: Random House, 1964), 10 and passim.

4. Jennifer Hochschild, *The New American Dilemma* (New Haven: Yale University Press, 1984), 5–6.

5. Andrew Hacker, *Two Nations: Black and White, Separate, Hostile, and Unequal* (New York: Scribner's, 1992).

6. Alexis de Tocqueville, *Democracy in America,* trans. George Lawrence (Garden City, N.Y.: Anchor Books, 1969), 340–396.

7. For a deep meditation on the complexities of ethnic assimilation, see Michael Walzer, *What It Means to Be an American* (New York: Marsilio Books, 1992), 23–49.

8. W.E.B. Du Bois, *The Souls of Black Folk,* in *Writings* (New York: Library of America, 1986), 364–365. For a searching discussion of Du Bois's concept of "two-ness" by a contemporary black theorist, see Adolph Reed, Jr., "Du Bois's 'Double Consciousness': Race and Gender in Progressive Era American Thought," *Studies in American Political Development* (Spring 1992), 37–92. See also Kwame Anthony Appiah, *In My Father's House: Africa in the Philosophy of Culture* (New York: Oxford University Press, 1992), 28–46. By no means all blacks or black intellectuals have seen their lives in terms of Du Bois's dualism. For a fascinating collection loosely related to the theme, see Gerald Early, ed., *Lure and Loathing* (New York: Allan Lane, 1993). Molefi Kete Asante, for example, altogether rejects the distinction. See "Racism, Consciousness, and Afrocentricity," in ibid., 127–143. Du Bois's political thought went well beyond the "two-ness" theme. For a general assessment, see Adolph Reed, Jr., "W.E.B. Du Bois: A Perspective on the Bases of His Political Thought," *Political Theory* (August 1985), 431–456.

9. Baldwin's later work was of a much lower order; I also feel that his fiction was less important than his essays, in which form he was an American master. For this study I have

used *Notes of a Native Son* (Boston: Beacon Press, 1955), *Nobody Knows My Name* (New York: Delta Books, 1962), and *The Fire Next Time* (New York: Dial Press, 1963). On the importance of early versus late Baldwin, see Henry Louis Gates, Jr., "The Fire Last Time," *New Republic* (June 1, 1992), 37–43.

10. The following discussion of Baldwin draws heavily on my book *The Politics of Affluence* (San Francisco: Chandler, 1968), 176–187. It is startling and quite depressing to me how little of my discussion of race in the 1960s needed to be changed today. Some sociological changes had to be taken into account and some ideological positions have been altered, but the basic alternatives remain much the same.

11. Baldwin, *Notes of a Native Son*, 6–7.

12. Ibid., 135–137; Baldwin, *Nobody Knows My Name*, xiii.

13. Baldwin, *Notes of a Native Son*, 25.

14. Ibid., 71.

15. Baldwin, *Fire Next Time*, 108, 24. Later he added: "And I repeat: The price of the liberation of the white people is the liberation of the blacks—the total liberation, in the cities, in the towns, before the law, and in the mind. Why, for example—especially knowing the family as I do—I should *want* to marry your sister is a great mystery to me" (111).

16. Baldwin, *Notes of a Native Son*, 9, 166.

17. Baldwin, *Fire Next Time*, 72.

18. Ibid., 117.

19. Ibid., 108.

20. Baldwin, *Nobody Knows My Name*, 75.

21. One should also by no means overlook the influence of the southern black churches. On the intellectual sources of King's thought, see "Martin Luther King, Jr., and the Black Folk Pulpit," *Journal of American History* (June 1991), 120–123; Clayborn Carson et al., "Martin Luther King, Jr., as Scholar," *Journal of American History* (June 1991), 94; and Eugene D. Genovese, "Pilgrim's Progress," *New Republic* (May 11, 1992), 33–40. King's own discussion of his intellectual genealogy is widely scattered, but see his book *Stride Toward Freedom,* in *A Testament of Hope: The Essential Writings of Martin Luther King,* ed. James M. Washington (San Francisco: Harper and Row, 1986), 417–490.

22. Baldwin, *Nobody Knows My Name*, 76.

23. George M. Fredrickson, "African Americans and African Africans," *New York Review of Books* (September 26, 1991), 32–33. I am much indebted to this fine article, which makes important comparisons between the United States and South Africa.

24. Ibid., 33.

25. Baldwin, *Fire Next Time*, 96.

26. Ibid., 64–65.

27. Ibid., 96.

28. Malcolm X, "The Ballot or the Bullet," in *What Country Have I?: Political Writings by Black Americans,* ed. Herbert J. Storing (New York: St. Martin's, 1970), 141–163.

29. This surely is part of the message of Spike Lee's controversial and ambiguous film *Do the Right Thing.* I have no need to enter into the controversy over which side, if either, Lee took in his film. Stanley Crouch's acerbic analysis of the picture and Lee's subsequent statements suggests that he clearly sided with Malcolm. See Stanley Crouch, "Do the Race Thing," in *Notes of a Hanging Judge* (New York: Oxford University Press, 1990), 237–244. The dichotomy of King and Malcolm is potentially useful in the way that any ideal type may be useful, but of course, it oversimplifies reality, particularly as presented in Lee's film. On the analytical limits of this pairing, see Adolph Reed, Jr., "The Allure of Malcolm X and the Changing Character of Black Politics," in *Malcolm X: In Our Own Image,* ed. Joe Wood (New York: St. Martin's, 1992), esp. 223–227.

30. Perhaps the classic statement was Stokely Carmichael and Charles Hamilton, *Black Power* (New York: Random House, 1967). For all its sometimes flamboyant rhetoric, this book remained within the limits of American pressure-group politics; the shock came when blacks began to play the game.

31. Storing, *What Country Have I?* 165. Storing noted the generally moderate tone of the book.

32. See Christopher Lasch, *The True and Only Heaven* (New York: Norton, 1991), 386–412. Lasch heartily disapproves of this development in King's politics. He is disturbed by the substitution of distribution for participation as the central issue of the movement (see 404). One can only observe that it is hard to participate if one is hungry. As a young man, King was drawn toward a kind of Christian socialism, and later his interest in Marx grew, though he never accepted any of Marx's materialist philosophy. See Eugene Genovese, "Pilgrims Progress," *New Republic* (May 11, 1992), 37.

33. William Julius Wilson, *The Declining Significance of Race*, 2d ed. (Chicago: University of Chicago Press, 1980).

34. Some object to the very term *underclass* on the ground that it is demeaning. Jennifer Hochschild referred instead to the "estranged poor" in a symposium on William Julius Wilson published in *Ethics* (April 1991). See Hochschild, "The Politics of the Estranged Poor," Bernard R. Boxill, "Wilson on the Truly Disadvantaged," and Wilson, "The Truly Disadvantaged Revisited: A Response to Hochschild and Boxill," 560–609. The study discussed in the symposium was W. J. Wilson, *The Truly Disadvantaged: The Inner City, the Underclass, and Public Policy* (Chicago: University of Chicago Press, 1987). Wilson later abandoned the term in favor of urban poor for fear of lending support to conservatives. See Nicholas Lemann, *The Promised Land* (New York: Knopf, 1991), 290.

35. For a good survey of Wilson's recent work and its critics, see Neil McLaughlin, "Beyond 'Race vs. Class,'" *Dissent* (Summer 1993), 362–367.

36. Wilson, "Truly Disadvantaged Revisited," 595–596.

37. William Julius Wilson, "Race-Neutral Programs and the Democratic Coalition," *American Prospect* (Spring 1990), 72–81. See the dissent by Kenneth S. Tollett, "Racism and Race-Conscious Remedies," *American Prospect* (Spring 1991), 91–93, and the further responses by Wilson and Cass Sunstein, 93–96.

38. Michael Walzer, *Spheres of Justice* (New York: Basic Books, 1983), 152–153.

39. Michael Walzer, *Radical Principles* (New York: Basic Books, 1980), 255.

40. Nathan Glazer, *Affirmative Discrimination: Ethnic Inequality and Public Policy* (Cambridge: Harvard University Press, 1987), 196–197.

41. Harvey Mansfield, Jr., *America's Constitutional Soul* (Baltimore: Johns Hopkins University Press, 1991), 87–88. In discussing affirmative action, Mansfield does not consider women and Hispanics; in his view, the latter were doing well; as for women, the discrimination against them could not begin to compare with that inflicted upon blacks. In general, the Straussian school of conservatism, which Mansfield represents, was not sympathetic to feminism. Allan Bloom was the leading critic of it. See Bloom, *The Closing of the American Mind* (New York: Simon and Schuster, 1987), 97–108, and *Love and Friendship* (New York: Simon and Schuster, 1993), 26–28.

42. Mansfield, *America's Constitutional Soul*, 88–93. Quote at 93.

43. Ibid., 87.

44. Ibid., 91.

45. Glenn C. Loury, "'Matters of Color': Blacks and the Constitutional Order," *Public Interest* (Winter 1987), 114, and "A New American Dilemma," *New Republic* (December 31, 1984), 14.

46. Loury, "'Matters of Color,'" 109–123, and "New American Dilemma," 14–18, passim.

47. Stephen L. Carter, *Reflections of an Affirmative Action Baby* (New York: Basic Books, 1991), esp. 143–168.

48. Shelby Steele, *The Content of Our Character* (New York: St. Martin's, 1990).

49. Carter, *Reflections of an Affirmative Action Baby*, 163–164.

50. For a similar analysis, see Cornell West, *Race Matters* (Boston: Beacon Press, 1993), esp. 55–58. On the black conservatives more generally, see 49–59. West too stresses the relation of black conservatism to forms of liberalism.

51. Peter Applebome, "Black Conservatives: Minority Within a Minority," *New York Times* (July 13, 1991), 1, 13.

52. Ibid., 7; and Carter, *Reflections,* passim. One can only add that the Republican Party may be missing a great opportunity. To capture it, however, the party would have to make some serious effort to appeal to blacks. Instead, as Carter shows, it has spurned the chance, leaving rational black voters little choice but to vote Democratic.

53. For an analysis of Malcolm X and the crisis in the black community out of which his present status arose, see Reed, "Allure of Malcolm X," 203–232. See also West, *Race Matters,* 95–105. On the tendency to downgrade King even in the historiography of the civil rights movement, see George Fredrickson, "What Is the New History?" *Dissent* (Summer 1991), 431.

54. Reed, "Allure of Malcolm X," 219–224. Reed's essay is very stimulating and refreshingly free from cant, but I think he seriously underrates King. He is right to point out that King was not the sum total of the civil rights movement, but to suggest that his legacy was "fictitious" goes too far. Malcolm's achievements in his lifetime were negligible, whereas King's were immense, even if we concede that he had reached his political limit at his death.

55. Ibid., 218.

56. Ibid., 212, 226.

57. Todd Gitlin, "The Rise of 'Identity Politics,'" *Dissent* (Spring 1993), 172–177.

58. Lena Williams, "In a 90's Quest for Black Identity, Intense Doubts and Disagreements," *New York Times* (November 30, 1991), 26. West, *Race Matters,* 11–20. Quote at 14 (italics in the original).

59. Walzer, *What It Means to Be an American,* 19; Arthur Schlesinger, Jr., *The Disuniting of America: Reflections on a Multicultural Society* (New York: Norton, 1992). Schlesinger's polemic has some value, but it is often overheated.

60. Quoted in Williams, "90's Quest for Identity," 26.

61. Orlando Patterson, "Toward a Study of Black America: Notes on the Culture of Racism," *Dissent* (Fall 1989), esp. 482–486.

62. West, *Race Matters,* 23–32. On Thomas and Hill, see Toni Morrison, ed., *Rac-ing Justice, En-Gendering Power* (New York: Pantheon, 1992). The contribution of Federal Judge Leon Higginbotham is particularly useful. See "An Open Letter from a Federal Judicial Colleague," 3–39. Another example of the dangers of an exclusive focus on race can be seen in the second edition of Carmichael and Hamilton; Stokely Carmichael, who changed his name to Kwame Ture, has become fixated on a militant pan-Africanism that has no conceivable relation to the problems of American blacks. See his afterword, 1992, in Ture [Carmichael, pseud.] and Hamilton, *Black Power* (New York: Vintage, 1992), 187–199. Hamilton, in his afterword, clings to his sense of political reality in spite of his manifest discontent with what the past twenty-five years have brought.

63. My treatment owes a general debt to a number of recent studies of feminist theory. See Susan Moller Okin, *Women in Western Political Thought,* 2d ed. (Princeton: Princeton University Press, 1992), esp. 309–340; Jean Bethke Elshtain, *Public Man, Private Woman,* 2d ed. (Princeton: Princeton University Press, 1993); Sondra Farganis, "Feminism and Postmodernism," in *Postmodernism and Social Inquiry,* ed. Andrea Fontana and David Dickins (New York: Guilford Press, 1993), 107–126; Elizabeth Fox-Genovese, *Feminism Without Illusions: A Critique of Individualism* (Chapel Hill: University of North Carolina Press, 1991); and Anne Philips, *Engendering Democracy* (University Park: Pennsylvania State University Press, 1991). The last is particularly notable for the way in which it engages the themes of liberalism, civic republicanism, and social democracy, which are central to my study.

64. Jean Bethke Elshtain, "Feminism," in *Blackwell's Encyclopaedia of Political Thought,* ed. David Miller et al. (Oxford and New York: Blackwell, 1987), 151–153.

65. Farganis, "Feminism and Postmodernism," 102.

66. Susan Moller Okin, *Justice, Gender, and the Family* (New York: Basic Books, 1989), 6.

67. See Fox-Genovese, *Feminism Without Illusions,* 70–72, for a clear example of an attempt to ostracize a prominent feminist historian because of her unconventional position on a major affirmative action suit. Or consider what would happen to the feminist credentials of

a woman who announced herself to be against abortion, no matter how militant her position on other issues.

68. Sara Evans, *Personal Politics: The Roots of Women's Liberation in the Civil Rights Movement* (New York: Vintage, 1980). See also Todd Gitlin, *The Sixties* (New York: Bantam Books, 1987), 362–376.

69. Carole Pateman, "Feminist Critiques of the Public/Private Dichotomy," in *The Disorder of Women* (Stanford: Stanford University Press, 1989), 118–140; Okin, *Women in Western Political Thought*, 314–315; and Farganis, "Feminism and Postmodernism," 6–7. Perhaps the best recent theoretical treatment of this problem is Elizabeth Fox-Genovese, "From Separate Spheres to Dangerous Streets: Postmodernist Feminism and the Problem of Order," *Social Research* (Summer 1993), 235–254.

70. Elshtain, *Public Man, Private Woman*, 124; and Okin, *Women in Western Political Thought*, 200; John Locke, *Two Treatises of Government*, ed. Peter Laslett (New York: Mentor Books, 1965), II, 84. See also Philips, "Introduction," *Feminism and Equality*, ed. Anne Philips (New York: New York University Press, 1987), 12–18. For a less critical interpretation of the relation of Locke to feminist concerns, see Melissa Butler, "Early Liberal Roots of Feminism: John Locke and the Attack on Patriarchy," in *Feminist Interpretations in Political Theory*, ed. Mary Lyndon Shanley and Carole Pateman (University Park: Pennsylvania State University Press, 1991), 74–94.

71. Philips, "Introduction," 14.

72. Elshtain, *Public Man, Private Woman*, 127.

73. Ibid., 217–218.

74. Ibid., 208, 219. Elshtain's critique of Brownmiller should not obscure the importance of the role of the latter in changing prevailing attitudes toward rape.

75. For Elshtain's critique of radical feminism in general, see ibid., 204–228. Among the positions she considers are those of Ti-Grace Atkinson, Mary Daly, Shulamith Firestone, Monique Wittig, and Kate Millett. Elizabeth Fox-Genovese also does much to explain the resistance of so many women to feminist ideas. See "From Separate Spheres to Dangerous Streets," esp. 250–252. See also Wendy Kaminer, "Feminism's Identity Crisis," *Atlantic Monthly* (October 1993), 51–68. Christina Hoff Sommers, *Who Stole Feminism?* (New York: Simon and Schuster, 1994), offers a cornucopia of "politically correct" feminist positions that may provide ammunition to the enemies of feminism, but she gives no real alternative, in spite of the fact that she proclaims her own feminism. Elshtain presents her view of Sommers and of Gloria Steinam in "*Sic Transit Gloria*," New Republic (July 11, 1994), 32–36. Sondra Farganis, *Situating Feminism: From Thought to Action* (Thousand Oaks, Calif.: Sage, 1994), provides a very sophisticated discussion of the tensions within feminism.

76. Farganis, "Feminism and Postmodernism," 6–7. Fox-Genovese is particularly insistent on the last point about the avoidance of communal responsibility. See *Feminism Without Illusions*, 33–54.

77. Carol Gilligan, *In a Different Voice* (Cambridge: Harvard University Press, 1982).

78. Farganis, "Feminism and Postmodernism," 105.

79. Philips, "Introduction," 19.

80. For a survey of humanist liberalism, see Okin, *Women in Western Political Thought*, 319–325; and Susan Moller Okin, "Humanist Liberalism," in *Liberalism and the Moral Life*, ed. Nancy Rosenblum (Cambridge: Harvard University Press, 1989), 39–53. For Okin's fullest statement, see *Justice, Gender, and the Family*. For Fox-Genovese see *Feminism Without Illusions*, 256.

81. Fox-Genovese, *Feminism Without Illusions*, 75–80.

82. See Walzer, *Spheres of Justice*, 165–183, for an important discussion of compensation for hard, dirty work as a problem in distributive justice.

83. Fox-Genovese, *Feminism Without Illusions*, 79. Though Fox-Genovese has been a sharp critic of liberalism because of its ties to individualism, it seems to me that her argument is quite compatible with Okin's position, though a world without gender leaves Fox-Genovese "cold" (52).

84. Okin, *Women in Western Political Thought,* 326.

85. Fox-Genovese, *Feminism Without Illusions,* passim, esp. 18–22.

86. Philips, *Engendering Democracy,* 58. Cf. 155.

87. Farganis, "Feminism and Postmodernism," 117.

88. On the importance of distinguishing between liberal theory and liberal practice, see Stephen Holmes, *The Anatomy of Antiliberalism* (Cambridge: Harvard University Press, 1993).

89. Farganis, "Feminism and Postmodernism," 120. Farganis draws on Iris Marion Young, *Justice and the Politics of Difference* (Princeton: Princeton University Press, 1990), 100, 157–158.

90. Stephen K. White, *Political Theory and Postmodernism* (Cambridge: Cambridge University Press, 1991), esp. 1–12. I have relied in what follows on White's excellent and sober summary; the latter quality is not always found in postmodernist circles. For an excellent selection of texts and a useful introduction, see James Farganis, *Readings in Social Theory: The Classic Tradition to Postmodernism* (New York: McGraw-Hill, 1993), 363–399.

91. White, *Political Theory and Postmodernism,* 4–5.

92. Ibid., 6.

93. Ibid., 7–8.

94. Ibid., 8–10.

95. Ibid., 10–12.

96. Farganis, "Feminism and Postmodernism," 32.

97. See Linda J. Nicholson, ed., *Feminism/Postmodernism* (New York: Routledge, 1990). For a standard treatment, see Nancy Fraser and Nicholson, "Social Criticism Without Philosophy: An Encounter Between Feminism and Postmodernism," in ibid., 19–38. See also Seyla Benhabib, "Feminism and the Question of Postmodernism," in *Situating the Self* (New York: Routledge, 1992), 203–241.

98. Farganis, "Feminism and Postmodernism," 107.

99. Ibid., 109.

100. Ronald Beiner, *What's the Matter with Liberalism?* (Berkeley: University of California Press, 1992), 18. More generally see Holmes, *Anatomy of Antiliberalism,* 190–197.

101. Ann Scales, quoted in Jean Bethke Elshtain, "Trial by Fury," *New Republic* (September 8, 1993), 32.

102. Ibid., 32–33; and Wilson Carey McWilliams, personal communication to author.

103. Benhabib, "Feminism and the Question of Postmodernism," 228–230; and Farganis, "Feminism and Postmodernism," 121–122.

104. Farganis, "Feminism and Postmodernism," 122.

105. Fox-Genovese, "From Separate Spheres to Dangerous Streets," 240, 240–245.

106. Ibid., 253.

107. Ibid., 247–248.

108. Walzer, *What It Means to Be an American,* esp. 23–49. See also Benjamin Barber's paper "To Be an American," in his book *An Aristocracy of Everyone: The Politics of Education and the Future America* (New York: Ballantine, 1992), 40–77; and Nathan Glazer and Daniel Patrick Moynihan, *Beyond the Melting Pot* (Cambridge: MIT Press, 1963).

109. Barber, *Aristocracy of Everyone,* 41.

110. John Higham, "Multiculturalism and Universalism: A History and a Critique," *American Quarterly* (June 1993), 197. Higham's article is part of a stimulating symposium, with commentaries on his contribution by Gerald Early, Gary Gerstle, Nancy A. Hewitt, Vicki L. Ruiz, and a reply by Higham. See 195–256.

111. Ibid., 195–196.

112. Charles Taylor, "The Politics of Recognition," in *Multiculturalism and "the Politics of Recognition,"* ed. Amy Gutmann (Princeton: Princeton University Press, 1992), 25, 27.

113. William E. Connolly, *Identity/Difference: Democratic Negotiations of Political Paradox* (Ithaca: Cornell University Press, 1991), 67.

114. Ibid., 73–74.

115. George Kateb, *The Inner Ocean: Individualism and Democratic Culture* (Ithaca: Cornell University Press, 1992), 238. Connolly is much more sympathetic to Kateb's version

of individualism than to that of other liberals, arguing that it provides a useful ethic, though still with a defective politics. See Connolly, *Identity/Difference*, 75–87. I have my own disagreements with Kateb's important book, but I wish to defer them until Chapter 15.

116. Kateb, *Inner Ocean*, 32. For a more recent discussion, see George Kateb, "Notes on Pluralism," *Social Research* (Fall 1994), 511–538.

117. Sheldon S. Wolin, "Democracy, Difference, and Recognition," *Political Theory* (August 1993), 465. Though I have some disagreements with it, I think it is a deeply penetrating article.

118. Ibid., 467.

119. Ibid., 471–472; quote on 472.

120. Ibid., 470.

121. Ibid., 471.

122. Ibid., 466, 481. Note Robert A. Dahl's observation that from a Tocquevillian point of view, the existence of equality is now as problematic as that of liberty. Dahl, A *Preface to Economic Democracy* (Berkeley: University of California Press, 1985), 51. Wolin's article is notable since he seems to concede so much to liberalism after thirty-five years as one of its most profound critics. A fuller assessment of his work must be deferred until Chapter 16. For an argument similar to Wolin's, though couched in rebarbitive postmodernist jargon, see Wendy Brown, "Wounded Attachments," *Political Theory* (August 1993), 390–410.

123. See esp. Higham, "Multiculturalism and Universalism."

124. Walzer, *What It Means to Be an American*, 18.

125. John Burt, "Tyranny and Faction in the Federalist Papers," *Raritan* (Fall 1993), 56–57. This paragraph draws extensively on Burt's brilliant article.

126. Rogers Smith, "Beyond Tocqueville, Myrdal, and Hartz: The Multiple Traditions in America," *American Political Science Review* (September 1993), 549–566. Though writing in an entirely different context, William Ian Miller uses "official" in much the same sense I do here. See *Humiliation* (Ithaca: Cornell University Press, 1993), 209: "By 'official' I mean to indicate a position that claims a certain privilege for itself independent of whether in fact that position represents an accurate description of motive or behavior. The official claims the ground of legitimacy often backed by public institutions. Its style is often aspirational, sometimes hortatory; it also claims for itself the realm of the moral as that is defined in the society's dominant institutions. Official discourse can be complacent in tone, the kind of thing we understand as represented by the paying of lip service. Yet it would be wrong to think of official as a kind of sham. The official represents those kinds of public statements in which a culture images itself, and as such it bears no small role in reproducing the culture that produces such official discourses."

127. Walzer, *What It Means to Be an American*, 18. I myself would prefer to emphasize a certain partial assimilation while still stressing that the old melting pot metaphor is clearly outmoded. To be Americanized is to be assimilated in some sense. For Walzer's more recent reflections on these themes, see Michael Walzer, "Multiculturalism and Individualism," *Dissent* (Spring 1984), 185–191.

128. Taylor, "The Politics of Recognition," 64–73 and passim. For a postmodernist critique of Taylor, see Thomas L. Dumm, "Strangers and Liberals," *Political Theory* (February 1994), 167–175.

129. Catharine MacKinnon, *Only Words* (Cambridge: Harvard University Press, 1993), 71.

130. This is the title of a collection of essays deeply influenced by MacKinnon. See Mari J. Matsuda et al., *Words That Wound: Critical Race Theory, Assaultive Speech and the First Amendment* (Boulder: Westview Press, 1993).

131. MacKinnon, *Only Words*, 13.

132. Henry Louis Gates, Jr., "Let Them Talk," *New Republic* (September 20 and 27, 1993), 48. Gates's discussion of Matsuda et al., *Words That Wound*, and, inter alia, of MacKinnon is a brilliant analysis that shows, among other things, that law is too important to be left to lawyers. See also Ruth Rosen, "Not Pornography!" *Dissent* (Summer 1994),

343–345, for another discussion of how the furor over pornography diverts feminists from more pressing social issues such as child care, family leave, and domestic violence, extending to transgender considerations such as higher minimum wages and nonpunitive welfare.

133. Gates, "Let Them Talk," 45, 44.

134. For an extensively documented illustration of this phenomenon, see Lee Rainwater, ed., *The Moynihan Report and the Politics of Controversy* (Cambridge: MIT Press, 1967).

135. Jonathan Rauch, *Kindly Inquisitors: The New Attacks on Free Thought* (Chicago: University of Chicago Press, 1993), is a brilliant polemic in defense of the critical skepticism at the heart of liberal free speech theory.

136. Cass R. Sunstein, *Democracy and the Problem of Free Speech* (New York: Free Press, 1993), 215. It should be noted that Sunstein favors moderate censorship of pornography, even though in that case we might have to accept overbroad regulation. See 216–217.

137. Gates, "Let Them Talk," 42.

138. For a mainstream liberal critique of MacKinnon's *Only Words*, see Ronald Dworkin, "Women and Pornography," *New York Review of Books* (October 21, 1993), 36–42; for a libertarian view, see Richard Posner, "Obsession," *New Republic* (October 18, 1993), 36; for a left-liberal position, see Carlin Romano, "Between the Notion and the Act," *Nation* (November 15, 1993), 563–570. For a critique that may be somewhat more surprising, see the conservative view by George Will, "PC Has No Sense of the Ridiculous," *Binghamton Press and Sun-Bulletin* (October 28, 1993), 8A. For another interesting perspective on the legal and ideological aspects of censorship, see Kathleen Sullivan, "The First Amendment Wars," *New Republic* (September 28, 1992), 35–40.

139. Stanley Fish, *There's No Such Thing as Free Speech: And It's a Good Thing Too* (New York: Oxford University Press, 1993); for Sunstein see *Democracy and the Problem of Free Speech*. Fish, MacKinnon, and Sunstein were jointly reviewed in Calvin Woodward, "Speak No Evil," *New York Times Book Review* (January 2, 1994), 11–12.

140. My thinking on this point has been advanced by correspondence with Wilson Carey McWilliams.

Chapter 14

1. Samuel P. Huntington, "Conservatism as an Ideology," *American Political Science Review* (June 1957), 454–456 and passim.

2. Russell Kirk, *The Conservative Mind* (Chicago: Gateway Books, 1954), 7–8.

3. Huntington, "Conservatism as an Ideology," 456.

4. Joseph A. Schumpeter, *Capitalism, Socialism, and Democracy,* 3d ed. (New York: Harper, 1950), 83, 81–86.

5. For a discussion and a fuller bibliography, see James P. Young, *The Politics of Affluence* (San Francisco: Chandler, 1968), 85–144. For a more extensive treatment, see M. Morton Auerbach, *The Conservative Illusion* (New York: Columbia University Press, 1959). For a more general discussion of the whole tradition, see Clinton Rossiter, *Conservatism in America: The Thankless Persuasion,* 2d ed. (New York: Vintage Books, 1962).

6. J. David Hoeveler, Jr., *Watch on the Right: Conservative Intellectuals in the Reagan Era* (Madison: University of Wisconsin Press, 1991), 29. This is a good source on Buckley as well as on the publicists among contemporary conservatives. It is less useful on issues of theory or philosophy. It is interesting to note that many of the *National Review* stalwarts, such as Frank Meyer, James Burnham, and Whittaker Chambers, were ex-Communists who attacked their former faith with all the fury of apostates. On this see John P. Diggins, *Up from Communism* (New York: Harper, 1977).

7. Hoeveler, *Watch on the Right,* 24.

8. Donald Devine, quoted in E. J. Dionne, Jr., *Why Americans Hate Politics* (New York: Simon and Schuster, 1991), 161.

9. The tensions emerged early and are well described in ibid., 157–169. See also Young, *Politics of Affluence.*

10. Dionne, *Why Americans Hate Politics,* 157.

11. Ibid., 178. It is also worth noting that among the authors of Goldwater's controversial acceptance speech was the well-known Lincoln scholar and Straussian political philosopher Harry Jaffa. For more on the Straussian position, see later in Chapter 14.

12. Harvey Mansfield, Jr., "The 1980 Election: Toward Constitutional Democracy?" in *America's Constitutional Soul* (Baltimore: Johns Hopkins University Press, 1991), 23. On these forces, Dionne's *Why Americans Hate Politics* is very useful. Dionne, a journalist, is unusually sensitive to the interplay between social moods, ideologies, and politics. Steve Fraser and Gary Gerstle, eds., *The Rise and Fall of the New Deal Order* (Princeton: Princeton University Press, 1989), is also useful. For a series of studies of presidential elections beginning in 1976, see the volumes produced by a team of Rutgers political scientists. Each was published early in the year following the election: Thus Gerald Pomper et al., *The Election of 1976* (Chatham, N.J.: Chatham House, 1977), et seq. Mansfield gives his own interpretation of U.S. congressional and presidential elections from 1980 to 1988 in *America's Constitutional Soul,* 21–69. For the 1992 election, see also Mansfield, "Change and Bill Clinton," *Times Literary Supplement* (London) (November 13, 1992), 14–16. Political theorist Wilson Carey McWilliams has collected his contributions to the Pomper series and added an introduction plus a comment on the 1994 congressional election: McWilliams, *The Politics of Disappointment* (Chatham, N.J.: Chatham House, 1995).

13. Mansfield, *America's Constitutional Soul,* 77.

14. I have borrowed this typology from Harvey Mansfield, though I embellished it somewhat. See "Pride Versus Interest in American Conservatism," in *America's Constitutional Soul,* 73–83. Mansfield's typology is useful both for its merits and because he himself is a conservative. He also achieves a certain distance from the movement and offers many criticisms with which I agree, though in the end we are politically and theoretically far apart. Another useful typology that overlaps Mansfield's and mine is David Spitz, "How New Are the New Conservatives?" in *The Real World of Liberalism* (Chicago: University of Chicago Press, 1982), 198–212.

15. Mansfield, "Pride Versus Interest," 79–80.

16. Ibid., 76–77. Quotes on 76.

17. Ibid., 77.

18. Friedrich Hayek, *The Road to Serfdom* (Chicago: University of Chicago Press, [1944] 1957), 35. My remarks on Hayek draw on a fuller treatment in my *Politics of Affluence,* 126–137. I would now not fully endorse the theory of democracy I followed in that study, though I stand by my critique of Hayek. Today Milton Friedman is much better known than his Chicago predecessor, but it seems to me that Hayek had a much finer mind as a social theorist. I am unable to judge their technical qualities as economists and note only that both are Nobel laureates. For Friedman see his *Capitalism and Freedom* (Chicago: Phoenix Books, 1963).

19. Hayek, *Road to Serfdom,* 71.

20. Karl Polanyi, *The Great Transformation* (Boston: Beacon Press, [1944] 1957).

21. Robert Nozick, *Anarchy, State, and Utopia* (New York: Basic Books, 1974), ix.

22. George Kateb, "The Night Watchman State," *American Scholar* (Winter 1975–1976), 819; and Nozick, *Anarchy, State, and Utopia,* 163.

23. Nozick, *Anarchy, State, and Utopia,* 163, 169.

24. Ibid., 3–4.

25. Ibid., 6–9.

26. Kateb, "Night Watchman State," 820.

27. Benjamin Barber gives a fine analysis of the economistic, apolitical nature of Nozick's theory. See *The Conquest of Politics* (Princeton: Princeton University Press, 1988), 91–119.

28. Ibid., 115.

29. Kateb, "Night Watchman State," 822.

30. Ibid., 825. Another potent critique of Nozick is David Spitz, "Justice for Sale: The Justice of Property vs. the Property of Justice," in *Real World of Liberalism*, 139–162.

31. Mansfield, "Pride Versus Interest," 77.

32. William Riker, *Liberalism Versus Populism* (Prospect Heights, Ill.: Waveland Press, 1982); and Jon Elster, *Making Sense of Marx* (Cambridge: Cambridge University Press, 1985). For a quizzical commentary on Elster's quixotic effort to process Marx through the filter of methodological individualism and rational choice theory, see Michael Walzer, "What's Left of Marx?" *New York Review of Books* (November 21, 1985), 43–46.

33. Theodore J. Lowi, "The State in Political Science: How We Became What We Study," *American Political Science Review* (March 1992), 3. Lowi's views are controversial. See the sharp exchange between Lowi and Herbert Simon, *PS: Political Science and Politics* (March 1993), 49–52. Readers of this debate should understand that Lowi and Simon are in essential agreement about the limitations of rational choice theory. They disagree mainly over Simon's relation to its development.

34. Joan Robinson, quoted in Lowi, "The State in Political Science," 5.

35. Ibid.

36. Daniel Bell, *The Coming of Post-Industrial Society*, 2d ed. (New York: Basic Books, 1976), 297. For a general treatment, see 269–298. I have drawn here on James P. Young, "The Prophet of Post-Industrialism v. the Politics of Nostalgia," *Polity* (Winter 1975), 272.

37. Bell, *Coming of Post-Industrial Society*, 367.

38. Mansfield, "Pride Versus Interest," 77. For Mansfield's other animadversions on economics, see "The 1982 Congressional Election," and on public choice theory, "Social Science and the Constitution," in *America's Constitutional Soul*, 43–45 and 157–162 respectively.

39. Mansfield, "Pride Versus Interest," 77. It might be noted that both Hayek and Friedman insisted that they were not conservatives, but true liberals who had been betrayed by the statist orientation of modern liberalism. Conrad P. Waligorski, *The Political Theory of Conservative Economists* (Lawrence: University Press of Kansas, 1990), is a very useful study that focuses on Hayek, Friedman, and James Buchanan. Other notable figures are also discussed. Although the men in question could be said to form a school, Waligorski pointed out that they were not in complete agreement—not even on the value of the market.

40. Michael Walzer, "Nervous Liberals," in *Radical Principles* (New York: Basic Books, 1980), 92–106. Other important treatments of this group are Sheldon S. Wolin, "The New Conservatives," *New York Review of Books* (February 3, 1976), 6–11; Peter Steinfels, *The Neo-Conservatives: The Men Who Are Changing American Politics* (New York: Simon and Schuster, 1979); and Louis A. Coser and Irving Howe, eds., *The New Conservatives: A Critique from the Left*, rev. ed. (New York: Meridian Books, 1977).

41. The editor of *Commentary* was Norman Podhoretz, whose memoir of the move from left liberal to moderate conservative to the farther right was offered, not without bias, but still informatively, in Podhoretz, *Breaking Ranks* (New York: Harper and Row, 1979).

42. Mansfield, "Pride Versus Interest," 80.

43. Nathan Glazer, *The Limits of Social Policy* (Cambridge: Harvard University Press, 1988), 1–17. (This chapter was originally published as an essay in 1971.) See also Charles Murray, *Losing Ground* (New York: Basic Books, 1984). Glazer also staked out a strong position against affirmative action in *Affirmative Discrimination* (Cambridge: Harvard University Press, 1987).

44. Albert O. Hirschman, *The Rhetoric of Reaction: Perversity, Futility, Jeopardy* (Cambridge: Harvard University Press, 1991), 7, 33–35.

45. Paul Starr, "The Price of Pessimism," *New Republic* (January 23, 1989), 32–35.

46. John Schwartz, *America's Hidden Success* (New York: Norton, 1982).

47. James Q. Wilson, *On Character* (Washington, D.C.: American Enterprise Institute, 1991), 11–13, quote at 12–13.

48. Ibid., 5, 108.

49. For the most sweeping and philosophically grounded of Wilson's statements to date, see James Q. Wilson, *The Moral Sense* (New York: Free Press, 1993). See also Wilson, "The Moral Sense," *American Political Science Review* (March 1993), 1–11.

50. Wilson, *On Character,* 139–148.

51. Irving Kristol's major essays are collected in three volumes: *On the Democratic Idea in America* (New York: Basic Books, 1982), *Two Cheers for Capitalism* (New York: Basic Books, 1978), and *Reflections of a Neoconservative* (New York: Basic Books, 1983). Two good general commentaries on Kristol's work are Hoeveler, *Watch on the Right,* 81–114; and Steinfels, *The Neo-Conservatives,* 81–107.

52. Kristol, *Two Cheers,* x-xii. Quote at xi.

53. Ibid., 257–259.

54. Ibid., 259–262.

55. Ibid., 263–265.

56. Ibid., 270. This point reflects the influence of Leo Strauss, about whom more later in Chapter 14.

57. Kristol, "An Obituary for an Idea," in *Reflections,* 114.

58. Ibid., 116.

59. Daniel Bell, *The Cultural Contradictions of Capitalism,* with new foreword (New York: Basic Books, 1978). On culture see xxx–xxxi. For a good discussion of Bell, see Steinfels, *The Neo-Conservatives,* 161–187.

60. On the technoeconomic order, see Daniel Bell, *The Coming of Post-Industrial Society,* with new introduction (New York: Basic Books, 1976). For my reflections on this study, see Young, "Prophet of Post-Industrialism v. the Politics of Nostalgia," 269–285.

61. Bell, *Cultural Contradictions,* 54–76.

62. Ibid., 76.

63. Ibid., 55.

64. Ibid., 71.

65. Ibid., xi.

66. Kristol published two lists of neoconservative principles, one more oriented to public policy and the other more theoretical. Since they are not inconsistent, I have woven them together. See I. Kristol, "What Is a 'Neo-Conservative'?" *Newsweek* (January 19, 1976), and "Confessions of a True, Self-Confessed—Perhaps the Only—Neoconservative," in *Reflections,* 73–77. All quotes are from these two sources. *Reflections* includes a very harsh critique of Steinfels. For a quite different view of Steinfels, see Walzer, "Nervous Liberals."

67. I. Kristol, "My Cold War," *National Interest* (Spring 1993), 143. It is interesting and disturbing to read Kristol's comments on the common soldiers with whom he served during World War II. Many, he told us, were "thugs or near-thugs," which persuaded Kristol that democratic socialism was a fantasy. His attitude does not fit with democracy.

68. Samuel P. Huntington, "The Democratic Distemper," in *The American Commonwealth: 1976* (New York: Basic Books, 1976), 9–38. Huntington generalizes this article into a full-scale interpretation of U.S. history and politics in *American Politics: The Promise of Disharmony* (Cambridge: Harvard University Press, 1981).

69. Huntington, "Democratic Distemper," 9, 11.

70. Ibid., 15.

71. Ibid., 23.

72. Ibid., 37, 35–38.

73. Huntington, *American Politics,* 14–15, 154.

74. Ibid., 39.

75. These responses are neatly summarized in a table: ibid., 64.

76. Ibid., 64–65.

77. These are the most important features of creedal passion for the purposes of this discussion. For a fuller list, see ibid., 86–87.

78. Samuel H. Beer, "The Democratic Temper," *New Republic* (November 11, 1981), 30–33. Much of this paragraph is based on Beer's discussion.

79. Huntington, *American Politics*, 236–262.

80. William Nelson, "Huntington on Democratic Politics," *Philosophy and Public Affairs* (Winter 1984), 92.

81. Huntington, *The Soldier and the State* (Cambridge: Harvard University Press, 1957), 464–466.

82. Huntington, *American Politics*, 129. For a good commentary on Huntington's antidemocratic leanings, see John Wallach, "Fearful Establishment," *democracy* (Winter 1983), 117–128.

83. Dionne, *Why Americans Hate Politics*, 212–219. For a much harsher view of fundamentalism in American life, see Richard Hofstadter, *Anti-Intellectualism in American Life* (New York: Knopf, 1963), 117–141. For a less jaundiced view, see the thoughtful, quirky, and unsystematic book by Garry Wills, *Under God: Religion and American Politics* (New York: Simon and Schuster, 1990). See also Michael Lienesch, *Redeeming America: Party and Politics in the New Christian Right* (Chapel Hill: University of North Carolina Press, 1993).

84. Dionne, *Why Americans Hate Politics*, 211.

85. Mansfield, "Pride Versus Interest," 78–79.

86. Daniel Bell, "The Revolt Against Modernity," *Public Interest* (Fall 1985), 55. For a discussion by Hofstadter with the same title, see *Anti-Intellectualism*, 117–143.

87. For the distinction between interest and cultural politics, see Richard Hofstadter, "Pseudo-Conservatism Revisited—1965," in *The Paranoid Style in American Politics* (New York: Knopf, 1965), 66–67 and vii–xiv. On the importance of fundamentalists in the Radical Right of the 1960s, see 72–82. See also Bell, "Revolt Against Modernity," 56.

88. See Michael Walzer, "Social Origins of Conservative Politics," in *Radical Principles*, 84–88. For a full-scale analysis of voting patterns, see Michael Paul Rogin, *The Intellectuals and McCarthy* (Cambridge: MIT Press, 1967). Note that Walzer wrote his essay before Hofstadter's subtle revision of his own position was published. Note also that Walzer too found roots of the Goldwater phenomenon in the social conditions of modernity.

89. James Davison Hunter, *Culture Wars: The Struggle to Define America* (New York: Basic Books, 1991).

90. Alan Wolfe, "Politics by Other Means," *New Republic* (November 11, 1991), 39.

91. Hunter, *Culture Wars*, 108–118.

92. Ibid., 63.

93. Ibid., 49.

94. Wolfe, "Politics by Other Means," 42.

95. Ibid., 40.

96. Ibid., 41.

97. Wilson Carey McWilliams, "The Meaning of the Election," in Gerald Pomper et al., *The Election of 1992* (Chatham, N.J.: Chatham House, 1993), 207. McWilliams was the source of the Baker quote. For further comments on the limits of permissiveness from the "near" Left, see Walzer, "Introduction," *Radical Principles*, 6–7.

98. Schumpeter, *Capitalism, Socialism, and Democracy*, 81–86.

99. Two collections of papers by Strauss serve as the best introduction to his outlook: Leo Strauss, *Political Philosophy: Six Essays*, ed. Hilail Gilden (Indianapolis: Pegasus Books, 1975), and *The Rebirth of Classical Political Rationalism*, ed. Thomas L. Pangle (Chicago: University of Chicago Press, 1989). See also Strauss, *Studies in Platonic Political Philosophy*, ed. Thomas L. Pangle (Chicago: University of Chicago Press, 1983). Other important studies include Strauss, *The Political Philosophy of Hobbes*, trans. Elsa Sinclair (Chicago: University of Chicago Press, [1936] 1963), *Natural Right and History* (Chicago: University of Chicago Press, 1953), *Thoughts on Machiavelli* (Glencoe, Ill.: Free Press, 1958), *The City and Man* (New York: Rand McNally, 1964), *Liberalism Ancient and Modern* (Ithaca: Cornell University Press, 1968), and *On Tyranny*, ed. Victor Gourevitch and Michael Roth, rev. and expanded (New York: Free Press, 1991). The last-named edition is of particular interest because it contains a commentary on the book by Strauss's friend and theoretical adversary Alexandre Kojeve as well as a response to Kojeve by Strauss and the extended correspondence between

the two. There is also a very large, collectively written *History of Political Philosophy,* ed. Strauss and Joseph Cropsey, 3d ed. (Chicago: University of Chicago Press, 1987). This posthumous edition is notable because it contains a chapter on Strauss: Nathan Tarcov and Thomas Pangle, "Epilogue: Leo Strauss and the History of Political Philosophy," 907–938. The most important studies of the United States by students and followers of Strauss include Harvey Mansfield, Jr., *Taming the Prince* (New York: Free Press, 1989), *The Spirit of Liberalism* (Cambridge: Harvard University Press, 1978), and *America's Constitutional Soul;* Ralph Lerner, *The Thinking Revolutionary* (Ithaca: Cornell University Press, 1987); Martin Diamond, *As Far as Republican Principles Will Admit,* ed. William A. Schambra (Washington: American Enterprise Institute, 1992); Marvin Zetterbaum, *Tocqueville and the Problem of Democracy* (Stanford: Stanford University Press, 1968); Harry V. Jaffa, *Crisis of the House Divided* (New York: Doubleday, 1959) and *Equality and Liberty* (New York: Oxford University Press, 1965); Walter F. Berns, *Freedom, Virtue, and the First Amendment* (Chicago: Gateway Books, 1965) and *Taking the Constitution Seriously* (New York: Simon and Schuster, 1987); David F. Epstein, *The Political Theory of the Federalist* (Chicago: University of Chicago Press, 1984); Herbert J. Storing, *What the Anti-Federalists Were For* (Chicago: University of Chicago Press, 1981); Morton J. Frisch and Richard G. Stevens, *American Political Thought,* 2d ed. (Itasca, Ill.: F. E. Peacock, 1983); Thomas L. Pangle, *The Spirit of Modern Republicanism* (Chicago: University of Chicago Press, 1988); Lorraine Smith Pangle and Thomas L. Pangle, *The Learning of Liberty* (Lawrence: University Press of Kansas, 1993); Allan Bloom, *The Closing of the American Mind* (New York: Simon and Schuster, 1987), and Bloom, ed., *Confronting the Constitution* (Washington: American Enterprise Institute, 1990); and Joseph Cropsey, *Political Philosophy and the Issues of Politics* (Chicago: University of Chicago Press, 1977). The Straussians have begun to take on the characteristics of an ideological movement, replete with factional in-fighting, a phenomenon that Strauss, who despised ideology, would have abhorred. For a sense of the conflicts, see Harry Jaffa, "Crisis of the Strauss Divided," *Social Research* (Autumn 1987), 579–603.

100. For commentaries favorable to Strauss, see Tarcov and Pangle, "Epilogue"; Pangle, "Introduction," *Studies in Platonic Political Philosophy,* 1–26, and Editor's Introduction in Strauss, *Rebirth of Classical Political Rationalism,* vii–xxxviii; Walter F. Berns et al., "The Achievement of Leo Strauss," *National Review* (December 7, 1973), 1347–1357; Allan Bloom, "Leo Strauss," in *Giants and Dwarfs* (New York: Simon and Schuster, 1990), 235–255; Nathan Tarcov, "Philosophy and History: Tradition and Interpretation in the Work of Leo Strauss," *Polity* (Fall 1983); Victor Gourevitch, "Philosophy and Politics I," *Review of Metaphysics* (September 1968), 58–84, and "Philosophy and Politics II," *Review of Metaphysics* (December 1968), 281–328; and Robert P. Pippin, "The Modern World of Leo Strauss," *Political Theory* (August 1992), 448–472.

The most extended account of Strauss, Shadia B. Drury, *The Political Ideas of Leo Strauss* (New York: St. Martin's, 1988), is highly critical. It has an invaluable annotated bibliography. See also an article by Drury that was followed by two commentaries: Drury, "Leo Strauss's Classic Natural Right Teaching," H. Jaffa, "Dear Professor Drury," and Fred Dallmayr, "Politics Against Philosophy: Strauss and Drury," *Political Theory* (August 1987), 299–337. See also M. F. Burnyeat, "Sphinx Without a Secret," *New York Review of Books* (May 30, 1985), 30–41; Stephen Holmes, *The Anatomy of Antiliberalism* (Cambridge: Harvard University Press, 1993), 61–87; Charles Larmore, "The Secrets of Philosophy," *New Republic* (July 3, 1989), 30–35; John G. Gunnell, "The Myth of the Tradition," *American Political Science Review* (March 1978), 122–134, and "Political Theory and Politics: The Case of Leo Strauss," *Political Theory* (August 1985), 338–361; Gordon S. Wood, "The Fundamentalists and the Constitution," *New York Review of Books* (February 18, 1988), 33–40; John H. Schaar and Sheldon S. Wolin, "*Essays on the Scientific Study of Politics:* A Critique," *American Political Science Review* (March 1963), 125–150 (includes responses by Strauss and his coauthors). On Bloom's *Closing of the American Mind,* see Richard Rorty, "That Old-Time Philosophy," and the reply by H. Mansfield, "Democracy and the Great Books," *New Republic* (April 4, 1988),

28–37. The reviews of Bloom have been collected in Robert L. Stone, ed., *Essays on the Closing of the American Mind* (Chicago: Chicago Review Press, 1989). This note is limited to studies that look at Strauss's work as a whole. For studies of particular items, see the bibliography and notes in Drury, *Political Ideas of Strauss.*

101. Strauss, "What Is Political Philosophy?" in Six Essays, 21–22. For Strauss's estimate of Weber and Heidegger, see Strauss, "An Introduction to Heideggerian Existentialism, in *Rebirth of Classical Political Rationalism,* 27–32. Nevertheless, Strauss remained deeply indebted to Heidegger. See Holmes, *Anatomy of Antiliberalism,* 76–77. For some autobiographical and historical reflections on Weimar, see Strauss, "Preface to Spinoza's Critique of Religion," in *Liberalism Ancient and Modern,* esp. 224–231.

102. Strauss, "What Is Political Philosophy?" 40–41.

103. Ibid., 49.

104. Strauss, *Political Philosophy of Hobbes,* 156. Quote on 156. This passage is one of the very rare instances in which Strauss cited a modern authority, Sir Ernest Barker, to support a position. See also Strauss, *Natural Right and History,* 166–202.

105. Strauss, "What Is Political Philosophy?" 50. I do not comment here on the adequacy of Strauss's historical observations. In Chapter 2, I attacked his reading of Locke. For Strauss on Locke, see *Natural Right and History,* 202–251.

106. For an important discussion of this problem, see Stephen Salkever, "Virtue, Obligation, and Politics," *American Political Science Review* (March 1974), 78–92. Salkever was notable among students of Strauss for his willingness to take other theoretical views into account. See also Pippin, "Modern World of Strauss"; and Stephen Taylor Holmes, "Aristippus in and out of Athens," *American Political Science Review* (March 1979), 113–128, and the exchange between James H. Nichols, Jr., and Holmes, which followed, 129–138.

107. Strauss, "What Is Political Philosophy?" 52.

108. Ibid., 51–56. Quotes on 52, 53, 56.

109. Strauss, "Three Waves of Modernity," in *Six Essays,* 94–97.

110. Ibid., 98.

111. Ibid. In *Political Ideas of Strauss,* Drury attempts to show that Strauss's greatest intellectual debt was to Nietzsche. Her argument is deeply interesting and I think she might be right, but for my purposes it is enough to stay on the surface and consider Strauss's exoteric teaching, which is influential in its own right.

112. Strauss, *City and Man,* 1.

113. Ibid., 11.

114. Ibid., 12, 3.

115. Strauss, *Natural Right and History,* 118, 135. On this general topic, see also "On Natural Law," in Strauss, *Studies in Platonic Political Philosophy,* 137–146.

116. Strauss, *Natural Right and History,* 142–143.

117. Ibid., 142. I leave aside the question whether the best regime is attainable. That question is not central here, and Strauss seemed to have changed his mind over time.

118. Drury, *Political Ideas of Strauss,* 97–98.

119. Strauss, *Natural Right and History,* 157.

120. Ibid., 157–158.

121. Ibid., 162.

122. Strauss, *Liberalism Ancient and Modern,* 28–29, iv.

123. Ibid., 4.

124. Ibid., 4–5.

125. The best-known book in the Straussian mode on this theme is Allan Bloom's surprising best-seller, *Closing of the American Mind.* One wonders whether this book became so popular because of its exposition of a Straussian theory of education and the history of political theory, or if people were simply drawn to its denunciation of contemporary youth culture, from rock to sexual mores.

126. Strauss, *Liberalism Ancient and Modern,* 24.

127. I have drawn this characterization of modern liberalism from Strauss's article, "The Liberalism of Classical Political Philosophy," in *Liberalism Ancient and Modern*, 26–64. This article is a scathing critique of Eric Havelock, *The Liberal Temper in Greek Politics* (New Haven: Yale University Press, 1957).

128. Strauss, *Liberalism Ancient and Modern*, 29, 64. The internal quote is from Havelock, *Liberal Temper*.

129. Cropsey, "The United States as Regime and the Sources of the American Way of Life," in *Political Philosophy and the Issues of Politics*, 9, 5, 7.

130. Ibid., 15.

131. The fullest analysis is Pangle, *Spirit of Republicanism*, 25–39 and passim.

132. Strauss, *Liberalism Ancient and Modern*, 16; Strauss, *Natural Right and History*, 1.

133. Strauss, *Liberalism Ancient and Modern*, 16–18.

134. The most extensive recent Straussian treatment of Locke is Pangle, *Spirit of Republicanism;* it is, for the most part, similarly hostile.

135. Cropsey, "On the Relation of Political Science and Economics," in *Political Philosophy and the Issues of Politics*, 32–43, quote at 43. See also the devastating critique of welfare economics in Cropsey, "What Is Welfare Economics?" in ibid., 19–31.

136. Cropsey, "What Is Welfare Economics?" 29.

137. Cropsey, "United States as Regime," 9–10. In his comments on Locke, which on the whole are typically Straussian, T. Pangle suggests the possibility of a high degree of government regulation of property and even of public ownership. This is consistent with my discussion of Locke in Chapter 2. See Pangle, *Spirit of Republicanism*, 169. In his review of Pangle, Richard Ashcraft suggests that here and elsewhere there is an esoteric text underlying the overt conservative message of the book. See Ashcraft, *Political Theory* (February 1990), 159–162.

138. Quoted by William Schambra, "Editor's Introduction," in Diamond, *Republican Principles*, 6.

139. Diamond, "Ethics and Politics the American Way," in ibid., 355.

140. Ibid.

141. Ibid., 259–360.

142. Mansfield, *America's Constitutional Soul,* ix; Walter Berns, "Does the Constitution 'Secure These Rights'?" in *How Democratic Is the Constitution?* ed. Robert A. Goldwin and William Schambra (Washington: American Enterprise Institute, 1980), 59.

143. Quoted by Schambra, in "Editor's Introduction," in Diamond, *Republican Principles*, 4.

144. Diamond, "Democracy and *The Federalist:* A Reconsideration of the Framers' Intent," in ibid., 20. This article, originally published in 1959, may well be the most frequently cited article in the literature of American political thought. Although I do not necessarily agree with its politics, I do believe its analysis of *The Federalist* is essentially correct. My treatment will be brief here because my discussion of constitutional theory in Chapter 4 relied on it heavily. I use it here as an example of the Straussian approach to democracy. There is a very interesting critique of Diamond's reading of *The Federalist* in Alan Gibson, "The Commercial Republic and the Pluralist Critique of Marxism: An Analysis of Martin Diamond's Interpretation of *Federalist* 10," *Polity* (Summer 1993), 497–528. This is followed by Jeffrey Leigh Sedgwick, "Martin Diamond's Interpretation of *Federalist* 10: A Response to Alan Gibson, with a further response by Gibson," 529–545.

145. Diamond, "Democracy and *The Federalist*," 32.

146. Diamond, "Ethics and Politics," 363.

147. Wilson Carey McWilliams, Review of *America's Constitutional Soul, Political Theory* (August 1992), 518.

148. Ibid., 521.

149. Mansfield, *America's Constitutional Soul,* ix–x.

150. Wood, "Fundamentalists and the Constitution," 39; Sheldon S. Wolin, *The Presence of the Past* (Baltimore: Johns Hopkins University Press, 1989), 3.

151. Mansfield, *Taming the Prince.*

152. Ibid., 13.

153. Ibid., 71.

154. Ibid., 205.

155. Ibid., 289–290.

156. Ibid., 294.

157. Sheldon S. Wolin, "Executive Liberation," in *Studies in American Political Development* (Spring 1992), 213. My analysis of Mansfield's book is deeply indebted to Wolin's critique. Mansfield responded in the same issue. See "Executive Power and the Passion for Virtue," 217–221.

158. It is possible that a way out will be offered by a surprising source. The ex-Marxist, ex-socialist historian Eugene Genovese has begun to write warmly of the southern conservative tradition, paying special attention to its skepticism about capitalism. He admires southern theories of hierarchy and decries radical egalitarianism, while also, it should be stressed, repudiating southern racism. However, Genovese denies he is a conservative and continues to style himself a member of the democratic Left, though it is unlikely his views will be well received there. In any case his position is unusual and still developing. It will be interesting to watch its course. See Genovese, *The Southern Tradition: The Achievement and Limitations of an American Conservatism* (Cambridge: Harvard University Press, 1994).

159. George Kateb, "On the 'Legitimation Crisis,'" *Social Research* (Winter 1979), 704–706. Kateb refers to the Straussian position as "the authoritarianism of moral elitism," in the end a form of paternalism. See also the comment on Walter Berns, 710. Note that Kateb also perceived a threat to legitimacy in Samuel Huntington's "authoritarianism of order" (701–702). Writing in 1979, Kateb believed the ideas of the authoritarian Right more often seemed within the frame of constitutional democratic principles than did those of the radical Left. However, he noted that the United States was "hugely" more likely in practice to lapse to a right-wing rather than a leftist position (711). The events of the intervening years seem to have borne this out.

Chapter 15

1. Thomas L. Haskell, "The Curious Persistence of Rights Talk in the 'Age of Interpretation,'" *Journal of American History* (December 1987), 984–1020.

2. Alexander Hamilton, *Federalist 84,* in *The Federalist Papers,* ed. Clinton Rossiter (New York: Mentor Books, 1961), 510–520.

3. James Madison, quoted in Gordon S. Wood, "The Origins of the Bill of Rights," *Proceedings of the American Antiquarian Society* 10, pt. 2 (1991), 272.

4. The above sketch has relied heavily on Wood, "Origins of the Bill of Rights," 255–274. Oddly, Wood does not stress the radical implications of the first ten amendments in his important study, Gordon S. Wood, *The Radicalism of the American Revolution* (New York: Knopf, 1992). For a full-length study that traces the explosive power of rights in American politics, see James MacGregor Burns and Stewart Burns, *A People's Charter: The Pursuit of Rights in America* (New York: Knopf, 1992). Sean Wilentz comments on Wood, the Burnses, and other recent studies while assessing the politics surrounding the drafting of the amendments. See Wilentz, "The Power of the Powerless," *New Republic* (December 23 and 30, 1991), 32–40. I have also been much influenced by this article. For a fuller treatment, see Robert Allan Rutland, *The Birth of the Bill of Rights: 1776–1791* (Boston: Northeastern University Press, 1991). For a documentary record of the debates in the First Congress, see Helen E. Veit et al., *Creating the Bill of Rights* (Baltimore: Johns Hopkins University Press, 1991). For additional analysis of the role of the Anti-Federalists, see Richard E. Ellis, "The Persistence of Antifederalism After 1789," in *Beyond Confederation: Origins of the Constitution and American National Identity,* ed. Richard Beeman et al. (Chapel Hill: University of North Carolina Press, 1987), 297–300.

5. See the important article by Joyce Appleby, "The American Heritage: The Heirs and the Disinherited," *Journal of American History* (December 1987), 798–813, esp. 805, 807–808.

6. John Rawls, *A Theory of Justice* (Cambridge: Harvard University Press, 1971).

7. For other works in the same vein, see Ronald Dworkin, *Taking Rights Seriously* (Cambridge: Harvard University Press, 1977); and Bruce Ackerman, *Social Justice in the Liberal State* (New Haven: Yale University Press, 1980). Robert Nozick's *Anarchy, State, and Utopia* (New York: Basic Books, 1974), discussed in Chapter 14, is a rightist version of the same mode of analysis, though it has an absolutism based on the assertion of a Lockean theory of natural rights that many others in the school would reject. For a brief characterization of the school, see Michael Walzer's review of Ackerman's *Social Justice, New Republic* (October 25, 1980), 39–41, esp. 39. For a highly critical discussion of this tendency in political philosophy, see John Gray, "Against the New Liberalism," *Times Literary Supplement* (London) (July 3, 1992), 13–15.

8. The literature on Rawls is enormous. A simple bibliographical listing would occupy the space of a substantial article. Among the items I have found the most helpful are Benjamin Barber, "Justifying Justice: John Rawls and Thin Theory," in *The Conquest of Politics: Liberal Philosophy in Democratic Times* (Princeton: Princeton University Press, 1988), 54–90; Allan Bloom, "Justice: John Rawls Vs. The Tradition of Political Philosophy," *American Political Science Review* (June 1976), 648–662; Stuart Hampshire, "A New Philosophy of the Just Society," *New York Review of Books* (February 24, 1972), 34–39; John H. Schaar, "Reflections on Rawls's *A Theory of Justice*" and "Equality of Opportunity and the Just Society," in *Legitimacy and the Modern State* (New Brunswick, N.J.: Transaction Books, 1981), 145–166 and 211–230; Alan Ryan, "John Rawls," in *The Return of Grand Theory in the Social Sciences,* ed. Quentin Skinner (Cambridge: Cambridge University Press, 1985), 103–119; and Ian Shapiro, *The Evolution of Rights in Liberal Theory* (Cambridge: Cambridge University Press, 1986), 204–270. Also useful is Norman Daniels, ed., *Reading Rawls* (New York: Basic Books, 1975). Much of the communitarian literature to be discussed in Chapter 16 is implicitly or explicitly critical of Rawls. For the limitations of treating Rawls explicitly as a contractarian, see Spencer Carr, "Rawls, Contractarianism, and Our Moral Intuitions," *Personalist* (Winter 1975), 83–95.

9. Rawls, *Theory of Justice,* 12. Susan Moller Okin chides Rawls for not including gender among the list of unknown qualities and quite rightly argues that it would have been plausible for him to have done so. See Okin, *Justice, Gender, and the Family* (New York: Basic Books, 1989), 91–92.

10. Rawls, *Theory of Justice,* 11–13. Quote at 12.

11. Ibid., 60.

12. Ibid., 60–62. For a fuller formulation of the principles, see 302–303.

13. Schaar, "Equality of Opportunity and the Just Society," 220.

14. Robert Amdur, "Rawls and His Radical Critics: The Problem of Equality," *Dissent* (Summer 1980), 325–326. Schaar, in "Reflections," 156–158, also stresses Rawls's deep egalitarianism, though Schaar is much more ambivalent about it than Amdur.

15. Amy Gutmann, "The Central Role of Rawls's Theory," *Dissent* (Summer 1989), 339.

16. Ryan, "John Rawls," 105.

17. Rawls, *Theory of Justice,* 258.

18. Barber, "Justifying Justice," 81.

19. Schaar, "Reflections," 150.

20. On this theme see Charles R. Morris, "'It's Not the Economy, Stupid,'" *Atlantic Monthly* (July 1993), 49–62. On the penetration of economics into political science, see Theodore J. Lowi, "The State in Political Science: How We Become What We Study," *American Political Science Review* (March 1992), 1–7. See the discussion of these themes in another context in Chapter 13.

21. Schaar, "Reflections," 163–164.

22. Shapiro, *Evolution of Rights,* esp. 251–270.

23. Rawls, *Theory of Justice,* 226–227. Cf. Barber, "Justifying Justice," 55, 77.

24. Rawls, *Theory of Justice,* 228. Cf. Schaar, "Reflections," 162.

25. Barber, "Justifying Justice," 78; Schaar, "Reflections," 148.

26. Schaar, "Reflections," 160.

27. Rawls, *Theory of Justice,* 226.

28. Gray, "Against the New Liberalism," 13. Gray's attack is exceptionally harsh. Although I am in general agreement with him, I do not subscribe to all the particulars of his critique of academic political theory.

29. John Kenneth Galbraith, *The New Industrial State* (Boston: Houghton Mifflin, 1967). In my discussion of Galbraith, I draw on my earlier analysis in *The Politics of Affluence* (San Francisco: Chandler, 1968).

30. For an analysis, see Galbraith, *New Industrial State,* 27ff.

31. Ibid., 320.

32. Ibid., 393.

33. Ibid., 399.

34. See Sheldon S. Wolin, *The Presence of the Past* (Baltimore: Johns Hopkins University Press, 1989), esp. 58–65.

35. Wilson Carey McWilliams, "Science and Freedom: America as the Technological Republic," in *Technology in the Western Political Tradition,* ed. Arthur M. Melzer, Jerry Weinberger, and M. Richard Zinman (Ithaca: Cornell University Press, 1993), 107. My purposes do not permit a full assessment of Galbraith's large and impressive body of work. *The Affluent Society* and *The New Industrial State* must be seen as part of a trilogy, the concluding volume of which is *Economics and the Public Purpose* (Boston: Houghton Mifflin, 1973). That is perhaps the most critical of Galbraith's studies and the one in which he pushed closest to socialism. For a survey of Galbraith's work as a whole, see Loren J. Okroi, *Galbraith, Harrington, Heilbroner: Economics and Dissent in an Age of Optimism* (Princeton: Princeton University Press, 1988), 29–108, for present purposes, esp. 59–108.

36. The major works are Robert A. Dahl and Charles E. Lindblom, *Politics, Economics, and Welfare,* 2d ed. (Chicago: University of Chicago Press, 1976); Lindblom, *Politics and Markets* (New York: Basic Books, 1977); Dahl, *Dilemmas of Pluralist Democracy* (New Haven: Yale University Press, 1982) and *A Preface to Economic Democracy* (Berkeley: University of California Press, 1985). For a commentary on most of this work that argues that it takes insufficient notice of the place of class, see John Manley, "Neo-Pluralism: A Class Analysis of Pluralism I and Pluralism II," *American Political Science Review* (June 1983), 368–283, and the responses by Lindblom and Dahl, 384–389.

37. Dahl and Lindblom, *Politics, Economics, and Welfare,* xxxvi–xxxvii.

38. Ibid., xxix–xxxii.

39. Ibid., xli–xlii.

40. Ibid., xxi.

41. Lindblom, *Politics and Markets,* 172.

42. Harold Brayman, quoted in ibid., 175, 178–179.

43. Ibid., 187.

44. Ibid., 201–206. For these relationships Lindblom uses the somewhat awkward term *circularity.* For his full discussion on corporate privilege and power, see 170–221. It should be noted that Dahl has serious doubts about Lindblom's circularity hypothesis. See "Comment on Manley," *American Political Science Review* (June 1983), 386.

45. Dahl, *Dilemmas,* 176–178.

46. Richard Hofstadter, *The Age of Reform* (New York: Knopf, 1955), 23ff.; and Dahl, *Dilemmas,* 178–181.

47. Dahl, *Dilemmas,* 201, 198–202.

48. Ibid., 204. See also Lindblom's remarks in his suggestively titled article, "The Market as Prison," *Journal of Politics* (May 1982), 324–336. Other significant revisionist papers by

Lindblom are collected in Charles E. Lindblom, *Democracy and the Market System* (London: Norwegian University Press, 1988), especially his APSA presidential address, "Another State of Mind," 279–304.

49. John Rawls, "Justice as Fairness: Political, Not Metaphysical," in *The Self and the Political Order*, ed. Tracy Strong (New York: New York University Press, 1992), 95–119.

50. Ibid., 97.

51. Ibid., 101.

52. John Rawls, *Political Liberalism* (New York: Columbia University Press, 1993), 44–46. *Political Liberalism* is a synthesis of the work Rawls did starting in the 1980s to respond to his critics and adjust the argument of his earlier book. There will no doubt be a large literature comparing the two books and assessing whether Rawls significantly altered his previous position. For discussions of the articles that culminated in the book, see William Galston, *Liberal Purposes* (Cambridge: Cambridge University Press, 1991), esp. 140–162; George Klosko, "Rawls's 'Political' Philosophy and American Democracy," *American Political Science Review* (June 1993), 348–359; and Georgia Warnke, *Justice and Interpretation* (Cambridge: MIT Press, 1993), 38–59. For early discussion and reviews of *Political Liberalism,* see Stephen Holmes, "The Gatekeeper," *New Republic* (October 11, 1993), 39–47; Bernard Williams, "A Fair State," *London Review of Books* (May 13, 1993), 7–9; John Gray, "Can We Agree to Disagree?" *New York Times Book Review* (May 16, 1993), 35; Stuart Hampshire, "Liberalism: The New Twist," *New York Review of Books* (August 12, 1993), 43–47; Perry Anderson, "On John Rawls," *Dissent* (Winter 1994), 139–144; and Jeremy Waldron, "Justice Revisited," *Times Literary Supplement* (June 18, 1993), 5–6. For the turn toward interpretation in political theory, see Warnke, *Justice and Interpretation.* For a survey of the range of political theories in opposition to Rawls, see Ian Shapiro, *Political Criticism* (Berkeley: University of California Press, 1990), esp. 3–16. For Walzer see my discussion in Chapter 16.

53. Gray, "Can We Agree to Disagree?" 35. Gray compares Rawls's book unfavorably with Judith Shklar's "liberalism of fear." See further discussion in this chapter.

54. Shklar, perhaps best known for her distinguished studies of the European Enlightenment, turned toward her adopted country in part to fill the gap left by Louis Hartz's departure from Harvard. To date the most important of her published works on American thought is Shklar, *American Citizenship: The Quest for Inclusion* (Cambridge: Harvard University Press, 1991). See also Shklar, *The Faces of Injustice* (New Haven: Yale University Press, 1990), "Redeeming American Political Theory," *American Political Science Review* (March 1991), 3–15, "The Liberalism of Fear," in *Liberalism and the Moral Life,* ed. Nancy Rosenblum (Cambridge: Harvard University Press, 1989), 21–38, and portions of *Ordinary Vices* (Cambridge: Harvard University Press, 1984). The full measure of Shklar's contribution to American political thought has yet to be taken. Much of her work is widely scattered and some is still unpublished. Its posthumous collection will be a major event. For three very early assessments, see Alan Ryan, "Philosophy and Public Life," *Dissent* (Summer 1991), 435–438; Bernard Yack, "Injustice and the Victim's Voice," *Michigan Law Review* 89 (1991), 1334–1349; and Seyla Benhabib, "Judith Shklar's Dystopic Liberalism," *Social Research* (Summer 1994), 477–488.

55. Shklar, *Ordinary Vices,* 7–44, and "Liberalism of Fear." The "ordinary vices" are drawn from Montaigne and include treachery, disloyalty, and tyranny, to which Shklar would add snobbery, dishonesty, and hypocrisy. George Kateb suggested that all her books, even the historical studies, were preoccupied one way or another with physical cruelty, against which she fought a lifelong intellectual battle. Kateb, "Judith Shklar: 1928–1992," *CSPT Newsletter* (November 1992), 1.

56. Shklar, "Liberalism of Fear," 29.

57. Shklar, *Faces of Injustice,* 16.

58. Ibid., 13–14.

59. Ryan, "Philosophy and Public Life," 436.

60. Barrington Moore, Jr., *Reflections on the Cause of Human Misery* (Boston: Beacon Press, 1972). See also Benhabib, "Shklar's Dystopic Liberalism," and Michael Walzer, "On Negative

Politics," in a memorial Festschrift for Shklar, *Liberalism Without Illusions* (Chicago: University of Chicago Press, forthcoming).

61. Shklar, American *Citizenship,* 2–3.

62. Ibid., 17.

63. George Kateb, *The Inner Ocean: Individualism and Democratic Culture* (Ithaca: Cornell University Press, 1992), 6. Kateb's book is a series of probing papers, published over a period of time and bound together by a set of common themes and ideas. The most general statement of his position is in "Introduction: Individual Rights and Democratic Individuality," 1–35. My understanding of his work has been enhanced by the review of *The Inner Ocean* by Michael A. Mosher, *Political Theory* (August 1994), 511–517; and by Leslie Paul Thiele, "Twilight of Modernity: Nietzsche, Heidegger, and Politics," *Political Theory* (August 1994), 480–485.

64. Kateb, *Inner Ocean,* 1 and 1–9 passim.

65. Ibid., 6–7. Quote on 7. For Rawls see *Theory of Justice,* 56.

66. Kateb, *Inner Ocean,* 8–9. Kateb accepts a strong form of Nietzsche's thesis of the death of God. In one paper he relies heavily on Nietzsche and Heidegger for his defense of the sanctity of human life in the face of the nuclear peril. This use is very limited; he believed that almost every direct remark either philosopher made on politics was "silly or wicked." See *Inner Ocean,* 135 and 127–151 passim. Kateb is aware of the danger of relying on these antidemocratic thinkers. I leave aside the question of whether they help his general case. For the most part, I think they are not needed to consider the questions in this study, nor am I convinced that they are needed for his argument. I think that Kateb is not essentially a postmodernist, but his recourse to Nietzsche and Heidegger makes his one of the most interesting attempts to put postmodernism to some constructive use. On the place of these thinkers, see Mosher's review of *The Inner Ocean* and Thiele, "Twilight of Modernity."

67. Kateb, *Inner Ocean,* 3. See also George Kateb, "On the Legitimation Crisis," *Social Research* (Winter 1979), 695–727. More generally see *Inner Ocean,* 57–76. Of course Kateb is not alone among rights theorists in his interest in the law. Cf. Ronald Dworkin, *Taking Rights Seriously* (Cambridge: Harvard University Press, 1977) and *Matters of Principle* (Cambridge: Harvard University Press, 1985). In fact, as a lawyer, Dworkin delves more deeply into case law than Kateb, but the latter's concerns are closer to those of this study.

68. Kateb, *Inner Ocean,* 1, 10.

69. Ibid., 82. In a book that appeared too late for me to consider here, Kateb extends his analysis of democratic individuality. See *Emerson and Self-Reliance* (Thousand Oaks, Calif.: Sage Publications, 1994). Morton Schoolman contributes a fine introduction on Kateb's developing theory. See x–xxii. For another look at the importance of the Emersonians from a very different point of view, see Irving Howe, *The American Newness* (Cambridge: Harvard University Press, 1986).

70. Kateb, *Inner Ocean,* 226.

71. Ibid., 87–88. See Ralph Waldo Emerson, "Politics," in *Emerson: Essays and Lectures* (New York: Library of America, 1983), 559, 563.

72. Kateb, *Inner Ocean,* 88–92. Regarding self-creation, Kateb quoted Thoreau on the need to "live deliberately" so that when it comes time to die, one does not discover that one has not lived (see 90). See also Nancy Rosenblum, *Another Liberalism: Romanticism and the Reconstruction of Liberal Thought* (Cambridge: Harvard University Press, 1987), 121.

73. Rosenblum, *Another Liberalism,* 103, 103–124. The "individualism of the strong" was attributed to Locke by Judith N. Shklar, *Men and Citizens: A Study of Rousseau's Social Theory* (Cambridge: Cambridge University Press, 1969), 41. Rousseau, in her view, represented the individualism of the weak.

74. Kateb, *Inner Ocean,* 22.

75. Ibid., 36–37.

76. Ibid., 39–40.

77. Ibid., 42–43.

78. Ibid., 47.

79. Ibid., 52–54, quote at 54.

80. George Kateb, "Disguised Authority," *democracy* (July 1982), 119.

81. Kateb, *Inner Ocean,* 56.

82. Ibid., 102–103, 51. See also the comment on Martin Luther King, Jr., on 30.

83. Ibid., 28. The term *possessive individualism* comes, of course, from C. B. Macpherson, *The Political Theory of Possessive Individualism:* Hobbes to Locke (Oxford: Oxford University Press, 1962).

84. Kateb, *Inner Ocean,* 2.

85. Ibid., 15–16.

86. Ibid., 96–97, quote at 97. Kateb seems to have softened his position on socioeconomic issues since he first published chapter 4 of *Inner Ocean.* See the original "Nuclear Weapons and Individual Rights," *Dissent* (Spring 1986), 161–172; and the subsequent exchange with Erazim Kohak, Jean Cohen, and Michael Sandel in *Dissent* (Summer 1986), 357–366. There Kateb attributed to the democratic leftist journal *Dissent* a higher degree of egalitarianism than seems warranted. In fact, it may be doubted whether any socialist theorist, including Marx, ever advocated as complete a program of equalization as Kateb feared. *Dissent* very carefully walks the line that distinguishes left reform liberals from moderate democratic socialists. In this connection, it is interesting to note that in a recent symposium devoted to the condition of the Left, in the wake of the apparent collapse of Marxism and the fortieth anniversary of *Dissent,* Paul Berman held up Walt Whitman as a possible source of radical democratic values for a new age. See Berman, "The Left After Forty Years," *Dissent* (Winter 1994), 9.

87. Kateb, *Inner Ocean,* 51.

88. Joseph A. Schumpeter, *Capitalism, Socialism, and Democracy,* 3d ed. (New York: Harper, 1950), 283, 302.

89. George Kateb, "The Night Watchman State," *American Scholar* (Winter 1975–1976), 816–826. For discussion see Chapter 14 herein.

90. Lindblom, *Politics and Markets,* 356.

Chapter 16

1. Theodore J. Lowi, *The End of Liberalism: The Second Republic of the United States,* 2d ed. (New York: Norton, 1979). The first edition appeared in 1969. A brief, but very stimulating, review of Lowi's book was offered by John Schaar, who will be discussed in this chapter. See *American Political Science Review* 64 (1970), 1258–1259.

2. J. Peter Euben, "The Battle of Salamis and the Origins of Political Theory," *Political Theory* (August 1986), 362. This paragraph and parts of the next are based on my article: J. P. Young, "The Theory of the Liberal Consensus and the Politics of Interpretation," in *Liberale Democratie in Europa und den USA,* ed. Franz Gress and Hans Vorländer (Frankfurt/New York: Campus Verlag, 1990), 34–48.

3. For the first point, see Michael Sandel, "The State and the Soul," *New Republic* (June 10, 1985), 39–40; for the second, see John P. Diggins, *The Lost Soul of American Politics* (New York: Basic Books, 1984).

4. J.G.A. Pocock, "The Machiavellian Moment Revisited: A Study in History and Ideology," *Journal of Modern History* (March 1981), and "Between Gog and Magog: Between the Republican Thesis and the Ideologia America," *Journal of the History of Ideas* (April-June 1987), 325–346.

5. For instance, see Thomas L. Pangle, *The Spirit of Modern Republicanism* (Chicago: University of Chicago Press, 1988).

6. Don Herzog, "Some Questions for Republicans," *Political Theory* (August 1986), 473–493; and Steven M. Dworetz, *The Unvarnished Doctrine: Locke, Liberalism, and the American Revolution* (Durham, N.C.: Duke University Press, 1990). Isaac Kramnick,

Republicanism and Bourgeois Radicalism (Ithaca: Cornell University Press, 1990), 35–40, provides an important account of the ideological dimension of this historical controversy.

7. Michael Sandel, *Liberalism and the Limits of Justice* (Cambridge: Cambridge University Press, 1982), "The Procedural Republic and the Unencumbered Self," in *The Self and the Political Order,* ed. Tracy Strong (New York: New York University Press, 1992), 79–94, "Morality and the Liberal Ideal," *New Republic* (May 7, 1984), 15–17, and "Introduction," in *Liberalism and Its Critics* (New York: New York University Press, 1984), 1–11. Other important works from the school include Benjamin Barber, *Strong Democracy: Participatory Politics for a New Age* (Berkeley: University of California Press, 1984) and *The Conquest of Politics: Liberal Philosophy in Democratic Times* (Princeton: Princeton University Press, 1988); Robert Bellah et al., *Habits of the Heart: Individualism and Commitment in American Life* (Berkeley: University of California Press, 1985) and *The Good Society* (New York: Knopf, 1991); William A. Galston, *Liberal Purposes: Goods, Virtues, and Diversity in the Liberal State* (Cambridge: Cambridge University Press, 1991); and Alasdair MacIntyre, *After Virtue* (South Bend, Ind.: University of Notre Dame Press, 1981). Among the major studies of the communitarians are Robert Booth Fowler, *The Dance with Community: The Contemporary Debate in American Political Thought* (Lawrence: University Press of Kansas, 1991); Derek L. Philips, *Looking Backwards: A Critical Appraisal of Communitarian Thought* (Princeton: Princeton University Press, 1993); and Amy Gutmann, "Communitarian Critics of Liberalism," *Philosophy and Public Affairs* (Summer 1985), 308–322.

8. Sandel, *Liberalism and Limits of Justice,* 153.

9. Sandel, "Introduction," 5–6.

10. Sandel, "Morality and the Liberal Ideal," 15.

11. Sandel, "Procedural Republic and the Unencumbered Self," 81–82, and *Liberalism and Limits of Justice,* 9.

12. Sandel, "Procedural Republic and the Unencumbered Self, 87.

13. Mary Ann Glendon, *Rights Talk: The Impoverishment of Political Discourse* (New York: Free Press, 1991).

14. Ibid., 8.

15. Cass R. Sunstein, "Rightalk," *New Republic* (September 2, 1991), 33–36. It is worth noting that Sunstein is by no means a rights absolutist and has communitarian, civic republican leanings himself. The above paragraph is much indebted to Sunstein's critique of Glendon.

16. Sandel, "Introduction," 6.

17. Ibid., 6–7.

18. Michael Walzer, "Constitutional Rights and Civil Society," in *What It Means to Be an American* (New York: Marsilio Books, 1992), 109–110.

19. Ibid., 111, 117–118.

20. Ibid., 118, 122–123. Benjamin Barber makes a similar analysis, though his communitarianism is much more thoroughgoing than Walzer's, and Barber is more worried about the subversion of duty and the counter-majoritarian aspect of rights theory than his fellow radical democrat. See Barber, "The Reconstruction of Rights," *American Prospect* (Spring 1991), 36–46.

21. Michael Walzer, "The Communitarian Critique of Liberalism," *Political Theory* (February 1990), 6–23. The following two paragraphs are based entirely on Walzer's essay. Walzer's own position is hard to define. He has been called a liberal, a communitarian, a social democrat, a democratic socialist, and an "unreconstructed democrat." The last is his own term, but it is not clear that it is an exhaustive description of his position. The fullest communitarian attempt to develop a theory of a nonneutral state dedicated to a theory of the good is Galston's *Liberal Purposes.* However, this book, though very valuable as a commentary on much of the current literature, is lacking in specificity. Thus liberal goods should include life, the normal development of basic capacities, freedom, rationality, a recognition of significant social relations such as family, friends, voluntary organizations, intense collective efforts, and the like. See 173–177. This is laudable but very abstract. Galston's views are of interest

because he is a founder of a communitarian journal, the *Responsive Community*, and because he has been a member of President Clinton's domestic policy staff. The communitarians have become a movement with a manifesto, "The Responsive Communitarian Platform." Its principal author was sociologist Amitai Etzioni, who had extensive help from Galston and Mary Ann Glendon. The manifesto appeared as an appendix in Etzioni's programmatic book, *The Spirit of Community: Rights, Responsibilities, and the Communitarian Agenda* (New York: Crown, 1991), 250–267.

22. Walzer, "Communitarian Critique," 12, 14, 15. These remarks seem to me to dispose of Galston's fears that Walzer would risk democratic tyranny rather than restrict democratic authority. See Galston, *Liberal Purposes*, 54.

23. Walzer, "Communitarian Critique," 15–19. This, I think, is Walzer's only direct reference to Dewey, who seems to me very much a kindred spirit, in content, though not remotely in style.

24. Sandel, "Procedural Republic and the Unencumbered Self," 89–92. The next several paragraphs are based on and all quotations are taken from these pages. For Kateb's position, see "Disguised Authority," *democracy* (July 1982), 116–124.

25. Sandel drew on an early study by Samuel Beer. That has now been superseded by Beer, *To Make a Nation* (Cambridge: Harvard University Press, 1993).

26. Sandel, "Procedural Republic and the Unencumbered Self," 92.

27. The Berkeley connection is important. One of the characteristics of this school of thought is a deep, though not uncritical, sympathy for the New Left ideal of participatory democracy, a sympathy that emerged partly as a response to large bureaucratic institutions such as the multiversity. See Sheldon S. Wolin and John Schaar, *The Berkeley Rebellion and Beyond: Essays on Politics and Education in the Technological Society* (New York: Vintage, 1970).

28. John Schaar, "Liberty/Authority/Community in the Political Thought of John Winthrop," *Political Theory* (November 1991), 493–518; and Wilson Carey McWilliams, *The Idea of Fraternity in America* (Berkeley: University of California Press, 1973), 112–149. See also Joshua Miller, *The Rise and Fall of Democracy in Early America: 1630–1789* (University Park: Pennsylvania State University Press, 1991), esp. 21–49. Though he lacked a direct connection, the work of Christopher Lasch is a close relative of that of the Berkeley school. He became a regular contributor to *democracy*, a journal of opinion founded by Wolin. See Lasch, *The True and Only Heaven: Progress and Its Critics* (New York: Norton, 1991), where he advocated a middle- or lower-middle-class populism. For a harsh liberal reply to Lasch, see Stephen Holmes, *The Anatomy of Antiliberalism* (Cambridge: Harvard University Press, 1993), 122–140. For a social democratic response, see Jeffrey Isaac, "On Christopher Lasch," *Salmagundi* (Winter 1992), 82–97, and the reply by Lasch, 98–109.

29. McWilliams, *Idea Of Fraternity*, 96. In my discussion of McWilliams, I drew on my article J. P. Young, "The Prophet of Post-Industrialism v. the Politics of Nostalgia," *Polity* (Winter 1975), esp. 278–281.

30. McWilliams, *Idea of Fraternity*, 7–8.

31. Ibid., 107.

32. Ibid., 620.

33. Ibid., 99.

34. Ibid., 109–110.

35. Ibid., 185–193 on *The Federalist*, and 74.

36. Ibid., 74, 109.

37. Wolin's major work on the history of Western political theory is *Politics and Vision: Continuity and Innovation in Western Political Thought* (Boston: Little, Brown, 1960). His most important statements of method are Sheldon Wolin, "Political Theory as a Vocation," *American Political Science Review* (December 1969), 1062–1082, and "Paradigms and Political Theories," in *Politics and Experience*, ed. Preston King and B. K. Parekh (Cambridge: Cambridge University Press, 1968). To date his major work on American politics is Wolin, *The Presence of the Past: Essays on the State and the Constitution* (Baltimore: Johns Hopkins

University Press, 1989). This should be supplemented by two closely related papers: Wolin, "The American Pluralist Conception of Politics," in *Ethics in Hard Times,* ed. Arthur L. Caplan and Daniel Callahan (New York: Plenum Press, 1981), 217–259, and "The Idea of the State in America," in *The Problem of Authority in America,* ed. John Diggins and Mark E. Kann (Philadelphia: Temple University Press, 1981). Other works will be cited as needed.

38. See J. Peter Euben, "Introduction," in *Greek Tragedy and Political Theory,* ed. Euben (Berkeley: University of California Press, 1986), 32–34.

39. Sheldon Wolin, "Editorial: Why *democracy?*" *democracy* (January 1981), 3. This is from the editorial statement of the first issue of a quarterly journal Wolin founded and edited for three years until its source of funds was cut off. Note that the subtitle of the magazine was "A Journal of Political Renewal and Radical Change." Wolin published a number of his major articles in it, and each issue had an editorial note that when read together, constitute a running critique of the early Reagan years.

40. Wolin, "Contract and Birthright," in *Presence of the Past,* 141–142, quote at 142.

41. Sheldon Wolin, "The People's Two Bodies," *democracy* (January 1881), 11. The most general statement of the theory of collective identity is Wolin, "Collective Identity and Constitutional Power," *Presence of the Past,* 8–31.

42. Wolin, *Presence of the Past,* 10.

43. Wolin, "People's Two Bodies," 12–13. Note that Wolin, in spite of his serious criticisms of liberalism, holds a rather favorable view of the thoroughly Lockean liberal Declaration of Independence here.

44. Ibid., 13–16; and Wolin, "Idea of the State," esp. 45–47. Note the sharp difference between Wolin's view of the intent of the Framers and Martin Diamond's Straussian account, which argues for their democratic motives. See Martin Diamond, "Democracy and *The Federalist:* A Reconsideration of the Framers' Intent," *American Political Science Review* (March 1959), 52–68. See also the discussion in Chapter 4.

45. Wolin, "Idea of the State," 48, and "American Pluralist Conception of Politics," 225–226.

46. Wolin, "American Pluralist Conception of Politics," 256–257.

47. Wolin, "Idea of the State," 52; and Schaar, *Legitimacy in the Modern State* (New Brunswick, N.J.: Transaction Books, 1981), 15–51.

48. Wolin, "Tending and Intending a Constitution," in *Presence of the Past,* 82–99, esp. 88–90. The term *tending* is introduced to suggest tending an organic growth as opposed to imposing an artificial, theoretical construct.

49. Wolin, "Democracy and the Welfare State," in *Presence of the Past,* 154.

50. Hannah Arendt, *The Human Condition* (Chicago: University of Chicago Press, 1958). Wolin was much influenced by Arendt, though he became very critical of some aspects of her work. See Sheldon Wolin, "Hannah Arendt and the Ordinance of Time," *Social Research* (Spring 1977), 91–105.

51. Sheldon Wolin, "E Pluribus Unum: The Representation of Difference and the Reconstitution of Collectivity," *Presence of the Past,* 135–136; Wilson Carey McWilliams, "Democracy and the Citizen: Community, Dignity, and the Crisis of Contemporary Politics in America," in *How Democratic Is the Constitution?* ed. Robert A. Goldwin and William A. Schambra (Washington, D.C.: American Enterprise Institute, 1980), 91–96, and "The Anti-Federalists, Representation and Party," *Northwestern University Law Review* (Fall 1989), esp. 26–32; and Miller, *Rise and Fall of Democracy,* 81–103.

52. Wolin, "People's Two Bodies," 16–17, 21.

53. Wolin, "Why Democracy?" 3, and Sheldon Wolin, "Counter-Enlightenment: Orwell's *1984,*" in *Reflections on America: 1984,* ed. Robert Mulvihill (Athens: University of Georgia Press, 1984), 113.

54. Sheldon Wolin, "The New Public Philosophy," *democracy* (October 1981), 23–36, quote at 33. In particular, Wolin derides the claim of the Reagan administration to be conservative, saying that it was not true in any meaningful sense.

55. Sheldon Wolin, "From Progress to Modernization: The Conservative Turn," *democracy* (Fall 1983), 9–21. Modernization, John Schaar tells us, "is our version of Hegel's idealization of the Prussian state." See Schaar, "The Case for Patriotism," in *Legitimacy in the Modern State,* 303.

56. Schaar, "Decadence and Revitalization: Reflections on the Present Condition," in *Legitimacy in the Modern State,* 355.

57. Ibid., 346, 344. Schaar did point out that his attack on the Left should not be misconstrued; the Right escaped because it has had "for many decades nothing to offer that even merits critical attention" (347).

58. Wolin, "Hannah Arendt and the Ordinance of Time," 104; "Reason in Exile: Critical Theory and Technological Society," in Arthur M. Melzer et al., *Technology in the Western Political Tradition* (Ithaca: Cornell University Press, 1993), 170. The whole article is useful as an assessment of the Frankfurt school, of which Herbert Marcuse was the leading American exponent. Whatever Marcuse's defects, the school is important and the Berkeley school seems, in some respects, like an Americanized version. See generally 162–189. See also Wolin, "Max Weber: Legitimation, Method, and the Politics of Theory," *Political Theory* (August 1981), 401–424.

59. Wilson Carey McWilliams, "Fraternity and Nature: A Response to Philip Abbott," *Political Theory* (August 1974), 329, and "Science and Freedom: America as the Technological Republic," *Technology in the Western Political Tradition,* 85; Schaar, "Decadence and Revitalization," 343. For the fullest Berkeley school statements on technology, see Langdon Winner, *Autonomous Technology: Technics-out-of-Control as a Theme in American Thought* (Cambridge: MIT Press, 1977) and *The Whale and the Reactor: A Search for Limits in an Age of High Technology* (Chicago: University of Chicago Press, 1986).

60. Schaar, "Equality of Opportunity and the Just Society," *Legitimacy in the Modern State,* 223; Wolin, "Democracy and the Welfare State," *Presence of the Past,* 151–152, 151–179 passim. For a similar view, see Theodore J. Lowi, "Two Roads to Serfdom: Liberalism, Conservatism, and Administrative Power," in *A New Constitutionalism,* ed. Stephen L. Elkin and Karol Edward Soltan (Chicago: University of Chicago Press, 1993), 171. In spite of his concerns about the welfare state, Wolin does accept the need for it in passing remarks. See Wolin, "Contract and Birthright," 147–148.

61. Sheldon Wolin, "Democracy, Difference, and Re-Cognition," *Political Theory* (August 1993), 464–483. For a fuller discussion, see Chapter 13.

62. Sheldon Wolin, "'Fugitive Democracy,'" *Constellations* (April 1994), 11.

63. Wolin, "Contract and Birthright," 149–150.

64. Wolin, "'Fugitive Democracy,'" 11, 19, 23, and 11–25 passim.

65. Sheldon Wolin, "What Revolutionary Action Means Today," *democracy* (Fall 1982), 25–26.

66. Wolin, "Revolutionary Action Today," 27, and "'Fugitive Democracy,'" 23. See also Hanna Fenichel Pitkin and Sara M. Shumer, "On Participation," *democracy* (Fall 1982), 55–65. For a book-length treatment of locally based politics from a position close to the Berkeley school, see Sara M. Evans and Harry C. Boyte, *Free Spaces: The Sources of Democratic Change in America* (Chicago: University of Chicago Press, 1992). For another interesting list of direct, participatory political activities, both historical and contemporary, see Miller, *Rise and Fall of Democracy,* 141–145.

67. Schaar, "The Case for Patriotism," *Legitimacy in the Modern State,* 307. For my brief reflections on Schaar, on which I have drawn a little, see J. P. Young, "A Critique of the Welfare State," in *Dissent* (Summer 1982), 379–380.

68. Wolin, "Revolutionary Action Today," 27–28, and "'Fugitive Democracy,'" 24–25. It might appear that an appeal to a wider group for support would lessen homogeneity, but Wolin aptly called attention to the disparate, yet temporarily united, Solidarity movement in Poland, surely one of the great successes in the recent history of peaceful revolution.

69. Sheldon Wolin, "On the Theory and Practice of Power," in *After Foucault,* ed. Jonathan Arac (New Brunswick, N.J.: Rutgers University Press, 1988), 179–201.

70. Wolin, "'Fugitive Democracy,'" 13. For a fuller and more recent statement by Sheldon Wolin on constitutionalism, see "Norm and Form: The Constitutionalizing of Democracy," in *Athenian Democracy and the Reconstruction of American Democracy,* ed. J. Peter Euben, John R. Wallach, and Josiah Ober (Ithaca: Cornell University Press, 1994), 29–58. This volume appeared too late for me to use fully. Wolin seems to have been a major influence on it; Euben and Wallach were his students.

71. Kateb, "Individualism, Communitarianism, and Docility," in *Inner Ocean,* 231.

72. Sar Levitan and Robert Taggert, *Promise of Greatness* (Cambridge: Harvard University Press, 1976); and John Schwartz, *America's Hidden Success* (New York: Norton, 1983).

73. George Armstrong Kelly, *Hegel's Retreat from Eleusis* (Princeton: Princeton University Press, 1978), 231, 222. It should be stressed that Kelly by no means saw the state as any sort of panacea.

74. Henry Kariel, *The Promise of Politics* (Englewood Cliffs, N.J.: Prentice-Hall, 1966), 66.

75. James A. Morone, *The Democratic Wish: Popular Participation and the Limits of American Government* (New York: Basic Books, 1990), 1–30. For a critical appreciation of this book by Wilson Carey McWilliams, see "Democracy and Power in America," *Review of Politics* (Spring 1992), 335–338.

76. These remarks on the relation of Wolin to Strauss owe a great deal to exchanges with Carey McWilliams and Michael Walzer. For some hints of Wolin's early antirationalist skepticism, see Sheldon Wolin, "Hume and Conservatism," *American Political Science Review* (December 1954), 999–1016, and "Richard Hooker and English Conservatism," *Western Political Quarterly* (March 1953), 28–47. Nothing said in those articles should be taken to indicate a complacent hostility to change on Wolin's part. It is also interesting to note a greater sympathy for constitutionalism there than in his later work.

77. In addition to *What It Means to Be an American,* already cited, Michael Walzer's major works include *Obligations: Essays on Civil Disobedience, War, and Citizenship* (Cambridge: Harvard University Press, 1970), *Radical Principles: Reflections of an Unreconstructed Democrat* (New York: Basic Books, 1980), *Spheres of Justice: A Defense of Pluralism and Equality* (New York: Basic Books, 1983), and *Interpretation and Social Criticism* (Cambridge: Harvard University Press, 1987). M. Walzer, "Exclusion, Injustice, and the Democratic State," *Dissent* (Winter 1993), 55–64, is a reflection on the themes of *Spheres of Justice* after ten years. Other works will be cited as needed.

78. The literature on Walzer has become very large. The most important items include Joshua Cohen, "Review of *Spheres of Justice,*" *Journal of Philosophy* (August 1986), 457–468; Nancy L. Rosenblum, "Moral Membership in a Postliberal State," *World Politics* (July 1984), 581–596; Ronald Dworkin, "To Each His Own," *New York Review of Books* (April 14, 1983), 4–6, and the exchange between Dworkin and Walzer in the *Review* (July 21, 1983), 43–46; Ian Shapiro, *Political Criticism* (Berkeley: University of California Press, 1990), 55–120; Emily Gill, "Walzer's Complex Equality: Constraints and the Right to Be Wrong," *Polity* (Fall 1987), 32–56. (This is an especially useful article because Gill sees connections that others do not. She helped guide me to passages I might otherwise have missed.) Other studies include Lyle A. Downing and Robert B. Thigpen, "Beyond Shared Understandings," *Political Theory* (August 1986), 451–472; Galston, *Liberal Purposes,* 44–54. From the point of view of the Berkeley school, see John H. Schaar, "The Question of Justice," *Raritan* (Fall 1983), 107–129, which is mostly sharply critical; and J. Peter Euben, "Walzer's *Obligations,*" *Philosophy and Public Affairs* (Summer 1972), 438–459, and "Fanfare for the Common Complaints," *New York Times Book Review* (January 8, 1989), 18, both of which are more sympathetic than Schaar but by no means uncritical. For an article that compares several of the leading theories of justice, see Chantal Mouffe, "American Liberalism and Its Critics:

Rawls, Taylor, Sandel, and Walzer," *Praxis International* (July 1988), 193–206. This is a useful article, somewhat marred by the author's exaggeration of Walzer's communitarianism.

79. Walzer, *Radical Principles*, 302.

80. Michael Walzer, "Liberalism and the Art of Separation," *Political Theory* (August 1984), 315–320.

81. Ibid., 324.

82. Walzer, *Obligations*, 205; Michael Walzer, "Must Democracy Be Capitalist?" *New York Review of Books* (July 20, 1978), 40. This article is a discussion of Lindblom's *Politics and Markets* (New York: Basic Books, 1977).

83. Walzer, *Obligations*, 7, 5. Euben argues that Walzer does not escape reliance on tacit consent. "Walzer's *Obligations*," 447–449. This argument may say more about the difficulty of doing without the idea of tacit consent in the modern state than it does about Walzer.

84. Walzer, *Obligations*, 227.

85. Ibid., 142.

86. Ibid., 227–228. Peter Euben criticizes Walzer for his acceptance of these limitations: To surrender to them is to concede too much to liberalism. The terms *high* and *chastened citizenship* come from Richard Flathman. See *Toward a Liberalism* (Ithaca: Cornell University Press, 1989), 65–108.

87. Walzer, *Spheres of Justice*, 68.

88. Ibid., 84.

89. Walzer, *Radical Principles*, 28–30. What might be done to improve the welfare state in the relatively short run is suggested by Michael Walzer in "Socializing the Welfare State," in *Democracy and the Welfare State*, ed. Amy Gutmann (Princeton: Princeton University Press, 1988), 13–26.

90. Walzer, *Radical Principles*, 10–11, 17.

91. Walzer, "Liberalism and Separation," 321, 328.

92. Walzer, quoted in Robert Leitner, "Unorthodox Leftist," *Present Tense* (January-February 1987), 33.

93. Walzer, *Spheres of Justice*, xiv.

94. This and the previous paragraph follow ibid., 13–20, quote at 20.

95. Ibid., xiv, 7–10.

96. Ibid., 64, 75–79.

97. Ibid., 83.

98. Ibid., 83, 86–90.

99. Ibid., 91–94.

100. Ibid., 95, 100–103.

101. Ibid., 107, 109.

102. Ibid., xi.

103. Robert E. Lane, *Political Ideology* (Glencoe, Ill.: Free Press, 1962), 57–81.

104. Walzer, *Spheres of Justice*, 281–282.

105. Ibid., 282–284.

106. Ibid., 285–286. See also Michael Walzer, "Deterrence and Democracy," *New Republic* (July 2, 1984), 16–21; and Robert A. Dahl, *Controlling Nuclear Weapons* (Syracuse: Syracuse University Press, 1985), for a defense of democratic decisionmaking in what is perhaps the most technical, and potentially the most dangerous, of all areas of expertise. Following Plato, Dahl coins the term *Guardianship* to apply to the rule of experts. The worry about control by technocratic experts and about the place of technology in American society is also central to the concerns of Wolin, Schaar, and McWilliams.

107. Walzer, *Spheres of Justice*, 303–304.

108. Ibid., 308–310.

109. Ibid., 129–131.

110. Ibid., 152.

111. Ibid., 153.

112. Ibid., 154. I have said that Walzer has written more about ethnicity than race. For his longest statement on race to date, see ibid., 151–154.

113. Ibid., 318.

114. Walzer, *Radical Principles,* 46; "Exclusion, Injustice, and the Democratic State," p. 56.

115. Walzer, "Exclusion, Injustice, and the Democratic State," 63.

116. Walzer, *Radical Principles,* 68–72. Apropos my remark about the declining civility of American politics, I note that Walzer has reprinted this essay, "Civility and Civic Virtue in Contemporary America" (first published in Dissent in 1974), unchanged in *What It Means to Be an American.*

117. Walzer, *Radical Principles,* 46–47.

118. Michael Walzer, "The Idea of Civil Society," *Dissent* (Spring 1991), 294–298. Joshua Cohen, in his review of *Spheres of Justice,* criticizes Walzer for abandoning the pluralist emphasis on groups as bearers of value so characteristic of *Obligations.* I think this misses much of the point of Walzer's argument, but the shift in emphasis in the work on civil society is worth noting. Cohen, "Review," 459. Much of Cohen's critique founders on his assumption that Walzer is a much more thoroughgoing communitarian than he actually is.

119. Walzer, "Civil Society," 298.

120. Ibid., 298–299.

121. Ibid., 300.

122. Ibid., 301–302.

123. Walzer, *Spheres of Justice,* 312–315.

124. The paradigm case is Dworkin, "To Each His Own."

125. Cohen, "Review," 466.

126. Dworkin, "To Each His Own," 6.

127. Michael Walzer, "Philosophy and Democracy," *Political Theory* (August 1981), 379–397, quote at 397. Walzer walks a fine line here. In *The Conquest of Politics,* Benjamin Barber made a similar argument, which Walzer criticized for its too complete rejection of the utility of philosophy. See M. Walzer, "Flight from Philosophy," *New York Review of Books* (February 2, 1989), 42–44. I briefly sketched a view of the place of political theory in J. P. Young, "Socialism and Its Critics," *Dissent* (Spring 1986), 245.

128. Walzer, *Spheres of Justice,* 316, 250, xv.

129. Michael Walzer, "Moral Minimalism," in *From the Twilight of Probability,* ed. William Shea and Antonio Spadafora (Canton, Mass.: Science History Publications, 1992), 3–4. For other arguments along these lines, see M. Walzer, "Two Kinds of Universalism," in *The Tanner Lectures* (Salt Lake City: University of Utah Press, 1990), 509–532, and "Objectivity and Social Meaning," in *The Quality of Life,* ed. Martha Nussbaum and Amartya K. Sen (New York: Oxford University Press, 1993). For a fuller statement of Walzer's current position, which includes his essay on "moral minimalism," see M. Walzer, *Thick and Thin* (South Bend, Ind.: University of Notre Dame Press, 1994). Here Walzer shows the influence of anthropologist Clifford Geertz's concept of "thick description," which Walzer has transformed into a thick description of political ideas and shared understandings. Cf. particularly Geertz, *The Interpretation of Cultures* (New York: Basic Books, 1973).

130. Walzer, "Moral Minimalism," 4–6. Though they missed Walzer's remarks about life and liberty in *Spheres of Justice,* Downing and Thigpen were on the right track when they argued that there were implicit standards of justice that were not merely conventional. See Downing and Thigpen, "Beyond Shared Understandings," 456 and passim. Emily Gill, working without the benefit of Walzer's recent writings, understood that he moved from the particular to the general, just the reverse of Dworkin. See Gill, "Walzer's Complex Equality," 52–53 and passim.

131. For some reflections along these lines, see the neglected book by Charles Frankel, *The Case for Modern Man* (Boston: Beacon Press, 1959), esp. 74–84. David Mapel, *Social Justice Reconsidered: The Problem of Appropriate Precision in a Theory of Justice* (Urbana: University of Illinois Press, 1989), is a useful exploration of the problem of precision in political theory. I

agree with his general point of view, though he exaggerates both Walzer's relativism and his communitarianism.

132. Walzer, *Spheres of Justice*, 8.

133. Ibid., 313. Cohen complains that Walzer does not show how this point could be integrated into the rest of his argument, but the implications seem clear, as I try to suggest. See Cohen, "Review," 466.

134. Euben, "Walzer's *Obligations*," passim. Euben also worries that Walzer has not taken up such problems as the impact of technical rationality on contemporary society or the possibility of manipulating consent through the mass media. These are accurate statements, though it should be said that *Obligations* is an early book and that Walzer addresses these problems to one extent or another in later writings. He has not been uncritical of modernity, though he is less so than Wolin and Schaar, and he is as critical of modernization theory as they are. See "Modernization," in *Radical Principles*, 189–200. And see below for his jaundiced view of electoral politics. Still, Euben's criticisms are worth noting because Walzer's approach is to start his social criticism from within the liberal tradition.

135. Walzer, *Interpretation and Social Criticism*, 3–16.

136. Ibid., 61, 59.

137. Ibid., 48–49. For a further development of his thought on social criticism, see Michael Walzer, *The Company of Critics* (New York: Basic Books, 1988).

138. Shapiro, *Political Criticism*, 75, 85.

139. Schaar, "The Question of Justice," 119, 122–123.

140. Walzer, "Exclusion, Injustice, and the Democratic State," 61. Christopher Lasch offered an argument against economic inequality that went beyond Schaar. Though generally sympathetic to the structure of Walzer's argument, Lasch argued, "Economic inequality is intrinsically undesirable, even when confined to its proper sphere. Luxury is morally repugnant, and its incompatibility with democratic ideals, moreover, has been consistently recognized in the traditions that shape our political culture. The difficulty of limiting the influence of wealth suggests that wealth itself needs to be limited." See Christopher Lasch, *The Revolt of the Elites* (New York: Norton, 1995), 21–22, quote at 22. This position has some appeal, and Lasch's point about the difficulty of the politics inherent in Walzer's position is important, but it does not meet his argument that equally distributed wealth would be unequally distributed a week later. This too is an aspect of the political reality egalitarians face.

141. Schaar, "Question of Justice," 128. To his reading list Schaar would add, in addition to Walzer and Lincoln—and I infer Rawls as well—the ideas of the Farmers' Alliance, the early Populist Party, Martin Luther King, Jr., and the New Testament. But Lincoln's writings are the definitive text. Note that even Wolin uses Locke's liberal theory of revolution as a model for us today. See Wolin, "What Revolutionary Action Means Today."

142. J. Peter Euben, "Fanfare for the Common Complaints," *New York Times Book Review* (January 8, 1989), 18. For the full quotation by Walzer, see my Introduction. Euben's article is a review of *The Company of Critics*.

143. Mouffe, "American Liberalism and Its Critics," 201.

144. Samuel Huntington, *Political Order in Changing Societies* (New Haven: Yale University Press, 1967), 344–345.

145. John Stuart Mill, *Considerations on Representative Government* (London: J. M. Dent, 1910), 253.

Chapter 17

1. Documentation for most of the historical arguments in this final chapter can be found in the body of the book.

2. Walter Dean Burnham, "The Politics of Repudiation, 1992: Edging Toward Upheaval," *American Prospect* (Winter 1995), 22–33.

3. See the remarks of the formerly conservative journalist Michael Lind, "Why Intellectual Conservatism Died," *Dissent* (Winter 1995), 42–47. See also James Atlas, "The Counter Counterculture," *New York Times Magazine* (February 12, 1995), 32–38ff.

4. See Garry Wills, "The Visionary," *New York Review of Books* (March 23, 1995), 4–8, for a discussion of the peculiarities of Gingrich's conservatism.

5. William E. Connolly, *Identity/Difference: Democratic Negotiations of Political Paradox* (Ithaca: Cornell University Press, 1991); and Stephen K. White, *Political Theory and Postmodernism* (Cambridge: Cambridge University Press, 1991). Connolly seems engaged in an attempt to rescue the liberal conception of personal identity from itself. On this see Geoffrey Hawthorne, "Is Postmodern Politics Politics?" *History of the Human Sciences* (August 1992), 93–97.

6. Sheldon S. Wolin, "On the Theory and Practice of Power," in *After Foucault*, ed. Jonathan Arac (New Brunswick: Rutgers University Press, 1988), 179–201; and Michael Walzer, *The Company of Critics* (New York: Basic Books, 1988), 191–209.

7. Richard Rorty's major political writings include "The Priority of Democracy to Philosophy" and "Postmodernist Bourgeois Liberalism," in *Objectivity, Relativism and Truth* (Cambridge: Cambridge University Press, 1991), 175–196 and 197–202, "Thugs and Theorists: A Reply to Bernstein," *Political Theory* (November 1987), 564–580, and "Human Rights, Rationality, and Sentimentality," in *On Human Rights: The Oxford Amnesty Lectures: 1993*, ed. Stephen Shute and Susan Hurley (New York: Basic Books, 1993), 111–134.

8. Richard Bernstein, "One Step Forward, Two Steps Backward: Richard Rorty on Liberal Democracy and Philosophy," *Political Theory* (November 1987), 538–563; and Charles Anderson, "Pragmatism and Liberalism, Rationalism and Irrationalism: A Response to Richard Rorty," *Polity* (Spring 1991), 357–371.

9. Sheldon S. Wolin, "Democracy in the Discourse of Postmodernism," *Social Research* (Spring 1990), 5–30; and Bernstein, "One Step Forward." See also Richard Bernstein, "Rorty's Liberal Utopia," *Social Research* (Spring 1990), 31–72; and Rorty, "Human Rights, Rationality, and Sentimentality." There are signs that the more direct postmodernist engagement with American politics called for here is beginning. See Thomas Dumm, *united states* (Ithaca: Cornell University Press, 1994); and Frederick M. Dolan, *Allegories of America: Narratives, Metaphysics, Politics* (Ithaca: Cornell University Press, 1994). These studies appeared too late for me to consider here. See also F. M. Dolan and T. Dumm, eds., *Rhetorical Republic: Governing Representations in American Politics* (Amherst: University of Massachusetts Press, 1993), which has interesting materials but lacks a sustained analysis; and Anne Norton, *Republic of Signs: Liberal Theory and American Popular Culture* (Chicago: University of Chicago Press, 1993), which contains some interesting material on constitutionalism but is too narrowly focused on popular culture to be relevant to the work considered in this study. I hope to return to these works on another occasion.

10. Francis Fukuyama, *The End of History and the Last Man* (New York: Free Press, 1992). On whether there is a postmodern world qualitatively different from the modern world, see Anthony Giddens, *The Consequences of Modernity* (Stanford: Stanford University Press, 1990), esp. 112–150. See also Todd Gitlin, "Postmodernism: Roots and Politics," *Dissent* (Winter 1989), 100–108; and Michael Rustin, "Incomplete Modernity: Ulrich Beck's 'Risk Society'" *Dissent* (Summer 1994), 394–400.

11. The classic commentary on these matters is George Armstrong Kelly, "Hegel's America," in *Hegel's Retreat from Eleusis* (Princeton: Princeton University Press, 1978), 184–223, esp. 189.

12. John P. Diggins, "Knowing and Sorrow: Louis Hartz's Quarrel with American History," *Political Theory* (August 1988), 362, 375; and Theodore J. Lowi, "Europeanization of American Politics?" in *Nationalizing Government: Public Policies in America*, ed. Lowi and Alan Stone (Beverly Hills, Calif.: Sage Publications, 1978).

13. Burnham, "The Politics of Repudiation." Jean Bethke Elshtain also worries about legitimacy. See "Issues and Themes: Spiral of Delegitimation or a New Social Contract," in

The Elections of 1992, ed. Michael Nelson (Washington, D.C.: Congressional Quarterly Press, 1993), 109–124.

14. See Theodore J. Lowi and Benjamin Ginsberg, *Embattled Democracy: Politics and Policy in the Clinton Era* (New York: Norton, 1995), 80–85; and Wilson Carey McWilliams, *The Politics of Disappointment* (Chatham, N.J.: Chatham House, 1995), 5. Lowi's major book, *The End of the Republican Era* (Norman: University of Oklahoma Press, 1995), appeared too late for me to use fully. He predicts not only the demise of the Republican coalition, but the possible end of a two-hundred-year era of history as well. In an analysis of the portions of the Contract with America that had been acted on, in whole or in part, by June 1995, Louis Fisher finds a degree of incrementalism that belies the rhetoric on both sides, and he also sees a weakening of government, particularly Congress. See "The 'Contract with America': What It Really Means," *New York Review of Books* (June 22, 1995), 20–24.

15. Quoted in Robert A. Dahl, "Ills of the System," *Dissent* (Fall 1993), 451.

16. Theodore J. Lowi, *The Personal President: Power Invested, Promise Unfulfilled* (Ithaca: Cornell University Press, 1985).

17. For what follows, I have been aided in working out my ideas by discussions with my student and research assistant, Kimberly Maslin-Wicks.

18. Closely adapted from Morris Janowitz and Dwaine Marvick, *Competitive Pressure and Democratic Consent: An Interpretation of the 1952 Presidential Election* (Chicago: Quadrangle Books, 1964), 5–8.

19. Michael Walzer, *Spheres of Justice* (New York: Basic Books, 1963), 307.

20. Ibid., 308. The Iowa caucuses, though they may have had too much influence over the final selection of presidential candidates, are in some ways models of grassroots politics.

21. On the problems of local revitalization, see Jeffrey Isaacs, "Going Local," *Dissent* (Spring 1995), 184–188.

22. See Wilson Carey McWilliams, "Parties as Civic Associations," in *Party Reform in America: Theory and Practice,* ed. Gerald Pomper (New York: Praeger, 1980), 51–68, "Politics," *American Quarterly* (1983), 19–38, "The Anti-Federalists, Representation, and Party," *Northwestern University Law Review* (Fall 1989), 12–38, and "Tocqueville and Responsible Parties: Individualism, Participation, and Citizenship in America," in *Challenges to Party Government,* ed. John K. White and Jerome M. Mileur (Carbondale: Southern Illinois University Press, 1992), 190–211. Schaar is skeptical about new parties; he thinks the crisis runs much deeper than that. See John Schaar, *Legitimacy in the Modern State* (New Brunswick, N.J.: Transaction Books, 1981), 348.

23. McWilliams, "The Anti-Federalists, Representation, and Party," 37.

24. Donald A. Robinson, "The Place of Parties in Democratic Ideas," in Pomper, *Party Reform in America,* 28.

25. Dahl, "Ills of the System," 454.

26. Lani Guinier, *The Tyranny of the Majority: Fundamental Fairness in Representative Democracy* (New York: Free Press, 1994). For good discussion, see Alan Wolfe, "Redesigning Democracy," *New York Times Book Review* (March 13, 1994), 6–7; Cass Sunstein, "Voting Rites," *New Republic* (April 25, 1994), 34–38; and Randall Kennedy, "Lani Guinier's Constitution," *American Prospect* (Fall 1993), 34–47.

27. George Will, *Restoration: Congress, Term Limits, and the Recovery of Deliberative Democracy* (New York: Free Press, 1992); Sean Wilentz, "Over the Hill," *New Republic* (October 12, 1992), 40–45; and Dahl, "Ills of the System," 452–453.

28. For historically informed perspectives on the Perot phenomenon, see Alan Brinkley, "Roots," *New Republic* (July 27, 1992), 44—45; and Sean Wilentz, "Pox Populi," *New Republic* (August 9, 1993), 29–35.

29. Theodore J. Lowi, "It Is Time for a Third Major Party in American Politics," in *Controversial Issues in Presidential Selection,* ed. Gary L. Rose, 2d ed. (Albany: State University of New York Press, 1992), 243–250, and "The Party Crasher," *New York Times Magazine* (August 23, 1992), 28 and 33. Robert Dahl is also tempted by a third party. See "Roundtable

Discussion: Politics, Economics, and Welfare," in *Power, Inequality, and Democratic Politics: Essays in Honor of Robert A. Dahl*, ed. Ian Shapiro and Grant Reeher (Boulder: Westview Press, 1988), 166. The difficulty of keeping third-party movements out of the hands of extremists is illustrated in Micah L. Sifry, "From Perot to Fulani," *Nation* (May 30, 1994), 746–747. Carey McWilliams points out the enormous difficulties faced by challengers to the two-party system as long as the electoral system is based on winner-take-all single-member districts (*Politics of Disappointment*, 11).

30. For an enlightening series of case studies of corporate misbehavior, see Alan F. Westin, ed., *Whistle-Blowing! Loyalty and Dissent in the Corporation* (New York: McGraw-Hill, 1980).

31. Michael Walzer, "The Idea of Civil Society," *Dissent* (Spring 1991), 302.

32. Robert A. Dahl, *A Preface to Economic Democracy* (Berkeley: University of California Press, 1985), 111.

33. Ibid. is filled with information on the successes and failures of this form of economic government. On the problem of consciousness, see Robert Dahl, *Dilemmas of Pluralist Democracy* (New Haven: Yale University Press, 1982), 138–165.

34. Sidney Blumenthal, "Christian Soldiers," *New Yorker* (July 18, 1994), 31–37. For a full exposure of Robertson's anti-Semitic and other conspiracy theories, see Michael Lind, "Rev. Robertson's Grand International Conspiracy Theory," *New York Review of Books* (February 2, 1995), 21–26. For further material see ibid. (April 20, 1995), 67–71. Some of the theories Robertson is recycling have been around for at least two hundred years. For a classic treatment, see Richard Hofstadter, *The Paranoid Style in America Politics* (New York: Knopf, 1965), esp. 3–40.

35. Jennifer Hochschild and Monica Herk, "'Yes But . . . ': Principles and Caveats in American Racial Attitudes," in *Majorities and Minorities: Nomos XXXII,* ed. John W. Chapman and Alan Wertheimer (New York: New York University Press, 1990), 308–335; and J. Hochschild, "The Political Contingency of Public Opinion, or, What Shall We Make of the Declining Faith of Middle-Class Americans?" *PS* (March 1994), 35–38.

36. Daniel Bell, *The Coming of Postindustrial Society* (New York: Basic Books, 1973).

37. Jürgen Habermas, *Legitimation Crisis* (Boston: Beacon Press, 1975), 13, 7, 4.

38. George Kateb, "Imperfect Legitimacy," in *The Open Society in Theory and Practice,* ed. Dante Germino and Klaus von Beyme (The Hague: Martinus Nijhoff, 1974), 166–168. Kateb notes (169) that it is a mystery why the social scientists who described the American system seemed blind to the implications of their analysis..

39. Michael Walzer, "Must Democracy Be Capitalist?" *New York Review of Books* (July 20, 1978), 41. Walzer made this remark in a review of Lindblom's *Politics and Markets* (New York: Basic Books, 1977).

40. Annual Message to Congress, December 1, 1862, in *Lincoln: Selected Speeches and Writings: 1859–1865,* ed. Don Fehrenbacher (New York: Library of America, 1989), 415.

About the Book and Author

Forty years ago Louis Hartz surveyed American political thought in his classic *The Liberal Tradition in America*. He concluded that American politics was based on a broad liberal consensus made possible by a unique American historical experience, a thesis that seemed to minimize the role of political conflict.

Today, with conflict on the rise and with much of liberalism in disarray, James P. Young revisits these questions to reevaluate Hartz's interpretation of American politics. Young's treatment of key movements in our history, especially Puritanism and republicanism's early contribution to the Revolution and the Constitution, demonstrates in the spirit of Dewey and others that the liberal tradition is richer and more complex than Hartz and most contemporary theorists have allowed.

The breadth of Young's account is unrivaled. *Reconsidering American Liberalism* gives voice not just to Locke, Jefferson, Hamilton, Madison, Lincoln, and Dewey but also to Rawls, Shklar, Kateb, Wolin, and Walzer. In addition to broad discussions of all the major figures in over 300 years of political thought—with Lincoln looming particularly large—Young touches upon modern feminism and conservatism, multiculturalism, postmodernism, rights-based liberalism, and social democracy. Out of these contemporary materials Young synthesizes a new position, a smarter and tougher liberalism not just forged from historical materials but reshaped in the rough and tumble of contemporary thought and politics.

This exceptionally timely study is both a powerful survey of the whole of U.S. political thought and a trenchant critique of contemporary political debates. At a time of acrimony and confusion in our national politics, Young enables us to see that salvaging a viable future depends upon our understanding how we have reached this point.

Never without his own opinions, Young is scrupulously fair to the widest range of thinkers and marvelously clear in getting to the heart of their ideas. Although his book is a substantial contribution to political theory and the history of ideas, it is always accessible and lively enough for the informed general reader. It is essential reading for anyone who cares about the future of U.S. political thought or, indeed, about the future of the country itself.

James P. Young is professor emeritus of political science at Binghamton University in Binghamton, New York, and now an independent scholar working in Ann Arbor, Michigan. He is the author of *The Politics of Affluence* and editor of *Consensus and Conflict: Readings in American Politics*. He is the author of many articles and reviews in both professional journals and popular journals of opinion on political theory and thought.

Index